REBUILDING
A
NATION

Philippine Challenges
and American Policy

The Washington Institute for Values in Public Policy

The Washington Institute sponsors research that helps provide the information and fresh insights necessary for formulating policy in a democratic society. Founded in 1982, the Institute is an independent, non-profit educational and research organization which examines current and upcoming issues with particular attention to ethical implications.

ADDITIONAL TITLES

REBUILDING
A
NATION

Philippine Challenges
and American Policy

Edited and with an introduction by
Carl H. Landé

A Washington Institute Press book

Published in the United States by
The Washington Institute Press
Suite 200
1667 K Street, NW
Washington, DC 20006

A Washington Institute Press book

Cover design by Catherine Nesbitt

Cover photos: Cory Aquino/by Christopher Morris/Black Star
               Marcos Monument/Photoreporters

Library of Congress Cataloging-in-Publication data:

Rebuilding a nation.

   Product of a conference held in Apr. 1986, sponsored by the Washington
Institute for Values in Public Policy.
   Includes index.
   1. Philippines—History—1986   —Congresses.
2. Philippines—History—1946–1986—Congresses.
3. United States—Relations—Philippines—Congresses.
4. Philippines—Relations—United States—Congresses.
I. Landé, Carl H. (Carl Herman)   II. Washington Institute
for Values in Public Policy.
DS686.614.R42   1987   959.9'04   86-32610
ISBN 0-88702-023-2
ISBN 0-88702-024-0 (pbk.)

Table of Contents

III. Social Change, Social Needs, Social Policy

IV. Government and Politics

V. Internal War and Defense

VI. United States Policy and the Philippines

NOTES ON THE CONTRIBUTORS

HISTORY

CARL H. LANDÉ is professor of political science and East Asian studies at the University of Kansas. He is author of *Leaders, Factions and Parties, the Structure of Philippine Politics* (1965) and *Southern Tagalog Voting, 1946-1963: Political Behavior in a Philippine Region* (1972). He is production editor of *Pilipinas, A Journal Of Philippine Studies* and has served on study missions to the Philippines for the Rockefeller Foundation and the Asia Society.

EMMANUEL M. PELAEZ is the Philippine ambassador to the United States. He has held the positions of senator, vice president, secretary of foreign affairs, and member of the executive committee and has been extensively involved with U.S. military base negotiations.

STEPHEN J. SOLARZ is United States representative from the thirteenth district of New York and chairs the House Foreign Affairs Committee's Subcommittee on Asian and Pacific Affairs. He has written extensively for *Foreign Affairs, Foreign Policy,* the *New York Times,* the *Christian Science Monitor,* and the *Wall Street Journal.*

THEODORE FRIEND is president of the Eisenhower Exchange Fellowships, Inc., and former president of Swarthmore College (1973-1982). His first book, *Between Two Empires: The Ordeal of the Philippines* (1965), won the Bancroft Prize in American History. He has also published *The Philippine Polity: A Japanese View* (1967). His next book on Southeast Asia, a comparative study of Indonesia and the Philippines under Japanese occupation, will be published in 1987.

THE ECONOMY

WILLIAM H. OVERHOLT is vice president in the International Economics group of Bankers Trust, based in Hong Kong and a former member of the Hudson Institute. He is the author of numerous books on Asian and international affairs and editor of *Global Assessment*.

GUSTAV RANIS is Frank Altschul Professor of International Economics at Yale University and an associate of the Philippine Institute of Development Studies. He was chief of the ILO Comprehensive Employment Strategy Mission to the Philippines in 1973 and the principal author of its report, *Sharing in Development: A Programme of Employment, Equity and Growth for the Philippines* (1974). He has served in administrative or advisory positions for numerous academic, governmental, and international economic research organizations.

CHARLES W. LINDSEY, associate professor of economics at Trinity College, Hartford, Connecticut, has been visiting professor at Ateneo de Manila University, the University of the Philippines, and was a research fellow at the Institute of Southeast Asian Studies in Singapore. He is review editor of *Pilipinas, A Journal Of Philippine Studies*.

DAVID REINAH is president of Ragus Trading Corporation and a vice president, director, and Sugar Committee chairman of the Philippine American Chamber of Commerce, New York. He has been active in seeking more favorable treatment for Philippine sugar in the United States.

BRUCE M. KOPPEL is a research associate at the East-West Center in Honolulu. He has been a visiting professor at the University of the Philippines at Los Banos and served as a consultant in the Philippines for the Asian Development Bank, the International Labour Organization, the United Nations Development Program, the United States Agency for International Development, and the World Bank.

RICHARD HOOLEY is professor of economics and public policy at the Graduate School of Public and International Affairs, the University of Pittsburgh. He is the author of *Saving in the Philippines, 1951-1960* (1963) and *Productivity Growth in Philippine Manufacturing: Retrospect and Future Prospects* (1985). He has been an advisor to various Southeast Asian governments and to the United States government.

SOCIAL CHANGE, SOCIAL NEEDS, SOCIAL POLICY

BENEDICT J. TRIA KERKVLIET is professor of political science and a member of the Center for Asian and Pacific Studies at the University of Hawaii. He has been a visiting scholar at Australian National University and the Woodrow Wilson International Center. He is author of *The Huk Rebellion: A Study of Peasant Revolt in the Philippines* (1977) and is currently writing a book on everyday politics in a central Luzon village.

ROBERT A. AND BEVERLY H. HACKENBERG are research associates of the Institute of Behavioral Science at the University of Colorado. Robert Hackenberg is also professor of anthropology at that institution. They serve as co-directors of the Davao Research and Planning Foundation, Inc., Davao City, Philippines, through which the data presented in their paper was obtained. Robert Hackenberg is co-author, with Henry Magalit, of *Demographic Responses to Development: Sources of Declining Fertility in the Philippines* (1985).

BENJAMIN N. MUEGO is associate professor of political science at Bowling Green State University and adjunct lecturer at the School of Area Studies of the Foreign Service Institute. He is currently a visiting Fulbright professor in the Philippines.

JUSTIN J. GREEN is professor of political science at Villanova University. He is co-author of *Asian Women in Transition* (1980) and *Political Stability in the Philippines: Framework and Analysis* (1986).

DANIEL F. DOEPPERS is professor of geography at the University of Wisconsin, Madison. He is author of *Manila 1900-1941: Social Change in a Colonial Metropolis* (1984).

GOVERNMENT AND POLITICS

GUY J. PAUKER is the senior specialist on Southeast Asia of the Rand Corporation. He has been a faculty member of Harvard University and the University of California, Berkeley, and a research associate at the Massachusetts Institute of Technology, California Institute of Technology and the East-West Center in Honolulu. He has published extensively on Southeast Asia and the third world.

ROSS MARLAY is associate professor of political science at Arkansas State University and has been a Fulbright senior lecturer at several Philippine universities. Earlier he served as a Peace Corps volunteer in Bataan province, Philippines. He is the author of *Pollution and Politics in the Philippines* (1977) and is articles editor of *Pilipinas, A Journal Of Philippine Studies*.

DAVID A. ROSENBERG is professor of political science at Middlebury College. He is editor and co-author of *Marcos and Martial Law in the Philippines* (1979) and author of *Landless Peasants and Rural Poverty in Indonesia and the Philippines* (1980).

ROBERT L. YOUNGBLOOD is associate professor of political science and a research associate of the Center for Asian Studies at Arizona State University. He has been a senior Fulbright-Hays research fellow in the Philippines. He has published extensively on the Philippine church in various journals.

RICHARD J. KESSLER is a senior associate with the Carnegie Endowment for International Peace and a former fellow of the Georgetown University Center for Strategic and International Studies. His book, *Politics of Rebellion in the Philippines*, will be published in 1987.

LINDA K. RICHTER is associate professor of political science at Kansas State University and has been a visiting research associate at the College of Public Administration of the University of the Philippines. She is the author of *Land Reform and Tourism Development: Policy-Making in the Philippines* (1982).

INTERNAL WAR AND DEFENSE

LARRY A. NIKSCH is a specialist with the Congressional Research Service, concentrating on United States security policy, internal political conditions, and general foreign policy developments in East Asia and the Western Pacific. He served as an official U.S. observer to the Philippine presidential election in February 1986.

LELA GARNER NOBLE is associate academic vice president for faculty affairs and professor of political science at San Jose State University. She is the author of *Philippine Policy Towards Sabah* (1977) and co-author of *Ethnic Conflict in International Relations* (1977). She has contributed articles and chapters on Philippine Muslims to numerous journals and books.

WILLIAM M. WISE, a United States Air Force lieutenant colonel, is assistant for regional policy and congressional affairs, East Asia and Pacific region, in the office of the Secretary of Defense, with responsibility for analysis and development of political-military policy in the region.

ALVA M. BOWEN, Jr., captain USN (Ret.), is a specialist with the Foreign Affairs and National Defense Division of the Congressional Research Service. He is the author of *Philippine Bases: U.S. Redeployment Options* (1986). A veteran of many years of operating experience in the Western Pacific, he has written on naval affairs and the Asia-Pacific and Indian Ocean regions for various professional journals.

ROBERT N. SMITH, lieutenant general, USAF (Ret.), last served before his retirement from the U.S. Air Force as chief of staff of the United Nations Command in Korea. Subsequently, he was Far East regional vice president for a Dallas-based electronics firm. From 1977 until 1980 he lived and maintained an office in Manila. He is now president of Trans-Pacific Consultants and a trustee of the Washington Institute.

UNITED STATES POLICY AND THE PHILIPPINES

WILLIAM C. HAMILTON was deputy chief of mission and sometime chargé d'affaires at the United States embassy in Manila from 1971 to 1973. A specialist on political and national security affairs in East Asia and Western Europe, he served also as a foreign service officer in Burma, Laos, Thailand, and Sweden. He was director of International Affairs at the National War College. Prior to his government service he taught at Douglass College of Rutgers University.

LEE T. STULL was deputy chief of mission and sometime chargé d'affaires at the United States embassy in Manila from 1975 to 1978.

He has served as political counselor at the United States embassies in Pakistan, India, and Germany. At present he is managing director of the Greater Philadelphia International Networks, Inc.

JOHN F. MAISTO served as director of the Office of Philippine Affairs in the U.S. Department of State from 1982 to 1986. He served previously at the U.S. embassy in Manila. Currently he is deputy chief of mission in Panama.

WILLIAM H. SULLIVAN was United States ambassador to the Philippines from 1973 to 1977. Earlier he served as political advisor to General Douglas MacArthur during the Korean War, helped to negotiate the agreements for the neutralization of Laos where he was U.S. ambassador and was Henry Kissinger's immediate deputy in negotiating the Vietnam agreements in 1972. He was the last U.S. ambassador to the Shah of Iran and is author of *Mission to Iran* (1981). After his retirement from the foreign service he was from 1979 to 1986 president of the American Assembly.

PAUL M. KATTENBURG was director of the Office of Philippine Affairs in the U.S. Department of State from 1965 to 1966. Earlier he served as political officer at the Manila embassy from 1956 to 1959. At present he is professor of government and international studies at the University of South Carolina in Columbia, where he specializes in United States foreign policy.

FRANCIS T. UNDERHILL was political counselor at the U.S. embassy in Manila from 1968 to 1971. He has served as the head of the political section in the U.S. embassy in Indonesia, as deputy chief of mission in Korea, and as United States ambassador to Malaysia.

PREFACE

Morton A. Kaplan

This extremely timely volume, *Rebuilding A Nation: Philippine Challenges and American Policy,* has been carefully crafted from papers first presented at a major conference on "The Philippines and U.S. Policy" convened in Washington, D.C., two months after the fall of the Marcos government. The Washington Institute for Values in Public Policy sponsored the conference under the chairmanship of Carl H. Landé.

When we began planning the conference in mid-1985, our first and vital task was to select the most eminent American Philippines scholar to be chairman. We were most impressed by the more than 30 years of scholarship on the Philippines of Carl Landé, professor of political science at the University of Kansas. We were fortunate that he could make himself available both as chairman of the conference and subsequently as editor of this book. Although we chose Carl Landé for this task while it seemed likely that Marcos would remain in office, we did not know where he stood on this crucial question until he had agreed to serve as chairman. We asked only that a spectrum of positions be presented.

The original intention for the conference was to illuminate American alternatives with respect to Marcos. But before we were able to meet, Marcos had been deposed. Carl Landé then switched gears almost immediately and produced a conference that explored the background of the revolution and its prospects.

The conference included academics whose thoughts and writings tend to be oriented toward long-term problems and diplomats and practitioners who are apt to be more carefully attuned to practical requirements and those immediate facts of life that make so many good theories inapplicable. We hoped that their intellectual intercourse would leaven the discussions, as it did, although of course the absolute dichotomy that this formulation suggests does justice neither to academics nor practitioners.

Rebuilding A Nation explores the history, the economy, social change, the Marcos regime and the Aquino succession, the insurgency, and American policy. His Excellency, Emmanuel M. Pelaez, the new ambassador from the Philippines, gave his first public address to the conference. Congressman Stephen Solarz, who played an active role during the succession, also addressed the conference.

The book speaks for itself. The travail of the Philippines continues. We can hope only that the competing forces, such as the contest of nerves between Cory Aquino and her former minister of defense, Juan Ponce Enrile, do not jeopardize the successful transition of the Philippines to a democracy whose economy and society strengthen it against internal and external threats.

Morton A. Kaplan,
Professor of Political Science
University of Chicago
       and
Chairman, Program Advisory Board
The Washington Institute for Values in Public Policy

REBUILDING A NATION

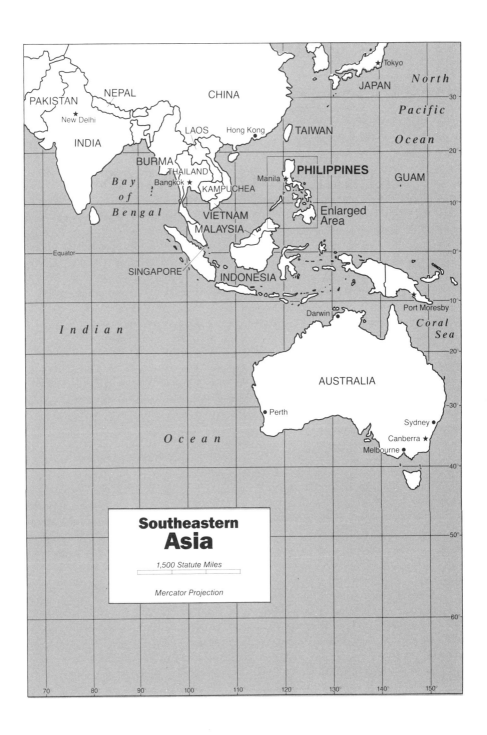

PAKISTAN
NEPAL
CHINA
★ New Delhi
INDIA
LAOS
Hong Kong
TAIWAN
BURMA
THAILAND
Bangkok ★
KAMPUCHEA
Manila ★
PHILIPPINES
GUAM
Bay of Bengal
VIETNAM
MALAYSIA
Enlarged Area
Equator
SINGAPORE
INDONESIA
Indian
Darwin
Port Moresby
Coral Sea
AUSTRALIA
Ocean
● Perth
Sydney ●
Canberra ★
Melbourne ●
Tokyo ★
JAPAN
North Pacific Ocean

Southeastern
Asia

1,500 Statute Miles

Mercator Projection

The
Philippines

150 Statute Miles

● Major Provincial Capitals
● **Other Large Cities**

Lambert Conformal Conic Projection

Luzon Strait

South China Sea

● Laoag
Tuguegarao
● Vigan
Ilagan
Bontoc
San Fernando ●
LUZON
● **Baguio**
Lingayen
Baler
Iba ●
● Palayan
Clark Air Base (U.S.) ▢
San Fernando
U.S. Facility Subic Bay ▢
● **Quezon**
▲**Manila**
Cavite ●
Lucena ●
● Daet
● Batangas
Boac ●
Naga
Mamburao ● Calapan
Legaspi ●
Virac
MINDORO

Philippine Sea

Masbate ●
Catarman
Catbalogan
Kalibo ●
MASBATE
SAMAR
Roxas ●
● Borongan
PANAY
Cadiz ●
Tacloban ●
Iloilo
PALAWAN
San Jose ●
● Bacolod
LEYTE
Cebu ●
CEBU
Maasin ●
NEGROS
BOHOL
Surigao ●
Puerto Princesa ●
Tagbilaran ●
Dumaguete ●
Bohol Sea
Butuan
Tandag
Sulu
Dipolog ●
● Cagayan de Oro
● Malaybalay
Pagadian ●
MINDANAO
Sea
● Tagum
● Sultan **Davao**
Zamboanga ●
Cotabato ● Kudarat
Mati ●
Digos ●
Isulan ●
● Koronadal

MALAYSIA
SULU
ARCHIPELAGO
Celebes Sea

3

I. History

1

Introduction:
Retrospect and Prospect

Carl H. Landé

INTRODUCTION

This book is the product of a conference on "The Philippines and U.S. Policy" sponsored by the Washington Institute for Values in Public Policy. The conference, held in Washington on April 30 and May 1, 1986, was designed to bring together present and former American policy makers as well as academic specialists on the Philippines. It consisted of five sessions, devoted to the Philippine economy, society, government and politics, internal war and defense, and United States policy towards the Philippines.

The papers presented at these sessions, and two papers written later, have been revised and form five sections of this book. Each section ends with a report on the discussion which followed the presentation of the papers. As all of the rapporteurs are established Philippines specialists, they were encouraged to incorporate their own views into their reports. A sixth section entitled "history," placed at the beginning of the book, contains two papers presented by distinguished guest speakers, as well as two papers designed to provide a historical introduction to the Marcos years and to the events that preceded and followed the coming to power of the Aquino government.

Planning for the conference began in 1985, at a time when many in the executive and legislative branches of the American government had come to the conclusion that the Marcos administration had become a liability for both his own country and for the United States. When the conferees assembled in April 1986, Marcos had fallen, and the new government of Corazon Aquino was in its place. On both sides of the Pacific, that government inspired much hope as to its ability to reestablish a stable democracy, revive the Philippine economy, and persuade at least the "soft" adherents of the communist-led New Peoples Army to abandon violence and work peacefully for social reform. As the anniversary of the February Revolution approaches, the admiration for Cory Aquino is still there and hopes for the success of her government remain strong. But they have been tempered by a recognition of the difficulties that face her government and the Filipino people. Solutions will not be found easily, nor will they be achieved quickly.

While these solutions will be Filipino ones, designed and carried out by Filipinos, friends of the Philippines abroad, both governments and individuals, can play a useful part. In attempting to help, they must be sensitive to Filipino values and aspirations, and especially to the strong sense of Philippine nationalism. This volume, which brings together the knowledge and suggestions of many American Philippines specialists is designed to contribute to informed policy making in the United States. We hope that it will be useful to our Filipino friends as well.

THE LEGACY OF THE PAST

The Democratic Tradition in the Philippines

To understand why Ferdinand Marcos was overthrown by a peaceful, democratic revolution—a rare occurrence in the Third World—one must be familiar with the Philippine past. That past includes the revolution of 1896, the last of many more localized revolts against Spanish colonial rule, which culminated in the establishment in 1899 of the short-lived Malolos Republic. These events, and the subsequent resistance to the ultimately successful imposition of American colonial rule in place of that of Spain, remain for Filipino historians the proudest time in their nation's history. They symbolize both the Filipino people's nationalism and their desire for constitutional democracy. It is no accident that Filipinos who are conscious of that history have called the events of February 1986 the "Second Philippine Revolution." For in February, Filipinos again asserted both their patriotism and their wish to be governed democratically.

Also important for an understanding of the February revolution, as it is more commonly called, is a recognition of several features of the American colonial presence which began in 1898 and lasted until the Japanese occupation of 1942-1945. Despite its violent beginning, American rule gave to Filipinos extended practice in the workings of competitive democratic politics. As early as 1907 Filipinos elected the first lower house of a national legislature. By 1916 they were electing the upper house as well. In 1935, having been promised complete independence ten years later, they elected their first president, Manuel Quezon, under a constitution modeled upon that of the United States. Some writers have suggested that Quezon, who from 1922 until his death in 1943 was the preeminent figure of Philippine politics, provided a precedent for Marcos' dictatorial rule. One of the contributors to this book, Theodore Friend, rejects that view, pointing out that Quezon never would or could silence his critics and never took steps towards totalitarianism.

While Quezon's *Partido Nacionalista* dominated pre-independence politics, in part because of its strident nationalism, opposing parties always won some seats in the legislature. After 1946, when a closely competitive two-party system took hold, and until Marcos imposed martial law in 1972, control of the presidency changed from one party to the other roughly once every eight years. During that long span of time, the political parties adapted themselves to the evolving conditions and needs of their country by formulating policies likely to win approval of a changing socio-economic elite and the votes of a changing mass electorate.

The long history of close and peaceful competition between two equally legitimate political parties helps to explain why most educated Filipinos were repelled by Marcos's attempts to suppress his political opponents and by his destruction of the existing system of checks and balances. It explains why the leading figures of the two old political parties, many of whom were imprisoned by Marcos during the early years of martial law, maintained their influence after 1972. The legal and political skill of these veteran leaders, their moderation on questions of public policy, and their preference for nonviolent methods of political change helped to make possible the candidacy and the triumph of Corazon C. Aquino. One of those leaders was her late husband, Senator Benigno Aquino, Jr.

A second legacy of American colonialism was the early establishment of a system of free public primary education modeled upon the public school systems of the American states, using English as the language of instruction, and stressing the extension of literacy, citizenship education, and vocational and physical training. Also introduced was a state-supported system of secondary and tertiary education. Maintained and expanded after independence, this public educational system, together with a number of church-related private schools dating from Spanish colonial times, gave the Philippines a more literate voting public and a larger indigenous professional and entrepreneurial class than could be found in any other Southeast Asian society. It has produced a large body of full and part time students, concentrated in the national capital city of Manila. Their aspirations are examined by Benjamin N. Muego. They played a major part in Philippine politics in the years preceding martial law, during the period of the Marcos dictatorship, and in the February revolution which overthrew the former president. Whether as supporters or radical critics of the new government, students remain a force to be reckoned with in the future.

A less happy inheritance from both Spanish and American times was a highly unequal system of agricultural land tenure which, especially in the main rice-growing regions, placed a large class of agricultural tenants under the dominance of and open to exploitation by a politically powerful landowning class. Several Philippine presidents have attempted to alleviate peasant grievances with programs of land reform, but usually have found these efforts blocked by a conservative congress. The condition of the peasantry and the history and prospects for land reform are discussed by two of the contributors to this volume, Benedict J. Tria Kerkvliet and Bruce Koppel.

Finally, despite the historic Filipino aspirations for democracy and an extended national experience in the management of democratic institutions, there also is to be found in the Philippines a long tradition of authoritarianism. Finding its model in the hierarchically structured Filipino family, a topic explored at length by Justin Green, it has produced a long line of domineering political leaders and office holders at both local and higher levels of government. It was to this tradition that Ferdinand Marcos pointed for justification when he established his new system of "constitutional authoritarianism." The widespread Filipino desire for a strong leader remains both a threat and a challenge to President Corazon Aquino.

The Origins of Marcos's New Society

When Marcos imposed martial law in 1972, near the end of his second term as a democratically elected president, his action won widespread public acceptance if not approval. For several years Manila had been rocked by student demonstrations which inconvenienced the city's non-student population. These demonstrations, as well as the nationalistic measures passed by the Philippine congress and endorsed by the courts, had provoked some foreign disinvestment.

Lawlessness in the countryside, much of it the work of armed "goons" employed by local politicians and members of congress, had forced many rural residents to seek refuge in the larger towns. Pre-martial law efforts of the president and his technocrats to adopt programs of economic development had been hampered by a lack of funds resulting from widespread tax evasion. Two incipient rebellions, one by the Communist party's recently formed New Peoples Army, the other by the secessionist Moro National Liberation Front among the Muslim minority of the far South, were causing increasing public concern. The present state of these rebellions, the former still growing, the latter now largely spent, are discussed by Larry A. Niksch and Lela Garner Noble.

To many Filipinos, with the notable exception of the radical left, of some nationalistic businessmen, and of those legislators who found themselves under arrest or deprived of their positions as a result of the abolition of the congress, the reforms imposed by Marcos during the early years of martial law seemed worth the price of a temporary loss of their political liberties. The confiscation of "loose firearms" met with almost universal approval, except among the Muslims, who saw it as designed to leave them defenseless against the continuing influx of Christian settlers into their homeland.

An amnesty for tax-evaders, followed by stiff penalties for those who then failed to pay their taxes, brought about a sharp increase in government revenues. These in turn made possible the institution of an impressive rural infrastructure program which Robert and Beverly Hackenberg call the best and perhaps only lasting achievement of Marcos's New Society. A program of land reform for rice and corn land, more radical than any that the old congress had been willing to approve, was imposed by presidential decree, winning applause from both agricultural tenants and middle class reformers. How many tenants actually benefitted from this reform remains a matter of dispute. Bruce Koppel estimates that only five percent of the rural work force was covered by the program.

In the cities an aggressive program of industrialization, financed in part by heavy government borrowing abroad, seemed to promise a period of rapid economic growth. The president's overruling of some nationalistic economic legislation and court decisions led to a reversal of the earlier outflow of foreign capital. Still, as William Overholt reports, the growth of American investment in the Philippines during

Marcos's New Society years lagged far behind its rate of increase in other Southeast Asian countries.

The Decline of the Marcos Government

Despite the initial acceptance of martial law and the early popularity of many of its reforms, public opinion by the mid-1970s had begun to turn against Marcos. By the last years of that decade he had become widely unpopular. When in 1978 Marcos held the first legislative elections under martial law, Manila was almost solidly in opposition. Had the votes been counted honestly, the imprisoned Senator Aquino, not Mrs. Marcos, would have been declared the front runner in the capital city. At the time of the senator's assassination in August 1983, the country was ready for a massive outburst of protest against the Marcos government.

Why did this drastic shift in public opinion come about so quickly? In part it was due to the nature of Marcos's new political system, a topic discussed by David A. Rosenberg, Ross Marlay, and Linda K. Richter. Criticism of that system came almost immediately from the country's many lawyers. The new form of government, described by Marcos as "constitutional authoritarianism," was alleged to be in harmony with Philippine tradition while retaining the essentials of Western constitutional government. It certainly was authoritarian in giving unusually great powers to the head of state. But it was not "constitutional" in the true sense. Though emblazoned with legalistic forms reflecting Marcos's background as a "bar top-notcher," it lacked the essential features of constitutional government: That it protect the basic rights of citizens against the state; that it serve as a sea-anchor providing stable institutions and procedures in a turbulent sea of legislative change; and that it be supported by a national consensus that crossed party lines.

Almost from its beginning, the new form of government was flawed by the manner of its adoption. That relied, at critical junctures, upon the bribing of members of the 1971-1973 constitutional convention with offers of cash or assured seats in a projected Interim Assembly. It was ratified by the voters by "acclamation" at open public meetings rather than through secret balloting in a plebiscite as was required under the previous constitution. These dubious procedures, evidently designed to assure the ratification of the new instrument in the possible absence of real majority support, undermined its claim to legality in the minds of respected members of the legal profession and led to the resignation of an outraged chief justice. Subsequent changes in the constitution, all of them seemingly designed for the convenience of the president, were ratified at hastily called referenda which left little opportunity for discussion or opposition.[1]

In its final form, after constitutional amendments pushed through in 1981, Marcos's system of government resembled that of the French Fifth Republic. There was an elected president with broad powers to issue decrees in place of law. A prime minister and cabinet, wholly dependent upon the president's favor, executed his wishes. A weakened legislature could neither block the president's emergency decrees nor control his prime minister and cabinet.

But resemblance to the system of government devised by Charles de Gaulle was more apparent than real. In France, the most executive-dominated country of Western Europe, the president's power has been restrained by the knowledge that elections will be contested freely and the results subjected to honest counting, that the press remains free, and that citizens can exercise their civil and political rights without fear of violence at the hands of the state or of private agents of the ruler. In the Philippines under Marcos none of these were the case. Marcos governed as he pleased, using his new emergency power under the 1973 constitution to issue a flood of sometimes secret decrees, as well as orders and letters of instruction, many of them favoring his family and friends but protected by the appearance of legality.

Aside from Benigno Aquino, other elected officials and journalists known to be outspoken critics of the regime were murdered by persons unknown. Suspicion rested both with the officially authorized or protected death squads of the paramilitary "lost command" in the South and the plain-clothed "secret marshals" in Manila, as well as with the "sparrow" assassination squads of the communist NPA. A formerly bipartisan and vigorously independent Commission on Elections was transformed by Marcos from being the guarantor of fair elections into what the opposition saw as a body tolerant of if not actively engaged in electoral fraud in favor of the ruling party.

[1]For a detailed account of the events and legal controversy surrounding the adoption of the 1973 constitution, see Rolando V. del Carmen, "Constitutionality and Judicial Politics," in David A. Rosenberg, ed., *Marcos and Martial Law in the Philippines* (Ithaca, N.Y.: Cornell University Press, 1979), pp. 85-112.

13

Also among the reasons for the growing disaffection with Marcos was a mismanaged economy which, during his last two years in office, showed negative rates of growth. This brought increasing unemployment and declining real incomes to the rural and urban working class. Among the professional and property-owning classes, it produced a large-scale flight of skill and capital abroad. The economic legacy of the Marcos years, the options for Aquino, as well as the special problems of the sugar industry, are discussed by six of our contributors, William H. Overholt, Gustav Ranis, Charles W. Lindsey, David Reinah, Bruce M. Koppel, and Richard Hooley.

Gustav Ranis traces the country's economic problems to the decision, taken in the 1960s, to pursue a narrow strategy of capital-intensive "secondary" import substitution. Meanwhile, opportunities for the expansion of agricultural and nonagricultural production in the countryside and for export-oriented labor-intensive manufacturing were neglected. These errors were exacerbated during the years of Marcos's absolute rule by a growing foreign debt and by the misdirection of borrowed funds to unproductive governmental prestige projects, to sweetheart loans for inefficient "crony capitalists," to costly election campaigns, and to the pockets of members of the regime.

The Military Under Marcos

One of the most noticeable features of the Marcos years was the increasing role of the military in governmental affairs. Since taking office in 1966 as an elected president, Marcos had favored the armed forces in various ways. When he imposed martial law in 1972, that step was prepared with the help of a group of his senior officers. However, a few generals opposed the president's move. One of them, General Rafael Ileto, has become President Aquino's new minister of defense.

While the armed forces grew in numbers under Marcos and increased their role in government, their quality as a fighting force deteriorated. Increasingly, promotions were determined by personal loyalty to Marcos and to his chief of staff, General Fabian Ver, instead of by seniority and combat performance. A greatly expanded Manila-based Presidential Security Command and Ver's National Intelligence and Security Agency became the armed forces privileged elite. Meanwhile, troops in the field, assigned to the less rewarding task of combating communist and Muslim insurgents, found themselves starved for supplies, without adequate transportation and communications or periodic re-training, and forced to live off the land when their pay was delayed. As a result, in the view of an American military observer, not more than one in eight combat units were properly prepared to take the field against the communist New Peoples Army when Marcos fell. The present state of the military's readiness is a matter of concern both to the Aquino government and to its American ally. That topic is discussed at length by William Wise.

These conditions led to the formation in 1985 of the Reform the Armed Forces Movement (RAM), an informal group of field and company-grade officers committed to restoring professionalism in the armed forces. While denying any intention of rebellion (a claim not taken seriously by Marcos, and disproved by later events), and making no effort to keep their organization a secret, RAM officers pledged themselves to report instances of military misbehavior to their immediate superiors, to President Marcos, and, if that proved ineffective, to "the Filipino people."

Many of the members of RAM including their leaders, Army Colonel Gregorio Honasan and Navy Captain Rex Robles were on the staff of Defense Minister Juan Ponce Enrile. Evidently, Enrile saw RAM as a potential source of support in the internal politics of the Marcos regime. A long-time friend and college fraternity brother of Marcos, Enrile had been defense chief since the beginning of Marcos's presidency. He had played an important part in making the plans for the martial law and, as he has since revealed, helped to stage the mock attack upon his car that served as a pretext for its imposition in 1972.

In recent years however Enrile had been the loser in a contest for influence with General Ver. Marcos favored Ver, leaving Enrile as the nominal administrative head of his ministry but excluded from the chain of command. Another loser in the contest with Ver was Vice Chief of Staff General Fidel V. Ramos. Though a West Point graduate, widely respected for his personal integrity and military professionalism and like General Ver a relative of Marcos, Ramos had been passed over in his quest for the post of chief of staff when Marcos selected the ROTC-trained Ver instead. Ramos too had ties with RAM. Those ties were to become vitally important in February 1986.

The Growth of the New Peoples Army

Contributing to the fall of the Marcos government was the growth of the communist-led New Peoples Army. The communist threat had been

Marcos's main justification for imposing martial law. But his prescription aggravated the disease it was designed to cure. By the end of 1985, after thirteen years of Marcos's authoritarian government, the New Peoples Army had grown from a small band of fewer than a thousand novice guerrillas into a seasoned force of some twenty thousand. Marcos's ineffectiveness in stemming this growth accounts to a large degree for the loss of what had seemed to be his most loyal sources of support: the Philippine armed forces and the Reagan administration.

The rapid growth in the strength of the CCP-NPA cannot be blamed wholly on the Marcos administration. Its causes are varied. Some involve communist leadership and strategy, notably a deliberate effort to attract new sources of support. And some can be traced to long-standing ills of Philippine society which have become more serious, in part because of Marcos's misgovernment.

Communism has a long history in the Philippines, beginning with the founding of the Partido Komunista ng Pilipinas (PKP) in 1930. Until the mid-1960s, however, its only substantial source of support were the peasants of central and southern Luzon, a large, densely populated rice-growing region surrounding Manila. That region was noted for its extraordinarily high rates of absentee landownership and of sharecropping by landless agricultural tenants. Tenant unions under communist or socialist leadership had existed in central and southern Luzon since the 1930s. It was this region, comprising roughly one-fifth of the country's provinces that, under a communist-led popular front, nurtured the "Hukbalahap" guerrilla army of the 1940s. The Huks combined resistance to the Japanese occupation with the seizure of lands from landowners accused of collaboration with the Japanese.

Although the Huks were disarmed by General MacArthur on his return to the Philippines in 1945, Huk leaders or sympathizers won six congressional seats at the first postwar elections in 1946. When they were denied seating by the congress on the grounds that they had been elected through force and intimidation, the Huks turned once again to guerrilla warfare. By the late 1940s, Huk units were operating near the gates of Manila. Their subsequent defeat in the early 1950s can be attributed in large part to the skill of a young former congressman who as secretary of national defense and then as president devised —with some help from American advisors—an anti-Huk strategy of "all-out friendship and all-out force." That strategy combined grants of frontier homesteads to surrendered Huks and promises of land reform for agricultural tenants in general with an intensified military drive against Huk units in their central Luzon redoubts by the newly invigorated armed forces.

In a limited geographic area suited for the application of concentrated military force, among a peasantry whose grievances were addressed by a sympathetic and immensely popular new president, and during a time of rapid economic growth, Magsaysay's strategy yielded striking results. By the mid-1950s the Huk threat had abated. Most of the members of the Moscow-oriented Politburo had been captured. Other communist leaders surrendered in later years. The majority of Hukbalahap guerrillas had returned to their farms. Some Huk units remaining in the field, or units claiming to be Huks, degenerated into simple bandits and protection racketeers.

The Philippine communist movement took a new and more formidable turn with the formation in the mid-1960s of a break-away "Maoist" Communist Party of the Philippines (CPP). Its history and present role are examined by Larry K. Niksch. Led by a group of university instructors and students, the Maoist party turned once again to armed revolution. At the same time it set out to broaden its base beyond that of its old Soviet-oriented predecessor and competitor. It began to infiltrate the leadership of organized labor and the working press and to create a powerful though ostensibly noncommunist youth organization, the *Kabataang Makabayan* or Nationalist Youth. At the same time, the new party made efforts to extend its rural base beyond central and southern Luzon, where Marcos's land reform had reduced the incidence of share tenancy, by sending student activists to all parts of the country to organize peasants in their home provinces while on vacation from their universities and colleges in Manila.

One reason for the ability of the Communist party to win widespread adherence among Filipino intellectuals is that there was little serious competition from other movements of the left. As the colonial subjects of a predominantly Protestant country that itself had been little touched by Marxist thought, pre-independence Filipinos studying in the United States or taught by American teachers in the Philippines received little exposure to the Christian Democratic movements that have produced strong non-Marxist reformist parties in Catholic Europe and Latin America. Also, few Filipinos had the opportunity to acquaint themselves with the nonrevolutionary tradition of democratic socialism that captured the minds of students in former British and French colonies.

(A small Central Luzon-based socialist party had disappeared after being absorbed into the communist-led popular front in the 1930s.)

Therefore, when communism became fashionable among Filipino intellectuals in the 1960s, it confronted no rival social democratic party and faced only weak competition from the embryonic Christian Democratic movement led by Senator Raul Manglapus that was belatedly attempting to win followers at church-related private colleges attended mainly by students from the prosperous classes. In this vacuum on the left, Marxism thrived. As a mode of analysis that had been withheld from Filipinos by their American teachers, Marxism had the additional attraction of representing for its new converts a rejection of the intellectual tutelage of the former colonizing power.

Another reason for the Communist party's success in winning adherents among students and other intellectuals, and thus in bringing into their movement a large body of well-educated and dedicated activists with familial connections among well-placed members of the middle and upper classes in all parts of the Philippine archipelago, was the party's skill in placing itself at the head of a powerful nationalist movement that swept the country during the 1960s and that continues to be a strong force in the Philippines today.[2] Finally, CPP/NPA growth can be attributed also to their ability to persuade many noncommunist Filipinos that the NPA alone was ready and able to employ a method that could bring an end to the Marcos government. That method was "armed struggle."

Among the peasants and working class, a strong reason for joining or supporting the NPA was the condition of their livelihood. As noted earlier, when Ramon Magsaysay defeated the Hukbalahap rebellion, the economy was on the upswing. During most of the Marcos years, the opposite was the case. The reasons for this, including the Marcos government's contribution to this economic decline, have been mentioned. The effects of the ailing economy upon the rural and urban poor are described in detail by Benjamin Kerkvliet and Robert and Beverly Hackenburg. For the NPA, the result has been a steady stream of recruits, especially among the young landless and unemployed rural poor.

---

[2]For a brief discussion of the politics of nationalism during the postwar years, see the writer's contribution to John Bresnan, ed., *Crisis in the Philippines, The Marcos Era and Beyond* (Princeton, N.J.: Princeton University Press, 1986), pp. 126-129.

The Church in Opposition

In this predominantly Catholic society, the Catholic church, through its premier cardinal, its bishops, its clergy, and its laymen, played an important part in the events that led to the fall of Ferdinand Marcos and the coming to power of Corazon Aquino. That marked a break in the nature and degree of the church's involvement in political affairs. Under Spain, the church had been the state's partner in the dual mission of extending the empire and spreading the faith. Parish priests in each locality oversaw the management of local affairs by a native elite. American colonial rule brought a separation of church and state. That separation continued after independence, except on the relatively rare occasions when the church mobilized its laymen to defend itself against hostile governmental action. When members of the clergy took positions on public matters, they were usually on the side of conservatism.

All this changed after martial law, albeit in an incremental fashion. From 1972 onwards some individual members of the clergy, and Task Force Detainees sponsored by the superiors of the major religious orders, criticized the Marcos government for its mistreatment of political prisoners and for its habit of riding roughshod over the interests of the urban poor. The political involvement of the hierarchy of the Philippine church however can be traced through the actions of Manila's Jaime Cardinal Sin and through the pronouncements of the Council of Bishops. That involvement grew slowly, beginning with protests by the cardinal against the arrest of politically active members of the clergy, moving to increasingly broad criticism of other policies of the regime, and after Benigno Aquino's assassination, to open appeals to the president to step down. Finally, after Marcos announced that a presidential election would be held in February 1986, Cardinal Sin played a decisive role in bringing together the united opposition slate and later in mobilizing the "people power" that helped to bring an end to the Marcos regime. Churchmen and Catholic laymen continue to exercise a significant if less visible political influence today. A full account of the church's role is given by Robert L. Youngblood.

The End of the Marcos Government: February Elections, February Revolution

During the first six years of martial law, Marcos governed without a legislature. In 1978, however, he held elections for an Interim Legislative Assembly. Six years later, in 1984, a regular legislative assembly was elected. Elections for local and provincial offices had been held in 1980. As for the presidency itself, after serving for twelve years without a renewed mandate from the voters, Marcos in 1981 called a new presidential election. At all of these elections, the president or his KBL party supporters won handily. Each time, however, there were bitter charges by the president's opponents that his victories were made possible only by large-scale electoral fraud. In 1981, in fact, the major opposition parties ran no presidential candidate against Marcos because of their conviction that the procedure would not be fair.

On November 3, 1985, with more than a year remaining of his latest presidential term but beset by a rising tide of criticism both at home and abroad, Marcos acted to once again demonstrate his political strength by calling a "snap" presidential election. The date finally set for the election, February 7, gave a seemingly divided opposition little time to decide on a single champion and to organize their campaign. To the surprise of skeptics, they managed to do both.

The candidate chosen was Corazon Aquino. Because of her unique position as the courageous widow of a martyred popular hero, "Cory" as she is affectionately called by her many admirers, was recognized as the only figure who could unite the opposition and hope to defeat the incumbent president. More than anyone else, she symbolized the grievances of the nation. In campaigning against her, Marcos would be obliged to exercise some restraint, leaving criticism of his opponent to another woman, the by then widely unpopular Imelda Marcos. Assessments of the personal qualities of the new president are presented by two of our contributors, Guy Pauker and William H. Overholt.

In her election campaign Mrs. Aquino was supported by a broad array of opposition groups. These included the remnants of the two pre-martial law political parties, the Nacionalistas and Liberals, as well as several new parties which had been organized to contest the Assembly elections of 1978 and 1984. Some time earlier, the diverse parties had formed themselves into two "umbrella" groups, UNIDO and PDP-Laban. UNIDO's leader was Salvador Laurel. Because of PDP-Laban's association with her late husband, it chose Corazon Aquino as its champion. Thus the Aquino-Laurel presidential-vice presidential ticket represented an alliance of the two umbrella groups.

An important part in the election was played by the National Movement for Free Elections (NAMFREL). This citizen's organization traced its roots to the early 1950s when it helped the official Commission on Elections (COMELEC), to keep elections clean. In recent years, beginning with the Legislative Assembly elections of 1984, NAMFREL was not COMELEC's helper but its rival. With COME-LEC obviously biased in Marcos's favor, the opposition in February could look only to NAMFREL's 400,000 to 500,000 volunteer election watchers for protection. Marcos accused NAMFREL of sympathizing with the opposition. That charge was certainly true. But in view of the obvious determination of both the government and COMELEC to manipulate the election in Marcos's favor, no Marcos follower was likely to help NAMFREL in its effort to assure an honest counting of the votes. At forthcoming elections, supervised by a cleansed and genuinely independent COMELEC, NAMFREL presumably will have a smaller and more neutral part to play.

No Philippine election has been contested more intensely than that of February 7, 1986. For Marcos it was a battle for survival. His private pre-election surveys, it was reported, had given him the unexpected news that in most regions of the country, he was running far behind his challenger. Ross Marlay reports that he was being deserted by many of his local leaders who were ashamed to be associated with his regime. Perhaps the underlying reason for Marcos's unexpectedly dim electoral prospects in the provinces, once his strongest source of support, was deepening rural poverty. Still, Marcos was determined to win at any cost, and marshalled his forces to make certain of victory.

Opposition leaders were equally determined to win. They and their followers knew that this was their last opportunity to restore democracy. Had Marcos prevailed, the prediction of the left that he could be ousted only by revolution would have been confirmed. That would have driven many supporters of the democratic opposition into the communist camp. No moderate leader would have asked his followers to risk their lives again in a futile election campaign. That explains the eagerness of so many Filipinos to carry the day for Cory Aquino and their later determination not to let her be cheated of her victory.

The president's campaign to win by any means was carried out on a truly massive scale. The methods used, some of them not seen before at Philippine elections but almost identical in various parts of the country, leave little doubt that they were centrally directed and coordinated. An immense amount of money was distributed, much of it newly printed currency. Cheating took place at many stages of the election process, each stage adding further distortion to the final outcome. It began long before the day of the election with the preparation of voters lists. There was large-scale multiple registration of Marcos followers who on election day appeared as "flying voters." At the same time, the names of many known Marcos opponents were either deleted or transferred from one precinct register to another. On election day many could not find out where they were supposed to vote.

During the weeks preceding the election, large numbers of extra ballot boxes were manufactured and stuffed with pre-marked ballots. On election day these were forcibly substituted for the proper boxes by gangs of armed men. Finally, some time before the election, public school teachers throughout the country, who traditionally serve as local polling officials because of their presumed integrity, were offered large sums of money to sign their names to blank tally sheets.

When election day arrived, it was marked by violence or fraud at every stage: during the voting, the counting, the transporting of ballot boxes from remote villages to the municipal halls, and, according to the testimony of a group of courageous women computer operators at COMELEC, in the reporting of the incoming results by that sadly flawed institution itself. Surprisingly, much of the most blatant cheating took place in Greater Manila, in full view of a large foreign press corps.

Several conclusions seemed unavoidable: For such cheating to have been carried out on any but the smallest scale, it was necessary that the perpetrators be in exclusive control of the election machinery, or that they must have had large numbers of men under arms. Marcos's followers met both of these conditions. The democratic opposition met neither of them. The NPA, which had men under arms, boycotted the election. The second conclusion is that, in view of the multi-stage process of the cheating, even NAMFREL's count of the votes was seriously distorted in Marcos's favor. By the time NAMFREL's observers were allowed to see the tally sheets, much of the manipulation of the final outcome had already been accomplished. In this observer's opinion, had the election procedures been honest at every stage, Aquino and Laurel would have won by a landslide instead of by the fairly narrow majority tabulated by NAMFREL.

The Commission on Elections, however, reported a Marcos victory and on February 15 the Legislative Assembly duly declared him the winner, together with his vice-presidential running mate, Arturo Tolentino. But that was not to be the end of the matter. Corazon Aquino, with a display of self-assurance, simple eloquence, and courage that became infectious, declared that she had won the election and called on Marcos to hand over power forthwith. If he did not, she would call on the people to demonstrate or to join her in passive resistance until he complied. Two tension-filled weeks were to pass, however, between the election and the "four day revolution" which marked the end of the Marcos government.

In the meantime, Marcos and General Ver were preparing a harsh crackdown against the president's opponents, including members of the Reform the Armed Forces Movement. For this, it is reported, they would employ not only elements of the military but also bands of armed "goons," some of them recruited in the criminal underworld and released from prison for that purpose. As a preemptive countermove, members of RAM made plans to seize the presidential palace, with the help of Presidential Security Command units inside the palace compound. Their intention, it is reported, was to set up a revolutionary government under a military junta headed by Enrile and Ramos.

Hearing of their plan, General Ver moved to arrest the members of RAM. The first to be arrested, early on February 22, were some of Enrile's Security Group, who had been assigned as body guards to Marcos's Trade and Industry Minister Roberto V. Ongpin, brother of Aquino's Finance Minister Jaime V. Ongpin. Ongpin complained to Enrile, who thus learned that Ver had begun to move against RAM, and presumably against himself and Ramos as well. Thus began the revolt that toppled Marcos. Enrile hastened to his headquarters at Camp Aquinaldo and alerted Ramos at Constabulary Camp Crane. At a press conference in the afternoon of February 22, they announced their break with the president, giving among other reasons their belief that the election had been won by Corazon Aquino.

The success of the revolt, which began with a mere 250 officers and men, was made possible in large part by "people power," in the form of the massed civilians who answered the call of Cardinal Sin to rally to protect the rebels. Near the end of the revolt, their numbers were estimated at more than a million. They were good-natured and included members of all social classes as well as many members of the clergy. Notably absent were the usual strident demonstrators of the radical left. Had these been in the forefront, Marcos's soldiers might not have held their fire. The "people power revolution" was a triumph of the political moderates and of the church, an all too rare occurrence in the Third World.

The revolt succeeded also because of the cohesiveness of an officers corps whose members were unwilling to combat each other to defend a tottering regime. From the beginning of the revolt, rebellious officers had been in telephone contact with fellow officers still under Ver's command with appeals to join or at least not to suppress the revolt. As a tide of defecting units increased, Marcos's position deteriorated. Had he ordered an attack on the rebels when the revolt began, it could have been crushed easily. But by February 24, which saw the defection of major operational units of the air force as well as of the navy, the tide had turned decisively against the president.

On February 25, abandoned by several members of his cabinet, his armed forces, and the United States, Marcos took his oath of office at the palace, while Aquino took hers at Club Filipino. A day later, having been refused his request that he be flown to his native Ilocos, where he could have rallied his forces, Marcos was on his way to Guam.

AQUINO'S FIRST YEAR

Achievements and Persisting Problems

Since the February revolution, much has changed for the better in the Philippines. A dictatorial government too long in power has been replaced by the government of a popular new leader. Filipinos, who brought this about through a collective display of courage, have a renewed sense of pride in their shared achievement. Civil liberties have been restored and political prisoners released. The press is free once again. A new constitution, designed to prevent a recurrence of some of the abuses of the past, is to be submitted for ratification to the Filipino people. The prospect of elections free of governmental intimidation has created a ferment of political activity.

The new government's economic policies have been set and some progress has been made toward their implementation.[3] To deal with the

---

[3]For information on the current state of the Philippine economy, and on the government's economic plans and performance, the writer is indebted to Mr. Omar T. Cruz of the Center for Research and Communication, Manila.

present crisis, an emergency employment program has been adopted, though its effects are yet to be felt. For the future, however, the private sector is to be the "engine of growth" while the government's role will be reduced. Rural growth is to be encouraged through an emphasis on small-scale, labor-intensive, rural-based industry. Industrial efficiency and consumer welfare are to be fostered through import liberalization, applied so far to over 700 products, and through the ending of special privileges for favored entrepreneurs. Monopolies in sugar, coconuts, and grains are being dismantled. Unproductive government firms are to be privatized. Foreign investment will be encouraged except in some industries partly or wholly reserved for Filipinos. In all this the government is moving deliberately, consistent with Gustav Ranis' advice that it is wiser to develop a consistent, carefully sequenced package of reforms than to act precipitously in order to satisfy a popular demand for action.

Despite these accomplishments, President Aquino's first year in office has not been a time of smooth sailing. The euphoria of the early months has turned into a sober recognition that much that was hoped for under a new government has not yet been realized.

A major disappointment for the new president is the continuing communist rebellion. With Marcos gone, together with General Fabian Ver, and with the military under the command of a respected professional soldier, General Fidel Ramos, it was hoped that many of the less ideologically committed New Peoples Army guerrillas would come down from the hills and give their support to the new government. Mrs. Aquino on taking power released Jose Maria Sison, founder of the CCP, and Bernabe Buscayo, his leading military commander, who had been captured and imprisoned some years earlier. By treating them as fellow victims of Marcos instead of as enemies of the state, she hoped to encourage them to call a halt to the rebellion and to enter the political arena as peaceful contestants for elective offices.

To date, NPA defections have been disappointingly few in number. Except where a local guerrilla leader has chosen to negotiate the surrender of his unit, few NPA members have surrendered. To what degree this is to be explained by the guerrillas' ideological commitment and sense of comradeship, by NPA threats of retaliation against defectors and their families, or by the government's failure to devise safe-conduct procedures for those who wish to surrender, is not clear.

As for the communist leadership, Jose Maria Sison has used his freedom to help to organize the *Partido ng Bayan* (Peoples Party) as a legal surrogate for the still-illegal Communist party, while at the same time proclaiming that armed revolution remains the main strategy of the CCP. Having thus gained admission to the legal political arena before abandoning the battlefield, the communists would seem to have little incentive to lay down their arms.

Still, Mrs. Aquino has committed her government to seeking a peaceful end to the rebellion through negotiations with its leaders. Only if this fails will she turn to the military option. On December 10, as a preliminary step to such negotiations, she began a sixty day cease-fire with the the NPA. In these efforts she has the understanding and public support of her military leaders and of the American government. Faced with the many other problems left to her by her predecessor, the Philippine president cannot be blamed for not wishing to inherit a fratricidal war as well.

The economy too has brought its share of disappointments. While foreign exchange rates have been stabilized, inflation and interest rates have been reduced, and capital flight has ceased, a major source of frustration for the new administration has been the slow pace of returning investment. The flight of Filipino capital abroad between 1965 and 1985 has been estimated as between ten and thirty billion dollars.[4] Such a sum dwarfs anything that the Philippines can realistically expect in the form of new foreign aid or investment. A substantial part of this Filipino money abroad is believed to belong to the Marcoses and their cronies. But large sums also were sent out by Filipinos who saw no hope for profit-making while Marcos and his friends monopolized the best business opportunities in the Philippines.

Despite their overwhelming election-time support for Corazon Aquino, the Philippine business community, both Filipino and resident Chinese, have been reluctant to make new business investments. With a high rate of unemployment, the market for consumer goods remains dead. Many existing firms are operating at half-capacity. Few businessmen have money to invest. And there is concern about the effects of trade liberalization as well as about the continuing threat from the NPA. All these may be good reasons for caution, but until Filipinos display a readiness to invest in their own country, foreigners will be

---

[4]Estimate by the Center for Research and Communication, Manila.

reluctant to bring their capital to the Philippines.

More heartening for the Aquino government has been the level of foreign financial assistance. Some of this was expected to come from the United States. On January 30, a week before the February election, President Reagan had announced:

> If the will of the Filipino people is expressed in an election that Filipinos accept as credible—and if whoever is elected undertakes fundamental economic, political and military reforms—we should consider, in consultation with the Congress, a significantly larger program of economic and military assistance for the Philippines for the next five years. This would be over and above the current levels of assistance we are providing.

While the increase in United States aid to the Aquino government has been relatively modest—$350 million in extra economic aid and military assistance added to regularly programmed support—the total new grants and loans from all foreign governments and international financial institutions amount to somewhat under two billion dolars.[5] This the Aquino government hopes to supplement with what can be recovered of wrongfully acquired wealth sent abroad by the Marcoses and their associates.

Changing the Guard

Proclaiming her government as "revolutionary in origin and nature, democratic in essence, and essentially transitory in character," President Aquino a month after taking office abolished the 1973 Marcos Constitution and proclaimed a new, interim "Freedom Constitution" which was to remain in force until a new permanent constitution could be written and adopted. This interim constitution placed all govern-

---

[5]Japan, which is the Philippines' largest aid donor, averaging $350 to $400 million yearly, pledged an additional $650 million as a result of President Aquino's November visit. The European Economic Community, together with West Germany, Canada, and Australia, pledged between $50 and $60 million. The World Bank has signed a $300 million economic recovery loan, the International Monetary Fund a $508 million standby agreement, and the Asian Development Bank a $100 million loan. In addition, efforts are being made to promote foreign investment in and increase foreign markets for the Philippines.

mental powers in the president's hands, though guaranteeing respect for the previous constitution's Bill of Rights. Using her new power, the president moved quickly to remove Marcos followers from important positions in both central and local government. At the center, she dissolved the Legislative Assembly, with its two-thirds majority of Marcos supporters which had been elected in 1984. At the local level she instructed her minister of local government to discharge large numbers of elected provincial and municipal government officials who were Marcos followers and to replace them with temporary "officers in charge." Many other officials appointed under Marcos were removed as well, including some judges.

These changes have provoked angry protests from officials who have lost their jobs, as well as from their friends and supporters. They point out that in her election campaign Mrs. Aquino promised to restore democracy and the rule of law. By removing elected local officials, they charge she has ignored the will of the voters and thus is as dictatorial as her predecessor. By removing judges with lifetime tenure, they assert, she undermines the independence of the judiciary. In the same vein Mrs. Aquino has been criticized for abolishing the constitution under which she was elected.

While these arguments appear reasonable, the drastic measures taken by the new president would seem to have been unavoidable. Had Aquino recognized the Marcos Constitution, she would have had to accept the legality of all of Marcos's dictatorial actions, including innumerable interventions in the economy under his power to issue decrees. Had she not removed many Marcos loyalists in the judiciary, these could have blocked the new government's attempt to confiscate the ill-gotten wealth of the former president and his cronies. Had she kept the Legislative Assembly in being, its pro-Marcos majority could have denied her the measures she needs for governmental and social reform. Had she left pro-Marcos local officials in place, these could have sabotaged her rural programs.

When coming from Marcos and his supporters, complaints about the new government's removal of officials seems hypocritical, since the former president gave himself the power to appoint and remove all governmental officials at will. But criticism has come from other quarters as well. There is intense and sincere disagreement on this issue because of the peculiar nature of the Marcos regime. Marcos behaved dictatorially, and held on to his position by highly dubious means. But, especially at lower levels of government, the system had both dictatorial and democratic features. Assemblymen and local officials were elected to their offices. Many won their posts only with the help of Marcos's "guns, goons and gold," and then misused their power. But other Marcos men were genuinely popular leaders who would have won even in honest elections. Their abrupt removal, and the uneven quality of their replacements, has weakened some local governments. The controversy will continue until local and congressional elections are held in 1987. Then popular leaders, discharged because of their past connection with Marcos, will have the opportunity to vindicate themselves by winning election once again.

To non-Filipinos familiar with the fate of those associated with overturned dictatorships in other countries, Aquino's treatment of Marcos's followers does not appear to be overly vindictive. If she has erred, it would seem, it has been on the side of excessive leniency. From the beginning, her aim has been reconciliation. She has, it is true, appointed commissions to recover any illegally acquired wealth of the Marcoses and their cronies and to investigate abuses of civil rights. Whether such investigations will lead to many prosecutions remains to be seen. At the same time, the president has welcomed into her government and appointed to the constitutional commission not a few members of the previous regime. Furthermore, some of its most blatant offenders remain untouched. Thus the officer most notorious for abusing political prisoners remains free. He showed his gratitude by taking part in the Manila Hotel escapade but again was not punished.[6] At the other ideological extreme, an officer who in Marcos's time defected to the New Peoples Army has been reinstated, promoted, and now is celebrated as the "first reform officer." Most astounding to non-Filipinos has been a government prosecutor's announcement that General Ver will not be among those retried for the murder of Benigno Aquino. The reason: His return from abroad to face trial would provoke "mischief" among the military.

Mrs. Aquino's policy of reconciliation reflects her own Christian

---

[6]The decision to forgive the Manila Hotel rebels reportedly was taken by Defense Minister Enrile. Then Deputy Defense Minister Rafael Ileto's opinion was that "she should have come down hard on those guys." *The Christian Science Monitor*, November 12, 1986.

beliefs as well as the fact that some important Marcos followers helped in the overthrow of Marcos. It also reflects the habits of a society in which men of status and influence are almost never held to account for their offenses against lesser persons or against the state but claim the right to share their own immunity with their dependents. Such a society can quickly put past conflicts behind it. In that respect the speedy post-World War II reentry into politics of those who collaborated with the Japanese foretells a similar post-Marcos accommodation. Still, this cultural bent for assaults upon the public interest obliges one to ask whether Philippine society, or the Aquino government, can recognize and defend itself against the genuine enemies of its reestablished but still fragile democracy.[7] This having been said, one cannot fail to be impressed by the solidarity shown in the critical days of February among both soldiers and civilians. As Ross Marlay suggests, the Filipino inclination towards forgiveness and reconciliation can be a source of strength for the Filipino people in the difficult times that lie ahead.

The New Constitution

A constitutional commission, appointed by the president to draft a new constitution, finished its work in October. The draft is to be submitted to the people for ratification in a referendum on February 2, 1987. As in other countries when new constitutions are written in the shadow of a traumatic past, it was designed to guard against the recurrence of a variety of specific previous abuses.

The new constitution abandons the constitutional innovations of the martial law period—which first promised Westminster-style parliamentary democracy but soon replaced this with a presidentially dominated autocracy. Instead, it will restore the 1935 constitution's American-style presidential-congressional system with its institutionalized checks and balances. That earlier constitution's checks against the arbitrary exercise of presidential power are augmented by provisions narrowing the conditions permitting the suspension of the writ of *habeus corpus* or

---

[7]Samuel Huntington defined the public interest as the interest of governmental institutions and processes. A society that does not preserve the integrity of these can maintain neither unity nor order. Samuel P. Huntington, *Political Order in Changing Societies* (New Haven: Yale University Press, 1968), pp. 24-32.

the proclamation of martial law and giving to both the congress and the supreme court the power to revoke such presidential actions.

Also designed to make more difficult the establishment of a new dictatorship are a one-term six year presidency. There are also limits on the number of consecutive terms for which sitting senators, congressmen, and local officials can seek reelection. There are new safeguards against the infringement of civil liberties by the state. At the same time, the new constitution seeks both to protect citizens and to strengthen the legal authority of the state by prohibiting the maintenance of private armies, one of the main reasons for the breakdown of rural law and order in the past.

As a reaction to the centralizing measures of the Marcos era, the new constitution increases the taxing powers of local governments and grants some degree of autonomy to Muslim and tribal regions. Reflecting the views of its business supporters, it commits the state to a private enterprise economy controlled by Filipinos. Reflecting the interests of the peasant and trade union members of Aquino's constituency, it incorporates commitments to agrarian reform and to the welfare of labor. While reaffirming the separation of church and state, the constitution reflects the influence of the church by committing the state to equally protecting the life of the mother and the unborn from conception. It permits religious teaching in public schools with parental permission, and allows state aid to students, in both public and private schools.

When she appointed the constitutional commission, Mrs. Aquino instructed its members to design a new legislature but not to do that legislature's work for it. At the same time, she promised not to interfere with their work or to overrule it. Disregarding her instructions and assuming she would adhere to her promise, CONCOM wrote numerous substantive policy prescriptions into the constitutional draft. These may limit the options of future presidents and congresses in matters of domestic and foreign policy.

The return to the presidential-congressional form of government avoids a disadvantage of parliamentary government: The danger of unstable coalition cabinets under what could have become a highly fragmented multi-party system. An elected presidency is likely to limit the number of political parties to those that have a serious chance of winning the presidency. The result could be a two-party or three-party system, though one marked by clearer ideological divisions than those which distinguished the two major parties before martial law.

Still, some minor party representation in the House of Representatives is assured by a constitutional provision requiring that one-fifth of its members be elected under a party list system.

Whether the constitutional checks against the misuse of executive power will prove to be effective will depend less on the wording of the new constitution than on the political setting in which the Philippines finds itself in future years. That setting also will determine whether major social reforms mandated by the constitution can be achieved. Checks and balances are most secure in normal times. In a national emergency, they may buckle under the demands of a ruler who believes that he alone can save the nation. Social reformist goals enshrined in a constitution can only be realized if they have the legislative and budgetary support of a future congress. That will depend upon the desires of the voters and upon the financial resources of the state.

Divisions in the Aquino Government

The broad "Cory coalition" was designed to win the election that ousted Marcos. President Aquino gave all of its elements some representation in her cabinet. Thus, unlike the one-party cabinets of previous presidents, her cabinet includes members of both PDP-Laban and UNIDO. In addition, she brought into her governing coalition the two Marcos subordinates whose revolt against their chief helped her to assume the presidency, Defense Minister Enrile and General Fidel Ramos.

Such a diverse coalition is not as well suited to governing as to winning an election. It has been troubled by disagreements over public policy as well as by the rival political ambitions of some of its members. The issues that divide the cabinet involve both domestic and foreign policy, a fact that is reflected in the way different groups in the cabinet are described by political commentators. One group has been labeled the "progressives" or "nationalists," the others the "conservatives" or "pro-Americans."[8]

---

[8]*Ang Katipunan,* a news magazine expressing the views of the radical left, in describing the members of the government who accompanied President Aquino to Washington in September grouped them as follows: "Progressives"—Audit Minister Teofisto Guingona, National Economic and Development Authority chief Solita Monsod, Press

In domestic matters, the conservatives favor a free market economy, foreign trade liberalization, and policies designed to attract foreign investment. The progressives too accept a free market economy, but are more inward looking. They stress the need to protect Filipino manufacturers against foreign competition and give high priority to the welfare of the poor and the working class, if need be at the cost of export competitiveness. Yet there is more consensus on economic goals than meets the eye. Both conservatives and progressives agree on the importance of balancing urban and rural development. Both recognize that there is a critical need for economic growth as well as for increased equity. How they will manage to make progress towards both equity and growth remains the overriding problem for the Aquino government.

In foreign policy there is less unity and less room for compromise. The conservatives believe that it is important to maintain the American alliance and to keep the American military bases, though with modifications to ensure Filipino control over their use and to increase the American rental payments. Progressives favor a nonaligned foreign policy and the abrogation of the bases agreement when it expires in 1991.

Recognizing her own limited experience in matters of public policy, President Aquino has relied heavily on the members of her cabinet to help her formulate her program. She has encouraged them to argue their diverse positions at cabinet meetings so that she may learn from them before arriving at her own decisions. The fact that these arguments have continued outside the cabinet room into full view of the public, with disagreements trumpeted by a newly liberated, highly partisan press, has contributed to an image of cabinet disunity and of an overly permissive president.

Secretary Teodoro Benigno, Presidential Spokesman Rene Saguisag, personal counselor and former Information Minister Teodoro Locsin; "Nationalist"—Deputy Foreign Minister Leticia Ramos Shahani; "Conservatives"—Finance Minister Jaime Ongpin, Central Bank Governor Jose Fernandez, Trade and Industry Minister Jose Concepcion. Remaining behind in Manila were Vice-president and Foreign Minister Salvador Laurel, described as "strongly pro-U.S." and Defense Minister Juan Ponce Enrile, who was described as "neo-fascist." *Ang Katipunan,* Vol XII, No. 11, October 1986. p. 13. Executive Secretary Joker Arroyo and Labor Minister Agusto Sanchez, who also remained in Manila, would certainly be counted among the progressives.

President Aquino has dealt with the mavericks in her cabinet in typically Filipino fashion. In several cases she appointed deputy ministers of her own choosing whose views on policy were close to her own and whose loyalty to her was beyond question. When undisciplined ministers exceeded the generous limits of her tolerance, competent replacements were ready to take over.

The most extreme example of cabinet indiscipline was provided by Defense Minister Enrile. As a holdover from the Marcos government, as the former jailer of several of his cabinet colleagues, and as a skeptic about the prospects for an acceptable negotiated settlement with the New Peoples Army, Enrile since the early months of the new government found himself under attack by cabinet progressives who made no secret of their hope that he would leave or be dropped from the cabinet.

Enrile's response was to counterattack, first against his critics and then in October against the president herself. Having had a major part in enabling Aquino to take office, he saw himself and the military who supported him in the February revolution not as mere subordinates of the president but as partners in a civilian-military coalition. Such a view was in conflict with the principle of civilian supremacy, as well as with that of presidential government. Enrile warned darkly that, having made a government, the military could unmake it as well. More realistically, it was clear that he wanted a larger voice in policymaking. In particular he urged the president to unleash the military against the NPA.

In challenging Aquino, Enrile also was positioning himself to succeed her in the presidency. But he could not have been pleased with the prospect of waiting five years until the expiration of her presidential term. Therefore he attempted to pressure her into holding an earlier presidential election by publicly questioning the legality of the abrogation of the Marcos constitution, and by challenging the president to test her claim to office by calling new presidential elections in 1987. In the meantime, he continued to seek support for his own presidential bid among the former followers of Marcos. Aquino however rebuffed Enrile's call for an early presidential election. Enrile and his RAM allies responded by escalating talk of a coup.

In a society that admires courage and flamboyance in its leaders, Enrile won many supporters. The president also played a culturally conditioned role of the equally determined female. Her move to rid herself of Enrile showed both firmness and *delicadeza*. On her return from a state visit to Japan in November, she asked for the resignation of her entire cabinet, thus leaving herself free to make a number of replacements. Enrile, though the first to have his resignation accepted, was spared the embarrassment of being singled out for dismissal. His deputy, the highly respected General Rafael Ileto, was made defense minister in his place. Together with General Ramos, who rallied the armed forces behind the president in what must have been for Ramos a painful break with his comrade of the February revolution, Ileto provides a solidly professional military backing for the Aquino government.

At the same time, the president has used the resignation of her cabinet to make some other needed changes. The first to be replaced after Enrile were Natural Resources Minister Ernesto Maceda and Public Works Minister Rogaciano Mercado. Both were reputed to be tainted with or tolerant of corruption. The next to be replaced was local government minister Aquilino Q. Pimentel, who had made himself unpopular by his manner of replacing local officials. He remains in the cabinet as a special advisor on national affairs.

Still in doubt as this book goes to press is the reappointment of Labor Minister Agusto Sanchez. Considered too far to the left by the military, and too pro-labor by the business community, he is strongly defended by his friends in the labor movement and by the political left. Unlike those who have been sacked for insubordination, corruption, or bad political judgment, Sanchez' possible replacement involves issues of substantive policy and will affect the nature of the government's support among the public at large. On balance, however, these cabinet changes will strengthen the Aquino government.

PROSPECTS FOR THE FUTURE

The May 1987 congressional elections, the first after Marcos, will reveal much about the Philippine political landscape that was unclear before. The last Marcos-era elections of February 7, 1986, which brought Corazon Aquino to power, divided the voters into but two camps: Those who were with Marcos and those who were against him. That simple bifurcation fails to describe important changes in the pattern of Filipino political affiliation that had occurred since the two-party presidential contests of pre-martial law years.

The 1986 election marked more than the restoration of genuinely competitive politics after a thirteen-year hiatus. It also signaled an unprecedented mobilization of new political forces after the August 1983 assassination of Benigno Aquino. Hidden behind the rivalry of two wealthy presidential candidates in February was an explosion of organized participation by a variety of minor parties and newly organized "sectoral" and "cause-oriented" groups. This new phenomenon, which is discussed by Richard Kessler and Daniel Doeppers, will permanently alter the character of electoral competition in the Philippines.

Some of the new groups receive guidance from the Catholic church or the Communist party. Other groups are more autonomous, including some formed by members of the business and professional communities. Many of the new groups were active in the February elections and in the subsequent display of "people power." All are likely to remain actively involved in politics, though not necessarily as uncritical supporters of any political party or leader.

The spectrum of participating groups will be widened further at the May 1987 elections by the almost certain participation for the first time on a nationwide scale of candidates supported by the Communist Party of the Philippines. That party and most of the groups under its influence boycotted the February election, asserting that it was a meaningless contest between two "bourgeois" candidates which Marcos would win in any case. It does not appear that the boycott dissuaded more than a small proportion of the party's sympathizers from casting votes. To most Filipinos, right, left, or center, the contest between Marcos and Aquino promised to be a pivotal event in their country's history, in which they were eager to play a part.

Since then, the CPP has recognized its mistake and, after some internal self-criticism, moved quickly to recapture lost ground by claiming—with some justification—that its guerrilla war, which Marcos seemed unable to contain, helped to discredit him and to prepare the ground for the election and the military revolt that led to his downfall. Since the fall of Marcos, as has been noted, communist leaders have been involved in the creation of the *Partido ng Bayan*, the latest in a succession of such front organizations. In one or another form, the CPP will play an important part at future elections.

Former Marcos followers, some of them members of the defunct National Assembly and some former local and provincial officials who were replaced by pro-Aquino Officers in Charge, also will be active in future elections with a view to maintaining or rebuilding their personal "power bases." As Richard Kessler suggests, their best hope lies in organizing themselves into a cohesive party with a genuinely conservative ideology. Anti-communism is likely to be their battle cry.

Taken together, the elections of February 1986 and of May 1987 will replace what before martial law had been a quadrennial contest between two similar clientelistic parties, by a more meaningful but also more bitter contest among a number of ideologically distinctive political parties.

There is reason to fear that the May 1987 elections may be not only divisive in their ideological appeals but violent as well. If the Communist party runs or supports candidates for national and local offices while its New Peoples Army remains in armed control of portions of the countryside, it will find it hard to resist the temptation to use its arms to help its candidates and to impede the electioneering efforts of their rivals. That would provoke counterviolence in turn. In such an event the constitutional prohibition against the formation of private armies, a prohibition also included in the NPA's latest negotiating demands, would go by the boards. The May elections therefore may confront NAMFREL and a newly reconstituted Commission on Elections with problems very different from those that they faced when the main source of electoral intimidation was the government itself.

While the elections will be bitterly contested, there is reason to hope that a post-election legislative impasse between ideologically hostile parties can be avoided. If Mrs. Aquino can win enough loyal adherents from both the moderate left and the moderate right for a strong social reformist but growth-oriented party of the center, such a party might control the congress and relegate parties of the extreme right and left to minor positions, while providing support for the president's legislative programs for the remainder of her term. The president has resisted suggestions that she form such a party, but has said that she will endorse individual candidates who meet her approval. However, her brother, Jose Cojuangco, Jr., is forming a "party coalition," *Lakas ng Bansa* to support her. Most cabinet members have joined *Lakas* and have become its regional chairmen. They include some members of UNIDO. Several prominent members of Marcos's KBL also have been welcomed into the new group, and more are likely to follow. After the president's display of firmness against Juan Ponce Enrile, party "turncoatism," a well-established practice in the Philippines, is in full swing. Mrs. Aquino's problem will not be to attract followers to her bandwagon but to separate her real supporters from the opportunists.

AMERICAN POLICY TOWARDS THE PHILIPPINES

The United States and Marcos

Until September 1972, few Filipinos doubted that their former colonial mentor had a strong interest in the preservation and perfection of what Americans called their "show window of democracy in Asia." Between 1972 and 1986, however, that assumption came to be widely questioned in the Philippines. American policy toward the Philippines after the imposition of martial law is the topic of seven of our contributors, all of whom have been directly involved in the making of United States Philippine policy. Representative Stephen J. Solarz is chairman of the congressional subcommittee most strongly concerned with the Philippines. William C. Hamilton, Lee T. Stull, John Maisto, William H. Sullivan, Paul M. Kattenburg and Francis Underhill are present or former members of the American foreign service. A Filipino perspective is presented by Ambassador to Washington Emmanuel Pelaez.

From the beginning of martial law, the relationship between the United States and Marcos was a subject of intense interest in the Philippines. Ultra-nationalists, notably the communists, claimed to see an unmistakable American hand in Marcos's decision to impose martial law. For them, "fascism, feudalism, and imperialism" were necessarily linked. The enemy was the "US-Marcos dictatorship." Without American support, they insisted, Marcos would quickly fall.

Non-Marxist opponents of Marcos were also strongly if less stridently critical of American policy. In their view, Washington's actions to distance itself from Marcos were too hesitant, too little, and were very long delayed. This, they argued, reflected a self-serving preference for Marcos as the reliable defender of American interests at the expense of those of the Philippines.

A kinder explanation of American policy would be that the evolving attitudes of the United States, like those of the Philippine church and business community, reflected the changing nature and stability of the Marcos government. In that view, American pressure on Marcos, like pressure from the church and later pressure from the business community, began with cautious criticism of his government's human rights abuses in the mid-1970s. It ended with a determined effort to help to bring an end to the Marcos regime in the latter part of February 1986.

Before martial law was declared the American ambassador, Henry Byroade, suspecting what Marcos had in mind, had urged him not to take unconstitutional action. When martial law was imposed nonetheless, Washington, urged by the Embassy to react strongly, made but a mild response. An explanation for this, given by an American official at the time, was that the United States could hardly protest more strongly while much of Philippine opinion welcomed martial law and applauded its early accomplishments. Another explanation was that, with the impending American withdrawal from Indochina, the United States could not afford to alienate one of the remaining friendly rulers in Southeast Asia. Thus United States policy, as one American diplomat put it at that time, was to "support the Philippines, but to neither support or to not support martial law." This policy proved to be easier to follow in theory than in practice, for opponents of the Philippine president saw American aid, and especially military aid, to the Philippine government as support for Marcos himself, an interpretation the latter took pains to foster.

Still, American officials from the beginning saw danger in an extended period of dictatorship. They repeatedly called Marcos's attention to specific human rights violations and urged him to restore democratic processes. In this their position differed little from that of the Catholic church. But American military and economic aid continued to flow to the Philippines, which led critics to argue that such assistance was a more telling expression of American policy than were Washington's attempts at persuasion or condemnation.

The reluctance to apply harsher pressure against Marcos during the first years of martial law could be explained in part by his record of support for the United States and its policies at a time when many of his critics, including those who called most insistently for American sanctions, had been among those Filipinos most vocal in their hostility to the United States. Later, the reluctance to "dump" Marcos could be explained also by memories of the consequences of withdrawing support from the Shah and General Somoza.

President Reagan, who criticized his predecessor on this score, seemed especially unwilling to abandon a pro-American Filipino leader with whom he had formed a personal friendship while he was governor of California. On becoming the American president in January 1981, Reagan invited Marcos for a state visit to Washington, a gesture much desired by Marcos, which had been denied him by all previous American presidents after the imposition of martial law. It was made easier by the formal lifting of martial law a few days before the inauguration of the Reagan administration and of a papal visit to the Philippines.

In any case, while Marcos's management of the economy was bringing substantial benefits to his country and while he still held the support of important sectors of Philippine society, pressure from either his domestic critics or from a foreign government could have little impact upon the Philippine president.

Not until his policies began to fail spectacularly, bringing new groups, among them the Philippine business community, into an increasingly vocal opposition and hardening the stand of old critics such as the church, was American pressure likely to move Marcos in directions not of his own choosing. Those conditions were not present until 1983, the year of the assassination of Benigno Aquino.

It was that event, together with the resulting outburst of Philippine public protests, the Philippine government's inability to service its foreign debt, and the rapid growth of the New Peoples Army, that led the Reagan administration to cancel a planned presidential visit to Manila and to dispatch a series of high-level presidential emissaries to attempt to persuade Marcos to undertake drastic reforms.

These missions had little effect. Marcos appears to have believed that they represented the views of the State Department, not of the American president. By the middle of 1985, therefore, a consensus had formed among American policy professionals that a prolonged continuation of the Marcos regime would have disastrous consequences for the Philippines as well as for American interests. An important contribution to the emergence of that consensus was the visit to the Philippines of the subsequently appointed chairman of the Joint Chiefs of Staff, Admiral William Crowe, who received from American military commanders there a grim assessment of the Philippine government's performance against the NPA.

To a degree unusual in United States foreign policy discussions, that assessment was shared in the Manila embassy and in Washington, among State Department professionals and military men, in the executive branch and among members of Congress most directly concerned with Philippine affairs. Marcos, all were convinced, could not or would not make the fundamental economic, military, and political changes that could restore business confidence in the economy, stem the alarmingly rapid growth of the insurgency, and restore popular confidence in the political system.

There was disagreement, however, as to what the United States could do to bring about a peaceful end to the Marcos regime. Some believed that he should be told bluntly that it was time to go. Others argued that this would only stiffen Marcos's resistance and that in any case President Reagan would not be willing to send such a strong message to his Philippine counterpart. Thus, for a time, Washington held back from such a harsh course. That message to Marcos was not to come, and perhaps could not have come, until a later stage in the unfolding Philippine drama. Instead, the White House in October sent another presidential emissary, Senator Paul Laxalt, to make it plain to Marcos that President Reagan shared the view of his subordinates that serious reforms were urgently needed.

Thereafter, American actions were shaped by events as much as they shaped events in the Philippines. Marcos reacted to the Laxalt mission by calling a snap presidential election designed to show to both domestic and foreign observers that he still enjoyed popular support. To this the United States responded a week before election day with a presidential statement stressing the need that the elections be fair, endorsing the efforts of NAMFREL, but avoiding any show of favoritism for either slate of candidates.

Marcos has said that his greatest mistake was to call the February elections. Another mistake, surely, was to invite foreign observers, including several missions from the United States. The most prominent member of these missions was U.S. Senator Richard Lugar. Arriving with an open mind, Lugar by the end of election day was convinced that the election process was fatally flawed by massive government cheating. Hastening back to Washington, he played a crucial part in persuading President Reagan of that fact. Equally damaging to Marcos's cause was the presence of the overseas print and electronic media, who brought the outrage of ordinary Filipinos over the blatant manipulation of the elections to millions of foreign viewers.

In the end, the Reagan administration helped to bring a relatively bloodless finale to the Marcos administration. Its role in that event has been cast into doubt in Filipino eyes by some extraordinarily careless high-level comments in Washington. For some days after the elections, the American president waffled with a series of off-the-cuff statements that incensed Aquino supporters at a time when many feared for their lives from an expected Marcos crackdown. Most incredible to those in the Philippines was the president's comment that "there might have been cheating on both sides." Like Vice-president Bush's 1981 accolade to Marcos, "We love your adherence to democratic principles and practices," that remark will be long remembered in the Philippines.

American policy came together after an urgent postelection visit to the Philippines by special presidential envoy Ambassador Philip Habib. Then the American president recognized that cheating was "mainly" on the government's side, and that it was sufficient in scale to invalidate the elections. When Enrile and Ramos made their move, American pressure was applied alongside "people power" to dissuade Marcos and his loyalists from crushing the rebellion by force. On February 24, Washington sent Marcos both through his emissary to Washington, Labor Minister Blas Ople and through U.S. Ambassador Bosworth the unmistakable message that it was time for him to step aside and prepare the way for a transition government, under a formula developed by Filipino leaders themselves. If violence were employed against elements of the Philippine armed forces, the United States would not be able to continue military assistance. In addition, there would be strong, perhaps irresistible, pressures from Congress to suspend economic aid as well. That this was President Reagan's personal position was confirmed by Senator Paul Laxalt when the Philippine president made his final telephone call to Washington.

The United States and the Post-Marcos Philippines

During the early months of the new government, Filipinos had some doubts about the strength of American support for Mrs. Aquino. These were caused by the noticeable lack of warmth shown by President Reagan for the new Philippine president. Clearly it was painful for Reagan, who tends to personalize international relations, to turn against an old friend and to embrace his successor. Filipino doubts were fueled by the relatively small-scale and slow pace of American economic assistance to an economy in great need of the injection of substantial foreign aid.

The warmth of the relationship has been restored in large part by the efforts of Secretary of State George Schultz, by the strong support for the Aquino government from numerous members of the United States Congress, as well as by the grace of the Philippine president. Her September visit to the United States, including an extended personal meeting between the two presidents and an enthusiastic reception by the Congress was a striking success. Strong American support for Aquino at the time of Minister Enrile's challenge was welcomed by her supporters in the Philippines. Clearly the American administration is persuaded that the success of the Aquino government offers the best hope for the survival of a stable Philippine democracy and for the endurance of the Philippine-American relationship.

The Military Bases and Philippine-American Relations

Perhaps the most controversial issue in Philippine-American relations is the future of the American military bases. The bases issue is explored by five of our contributors. Four of them, Alva M. Bowen, Jr. Robert N. Smith, William H. Sullivan and Paul M. Kattenburg, express differing American opinions as to the desirability of maintaining United States bases in the Philippines. Ambassador Pelaez discusses the bases from a Filipino point of view.

The bases received much criticism from Philippine nationalists, even before martial law, as an infringement of Philippine sovereignty and as a magnet for potential Soviet attack. After 1972 they were criticized further as enabling Marcos to extract both political and financial support from the United States. President Aquino on taking power announced her intention to honor the bases agreement until its expiration in 1991. After that, she has stated, she will "keep her options open."

The United States for its part has a heavy investment in its Philippine bases. The naval and air force installations at Subic Bay and Clark Field are among its largest and finest service facilities anywhere in the world. Their strategic importance is obvious in view of the Soviet navy's presence at Vietnam's Cam Ranh Bay. The United States leases the bases from the Philippines under an agreement that expires in 1991 at a rental equivalent to approximately $180 million per year. Subic Bay alone has an on-base workforce of 34,000, including highly skilled workers capable of servicing everything from diesel engines to advanced radar systems, on a wage scale of $1.80 an hour. It has been estimated that it would take up to eight years to replace these facilities elsewhere in the region at a price tag of approximately $5 billion. Additional yearly operating costs elsewhere could reach $500 million. Costs of procuring additional air and naval squadrons necessary for reaching Southeast Asian chokepoints from the more distant bases could easily run several times the new bases construction costs, and possibly much more. To finance an expenditure of $20 billion, for example, would require the equivalent of a tax of $250 on every American household.[9]

The bases remain a matter of contention within the Aquino cabinet. The Communist party has made their abrogation one of its negotiating demands. The Constitutional Commission, after rejecting nationalist proposals to ban foreign military bases from Philippine territory, adopted a compromise provision that would require any extension of the bases agreement to take the form of a treaty, requiring ratification by the Philippine Senate. The Congress would have the option of submitting such a treaty to a national referendum. An additional provision included in the draft constitution states that the Philippines,"consistent with the national interest, adopts and pursues a policy of freedom from nuclear weapons in its territory." That leaves open the possibility of a "New Zealandization" of the Philippine-American defense relationship. It seems certain, therefore, that the bases will remain a highly visible issue in Philippine politics.

CONCLUSION

In the Aquino government lies the Philippines' best hope for reformist democracy. To help strengthen that democracy against the extremes of both left and right, the United States may be called upon to increase its economic and military aid. Military support, unless limited to funding, supplies and advice, entails serious risks. It would be a tragedy for both countries if once again, as in the early years of the century, American soldiers fought against Filipino "insurgents." Increased economic aid, which to the degree that it helped revive the Philippine economy would lessen the need for military aid, entails no comparable risk. It would be welcomed by the vast majority of Filipinos.

[9]For these calculations, the writer is indebted to Richard Hooley.

2

The Philippines and the United States

Emmanuel M. Pelaez*

THE HISTORIC ENCOUNTER

Ever since the fateful Battle of Manila Bay on May 1, 1898, that culminated in the formal Spanish surrender in Intramuros by August 13, and the cession of the Philippines to the United States under the terms of the Treaty of Paris of December 10, 1898, the destiny of the Filipino nation has been closely linked with the Asian-Pacific policies of the United States government. The Philippine Islands became a colony ruled by American administrators until Philippine independence (which had been won by the Filipinos from Spain and proclaimed by General Emilio Aguinaldo on June 12, 1898) was restored in accordance with United States law on July 4, 1946, in a postwar setting of devastation.

In the early 1900s, when the Americans started to consolidate their control over the Philippine Islands, the Filipinos could not have foreseen that their new Caucasian conquerors would become in a few decades the most powerful nation on earth. But the record shows that as the United States proceeded through World War I and World War II to become the world's foremost industrial and military power, Filipinos remained steadfast in their nationalistic aspirations. True to the rich

*Paper delivered by Ambassador Emmanuel Pelaez at the Conference on the Philippines sponsored jointly by the Fletcher School of Law and Diplomacy, the Asia Foundation, Center for Asian Pacific Affairs, the Philippine Council for Foreign Relations, the Academy of ASEAN Law and Jurisprudence, and the Asia Society, Tufts University, Medford, Massachusetts, October 5-7, 1986. With the kind permission of the Fletcher School and Ambassador Pelaez, this paper replaces one delivered by him at The Washington Institute Conference.

legacy of patriotism they inherited from Jose Rizal, Andres Bonifacio, and Apolinario Mabini, Filipino leaders like Manuel Quezon and Sergio Osmena yearned and worked for the day when Filipinos could operate a democratic government by themselves in their own country.

But the historic colonial encounter certainly left its deep imprint on the life, culture, and modes of political and economic organization adopted by the Filipino people. Filipinos have inherited a wealth of influences from America, such as certain liberalist democratic precepts and the free enterprise model for generating economic growth. Public administration, law, jurisprudence, education, medicine, the natural and social sciences, and English are but a few of the areas in which America can be said to have contributed decisively to the shaping of Philippine institutions. While some Filipinos may resent these contributions as vestiges of colonialism, they may be more constructively viewed as tools of enrichment by which Filipinos can equip themselves to proceed with the task of building a nation in this modern world in accordance with their ideals and aspirations.

The meeting of the Filipino and American nations, unlike the experience of fire and bloodshed in other cases of colonization, resulted basically in lasting bonds of goodwill between the two peoples. On the government-to-government level, the encounter had as a consequence the forging of close friendship and alliance. The Japanese conquest of the Philippines in World War II provided at the time a terrifying lesson in the importance of strong external defense. This and the requirements of reconstructing a country badly ravaged by war were factors that led the leaders of the new republic to sign key agreements with the United States in the postwar period. These agreements, such as the Philippine Trade Act of 1946, the Military Bases Agreement of 1947, the Mutual Defense Treaty of 1951, and the Laurel-Langley Trade Agreement of 1955, reinforced existing preconditions out of the colonial past for shaping Philippine economic and security policies within the scope of broader United States policy. It is this early patron-clientelist mold of United States economic "nurture" and external protection (or exploitation and imperialist design as others would view it) which both American and Filipino officials must, it seems, outgrow today.

The slanting of Philippine foreign policy towards the United States at the time represented both a sequel to the colonial relationship and a decision reached in accordance with the assessment by Filipino leaders like Manuel Roxas and Elpidio Quirino of the hard choices which had to be made in pursuit of Philippine national interests. But one fact seemed certain and was well understood early on. And that is, after the mantle for governing the nation fell solely on the shoulders of Filipinos, the agenda and priorities of the United States as a superpower and the interests of the Philippines as a young state anxious to assert its sovereignty could not for long remain the same.

THE COMPLEX NATURE OF PHILIPPINE-UNITED STATES RELATIONS TODAY

Many Americans and Filipinos tend to adopt a rather simplistic view of Philippine-United States relations: a rich "Uncle Sam," a former colonial master, needs to extend economic and military assistance to a beleaguered former colony but prefers to have the latter adhere to conditions proferred by the former. Some others would simplify the relationship even further and see it mainly in terms of the United States tying assistance to the anti-Communist efforts of the Philippine government and its attitude toward the United States military bases in the Philippines. Such a perspective, by focusing on the "aid" aspect of the relationship, not only disregards the depth of nationalist sentiments among Filipinos but also the various other ramifications of an unequal relationship.

The following are a few points to suggest some complexities in the United States-Philippine relationship:

1. *The divergent agenda of the Philippines and the United States.* The United States is a superpower engaged in an adversary relationship with the Soviet Union. It has global security interests and stations 721,000 men in forty countries and on the world's major seas. Its $3.06 trillion GNP means it produces one-fourth of the world's wealth in goods and services. Its economic-financial dominance continues to make or break international regimes that form the basis for global economic cooperation and interdependence. It is the largest market in the world and the biggest aid donor to developing countries. It thus has global goals and interests and is likely to place all its bilateral ties in the context of a world view.

   On the other hand, the Philippines is a developing country whose GNP of around $40 billion is but 1.3 percent of the United States GNP. The Philippines needs to spend at least $2 billion annually, or about one-half of its export receipts, to pay interest on a $26.3 billion foreign debt. About two-thirds of Filipinos now live below the poverty line as a result of falling real incomes under the previous regime. Almost 70,000 Filipinos have died from internal strife, especially during the intensification of the Mindanao conflict in the mid-1970s.

In short, the Philippines faces an agenda of development and national-interest concerns basically different from the priorities the United States faces as an immense economic-military power.

2. *The gross imbalance between the positions of the Philippines and the United States.* While United States policies can exert powerful effects on the Philippines, Philippine policies—except possibly regarding the bases—can hardly move the United States. This imbalance appears clearest in the economic sphere. The United States is the Philippines' largest trading partner, accounting for around 35 and 27 percent of Philippine exports and imports, respectively, over the past ten years. On the other hand, United States trade with the Philippines comprises only 2 percent of its trade with the Asia-Pacific region alone. Thus in 1984 the two-way United States-Philippine trade of $3.6 billion, while representing one-third of Philippine trade, was only 2.1 percent of the United States-Asia-Pacific trade of $168.6 billion. Philippine-United States trade was less than .07 percent of the total United States world trade valued at $543.6 billion in 1984. Also, the Philippines derives 40 percent of its GNP from trade. Only 17 to 18 percent of the United States GNP comes from its trade with the world. (Table 1 will highlight aspects of this imbalance.)

Table 1
United States-Philippine Trade Relative to United States-Asia Pacific and United States World Trade
1984

	TOTAL U.S. WORLD TRADE	U.S. TRADE WITH ASIA/PACIFIC	U.S.-PHILIPPINE TRADE
VALUE	$543.6 Billion	$168.6 Billion	$3.6 Billion
PERCENTAGE	100.00	31.01	.066

Furthermore, while total United States investment in the Philippines since 1970, around $3 billion, represents approximately 50 percent of all investments in the Philippines, this is only 8.57 percent of United States direct investments in the Asia-Pacific region, around $35 billion in 1984 alone, and only 1.3 percent of United States direct investments worldwide, valued at $233.4 billion in the same year.

Clearly, therefore, the Philippines' ties with the United States comprise its single most important bilateral relationship. The economic recovery efforts of the Philippines can be helped or harmed by United States trade policies, and a healthy United States economy is as much in the interest of the Philippines as it is vital to the United States itself.

3. *The Philippines as an Asian nation that shares common concerns with the Third World and wishes to broaden its ties with socialist countries.* This facet of Philippine foreign relations springs from the Philippines' aspirations to be a truly sovereign nation that perforce must pursue its own national interest. It is another point that should be stressed to illustrate a further dimension in Philippine-United States relations.

The Philippines is an Asian nation, and its desire to connect with its Asian neighbors goes back to the 1960s, when it joined with Thailand and Malaya in forming the Association of Southeast Asia. After ASA failed, the Philippines continued to pursue its objective of forging a regional grouping with its neighbors. This time, in 1966, it succeeded in creating with Indonesia, Malaysia, Thailand, and Singapore the Association of Southeast Asian Nations. Today, twenty years afterward, reinforced by the entry of Brunei in 1984, ASEAN is a strong and influential regional grouping that is contributing much to the security and stability of the Southeast Asian region.

The Philippines' identification with the concerns of Third World countries—for economic development, sovereignty, and dignity—also goes back to the Bandung Conference of 1955. As a developing country, the Philippines has much in common with members of the Third World, especially in regard to north-south issues. Furthermore, in pursuit of its developmental goals and the concretization of its sovereignty, the Philippines desires to broaden its ties with other countries of the world regardless of their political and economic systems. In this regard, the opening up of the Philippines to diplomatic, cultural, and economic associations with the socialist countries in the 1970s was one of the few positive legacies of the previous regime.

While many United States policymakers have understood factors such as those enumerated here that make United States-Philippine relations more complex than some would think, there are those who still appear to view such ties in purely strategic-security terms. The so-called "love-hate relationship" between the Philippines and the United States might be better explained and understood through an in-depth examination of Philippine nationalism, the divergent priorities of the two states, the asymmetrical nature of one state's salience to the other, and the Philippines' identification with Asia and the Third World and its desire to broaden its relations with socialist countries.

THE OLD FORMAT OF UNITED STATES-PHILIPPINE RELATIONS

The format of United States-Philippine relations that existed throughout much of the past forty years may be described as that of "special relations." This was a relationship characterized by a considerable degree of Philippine economic dependence on the United States and the existence of United States extraterritoriality on the Philippine military bases. The Philippines' economic dependence was manifested largely through the Philippine Trade Act of 1946, the Parity Rights Amendment to the Constitution, and the Laurel-Langley Agreement previously mentioned. A feature of this dependence was the lack of export diversification, on the one hand, and a narrow focus on the United States as trading partner, on the other.

The American flag's flying over Philippines military bases—alone from 1947 to 1957, and together with the Philippine flag from then until 1979—symbolized the absence of Philippine sovereignty over the bases. For many years, Olongapo City (adjacent to the bases) was virtually governed by American naval authorities. This was another feature of "special relations."

Complementing these characteristics was the fact that the Philippine-United States military alliance under the Mutual Defense Treaty and the Military Bases Agreement tended to restrict the options of the Philippines with regard to the formulation of foreign policy and the establishment of diplomatic relations with the various countries of the world. This was especially so in the 1950s and the 1960s when the East-West conflict represented by the cold war was at its height, and when China as a Communist state was seen as an overt threat to the Philippines.

The prime characteristic of "special relations" which must be noted is that the relationship was one of unequals. Many in United States officialdom viewed the Philippine state, as it were, as a United States ward whose aspirations for authentic sovereignty were negligible and where nationalist sentiments were anathema to American interests.

Under the Marcos presidency, especially in the final ten years of his rule, with the termination of the Laurel-Langley Agreement and Parity Rights in 1974 and the new amendments to the Military Bases Agreement in 1979 and 1983, "special relations" were supposed to have ended. But the relationship that increasingly took shape, coinciding with Marcos's plan to stabilize one-man rule with the trappings of a Philippine-styled "democracy," was that of a symbiosis in which the Marcos regime and the United States administration supported close relations for inherently conflicting reasons and during which popular support for Marcos's political experimentation was basically suspect.

This symbiosis was at its height just before the assassination of Benigno Aquino, Jr., in 1983. The Reagan administration had come to power in Washington in 1981 when Marcos was facing mounting violent and nonviolent challenges at home, when his envisioned Philippine-styled "democracy" with him as president-for-life was meeting widespread popular apathy or opposition, and when he needed American assistance in addition to an American imprimatur on the legitimacy of his "New Republic."

On the other hand, Marcos appeared particularly suited to serve as a prototype for the United States New Right's desire to get American allies to play a more active role in the effort to counteract a perceived Soviet threat and the adventurism of the Soviets and their proxies. Securing the United States military facilities in the Clark and Subic Bases under a stable ruler seen as in firm control of the Philippine political situation and very friendly to the United States became a United States desideratum. It was not surprising that the United States endorsed Marcos's rule during Vice-President George Bush's visit to Manila in 1981 and Marcos's state visit to the United States in 1982. American policy makers at the time evidently believed that Marcos was in power for good, and that the key to ensuring United States access to Philippine bases was to support and befriend the Marcos regime despite its growing track record of economic policy failures and human rights abuses. Marcos astutely cultivated this symbiosis by threatening to reach a modus vivendi with the Soviet Union or to renegotiate the bases agreement whenever he felt peeved by the efforts of some members of the U.S. Congress to link the appropriation of base rentals to his human rights record.

An outstanding characteristic of such a flawed format for Philippine-United States relations, therefore, was the complementary existence of basically opposing motivations. On the one hand, Marcos was motivated by an obsession to remain in power for life, to the detriment of his own country's economic health and political stability, and for which he needed United States assistance and support. On the other, the United States wished to establish close relations with Marcos for basically strategic security reasons, although Marcos's political innovations and economic policies contrasted with the democratic ideals and the free enterprise tenets for which the United States has historically stood.

TOWARD A NEW FORMAT IN UNITED STATES-PHILIPPINE RELATIONS

President Corazon Aquino has inherited a huge and complex task of reconstruction, greater than any newly elected president before her (including Marcos in 1965) has ever faced. But the Philippines should now represent less of a policy dilemma for the United States, considering the sincerity and integrity of the Aquino administration.

It is certainly noteworthy that the Reagan administration today, despite the severe restraints imposed by the huge United States budget deficit, understands the unique opportunity Mrs. Aquino represents for the economic recovery, the internal peace, and the political stabilization of the Philippines.

During his meeting with President Aquino at the White House on September 17, 1986, President Reagan expressed his support for the Aquino government in a way that should dispel once and for all any remaining cloud of doubt among some Filipinos about his previous backing for Marcos. The public remarks of President Reagan after that meeting might be repeated here: "The United States stands ready to assist President Aquino in her quest to create a stable and secure land, as well as in her commitment to invigorate the Philippine economy."

The Philippine government notes with gratitude that, despite the constraints of the Gramm-Rudman Act, the U.S. House of Representatives expeditiously moved to implement this pledge of support, followed not long after in the U.S. Senate, by resoundingly voting a grant of $200 million as additional assistance to the Philippines and providing for the increase of the Philippines' sugar quota.

We now have a reason to believe that a new era of Philippine-American relations under a new format is emerging.

This format refers to the government's choice among several possible options for the formulation of its United States policy. There is the neutralist-isolationist option under which the Philippines, as an expression of nationalism and nonalignment, would have restricted political and economic linkages with both the East and West as it continued to exist in relative isolation. There is also the radical nationalist option that would place nonalignment as its foreign policy centerpiece, terminate the alliance relationship with the United States, and place heavy emphasis on economic nationalism, state control of the economy, and "self-reliance." There is also the "special relations" option which basically entails a return to the classic postwar model noted for its having been a relationship of "non-equals" and thus criticized by some as "neo-colonial."

The new government of President Aquino has chosen the path of what might be known as the moderate nationalist option, under which the Philippines will maintain close relations with the United States on the basis of mutual respect and benefit even as it strives to build a real democracy, adopt the free enterprise developmental model while being committed to battling poverty and social inequality, and seek internal stability by first trying out the path of negotiation.

Underlying this option—as well as the others mentioned—is the fact that nationalism is a powerful force in the Philippines today, that the Philippines, like any other independent state, has its interests to pursue, that the Philippines wishes to stress its nature as an Asian nation, that it desires treatment as an equal, and that it needs to assert the authenticity of its independence, sovereignty, and dignity. This the Philippines can do without necessarily becoming anti-American or breaking the historic friendship that has bound the two countries and peoples together for much of this century. Instead, the Philippines would like to believe that its historic encounter with the United States constitutes a comparative advantage giving it an edge over others in getting the assistance it now seeks. Such assistance the Aquino government needs as it addresses the huge financial, socio-economic, political, and internal security problems it inherited from Marcos. But obviously, such requests for assistance, especially at this time of rehabilitation and reconstruction, are but one element in a relationship of many dimensions.

As earlier intimated, the relationship between a small developing country with its own agenda of concerns and a huge superpower with global security, political, and economic interests will necessarily be complex. The task of formulating a Philippine policy towards the United States has become to some extent that of reconciling Filipino aspirations with American concerns as a superpower which nevertheless represents common values or a sharing of interests.

This means, for instance, an effort to blend Filipino nationalist aspirations for sovereignty, economic prosperity, and modernization, on the one hand, with the United States' interest in preserving the integrity of the world economic system and the perpetuation of democratic values under a condition of world peace, on the other. The effort to pursue Philippine nationalist and developmental goals within a broader international framework consistent with United States interests and redounding to the benefit of the world as a whole is a complex and difficult one. But it is on the basis of this endeavor that a genuine closeness in Philippine-United States relations can be forged today.

Under Mr. Marcos, as pointed out, a symbiotic relationship had emerged by mid-1983 based on the narrow convergence of basically incompatible interests. Under President Aquino, with an element of understanding on both sides, a new closeness between the two countries can be built on stronger foundations: a real long-term convergence of interests in rebuilding democracy and achieving economic recovery for the Philippines, cultivating global interdependence under market forces, and maintaining regional and international security as a common concern. Such closeness would be in consonance with the historic relationship between our two peoples. Khalil Gibran's metaphor comes to mind: "The mother country the bow, the young developing state the arrow—designed to fly free and reach the zenith of its own aspirations."

I would like to conclude by reiterating President Corazon Aquino's challenge: "Join us, America, as we build a new home for democracy, another haven for the oppressed, so it may stand as a shining testament of our two nations' commitment to freedom."

3

A New Era:
An Auspicious Beginning

Stephen J. Solarz

The miracle in Manila which took place a few months ago constitutes one of the few authentic democratic revolutions of our time. With awe and amazement, I watched the unfolding human and political drama which was taking place before our eyes on American television. I alternately thrilled and trembled at the sight of ordinary people laying their lives on the line for democracy. I trembled with fear at the possibility of massive bloodshed, and possibly even civil war. But I felt delighted at the sight of nuns and ordinary people turning back tanks with nothing more than their prayers and their presence.

In Washington, there has been entirely too much self-congratulation about the role of the U.S. in the restoration of democracy in the Philippines. It was, after all, the people of the Philippines themselves, through the remarkable manifestation of what has come to be known as "people power," who ultimately made possible this stunning triumph over tyranny.

It was the people of the Philippines, not the United States, who protected the sanctity of the ballot box with their very lives. It was the people of the Philippines who surrounded Camp Crame at a critical moment when the balance of power in Manila was very tenuous. It was the people of the Philippines who put their lives on the line for democracy and it is they, therefore, who deserve the credit.

In those climactic days, the President of the United States said on national television that he thought both the government and the opposition were responsible for the fraud which took place. I remember vividly a meeting in my own office with two of the leading Administration policy makers on the Philippines—only a few days before Johnny Enrile and Eddie Ramos decided to break ranks with Mr. Marcos. The two policy makers pleaded with me not to go forward in my subcommittee with legislation scheduled for consideration on the following day. This legislation would have put all our unobligated military assistance to the Philippines into an escrow account pending the establishment of a legitimate government which had the confidence of the Filipino people.

The fact that we were able to get a unanimous vote in our subcommittee the next day in support of that legislation reflected the emerging consensus within the Congress and the country, that the time had come for the United States to definitively disassociate itself from a corrupt and discredited regime. By virtue of the theft of the election, the Marcos regime lost its residual legitimacy. We were then able to signal to the ruling establishment of the Philippines and the people of that country that the United States was in the process of clearly putting itself on the side of democracy rather than dictatorship. The Administration did, in the 59th minute of the 23rd hour, take the appropriate position, and the interests of the United States were thereby served.

During this time one of the most significant things we did was to offer Mr. Marcos an exchange: he might come to the United States if he were willing to peacefully relinquish power. I wasn't enthused or excited about having Mr. Marcos and his wife in our country, but I felt very strongly that President Reagan made the right decision. If the price of avoiding civil war was to allow him to come here, then it was a price worth paying.

But where do we go from here in our relationship with the new government of the Philippines, given our significant stake in its success?

No one ought to be under the illusion that the restoration of democracy in the Philippines is a panacea for the problems which continue to confront that country. The insurgency will not disappear overnight. The economy, ravaged by a decade of crony capitalism and government-led capital flight, will not instantly recover. It will take all of the new government's skill and determination to cope with these problems.

Its success will depend largely, although not exclusively, on its willingness to undertake fundamental political, military and, most of all, economic reforms. Several hundred years after the Spanish first arrived on its shores, the Philippines still retains many of the characteristics of a semi-feudal society. The insurgency in the Philippines was a reflection of much more than dissatisfaction or discontent with the corruption and repression of the Marcos regime. It was also a reflection of a profound upheaval by an underclass in the Philippines that has historically been denied access to the material benefits of the society.

Although the departure of Mr. Marcos and the transition from dictatorship to democracy will facilitate a restoration of confidence in the economy, these events alone will not be sufficient to achieve the kind of economic growth or equitable redistribution of income required to counter and contain the communist appeal.

The New People's Army (NPA) has certainly suffered a blow from recent developments in the Philippines. But if the new government cannot bring the fruits of freedom to the majority who live in the countryside, it will only be a matter of time until the insurgency recovers lost ground and renews its very serious challenge.

What is required? First and foremost, fundamental reform. Still, breaking up monopolies, promoting development of the rural sector and establishing a high standard of public trust and accountability will not be sufficient. The Philippines will require additional resources from both bilateral donors and multilateral lending institutions. From the point of view of the United States, even in this era of Gramm-Rudman —when foreign aid is not exactly the most popular program, and substantial reductions are going to have to be made in all sorts of important domestic programs—it would be penny-wise and pound-foolish for us not to provide the kind of additional assistance the Philippine government will need to effectively implement many of the necessary reforms.

In the short run, the government of the Philippines requires a significant and immediate transfusion of cash assistance. Before the election, President Reagan pledged to increase the level of U.S. aid to the Philippines if the election was free and fair and if the new government was prepared to implement fundamental reforms. That is precisely the direction in which we should be heading.

The Administration has announced a program which calls for approximately $171 million in new aid, and for the expedited disbursement of about $200 million in aid that has already been authorized and appropriated but which, under ordinary circumstances, might take several years to disburse.

The strategic significance of U.S. facilities at Clark Field and Subic Bay is clear. The bases have a very important role in enabling us to preserve the peace and stabilize the balance of power in Asia. If the United States were deprived of access to the bases, shock waves would reverberate throughout the region. Virtually every one of our friends in the area would be deeply concerned because they all depend on us, to a greater or lesser extent, to use the bases to fulfill our explicit and implicit defense commitments to them.

If the communists came to power, it is doubtful whether we could maintain our access to the bases. But with democracy restored in the Philippines, there is every reason to believe that we will reach a satisfactory agreement when the base negotiations occur.

The transition from the Marcos regime to the Aquino government was therefore clearly in the interest of the United States. If Mr. Marcos had remained in power, it would only have been a matter of time before the communists triumphed. That would have been a political disaster for the Filipino people, as well as a strategic debacle for the United States. I am certain that the present government in the Philippines will be a part of the solution rather than, as the Marcos government was, a part of the problem.

Two weeks after Mr. Marcos left Manila I was privileged to meet with President Aquino. She is one of the most impressive political figures I have ever met, in her own very nonpolitical way. I have met dozens of heads of state, foreign ministers and other dignitaries, but she is unique in exuding a palpable sense of purpose and of principle. She struck me as the complete antithesis of Mr. Marcos. Where he was totally corrupt, she is honest. Where he was invariably devious, she is completely straightforward. Where he was concerned about himself and his cronies, she is interested only in the welfare and well-being of her people.

I realize that she brings to her office little prior political or governmental experience. Yet I also know that she brings honesty, integrity and a driving determination to do justice—characteristics which have unfortunately been in short supply among Philippine leaders in the last two decades. These are qualities which will be extraordinarily important in the difficult days ahead.

This is a woman who has progressed enormously in the last year. She combines great moral authority with an incredible political charisma. The first comes from being the widow of the man whose martyrdom made restoration of democracy possible in the Philippines, and the second is by virtue of her own courageous campaign for the presidency in the Philippines. She can, on 24 or 48 hours notice, assemble a crowd of over a million people in Luneta Park, a crowd which simply comes to hear what she has to say.

On balance, I am very hopeful about the future of the Philippines. I recognize that Cory Aquino and her government face a daunting task. The challenges are enormous; the problems are great. Yet she brings to the job the kind of determination and integrity which is needed so badly at the present time. If friends in the United States and elsewhere around the world are willing to provide the additional assistance necessary, and if the new government is prepared to undertake the reforms to which they say they are committed, we may be at the dawn of a new era in the Philippines. A consolidation of democracy could then be possible, and the great majority of the Filipino people might finally have access to the benefits of progress and prosperity which they have historically been denied.

QUESTIONS AND ANSWERS

Q. What if the democratic Philippines decides to limit our ability to use the strategic and tactical aircraft and naval vessels out of those bases, or what if they decide democratically to let the leases run out?

CONGRESSMAN SOLARZ: If they make that decision, I think we have no alternative but to respect it. I think the chances that such a decision will be made, that we will be denied access to our facilities, or be deprived of the ability to effectively use them, are much less than they would have been if Mr. Marcos had remained in power.

There were two threats to our continued access to the bases while Marcos was in power. The first was the very real possibility that the communists would prevail. The second was that even if the communists didn't prevail, by virtue of the assistance we were providing the government in the Philippines pursuant to the base agreement, we were in the process of alienating significant sectors of Filipino society. There was a growing feeling on the part of many Filipinos that our aid to the Marcos regime was helping to prop up a dictatorship which had lost its confidence. If the bases weren't there, we wouldn't be providing the aid, and if we weren't providing the aid, Marcos wouldn't be able to remain in power.

Leaving aside the validity of that analysis, I think the perception was accurate, and now that Marcos is gone, the aid that we provide will no longer be seen as aid which is keeping a corrupt regime in power. It's much more likely to be seen as aid which is genuinely helping the Filipino people.

Therefore, I think the prospects for a healthy long-term relationship between the people of the Philippines and the United States will be greatly enhanced. In the long run, our ability to remain at Clark and Subic, which depends on the willingness of the Philippine people to have us there, will be increased.

Now, I believe we are going to see more Filipino nationalism. That's to be expected. Still I don't think that is in any way incompatible with a constructive relationship between our two countries.

I believe that the Association of East Asian Nations (ASEAN) countries see our facilities at Clark and Subic as playing a very important role in stabilizing the region. I think their views will clearly be taken into account by the new government. I would think that the Chinese Ambassador to Manila is also probably quietly sharing the thought that the Peoples Republic of China (PRC) would like to see the bases remain.

If, in 1991 when the base agreement expires, the new government decides to give us one year's notice under the terms of the agreement that they want to abrogate it, that is their right. The Philippines is a sovereign and independent country. We would then have to dig deep into our pockets and find the resources to develop alternative facilities in the region.

At the end of the day, we won't be in as good a position as we are now, but the United States is, and will remain, a Pacific power, whether we stay at Clark and Subic or whether we leave our bases there. I hope we remain at those bases, but one way or the other, we're going to remain in the Pacific.

Q. You and Senator Dole have suggested that we search for alternatives to the bases in that region. Now it appears that we will have a grace period for a few years. Wouldn't it be the ideal time now, to try to lessen the rhetoric and bring down the stakes for both the Philippines and the U.S. by exploring those alternatives seriously?

CONGRESSMAN SOLARZ: I fully agree with you. I think it is a mistake to put all our eggs in one basket under any circumstances. In addition, I have every expectation that when 1989 arrives and the time for the renegotiation of the base agreement is upon us, Cory Aquino is going to drive a very hard bargain. I think that's not only her right, I think that's her responsibility.

To the extent that we can demonstrate that we do have viable alternatives available, I think that enhances our negotiating position. I think that it is in our interests to explore these possibilities, both as a hedge against the possibility that we may not be able to utilize these bases in perpetuity, and also as a way of enhancing our bargaining position in those negotiations.

Q. Some people seem to have a different view of the insurgency than the one you have been expressing. They have begun to question the U.S. estimates of NPA strength. Some people are questioning the assessment of the Pentagon and the intelligence community that there are 20,000 regulars in the NPA.

There's also a view that the movement is much less centrally organized, and is generally softer and much more susceptible to falling apart through divisions or through a general lack of organization. Vice President Laurel has predicted that it will collapse in three to six months, and there are many Filipinos who share this view.

Are you convinced that the intelligence community is providing you with the right data on this, and what is behind your perception of the formidable threat that you seem to portray of this movement?

CONGRESSMAN SOLARZ: I am more convinced that the Marcoses owned $350 million worth of prime real estate in Manhattan than I am that all my judgments on the NPA should be carved in stone. Nevertheless, I have a good deal of confidence in my conclusions, which are based on discussions in the Philippines as well as on the intelligence I have received here in Washington.

My impression is that, if anything, the NPA has substantially more than 20,000 men under arms rather than substantially less than that number. If there is any mistake in the figures, I think it's that they understate the degree of armed strength on the part of the NPA.

However, we must distinguish between the number of full-time fighters who are working for the NPA and the other Filipinos on whom the NPA can draw for sympathy and support. I think in terms of the long-term prospects for the insurgency, it's the latter group that is by far the more significant.

In addition to the 20,000 to 30,000 full-time fighters in the NPA, there are another million Filipinos who can be mobilized through the National Democratic Front (NDF) for demonstrations on behalf of the Communist party of the Philippines, which controls the NDF and the NPA. There are another five million or more Filipinos who constitute a kind of mass base for the NPA. They are prepared to provide sanctuary, food, intelligence and other support to the full-time cadre of the NPA.

In the absence of a negotiated settlement between the Communist party and the government, it seems unlikely that a very large number of the full-time, hard-core cadre of the NPA will lay down their arms. I think several hundred, maybe even a few thousand might.

The bulk of them will probably continue the armed struggle in the absence of a negotiated settlement, but the real test is what happens to the mass base. If the government can deliver on its promises of fundamental reforms, and if the economy can be reversed now that democracy has been reestablished, there's a very real possibility that there will be substantial defections from the mass base. In that case, millions of Filipinos who were previously sympathetic to the NPA may now be willing to give their sympathy to a new government which clearly has their interests at heart.

What happens to that mass base will, more than anything else, determine the future of the insurgency in the Philippines.

There is another issue which is often raised in connection with the NPA, and it has to do with an article by Ross H. Munro in the December 1985 issue of *Commentary*. He portrayed the New People's Army as a kind of Filipino version of the Khmer Rouge. I fundamentally disagree with two propositions in that article, one implicit and one explicit.

The explicit proposition was that the NPA and the Khmer Rouge were virtually identical. I do not believe that Ross Munro produced any evidence in that article which would convincingly demonstrate that if the NPA came to power, it would, like the Khmer Rouge, evacuate all of the cities, abolish the monetary economy, systematically exterminate everybody who had a fifth-grade education or higher, and transform the entire Philippine archipelago into a kind of Asian Auschwitz in the way that Pol Pot transformed Cambodia.

He did demonstrate that they are a ruthless bunch of characters and that they don't hesitate to commit murder, assassination and terror to advance their interests, but that is usually par for the course for revolutionary movements.

They are a bad bunch, and I have no doubt that they would attempt, if they came to power, to establish a totalitarian society. But my guess is it would probably be more akin to the Vietnamese model than to the Cambodian model.

The second objection I had to the article was the implicit suggestion that it was only because the NPA was as bad as the Khmer Rouge that their triumph is something which needs to concern us. I disagree because even if the NPA is no worse than the Vietnamese communists, that's bad enough. That would be a tragedy for the Philippines, and it would be a tremendous setback for us.

It would eliminate all hope for the restoration or the resumption of democracy. It would doom the Philippines to an economic disaster and, therefore, I think it is a tragedy to be avoided at all costs. I don't think that one has to believe that the NPA is as bad as the Khmer Rouge to assume that its triumph would be unwanted and unfortunate, and I think Munro's article lends itself to that interpretation. He tries to prove too much and, therefore, makes a continuously flawed argument.

Q. Up until now, the NPA has not killed any Americans in the Philippines, at least willfully. As we move toward a closer relationship with the Aquino government, are you concerned that the NPA might see that movement as a threat? If we begin to strengthen the capability of the Armed Forces of the Philippines (AFP) and boost their morale, the NPA may feel more threatened than before when the AFP was demoralized and had a live-and-let-live attitude. Americans, especially in Subic and at Clark, could become targets of NPA terrorism. If so, what should we do about that?

CONGRESSMAN SOLARZ: As you point out, they have very carefully avoided targeting Americans until now. I would be hesitant to predict what they will do in the future, because there is a very fluid situation in the Philippines, and my sense is they don't know themselves how to react to the departure of Marcos. With Marcos's departure from the Philippines, the NPA lost its major recruiting agent: Mr. Marcos. They are reeling from the blow.

Now there are two possibilities. The government may succeed in its efforts to improve the economy, and may be able to consolidate democracy. Or it may fall flat on its face and come apart because of internal squabbling, and be unsuccessful in revitalizing the economy. Each of these situations poses very different problems for the NPA.

It's very hard to speculate about this, because they might conceivably decide that it was in their interest to provoke an American response to bring in the United States. This would give them an opportunity to try to seize the nationalist issue. It's difficult to predict what desperate people will do.

My real answer to your question is, I don't know if they are going to do this. It's not likely but it cannot be precluded.

Q. What do you predict will be President Aquino's ability to consolidate power, given the disparate group of supporters, including the last-minute converts as well as the Marcos holdovers in the local governments?

CONGRESSMAN SOLARZ: I'm very hopeful because I'm enormously impressed by her. It was symbolically significant that she chose not to live in the Malacanang, because she said she thought it was inappropriate for the president of a country afflicted by as much poverty as the Philippines to be living amidst such splendor. I think that you need to lead by example, and I think she is prepared to set the kind of example which can be an inspiration for the people of her country.

There comes a point where you have to be willing to put some faith in people, and just as I had a very good feeling about Josea Napoleon Duarte in El Salvador, who had, really, the right instincts, I have a comparable faith in her.

Now, many of the problems in El Salvador still exist. The war continues, and the economy is still suffering significantly. But if Duarte hadn't been elected, it would have been a disaster. Similarly, if she hadn't come to power, it would have been a disaster for the Philippines. I am hopeful, but it wouldn't amaze me if the government fell apart. The problems really are daunting.

There is a very real importance in providing the new government of the Philippines with whatever help we can, and to further its efforts to recover the hidden wealth of the Marcoses in the United States.

This is not just a matter of simple justice; it's also a matter of simple arithmetic. The value of the real-estate properties controlled by the Marcoses in the New York area alone is worth more than twice the annual level of American economic assistance to the Philippines. It would obviously be very helpful to the new government if they could effectively recover those resources. I hope that, while this matter is in the courts, we will take whatever steps are requested to facilitate their task in recovering these assets.

4

The "Yellow Revolution": Its Mixed Historical Legacy

Theodore Friend

THE YELLOW REVOLUTION IN GLOBAL PERSPECTIVE

The Yellow Revolution in the Philippines, 1983-86, already begins to recede in time. The question is whether or not its basic hue will hold fast in the fabric of Philippine life. President Aquino finds it acceptable now to wear dresses of a greater variety of colors, her wardrobe suggesting the opportunities, as well as the pressures, of normality. The institutions, ideas, and alliances which will be her legacy are still developing. And both form and style of government in the Philippines are in the remaking. Will they settle out as legislative and libertarian as they did in one revolution of 1896, or will they this time crystallize as executive and authoritarian? Or will circumstances drive them toward the dictatorial? Historical perspective on Mrs. Aquino's situation and her problems may be helpful.[1]

A one-man, one-party state such as President Marcos developed before her, with an increasingly militarized bureaucracy and a tendency to rule through appanage or crony-patronage, is hardly unknown in Southeast Asia. The interesting questions are to what degree such systems provide food, jobs, education, and enhanced real social opportunity, as distinct from management of malnutrition and underemployment combined with indoctrination and manipulation of hopes. Marcos' regime, while perhaps marginally constructive from 1965 to 1975, clearly tilted toward the destructive sometime after that and

---

[1] I find two recent articles in *Foreign Affairs* particularly helpful, one regional and one country-specific: Richard Holbrooke, "East Asia: the Next Challenge," 64, 4 (Spring, 1986), 732-51, and Carl H. Landé and Richard Hooley, "Aquino Takes Charge," 64, 5 (Summer, 1986), 1087–1107.

toppled from power when its rot and inertia were tested by an aroused populace.

The forces that pressed for Marcos' downfall, however—leaving aside the contribution of his own errors and hubris—are not found in clear confluence anywhere else in Southeast Asia. They could be generalized as consisting of bourgeois, intellectual, and clerical. But all those terms suffer from intellectual bloat. More accurately, the forces for change arose from businessmen, educated middle and upper middle classes, and activist priests and nuns. Individuals from those groups came together in a rare and new coherence, joined by the votes and energies of the hungry, and produced the change.

One may detect resemblances to forces in Latin America which have brought about the surprising democratic resurgences there since 1980. "Only the most optimistic observers imagined five years ago that South America would enter the second half of the 1980s with 94 percent of its population living under civilian and constitutional regimes. . . ."[2] The temptation arises to look for predictable patterns in Iberian-American history and to fit the Philippines into those shapes. Such analyses would be misleading, however—first, because of the Malay ethnic base to Philippine history, and second, because of the American superstructure to it.

For an understanding of the recent past, and a sense of probable futures, one does better to look at Philippine history itself since 1896, which leads inevitably to examining the patterns and latent probabilities in the bilateral relationship with the United States.[3]

---

[2] Abraham F. Lowenthal, "Threat and Opportunity in the Americas," *Foreign Affairs* 64 (1985), No. 3, 539–61; quotation p. 544.

[3] I have examined that subject at some length in "Freedom, Independence, and Development: Philippine-American Tensions in History," John Bresnan, ed., *Crisis in the Philippines: the Marcos Era and Beyond* (Princeton: Princeton University Press, 1986). I have also written an article for a Japanese audience, translated into Japanese by Professor Miwa Kimitada, appearing in *Chūō, Kōron*, September 1986, pp. 212–222: *"Philippine shin sei ken no sen taku: Kenishugi no Saikōchiku wa Kanōka?"* (original English title: "Can the Philippines Mix Authority with Democracy and Make Them Work?").

INITIATIVES AND PHASE-CHANGES IN PHILIPPINE-AMERICAN HISTORY

In transnational perspective, Philippine-American history of the last ninety years may be seen as containing five fundamental initiatives. The first three were American, and the most recent two Filipino. Each, inescapably, became a series of bilateral processes, lurching forward in directions intended by the initiators, then fading away; ricocheting off counter-forces; partially recaptured and finally reshaped into the sedate facts and accepted data which are thought of as "history."

All analytic periodizations are arbitrary. The following list of initiatives and phase-changes may summarize a complex history in a new and suggestive way.

1898–1901: American conquest and assimilation: American dominance was established, the principles of constitutional government were laid down, and lines of imperial culture were laid out.

1929–1934: American approaches to devolution: Pressure from American farm and labor lobbies, recognition of strategic jeopardy, and resurgence of anti-imperial principle led to accelerated Filipinization of the government, American determination of eventual independence, and scheduling of Philippine sovereignty for 1946.

1942–1949: American defense of the binational achievement and assertion of neo-mercantilism: The Fil-American joint loss to Japan in 1942 and joint triumph in 1945 led to trade, aid, and basic agreements, 1946-49, overshadowing the fact of Philippine sovereignty.

1955–1965: Philippine economic nationalism: The Laurel-Langley agreement of 1955 revised terms of trade and was accompanied and followed by entrepreneurial initiatives in Philippine legislation and regulation.

1972–1981: Philippine martial law government: This experiment in "constitutional authoritarianism" lost its economic

71

productivity as early as 1975, though it caused continued dilution of national institutions and civil rights into 1986.

The Yellow Revolution clearly initiates another phase-change, but one that can only be partly described. Until time allows better definition, looking back will serve to help clarify the present.

CONTRADICTORY FORCES IN THE PHILIPPINE POLITY

To Americans who care and to Filipinos proud of a binational tradition, it is a matter for chagrin that a former colony of the United States, with mass education, high literacy, and free institutions, should go into a period of show-of-hands constitution making, buttoned lips regarding governmental fallibility, and eyes averted from invasions of privacy, abrogation of rights, and destruction of human life. There were, of course, masses of Americans who did not know enough to care. In addition to its recognition of the fact that the Philippines had been for a quarter century a sovereign nation, privileged to make its own mistakes, in 1972 the American government was preoccupied with extracting itself from Vietnam. There were also many Filipinos who did not "care" in the sense that their libertarian tradition was passive and ideal, and their authoritarian heritage more concrete and real—a daily matter of home, school, and church.[4] This last may be a vital fact underappreciated by American journalists and officials.

Little of Spanish rule in the sixteenth century through nineteenth century conveyed a sense of individual rights to Filipinos. The government was foreign, imperial, and monarchical. Geography and the structure of government strongly constrained against the expression either of individual conscience or of collective will in public affairs. Whether one looks high or low in formal power, *governador* or *cabeza de barangay*, or at the *principales* holding local influence, one tends to

---

[4]This is by no means a new discovery; see Rex Drilon et al., "Philippine Democracy Reexamined," pamphlet based on Philippine *Historical Bulletin* 6 (December 1962). Alfred W. McCoy's paper, "Quezon's Commonwealth: The Emergence of Philippine Authoritarianism" (presented to the Association for Asian Studies, Philadelphia, March 1985) does an excellent job of showing extension of dyadic ties from Manila to Washington. To speak of the "emergence" of Philippine authoritarianism in 1935–41, however, is to slight its cultural presence and its potency in most of recorded modern history.

find power and resources focused in single persons. Only as European liberalism slowly and belatedly percolated into the consciousness of many Philippine-born *ilustrados* were counter-expectations developed.

Revolution broke out against Spain in 1896, but it was riven with factionalism and in retreat by 1898. Its key general, Emilio Aguinaldo, was exiled in Singapore when American arrival in Manila ensured both defeat of Spain and a new confrontation: young expanding empire against young would-be nation. In the Philippine-American war that followed, three strains of Filipino political thinking can be identified. First was the autocratic: Aguinaldo announced a "dictatorial government," which revealed his true instincts but alienated many potential followers. Second was the authoritarian, as represented by Apolinario Mabini, a romantic nationalist who favored a strong executive for the discipline necessary to social regeneration. Third was the libertarian, favored by the cosmopolitan *ilustrados*, who mistrusted both Aguinaldo and Mabini and wished a strong legislature instead. The third element prevailed politically in 1898–99 and eventually articulated and managed the compromises with the United States that brought about peace and assimilation politics, 1899–1901.[5]

All three elements can be detected in subsequent history. The American presence ensured libertarian dominance. But authoritarian elements came in as an undercurrent during Quezon's presidency of the commonwealth in 1935–41; military-executive fiat prevailed under the Japanese, 1942–45; and native dictatorship, emboldened as an experiment in regional dynasticism, prevailed after Marcos announced martial law.

At first, however, American organic laws and educational policy drew the Filipinos deep into modern constitutionalism and cultural liberalism, far beyond their own revolutionary document. On top of the Roman Catholic concept of the precious individual soul, which could be saved or damned, American culture strengthened new notions: Individual social dignity could be educated in its own self-expression, and individual secular ambition could be equipped for gathering economic momentum and political influence. If that sometimes led to

[5]David Steinberg et al., *In Search of Southeast Asia* (New York: Praeger, 1971), pp. 262–66. For the view of an Hispanic Filipino on the same events, see Antonio M. Molina, *Historia de Filipinas* (Madrid: Instituto de Cooperacion Iberoamericana, 1984), 2, 329–511.

factionalistic squabbling or near-anarchic competition, such might be the price of modernization, American style.

In restraint, there were still American colonial officials to cope with regression in standards of health and finance, such as were found by the Wood-Forbes Commission of 1921. An American majority prevailed on the Supreme Court even into the commonwealth period. After 1935, an American high commissioner might still curb the excesses of the popularly elected president.[6] The job was transitional and performance varied with the men who did it: Frank Murphy, tactful and cooperative; Paul McNutt, vigorous in pursuit of American interests; Francis Sayre, principled and stilted. Quezon, as time went on, found the power of the high commissioner a snafflebit. It restrained him, and he could not spit it away. Then a new invasion forced him into exile.

The Japanese occupation, 1941–45, brought great loss of life, as well as material and moral damage to the Philippines. On the positive side, Tagalog as the basis for a national language was strengthened, and so was pride in native values clearly Asian. National identity, however, strongly resisted a proffered pan-Asian identity with Japanese overlordship. And the form of presidency which the Japanese promoted, an authoritarian executive backed by the potential *diktat* of their own military, was accepted only because imposed. Jose P. Laurel as the bearer of that office, 1943–45, was acceptable to Filipinos as a buffer against the Japanese. And he did what little he could to use Fil-American legal principles to constrain the new conquerors. At the same time, a Mabiniesque concern for leader-inspired social regeneration flared out in him, just as genuine as his Yale-taught concern for due process of law.[7]

A strong mood of restoration after the war reestablished the political ethos of the Philippines in its now fundamental tension between the amalgam of Hispano-Catholic values with the Filipino family system on one side and the American matrix of constitution-civil service-representative elections-and education for citizenship on the other.

---

[6]The best description of Philippine public institutions in this period remains Joseph Ralston Hayden, *The Philippines: A Study in National Development* (New York: Macmillan, 1947).

[7]Theodore Friend, "Revolution and Restoration: Java, Luzon and Japanese Impact, 1942–1945," (Princeton University Press, estimated date of publication, 1987).

A thoughtful Filipino sociologist has written of his countrymen's "Split-Level Christianity."[8] By the same token, one may speak of split-level democracy in the Philippines. In the same nation, and sometimes in a single individual, there is genuine feeling, even passion, for democratic values; powerful rhetorical expression, both sincere and insincere, of those values; and frequent avoidance of democratic processes in action. Even the avoiders may feel distress at any profound public estrangement from a core democratic credo. Private comfort with authoritarian values in home, school, and church may be profound, but will still not guarantee an easy time for statist behavior. Thousands of crypto-democrats may come out and express themselves in ways countervailing to the state, should government dispose itself in too authoritarian a manner.

"NOON AND DARKNESS"

The American colonial presence apparently required a one-party system as a nationalistic rallying point. Quezon's success in keeping that party together and in exploiting nationalistic issues helps explain his twenty-one years of power, from 1922 until his death in 1943. Postwar devolution of sovereignty, however, led to a series of one-term presidents, 1945–65—Roxas, Quirino, Magsaysay, Garcia, and Macapagal.[9] All were chosen through close elections in a fluid two-party system, plastic, factional, and personalistic.

Ferdinand Marcos snapped the string. Elected in 1965 over Macapagal, he won again in 1969 to become the first twice-elected president of the Philippines. Two terms, however, were the limit constitutionally allowed. So Marcos in 1972 yanked the cord on martial law, and changed the rules to perpetuate his regime. Other essays in this volume tell what followed, until Marcos' presidency ended.

Marcos' twenty-year primacy in Philippine politics (1966–86) nearly equalled that of Quezon's (1922–43) in duration, and probably exceeded it in impact. Attempts have already begun to link and liken their periods of rule, to analogize them in style as spendthrift autocrats.

[8]Jaime Bulatao, S.J., "Split-Level Christianity," and Vitaliano Gorospe, S.J., "Christian Renewal of Filipino Values" (Quezon City: Ateneo University Press, 1966).

[9]Roxas and Magsaysay both died in office. They were strong presidents who might conceivably have been reelected had they lived.

Some would imply that the "U.S.-Marcos dictatorship" was prefigured in what could be called the "U.S.-Quezon puppet show." In this view, America held the strings in the commonwealth period and pulled them when necessary for American interests, but they were basically indifferent to Quezon's enforcement of an extravagant power-appetite upon a subdued people. Forty years later, the political wires that animated and controlled from above were simply replaced by economic lifelines that sustained from abroad. America would succor Marcos while Marcos suckered America.

That picture, however, is grossly overdrawn. An eminent Filipino, a cultural critic and public servant who lived through both regimes, says, "Quezon and Marcos? They were as different as noon and darkness." Quezon he found clear and open in style (the commentator pointed to his heart as he talked); but Marcos was obscure, manipulative, calculating (he pointed to his head while frowning and narrowing his eyes).[10]

The dramatic difference in style is important. Allied to it are basic differences in value and procedure. Quezon's lineage was in part from Mabini, in that authoritarianism coexisted with romantic nationalism. But both remained under authentic discipline of law. Marcos, however, used the law tactically, without conviction as to its historic and social value. As a result his style approached Aguinaldo's in its dictatorial nature but was dextrous where Aguinaldo's was awkward. At the same time he found an allure in the magic personalism of some neighboring potentates and in monuments and dynasticism far exceeding anything expressed by Quezon. Basic distinctions drawn, it is revealing to pursue the thoughts of the two leaders.

QUEZON'S THEORY OF A PARTYLESS DEMOCRACY

Among leaders of colonized peoples before the Great Pacific War, Quezon was the only man styled as a president, and receiving a nineteen-gun salute. As he looked forward to twenty-one guns, he gave thought to the future shape of the Philippine polity and its leadership. In 1940 three speeches laid out a rough "Theory of a Partyless Democracy."[11] Quezon was at the height of his powers, and the Japanese

---

[10]S.P. Lopez, in conversation with the author, June 8, 1986.

[11]"Addresses of His Excellency, Manuel L. Quezon, President of the Philippines, on the Theory of a Partyless Democracy," (Manila: Bureau of Printing, 1940).

threat, while felt, was still sixteen months away from becoming an invasion. In a speech at the University of the Philippines, he criticized dictatorships, including dictatorship of the proletariat, and lauded democracy of the Lincolnian kind, "of, by, and for the people." This rhetorical opening preceded a series of sallies against old ideas of the scope of governments, which accented too much the sacredness of property and contracts and recognized too little the social obligations of men living under the same system.[12] Quezon proceeded to attack as "fetishes" the concept of political parties and the idea that individual liberty must not be restricted,[13] while heading towards his conceptual and practical goal: governmental initiatives in behalf of social justice.

Quezon made the metaphorical point that a nation is like a family, in which the father and the children cannot be at cross purposes. Nobody challenged his figure of speech. Quezon did not sound to his audience like a wayward Confucian from Northeast Asia; he was in fact touching the heart of some prominent values in the Philippines which were common to Greater Malaysia.[14]

But nearly everything else Quezon said that day was challenged—by students, professors, journalists, jurists, and the Civil Liberties Union. The latter organization raised fears of a "tyrant." Quezon, undaunted, reentered the fray with another speech, in which he clarified his

---

[12]Quezon, "The Essence of Democracy," in Ibid., pp. 1–16. Quezon had earlier elaborated his criticism of excessively privileged defense of property rights in a candidly recorded "Conference given by the President to the Representatives of Foreign and Local Press held at Malacanan February 2, 1939, at 10 A.M." (32 pp.), transcript in Quezon Collection, National Library, Manila.

[13]In these comments one can now see analogy to Sukarno's attack on "free-fight liberalism" in the Indonesia of the 1950s and 1960s. Quezon's critique of party politics as causing inefficiency, delay, and lack of direction preceded Sukarno's attempt to lower the profile of parliamentary democracy in Indonesia. In that effort, the Suharto government since then has steadily persisted, and more solidly succeeded, while also achieving some economic goals which Sukarno never even tried to formulate.

[14]Quezon's reasoning towards restriction of individual liberties anticipated themes that Jose P. Laurel, Sr., and Benigno Aquino, Sr., would voice during the Japanese occupation of the Philippines. They were prompted certainly by their new conquerors, but they spoke with a conviction consistent with the rest of their careers in behalf of social duties as prior to and inseparable from individual rights. Quezon, onstage, dominated Philippine politics. When he was offstage in exile, a number of politicians made statements and uttered criticisms they had not previously expressed.

principles and stressed his major aim of social justice. The second speech further reveals both his attempt to clear theoretical ground so that the Philippines might catch up with the New Deal in the United States and with the reforms of Miguel Aleman in Mexico, and his effort to ride past the high-handed *hacendero* mentality which he disliked.[15] He was not of that class; he could get along with it though he might seek and get its support in some matters; but he could still see its self-indulgence and social hierarchism as dangerous to the Philippines.

To the criticism that he wanted to do away with all "fiscalizers" (critics), Quezon said that nobody feared to speak out in the Philippines. The evidence was that so many had done so against him: "Your Constitution offers you all the checking you need, except the checking of the opposition." He wished to make the basic point that executive power was required to effect social justice. This the opposition was trying to block. He would be content, however, to succeed in less—to "show the world that this totalitarian ruler is known enough in the government university, known well enough in fact for everybody to feel that he can disagree with him, and neither lose his job nor go to jail, that is enough for me."

Quezon had difficulty only in answering the observation of President Bienvenido Santos of the University of the Philippines that abolishing political organizations would lead to stronger class consciousness and to political control by a small and well-organized minority, both of which were bigger evils than political organizations as they then existed. Quezon did not effectively refute the point, but he restated his belief that a carping opposition was the major obstacle to Philippine progress.[16]

In a third and final speech at Far Eastern University, Quezon carried his themes further. He stressed the great value of a nation of critical individuals, as distinct from opposition parties. Partyless government, he said, presupposes an educated citizenry, an independent and honest press, an "extended radio service that is not controlled either by the government or special interests," and a community without privileged classes.

[15]"A Partyless Government in a Democracy," in Quezon, "Theory of a Partyless Democracy," pp. 17–40.

[16]Ibid.; quotations, pp. 30, 26.

Idealized and modernized Athenian democracy was more to the taste of his university audience. But Quezon had to come back to the practical. He acknowledged criticisms of the Philippines' "one-party system" by likening it to the southern states in the United States or the Irish Free State, where such things existed in ways that were democratic, and certainly not devoid of struggle. He concluded that the direction in which to move was not toward a system of two well-balanced parties, but toward a system in which parties were unnecessary. Far more education of the public would be required, however, to approach that desirable point. Quezon concluded more than a month of public debate by admitting that "it would seem to be rash to try and experiment now with a partyless government."[17] By this public admission, Quezon displayed his talent for acknowledging frustration without admitting defeat. Even when his ideas created shivers of apprehension, his candor in advocacy and openness in debate could serve actually to enhance public trust in him.

An earlier speech shows how deep Quezon's concerns actually went—to the deepest levels of national character.

> The Filipino of today is soft, easy-going. . . . He is uninclined to sustained strenuous effort. . . . Face-saving is the dominant note in the confused symphony of his existence. His sense of righteousness is often dulled by the desire of personal gain. His norm of conduct is generally prompted by expediency rather than by principle. . . .[18]

Apologizing for the severity of what he was saying, he called upon memories of the heroes of the past, Bonifacio, both del Pilars, Mabini, Luna, and above all Rizal. Why wait for an emergency to awaken the

[17]Quezon, "The Elimination of Partisanship in a Democracy," in Ibid., pp. 41–58; quotations, pp. 43, 58.

[18]"Policies and Achievements of the Government and Regeneration of the Filipinos" [Delivered before the faculties and student bodies of public schools, colleges, and universities, at the Jose Rizal Memorial Field, August 19, 1938], *Messages of the President* (Manila: Bureau of Printing, 1938), *4*, part 1, 146–157; quotation, p. 152. This speech also exists, with pp. 1–2 missing, in draft typescript in the Quezon Collection, National Library, Manila.

flame of their spirit? To endow the Filipino with optimism and valor, to refashion the culture and character is an urgent "task of national spiritual reconstruction." To ensure its accomplishments,

> we shall formulate and adopt a social code—a code of ethics and personal conduct—a written Bushido—that can be explained in the schools, preached from the pulpits, and taught in the streets and plazas. . . . We shall indoctrinate every man, woman, and child in its precepts. . . .
>
> Every official of the government will cooperate, and ignorance of, or failure to live up to, the rules of conduct established, will be a bar to public office. There will be some superficial men, those who claim and believe that they know it all, who would brand this as the first step toward totalitarianism. Let them bark at the moon.[19]

An astonishingly candid speech, defiant of ordinary political prudence. What does it signify? Certainly it shows some of the inner operations and colorings of Quezon's mind. His deep comprehension of the national character, usually expressed in compassionate patience, or voluble frustration, or humor, here takes the shape of imagining complete "spiritual reconstruction" once and for all. Such visions are not livable by whole peoples, or practicable by realistic leaders. Quezon's utterances here, particularly the reference to a "written Bushido," show his apprehension over the encroaching energies of Japan. And indeed, within four years Laurel would be at the president's desk uttering similar thoughts with Japanese advisors at his shoulder. But Quezon apparently did not dare initiate his program of Philippine social Bushido. When he did nerve himself up to pursue an unpopular message, it took the form of criticism of what he saw as the irresponsible and fruitless carping of the opposition parties. And he backed down gracefully, with himself in the limelight.

The first Filipino steps toward totalitarianism were not taken by Manuel Quezon. They were taken by Ferdinand Marcos, a full generation afterwards.

[19]Ibid., pp. 15–16.

MARCOS' "IDEOLOGY FOR FILIPINOS"

The course from declaring martial law to ruling by presidential decree went rather smoothly for Marcos. There was a splutter of protest at the beginning. But many misgivings gave way to relief, and, en masse, to passivity. "The President was able to paralyze Congress in 1972, and then pulverize it in 1973, and finally resurrect it in caponized form in 1976." The Supreme Court, unable to stand alone against an assertive presidency, bowed before it until the assassination of Aquino, when it began to yield rights to demonstrators.[20]

The resulting government was authoritarian by anybody's definition —autocratic in its initiative, cronyistic in its preferments, and oppressive in its impact. Where did it come from? It came, inescapably, from Philippine history and character. It could also be said to borrow, in part, from Madison Avenue for its public relations techniques, from Sukarno for its verbalism and glib Third Worldism,[21] from Suharto for its reliance on the military and on police surveillance and censorship. But it surely did not come in inspiration or example from Manuel Quezon.

By the time the ruling theories of Ferdinand Marcos (or his staff writers' reactions of them) had ripened,[22] he was dismissive of pre-World War II democracy in the Philippines. He rejected the era and never mentioned Quezon by name.[23]

One who knew and adhered to the 1935 Constitution and kept his distance from Marcos does not recall Marcos ever using Quezon's theories or stances as arguments or precedents for himself. Marcos swept on by Quezon, the constitution, everything. He once described his intention to former Senators Pelaez, Padilla, and Sumulong, to "subvert" Philippine society.[24] That he corrupted it instead should not

[20]Joaquin G. Bernas, S.J., "Constitutionalism after 1982," in Ramon C. Reyes, ed., *Budhi Papers, VI,* "Philippines After 1972: a Multidisciplinary Perspective" (Quezon City: Ateneo de Manila University, 1985), pp. 190–203, quotation p. 202.

[21]Ferdinand E. Marcos, *The Third World Challenge* (Manila: NMPC Books, 1976, 2nd printing 1980).

[22]Ferdinand E. Marcos, *An Ideology for Filipinos* (n.p., n.d., "second printing," copyright 1980).

[23]Ibid., p. 31.

[24]Author's conversation with Ambassador Emmanuel Pelaez, June 6, 1986; the incident spoken of was early in the martial law period.

obscure the fact that social justice was still at that time one of his objectives.

Quezon helped popularize the term "social justice" in Philippine political parlance, and he welcomed its introduction in the Constitution of 1935. He was largely frustrated, however, in achieving significant steps toward it by oligarchic skepticism, a caretaker colonial administration, and lack of allies. He spoke more sympathetically of the communist leaders, Cristanto Evangelista and Guillermo Capadocia, than he did of Filipino plutocrats and oppositionist lawyer-politicians.[25] But they could not help him. And he had neither the power, nor in the end the time, to do much for the vast classes of the Filipino needy.

Marcos in the martial law period pictured himself almost as a frustrated Marxist. He said he wished to take governing beyond "a political game played by the economic and intellectual elite." But he could not take it to the masses, because seventy percent of the population only knew consciousness of oppression and demonstrated loyalty to *particular* leaders. They would take up arms for or against a personalized enemy, but not against the system. Marcos concluded that "there cannot be any genuine class revolution in this country."[26]

There must, therefore, be a government-led revolution. Precisely what it would be for, who would get what, and who could give up what, were best left out of an ideology. But Marcos did declare that "democracy is the formulation of a national consensus on basic guiding policies born of free and responsible discussion."[27] In that there is a tinny echo of Sukarno and his stress on *musyawara/mufakat* in Indonesia.[28] There is also a loud contradiction. What is meant by free and

[25]Undated draft of 41-page transcript of [1939] press conference, pp. 1–5 missing; especially pp. 6–7; "Conference between his Excellency, the President and Mr. Wilkins of the Bulletin, February 9, 1939," pp. 7–9, 12–15, especially p. 13 (Quezon Collection).

[26]Marcos, "Ideology," pp. 32–33.

[27]Ibid., p. 40.

[28]J.D. Legge analyzes these concepts as advocated by Sukarno, as well as their flaws, in his excellent *Sukarno: a Political Biography* (New York: Praeger, 1972), especially pp. 283–85.

Sukarno first began his rise to power (1942) as Quezon was dying and his fall from power as Marcos was elected to the presidency (1965). The years between, in which the Philippines clung to two-party, fluid-faction, client-patron politics, were years in which Sukarno launched his critique of Western-style parliamentary liberalism, introduced his Guided Democracy, and elaborated his own brand of leader-dominated consensus.

responsible discussion in circumstances that Marcos had already defined as "a rapacious oligarchy and an electorate, enfeebled by poverty, open to corruption"?[29] Discussion under such conditions became leader-dominated. Deliberation (*musyawara*) is initiated and structured by the leader. Consensus (*mufakat*) is determined and announced by the leader. The process could conceivably, under a wise leader, produce fresh ideas, broad support, and social advances. But Marcos appears to have pursued his own instinct, and the promptings of his own cunning, to his own ends.

Marcos proudly stated that his constitution had advanced beyond that of 1935 regarding social justice—from it "*should* be the concern of the state" to the state "*shall* promote social justice."[30] The pride was no doubt real. But what were the accomplishments? Other essays in this volume will tell of the condition in which Marcos left the Philippines: hunger and malnutrition not seen since World War II, debt out of proportion to anything in Philippine history, and oligarchic rapacity (to use Marcos' words) developed by an in-group of presidential cronies with cynical intensity and to grandiose extent. His "ideology" was discredited as blatantly insincere, the palaver of a consummate tactician. The people felt police repressiveness of a brutality not seen since the Japanese *Kenpeitai*, in the service of ordained ideas and regulated discussion not seen since the days of the Spanish, and for the first time combined in the Philippines with modern electronic modes of surveillance.

QUEZON AND MARCOS: DISSIMILARITIES IN THE LIGHT OF THE PRESENT

In explaining how the Philippines brought Ferdinand Marcos on itself, it is tempting to look for a previous "dictator" in Manuel Quezon, and to say that the groundwork was laid before. But that would be grossly misleading as to basic processes. Quezon's theory of a partyless democracy clearly shows that he would have liked to head toward a no-party state. To the credit of his common sense, however, he backed off. After weeks of the freest possible kind of public criticism, he concluded that the time was not ripe. What Quezon had

---

[29]Marcos, "Ideology," p. 39.
[30]Ibid., pp. 54–58.

going during the commonwealth, in fact, was a one-party system, with an abundance of ill-organized "fiscalizers." They stung and annoyed him. But he could not and would not jail or silence them. Meanwhile, they could and did restrain him in his moments of ambitious imagination.[31]

What would have been the outcome had not there still been an American colonial presence as critic and counterweight to Quezon? Would he have overridden constitutional precepts or evaded his own wiser principles? Something different, no doubt, would have emerged, and less libertarian. But two points need to be firmly lodged in order to proceed to compare Quezon with Marcos. First: The United States was there, as a guarantor of a due process state and of civil liberties. Second: along with his abundant flaws, Quezon did have scruples. He rejoiced in winning open political combat through eloquence, flair, agility, fervor. He would summon money for victory whenever he needed. But he was not a liar. And he was not a killer.

The system that Ferdinand Marcos introduced under martial law could be called a "one-party dominant" system, replacing the two-party system of 1945–72, and superficially resembling what took shape in Quezon's pre-war presidency, 1935–41. The potential of one-party dominance for stability against coups has been shown to be greater than two-party systems.[32] The KBL could conceivably have worked better for the Philippines than the alternating currents and personalities of the Nationalist and Liberal parties.

But the key is to consider what is given up for stability. A quick answer for the Philippines, to be reassessed in the light of time and further research, is that martial law may have yielded the Philippines some developmental advantages through 1975 or 1976, after which the exchange of liberty for order and welfare began to become a poor trade. By the early 1980s, not only had liberties been lost, but well-being too; and even order was beginning to unravel.

Marcos' "ideology for Filipinos" in retrospect looks like a sham and a cover for corruption of power. Quezon's "theory of partyless democ-

[31]A provocative comparison of strengths and weaknesses between Quezon and another successor as president is Miguel A. Bernad, S.J., "Quezon and Magsaysay," in his *Tradition and Discontinuity: Essays on Philippine History and Culture* (Manila: National Book Store, 1983), pp. 77–94.

[32]Samuel P. Huntington, "Political Order in Changing Societies" (New Haven: Yale University Press, 1968), pp. 422–33.

racy," however, appears at worst to have been a trial balloon. The political winds were against him, not to mention a good deal of buckshot. He drew back. In that simple sequence one may visualize functioning democracy in the late American period. It was a one-party-against-the-colonists system, with occasional splintering into secondary parties. Quezon led it with panache and success. That success may be attributed not only to his own skill, but to America's stabilizing presence and its political utility to him as a benign adversary. The American presence also gave courage to his opponents and silently inhibited him from authoritarian experiments that he imagined in moments of frustration.

Marcos took the Philippines into a new world. It was not a bright one. To preserve his power, he invoked martial law, ruled by presidential fiat, and availed of a supine legislature through one prevailing party held together by patronage ties. He allowed or licensed favorites into what became unchecked debauchery of the economy. He diverted government funds to preferred individuals as well as making them concessionaires.[33] The "compadre colonialism" of Quezon's era was perhaps a sloppy cultural adjustment on both sides. But the "crony capitalism" of Marcos' time became rampantly erosive of the finances and institutions of the Philippines.[34]

Repairs of the damage of the Marcos era will take a long time. Most of the Aquino government apparently seeks to proceed in a style combining open politics with NAMFREL free enterprise and a modern Catholic religious spirit.[35] As it does so, it faces debt, insurgency, and a population beset by severe malnutrition and underemployment—all at once. Totalitarians in the cordillera and in the outer islands, Marcos

[33]The distinction is important. Government concessions are a mode of life in Indonesia, for instance; but preferment there does not decline into the direct and massive pilferage of the Marcos family and circle of cronies.

[34]Norman G. Owen, ed., *Compadre Colonialism: Studies on the Philippines Under American Rule* (Ann Arbor: Center for South and Southeast Asian Studies, theUniversity of Michigan, 1971); and David A. Rosenberg, ed., *Marcos and Martial Law in the Philippines* (Ithaca: Cornell University Press, 1979). In the latter volume, Robert A. Stauffer takes the view that American-inspired "refeudalization" of the Philippines is the real demon: "The Political Economy of Refeudalization," pp. 180–218.

[35]On the latter theme: Jaime Cardinal Sin, *Selected Writings on Church-State Relations and Human Development* (Manila: Centre for the Development of Human Resources in Rural Asia, 1984), 68pp.

loyalists in the streets and the Manila Hotel—together they make a difficult beginning for the new government. It proceeds with divided views but with hope and apparent integrity of spirit.

Americans in mid-1986 still tend to be jubilant at the renewal of what they conceive of as the best of the heritage that they offered to the Philippines. And Filipinos of many kinds—businessmen, professional people, ecclesiasts, educators, ordinary middle class, humble working class—rejoice in their own courageous overthrow of Marcos' armed autocracy. At the very same time, however, their Southeast Asian neighbors ask the Filipinos, "Why can't you make authoritarianism work?"

The question is chilling, but ignores the unique variety of alternatives latent in Philippine history. They include, without beginning to exhaust possibilities: militaristic dictatorship, whether Aguinaldo-clumsy or Marcos-adroit; romantic and authoritarian constitutionalism, whether derived from European traditions (Mabini) or Asian ones (Laurel); and guided democracy, Philippine style, whether finely tempered by American sense of due process, as in Quezon's years, or in some new indigenous form that Corazon Aquino and her counselors might evolve.[36] Out of a full stock of possibilities, it is only clear that they must evolve something credible, distinct, and effective.[37]

[36]In conversations with the late Benigno Aquino, Jr. (Philadelphia, 1982; Swarthmore, Pennsylvania, 1983), I asked what he would do with the emergency powers of the president if he should succeed Marcos. He answered on the first occasion that he would need to retain a great many of those powers in order to repair the mess Marcos had made. On the second occasion he repeated that answer, but added a specific statement that he would reinstate the writ of habeas corpus and do away with preventive detention orders. I presume that Mrs. Aquino, while following her own best judgment in the light of circumstances, will continue to be moved by her husband's imprisonment in a way so as not lightly to inflict such experiences on others and at the same time to attempt to exert power in a strong executive mode, as her husband would have done. Her own character, of course, adds still another variable, among many others.

[37]Octavio Paz, the Mexican poet-essayist, in writing about the United States, may also be illuminating about the Philippines. Paz sees the errors of the United States as "revealing of vices and faults inherent in plutocratic democracies." At the same time its achievements, energies, and self-criticism keep high its potential for others. What he concludes of America might also be said of its former colony: "The malady of democracies is disunity, mother of demagogism. The . . . road . . . of political health leads by way of soul-searching and self criticism: a return to origins, to the foundation of the nation . . . to make a new beginning. Such beginnings are at once purifications and mutations. With them something different always begins as well." "Notes on the United States," *The Wilson Quarterly*, Spring 1986, pp. 80–93; quotation, p. 93.

II. The Economy

5

Pressures and Policies: Prospects for Cory Aquino's Philippines

William H. Overholt

HISTORICAL BACKGROUND

The political forces that impinge on the Philippines' new political regime are of course the product of history and cannot be comprehended without brief reference to their historical genesis.[1]

Philippine Democracy: The Latin American Model

The democratic era of the Philippines, from 1946 to 1971, represents in its entirety a period of great achievement. Democracy and marginal economic reforms defeated the Huks. The colonial legacy of education was enlarged. Freedom was greater than in any other Third World country. Social peace was maintained with a remarkably small military. Economic growth was quite respectable.

But democracy had its failures too. A parliament with members drawn from the elite proved incapable of instituting effective land reform or other measures to ameliorate social inequality. An American-style court system was too complex to deal with crime and corruption, and its lawyers were too expensive to provide justice to the poor. Democratic party patronage enhanced corruption. Pressure-group politics prevented a shift of economic development strategy from import substitution to export-oriented growth. As import substitution opportunities dwindled, growth began to decline. The Philippine growth record began to slip from being one of Asia's best to being one of Asia's worst. Along with the glories of democracy came pervasive fear

---

[1]For a more detailed account of the history of this period, see William H. Overholt, "The Rise and Fall of Ferdinand Marcos," *Asian Survey* XXVI, 12 (November 1986).

of violence, widespread resentment of injustice, and concern over economic malaise.

The democratic Philippines was governed by a traditional Spanish-American coalition. A traditional landed elite dominated the congress. A backward and inefficient but politically assertive sector of highly protected industrialists played a strong secondary political role. A patronage-oriented (rather than merit-oriented) civil service controlled much of the formulation and implementation of policy. The landed elite vigorously opposed greater domestic competition, and the civil service successfully protected its role as a source of sinecures exchanged for political support. All these reactionary interests found ideological justification in leftist, anti-imperialist ideas promulgated by an academic and media left that defined nationalism in terms of import substitution based on high tariffs, restrictions on foreign investment, use of the civil service primarily to generate employment, and protection of the landed elite despite a great deal of lip service to land reform. The Philippines differed from such Latin American countries as Mexico primarily in having a weaker labor union movement; in many polities of this kind, a highly organized labor union elite uses its political clout to obtain high wages for members, at the expense of causing mass unemployment by pricing most workers out of the market. In the Philippines, there was strong ideological support for such policies, but the unions were in fact weak. The Philippines shared with its Spanish-American counterparts the central characteristic of the Spanish-American political economy: an unholy alliance of right-wing interest and left-wing ideology.

This unholy alliance has had the same consequences in the Philippines that it has had throughout Latin America. The civil service expands out of control and absorbs scarce resources. Political parties that have no ideological or policy differences compete almost exclusively on the basis of who can deliver the most patronage. Landlord interests block land reform, and industrialists block domestic and foreign competition, so the economy remains uncompetitive and inefficient, dependent for survival on ever-higher tariffs and subsidies. Excessive susceptibility to union pressures raises wages in a few industries at the expense of farmers and of the unemployed. Pursuit of the interests of the elite, justified by the academic nationalists, leads to heavy borrowing rather than foreign investment. The same interests, justified by Third World theories of self-reliance, emphasize heavy industry (steel and petrochemicals, for example) rather than light industry, at the cost of spiralling indebtedness and high unemployment. (By definition, capital-intensive heavy industry generates fewer jobs than labor-intensive light industry.) The result is an economy that cannot grow rapidly, cannot employ its people, cannot distribute income fairly, and eventually cannot pay its debts. In such a system, the ideas of dependency theory become self-fulfilling prophecy. "Nationalism" becomes a cover for protection of certain elites at the expense of the long-run national interest.

The Asian Model

Other Asian countries had earlier faced these same problems, usually in more acute form. South Korea and Singapore increasingly were regarded as models for their solution. The emerging Pacific Asian model pointed toward more decisive leadership, replacement of patronage with administrative and military reform, more open domestic and foreign investment policies, forceful replacement of import substitution policies with an export orientation, state leadership of economic and technological advance, and technocratic overriding of parliamentary elites in order to improve employment, to reform land ownership, and to enhance social justice. The overall pattern was superior performance toward a wide range of economic and social goals at considerable cost in terms of parliamentary democracy. In short, they delivered jobs, growth, social justice, and rapid technological advance, but limited democracy and liberty. So long as the limitations stayed within bounds and the performance remained impressive, the result was greatly enhanced regime stability.

Martial Law: Marcos Promises the Asian Model

Upon declaring martial law, Marcos promised all these economic and social achievements. He promised stability, growth, equality, and administrative reform. He collected guns, implemented a land reform, appointed some conspicuously bright technocrats, and for the first time built the roads with real cement. He promised to implement his program with less force than elsewhere; hence the phrase, "Martial Law, Philippine Style."

From 1972 to 1975, this program was widely accepted at face value. Despite the usual dissent from the press, the unseated congressmen, university-based intellectuals, and what was then a very small proportion of human rights-oriented clergy, along with Muslim groups who perceived the weapons collection program to be a Christian trick, the program received broad support. The bulk of the military was delighted to be able to collect guns and apprehend criminals effectively for the first time in a generation. (But note that key senior military officers could not stomach martial law and quietly left the service or were forced out.) Nearly everyone applauded improved law and order. The left was delighted with the land reform plans; Luis Taruc of the Huks and Jeremias Montemayor of the Federation of Free Farmers, along with many left-leaning intellectuals like Adrian Cristobal and labor leaders like Blas Ople, joined Marcos and eloquently spread the reformist word. The middle class and many other groups celebrated the building of the roads, most notably the highway north from Manila to Angeles and Baguio, with unadulterated cement that would not wash away in the rainy season. The business community as a whole adopted a wait-and-see attitude, but there were substantial pockets of enthusiasm.

Internationally, the reaction was similar. To many, the Philippines seemed to be jettisoning its democratic baggage of patronage, corruption, incompetent administration, crime, and inequality and following the lead of more economically and socially successful neighbors. The United States reacted with its usual division and ambivalence, but the American government certainly acquiesced quickly in the Marcos program. The World Bank and the IMF looked forward to funding another of the series of Pacific Basin economic miracles. International banks were delighted to have a major new customer, which initially had very little debt but was as voracious as South Korea once had been for development loans. Two years after Marcos declared martial law, OPEC's success created an international money glut, and banks desperately needed customers to match their Arab deposits.

Those large elements of the domestic Filipino left that backed Marcos have been anxious to repress memories of those days. Many Americans, divided ideologically between liberals who see all dictators as bad and conservatives who see all of them as loyal allies and sources of stability and are unable to understand the vital importance of economics, never understood Marcos's reformist appeal. But it was there. And in that appeal is a central lesson for Cory Aquino: Democracy will buy a few weeks or a few months, but the vast majority of Filipinos, like the vast majority of citizens almost anywhere in the

Third World, care more about economic and social reform than they do about politics. That is why, although almost all decolonized countries initially aspired to democracy, few have retained it. If she does not deliver economic growth, employment, and social justice, virtually all groups will quickly begin a search for a tough guy who will.

The late Senator Aquino understood this perfectly. Like all opposition politicians, he understood the appeal to democracy and human rights. He believed in those values. But he also understood the popular priority of economics. He could expound for hours on his experiences as the youngest reporter in the Korean War, on his pity for the Koreans, who were so much poorer than Filipinos and who, unlike Filipinos had virtually no exports. He deeply admired Park Chung Hee. He told this writer and Guy Pauker, over dinner in Boston, that what he needed to implement his economic program was "three years of full power." He meant power unrestrained by national assembly, courts, and other obstacles. In short, Senator Aquino was advocating the same program Marcos had promised, although like all Pacific model leaders out of power he found it useful to stress the themes of democracy and liberty in public debates and save the hard realities for private conversations. The difference between Benigno Aquino and Ferdinand Marcos was that, at least by the 1980s, Aquino would have implemented the program whereas Marcos used it as a smokescreen.

Marcos twisted each element of his reform program to serve personal rather than national interests. The Construction and Development Corporation of the Philippines (CDCP) was formed to build the roads with real cement, and initially did so, to great public acclamation. However, unlike the giant Korean conglomerates on which it was modeled, it never was faced with the rising domestic and international competition that are the only forces for increasing efficiency. Instead, presidential fiat protected it from all competition and extracted a share of the resulting monopoly profit. Likewise, land reform became a method for extorting land and imposing a Marcos political organization. Administrative reform never went below the top level and gradually twisted the technocrats to corrupt purposes.

In the process, Marcos corrupted and destroyed the parliament, the political parties, the courts, the military, and independent business. Whereas institution building was the hallmark of the regimes of Park Chung Hee and Lee Kwan Yew, and even of Suharto, institutional destruction became the lasting legacy of Marcos. Two indicators of institutional destruction will suffice. First, economic efficiency. In the average Pacific Asian country, it takes just two dollars of investment to generate an additional dollar of annual output. In corrupt and inefficient Indonesia, it takes four dollars. In more corrupt and more inefficient India, it takes six dollars. In the Marcos Philippines, it took nine to ten dollars. This obscure economic indicator, the capital-output ratio, is the best single measure of the Marcos legacy.

Second, military security. For comparison, Park Chung Hee took what was then regarded as one of the world's most corrupt and inefficient militaries and built it into a world-class force while reducing its budget to four percent of GNP. (The United States was spending nine to ten percent of GNP at the time.) Marcos took armed forces of only 60,000 men (army, navy, constabulary, and air force), who had kept the peace so well that they faced only 800 communist guerrillas (official estimate of the armed forces chief of staff at the time), and increased them to a quarter-million men who by 1983 were being defeated (piecemeal but systematically) by some 16,000 guerrillas. Marcos corrupted the leaders, transformed a force that was meritocratic and broadly based into one that was patronage-oriented and based primarily on Ilocanos, and encouraged the replacement of effective small-unit counter-guerrilla operations by multi-battalion operations that relied on massed heavy artillery. (One American attache referred to the 1972 tactics of the Marcos army as "nothing more than competitive ejaculation.") This new strategy wiped out villages but could not catch guerrillas. At enormous expense, noncommunist Southeast Asia's finest armed force was corrupted and effectively destroyed, not by its opponents but by its leader.

By destroying the country's competitive business, Marcos made economic growth unsustainable. By destroying its political institutions, he eliminated potential bases of opposition but also disconnected all the levers by which the country could be governed.

Erosion of Political Support

This destruction of institutions took its toll of Marcos's political support. The Catholic church, traditionally a supporter of the Philippine establishment, became disillusioned at a relatively rapid rate. The gradual movement of the country's Catholic clergy from support of Marcos to democratic criticism, from democratic criticism to radical denunciation, and, for many of the most active, from denunciation to left-wing organizing, proceeded at an accelerating pace through the Marcos years. By the spring of 1983, months before the assassination of Senator Aquino, many of the rural clergy were helping the NPA organize, and Cardinal Sin broke moderately, but officially and decisively, with Marcos when he promoted the idea of the church's sponsoring a weekly magazine which would spread the truth (as opposed to what the Marcos press was saying). The transformation of the vital elements of the Philippine Catholic church from the conservative institution that had been one of the key reasons for defeat of the Huks in the 1950s into a partially radicalized institution whose left wing was one of the key pillars of the NPA in the 1980s will be seen by future historians as one of the most important elements of the Marcos legacy.

The Philippine independent business community moved into opposition even faster than the Catholic church. The essence of the Marcos economic program was the creation of predatory monopolies that would use their monopoly profits and interest-free or government-guaranteed loans to gobble up independent businesses or drive them into bankruptcy. It was no accident that the Light a Fire movement was led by the editor of *Business Day*, the local equivalent of the *Wall Street Journal*, and that the subsequent bombing campaign was the creation of businessmen. Leading businessmen supported opposition to Marcos, sometimes including violent opposition. They protected friends who joined the NPA, sometimes just because they were friends but frequently because they themselves thought the NPA no worse than Marcos. Even the Marcos crony firms frequently had NPA members at fairly high levels. It was not unusual for young, successful executives to become disillusioned and either join the NPA or surreptitiously support it. The result was probably the most intellectually sophisticated and managerially experienced guerrilla leadership the world has yet seen. But more often businessmen supported the Makati Business Club's moderate criticism, which also came to a head in the spring of 1983.

The businessmen coordinated their opposition with the church. The bomb throwers had clerical advisors who encouraged them to throw their bombs late at night and not hurt anyone. The moderates also had clerical advisors, who gradually constructed a theological as well as a practical and democratic case for resistance to Marcos. In the Philippines, such a theological underpinning is vital to political success.

Regional opposition to the Marcos regime also developed steadily from an early date. One of the great virtues of the democratic system had been that every major region and group was well represented. And the democratic system had the virtue of its vices: everyone got a share of the patronage. Under Marcos, the Muslim areas felt terribly threatened, the Visayas were systematically neglected, and many other regions lost out, while Ilocos, Leyte, and Manila lived parasitically off the rest of the country. (Because of the Muslim uprising, Mindanao also came to receive a disproportionate share of national resources.)

Farmers were slower to become disillusioned, and indeed many rural areas benefited from land reform and agrarian reform in the early days of martial law. These benefits yielded political dividends: for a few years, dissidence nearly disappeared from central Luzon—truly an historic accomplishment given the history of the region. But as the Cojuangco and Benedicto monopolies began to squeeze the farmers (Marcos decrees prohibited Lever Brothers and Proctor and Gamble from purchasing directly from the farmers, since their higher payments would have driven Cojuangco out of the market), dissidence began to spread. The most noteworthy acceleration came in 1981, when the squeeze combined with low world prices to make much of that third of the Philippine nation which depends on coconuts suffer from real hunger. From that time, armed dissidence and NPA organization spread through the coconut-growing areas like wildfire; the NPA became a major force in Mindanao at this time.

Rural people continued to vote for Marcos and to support him in public opinion polls, and this deceived many Western poll watchers into believing that Marcos and his wife had strong rural support. Nobody who was aware of the rapidity with which Marcos punished villages for failure to support him could have made such a mistake. After the mid-1970s, most of the rural population was terrified, not supportive.

The lot of urban workers steadily deteriorated during the Marcos years, but they never became effectively organized to oppose Marcos, and Marcos regime studies correctly indicated less resistance to his rule among this group than among most others.

The domestic group slowest to become disillusioned with Marcos was the military. After an initial exit of the army's best and most democratic leaders, military officers took pride in their participation in the great Marcos reform program. The political commitment to this reform by some of the most able officers in the early years of martial law was so strong that it took many years to weaken in the face of the evidence. Meanwhile, Marcos corrupted the senior levels of the military, appointing generals who were almost exclusively Ilocanos, weeding out even those Ilocanos who proved hard to seduce with corrupt blandishments, and keeping control of the senior generals by allowing them to serve beyond retirement age, so they served successive six-month extensions at presidential prerogative.

But eventually disillusionment came even to the military. It started with the retired pre-martial law generals, who had been proud of their service and rued its destruction. It penetrated down to the captains, who were losing their friends unnecessarily in battles with the NPA run by incompetent Marcos friends. It spread to the colonels, who could not be promoted because of the overstaying Marcos generals. It pervaded the Philippine Military Academy, where the old ideals were still inculcated despite sharp contrast with contemporary practice. Eventually it reached even the colonels and young officers who had strongly supported Marcos but now discovered that competence counted for nothing in promotion to full colonel; only loyalty to General Ver counted. The reform movement started with "We Belong" and spread in countless conspiracies. At the time of the election, a cell movement at the captain level found seventy-five percent of those approached willing to take an oath to disobey illegal orders during the election. If Marcos had not called the snap election in February, he would probably have been assassinated by an Ilocano officer within the year. Many were speaking of the need for such an action.

In short, by the time martial law had revealed its true colors, Marcos's Spanish-American policies were supported only by a Spanish-American coalition. By 1983, his political base was limited to his cronies (a caricature of a Spanish-American protected and subsidized business elite), corrupt senior military officers, an agricultural elite that was narrower than before 1972, and the now-cynical former left of Luis Taruc, Adrian Cristobal, Blas Ople, and various expensively purchased former NPA and KM leaders.

Foreign support proved more reliable than local support. International financial institutions, official and private, were far slower than most domestic groups to become disillusioned. As noted, commercial banks needed customers and found it difficult to distinguish a Marcos, who was quite willing to destroy his country for personal benefit, from a Suharto, who enjoyed the full benefits of high Third World office but cut back family and friends quickly to save the country's honor when falling oil prices bankrupted other oil-producers. Confused by the caricatures that dominate much of American thought about the Third World (for Carter all dictators were corrupt, evil, and unstable, while for the early Reagan they were all noble sources of loyalty and stability), they even found it difficult to distinguish a nation builder like Park Chung Hee, who cared only about saving his country, from a nation destroyer like Marcos, who cared only about squeezing his country. In this respect, bankers simply shared in the general ideological confusion of their countrymen.

By the early 1980s some of the commercial banks were becoming worried about Marcos's management. But such worries were far rarer at the official institutions, the IMF and the World Bank. Filipinos had a special hold on these institutions. Notwithstanding the popularity of radical rhetoric about the harsh policies of these institutions as they crushed local sovereignty, the balance of influence was heavily on the side of the Philippine government. Filipinos pervaded these institutions. Cesar Virata and the other Marcos technocrats were intensely admired figures. It was not unusual for Filipinos to design programs and then for the Philippines to become the initial beneficiary. This did not of course imply any impropriety. Quite the opposite: it was a response to the competence and standing of Filipinos in the international financial institutions and of Prime Minister Virata and other key Philippine government figures throughout much of the international financial community.

The special standing that the Marcos government had with the IMF and the World Bank resulted in part from the impressive ability of key senior officials to prepare plans and make presentations. Everyone who has dealt with the Philippine government these past twenty years has experienced this. I was a consultant in the early days of land reform. The plans were extremely impressive by comparison, for instance, with their Taiwan counterparts. In part because of Filipino skills with the English language, and in part because of certain warm, humorous, and theatrical qualities of Philippine culture, their presentations were often magnificent. But implementation hardly existed. Anyone who looked into the plans for a huge waterfront development project in Mindanao had a similar experience. This was a special project of Imelda Marcos. The briefings in Manila, the artists' sketches, the architectural layouts, and the detailed economic plans were enormously impressive. But when one went to Davao to see the project, which had been under way for years, it was impossible to locate any significant development.

The World Bank played a special political role in supporting the Marcos economic program, quite aside from actual expenditures of funds. In most of the intense controversies over commercial bank lending to the Philippines that occurred in the early 1980s, those who believed the Philippine economy to be well run and creditworthy relied very heavily on quotations from key World Bank officials in charge of Philippine programs. Their arguments were sincere, and often subtle and forceful. What critics like myself saw as corrupt white elephants they perceived as important steps in industrialization and energy independence. What critics saw as patronage boondoggles for Imelda's province and friends they perceived as vital steps in decentralizing economic activity away from Manila. The authority of the World Bank greatly weakened Marcos's critics inside private banks and greatly strengthened advocates of increased lending.

The strong support Manila received from these international financial institutions led to proportionate disillusionment when, in the fall of 1983, they discovered the extent to which the Marcos regime had lied to the world about its external finances. A phantom $600 million of reserves, systematic falsification of trade figures, and other accounting scandals put a new face on the charming presentations and brilliant plans of the Marcos technocrats. From that time onward, Philippine statistics received a special scrutiny. The IMF programs for the Philippines subsequently had a hard edge—an edge that was fully deserved because the most important Philippine officials remained more interested in capital flight and bailing out cronies of the president than in reviving the economy.

Foreign, and especially American, business was far less enthusiastic about dealing with the Marcos Philippines than the financial community. This will surprise many readers. One of Marcos's great promises was to rationalize investment laws and attract foreign investment, and to create a more open trading system—as other Pacific Asian countries had done. His investment and trade reforms, however, followed the same pattern as his administrative and land reform. Effective protection increased during the Marcos years. Marcos used leftist, Group 77 rhetoric to justify squeezing the multinational corporations just as he squeezed domestic businesses. Thus, for instance, he used nationalist and pro-farmer social justice rhetoric to justify forcing Lever Brothers and Proctor and Gamble out of key roles in the coconut industry. But the real purpose was to safeguard the Cojuangco monopoly which paid the farmers only half what the Western corporations were paying.

The attitude of foreign investors is worth documenting. Here, from official U.S. Embassy records, are data on the growth of American investment in Asian countries during the Marcos years:

U.S. Investment, Millions of U.S. Dollars

	1972	1984	Growth Factor
Hong Kong	501	3799	7.58
Indonesia	563	4409	7.83
Malaysia	171	1153	6.54
Philippines	644	1185	1.84
Singapore	81	2232	12.33
South Korea	274	823	3.00
Taiwan	156	828	5.31
Thailand	147	967	6.58

These numbers speak for themselves. They refute Marcos's claims regarding his policies. They refute the claims of the Philippine and foreign left that Marcos opened the country to foreign investment and that the multinationals took over. When one subtracts the effects of inflation from these figures on growth of American investment in the Philippines, nothing is left. Marcos was noncommunist Pacific Asia's most antagonistic leader in dealing with multinational corporations. The reason the foreign investment and foreign trade-led model of development did not work in the Philippines is that it was never tried. Behind the rhetoric, Marcos's practice was protectionist, inward-looking, anti-investment, and socialist in the strict sense of radically increasing the state's ownership of the means of production. This contrasts sharply with trends in every other country of noncommunist Pacific Asia.

The left regarded with cynicism Marcos's claims to reform in every other area of social and economic life. But they swallowed his claim to have reformed trade and investment policy. The result is a widespread hostility to trying the economic policies that created the economic miracles elsewhere in Asia. The vast majority of economically aware Filipinos believes that the Philippines tried open, market-oriented, export-led, technocratically managed development and failed. The opposite is true, but erroneous views and mischievous interests on this point represent one of the greatest obstacles to economic success that the Aquino regime faces.

Returning to an analysis of pressure groups, the most durable support of the Marcos regime came from its own senior military officers and from the United States government. Even in the Carter years, when Assistant Secretary for Human Rights Patricia Derian's shrill and ineffectual denunciations of Marcos captured headlines, Marcos had solid support where it counted. The Reagan administration came to office determined to support American allies—defined in terms of leaders rather than peoples—and determined to treat the bases in the Philippines as America's principal interest there. (The bases are extremely important, but the long-term stability of the Philippines and of Philippine-American ties are far more important.) The early 1980s was the period when George Bush toasted Marcos, "We love your adherence to democratic principles and practices," when Ambassador Armacost was known as "Armaclose" for his policy of being close to Marcos, and as "Ourmarcos." Never since the time of Magsaysay had an American government tied relations with the Philippines totally to a single individual.

The assassination of Senator Aquino in August 1983 brought with it universal American revulsion at the act but a split in the practicalities of American policy. Liberals led by Congressman Solarz demanded concrete action against the Marcos regime. The embassy skillfully created diplomatic distance between itself and Marcos, but, under orders, continued to work closely with him on virtually all practical issues. The administration took the view that Marcos was the key to the solution of the problems and that the United States had to retain close ties to him while nonetheless creating some political distance from him. As evidence mounted of the seriousness of the problem, Washington's concern mounted. The administration demanded reforms and criticized some of Marcos's actions.

The key to any policy is the price one is willing to pay for it. One must understand United States-Philippine relations in this context. Washington demanded that Marcos designate a successor. Marcos complied by designating Speaker Iniguez, a virtually unknown figure with no political base. Washington accepted this.

Washington demanded military reform and the removal of General Ver. Marcos shuffled a few senior figures and called it reform. Marcos threatened to remove General Ramos if we kept the pressure on General Ver. Washington backed down.

Washington demanded reform of the system of monopolies. Marcos repeatedly shuffled names, titles, and corporate relationships but made no significant modification of the system. In complete contrast to its dealings with every other key friendly nation (Mexico, Brazil, Nigeria), Washington provided a completely open pipeline of financial assistance prior to the country's reaching agreement with the IMF.

By the summer of 1985, the United States government professionals had focused on the Philippine situation. Conservative or liberal, upper-middle level American government officials share a broad professionalism and respect for the facts. The facts showed that Marcos was deliberately destroying his country's economy for personal advantage. The facts showed that he was deploying his troops in Manila for political advantage rather than in Mindanao to fight the NPA. The facts showed that he was using senior military positions for political advantage at the cost of piecemeal defeat by the communists. The facts showed that his logistics system was designed to maintain personal political and financial advantages at the cost of losing battles. These facts indicated that Marcos was willing to see a communist Philippines rather than surrender short-term personal advantages. Recognizing this, virtually all the conservatives below the assistant secretary level joined the liberals in wishing Marcos a speedy exit.

Up to this point Washington had been immobilized from any policy other than firm support for Marcos by divisions between right and left. From August 1985 on, that division was healed. But the very top was never convinced. Top advisors were hesitant to insist to the president that a Marcos Philippines in 1987 meant a communist Philippines by 1990. The liberal congressmen wanted to act. The conservative colonels wanted to act. The preponderance of opinion at the U.S. Embassy wanted to act. (During the election, the American ambassador, Stephen Bosworth, maintained an extraordinarily fine balance between the diplomatic necessity for neutrality and the overwhelming sympathy of his staff for an Aquino victory. He was the picture of correctness; but the sympathies of the embassy staff showed vividly, and private Americans seeking to help Cory Aquino received a sympathetic smile rather than the reproach customary for private-sector intrusions into diplomacy. Bosworth's quiet but heroic professionalism deserves to be the subject of a detailed study.) The president did not want to act.

The United States ended up with a lowest-common-denominator compromise. It pressed for reform, but mainly with words. Economic and military aid continued. It did press for the one thing American conservatives and liberals could agree on: an election. Once again, Marcos trumped the American ace. He gathered a half-billion-dollar kitty, planned an election rigged so many ways that any Brazilian general would have been awestruck, and called a snap election which, after discounting for the effects of Christmas, gave a totally disorganized and divided opposition only two months to create an effective party and run a campaign. Against this opposition, Marcos had reason to believe he was a sure winner. Once again, he had taken on Washington and his domestic opponents and gained an assured victory.

But this time Marcos had not only outwitted Washington. He outwitted himself. His regime no longer had the cohesion to run a successful campaign. In the end, the Marcos regime collapsed for lack of support. When one reviews the preceding paragraphs, the outcome is clear: By 1983, Marcos's political base was perilously narrow. (This was the calculation that led Senator Aquino to return that year.) By the autumn of 1985, his political base hardly existed. The Marcos regime in 1985 was in the same position as the French monarchy in 1789, the Tsar in 1917, and the Shah in 1978. By that time not even the senior military officers, the cronies, or the Ilocanos offered full support. Even Marcos's closest political advisors were expressing total contempt for him in the last year of his rule. An election and the extraordinary figure of Cory Aquino were the instruments by which he fell. Had these instruments not been there, he would have fallen by more violent means. It would not have taken long.

FUTURE PROSPECTS

The Philippine economy appears unrelievedly bleak. Its institutions have been destroyed. Its export products, notably sugar, coconut products, and copper, yield low returns and have poor future prospects. Its debt is approaching the size of its GNP.

But the experience of other Pacific Asian countries teaches a central lesson: Raw materials are not the essence of development. Human capital is. Japan, Korea, Taiwan, Singapore, and Hong Kong have no copper, coconuts, or sugar, nor any counterpart of them. And Philippine human resources are as abundant and impressive as Korea's.

That experience also teaches another central lesson: exports can be increased, and even very large debts can be paid, even in a somewhat adverse international environment, with proper domestic policies.

The Philippine economy can make it. But it takes sound management of the kind other Pacific Asian countries have had. The question is whether the new government will have the ability to identify and (more importantly) to implement the appropriate policies. This will take strong presidential leadership, correct policies, a sound political base, and effective administration.

Leadership

Worries have been expressed about Cory Aquino's leadership skills and lack of toughness. These worries come mainly from Western reporters who take outward Filipino appearances at face value. Filipinos are taught from earliest childhood to be soft on the outside and tough on the inside. Cory Aquino exemplifies those qualities. No examination of her election performance, whipping the male political leaders into line, mounting a major campaign, overcoming some of the most ruthless government subversion of the electoral process the modern world has seen, and operating calmly under constant threat of death, can accept the accusation that Cory Aquino is weak.

Senator Aquino was a tough man, at least as tough as Marcos. In this light, another comment of his is apropos: He once told me, "Bill, if you think I'm tough, wait till you have to deal with Cory." He did not mean this in terms of a specific political or economic program, because the idea of her having a program had not arisen. He did offer this as an assessment, which was correct, of her strength of character.

Political Base

Moreover, Cory Aquino has broad political support. Her campaign was ultimately a revolt of the independent business community, supported by the Catholic church, against Marcos. The independent businessmen led the demonstrations, created the organizations, and penned the analyses that preceded Cory's rise to power. They were opposed by the superior power of Marcos's cronies' vast network of monopolies and by the whole apparatus of government tax men and regulatory authorities. They were terrified. But they became increasingly assertive because the only other choice was to be squeezed to death by Marcos's cronies on the right, and by the communists who grew in the cronies' soil on the left. Cardinal Sin desperately sought to remain persona grata with all parties, and to hold together a church divided among friends of Marcos, supporters of the NPA, and an increasingly despondent center; but he tilted ever farther toward providing moral support for the business opposition and their allies. The support of the business community and the church could have important economic as well as political consequences. When businessmen celebrate they invest. Church support enhances business and consumer confidence.

The traditional democratic politicians remained fractious, weak, devoid of an economic program, and impotent until the end. The country was repudiating Marcos, but no major social forces supported the old-style politicos.

Cory Aquino's support today remains based on the business community, the church, and the moderate left. She is opposed by the hard left and a good bit of the military. The leading old politicians do not like her disregard of their demands for patronage and are increasingly hostile to her. The moderate left's support is at best fickle.

Internationally, she has the strong support of the ASEAN governments, and of the United States and Japan. China is happy to see a potentially stable government. The Russians in the end bet on Marcos, giving medals to Ferdinand Marcos, money to Imelda Marcos and General Ver, and trade deals to Cojuangco, so they are deeply disappointed by Cory's success.

The IMF enthusiastically supports the new regime, and the World Bank people have responded with a slightly skeptical but very positive attitude. From these institutions and the ADB, and from the United States and Japan, the Aquino Philippines will receive a great deal of concrete support.

Most private international banks welcome the new regime, with its promise of greater honesty and sounder economic management. They know the new finance minister, Jaime Ongpin, and have the greatest respect for his integrity and competence; for them, Ongpin is the face of the new government, and they respond well to that face even though it tells them that they will have to pay for better management by making concessions and that paying them will be secondary to feeding Filipinos. Better management is their only hope for getting paid back in the distant future, and they are willing to negotiate a price for that. They are not disturbed by the advocates of repudiation or selective repudiation of the debt (by Solita Munsod, Leticia Ramos Shahanai, and many others) because they believe that Cory Aquino and Jaime Ongpin speak with a more sensible voice. And they know from their experience with Argentina and others that the Munsod policies have such unfortunate consequences that even an Alfonsin must quickly abandon them or lose his job. When the government compromises among its factions and says it will repudiate loans that can be proved corrupt, most foreign businessmen and bankers recognize the policies they themselves would employ in parallel circumstances.

While the banks welcome the new government and will support it with trade credits, reschedulings, and other concessions, they are overcommitted in so many countries like the Philippines that they will be unable to invest a great deal of new money until a good deal of adjustment has taken place.

Foreign investors will mainly sit on the sidelines waiting to see how things work out. They stayed away from the Marcos Philippines. They see opportunities if real reform occurs. But they will wait until they see reform actually happening. In the meantime, representatives of the left in the new cabinet, most notably the minister of labor, are doing their best to terrify new investors. However, despite the rhetoric of the left and the "wait and see" attitude of most of the business community, one can see at least the beginnings of an inversion of the early Marcos experience: with Marcos, investors held back and banks rushed in. If this trend continues (one cannot yet extrapolate with any confidence), it is auspicious. Whatever domestic investors do, foreign investors will follow. (The lesson for President Aquino is to create a favorable—but fiercely competitive—climate for domestic investors.)

President Aquino's reliable base therefore comprises the business community, the Catholic church, the official international financial institutions, and foreign governments. Her success depends on consolidating this base, extending it, creating reformed and competent administrative institutions, and turning the economy toward growth and social justice.

She faces vital problems in dealing with these issues.

She does not have an organized political base that is reliable. Salvador Laurel and his party, UNIDO, under whose banner she ran, are desperately unhappy over her nontraditional approach to patronage and over key appointments. The left, better organized than UNIDO, finds it useful to support her but would like an opportunity to characterize her as just another representative of a heartless wealthy elite and seize power from her. She cannot use the military as a substitute for an organized political base so long as her minister of defense and top general are ex-allies of Marcos and her policy of freeing jailed guerrillas and negotiating with the NPA induce skepticism at all levels of the military. By the end of 1986, whatever remains of her personal popularity will not suffice to cope with an organized left and with military units which already show all the classic indicators of preparation for a coup.

But in the meantime of course she has great political assets. She has a personal popularity that the traditional politicians as a group cannot compete with. She has partially domesticated the left by a democratic, reformist, peaceful, and compromising attitude which strips away from the hard left much of the well-meaning church and reformist support that under Marcos was migrating in despair from the center to the hard left.

President Aquino's broad but inchoate support give her a window of opportunity in which she can either create an organized civilian political base or create a military whose loyalty she can rely on as a partial substitute for an organized civilian base. But the window is small, and she has not yet moved decisively toward it. She probably has no more than a year in which to use her window. If she does not use it, economic disappointments will diminish her ability to mobilize mass outpourings of support. Then either the military or the left, or both, will move into the vacuum.

Administration

To implement policies, President Aquino must have a radically reformed civil administration. She has yet to create an effective administration. Military reform has proceeded, albeit slowly, but no agenda has yet appeared for equally important civilian administrative reform. She has made some very good top-level appointments. This is a good start, and putting good men in charge can make a big difference, but it is only a start; Marcos too named an impressive cabinet. Unlike Marcos, she has, however, avoided conspicuous nepotism and cronyism so far. She is staffing many key administrative and political posts with temporary "Officers in Charge," which represents a well-meaning and democratic response to the problem of preparing for elections in a hostile context; she displaces the Marcos people who were installed by undemocratic means and would otherwise manipulate local elections, but she refrains from imposing her own people permanently. But this worsens the problems of administrative disorder.

Cory Aquino's immediate political problem is to fill the Marcos vacuum. To repeat the earlier analysis: Marcos was not expelled by a powerful, well-organized movement. His regime collapsed from total lack of support. The genius of Cory Aquino was to move into the vacuum so deftly with a minimally organized movement, out-maneuvering the far better-organized military and the far better-organized pro-communist left. But the inchoate genius and personal popularity that enabled her to seize power will not suffice to retain it. She must quickly create some combination of an administrative base, an organized political base, or a military base, or she will lose power. She has moved into a vacuum but has not yet filled it. The lesson of Kerensky in Russia and Chang Myon (1960-61) in Korea is that politics abhors a vacuum and moves swiftly to fill it.

Economic Policy

If filling the vacuum is her most immediate problem, reviving the economy is her most serious problem. The lesson of Philippine democracy, and of early public support for Marcos, is that the Philippine public, along with its counterparts elsewhere in the Third World, cares more about poverty and inequality than about democracy. (I estimated during the campaign that democratic euphoria would buy President Aquino nine to twelve months of enthusiastic support; instead, it brought about nine weeks.)

The Aquino government has started in the right economic direction. Its foreign debt negotiations have been more smoothly handled than those of virtually any of its Latin American counterparts. It is giving priority to reviving agriculture. It is dismantling the Marcos monopolies. It has appointed some highly capable younger managers. It is trying to sell off the crippling burden of state firms accumulated by the Marcos administration, which not only seized the commanding heights of the economy but also a good many of the minor foothills. But this is only a beginning, and one cannot yet judge whether impressive policy statements will be followed by implementation. That will depend on political unity and upon capable administration.

President Aquino's problem of administrative and economic reform is complicated by a severely divided cabinet. She has in her cabinet only two technocrats of the kind who have reformed institutions and stimulated growth elsewhere in Asia. Jaime Ongpin, the leader of the technocratic managers, is a world-class manager, but has few comparable colleagues, in part because Cory is reacting strongly against the Marcos "technocrats." She appears to have some tendency to blame technocrats in general, rather then Marcos's twisted, corrupt use of technocrats, for the country's difficulties.

A second faction, along with the technocrats, is the traditional politicians. These have no economic program, by and large do not understand economics, and see vividly all the disadvantages of taking hard decisions to control spending, create more competition, sell off the government's portfolio of loss-making industries even at the cost of giving some "bargains," and so forth. They have the highest profile in the press, because they are professionals at using the press and because the American press likes democratic politicians, but they have negligible support among the public, which sees them as a self-seeking elite. Their pursuit of political coalitions helps keep President Aquino's inchoate coalition patched together, but it gets in the way of painful but regrettably vital economic choices.

A third faction is the left, which is better organized than the traditional politicians. The left would do all the things that Marcos did, using the same rhetoric: assert more government control over the economy, protect inefficient domestic industries, squeeze foreign investors in return for domestic political advantage, reject IMF reforms, and give advantages to organized labor at the expense of creating greater unemployment. Labor Minister Sanchez exemplifies this faction. Formally, he is minister of labor and employment, but his policies make him minister in favor of union power at the cost of rising unemployment. Leftist rhetoric, however, conveniently calls attention to conflicts between management and labor, while neglecting the vital conflict between union perquisites and national employment. Since urban and rural unemployment is the single greatest source of potential political instability, the prospects of President Aquino are in inverse proportion to the prospects of her labor minister.

Ultimately, Cory Aquino will create a reformist coalition, form an organized political base, and follow the economic policy examples of successful countries around her, or she will be ejected in favor of someone who will either impose such reforms by military force or who will create a leftist political organization that can suppress demands for economic betterment in the manner of Vietnam or (more likely) Burma.

Stepping back a bit more from the details of the current political and policy scene, one can offer a broader definition of the Philippines' dilemma. The successful countries of Pacific Asia have been led by a reformist coalition composed of reformist technocrats, modern army officers, farmers, and an emergent industrial/entrepreneurial class. They have created a more competitive, more open, more export-oriented economy and, in the more successful cases, also implemented drastic land reforms and urban reforms to equalize the distribution of income. This is the Asian pattern. Throughout both democratic and dictatorial periods, the Philippines has followed a different pattern, dominant in Spanish America. In that pattern, an unholy alliance of a traditional landed class, an inefficient and protected industrial right, and a pseudo-nationalistic left have combined to protect and subsidize a relatively uncompetitive and monopolistic economy, to emphasize import substitution, and to subsidize a labor elite at the expense of incredible unemployment and agrarian backwardness.

The Asian model takes modern methods to achieve the stated goals, growth and equity, of both left and right.[2] By achieving these goals, it dampens social conflict and further enhances growth. The Spanish-American model takes the rhetoric of the left to protect the traditional interests of the right. By using nationalist rhetoric as a cover for pursuit of narrow interests, it assures unemployment, bankruptcy, and escalating conflict. Cory Aquino's cabinet looks like a traditional Spanish-American cabinet. Her most dynamic ministers and the trend of her early decisions, however, have been consistent with the Asian model. The outcome remains uncertain.

Cory Aquino's historic task is to take the Philippines out of Spanish America and into Pacific Asia. On her success or failure at that task lies the future of the Philippines and the future of the Pacific balance of power.

[2]For an extended treatment of this thesis, see William H. Overholt, "The Moderation of Politics," in James Morley, ed., *The Pacific Basin* (New York: Academy of Political Science, 1986), pp. 35-45.

6

Marcos's Economic Legacy: Problems, Policies, and Prospects for President Aquino and How the United States Can Help

Gustav Ranis

HISTORICAL BACKGROUND: 1960S THROUGH MARCOS

As is well known, the Philippines is just emerging from a set of very serious financial and economic problems. For two years there have been massive declines in per capita income such that the economy is currently at roughly its 1975 level. Investment declined by more than 30 percent in 1984 and by another 15 percent in 1985, while inflation was rampant and exports tumbled.

This is the immediate heritage President Marcos left behind. But, since this record is by now quite well known, I don't intend to go into detail here on the precise dimensions of the present economic situation resulting from the last few years of the Marcos regime's policy and excesses. Rather, I take my task to be to examine the longer-term legacy which Mrs. Aquino inherited and with which she now has to deal.

Most of us would agree that the formidable array of current problems did not start with the Ninoy Aquino assassination, though this event admittedly focused worldwide attention on the Philippine problem. It did not even begin in the early eighties, when the Philippines became caught up in international economic events that impacted on many developing countries and attracted the sustained attention of the advanced countries, and especially advanced-country bankers, to the plight of the Third World. The problem did not even start in 1972, when Mr. Marcos assumed martial law powers, although it undoubtedly got worse during that decade.

The fact is that the current economic malaise of the Philippines has its origins in the 1960s, when it was decided that, after having gone through what economists call "easy" import substitution, the system would continue with a "not-so-easy," more capital-intensive, type of "secondary" import substitution. Unlike the situation in some of the other countries of Asia, this decision in the Philippines led to the severe neglect of two essential ingredients of successful development. For one, the Philippines has continuously failed to really mobilize its rural economy, both agricultural and, especially, non-agricultural, on behalf of the development effort; and, for another, the Philippines did not pursue strongly enough its involvement on a competitive basis in the international economy by exploiting its comparative advantage in labor-intensive industrial products, which could have been exported to the rest of the world in much larger quantities.

As a consequence of this two-sided failure, to obtain the full support of the rural economy's productivity growth and to explore the large opportunities existing in the exportation of labor-intensive industrial products, the Philippines fell further and further behind two peer groups of developing countries. First, in the 1960s, the so-called East Asian superexporters or "Gang of Four" stole a march on the Philippines; and then, in the 1970s and the 1980s, the less "special" and more similarly situated countries of Southeast Asia, for example, Thailand and Malaysia, moved consistently ahead of her in terms of their bottom-line economic performance. The Philippines could never have duplicated the performance of the Gang of Four—for that matter, no two countries are ever sufficiently alike to duplicate economic performance—but the Philippines clearly could have done much better than has actually been the case from the sixties onward.

Admittedly some efforts at fundamental change were made in the past, and these efforts need to be recognized and acknowledged. In fact, there are many people present at this conference who were active participants in the attempted reforms of the seventies. There was land reform in corn and rice, if not a perfect member of the species. There was a "green revolution" in agriculture, which was in fact a substantial success. There were some reforms in the foreign-trade and foreign-exchange regime as well as in the liberalization, to some extent, of money markets. However, after some halting starts, with the help of international advice and funding, the economy basically remained narrowly based, focused on the urban industrial sector and on large-scale, domestically oriented activities.

These rather half-hearted efforts at reform in the early seventies may be said to have foundered on the increasingly easy access to foreign capital which became a fact of life in the mid-seventies. The easy availability of OPEC dollar reflows, more than anything else, thwarted the reformers' efforts in the Philippines. The pressure was off, as it was now possible to simply bring in foreign commercial capital and maintain high growth rates without undertaking politically difficult reforms, inevitably painful for some vested interest groups, at least in the short term.

Commercial banks were eager to lend huge amounts of money to the Philippines in the seventies, and the government was anxious to circumvent IMF and World Bank tutelage. As a consequence the reforms were by and large blunted, and the Philippines continued on the very narrow urban industry-oriented growth path already outlined. This meant that the economy enjoyed reasonably good growth rates, around six percent per annum, fed mainly by good natural resources in the sixties and by debt in the seventies. But underneath all of that good performance there were in evidence increasingly festering problems of unequal participation, the worsening of an already-bad income distribution, underemployment of large and increasing proportions, and of course an insurgency gaining influence and fuel from these events.

While the picture was not one of unmitigated gloom, by the late seventies the bubble was ready to burst and the underlying problems, masked by the surface prosperity of the urban elite, began to assert themselves. When in the early eighties the international roof started caving in, as indexed by international terms of trade deterioration and recession abroad, and as the "third oil shock" hit and the commercial banks were suddenly unable to continue to finance rapidly growing import surpluses, the Emperor (Marcos) was all of a sudden perceived to have no clothes on. All this was compounded by shocks peculiar to the Philippines, including the Dewey Dee scandal and of course the cataclysmic events surrounding the Aquino assassination. But we should remember that both substantial financial and human capital flight had been going on for years. Those "in the know" had begun to lose confidence much earlier.

CURRENT CHALLENGES—DOMESTIC AND INTERNATIONAL

Mrs. Aquino is now clearly faced with a formidable task as she tries to put the pieces together. Of course she also has many things going for her. Most importantly, she benefits from a very substantial change in the atmosphere. In the last few years of the Marcos regime people at all levels, public and private, high and low, had really more or less "given up" in terms of expecting any real changes to be made. In fact, the policy pronouncements of those last few years of the Marcos regime were not very different, either in terms of the stated objectives or the policy reforms needed to get there, from what Mrs. Aquino and many of her advisors are now saying. But there existed a state of almost complete disbelief in what was going to be attempted or accomplished.

President Marcos' speech on the occasion of the opening of the Bataasan, for example, was unexceptional. Such statements were written by the National Economic Development Authority (NEDA), distributed by it, and that, everyone knew, would be the end of it. The critical question now is whether the statements currently being made are more meaningful in terms of future actions.

We can propose a specific list of actions that are now considered essential. I have my list, and others have theirs. But the crucial, and prior, issue is to recognize the importance of the new-found credibility of the government and that the critical challenge is how to maintain it. This means that it is just as important not to make serious mistakes as it is to move forward quickly. "Shooting from the hip" often means "shooting oneself in the foot"; and that can be very costly, especially at this early stage of the Aquino administration.

When it comes to accomplishments to date, we should remember therefore that the new government has been in power only a few months, without benefit of a transition period. The famous first one hundred days should really be viewed as just that. Accordingly, the first task now is to decide how to organize to make the necessary economic decisions in a reasonable, sequential way, and then to persevere with them and ensure that they are indeed carried out. As a consequence, when we are asked to prognosticate about the Philippines and about how the United States can best help, the answer is that it is not so much by providing large additional sums of aid or advice but in helping, if asked, to get the indigenous decision making process installed and functioning. This credibility of government is a tender plant, especially in the Philippines, given the past record of rhetoric, inaction, and cynicism, official and private. It is a plant well worth nurturing and preserving from the outset.

We know that there are some ministers in the new Aquino cabinet who propose something akin to the nationalization of industry. We know there are others who are talking about an increased market

114

orientation and of "getting the government off the backs of people," to use a familiar phrase. And there are still others who might be characterized as populist reformers who want to do things directly for people, mainly in the countryside. How all this is going to shake out or coalesce is still a very big question. But the important thing is that the Filipinos find a way to determine what particular internally consistent policy package seems to be in their own best interest after everyone, inside and outside, has had his or her say.

Moreover, any package of reforms that is ultimately adopted by the Philippine government must not only be consistent across sectors but also carefully sequenced, so as not to overload the circuits and avoid oscillations and pull-backs. The new government, still in its infancy, must in other words not only decide what it needs to do, but it must also be careful about what it does when, what it can bite off, and what it can chew. It must, for example, recognize that it can afford to tax its own consumers a bit longer via tariffs than foreign consumers, who will not be coerced as readily. The government must, to cite another example, understand that the pursuit of "hidden wealth" at some high level may be a political necessity, but that trying to chase after millions of illicit or near-illicit transactions may constitute a dangerous diversion of scarce energy.

The most important problem right now is how to organize the cabinet for this decision making process. In that connection it is encouraging to note that economic task forces have been established under the NEDA to, in fact, help undertake that job. Clearly, it cannot all be done by the minister of finance, although that is of course a key ministry; nor can it all be done under NEDA, because that is not an operating agency. All the economics-oriented ministries, from agriculture to industry and commerce, public works, natural resources, and land reform, must obviously be involved in putting together a viable, time-phased reform program. But NEDA should shift some of its energies from the usual construction of five-year resource-oriented plans, which are often not terribly useful—especially at a time of an important transition—and instead focus more of its attention and human resources on the evolution of a gradual, sequential plan for policy change.

The worst thing, in sum, is to choose to act too quickly or be forced to act too quickly by either internal or external pressures. Both of these pressures are very much in evidence at present—quite naturally. In the wake of the events of but a few months ago a certain euphoria is to be expected. Everybody both inside and outside the country is looking for big changes from the Marcos era— and quickly. Such expectations are bound to be unrealistic. On second thought most observers will recognize the need to give the government the time to organize itself and evolve an understood and agreed-on program of reform and recovery. To march off resolutely in some direction just because of these pressures—and then to have to retrench a few months later—could be very damaging at this stage of the game, when confidence and credibility represent especially precious assets. It is better to be accused a bit longer of being a "do nothing" regime than to become a "do wrong" regime, at least for the time being.

In the same vein, as far as the international community is concerned, the single most important consideration over the near term may well be to try not to overstrain the system and not to overcondition our assistance. The Consultative Group has presumably met once (in Tokyo) in informal session and will meet again more formally in the fall of 1986. Turning to the United States in particular, in these extremely difficult days of Gramm-Rudman-Hollings the additional or supplemental resources which can be made available—with the best of intentions—are severely limited. The United States is trying to provide as many additional resources as possible, and this general posture is reflected elsewhere as well; that is, the Japanese, the ADB, the World Bank, and the other bilateral donors are searching for ways to make more money available in the short term, over a one- or two-year period, without too many strings attached. How many of them can be as flexible as the United States in converting loans to grants and having the funds flow freely and quickly is another matter.

Getting control of the budgetary hemorrhaging of the recent past must come first, and addressing the neglect of the rural sector, second. The first requires a new view also of the role of the Central Bank; and, with respect to the latter, one must hope that there won't be undue delay in the establishment of a credible local government.

I know there are good reasons which have led the Aquino government to its present posture on constitutional revision and subsequent local elections; but from the economist's point of view, the hiatus in local government should be as short-lived as possible. If the most important issue in the Philippines is to mobilize the rural economy, as Mrs. Aquino has pointed out, this cannot be done from Manila but only by decentralizing both public and private decision making. Mobilizing

116

the rural economy means that the government has got to have faith not only in the basic ability of peasants who produce corn and rice, but also in the ability of medium- and small-scale entrepreneurs who might produce industrial products and services in the rural areas. It requires much more decentralization of decisions as to what infrastructure is applied where and who decides what is needed where. And this, in turn, requires a credible local government. It cannot be done from the center, whether the Manila government is democratic or authoritarian.

The initial problem will thus be one of achieving budgetary balance. Marcos' pre-election spending spree has contributed to the need to negotiate a new IMF package, with the budget brought back into some sort of balance. Although budget support normally does not sell too well in developed country parliaments, it is what the Philippines needs right now and it is apparently what the Philippines is going to be getting.

The only kinds of agreed-on constraints in negotiating with or on behalf of the Philippines would be to make sure that in fact at the end of this stabilization period of twelve to eighteen months, the budget deficit is in large part eliminated, mainly by collecting taxes currently on the books. Secondly, it should be ensured that interest rates, which have been markedly positive recently, remain positive and do not come down again to low or negative levels as in the past. This is extremely important from the point of view of priority access to the medium- and small-scale borrowers, rural and urban but especially rural, in both agricultural and non-agricultural activities.

Such liberalization of the financial markets might also yield higher savings rates, but the allocation effects are clearly the more important. Of course, such a shift to "on the table" explicit taxes and away from "under the table" inflation taxes is not going to be easy. Not much can be done in the short term in effecting further substantial cuts in public expenditures. The cutting off, privatizing, or sanitizing of some of the many parastatals which have come to rest in government hands as a consequence of the inflow of private foreign capital, its misallocation, and the exercise of government guarantees is unlikely to have large results quickly enough. Privatization, in particular, should not be raised to the level of a religion. For one reason, there are too many parastatals; for another, most are much too ill for sale or a quick recovery. Even with the help of the World Bank and IFC it will be difficult to sell off very many very soon, especially if the government is anxious to get rid of the worst, rather than the best, cases. On the other hand, one has to be very much encouraged by the appointments made by the new government to head up the PNB and the DBP. If it is humanly possible to make a dent in the problem, the right people are in place.

While expenditure cutbacks will thus be hard to come by, something can be done about raising taxes, just by better collections under the existing tax structure, possibly with the help of an amnesty. This would ensure that the use of foreign capital for budgetary support does not become a habit, which would neither be good for the Philippines nor acceptable to most donors.

There will presumably be a full Consultative Group meeting this fall, the Aquino government's first. Presumably that will be the time for the government to present the outline of its medium-term plan for recovery and reform. The most basic and stubborn issue beyond stabilization, as already mentioned, is the mobilization of the rural economy. This problem extends beyond increased productivity in agricultural staples, into secondary crops, and, most importantly, into the expansion of rural industry and service. In most developing countries the rural population earns 30, 40, or 50 percent of its income from non-agriculture, that is, from services and small-scale industry. In the Philippines, this percentage is very small, perhaps 10 percent, and I believe this is where much can be accomplished to increase growth, generate employment, and simultaneously improve the distribution of income.

The Philippines is a country of many islands, and its geography is a problem for spatially balanced development. Nevertheless, there are also certain advantages for rural industry and services to be derived from the natural protection of distance and transport costs. Over the years these advantages have been eroded by the system of linked foreign exchange, credit, and tax incentives, which have given a large advantage to urban, particularly Manila-based, activities. Consequently, even when the Philippines is compared with "like" countries in terms of size, topography, and so on, the absence of non-agricultural activities in the rural areas is striking. There continues to exist a lack of confidence in the entrepreneurial capacity of people in the private sector outside of Manila. Similarly, there continues to exist a lack of confidence in local government. Both of these deep-seated attitudes must change if the situation is to be basically redressed.

This is not so easy to do. Even the current minister of finance, whom

I admire for most of his policy pronouncements, seems to indicate that he wants to focus attention in some of the rural areas on large-scale plantation-type agriculture, in palm oil and possibly in other crops. There may be room for that in some places like Malaysia—perhaps even in some locations in the Philippines—but it is hardly the general answer for the problem of the extremely labor-surplus rural economy of the Philippines. Eighty percent of the rural population surely cannot be reached even with a carefully orchestrated plantation project, which is usually quite capital-intensive and likely to be costly. This comment is based not on a careful study of the diversification prospects on Negros but on general LDC experience, plus what little I know of the location endowment and distribution of land. What is important is that individual tenants and households be given access to resources, to fertilizer, credit, technology, and market information at market prices, that infrastructural allocations be restructured to favor rural areas, that allocations be increasingly entrusted to local governments and that the National Food Authority and all the other interventionist tentacles of the central government be prevented from interfering with the small would-be rural entrepreneurs.

Not everybody is a natural entrepreneur; there are going to be failures. But most observers who know the Philippines will agree that there are a lot of talented people in the rural areas. The government has not acted consistently with that fact in the past; most of these people have not had a chance to participate in a reasonably fair game. Most Filipino officials now seem to have confidence in the food-producing peasant, once considered unreliable and backward. But there still is not the same, equally necessary, confidence in the entrepreneurial and managerial capacity of these very same people outside of agriculture. Unless that changes, both in the public and private sectors, the Philippines is going to continue to make very slow progress.

THE UNITED STATES AND THE INTERNATIONAL COMMUNITY

What, in sum, can the United States and the other donors and institutions do to help? As already indicated, showing some patience and understanding is probably most important. We must not push on this fledgling government a lot of difficult conditions right off the bat. It is not ready for it. In the absence of a transition period, it is much more important to achieve a real consensus on what needs to be done than a surface agreement which will ultimately give way and undermine the very credibility of the process. Already many observers are complaining that "nothing is happening." It is entirely unrealistic to expect much to have happened. Many people are worried about how this cabinet is going to shake out and how decisions will be reached. But we do have to give it time, and we should be more concerned with the avoidance of false starts and oscillations than with quick actions to satisfy demands inside and outside the country.

It is to be hoped that President Aquino establishes a standing group of independent economic advisors she can call upon. Morover, she should use technocrats more fully. The current feeling in Manila that technocrats were too closely associated with Marcos and should therefore take a back seat is understandable, but it is an attitude that may prove costly. One has got to rely on technocrats at some level to try to bring various differing viewpoints together, or at least to show the costs and benefits of each. Ultimately President Aquino, having let everyone have his or her say, must evolve a reasonably consistent policy. There has to be a way of making quantitatively informed decisions, and, while that still hasn't taken place, it is hoped and expected that that process is now under way.

By this fall, the international community should be ready to act in support of a time-phased realistic program of recovery and reform over a three- to- five-year period. Capital inflows can be very helpful in diminishing the inevitable pains of adjustment for some of the affected parties in such a structural adjustment process. Capital inflows, as the experience of the seventies indicates, can also serve to weaken the hand of the reform elements and make it possible to stay longer with an inappropriate and self-defeating set of policies. The international community must be sure it chooses the first, if more difficult, path.

By this fall also the international community can begin to think beyond budget support and be ready to contemplate something bigger in the way of reform and in the way of providing additional resources. The *sine qua non* of all this, of course, is that the Filipinos decide, possibly with our help, on what needs to be done; that they articulate a three- to five-year restructuring agenda for their economy; and that they then approach the international community for help with that effort. This undoubtedly is the preferred way for any Baker Plan to operate on a country-by-country basis within the context of a multilateral Consultative Group structure. The United States will undoubtedly want to do its share. But to be truly helpful requires not a "quick fix" mini-Marshall Plan dispensation of aid—even if we could afford it—but the patient application of counsel and resources to a sequential package of reforms which the new government really believes in and is ready to implement over a three-to-five-year period.

7

The Nationalist View of the Philippine Economy: Criticisms and Proposals

Charles W. Lindsey

In this paper, the core ideas of Philippine economic nationalism will be discussed and nationalist criticisms of economic policies of previous Philippine governments will be examined. Particular attention will be given to the policies of the Marcos regime. I will also compare and contrast the economic programs of two major coalitions in the current political scene with a pre-martial law nationalist organization, and look briefly at the economic policies of Philippine President Corazon Aquino (as far as they are known). In beginning, however, it will be useful to look at the history of economic nationalism in the Philippines.

HISTORICAL CONTEXT

Filipino nationalists throughout this century have resisted efforts, particularly by the United States government and American business, to integrate the Philippines into the larger world political economy, fearing a detrimental effect on the (potential) sovereignty of the country and its economic development. For instance, in 1909 the Philippine Assembly passed a resolution petitioning the United States Congress not to establish free trade between the colonizer and the colony.[1] The 1935 Philippine constitution contained several provisions that restricted foreign economic activity in the Philippines: operation of public utilities, exploitation of natural resources, and ownership of public lands were limited to Filipinos or corporations controlled by Filipinos.[2] After the nation's independence, additional restrictive legis-

---

[1]Alejandro Lichauco, "Why the Philippines is Underdeveloped," n.p., n.d., p. 14.
[2]Soledad Cagampang-de Castro, *Foreign Business Enterprise in the Philippines: A Study of the Legal Framework of a Developing Economy* (Quezon City: Multiplex Publamark, Inc., 1977), pp. 16–17.

lation was enacted, although it tended to be directed more toward the resident Chinese community than Americans.

Washington was not particularly supportive of American economic interests in the Philippines during the colonial period.[3] In 1946, however, the United States forced the government of the newly independent Philippines to agree to maintain the nation's economy open to American business, ensuring the continuation of economic dependency at the time it was achieving nominal political sovereignty. This and other aspects of subsequent American policy towards the Philippines has generated considerable hostility towards the United States among Filipinos. Also, successive Philippine presidents have come under criticism for their willingness to comply with what nationalists consider dictates from Washington. The linking of former president Ferdinand E. Marcos and the United States with the slogan "U.S.-Marcos Dictatorship" is only the most recent formulation of this historical concern.

Attention is often drawn to the warmth in personal relations between Filipinos and Americans and the frequent reference by Filipinos to the special relationship between the two countries in suggesting that nationalist sentiments are not widely held in the Philippines. The argument is not persuasive. Both Americans and Filipinos make the distinction between Americans, on the one hand, and United States government policy and business interests, on the other. The leader of the nationalist struggle during the 1950s, Senator Claro M. Recto, made the point this way:

> It is evident that a "Filipino-first" policy is necessarily against American imperialism, and being Filipino or pro-Filipino is necessarily being anti-American imperialist. There is no anti-Americanism involved in this excepting in the eyes of those who would erroneously identify American imperialism with Americanism.[4]

---

[3]Frank Golay, "'Manila Americans' and Philippine Policy: The Voice of American Business," in *The Philippine Economy and the United States*, ed. Norman G. Owen, Michigan Papers on South and Southeast Asia, no. 22 (Ann Arbor: The University of Michigan, Center for South and Southeast Asian Studies, 1983).

[4]Quoted in Renato Constantino, *The Making of a Filipino* (Quezon City: Malaya Books, Inc., 1969), p. 284.

Economic nationalism grew increasingly popular in the period prior to the declaration of martial law by President Marcos in September 1972. Although stifled during much of the 1970s, it has gained currency again in the 1980s. Today it would be difficult to find influential Filipinos who would publicly disassociate themselves from a broadly nationalist perspective. For example, Proclamation No. 3, signed by President Aquino on March 25, sets forth the qualifications for members of the commission to be formed to draft the nation's new constitution: "natural born citizens of the Philippines, of recognized probity, known for their independence, *nationalism* and patriotism." (emphasis added).[5]

During the Marcos regime, a group of so-called technocrats were brought into the government, particularly in areas concerned with planning and implementing economic policies. They were to provide rational economic input to what was considered a highly politicized process. For this reason the technocrats were generally held in high regard.[6] Their hostility to economic nationalism provided important support for those in favor of a more open economy. However, events of recent years—the technocrats' continued association with Marcos-era policies (if not the former president himself), the economic crisis, and political revelations since the regime crumbled—have tarnished the technocrats' non-political image. It is doubtful that they or their successors will be able to successfully defend the economic policies of the new government on the basis of a purported economic rationality alone.

The economic policies of the Aquino government are still being formulated. To what extent they embody a nationalist perspective remains to be seen. The economy's manifold problems considerably constrain the range of alternatives. On the other hand, the severity of the situation has its advantages. Few will be willing to seriously challenge the new government. President Aquino has a reservoir of good will; also, there is a fear that the fragile situation might simply disintegrate if too much pressure is exerted. For this reason, the

[5]"The Freedom Constitution," *Philippine News*, April 2–8, 1986, p. 5.
[6]For a discussion of the emergence of the technocrats in the Philippines, their attitudes and approach to planning, and their ideas about politics and modernization, see Romeo B. Ocampo, "Technocrats and Planning: Sketch and Exploration," *Philippine Journal of Public Administration,* 15 (January 1971), pp. 31–64.

multilateral lending institutions and the United States government will probably be reluctant to strongly push their traditional prescription of lower tariffs, devaluation, and, in general, deflationary actions.

PHILIPPINE ECONOMIC NATIONALISM

Defining what is meant by economic nationalism is not all that easy. Like defining an elephant, the problem is really one of description. Further, nationalism is a political word; its meaning evolves as does the context in which it is used. Extracting definitions and enumerating policies and positions is, perforce, somewhat arbitrary. However, for purposes of discussion, there are certain figures and organizations in the Philippines which are widely perceived as having a nationalist orientation. Their writing can reasonably serve as a reference point in the following discussion.

One of the more articulate spokespersons of Philippine nationalism, Alejandro Lichauco, has put forth the following definition:

> [Nationalism] is a philosophy of power. It is an outlook borne of the perception that welfare, progress and security of a people lie, ultimately, in the unsullied integrity of their independence, and in the maximum enhancement of their collective power as a nation-state.[7]

A nationalist analysis focuses on the interplay of economic and social forces. The primary actors are nations, not individuals or social classes. Economic nationalism can therefore be distinguished from orthodox economic theory, where the individual person or producing unit is the object of study, and from classical Marxism, where social classes are the fundamental units of analysis. The theoretical perspectives may be combined as, for example, in dependency theory. However, in examining economic nationalism in the Philippines, it is useful to make the distinction.

Philippine nationalists view the interaction of nation-states, particularly the advanced capitalist nations with Third World countries, as being essentially a relationship of conflict. Imperialism, not compara-

---

[7]Alejandro Lichauco, "The National Situation: A Nationalist Interpretation," National Secretariat of Social Action, Justice and Peace, 1982, p. 2.

tive advantage, is the operative word. This is in contrast with neoclassical theory and its advocacy (under most circumstances) of free trade, but it is compatible with Marxism. The lack of economic development is a consequence of imperialism.

Underdevelopment is defined by nationalists in technological terms: "[it] is essentially a condition of incapacity: incapacity to create, or manufacture, the modern means of production."[8] Economic growth is part of the process, but its defining characteristic is industrialization. The primary cause of underdevelopment is seen neither in the absence of an ingredient—lack of capital, savings, investment, or entrepreneurship, nor in the domestic class structure of the society. If anything, these factors are seen as consequences. The problem is essentially one of powerlessness within the world economy, of American imperialism, and of an elite which submits to the outside demands.

> What we are undergoing today—the massive poverty of our people, their backwardness, the economy's continuing state of underdevelopment, our society's moral and economic decay, soaring international debts, ceaseless inflation, the social and psychological instabilities which this inflation is bringing about, the demolition of democratic practices and institutions, anarchy and pervasive breakdown of peace and order, overwhelming control of the economy by aliens and international agencies, among many others—are actually the cumulative and cumulating repercussions of (1) America's vicious anti-industrialization program, systematically pursued, since 1909, or almost a total of 75 years; (2) the dictatorship which has enforced that program during the last 10 years; and (3) a socio-political and economic system that has made that anti-developmental program, and that dictatorship, possible in this country.[9]

The comparison of economic nationalism as espoused by Lichauco with neoclassical economic theory and Marxism is useful for two reasons. First, it draws attention to differences in theoretical orienta-

---

[8]Lichauco, "Why the Philippines is Underdeveloped," p. 2.
[9]Lichauco, "The National Situation," pp. 19–20.

tion. Although there is plenty of room for debate over facts, much of the discussion about economic policy in the Philippines has taken place at the level of world view; opposing sides talk past each other. Second, individuals with a range of viewpoints may identify themselves as nationalists. In trying to sort through the arguments, it is useful to be able to place them in a theoretical context. As another prominent nationalist, Renato Constantino, points out, some approaches are more relevant to national development than others:

> It may be more rhetoric than substance; it may project the cultural aspect to camouflage the fact that the economy is being delivered to the transnationals. It may be the national-ism of the deprived local entrepreneurs and the discontented local partners of global corporations, or it may be the nationalism of wider sections of the population who see in imperialist dictation and transnational control the source of their poverty. The latter is the decisive form of nationalism in the overall transformation of the neocolonial system into a social order which will truly serve the needs of the major-ity of the peoples of the Third World.[10]

NATIONALIST CRITIQUE OF PHILIPPINE ECONOMIC POLICIES

Linking the Philippines' underdevelopment—poverty and lack of industrialization—to integration into the world economy and the ab-sence of sovereignty, nationalists focus on policies dealing with inter-national trade, foreign exchange, and foreign investment. It is interest-ing, and important, that both they and the technocrats and orthodox economists with whom they disagree point to 1962 as a decisive date in Philippine economic history.

During the 1950s the Philippines engaged in import licensing and foreign exchange controls to limit the size of the country's balance of trade deficit. In 1962, a devaluation of almost one hundred percent occurred, and import licensing ended. Nationalists claim that as a result

---

[10]Renato Constantino, *The Nationalist Alternative,* revised ed. (Quezon City: Founda-tion for Nationalist Studies, 1979), p. 6.

128

the government's ability to control the economy and channel development efforts was severely limited; tariffs that were erected in place of the import controls are considered a weak substitute. The nationalists believe that a successful industrialization process requires protection for national capitalists. The standard economic argument by technocrats, on the other hand, is that the erection of tariffs was a missed opportunity. The slower growth of the Philippines (relative to its neighboring countries) is a result of the continuation of protectionist policies until the early 1980s.

The 1962 devaluation and a later one in 1970 are seen by nationalists as examples of policies advocated by the IMF and the technocrats to destroy Filipino entrepreneurs and open the economy for foreign capital. The abrupt increase in the Philippine peso cost of foreign debt drove many Filipino businesses to the wall. The technocrats, on the other hand, point to what they believe is the continuing overvaluation of the Philippine peso and the resulting inefficiencies and misallocations of scarce resources. On each side there appears to be little interest in confronting the opposing argument.

Another area of controversy is the Philippine government's policy toward foreign investment. Nationalists claim that successive Philippine presidents have held the door open for transnational corporation (TNC) investment and that this has retarded Philippine economic development. "To a nationalist, economic power is political power. A people's political independence is meaningless and stripped of subsistence unless they control the vital seats of economic decision in their own country."[11] Others, particularly technocrats within the government, reject this view. Gerardo Sicat, former director-general of the National Economic Development Authority, puts it this way: "There is the contention that it is so much better to have an economy with less foreign investment because this would mean Filipinos would be in control of major enterprises. Only a blind chauvinist would entertain such a notion of economic development."[12]

[11]Alejandro Lichauco, "Nationalism, Economic Development and Social Justice," in *The Role of Nationalism in Economic Development and Social Action*, Report No. 20, Institute of Economic Studies and Social Action, Araneta University, Manila, October 1968, p. 27.
[12]Gerardo P. Sicat, "The Role of Foreign Investment in RP Economy," *The Fookien Times Yearbook 1972*, p. 82.

Criticism of government policy towards TNCs should not be interpreted as an argument for the total exclusion of foreign investment. The issue is one of the extent of control. Constantino argues that currently "the Philippine economy is controlled by foreigners, from banking and finance to the simplest consumer goods for everyday use."[13] A counterargument is that, relative to the economy as a whole, foreign investment in the Philippines was never large, and since the 1950s it has become increasingly less important. Legislative, administrative, and judicial actions have steadily reduced the area and range of economic activity in which foreigners could participate.[14] Part of the debate is statistical in nature.[15] It is also about the locus of nationalist efforts to restrict entry of foreign investment.

Prior to the declaration of martial law in 1972, nationalist legislation originated almost entirely within the Philippine congress. There was little support, and often considerable resistance, from the executive branch of the government. Ferdinand Marcos is not an exception; he was a consistent advocate of foreign investment and expressed continual willingness to provide lucrative incentives to encourage capital inflow.

At the onset of his authoritarian rule, Marcos closed legitimate avenues of opposition and dissent. Through presidential decrees and other measures Marcos removed or liberalized the application of restrictions on foreign investment imposed by the congress, regulatory rulings, and legal judgments. The regulatory environment, it was promised, was to be improved, additional incentives were to be given for investing in priority areas, labor peace was to be maintained, and wage rates were to be kept low. Marcos also concluded a commercial treaty with Japan, an agreement that nationalists in the Philippine congress had opposed for several years.[16] The change in economic

[13]Constantino, p. 11.

[14]Frank Golay, "Taming the American Multinationals," in *The Philippine Economy and the United States*, ed. Norman G. Owen, Michigan Papers on South and Southeast Asia, no. 22 (Ann Arbor: The University of Michigan, Center for South and Southeast Asian Studies, 1983).

[15]See Charles W. Lindsey, "The Philippine State and Transnational Investment," in *Transnational Corporations and the State*, ed. Robert B. Stauffer (Sydney: The Transnational Corporations Research Project, 1985). The following draws on the discussion there.

[16]For a compilation of rules and guidelines issued to accommodate foreign investment, see Policy Studies Group, Civil Liberties Union, *Obstacles to National Development*, CLU Policy Studies Series-1 (Quezon City: Karrel, Inc., 1983).

policies was dramatic, and those who had been in the nationalist camp reacted with some bitterness. "Before martial law, Congress had explicitly adopted 'the principles and objectives of economic nationalism.' Martial law betrayed this ideal."[17] On the other hand, Marcos's actions were supported by the United States government and the American business community.

NATIONALIST ECONOMIC POLICIES

Codifications of policies that flow from a nationalist perspective are not numerous. In the late 1960s an attempt to do so was made by the Movement for the Advancement of Nationalism (MAN). Below I examine its program and compare it with that of two major political coalitions that are currently on opposite sides of the political spectrum —the United Democratic Opposition (UNIDO), a center-right coalition led by Vice President Salvador Laurel, and the communist-led National Democratic Front (NDF).[18] The latter combines a nationalist and a Marxist, class-based analysis. Overview of these three programs should provide a reasonably good indication of the spectrum of views on economic nationalism in political discussion today.

1. *Sovereignty*. Here the difference in political orientation is most clear. The UNIDO document devotes one short paragraph to the subject: "The people have the right to shape their own destiny, free from domination by any man and from control by any foreign state." By contrast both the MAN and NDF documents make explicit reference to American imperialism in the Philippines. Among other things, they call for an end to unequal relations with the United States and an abrogation of disadvantageous treaties.

2. *Foreign investment*. The MAN document calls for Filipinization of strategic areas of the economy. The NDF program demands

---

[17]Civil Liberties Union of the Philippines, "The State of the Nation After Three Years of Martial Law," San Francisco, September 21, 1975, p. 13.

[18]The following discussion is based on three documents: "M.A.N.'s Goal: The Democratic Filipino Society" (n.p.: Malaya Books, Inc., 1969); "A Program for a Just Society in a Free and Democratic Philippines," proposed by the United Democratic Opposition (UNIDO) as an alternative to the "New Society" of the Marcos Dictatorship, n.p., n.d.; and "Program of the National Democratic Front," revised draft, January 1985.

more sweeping divestment by foreigners, but does allow for exemptions based on the national interest. National capitalists are called on to strengthen their economic positions. The UNIDO program lists the areas where the "Marcos dictatorship has disregarded the constitutional and legal safeguards of economic nationalism," and calls for a revision of policies toward foreign investment. However, so long as "Filipino control of the economy" is not impaired, foreign investment is welcome. No doubt the point where Filipino control of the economy is in jeopardy will remain a contentious issue.

3. *Foreign debt.* After noting that Marcos has left the Philippines with a backbreaking debt burden, the UNIDO document only makes reference to future loans and argues that they should be only for productive purposes and within the repayment capacity of the country. There is no discussion of repayment problems for the existing debt or of the fact that the world financial community supplied enormous sums to a corrupt dictator for questionable projects. The NDF position is stronger. "All foreign loans used to overburden and sabotage the Philippine economy, deepen the country's agrarian and non-industrial state and divert local resources into unproductive channels such as the IMF loans must be cancelled." Other loans can be renegotiated for easy payment terms. The MAN document is silent on the subject; in 1969 foreign loans were not a significant issue.

4. *Industrialization.* All three programs call for industrialization, where necessary under state control. The UNIDO and NDF programs make reference to the relationship between agriculture and industry. The UNIDO position is that the subordination of industry to agriculture as during the Marcos era should be rejected. The NDF document stresses the interdependence of agriculture and industry, seeing "national industrialization as the leading factor in economic development. This should complement agriculture, which is the main basis for economic development." Both programs emphasize the need for industry to utilize locally produced raw materials.

The MAN and NDF documents also address the relationship between international trade and industrialization; the UNIDO document does not. The earlier MAN program calls for the reinstitution of import and exchange controls (which existed prior to 1962). The NDF document goes further, calling for an end to the "import-export character of the present semi-colonial and semi-feudal economy," and for engaging, "whenever possible, in barter or counter-trade."

5. *Agriculture*. All three programs include provisions for extensive land reform, accompanied by government assistance—technology, production, credit, marketing. The UNIDO program calls for the transformation of corporate farms into cooperatives. The NDF program, on the other hand, argues for allowing capitalist farmers to continue their agricultural activities so long as they work to raise productivity and modernize their farms, while at the same time ceasing to exploit the workers. Only plantations owned and controlled by TNCs should be taken over by the state.

6. *Work and income distribution*. All three programs call for recognition of the workers' rights to employment, to a decent wage, and to organize and strike. All place the burden on the state to see that workers' basic needs are met, although the UNIDO program is rather vague on the subject. Both the UNIDO and MAN documents take a welfare orientation. By contrast, the NDF program focuses on involving individuals in production and seeing that resources are available. It also includes the provision of social services such as health care.

7. *State intervention in the economy*. All three programs call for economic planning by the government and for state ownership or control of some areas of productive activity. The UNIDO paper mentions distributional consequences of planning, the MAN program discusses the importance of planning to achieve development, and the NDF plan is concerned with imbalances in various sectors of the economy.

In the MAN document state intervention is limited to activities that are too risky to call forth Filipino capital. The UNIDO program goes further, arguing that, as a "general principle, key industries and public services essential to the national interest and common welfare should be owned or controlled by the state." Among the three, however, reliance on state control and participation is the greatest in the NDF program.

No doubt there are differences between political documents and the policies that may actually result from them. As stated, however, there are both major differences and some similarities between the UNIDO and NDF programs. Where there are differences, particularly in the areas relating to the world political economy—sovereignty, foreign investment, foreign debt, protection of the domestic economy—the NDF position is much closer to that of the nationalist tradition.

All three programs emphasize industrial development, with UNIDO and MAN placing agriculture in a position subordinate to industry. The NDF, on the other hand, see the need for a more symbiotic relationship. Also, all three see the necessity of land reform as a social issue, although here again the NDF program gives more attention to production requirements. Lastly, both the UNIDO and NDF programs call for considerable state intervention in the economy, more than the older MAN program.

The new regime of Corazon Aquino has yet to put out a comprehensive economic policy. The best we have to go on is a campaign speech presented to a meeting of influential business people.[19] No doubt the talk is an incomplete statement of her views, but it does include some policy statements that can be compared with the positions of UNIDO and NDF discussed above. In this way we can gain some insight as to the degree the new regime is oriented nationalistically.

In her speech President Aquino made no comment that would evidence concern about the sovereignty of the Philippines or imperialist intervention. The country's dependency on the world economy was mentioned only in passing. Foreign investment was welcomed as a supplement to domestic investment, except in the areas of public utilities and natural resources. The priority areas for investment activity were labor-intensive, rural-based, and small- and medium-scale enterprises, particularly those utilizing agricultural materials. Capital-intensive, urban-based industrial projects not self-sufficient in foreign exchange requirements would be postponed. There would be some protection, but the government "will not pamper the private sector." All of this places Aquino rather outside the position of economic nationalists, although concern with nonagricultural economic activity in rural areas was evidenced in the NDF document.

[19]The talk was given to the Management Association of the Philippines, the Makati Business Club, and the Bishops-Businessmen's Conference on Human Development on January 6, 1986. See "Building from the Ruins," *Veritas*, January 12, 1986, pp. 6–8.

According to President Aquino, land reform will be implemented, and necessary government services will be provided. The emphasis, as with the UNIDO program, is on addressing the aspirations of farmers, rather than on production. She also referred to the need to deal with the country's unemployment problems and the mass poverty of the people. Her solution is to rely on private enterprise: "My government will endeavor to create an economic structure that assures a decent life for [workers] and their families." However, no provisions were suggested for providing jobs or the meeting of basic needs in the event that private enterprise fails her expectations. To press for their rights and needs, workers should be given the right to organize and bargain. In her speech, however, President Aquino made no reference to the right to strike. Rather, she supported the right of workers "to exhaust all legal means for the redress of their legitimate grievances." Finally, in the area of state intervention in the economy, the president mentioned several times that government activity would diminish and that the private sector should be the engine of growth of the economy. Little was said about planning, although reference was made to investment priorities.

CONCLUSION

The nationalist tradition has a long history in the Philippines. It has not been a minor movement consisting of students, intellectuals, and a few politicians and business people. It was growing in strength in the 1960s but was thwarted both by the arguments of the technocrats and by Marcos's authoritarian rule. Resistance to Marcos, particularly in the 1980s, resulted in a resurgence of nationalism, some of which has moved in a more radical direction. Criticism of the Marcos regime's economic policies focused on openness to foreign investment and international trade and on the lack of protection for domestic industry. Support for Marcos by the United States and the American business community also came in for attack.

The authoritarian atmosphere of the past fourteen years severely constrained debate over economic priorities and policies. Economic programs of political organizations and coalitions are available, but it is too early for actual policies to have been worked out. It is obvious, however, that there is a range of positions, and the debate will be joined. The existence of clear, substantive differences among political groups (most are not yet parties) adds a new dimension to Philippine politics. The extent to which those who favor nationalist economic policies will prevail depends too much on the working out of larger political issues to venture predictions.

I examined the economic programs of two major political coalitions to determine to what extent they embodied nationalist policies. Both the NDF and UNIDO call for continued state intervention in the economy (of course, of a different variant than occurred during the Marcos era) and an emphasis on industrial development. However, the UNIDO document made little connection between the larger world political economy and the current Philippine situation; neither did President Aquino's program raise the dependency issue in a critical manner. On the other hand, the NDF document emphasized the relationship between the international and domestic economies. Although the NDF is not at present a legal entity, its views are shared by many organizations who are operating above ground. Whether they will thrive or wither in the new political atmosphere remains to be seen.

EPILOGUE

When this paper was originally written (April 1986), the Philippines' new government was still in the process of organization. Much of the public discussion, then as now (October), had to do with political issues. Debates over economic issues have been rather restricted. In part, this is because the new regime has had to formulate its economic plans and policies. Some issues, such as the foreign debt, were perforce addressed without reference to a larger plan. Recently, however, the overall program has been made public. During a recent conference on the Philippines at Tufts University, Minister of Planning Solita Monsod presented a paper outlining the government's economic policy.[20] It appears to be a distillation of a much larger report prepared by a number of Filipino economists, both within the government and outside.

In reading the document two features stand out. First, the major themes are the same as in Mrs. Aquino's economics speech referred to in the main body of this paper; there is an emphasis on the small and the rural, on the welfare of the mass of the population. Second, and

---

[20]"Policy Agenda for People-Powered Development," n.p., n.d.

perhaps of contradictory nature, there is the continuation of the central theme of the economists and technocrats that served the Marcos regime: the striving for economic efficiency as the means to achieve growth. At one level, efficiency means eliminating waste, duplication, corruption, favoritism, government intervention into the economy—that is, the mismanagement of the Marcos administration. At another level, efficiency is used in the more technically economic sense of not using government policy to "distort" prices from what they would be in a free market, including prices in the larger world economy.

In getting prices right, as the refrain goes, three main (interconnected) criticisms of existing policy are made. First, the international: Tariffs, other trade restrictions, and fixed exchange rates foster inefficient industry at the expense of agriculture and imports at the expense of exports. Thus, under the plan, trade restrictions will be eliminated over time, and the exchange rate will be allowed to fluctuate.

Second, the preceding as well as a host of other policies favor urban, generally large-scale industry over rural economic activity, both agricultural and industrial. The biases in these policies will be eliminated. In addition, other policies to assist small-scale economic activity will be installed. Examples are the provision of infrastructure, technical support, and training, and relevant market and other information.[21] Thirdly, subsidies on the utilization of capital equipment (that is, low interest rates, tax breaks, import rebates) and minimum wage legislation are seen as biasing the entire economy away from the use of labor, resulting in increasing un- and underemployment.

As the political process becomes more regularized, these policies will likely encounter substantial opposition, for all of them are at variance with the historical thrust of nationalist arguments. Large-scale industry will probably run into substantially increased competition from abroad as levels of protection are reduced, although this could be offset in part by a fall in the exchange rate. The agricultural sector will no longer be used to support industry; the latter will have to stand on its own feet. The plan's proponents are quite clear, however, in that the industrial development they envision is to be directed primarily toward

[21]It should be noted that those constructing the economic plan appear to see the provision of relevant and timely information as being a major equalizer among economic units of unequal power in a number of contexts.

needs of the rural economy and, secondarily, toward the production of light consumer goods. Heavy industry is to be placed on the back burner.

The distributional impact of the program between rich and poor, and between labor and capital, will likely generate controversy; in fact, it already has. Efforts to assist the small farmer, manufacturer, and businessman will probably not come under direct attack, although it will bear watching to see if, over time, the more economically powerful are able to turn the advantages to themselves.

More problematic issues are labor and land reform. The standard of living of workers is to be protected, in the first instance, through increased job provision. In the short run, this is to be accomplished through an emergency employment program. In the longer period, it is argued that the thrust toward rural development and labor-intensive activities will provide necessary jobs. Second, and more controversial, is the policy of the government to (a) support the rights of workers to organize and bargain collectively and (b) not intervene in wage setting.

The difficulty in implementing these policies is obvious from the most cursory reading of the press. The employment goal will require private business investment, but investor activity, both Filipino and foreign, is reported to be rather light, in part because of labor unrest and the influence of the left in the labor movement.[22] Mrs. Aquino's labor policies have not improved the situation. In a May Day speech, for example, she announced that strikes could be called with only a majority vote of union members, that a petition for certification of a union required only 20 percent of a firm's workers, and that the mandatory fifteen-day cooling-off period between strike notification and a strike could be foregone in cases of union busting. The response from business groups was predictable. In opposing the pro-labor policies of Aquino's minister of labor, Augusto Sanchez, American business in the Philippines has gone so far as to enlist the support of United States Secretary of State Shultz.[23]

The government hopes to use "tripartism" and a code of industrial harmony to create a climate in which labor and capital agree to settle

[22]Jose Galang, "The Economy Marks Time," *Far Eastern Economic Review,* August 28, 1986, p. 31.
[23]Jose Galang, "Troubled Relations," *Far Eastern Economic Review.* August 7, 1986, p. 54.

wage and other work-related issues without recourse to strikes, lock-outs, and so on. This will not be easy in Manila and other areas in which there is a history of union activity. It will be even more difficult elsewhere. (Currently, only 1.5 percent of total employment is covered by collective bargaining agreements.)[24] Government encouragement of unionization will receive active support from economic nationalists that are connected with the labor movement. The organizational efforts of labor, on the other hand, are predictably being resisted by capital, often by their labeling the unions communist.

In summary, a considerable portion of the economic program of the Aquino government is similar to the positions put forth by the techno-crats in the Marcos regime. Those policies were criticized by national-ists at the time; there is little reason to suspect they will not come under criticism now. The administration's labor policies are receiving a much more mixed response. When compared with the repressive policies of the Marcos dictatorship, the labor movement will find much that is favorable. The business community, nationalist or not, is much more critical.

[24]Ibid., p. 55.

8

Philippine Sugar Industry Market Considerations and United States Policy

David Reinah

PROBLEMS IN THE PHILIPPINE SUGAR INDUSTRY

The immediate problem facing the Philippine sugar industry is the same problem that is facing all less-developed sugar cane-producing countries—namely, the low price of sugar.

The cost of production of cane sugar is variously estimated at 11 cents to 16 cents per pound, free on board (FOB), stowed country of origin.

Production costs for beet sugar, normally from developed nations, range from 13 cents to 32 cents in Japan, and are as high as 38 cents in the Soviet Union.

Production cost estimates are stated in terms of United States currency; therefore, movements in the value of the dollar obviously affect the dollar equivalent of the local cost of production. This is particularly noticeable in the case of the European sugarbeet producers, who experienced consistent devaluations of their currencies against the United States dollar. As a result of these currency movements, European producers have become much more competitive with United States sugar producers, and to a lesser extent, with most other cane sugar exporters. Currency movements notwithstanding, however, part of the reductions observed must be due to productivity gains and adoption of new technology.

The world market price for sugar as of May 1, 1986, was approximately eight cents per pound. It had even reached in early April a level of about nine cents per pound on the basis of confirmation of Russian buying.

The price level of eight cents per pound is still quite remarkable, considering that world prices averaged just over four cents per pound in 1985, the lowest annual average price since 1970.

INTERNATIONAL SUGAR PRODUCTION

World sugar production, in accordance with USDA projections for the 1985/86 crop, is forecast at 98.0 million metric tons raw value (MMTRV). Of this total, 37.3 is beet sugar and 60.7 is cane sugar. World sugar consumption for the 1985/86 crop is expected to be 97.5 MMTRV. Ending stocks (carryover stocks from previous crops) are forecast at 46.2 MMTRV. Prices do not begin to strengthen significantly until stocks drop to 25 or 30 percent of consumption. Current stocks are expected to build, approaching 50 percent of consumption. The 25 or 30 percent rule of thumb implies that there needs to be a stock reduction in the area of 15 to 20 million tons. This will be difficult to achieve, given the apparent tendency for production to decline from one year to the next while consumption increases over the same period; yet we have still had an excess of production over consumption.

The USDA has indicated that burdensome ending stocks and corresponding depressed world prices are still not signaling producers to curtail production. Part of the reason for this is that producers are insulated from world market fluctuations through a variety of domestic support programs. Another part of the explanation is that the amount of sugar which is actually traded "freely" at world market prices is very small, about 10 percent of total world production.

USDA has recently estimated that in 1984, of total world net exports of 24.3 million tons, 11.6 million tons (or less) was actually traded at, or on the basis of, the average price of the number eleven contract (world sugar price) of the New York Coffee, Sugar and Cocoa Exchange, Inc. of just over five cents per pound. The rest was traded under long-term agreements and preferential arrangements. (The latter include the European Community's Lome Convention for African, Caribbean and Pacific (ACP) nations, barter trade between Cuba and the Soviet Bloc countries and various long-term contracts between major exporting and importing countries.)

The average price of sugar covered by these arrangements was 21 cents per pound. As a result, in 1984 sugar exports actually moved at an average of about 13.5 cents per pound. This is clearly not sufficiently depressed to encourage a dramatic decline in world production. Certainly in combination with domestic production supports, an average traded price of 13.5 cents per pound might actually encourage worldwide production increases. It might similarly be too high to lead to large increases in world consumption. It could even be argued that substitution of alternative sweeteners in developed countries coupled with an average traded price of 13.5 cents per pound translates into a stagnation in world consumption.

PHILIPPINE SUGAR CONSIDERATIONS

Philippine sugar production for the 1985/86 crop year is estimated at 1.3 million metric tons, down by more than 14 percent from 1985. The decline is the result of typhoon damage to the crop in Central Luzon, crop diversification in some of the traditional sugar areas—notably Negros Island—due to low sugar prices below the cost of production, and the absence of planting or fertilizing in the marginal areas. Domestic consumption during 1985/86 is estimated at just under 1.0 million metric tons. The balance of about 300,000 metric tons is allocated to the Philippines/United States quota, which for calendar year 1986 is 231,660 short tons raw value or approximately 203,000 metric tons. Any balance of production over consumption is held in reserve for any additional United States quota. This represents 13.5 percent of the total 1986 foreign offshore quota from December 1, 1985, to December 31, 1986, of just under 1.85 million short tons raw value. (Actually, the 13.5 percent is calculated on a lower base number of 1.772 million short tons raw value via a USDA formula.) Contrast the above with Philippine production for the 1973/74 crop year of 2.446 million metric tons with a Philippine/United States quota for 1974 under the Sugar Act of 1.472 million short tons raw value or 1.290 million metric tons. This represents 25.6 percent of the total 1974 foreign offshore quota of 5.744 million short tons raw value.

1974

On June 6, 1974, the United States Congress voted not to renew the Sugar Act (for what would have been a renewed quota period beginning January 1, 1975). This action came as serious blow to the Philippines. World market prices were rising even above United States quota prices. (World prices reached the highest price level recorded for sugar of 64.50 cents per pound.) Some quota-holding countries, after learning the news of the nonextension of the Sugar Act, actually welcomed this action as an opportunity not to fulfill all their United States quota for calendar year 1974. The Philippines, however, respected their commitment to the United States government and delivered fully for 1974 all their United States quota entitlement (which included deficit reallocations of some other nations).

Coincidentally, in June 1974, President Marcos decreed that the Philippine National Bank through its subsidiary, the Philippine Exchange Company, would be the sole agency responsible for the domestic distribution and foreign marketing of Philippine sugar.

On July 3, 1974, the Laurel-Langley Trade Agreement (Philippine Trade Act of 1946) expired. It was under this statute that the Philippines had a guaranteed annual minimum sugar quota to the United States of 980,000 short tons raw value. On July 4, 1974, Philippine sugar became totally dutiable.

1975–1981

The period of 1975–81 was difficult for the Philippine sugar industry.

The first export of Philippine sugar to the United States occurred in 1796, when the sailing ship *Astrea* from Salem, Massachusetts, carried from the Philippines a cargo of sugar, indigo and pepper for which a United States duty of $24,000 was paid.

During the last 50 years of Spanish rule, through independence on July 4, 1946, through the termination of Laurel-Langley and the Sugar Act of 1974, the Philippines enjoyed a "most favorable" and special treatment from the United States as far as sugar was concerned, both on a quota and duty-free and duty-reduction basis.

When the Sugar Act lapsed, at the end of 1974, the Philippines found itself confronted with the immediate problem of excess factory capacity as a result of the expansion program launched in 1965, with Philippine government support to ensure fulfillment of quota deficits of other countries supplying the United States. These deficits had been reallocated to the Philippines from year to year. When the Philippines found itself exposed entirely to the world free market in 1975, production stood at 2.5 million metric tons, while installed production capacity already exceeded 3.2 million metric tons under the expansion program then underway. Domestic consumption was about 850,000 metric tons.

During the period 1975 to 1981, the Philippines sold sugar mostly to international sugar-trading companies in the international market on an

FOB stowed basis with "free" destination (that is, unrestricted destination). The Philippines did sell on what is called a "participation contract basis" to several American refiners starting in 1976, for approximately two to three years.

In July 1977 the Philippine Sugar Commission (Philsucom) was formed. The National Sugar Trading Corporation (Nasutra), which took over the functions of the Philippine Exchange Company, was established in 1978.

Under the 1977 International Sugar Agreement (ISA), the Philippines were given a basic export tonnage of 1.4 million metric tons raw value with an 80 percent export quota to all destinations of 1.141 million tons. In April 1980, the United States joined the ISA as a member importing nation. In April 1980 and then again in November 1980, the price range of the agreement was set at a 13-cent floor and a 23-cent ceiling. The agreement provided for ISA export quota reductions and world special (buffer) stock accumulations when prices were low, with suspension of export quotas and release of special stocks when prices were high. The 1977 ISA was in place from 1978–1982 and not renewed.

Since most of the sugar sold by the Philippines during 1975–1981 was sold to unrestricted destinations, it stands to reason that when no United States quota existed, buyers tended to ship this sugar mainly to other destinations such as Japan, China, and Russia, which had a demand and more economic freight rates.

Again, in the absence of a United States quota, a lesser annual quantity than in previous years was shipped to the United States.

During this time more sugar from the Caribbean and Latin America —primarily from the Dominican Republic and Brazil—was shipped to the United States.

During the second half of 1981, prices ranged from 12 to 16 cents per pound.

On December 21, President Reagan signed the Agriculture and Food Act of 1981 (1981 Farm Bill), which established a support price for domestic cane and beet sugar at 16.75 cents per pound basis raw cane sugar. During the congressional debate that preceded this legislation being signed into law, the president's position regarding the sugar title of the bill was to advocate a free trading market philosophy for sugar.

However, the president needed the help of the so-called southern congressional "boll weevils" for passage of his tax legislation.

During the debate, therefore, following the 1981 Labor Day recess, the president changed his position to one of "neutrality"; he would not challenge the view of those senators and congressmen who advocated a five-year support program for domestic sugar.

During 1981, world sugar prices were declining. The expectation was rampant that some sort of protectionist sugar legislation would emerge, along with a commensurate restrictive quota, increased duty and/or import fee. Hence sugar from foreign producers poured into United States ports, especially during the final six months of 1981. This influx included volume imports from nearby countries such as the Dominican Republic.

The effect of this huge importation was a "catch-22." The more sugar that arrived in the United States for customs entry before the year's end—at the statutory minimum duty of .625 cents per pound and no import fee and no quota—the lower the United States domestic price, and the more pressure on the U.S. Congress by the domestic sugar industry and the domestic corn wet-milling industry to pass protectionist sugar legislation.

On December 23, 1981, President Reagan signed two proclamations pursuant to the newly enacted farm bill, raising the duty to its statutory maximum of 2.8125 cents per pound and imposing import fees on imported foreign sugar per his authority under Section 22 of the Agricultural Adjustment Act of 1933, as amended. On signing these two proclamations President Reagan stated:

> I personally regret the necessity for signing these proclamations. The sugar program enacted by Congress to protect higher-cost domestic producers will result in higher costs for all American consumers. I have directed that the import fees imposed by these proclamations be adjusted at least quarterly, so that they can be revised downward whenever possible, without incurring significant government purchases of sugar or encouraging forfeiture of sugar loans beginning in FY 83.

> In addition, I realize that the sugar duties and fees may have adverse effects on our major foreign sugar suppliers, particularly those in the Caribbean Basin. I have thus asked appropriate agencies to review this question on a priority basis to see what we can do to mitigate the effects.

By April 1982, prices declined to just under 10 cents per pound, and on May 5, 1982, President Reagan signed two more proclamations: one modifying the import fee proclamation and the other establishing a quota on all imported foreign sugar with specific percentage allocations to foreign countries supplying sugar to the United States.

On signing the quota proclamation, President Reagan stated:

> In arriving at this decision, we have taken fully into account the Caribbean Basin Initiative. The historical formula chosen to allocate quotas among countries fully reflects the traditional role of Caribbean Basin countries in our sugar market.
>
> In separate action, steps are also being taken to provide Carribbean Basin sugar producers with additional financial assistance during the remainder of this year beyond that already proposed in the Carribbean Basin Initiative legislation and normal budget requests.

The method chosen by the adminstration to calculate these percentages was to use the total quantities imported into the United States by each of the quota-holding countries during 1975 through 1981, drop the highest and the lowest year and quantitatively average the remaining five years.

The premise was to demonstrate the history of imports into the United States during a non-Sugar Act period.

As a result of this method, the percentages for the top four countries were:

Dominican Republic	17.6%
Brazil	14.5%
Philippines	13.5%
Australia	8.3%

These same percentages exist today!

In September 1982, during the official state visit by President Marcos to the United States, a position paper prepared by the Philippine Sugar Commission and dated Septmber 13, 1982, was given to the administration by the visiting Philippine delegation. This document recapitulated the Philippine sugar performance record with the United States from 1930–74 and the Philippine/United States government relationship during this period. This document recommended:

a. An increase in the Philippine/United States quota from 13.5 percent to 25 percent, based on Philippine historical performance to the United States.

b. A most-favored-nation treatment for sugar, equal to the benefits included for the Dominican Republic in the Caribbean Basin Initiative legislation that had been introduced in March 1982 and was still being debated.

On April 1, 1983, the Philippines were granted duty-free treatment on sugar imports for twelve months under the Generalized System of Preferences (GSP) provisions of the Trade Act of 1974, based on a "competitive need formula" pursuant to the Act. Brazil and the Dominican Republic remained dutiable.

On August 5, 1983, the Caribbean Basin Economic Recovery Act (CBI) was enacted. It granted the Dominican Republic, as well as Guatemala, Panama and a number of Caribbean and Central American countries, duty-free status on imports (including sugar) into the United States.

The act, which expires on September 30, 1995, gives the Dominican Republic a "special duty-free access for sugar to the United States market of 780,000 metric tons," or 890,000 short tons raw value, in the absence of a restrictive quota system (but under a domestic support program with a Section 22 proclamation in effect).

The calculation for this quantity was accomplished on the basis of 110 percent of the quantity imported by the Dominican Republic into the United States during 1979–81 (when Philippines/United States imports were the lowest).

UNITED STATES QUOTA

The United States sugar quota during the life of the Agriculture and Food Act of 1981 (for which the Philippines has a percentage allocation of 13.5 percent) is as follows:

Period	MillionShort TonsRaw Value (STRV)
October 1, 1982–September 30, 1983	2.8
October 1, 1983–September 30, 1984	2.952
October 1, 1984–November 30, 1985	2.552
December 1, 1985–December 31, 1986	1.850

On January 31, 1985, President Reagan signed a proclamation reducing the sugar duty from 2.8125 cents per pound to .625 cents per pound. On March 29, 1985, he signed a proclamation reducing the import fee on imported raw sugar to zero. The logic behind both these actions is quite simple: While a restrictive quota is in place to prop up domestic prices, a high duty and an import fee are unnecessary and only hurt the quota-holding country.

FOOD SECURITY ACT OF 1985

On December 23, President Reagan signed the Food Security Act of 1985 (1985 Farm Bill renewal). An effort to add to this legislation a "most-favored-nation" amendment for the Philippines was soundly defeated.

On signing this legislation into law, President Reagan stated that he would introduce legislation to liberalize the restrictive foreign quotas mandated by the bill, as the sugar title of the statute adversely affected the economies of the CBI countries and the Philippines.

On the president's trip to Grenada in February 1986, he reiterated his position of introducing legislation to liberalize foreign quotas.

It is unlikely in this 1986 congressional election year that major changes to this statute will be made. (The Food Security Improvements Act of 1986, approved March 20, 1986, includes technical changes rather than policy changes.)

The Food Security Act of 1985 includes Title IX Sugar. This Act will apply to the 1986 through 1990 domestic crop years, but for sugar it will also have a signficant effect on the 1985 crop. The Food Security Act generally left the major provisions of the 1981 Agriculture and Food Act in place and differed greatly from the original proposals suggested by the administration.

FORFEITURES

The most important sugar provision of the act deals with the problem of forfeitures of sugar loans to the Commodity Credit Corporation (CCC). For the 1986 through 1990 crops: "The President shall use all authorities available to the President as is necessary to enable the Secretary of Agriculture to operate the sugar program . . . at no cost to the Federal Government by preventing the accumulation of sugar acquired by the CCC." This language differs from the 1981 act in that it mandates the program be run at no cost to the government. The implication for the 1986–90 crop is that supplies be restricted to levels that would prevent forfeitures of sugar to the CCC.

IMPORT QUOTAS

Another provision of the sugar program dealt with the allocation of the sugar import quota. Beginning with the quota year after the 1985–86 quota year, no import quota would be allocated to a country that is a net importer of sugar unless it can prove that it does not import and then reexport Cuban sugar to the United States.

LOAN RATES

For the 1986–90 crop years, the loan rate for raw cane sugar has been set at no less than 18 cents a pound. The loan rate can be raised based on changes in the cost of sugar products, sugar production costs, and other circumstances affecting domestic sugar production. If the secretary finds that the loan rate should not be increased, a report with the data supporting his decision must be submitted to the House Committee on Agriculture and the Senate Committee on Agriculture, Nutrition and Forestry. The loan rate for raw cane sugar will be evaluated each crop year.

As in the 1981 Agriculture and Food Act, the Food Security Act of 1985 mandates that the price for domestically grown sugarbeets be supported "at such level as the Secretary determines is fair and reasonable in relation to the loan level for sugarcane." For the 1985 crop, the national average loan rate for raw cane sugar was 18 cents a pound and the national average loan rate for beet sugar was set at 21.06 cents. If the loan rate for raw cane sugar stays at 18 cents, the loan rate for beet sugar should also remain steady. The factors that would change the relationship between the beet and the cane loan rate are changes in fixed marketing expenses or the percentage net return from beet sugar to the raw sugar spot price. Consistent with the 1981 act, the secretary is obligated to announce the loan rates as early as possible. All loans made to sugar processors must be made after October 1 and mature before the end of the same fiscal year.

EFFECTS OF GRAMM-RUDMAN ON SUGAR LOANS

There is a great deal of uncertainty about the impact on the sugar program of the Balanced Budget and Emergency Deficit Control Act of

1985 (Gramm-Rudman Act). The uncertainty stems from how the act will be applied to sugar loans. Loans taken out in fiscal 1986 will not be affected, as they apply to the 1985 crop. It is still unclear if the 4.3-percent budget reduction being applied to the 1986 crop loans for some other commodities will be applied in fiscal year 1987 to the 1986 crop sugar loans.

CCC STOCKS

The USDA, pursuant to an expanded section 416 Food Aid Authority in the Food Security Act of 1985, has notified Caribbean nations hurt by lower United States sugar imports, that the United States will offer government-held CCC stocks as some compensation for the reduction.

USDA is now awaiting an indication from the Caribbean nations of their commodity needs.

This effort follows a pledge earlier in 1986 by President Reagan that Caribbean nations would be given compensation for a cut in United States sugar imports required by the act.

In early December 1985, the Philippine Sugar Marketing Corporation (Philsuma), a privately owned firm, was formed and began operation to replace the National Sugar Trading Corporation (Nasutra), which was government owned. The formation of Philsuma was part of the overall guidelines established by the International Monetary Fund to privatize government-run or government-owned agencies in the agricultural sector. Philsuma is composed of representatives from sugar millers and planters as well as government representatives.

The sugar quota for the Philippines for December 1, 1985, to December 31, 1986, is 231,660 short tons raw value (about 200,000 metric tons). According to USDA shipping patterns, this is to be shipped at regular intervals throughout the year in ten shipments of about 20,000 metric tons each (in bulk carriers). This sugar has already been sold by Philsuma for shipment to the United States.

The Philippine Sugar Commission, which functions as a governmental supervisory and regulatory body—including the signatory to "Certificates of Quota Eligibility" with USDA and the U.S. Customs Service—is expected to be replaced by another quasi-government agency.

There is talk of selling sugar to the United States for the 1987 quota through individual sellers rather than through a single seller such as Philsuma.

The highest realistic estimate being discussed for the 1987 quota (for twelve months) is 1.5 million short tons raw value. That does not mean that the Philippines, or any other country, receives its fixed percentage of this total quota. USDA and the United States Trade Representatives will first deduct from the total any adjustments or corrections and then make the percentage allocations.

WHERE DO WE GO FROM HERE?

The world market price for sugar remains at about the eight-cent level. This is clearly below the Philippine sugar production cost of about to 13 cents per pound, but certainly better than the 1985 average price of about four cents per pound.

Only time will tell when sugar prices will rise high enough to justify full-scale or even moderate-scale sugar production.

An increase in the Philippine/United States quota (which gives the Philippines an FOB return of about 17 cents per pound) would be a shot in the arm to the Philippine sugar industry. While an effort still exists in the Congress to accomplish this objective, the administration is reluctant to change any of the percentages assigned to quota-holding countries for fear of the adverse effects of upsetting the status quo.

ALTERNATIVE CROPS

In 1978, intercropping was introduced on an experimental basis in some sugar mill districts, to maximize income in sugar cane production by planting cash crops such as mungo bean or peanuts between sugarcane furrows. The provinces of Negros Occidental, Negros Oriental, Iloilo, Tarlac, and Pampanga were designated priority areas.

Today, there is talk of intercropping cacao and coffee in coconut-producing areas. Oil palm production has been suggested for Negros. So too has been the planting of Ipal Ipal trees, which yield a leaf used for cattle feed. White and yellow corn are candidates. Aquaculture is a realistic alternative to sugar cane, especially near the coastline in Negros. Prawns and shrimp produced in flooded cane land are exported primarily to Japan. Fishponds could be developed, with the production and export of shellfish encouraged.

Still needed, however, especially in areas of Negros, is assurance that the new plantings or, indeed, agriculture in general, can proceed without interruption by units of the National Peoples Army (NPA). Agriculture, social progress, the political climate, improvement of the economy, and the problems of the Philippine sugar industry are all interwoven.

CONCLUSION

Barring any major disruptions in production, world sugar prices, according to many analysts, should remain between 7 and 10 cents per pound through the end of 1986. The Philippines will have to consolidate sugar production so that only the most productive areas, sugar mills and sugar refineries are utilized. (The manufacture of ethanol does require capital investment. While not now suggested as an immediate alternative use of excess sugar cane, the facilities for such manufacture are best and most economically built or expanded alongside existing sugar mills).

The Philippines should continue to exert maximum efforts in the U.S. Congress and all other areas of interest and influence in the United States, to increase their share in the United States sugar quota program and renew their petition to the administration for duty-free treatment for sugar and other products under the Trade and Tariff Act of 1984.

The Philippines should vigorously pursue: Section 416 food aid assistance (for less-developed United States sugar-quota-holding countries); the entire $500-million "Philippine aid package" for economic and military assistance, as announced by the White House on April 23, 1986; and even further economic assistance requests for fiscal year 1987. The White House press release (April 23, 1986) specifically states that an element of the aid package is devoted to "the severely depressed sugar producing region of Negros Island."

The United States, for its part, should encourage friendly nations to assist the Philippines, especially in this time of need. Such influence can be channelled, in part, through the World Bank, the International Monetary Fund (IMF), the Asian Development Bank, Association of South East Asian nations (ASEAN), multilateral institutions and bilateral donors.

Aquaculture in the Philippines should be intensified. Although fishponds and prawn-producing areas by themselves are no panacea, relatively little in the way of capital investment is required for aquaculture, allowing for trial, error, and improvement. Greater areas of prawn production can receive pre-export financing by the receiving foreign buyers such as Japan and even the United States.

References (Statutes)

Section 22, Agriculture Adjustment Act of 1933 as Amended.
Agriculture and Food Act of 1981.
Caribbean Basin Economic Recovery Act.
Food Security Act of 1985.
Food Security Improvements Act of 1986.
International Sugar Agreement, 1977 (United Nations).
Philippine Trade Act of 1946 as Amended.
Sugar Act of 1946 as Amended.
Trade Act of 1974.
Trade and Tariff Act of 1984.

Bibliography

A U.S. Sugar Quota for the Philippines Commensurate with its Record as a Historical Supplier, Position Paper, (Philippine State Visit to U.S.). Manila: Philippine Sugar Commission, September, 13, 1982.

Atienza, J.C., *The Sugar Industry in the Philippines,* Sugar y Azucar, Manila, Philippines:International Society of Sugar Cane Technologists, XVII Congress, presented in January 1980.

Blamberg, Margaret, Ph.D., *The Political Economy of Sugar 1986 and Beyond.* New York: Anstar Corporation, November 21, 1985.

1985 Annual Report. New York: Coffee, Sugar & Cocoa Exchange, Inc., January 1986.

Second Estimate of World Sugar Production 1985/1986. Ratzeburg, Germany: F.O. Licht's International Sugar Report, January 23, 1986.

Harding, Ralph R., Advisor and Consultant Government Affairs, Philippine Sugar Commission, *Statement Before U.S. Senate Committee on Agriculture, Nutrition and Forestry* (1985 Farm Bill debate), Washington, D.C.: 1985.

Hoff, Frederick L., and Lawrence, Max. *Implications of World Sugar Markets, Policies, and Production Costs for U.S. Sugar,* Washington, D.C.: USDA ERS, November 1965.

Nuttall, John L., and Barry, Robert D., Chief, Sugar Group, FAS/USDA, *Outlook for Sugar, Annual Agricultural Outlook Conference,* Washington, D.C.: USDA, December 4, 1985.

Sugar, Molasses and Honey, World Sugar and Molasses Situation and Outlook, Washington, D.C.: U.S. Department of Agriculture, Foreign Agricultural Service, November 1985.

Sugar and Sweetener Outlook and Situation Report, Washington, D.C.: U.S. Department of Agriculture, Economic Research Service, September 1985 and March 1986.

Sugar, Report to the President on Investigation No. 22–45 Under Section 22 of the Agricultural Adjustment Act (Includes Presidential Proclamations), Washington, D.C.: U.S. International Trade Commission, Publication 1253, June 1982.

Announcement of Country-by-Country Sugar Allocations, Washington, D.C.: U.S. Trade Representative, September 13, 1985.

1985 Commodity Year Book, New York: Commodity Research Bureau, January 1986.

9

Agrarian Problems and Agrarian Reform: Opportunity or Irony?

Bruce M. Koppel

INTRODUCTION

The new Philippine government faces few problems that present a juxtaposition of historical legacy, socioeconomic complexity, and political risk on such daunting scales as does land reform. For essentially all of the twentieth century, and arguably a good portion of the many decades before, one issue has loomed largest in the development of the agrarian Philippines: land—who owns it, who can acquire it, who can use it.

No Philippine government since independence has approached the land issue with a clean slate. Always there has been something, however small and implicit, that simultaneously established a departure point and narrowed the possibilities for a destination point. One result has been a certain continuity and even progression. An example is change in perceptions of what was needed and why. What could not be done in 1935 (for example, establishing a process for transferring title to tenants) could be tried in 1975. What was acceptable in 1975 (limiting land reform to tenanted rice and corn lands) might not suffice in 1990. Another result has been a certain discontinuity and even regression. An example is change in when, how, and why opposition to agrarian reform is exercised. What was not widely attempted in 1935 (for example, use of regular military forces to support land stealing) could be openly employed in 1975.

For the Aquino government, the land reform challenge is laced with irony: the new government is in the position of inheriting *both* the most comprehensive land reform policy ever attempted in the Philippines (or anywhere else in Southeast Asia) *and* the most extensive record of extra- and paralegal manipulation of land rights to date. Just determining what happened and why since the early 1970s would be difficult and important enough, but determining enough to go forward will require coming to terms with what is now an incredibly complex situation of questionable titling, retitling, title reversion, occupancy by *force majeur,* and so on—all this at a time when the country's economic and political future is in jeopardy and is acknowledged to depend primarily on agricultural and rural development.

This chapter will briefly review past Philippine experience with agrarian reform, characterize the contemporary agrarian situation, and identify the major reform challenges it presents.

PHILIPPINE EXPERIENCE WITH AGRARIAN REFORM

When the United States began its colonial rule of the Philippines in 1898, prime agricultural land was largely controlled by the Catholic church and large private land grants. The United States increasingly saw this situation as incompatible with its interests in the Philippines. In its place, the United States sought to confer and confirm a more broadly based pattern of land ownership in order to create and strengthen a landed class that would support the American presence. Several steps were taken to bring this about. Initially, the large church holdings, or friar lands, were protected, but gradually efforts were initiated to break these up. Other steps included a homesteading act, measures to clarify and expand the existing Torrens land-titling system, and regulation of landlord-tenant relationships. The United States significantly enhanced its position in the Philippines through these agrarian reform tactics. However, most of the Filipinos who benefited were not cultivators. In fact, tenancy increased.

Under Commonwealth President Manuel Quezon, several programs were initiated to strengthen existing tenancy laws. For example, a Rice Share Tenancy Law, enacted in 1933, provided for fifty-fifty sharing. This period also saw a few examples of large private estate expropriation carried out under Article XII of the 1935 Constitution. Finally, efforts to deal with agrarian reform through resettling households from Luzon and the Visayas in Mindanao under homesteading laws were continued. These efforts coincided with an unsponsored migration of rural households from Luzon and the Visayas to Mindanao and Palawan.

After the Japanese occupation, limited agrarian reform resumed. For example, Republic Act 1119, enacted in 1950, mandated a seventy-thirty sharing arrangement. However, this was generally ignored. During the administrations of Presidents Roxas and Quirino, a Rural

Progress Administration (RPA) was established to purchase and redistribute large estates. Very little was accomplished, in part because the Philippine congress committed little money to the RPA. During the administrations of Presidents Magsaysay and Garcia, more funds were made available, and American pressure for tenure reform as an anticommunist strategy was felt. Agrarian reform legislation passed included establishment of The Agricultural Credit and Cooperative Financing Administration (1953), the Agricultural Tenancy Act (1954), and the Land Tenure Act (1955). A Land Tenure Authority was established. Some funds were made available for estate purchase, but the RPA's limited power of expropriation was reduced. Perhaps the major accomplishment of the period was the resettlement activity undertaken after the defeat of the Huk rebellion. The actual scope of the resettlement was not large, but its symbolic implications were substantial as evidence that tenants in central Luzon actually could become owner-operators. This possibility was not lost on opponents of land reform, one of whom denied the communist insurgency demanded land reform and asked:

> Don't we take pride in the fact that our countrymen who are generally poor can point with pride to foreigners that we also have a little of "the landed gentry" who live a little bit better than they do, and that we are not a nation of peasants?[1]

In 1963, during the administration of Diosdado Macapagal, the Agricultural Land Reform Code (Republic Act 3844) was passed. The code announced that agricultural share tenancy was "contrary to public policy and shall be abolished." Farmers were to become owner-cultivators. A Land Authority was created to administer the law and a Land Bank was formed to finance it. However, inadequate appropriations and other expressions of opposition from landlords made the code ineffective. In 1966, the new president, Ferdinand Marcos, declared twelve municipalities in Pampanga Province as a land reform area under the code, matching the twelve proclaimed by his predecessor.

---

[1]Frances L. Starner, *Magsaysay and the Philippine Peasantry: The Agrarian Impact on Philippine Politics, 1953-1956* (Berkeley: University of California Press, 1961).

The government later proclaimed other areas, but by 1970, it was apparent that very little progress was being made.

Five days after the declaration of martial law in September 1972, Marcos issued Presidential Decree (PD) No. 2 declaring the entire Philippines a land reform area. Shortly thereafter, on October 21, 1972, PD 27 was issued, the so-called "Tenants' Emancipation Act." Landholdings exceeding one hundred (eventually reduced to seven) hectares of rice and corn land were the target. Land would be purchased and then parcelled out to individual tenants with the price determined by the land's productivity. The amortizing tenant would pay this off at 6 percent interest on a fifteen-year term. A tenant could acquire up to three hectares of irrigated and five hectares of unirrigated land. In order to qualify, a tenant had to be a member of a *samahang nayon,* a village cooperative. If the farmer defaulted on amortization payments, the *samahang nayon* was supposed to pay.

Implementation was slow, limited, underfunded, and later openly subject to corruption and reversion. The program had consistent financial problems, with too little coming from the government given the stated task and scope and, later, through mismanagement of the program's principal fiscal instrument, the Land Bank, a draining of available reserves. PD 717, issued in 1975, indicated that banks had to set aside 25 percent of their loanable funds for agriculture and 10 percent of that for agrarian reform participants. However, there were so many exceptions that banks were not induced to finance the program.

Political commitment is best described as selective, with the programs being pursued vigorously in some places and completely ignored elsewhere. For example, in 1984, Marcos authorized the Ministry of Trade and Industry and the Board of Investments to prepare an intensive program for feedcorn and soybean production in which landowners who participated could be exempted from land reform. Judicial subterfuge, a problem in prior land reforms, remained a problem, with knowledgeable landowners able to sidetrack the land reform process through the notoriously slow Philippine judicial system. A range of other government support services directed towards rice and later corn production (especially the Masagana 99 rice production program) were coordinated with the *samahang nayons* during the first few years of martial law, but this linkage weakened as political endorsement of the *samahang nayon* system was eclipsed by the rise of other village-based political mobilization efforts (most notably the Kabataan Barangay movement), and the Masagana 99 system broke down under the weight of very low loan repayment.

More than one-third of the country's agricultural lands were excluded because they were not planted to rice or corn. The widely recognized rationale was that the productivity of export agriculture should not be undermined by subdivision into uneconomic sizes. Less widely recognized was that only about 5 percent of the rural work force was covered, that is, existing tenants on the portions of individually owned rice and corn land in excess of seven hectares. While the rural Philippines is not purely agrarian, the 95 percent who were excluded were not all town residents and nonagricultural employees. Among the others in the rural labor force who were excluded were tenants on agricultural land other than that devoted to rice and corn, most notably sugar and coconut, and also households dependent on fisheries and forestry; farmers cultivating rice or corn on untitled or imperfectly titled lands, most notably those who had occupied or otherwise gained access to public lands; farmers functioning as tenants on land that was not part of a holding exceeding seven hectares; farmers classified as workers *for* rather than tenants *of* a landowner on any agricultural land; and subtenants on rice and corn lands. Throughout the program, the number of farmers considered to be included in the program has greatly exceeded the number to receive a certificate of land transfer (which specifies the eligible land and assigns to the cultivator a "right" to purchase), which in turn has greatly exceeded the number actually entering the amortization process (which requires a final determination of price for the land).

Philippine experience with agrarian reform and the political objectives of the Marcos government made most of these characteristics unsurprising. In the words of David Wurfel:

> The political purpose of land reform and its ancillary policies was to create mass support for the new society and its leader, legitimize him abroad, and undermine support for alternative leadership on both the right and the left.[2]

---

[2]David Wurfel, "The Development of Post-War Philippine Land Reform: Political and Sociological Explanations," in Antonio J. Ledesma, Perla Q. Makil, and Virginia A. Miralao (eds), *Second View from the Paddy* (Manila: Ateneo de Manila University Institute of Philippine Culture, 1983), pp. 1-14.

However, the program has had two impacts that were not clearly foreseen by either critics or proponents. First, the exclusion of subtenants (which was explicit in the decree's failure to recognize the existence of subtenancy and implicit in the constraints placed on amortizing owners from taking on tenants or subdividing) contributed to a significant expansion of the rural landless labor force (estimates generally begin at 50,000 households). Land arrangements in the rural Philippines are very complex, especially where population densities are increasing, problems of landlessness already rising, and also where the importance of off-farm employment in household income is growing. Consequently, in some areas, subtenancy arrangements were multi-tiered, often seasonal, and in general very complex—sometimes reflecting immiseration and sometimes reflecting employment differentiation. PD 27, in the tradition of Philippine agrarian reform, did not recognize these diverse agrarian realities, with the result that making one tenant a candidate-owner could put several subtenants out of work and off the land.

Second, problems of amortization default coupled with mismanagement of the Land Bank had the ultimate effect in many cases of leading tenants to reactivate tenancy agreements with former landlords (which was foreseen). In other cases, however, the landlord role has effectively passed to the primary agency responsible for program administration, the Ministry of Agrarian Reform (a development that was not foreseen). In these circumstances, the tenant could be displaced, but MAR rather than the Land Bank or the original landlord would hold the land. The ministry could then participate in what has come to be an "aftermarket" in certificates of land transfer. This was especially common in the Bicol region, but could be seen in other regions as well.

THE CONTEMPORARY AGRARIAN SITUATION

Rice

Rice production is found throughout the Philippines, and it is really only among rice producers that any impact of PD 27 can be found. However, as implied earlier, the current situation is very confused in many places. During the last fifteen years, Philippine rice production has been the object of considerable public investment, foreign borrowing, and development assistance. This has provided for a significant expansion in irrigation facilities and a major improvement in roads.

The presence of the International Rice Research Institute in the Philippines has provided a significant source of technological innovation, principally for lowland irrigated rice. Average productivity increased (from approximately 1.8 metric tons per hectare in 1970 to 2.3 metric tons per hectare in 1983), and the Philippines temporarily moved from a position as perennial importer to marginal exporter in the early 1980s. However, yields remain considerably lower than elsewhere in Asia, yield growth has essentially stopped, several hundred thousand hectares of good rice production land have been taken out of rice production, primarily in Luzon, since the late 1970s (in some cases to avoid land reform); and in 1984 the Philippines resumed significant levels of rice imports. Recently it has become clear that levels of self-sufficiency may not have risen as much as was thought. Beginning in the late 1970s official per capita rice demand estimates were lowered from close to ninety-three kilograms to seventy-nine kilograms in 1985.

While the Philippines had some form of palay (rough unhulled rice) buying system before Marcos, government rice policy tended to focus on trying to control retail prices and periodically (usually before elections) importing estimated shortfalls. Under Marcos, the scope of government intervention grew far greater. High volumes of often subsidized production credit were made available, usually to the better-endowed irrigating farmers, increasing income differences between irrigating and rainfed rice producers. Important inputs, most notably fertilizer (which was in very high demand), were heavily taxed, a strategy that penalized farmers and ultimately weakened the domestic fertilizer industry. By the late 1970s, it was clear that private investment to improve milling and marketing was being squeezed out. By the early 1980s, the primary instrument for state intervention in the rice economy, the National Food Authority, had so overextended its operations that it had to "raid" other parts of the food economy (primarily controlling wheat imports and, later, flour distribution) to support its operations in rice and vegetables. With the onset of the external debt crisis in 1983, the primary sources of subsidized domestic agricultural credit dried up while other funds that had been available for rice production financing migrated to very high-interest Central Bank certificates of deposit. By the 1984-85 crop year, for example, Masagana 99 credit was down to approximately 250 million pesos, 20 percent of what it had been ten years earlier. By the same year, NFA essentially was unable to defend its own announced support price. Many farmers faced prices that were only half of their production costs.

Under World Bank and United States pressure, steps were taken toward the deregulation of retail rice prices in October 1985. Efforts to maintain support prices for farmers remain, but it is not clear how to finance these efforts. Fertilizer taxes have been lowered while inflation rates have dropped and weather has been favorable. The new government is talking about shifting attention to rainfed rice producers. Rice policy is clearly being "reformed," but the reform is unfolding in a problematic context. Today, complex rice land arrangements are complicated further by problems of indebtedness, low productivity, and outside of the most favored irrigated areas poor research, extension, and marketing support. Even within the irrigated areas, there is considerable evidence that productivity has leveled. With pressure to increase nonagricultural wages coming from more militant unions combined with the inevitable pressures to keep farm prices up and retail prices down that will accompany the approaching local elections, it is clear that the government is far from being off the hook on rice.

Corn

Corn production is concentrated outside Luzon, primarily on nonirrigated and highly tenanted lands. Corn producers have been practically untouched by land reform. Corn productivity in the Philippines is very low, although in the last few years this has begun to change (average yields were approximately .85 metric tons per hectare through most of the 1970s, rising to approximately 1.2 metric tons per hectare by the early 1980s). Government intervention has been present, principally in establishing support prices, but the price has not been seriously defended through buying activity. Some extension and credit assistance has been available. For example, a Masagana 99 program was introduced in 1981; however, with neither productive technology nor price inducements to offer, repayment rates ran about 52 percent. By 1984, the program ceased making loans. Support was also provided for higher-yielding hybrid corn production, but production costs were about four times higher than those for traditional corn. Few small farmers could qualify for these loans.

The bulk of government intervention in corn has run in a different direction than it has for rice. While in the southern Philippines white corn is a grain of preference for human consumption, the importance of yellow corn as a poultry and animal feed has increased dramatically in the Philippines during the last ten years. Demand for feedcorn has been increasing by more than 10 percent annually, while domestic production has been rising only about 5 percent per year. To meet this growing demand, the government initially chose to expand imports from the United States (averaging about $300 million per year) rather than make a serious commitment to improving domestic corn productivity. Later, in 1983, the government began supporting corporate feedcorn production through discounted loans and inputs. Levels of corn imports did decline after 1983 because of trade financing problems, although this slump was short-lived, with the U.S. Commodity Credit Corporation making available longer terms than were commercially normal (three years rather than one) at lower interest rates to maintain the United States corn market in the Philippines. This amounted to an export subsidy for American producers since it discounted the costs to the Philippines of financing corn purchases. Attention to small domestic corn producers has increased in the 1980s, but in general it is correct to say that corn production today is characterized by low productivity on very low-capitalized farms.

Sugar

Sugar and coconut are traditionally the Philippines' major agricultural exports. Under Marcos, significant reorganization affecting control of these industries was conducted. In the case of sugar, reorganization (which has really been ongoing since independence) accelerated and took the form of mill and plantation establishment and takeover, control of marketing and export operations, and control of production financing. As long as the Philippines had preferential access to the American market, could sell on a world market at high prices, or could negotiate favorable long-term contracts, problems of low productivity were downplayed. In the 1980s, all this unraveled and the basic weaknesses of the sugar industry, severely exacerbated under Marcos, were revealed. From 1980, the value of Philippine sugar exports *declined* at an annual rate of close to 21 percent. With Philippine production costs averaging twelve cents per pound and world spot prices hovering around four cents per pound by 1984, the sugar industry was losing over five billion pesos annually. By 1984, estimates were that only 5 percent of the country's sugar planters were self-financed. The rest were exposed to a near-collapse of the sugar production financing system. Eighty-five percent of the sugar growers were estimated to be in serious arrears on production loans from Republic Planters Bank (RPB), in part because they had not been paid for their 1983 sales to the National Sugar Trading Corporation (NASU-TRA). By 1985, RPB owed the Central Bank over two billion pesos and had virtually no loanable funds.

What is especially significant is that friends of Mr. Marcos, especially Mr. Roberto Benedicto and his associates, effectively controlled sugar financing, milling, and trading. Using what amounted to an export tax on the production of other producers and millers, the Benedicto interests were able to accumulate enormous funds with virtually no responsibility to account for what happened to these funds. The Benedicto interests also were able to shield themselves from many of the downside risks through preferential financing and trading. For example, NASUTRA was the only agency that could export. RPB was essentially the only bank that could finance production. Under pressure from the United States and the World Bank, and with growing support among sugar planters for the emerging political opposition to Marcos, sugar trading was "opened" in 1984. However, producers found themselves facing a difficult choice: if they did not sign a long-term (five-year) contract with NASUTRA, they were unlikely to receive production financing. In 1985, NASUTRA was abolished and a new agency formed with commissioners elected by eligible planters. The election rules ensured that while crony power would remain, representatives of other planters would have some influence. Even before Marcos fell, no one really appeared to be happy with this arrangement; but with the continuing decline of the sugar industry it was clear that the debts of NASUTRA and RPB alone were tending to hold policy hostage. The Aquino government still faces the same dilemma, even though Benedicto left with Marcos.

The country's most serious rural labor problem is in sugar production. Large-scale unemployment is coupled with very low wages. In 1984, Minister of Labor Blas Ople offered to "exempt" planters from having to pay minimum wages if they diversified away from sugar. In fact, it was no secret that minimum wages were not being enforced for sugar planters who did grow sugar. In the late 1970s, as the sugar economy began a serious decline, labor militancy began to increase; but there was virtually no tolerance for sugar labor organizers. Such people were called communists and were targets of the military. In addition, many plantation owners, especially those who were not politically "in," were first underpaid by the single government agency that had exclusive buying and exporting rights (NASUTRA) and then completely unpaid for their crops. Today, the position of the industry is one of excess milling capacity (by 1985, only ten of the country's forty-one mills were considered to be profitable), inefficient production, highly indebted producers, and a labor force of more than 500,000 workers with little or no work. The situation is worst in Negros Occidental, where the absence of alternative employment and land use opportunities has created a very bad situation. There is widely documented starvation, serious problems with very oppressive local political leadership, and probably the most rapidly growing NPA movement in the Philippines.

Coconut

The coconut story has similar themes: producers characterized by low productivity facing tightly controlled financing, marketing, and prices. Coconuts are grown throughout the Philippines, but this crop is especially important in eastern and southern Luzon, the eastern Visayas and northern and eastern Mindanao. The Philippines is a major world producer. However, the world coconut market is volatile, a result of high substitutability between coconut oil and other seed oils.

More than two million Filipino households are directly dependent, in one form or another, on coconut production. Unlike rice, corn, and sugar, coconuts are a perennial crop, depending on a standing crop of trees. Although most production occurs on small farms, most producers are in complex tenancy relationships with both landowners and copra superintendents. The point of control for the industry, however, is not in production but in marketing, milling, and pricing. These were the points where control was taken. The key instrument was a coconut levy, in pre-Marcos days a device to subsidize domestic coconut oil prices when world prices were high. Under Marcos, the levy, along with a bewildering variety of other export taxes and milling tolls, placed an average annual effective tax rate on the producers exceeding 40 percent, maintained even when world prices collapsed. The funds were supposed to have additional objectives, most notably financing a replanting scheme as well as welfare-oriented activities for coconut producers, but by and large they did neither. What happened to most of the levy funds is not certain, but it is apparent that the levy became a tool to finance enormous asset acquisitions by important cronies of Mr.

Marcos, including his defense minister.

As in sugar, under United States, IMF, and World Bank pressure, some significant government initiatives were taken in 1985 to open trading and rehabilitate financing. The Aquino government is attempting to continue this reform. However, the initiatives are more symbolic than substantive, illustrating the political limits on reform. The regulations "opening" export trading actually limit trading to those who held that monopoly before, the existing millowners. The Philippine Commission on Good Government (PCGG) sequestered over 90 percent of the shares of United Coconut Planters Bank. However, direction of the bank as well as the Philippine Coconut Authority still rests primarily with the pre-Aquino controllers of the industry. Today coconut farmers are tending aging trees (more than 25 percent of the trees are over sixty years old) that are losing productivity. Rates of out-of-school youth, already high in coconut areas, are growing, an important indicator of deepening rural distress. Not surprisingly, NPA activity is also high in many coconut areas.

Questionable Land Grants

During the Marcos years, land "grants" for a variety of export crop (palm oil, rubber, and fruits) and logging purposes were common, often at the price of forcibly dislocating large numbers of people. While in many instances the beneficiaries of these grants were Filipino associates of Mr. Marcos, there were also numerous instances when the effective beneficiaries were foreign investors, primarily American and Japanese. This problem was especially rampant in Mindanao where everything from land previously occupied by homestead settlers and the island's ethnic and tribal minorities to public land was, in one way or another, given away. In some cases, for example in the Cagayan de Oro area, farmers were not actually displaced but "re-employed" in contract agriculture. However, in many cases, displacement was the effect. One result has been to exacerbate communal violence in Mindanao. While problems of inter-ethnic relations and land conflict in Mindanao (and other areas such as northern Luzon) are not new, numerous activities that occurred during the Marcos years in the name of "resource development" dramatically increased these problems. In Mindanao, many of the displaced found their way to regional cities (especially Davao and Zamboanga), but as refugees rather than migrants.

The numbers of people affected by land stealing and granting are not really known. What is known is that public land designations bear little correspondence to actual land use. In Mindanao, Palawan, and many parts of Luzon, much of the public land has been logged, planted to a variety of exportables, or converted to ranches. In the past, problems of public land occupancy and deforestation were blamed on *kaingeros,* shifting slash-and-burn cultivators. This is a problem, but only a marginal one in comparison to the alienation of public lands as well as the takeover of other lands that has occurred throughout the "upland" Philippines. As population densities have increased in upland areas, where land titling arrangements were already unclear, a maze of occupancy arrangements have co-evolved, often with no "legal" recognition. Consequently, today there are literally thousands of conflicting claims based on everything from a Torrens title to an occupancy claim, an executive order, or a well-armed security force.

THE CHALLENGES OF AGRARIAN REFORM

Historically, resettlement has been an important element of Philippine agrarian reform, but since the mid-1960s, resettlement has declined in significance. This has been frequently attributed to a decline in the supply of "vacant" land suitable for small farmer development. However, as events under Marcos demonstrated, "vacancy" could be in the eye of the beholder. Instead of small farm resettlement, there was extensive small farm displacement and large farm development. At least since the early 1960s and arguably since well before that, the basic theme of Philippine approaches to agrarian reform has been purchase by government of tenanted rice and corn land and its resale to tenants. The successes and failures that characterize the Philippine agrarian reform experience have revolved around levels of political commitment and mobilization, problems and capacities associated with reform implementation (primarily administrative and judicial), and arguments about relationships between reform, productivity (usually stated in terms of economies of scale), and national economic welfare (usually stated in terms of not endangering export crop production).

The contemporary agrarian situation as a candidate for reform is the accumulation of this experience and its impacts, along with the changing agrarian situation itself. The intersection of these two themes presents an irony: a prime dimension of the contemporary challenge of land reform in the Philippines is that it is land reform and other aspects of change in landownership and land use already in existence that have to be clarified before the agrarian situation can be understood well enough to support a comprehensible statement of the agrarian reform challenge.

Any land reform program will have to be implemented in an economic, political, administrative, and judicial context that is very different from the context that existed in the early 1970s. Elements of this context will change under the new Aquino government, but it would be incorrect to assume that an entire agrarian situation, along with its political and administrative infrastructure, can somehow revert to some pristine pre-Marcos condition. What are some of the most important elements of this context from an agrarian reform perspective?

Rural Transformation

The rural Philippines today is much more than an agrarian Philippines. Consider, just as examples, the following factors affecting the rural Philippines today: diversification of the rural economic base beyond agricultural production to agriculturally based industries and beyond that to a range of service functions; expansion of urban labor, service, and transport markets, the growth of tertiary cities and the transition of larger *poblaciones* into rungs on an urban hierarchy, all with impacts on the organization, performance and autonomy of regional factor (including land and water) and product markets; continuing high levels of foreign remittances from the Middle East affecting savings and investments in rural housing and land; a changing role for rural women with growing proportions of women serving as farm operators. These sorts of patterns are distributed very unevenly across the rural Philippines. Today, for example, many parts of central Luzon have significantly more diverse economic systems than was the case fifteen years ago. It all means that a land reform strategy designed for an area that is predominantly agrarian may have very different implications and consequences if the same strategy is followed in an area where agrarian and rural differentiation have proceeded further. Land and labor values will differ, as will the impact of land reform rules regulating subdivision and inheritance. Also, there will be different implications for the composition and levels of public and private investment needed to provide support services required by a reform.

Environmental Degradation

The status of the natural resource base for Philippine agriculture has declined during the last fifteen years. Levels of land use intensity have generally mined rather than managed the natural resource base. This is true of deforestation and poor upland soil management (for example, upland rice and corn cultivation often have been highly erosive), with consequences for the productivity of the uplands as well as downstream siltation impact on water impoundment facilities and nearshore fisheries. It is also true of poorly designed and mismanaged irrigation, with consequences for the productivity of lowland areas subject to waterlogging and salt infiltration. Some elements of this picture *are* reversible, but the basic point is that agricultural and forest lands that once were productive can and have become less productive and even marginal. This has implications not simply for the socioeconomic arrangements that might be associated with higher productivity, but also for the socioeconomic arrangements that might be most consistent with resource conservation and production stability. Unfortunately, the last fifteen years tells much more about what does *not* work than about what does. Land use capability measures are available in the Philippines but not to support a serious assessment of land capability at the levels of disaggregation a reform might need.

The Agricultural Support System

In the Philippines agrarian reform has tended to be equated with land reform alone, and land reform has often been equated with converting tenants to owner-cultivators. However, high levels of administrative mobilization and political cooptation characterizing agricultural development in the 1970s have apparently shifted understanding of agrarian reform. Today it appears to be widely accepted that any agrarian reform will be considerably more than a shifting of land titles. Across the political spectrum, the assumption is shared that for a land reform program to work, a significant support system needs to be functioning that is able to provide technology, credit, and markets. Despite considerable investment in facilities and training during the last fifteen years, most observers agree that the Philippine public agricultural support system is weak and will need considerable time to reach required levels of performance. Extensive politicizing of the system, ranging from the operations of the Fertilizer and Pesticide Authority and the NFA to the compromising of the Ministry of Natural Resources by executive-sanctioned logging operations, to the utilization of agricultural extension services for voter mobilization purposes, to budget diversions and delays—all combined to undermine the growth of competence and morale.

There is a belief in some quarters that policy reform alone ("getting the prices right and the government out") will be enough to stimulate appropriate private activity in agricultural support services. It will certainly help, but it is not sufficient. At the least, such expectations ignore (1) deeply ingrained investment preferences for land holding rather than land improvement, (2) the inadequate supply of technology to bring small farm productivity to levels that would attract significant investments in farm services, and (3) the seriously indebted position of most producers. In this connection, it is important to note that the rural financial system, significantly built up during the 1970s, essentially collapsed in the 1980s. For example, of nearly one thousand rural banks functioning in 1985, less than fifty were judged solvent by the Central Bank. Although steps are already being taken to strengthen (not necessarily restore) the system, the larger problem remains: how will agricultural development be financed? High interest and inflation rates in 1984 revealed what many investors saw as the principal weakness of agricultural projects. In the words of one prominent investor, Vicente Lim:

> We are still looking for the agricultural project which can be made feasible at a 30% interest rate. The gestation periods and the risks of an agricultural project cannot stand the penalty.[3]

The issue is only slightly moderated by lower prevailing interest rates of 15 to 20 percent. However, since this issue alone has enormous implications for national budget and monetary management, how it is answered will have a significant influence on how any agrarian reform can be financed.

---

[3]"Finance Cited as Major Factor in Agricultural Productivity," *Business Day* (October 24, 1984), p. 10.

The Changing Food System

The Philippine food system has undergone some major changes during the last twenty years. At the same time that problems of malnutrition may have seriously increased for a majority of the overall population, meat, fish, and chicken consumption have risen dramatically, particularly among urban residents. Supplying large urban markets has had, and most likely will continue to have, significant effects on the food production and processing system. For example, in 1984 middleman mark-ups for rice started to climb. The NFA could not afford to buy enough local palay to defend the support price nationally and also undersell private retailers. Instead, the NFA imported rice (from China and Thailand). The result was that metro-Manilans enjoyed low-priced imported rice while people in provincial urban centers had to buy more expensive local rice stocks. Stability of urban food supplies traditionally has been a central food policy concern, reflected in rice import policy, but today more diverse urban demand has led to at least two important changes. First, imports other than rice have become quite important. The primary examples are yellow corn and wheat. Second, strengthening of vertical linkages from domestic production through processing to retailing, principally through direct and indirect state operations, has weakened the relative insularity of local food markets. Davao City can face food shortages because Manila can effectively lay first claim to food from Davao's own producing areas. All this has impact on farm prices, risk, and marketing options.

In this context, food security policy, already challenged by the high levels of malnutrition associated with declining real wages and the diversion of much food-producing land to agricultural export production, becomes very complex. At present, the capacity to administer a complex food security policy that does not rely on large-scale market intervention is not present. In the interim, one answer favored by agricultural development planners is for many agricultural producers to look beyond traditional grain production and marketing. Those who do may face a volatile market environment. For example, in the late 1970s and early 1980s, some rice farmers in central Luzon started growing onions. They faced very volatile markets, profitably pre-selling all their production one year and selling at tremendous losses the next. Many of the farmers could not withstand this and were forced to abandon their land. This raises a difficult question: how can an agrarian reform strategy be designed that does not freeze producers into a low-income but relatively lower-risk grain production trap during a long amortization period?

Political and Economic Recovery

The coming years will see attempts to restore more democratic principles in Philippine politics and to recover a reasonable degree of momentum in economic growth. This process will present crucial challenges to any agrarian reform agenda. For example, Mrs. Aquino appears committed to a constitutional format that offers a less powerful president, in effect shifting power back to a legislature and perhaps down to regional levels. To what degree will this open the political system and to what degree will this weaken Marcos crony power but restore a version of *ilustrado* power? What will be the implications for an agrarian reform program that challenges both crony and *ilustrado* interests?

For example, some members of the church hierarchy argue for highly decentralized and participatory management of agrarian reform. However, it is important to consider the experience of the Basic Christian Communities. As an outgrowth of the Second Vatican Council, several Filipino priests in the mid-1970s began arguing that the church had to go beyond its traditional focus on weekly masses and prayer to the building of small communities strongly dedicated to sharing, group decision making, striving to eliminate injustice, and reconciliation. In Negros, the NPA, the military, and local authorities all were upset with the increasing number of these communities. The results were large numbers of murders and assassinations, the forced departure of several foreign priests, and no visible improvement in the situation facing the people of Negros. Local opposition to agrarian reform can be very vigorous. Consequently, can an agrarian reform be effectively pursued without a strong and supportive executive?

It appears that in the coming few years, prospects are quite high for political factionalism, unstable party formation, and intense competition for political leadership positions. Can an agrarian reform be effectively sustained without a strong and continuing coalition's supporting it? Can the foundation for such a coalition be organized and maintained for a significant agrarian reform initiative, even before the coalition is otherwise institutionalized, or must the reform await a settling of the political dust? What if patterns of political mobilization and institutionalization refract more than reflect the interests of tenants, displaced settlers, the landless, and so on? This concern is most strongly expressed by the communists, even as they now admit their boycott of the February election was a mistake.

Economic recovery will have to face the challenge of economic reconciliation. Labor in manufacturing and service industries did not do well under Marcos. The recovery strategies being discussed may not offer much for labor. Policy liberalization (reducing government involvement in the economy) and tariff reform, urged by the IMF, may well *increase* unemployment in industries that matured in a more protected environment. Business people who are calling for selectively maintaining protectionism noticeably are not calling for a rise in minimum wages. The result in either case is likely to be increased labor militancy. One response will almost certainly be a demand to keep the costs of basic goods, most notably food, down. This poses a traditional food policy dilemma: how to keep urban wages down and keep farm prices at a level high enough to elicit high production. Can agrarian reform work in an environment where farmers face very low prices for their products (a major factor leading to CLT reversion), or where investments in processing and marketing are constrained by the prospect of inadequate returns?

Land Reform Choices

In one sense, the country has a limited number of agrarian reform choices. It can live within the PD 27 reform, improving rules and administration; it can draft a new land reform program to cover rice and corn land although it will still have to decide what to do with the PD 27 inheritance; or it can extend land reform based on PD 27 or something else to lands other than rice and corn. In another sense, however, there are an enormous number of choices—not only in the many operational details that define any agrarian reform program, but in the more difficult and continuing tasks of maintaining and translating political commitment for the program, and interpreting and administering the program.

Many factors combine to frame the choices. Some of the contextual ones have already been reviewed, the most notable being the very confused situation created during the last fifteen years by a broad but very unevenly implemented land reform program for rice and corn land, an elaborate pattern of title reversion and land stealing with connivance from a compromised judicial system, and the strengthening of the agricultural marketing and financial support systems as instruments to control rather than support rural producers. No matter what path the government chooses to follow, it will have to come to terms with these and other contextual factors. In fact, the argument can be made that it is precisely this "coming to terms" that will be the first task, before any other choices even can be considered.

Of course, the reality is that there are pressures to do more than come to terms. What are these pressures? There are two, in particular, that equate coming to terms with going well beyond the scope of PD 27. The most important of these is reflected in the NPA rebellion, but it is also seen in ethnic and tribal problems associated with land stealing. Here the call for land reform is fundamentally political and viewed by some as the most pressing item on the internal security agenda. A second, closely related pressure is a belief among many members of the urban middle classes (white-collar and professional) that a broader land reform will not only defeat the NPA, but will provide a viable foundation for dealing with rural poverty and low productivity and, not incidentally, will slow down rural-urban migration.

There are also pressures that say: coming to terms means reassessing, and possibly narrowing, the scope of PD 27. The most important example of this comes from the urban business classes who, along with many of the larger rural capitalists, were no longer Marcos beneficiaries when the regime fell. Their major spokesman within the government is the minister of finance, Jaime Ongpin. From this group come doubts about the economic viability of land reform and a preference instead for a combination of economic policy liberalization (on minimum wages, export taxes, and import tariffs for their inputs but not their products), technological improvement, and agribusiness investment as an engine to drive rural (and national) economic recovery. They see the NPA problem as a reaction to military abuse and political disaffection with Marcos. Consequently, they believe that with the fall of Marcos and reform in the military, the NPA problem will abate. They worry that a broad land reform carried out on lands other than rice and corn will undermine economic growth. They believe that the country's budget deficits mean the Philippines cannot afford to implement a very broad agrarian reform effort, and they are not enthusiastic about a program based on expropriation.

The pressures shaping the choices are complex—a mix of goals relating to national security, social welfare, economic reform, moral commitment, and political mobilization. However, not all pressures apply the same force. The issue is not so much whether there will be agrarian reform, but rather whose agrarian reform it will be. What is revealed here is the considerable continuity of Philippine politics. Agrarian reform "owned" by the political right, like agrarian reform of the 1950s, will tend to concentrate on national security and be very limited in its commitment to any other goals. Agrarian reform owned by the center, like the agrarian reform of the 1960s, will share the security concern but will add concerns for social welfare and some economic reform. Agrarian reform owned by the left, like some of what could be seen in NPA-controlled areas in the 1970s, will tend to emphasize economic reform. What all will share, however, is a legacy from agrarian reform of the 1970s, namely a recognition that agrarian reform can be both a powerful instrument for political mobilization and for depoliticizing agrarian conflict. All this should be kept in perspective when considering the major agrarian reform choices being discussed: living within PD 27, modifying PD 27, and going beyond PD 27.

Living Within PD 27

This option is the least that is likely to be considered as an agrarian reform option. Certainly the PD 27 strategy can be fine-tuned. There does appear to be wide support for doing what was supposed to be done. The problem here, as for any option, will be to clarify what has already happened and what current conditions are. With so many anomalies present, major fine-tuning would probably center on developing and implementing a streamlined adjudication process for clarifying and settling disputes. The fragile status of the Land Bank and, more generally, the system for financing land reform would also have to be evaluated. Here the issue would be how to create and maintain financial arrangements capable of supporting a land reform process. The rural bankers are already quite vocal in support of this clarification. The moribund status of the *samahang nayon* system would need to be assessed and the utility of attempting to revive it for land reform purposes considered. This will be a complex issue, involving both political questions related to local politics (an important point with local elections probable in early 1987) and economic questions related to various savings funds established under the *samahang nayon* system. Finally, the role of the Ministry of Agrarian Reform would have to be thoroughly reexamined. The functions required to support a land reform would need to be clarified, along with which of these functions can and should be performed by a national line agency (as compared to the executive, local government, or some other group), and what technical capacities and institutional strategies adequate performance demands.

Modifying PD 27

There is also significant sentiment for modifying or even replacing PD 27. This strategy cannot be pursued, however, without developing some way of clarifying the PD 27 inheritance. Modifying PD 27 would mean continuing to limit land reform coverage primarily to land currently being used for rice and corn cultivation, but possibly making at least three fundamental changes:

> 1. One change would involve making basic modifications in the criteria and policy instruments characteristic of PD 27. This could deal with matters such as land size, compensation bases, inheritance rules, and subtenancy and might introduce new adjudication mechanisms and financing arrangements.
> 2. A second possibility would involve a much more serious commitment to extend reform coverage to rice and corn lands in upland and rainfed areas, where land reform has not been widely applied and where problems in determining existing titles are often more complex. This could include addressing the problem of public land alienation to the politically favored, who subsequently may have taken tenants on to cultivate the land, and the stealing of homestead land, converting those already cultivating the land to tenants.
> 3. A third direction for modifying PD 27 would involve a commitment to retroactively cover former rice and corn lands that were exempted from PD 27 coverage through evasive subdividing of estates, conversion of tenants to employees, and the like.

Going Beyond PD 27

The option of going beyond rice and corn production lands is probably being discussed more seriously now than ever before. This reflects reaction to the scope of land use anomalies that went on under Marcos generally, the seriousness in the eyes of many of the NPA problem, and the depressions in the sugar and coconut economies. The situation in Negros Occidental, in particular, has heightened awareness of agrarian reform as a strategy that could go beyond rice and corn.

There are three major arguments being made. They share a recognition of the importance of export agriculture as a foreign exchange earner and supporter of Philippine economic growth but differ in their interpretation of why the industries are in trouble and what this means in turn for agrarian reform.

One argument accepts the importance of export agriculture and the necessity not to do anything that weakens these industries during difficult times. However, the case is made that, while the industries are not especially productive, efficient, or well-managed, their owners have grown wealthy nevertheless by poor treatment of labor and land. Experience in other parts of the world suggests that smaller-scale producing units for crops such as sugar, oil palms, and rubber are not inconsistent with productivity and efficiency, provided that input and product markets do not operate against producer interests.

A second argument says that the depression in many of the export agriculture industries is not short term nor is it necessarily a consequence of mismanagement. Instead, the case is made that the country faces a challenge to diversify its agricultural base. Proponents of this argument often conclude by advocating the economies of scale that come with larger-size and more heavily capitalized agricultural enterprises. Reform in this instance points to contract farming.

The third argument actually weaves through the other arguments and says that the industries were weakened by many factors, but that primary among these was excessive government intervention. In some cases, the damage done may be irreversible. Consequently, a significant degree of industry rationalization will need to occur. This should occur in a free-market environment with planning and implementation characterized by wide participation of those affected. This argument has been made by the Makati Business Club and others who now appear to have significant influence on economic thinking in the government.

An additional point over which there is growing debate has to do with how to value these lands and finance their acquisition and conversion. This has the potential to be a very complex and ultimately expensive problem. However, several examples typically come to the fore and suggest there are some short-term paths through the problem. The first is Hacienda Luisita, the six-thousand-hectare estate owned by the Aquino family. Suggestions are being made that the president could set an example of socially responsible land reform on that estate. The second is Negros Occidental, where it appears that a significant government response is going to be necessary. The third example is in Mindanao where notorious cases of land stealing and occupant dislocation exist.

In each of the cases, the argument is made that the way is open to do something in the short term if serious political commitment is present. For Hacienda Luisita, the president can simply do it—reach and implement a fair agreement selling the property to its tenants. In Negros, the chance exists to begin to mobilize a broad-ranged strategy directed at land reform, employment generation, and food security. In Mindanao and other places where significant land stealing occurred, there are real questions as to whether any compensation is required, or whether, for example, the Philippine Commission on Good Government (PCGG) can simply sequester the properties in question as an important first step in an agrarian reform scenario.

In the medium term (that is, over the next five years), some of the short-term possibilities are just that, short-term. Hacienda Luisita could be given away tomorrow. It might enhance the already bright moral aura around Mrs. Aquino, but such a gesture would be primarily a symbolic step having a short half-life as a resource for building medium-term political commitment. The same is true of the actions of the PCGG. Sequestering property, for example, is appealing as a demonstration of political will, but actually it may not mean very much in the absence of clear policy guidelines for reallocating that property. Already the earlier-noted experience of the PCGG with the PCA has revealed the limits of the sequestration strategy as a way to build political support for reform.

The Negros case appears to offer a more promising possibility of merging short-and medium-term strategies, but this is not inevitable. Certainly there does appear to be wide support for significant action in Negros. Filipinos of diverse political color were embarrassed by the international attention drawn to the specter of famine in Negros. Famine is not something Filipinos tend to associate with the country's problems. In the short term, therefore, the likely emphasis will tend to be on relief. In the medium term, however, relief will falter and become just another example of dispensation to worthy supplicants unless the support that exists to do something in Negros is translated into the political commitment to do something significant. Here those who would so act will have to resist the arguments made by many planters that their sugar operations are fundamentally sound and, although seriously weakened by the machinations of Benedicto and others, they can recover if they are paid what NASUTRA owes them, or if the United States restores the old sugar quota, or if the world sugar market rebounds, or something else.

BEYOND THE DEBATE

The major agrarian reform options currently being considered range from a more narrowly considered modification of the existing strategy to a broad extension of reform beyond rice and corn lands to estate-based export agriculture. The options are acknowledged across the political spectrum and are accordingly debated. There is always some recognition, however, that nothing can be done effectively without clarifying the existing situation and that nothing effective can be sustained without attention to the economic environment and techno-logical support system that reform beneficiaries would face.

These are all important considerations. However, there are very important agrarian reform challenges that one does *not* see considered in the current debate, or sees only in very carefully circumscribed form being forwarded by one group but with no serious response from other groups. Five examples are the issues of landless labor, foreign invest-ment, common property food production, the role of the United States, and the political management of land reform.

Landless Labor

The issue of landless labor *is* recognized in the Negros case, but the issue is not being acknowledged as a national problem. One reason is that the Philippine statistical system traditionally has not shown much interest in rural labor. Consequently, estimates of the landless labor problem vary widely. However, there is a deeper problem, namely an unwillingness to consider that a significant number of people are in the permanent economic limbo known as landlessness, a limbo many Filipinos associate with places like Bangladesh but not the Philippines.

In most discussions of land reform in the Philippines it is readily acknowledged that land reform is not a solution to problems of rural unemployment and underemployment. In fact, precisely this recognition is used by some to argue that a strategy other than land reform is needed. Recognizing landlessness, however, means going further than recognizing the conventional concepts of a labor force and limited employment opportunity. Landless households depend on the land for survival but do not have a secure relationship to the land. It is this fundamental insecurity that is sometimes missed. For example, in many parts of the Philippines landless laborers in the off-season might be very marginal inland fishermen. In such places that is how they are most often seen—as fishermen, characterized by low productivity. This being the case, the solution is to improve inland fishery productivity. Yet when this is done, these are not the people who benefit. One reason is that they were never really fishermen to begin with, but rather primarily landless laborers.

In the Philippine rural context, agrarian reform has been seen too narrowly as an adjustment of man-land relations between a landlord and a tenant with the government as intermediary. The image this evokes might still be appropriate for some rice and corn situations. It hardly applies, however, to relationships between hundreds of *sacadas* and their *haciendero*, or dozens of families tending coconut trees and a superintendent, or commonly owned ethnic and tribal lands occupied by Marcos cronies. Agrarian reform should be seen as an adjustment of complex ownership, cultivation, use, and labor relationships built on and around land, and also water and biomass. In the Philippine case, it would appear that in many parts of the country, this broader recognition will be essential *if agrarian reform is going to broaden participation in rural development*. Otherwise, reform runs the very real risk of making rural unemployment worse, as opponents of land reform sometimes claim, by only creaming the top of the socio-economic relationships dependent on the land, a risk that proponents of land reform tend to ignore.

Foreign Investment

While foreign investment in agriculture and other natural resources was present before Marcos, the level of investment grew under very active encouragement and facilitation by the Marcos regime. In several places, the issue of agrarian reform is quite often the issue of these investments. The problem here, of course, is how to deal with foreign investment in agriculture—investment already in the country, as well as future investment—in a manner that is consistent with the nation's agrarian reform objctives and, more broadly, its economic development orientation. With so much owed and with capital so short, can the government afford to give a signal that could be interpreted as meaning the Philippines does not want foreign investment in the future—or worse, that foreign investment already in the Philippines is not safe? This matter is further complicated by the belief held by many influential members of the business and financial communities that agricultural development will not go anywhere until there is a more active agribusiness dimension to Philippine agriculture. This means diversification, economies of scale, technological efficiency, and so on. Rather than chase the foreign agribusiness holdings out, the argument goes, such investment needs to be encouraged and emulated. Debate around these points is looming, but the more fundamental question of the role of foreign investment in agrarian reform has really not been addressed except by nationalist and communist groups.

Common Property Food Resources

In the wider debate on land reform, the traditional distinction drawn is between rice and corn on one side and export agriculture on the other. But there is a very important excluded middle, one that receives periodic attention, but somehow that attention is never systematically connected to agrarian reform. This excluded middle relates to land and farmers producing food other than rice and corn. The major example is inland and near-shore fisheries, but a variety of root crops and vegetables as well as noncommercial-scale forest product collection may also qualify.

Fish is a major source of protein for Filipinos, and a variety of forest products, most notably firewood and charcoal, represent the principal cooking fuels for the vast majority of rural households. One very important characteristic of production for fisheries and forest products that is loosely recognized is that often these are activities carried out in areas where clear titling does not exist. A second important characteristic is the incidence of common-property resource management, indigenous social arrangements that provide for collective determination and enforcement of how a specific natural resource (for example, a bay) will be exploited and maintained. This is very important, because unregulated overexploitation by some could deplete the resource for all. Inappropriate privatization in such cases can cause problems if it undermines the cooperation needed to prevent overexploitation. However, because common property regimes often occur in areas such as near-shore or inland water resources with unclear titling (more generally regulatory rights are assigned to a specific agency or local government unit), properly connected people can title or otherwise appropriate the area. This has happened, as any flight over Laguna de Bay makes clear, for many years.

Here is perhaps the clearest statement being made that agrarian reform does not always have to mean the privatization of natural resource management in the form of individual titles. It is a statement, however, that is not clearly heard because none of the major participants in the political debate on agrarian reform have adopted it: no one wants to open a Pandora's box of issues about collective ownership. Yet if conflict in Laguna de Bay ever became serious, Manila's food security would be quickly threatened. It is probable that the very visibility of the Laguna de Bay situation will generate a response that at last restores entry to the lake for hundreds of municipal fishermen, but the problem exists throughout the Philippines. Agrarian reform in these situations, or in situations where open access or communal rights currently function but need protection, has very different meaning from the land reform model usually discussed in the Philippines.

The Role of the United States

The United States will have an enormous impact on the prospects for agrarian reform in the Philippines, at least for all the reasons the United States influences other aspects of Philippine life. All parties to the agrarian reform debate appear to recognize this, but explicit discussion appears to be restricted to the left side of the political continuum. This is important because over the next few years agrarian reform discussions may well move in directions that would appear to challenge American interests and ideological preferences in the Philippines, such as questioning or restricting certain forms of foreign investment, utilization of lands in the areas around (and ultimately on) the American bases, encouraging domestic agricultural production that displaces American agricultural exports to the Philippines, even the possibility of collectivization in some places. The United States will be challenged to see these developments as positive expressions of a more self-confident and independent Philippines.

The new government appears to be accepting the United States-IMF notion that economic recovery is tied to an expansion of exports but is challenging the United States to open its markets to Philippine products. The United States, in turn, is challenging the Philippines not to restrict entry of American products. There is likely to be continuing tension along this axis, with more nationalist and protectionist-oriented parties in the Philippines concerned about the roles and impacts of American capital while the traditional exporting groups will worry about market reduction they may suffer as a result of domestic protection. Where the debate has not yet moved, however, is to an examination of relationships between trade policy and trade relations with major trading partners such as the United States (but also, for example, Japan and Korea, where high tariffs limit Philippine banana exports) and the prospects for domestic agrarian reform. Yet, there is little question that the two are closely intertwined, through Philippine interest in exporting agricultural (and manufacturing) products to the United States and American interest in exporting agricultural products to the Philippines.

If the United States wants to help more actively, there are a number of possibilities. Subsidizing agricultural exports to the Philippines should be halted. They only depress the possibilities for economic development in the Philippines and have had too much to do with the maintenance of state intervention in basic commodity markets. If investment is welcomed, then the United States should make efforts, along with Japan and other countries, to seriously consider implementing such investments in a way that is consistent with broader agrarian reform objectives. What must be halted is the "head in the sand" tactic of ignoring how land is acquired and what the social, economic, political, and environmental impacts of natural resource development are on local populations. American participation in official development assistance can be helpful by contributing to strengthening the agricultural support system, including the ability of the Philippines to implement an effective food security policy, and supporting innovative efforts to encourage rural enterprise formation, rural employment generation, and agricultural diversification.

The Political Management of Agrarian Reform

The predominant Philippine pattern of managing land reform has been to form an agency for that purpose and to assign the management functions to it. Executive intervention is limited to getting a land reform measure on the books and then, intermittently, to encouraging implementation. The scope of the PD 27 program demonstrated an important, indeed essential, limitation of this strategy. In the trench warfare among agencies, the agency managing land reform, the Ministry of Agrarian Reform, becomes just one more agency. Then the program just becomes one more program, along with farm-to-market roads, *kadiwa* centers, and so on.

The issue of the political management of agrarian reform draws attention to what is really the heart of the matter in Philippine agrarian reform. Is agrarian reform in the Philippines fundamentally social programming, addressing problems of social dislocation and unrest (but not challenging basic social arrangements defining agrarian society)? Is agrarian reform fundamentally economic reform, adjusting the economic system through modification or clarification of land ownership (but not challenging the basic economic arrangements that define the agrarian economy)? Is agrarian reform fundamentally an effort to influence the basic political characteristics of rural society (but not challenging the basic political arrangements that define the organization and use of agrarian power)?

Agrarian reform in the Philippines has been and is likely to remain a mixture of all three. The issue is the relationship among the three. Whatever the relationship, however, the political dimension is crucial because how far and fast the program moves is clearly a political outcome. Agrarian reform is therefore ultimately *politically* managed, not simply technically administered. Unfortunately, land reform management has really not yet been discussed in any detail by any group, except as a technical matter. But can technical matters and political matters be clearly distinguished?

An example of the mixing of political and technical management is the issue of phasing. Given the diversity of Philippine agrarian problems, with at last eight different groups of potential beneficiaries involved (rice and corn tenants, coconut farmers, sugar workers, tribal peoples, homestead settlers, fishermen, and agro-foresters), the case for phasing agrarian reform is obvious. But how will the phasing be determined? What are the political implications of both *how* phasing is decided as well as *what* is decided? Clearly, how the government chooses to *politically* manage an agrarian reform program tells much about the political commitment to the program. It is only a matter of time before this issue assumes center stage. The significant political

186

changes that are likely to occur in the Philippines over the next eighteen months will have an enormous impact on the political management of agrarian reform. For now, however, there is distressingly little open discussion of this.

OPPORTUNITY OR IRONY

Mrs. Aquino's rise to power is really a remarkable story. It bodes well for the resilience of democratic values in the Philippines. But the rural Philippines presents very fundamental agrarian problems, problems that can quickly make the euphoria of EDSA bittersweet. Agrarian reform *is* on the agenda, but it will be buffeted severely by the complex political and economic crosscurrents swirling around the new government. No other issue so directly tests the nature of the February revolution: no time has appeared better for a serious commitment to agrarian reform. Or has the problem become too serious for this kind of government to make and mobilize a broad commitment? That is the opportunity and the irony. Which will it be?

10

Report on the Discussion:
The Philippine Economy, Its Problems,
and Some Suggested Policy Approaches

Richard Hooley

The Philippines emerged from the era of martial law with serious production, financial, and international-debt problems that received attention and extensive discussion at this conference. The current somber view of the country's economic predicament is, however, a relatively recent development. As late as the early 1980s the country was in possession of a superior international-credit rating based upon what was then regarded as significant progress in agriculture and industry. Following the Aquino assassination the Philippines' economic image both at home and abroad began to unravel rapidly.

The central purpose of this session of the Washington Institute conference was to analyze the underlying causes of the economic failure and to suggest some policy approaches that will contribute to the construction of feasible and effective solutions. Given the wide-ranging nature of the discussion (which invariably occurs whenever economists discuss policy questions) it will not be possible to cover all the valuable points made during this session. We try to summarize the main lines of arguments in a systematic way and relate these to the main areas of interest targeted during the open discussions.

SHORT-RUN SOLUTIONS AND LONG-TERM PROBLEMS

Professor Ranis put forward the view in his paper that a useful way to approach current economic policy issues is to break them into short- and long-run problems. In the short run the most pressing issue is finding noninflationary ways to close the government budget deficit of nearly $2 billion. It is estimated that at least $500 million of outside money (World Bank, USAID, etc.) is necessary to get the deficit-closing process moving. Additional closure should come from expenditure cutting, as resources going into government corporations are reduced and measured to begin privatization are implemented. In addition, tax revenues should rise as business activity resuscitates. If the administration can renegotiate its foreign debt this would also have a beneficial effect on the immediate situation. The policies necessary to revitalize the Philippine economy over the short run are clear and relatively unambiguous.

The question was raised whether or not it is feasible to separate short-term stabilization policy from long-term reform policies. Some participants argued that not acting quickly on basic reforms runs the risk of missing a window of opportunity for fundamental corrective action, by allowing the old elite a chance to regain its grip on economic policy. Further, it was observed that short-term stabilization policy, involving the conclusion of agreements with the International Monetary Fund, foreign commercial banks, etc., involves commitments that may constrain the design of longer-term reform measures. On the other side it was argued that reform measures that are not well thought out may have the effect of destroying the government's fiscal credibility— an important asset in the present situation.

The longer-run economic problems faced by the Philippines today are not due primarily to the Aquino assassination, nor to the era of martial law, nor even to the style of the Marcos presidency itself, although they became deeper and much more complex during the Marcos years in office. The roots of today's economic problems go back to the late fifties and early sixties. We see several distinct causes of underlying economic atrophy. The first is the declining rate of agricultural growth due to the change in the country's resource base. In the quarter century before 1960, land under cultivation increased at 3 to 4 percent per year. This was substantially faster than the increase in population and provided the basis for both a steady growth in food supply and a rapid expansion in agricultural employment. Exports of agricultural products also grew rapidly, providing a steadily expanding base of foreign exchange receipts from primary-product exports. During the late fifties and early sixties this situation underwent a marked change. As outlying areas like the Cagayan valley and southern Mindanao became more fully populated, the expansion of land for agricultural use slowed from 3 to 4 percent to about 2 percent—significantly below the population growth rate. In recent years this figure has been further reduced, and at present is less than 1 percent per year. The expansion of land under cultivation will continue for many years to come, but the important point is that it alone can no longer provide the major source of agricultural growth as it did in the pre-1960s era.

AGRICULTURAL PROBLEMS

As Bruce Koppel points out, the price of this deterioration in the resource base has been an increase in tenancy in many parts of the country and a general deterioration of the economic situation of both peasants and agricultural workers. There is plenty of evidence of this, both from experienced observers as well as from surveys of household income and expenditure.

The full effects of this slowing down in land availability have been partially offset by increases in agricultural yields. The increase in yield per hectare has been achieved in two ways. There has been a shift from low-yield crops to higher-yield crops. For example, in 1950 palay rice accounted for half of crop production and nearly half of land area. By 1980 the fraction had fallen to one-quarter. Other crops, such as bananas and pineapples, where yield per hectare is far higher (and value of production per worker also much higher), accounted for the decline in palay production. But the new crops are not as labor intensive as palay, requiring more land and/or capital per worker. The second reason for rising agricultural yields has been technological change, popularly referred to as the "green revolution." However, modern agricultural technology is generally associated with increased use of nonlabor inputs. The net result of these changes is that agricultural employment has not grown commensurately with output, and farm-ownership patterns have undergone some shift. In 1950 agriculture employed nearly 60 percent of the country's work force. Today that figure is down to about 45 percent. Similarly, tenancy has been growing. In the pre-war Philippines, landless farmers were reported to constitute only 15 to 20 percent of all farm operators. Today the figure is reported at about one-third, in spite of the fact that areas of recent settlement (for example, Mindanao) are typically non-tenant-farm areas. In summary, the agricultural strategy that has emerged over the years has provided a steady growth of agricultural output, but at annual rates of around 3 percent per capita—not fast enough to provide either dynamic export growth or substantial reductions in the unit cost of food. Expansion of demand for employment has been severely restricted, and shifts in farm-ownership patterns have tended to produce a growing class of landless farmers.

Nowhere have these problems been more in evidence than in the sugar industry. As David Reinah's paper made clear, with world-market price at eight cents per pound, compared with an average cost of production in the Philippines of twelve cents per pound, most sugar operations are losing money. In addition, the sugar monopoly National Sugar Traders Association (NASUTRA) suppressed farm-gate sugar prices during the Marcos years even further. The result has been widespread financial distress among sugar owners and operators, low levels of output, high levels of unemployment and falling real wages. Real-farm wages have declined by 50 percent during the past fifteen years. The result is a rise of insurgency of major dimensions—particularly in the central sugar-growing region of Negros. The connection between economic and social distress on the one hand and insurgency activity on the other was commented on repeatedly.

FAILURE OF STRATEGY

A second root cause of the atrophy of the economic system is the strategy of industrial expansion followed during the post-war period. Up to 1960 Philippine industrial output expanded at about 8 percent a year, generating a rising demand for employment that offset any slack in the demand for agricultural labor. But the import-substitution strategy provided satisfactory industrial growth rates only through the early 1960s. By the middle and late sixties it was abundantly clear that domestic markets were fully saturated with local manufactures, and therefore the fruits of this prolonged import-substitution phase had been fully harvested. Nevertheless, the country continued along this narrow growth path, first fed by the relative largess of the country's natural resources, and later by the largess of foreign commercial banks, but continuously decelerating in terms of both growth of industrial production and in terms of the provision of employment opportunities.

The cost of the failure of industrialization policy to shift away from an easy import-substitution strategy can now be more fully appreciated not only for industry but for the entire economy. The slackened demand for agricultural labor after 1960 need not have set off such socially dislocating effects if the industrial sector had expanded output and employment rapidly enough to offset these trends in agriculture. However, high protection rates for industry had exactly the opposite effect. Growth rates of industrial output and employment both declined continually from 1960 to the mid-eighties. So the deceleration of output and employment in agriculture was reinforced and gradually became characteristic of the economy as a whole. Because labor demand in the Philippines is relatively inelastic, these trends were reflected in a sharp decline in real-wage rates beginning about 1960.

Besides its deleterious effects on production, employment, and worker incomes, continued allegiance to the narrow import-substitution strategy also shifted the domestic terms of trade against agriculture. The higher prices charged by protected manufacturing producers for their goods, when sold to agricultural workers, reduced the purchasing power of the latter's wages even further. Thus the full impact of continued reliance on an import-substitution strategy was not only to reduce the pace of growth of the industrial sector, but also to exacerbate the trends toward slower employment growth and more unequal distribution of income that were emerging independently in agriculture. The result was a dual decline in worker incomes in both agriculture and industry far deeper, more widespread, and much more socially dislocating than anything that had previously been experienced in this century.

Continuation of this import-substitution strategy after the early and mid-seventies was made possible in part due to the support of foreign commercial banks for the Marcos regime. Little apparent effort was made to carefully assess the "project prospects" of the country's economic machine. As the discussion brought out, there was a failure of the accountability process. It was never made clear for what purpose(s) many of the loans were made or who really benefited from them. Sovereign risk was thought to be minimal by foreign lenders, and so economic support in terms of increased (foreign) borrowings continued through the early eighties. On the one hand some conference participants expressed the view that foreign banks ought to bear some of the costs of readjustment of the country's international debt since the foreign banks were a contributing factor. One reply to this view is that "it takes two to tango," and therefore apportioning out "blame" in this situation is not really feasible. In reply, opponents of this view argue that tying up one-half of the country's annual foreign exchange earnings in debt-service payments is at least equally infeasible from the standpoint of long-term political stability in the borrowing country. Actually, the sharing of the burden of adjustment is likely to be largely determined by political power of the bargainers. The Philippines alone cannot fight the international banking community and win. But if other debtors manage to win favorable terms for radical restructuring of their debt, the Philippines can probably get similar concessions from its creditors.

SOME SOLUTIONS

Given this array of economic problems, what is to be done? One of the first items on any reform agenda is to restructure some economic institutions. Chief among these is the Philippine National Bank (the country's largest commercial bank) and the Development Bank of the Philippines. It is estimated that at least half, and perhaps even three-fourths, of these banks' loan portfolios are in arrears as to payments on principal and/or interest. Other parts of the country's financial system are in little better health. The nation's largest savings bank (Banco Pilipino) was declared bankrupt last year. A number of commercial banks and rural banks are in an extremely illiquid position. These problem cases will have to be resolved before extensive restructuring of industry and agriculture can be undertaken.

Efforts will probably be made to substitute the marketplace for the deadly hand of government intervention in the economy. However, it was observed that this assumes the country already has an adequate system of operating market institutions. In other words, macropolicy prescriptions intended to move the economy toward a system of free markets imply the existence of well-functioning competitive markets that can transmit correct signals to participants. The most basic of these is the "exit" function, which is absolutely essential.[1] Institution building beyond restructuring of financial institutions may be necessary to get all the markets functioning in positive directions.

Clearly, there has to be some reform in industry. Removal of, or at least significant reduction in, import tariffs on domestic manufactures is necessary, painful as this will be for many enterprises. In particular, the structure of duties that penalizes agricultural products while favoring domestic industrial products must be reformed. In addition, various types of quantitative restrictions on imports also require major modification or elimination. Major reforms of this kind will also require some institution building. Refurbishing of credit institutions is essential and

---

[1]Hirshman describes two contrasting responses to decline in firms as "exit" and "voice." Exit represents a scenario whereby the impersonal forces of the market provide a mechanism that rewards unsatisfactory performance with forced exit of the firm from the marketplace. In contrast, voice represents a more politicized scenario in which the firm struggles to stay alive through adroit manipulation of political channels. See Albert Hirschman, *Exit, Voice and Loyalty* (Cambridge: Harvard University Press, 1970.)

has already been mentioned. In addition, appropriate science and technology policies, which will enable industry to adapt the existing stock of technology to the availability of domestic inputs, is also needed. Later we discuss some specific institution-building examples suggested by this type of policy.

One of the biggest challenges of all is certainly in the agricultural sector. These is a consensus among most policymakers, including those attending the Washington Institute Conference, that agriculture will play a critical role in any strategy for revitalization of the economy. There is far less consensus, however, on exactly how agriculture fits into the total macro picture. One strategy, proposed by some (including members of the Aquino cabinet), views the agricultural sector as the cornerstone of any long-run revitalization strategy. They look to agriculture to provide stimulation for output growth (especially food products) and the alleviation of the employment problem. Those who propose this approach maintain that their primary concerns are feeding the people and providing employment rather than earning foreign exchange. They appear to be placing much of their hopes on the expansion of large farms, including estate-type agriculture.

There are questions about the feasibility of any strategy that relies too heavily on agriculture alone. A quarter century ago the Philippines was still a genuinely agricultural economy: half of the GNP was produced there and 60 percent of employment was accounted for by agriculture. Today, the contribution of agriculture to GNP has dropped to 29 percent (slightly less than that of industry) and the sector now accounts for only 45 percent of total employment, while the business sector accounts for about 30 percent and government services the remainder. Part of the decline in the importance of agriculture is due to the closing of the frontier. Part is due to unwise decisions on resource allocation in agriculture in recent years. In any event, the decline in the importance of agriculture in the Philippine economy is a fact that policymakers have to face up to. In addition, a strategy of agricultural expansion focused on estate-type agriculture runs the risk of being stranded on the shoal of capital intensity. A study of corporate agriculture some years back indicated that there was little difference between the capital-labor and capital-output ratios of agricultural corporations and large manufacturing corporations.

Even though the rural areas cannot pull the country ahead *alone*, the agrarian sector is still a critical element in the total policy approach. As made clear earlier in this paper on the situation in agriculture, there has been significant deterioration in the economic and social situation of rural-area dwellers. Tenancy has increased, farm debt is way up, real wages of farm laborers down, and income distribution deteriorating. Some action in the area of agrarian reform is required. In the past, agrarian reform has been equated with land reform, and the focus has therefore been a shifting of land titles. Today, however, it is understood that in order for a land-reform program to work, a comprehensive support system must be in place to provide farmers with technology, access to inputs, credit, and market information. This in turn requires significant mobilization of the political system. Past efforts at agrarian reform have not produced much change, partly due to low levels of political commitment, politicization of the administrative and judicial dimensions of the reform movement, and minimal capabilities of the administrative system. Future efforts at agrarian reform face these problems and some new ones as well, including a much more variegated rural industry structure, the need for a more complex agrarian support system, and more extensive deterioration of the resource base.

POLITICAL FACTORS

Charles Lindsey makes the point in his paper that the nationalists have gained ground as a result of the economic muddle that followed the Marcos years in office. Add the fact that Marcos presented his administration as solidly behind foreign investment and foreign participation in the economy, and the present economic dilemmas obviously play into the hands of the autarchic nationalists. But the discussion that followed on this point questioned whether present events have resulted in really strengthening the nationalists' position significantly. An alternative explanation is that Philippine economic nationalism has been developing over a long period of time—at least since the founding of the Philippine National Bank in 1916. It has broad-based support in various sectors of society and is not delimited by the position of one political party or one select group of persons.

One of the interesting pieces of political fallout emerging from the complexity and seriousness of the economic problems discussed at this conference is the weakened position of the country's traditional elite. It is well documented that before 1960 the Philippines was governed by a small number of powerful families—perhaps fifty in all—the Osmenas,

Lopezes, Cojuangco, among others. It is increasingly obvious that the old agricultural system together with a highly protected industrial sector cannot move a country of sixty million (ninety million by the end of this century) into the modern era. The traditional elite simply have not been able to give the nation any substantial hope of a new, progressive economic system capable of creating the goods and services needed by a modern nation. In a word, the old elite lost credibility to provide effective economic leadership. Marcos and his wife further reduced their power by ruthlessly destroying those families who opposed them, in the end decimating their number and substantially reducing their wealth.

The result has been the emergence of a number of groups who offer to fill this leadership vacuum. The more important of these groups include the military establishment and the Catholic church, revitalized under the leadership of Cardinal Sin. The intellectuals and young industrialists form another group, and the radical left, including radical nationalists and the New Peoples Army (NPA), constitute additional candidates. This obviously adds to the heterogeneity of the country's elite and substantially increases the political tasks of governing.

POPULATION GROWTH AND RURAL DEVELOPMENT

Rather surprisingly, the conference devoted little attention to the question of population growth. What discussion did occur, however, was relevant and informative. The increase in population has permanently changed the structure of the resource base in the Philippines. The population of the country at the beginning of the industrialization drive (early 1950s) of thirty million has now doubled; by the turn of the century it will be at least ninety million. The question naturally arises whether this society can support a population of this size, and what can be done to constrain the rate of population growth. It was pointed out that population growth is increasingly related to the female education level and to the growth rate of output. Thus, without positive action on these variables not much in the way of results can be expected from policies aimed at reducing birth rates. In regard to the latter, it is not clear yet precisely what the approach of the Aquino administration will be. Continued population growth at current rates will, however, increasingly complicate the solution to current problems by producing faster deterioration in the physical environment and by creating greater diversity in the rural output mix.

The rural areas today are much more than a crop-based economy. Over the past two decades the agrarian production base has diversified dramatically. We have already pointed out the shift in crop production. In addition, under pressure of increasing population and underemployment there has been an expansion of production into a variety of local industries, including small manufacturing, transportation, and service activities, and in the growth of tertiary cities and towns. These developments have suggested a long-term development strategy based on the expansion of rural industry. For example, there are now two million persons employed in manufacturing, but only about one-half of these, or one million persons, are employed in establishments of five workers or more. The remaining one million are employed in household industry, much of which is located in the rural areas. This shows the potential power of small industrial establishments to absorb labor. Moreover, since most of small industry is located in the rural areas, the employment generation associated with the expansion of small industry is also in rural areas.

Rural industry now produces primarily for domestic final demand in the provinces. The overwhelming concentration of these small firms is in a few industries—namely, food and beverage processing, apparel manufacture, wood products, and miscellaneous items, including handicrafts. The expansion of handicraft production for export in recent years demonstrates that rural industry has a potential for servicing foreign markets as well as domestic. Capital-labor ratios are low, so that output growth here has substantial employment-generating impact. However, output per worker is also low, partly reflecting relatively low levels of efficiency of many of these producers. Quality of products is often very uneven. Many of these small producers compete for the consumer's peso mainly on the basis of low wage rates. If efficiency could be improved, costs cut, and quality standardized, it is likely that output would expand much more rapidly than at present.

An intriguing question is to what extent rural industry might become the supplier of intermediate goods for the larger urban producers. In other developing countries—for example, Brazil—large firms depend heavily on supplies and services delivered by small firms. At the present time there is almost no connection between small rural firms and the large urban-based industries (including those located in export zones). Indeed, Philippine industry now imports nearly one-third of total intermediate inputs from abroad, constituting the largest single drain on the country's foreign-trade accounts. If the food, beverage, woodworking, and apparel industries are excluded, the dependence on imported intermediate goods rises to one-half. The potential benefits to the economy of shunting part of this urban-industry demand for intermediate products to rural industry include not only providing a major stimulus to the growth of rural income and employment, but also the damping of intermediate imports and the strengthening of the peso in the foreign exchange markets.

To realize these benefits from the development of rural industry will require a variety of supporting policies. First, research shows that the growth of rural industries is highly dependent on the growth of farm incomes. Undoubtedly one reason for the poor showing of rural industry during the past decade was the monopolization of major agricultural products, which shifted income away from rural households. Demonopolization of agricultural markets and the privatization of agricultural enterprises can significantly assist in stimulating rural industry growth. The elasticity of rural industry employment with respect to farm income is about $+3$. Therefore, any significant expansion of farm income can be expected to have a large positive impact on rural employment.

Second, the cost-price distortions that now exist in industry have to be corrected in order to provide incentives for large enterprises to utilize locally produced intermediate goods. Chief among these distorting agents is the existing tariff structure, which contains a high cascading effect. In other words, import duties on intermediate goods are often near zero, and sometimes even negative. Under such a price regime, local establishments are actually induced *not* to purchase from other local plants, and imported intermediate goods are substituted not only for local intermediate production, but also for labor and capital as well.

Third, some applied industrial research has to be undertaken on a systematic basis to determine what adjustments need be made in order that small enterprises can become both more economical from a unit-cost standpoint and more capable of producing output of standardized product-quality levels. There is also a need for research on adaptation of industrial processes. Large firms' intermediate input demand is heavily import dependent, partly because the technology itself is imported and no effort has been made to study the adjustments necessary to utilize local production. These new tasks suggest a need for an institution that would do for small industry what the agricultural research and extension institutions have done for the small rice farmer. It need not be a large institution, and it is our feeling it should not be exclusively owned and operated by the government. A semi-independent status with links to both private and government sectors would be our preference.

CONCLUSION

In this paper we observed that the Philippine economy has performed poorly during the recent past. We admit that certain aspects of the institutional and international economic environment—namely, martial law and Nutrasweet—have played a role in this outcome. The final assessment at the conference, however, is that remote causes already operating by 1960 or before are the main roots of the present economic distress. Three fundamental causes were mentioned. First, there is the pattern of economic growth and change in agriculture. The pattern of change has been characterized by increased reliance on technical innovation for specific crops and shifts of land among different crops—both aimed at raising yields per hectare. However, these changes have been unfavorable to labor absorption, and have helped fuel an increase in tenancy, a precipitous fall in real wages, and socially dysfunctional impacts on income distribution. These developments were exacerbated by the sharp fall in world primary-products prices after 1975.

The strategy of industrial development adopted in the late fifties exacerbated these trends. Protected industrial enterprises adopted production methods that were generally capital- rather than labor-intensive, and that often encouraged the substitution of imported intermediate-goods inputs for both labor and capital. The increased demand for labor emanating from local industrial establishments has been severely restricted, providing little or no offset to the weakening demand for agricultural labor. Finally, the higher prices of goods produced by local industry have adversely affected agricultural labor by turning the domestic terms of trade against agriculture. The net result of the interaction of agriculture and industry has been a decline in worker income and an adverse shift in the distribution of income and wealth that has proved much more detrimental to the society than any such previous development.

These economic changes have had important political impacts. They have tended to reduce both the power and credibility of the old elite and have stimulated new factions claiming a role in national policymaking: the church, the military, intellectuals and professional groups, and the radical left, among others. Hence, these changes have made political governance and policymaking considerably more difficult.

III. Social Change, Social Needs, Social Policy

11

Peasants and Agricultural Workers: Implications for United States Policy

Benedict J. Tria Kerkvliet

COMPOSITION

Households relying largely on agriculture constitute about half of the fifty million Filipinos. Roughly two-thirds are peasants; the other third are landless agricultural workers.[1] Peasant households have small amounts of land, most less than three hectares, on which they farm crops for home consumption and sale. (Pure subsistence producers are now rare.) A major problem for peasants is keeping enough of their earnings to meet basic household needs and provide for their children's future while also having enough to cover farming expenses (which for many includes mortgages and rent to landlords.) Typically the prices they get for commodities they produce compare unfavorably to what they must pay for purchased goods, farming inputs, rents, and so forth.[2]

Agricultural worker households have no land, not even as tenants, nor do they have reliable means of livelihood outside the agrarian sector. Even their agricultural work is seasonal; hence, underemploy-

---

[1]Neither Philippine census data nor other sources provide enough detail for one to determine accurately the size of the agricultural population in the country circa 1980 or the percentage of peasants (including tenants) and the percentage of landless agricultural workers. My rounded figures are extrapolated from the estimates reported in the following references: The World Bank, *The Philippines: Priorities and Prospects for Development* (Washington, D.C.: World Bank, 1976), 97–99; Philippines, National Census and Statistics Office, *Integrated Census of the Population and Its Economic Activities: Population, Philippines, 1975* (Manila, 1978), tables 11–15; and Filomeno Aguilar, Jr., "The Agrarian Proletariat in the Rice-Growing Areas of the Philippines," *Philippine Studies* 31 (Third Quarter, 1983): 342, 346–48.

[2]See the unfavorable terms of trade for rice producers from 1972 to 1982 in Hall Hill and Sisira Jayasuriya, "The Philippines: Growth, Debt and Crisis," Working Paper No. 85/3 (Canberra, A.C.T.: Development Studies Centre, The Australian National University, 1985), 26–28.

ment is one of their major problems. Most of these households scrounge for other ways to earn money, and they forage in the fields and waterways for edible plants and fish. Their second major problem is low wages, which in real value have been dropping (perhaps by as much as 50 percent) since the late 1960s.[3]

Both peasants and agricultural workers are poor. Only a small percentage enjoy what could be regarded in Philippine terms as a middle-class standard of living. A World Bank study says that in 1975, 47 percent of rural families live below or at the poverty line.[4] Given the worsening economic conditions since then, the percentage has probably increased. Life for this half of the rural people is an endless struggle to get enough food. They live, as some poor have told me, like frail, little birds, each day waking at dawn to look for grains of rice and flitting here and there all day searching for ways to feed their families. Living just slightly above the poverty line is not much better. Obtaining the basics—food, housing, a little education, good health, a bit of savings for emergencies—is often worrying. If one counts these households among the poor, then the percentage is close to three-fourths of the rural population.

While they share impoverishment, peasants and landless workers are divided by other conditions. Ethnolinguistic differences are somewhat divisive, although diminishing in importance and certainly not as significant as in neighboring Indonesia and Malaysia. More important are their different positions in the political economy. Relations between agricultural workers and peasants living in the same area are frequently tense because the laborers want higher wages whereas peasants for whom they work want to minimize their farming expenses by keeping wages low. Because the landless typically would like to farm, they sometimes can even be used by other interests—large landowners, corporations, government agencies—that are trying to squeeze peasants off the land, replacing them with the landless either as new tenants or hired laborers. Among the peasantry, slightly less than 60 percent own their fields. Virtually all the remainder are tenants. But about a third of the tenants also own a bit of land, and thus differ in that respect from those who own none. Some tenants rent land from large land-

[3]The World Bank, *Philippine Poverty Report,* 1980 draft, tables 4.3, 4.4, and 4.19. Also see Hill and Jayasuriya, "The Philippines," 46.
[4]The World Bank, *Philippine Poverty Report,* 1980 draft, table 1.8.

owners with whom they have few direct dealings and whom they see infrequently. Others rent from small landowners who are peasants like themselves, perhaps even their relatives, living in the same or a neighboring village. The specificities of tenant-landlord relations influence whether or not tenancy arrangements are antagonistic. Generally, antagonistic relations mean that one's tenure is uncertain and the threat of eviction is high. Also affecting the degree of tenure security is government policy. During the last decade the government has shown some concern for protecting rice- and corn-growing tenants against eviction and helping them convert from sharecroppers to leaseholders. The same has not been done for tenants who grow other crops and who frequently are threatened with eviction if not actually forced off their fields.

The crops they grow also make for notable differences among rural people. About 40 percent of the peasants and landless workers in the country are directly involved in farming rice, another 20 percent in farming corn.[5] These products are sold and consumed domestically. Coconut producers, half of whom are landowners and tenants and half wage laborers, compose about 20 percent of the country's farming population. Most of these people are concentrated in a few areas, especially southern Luzon, Bicol, parts of the Visayas, and areas in Mindanao. Most coconuts and coconut products are destined for the international markets; consequently, peasants and laborers in the coconut industry are more directly affected than are those in rice and corn by the volatile world prices for these commodities. The same is true for sugarcane, a second principal export crop. Although involving only a small fraction of the country's population, it, too, is concentrated in a few places, particularly Negros and Panay, and the world price of sugar directly affects the lives of the majority who live on those two islands.

POLITICAL VALUES AND ORIENTATIONS

Given the diversity among peasants and agricultural workers, it is risky to generalize about their political thinking; moreover, the litera-

[5]My approximate distribution of the agrarian population by major crops is based on figures in Philippines, National Census and Statistics Office, *Census of Agriculture, Philippines, 1971* (Manila, 1974); and Lorna Peña Reyes-Makil and Patria N. Fermin, *Landless Rural Workers in the Philippines: A Documentary Survey* (Quezon City: Institute of Philippine Culture, Ateneo de Manila University, 1978), 21–22.

ture is especially sketchy in this regard. Nevertheless, in order to discuss the implications of these sectors of Philippine society for United States foreign policies, I have to suggest three prominent political orientations of rural Filipinos.[6]

One is the high value placed on personal relationships. Having networks of people who know each other well or at least are known to each other through mutual acquaintances is important to most people in the Philippines. Without such networks it is exceedingly difficult, especially for poor people, to make claims on scarce resources. The wider and more far-reaching the networks, the greater are one's opportunities. Also, the higher up one's networks reach in the socioeconomic strata, the better one's prospects and the more protection one has.

While often based on relatives, networks also include ritual kin, workmates, village- and townmates, classmates, and people known well from other associations such as business dealings. In order to call upon people with higher socioeconomic standing, peasants and agricultural workers frequently try to have complex ties to large landowners, wealthy moneylenders, rich employers, and local government officials. These instrumental connections, known as patron-client relationships, impose obligations on the lower-class peasants and workers to the higher-class individuals but also obligate the latter to help and look after the former, hence providing peasants and workers with more protection than they would otherwise have.

---

[6]Carl H. Landé, *Leaders, Factions, and Parties: The Structure of Philippine Politics* (New Haven: Southeast Asian Studies, Yale University, 1964); Leonardo N. Mercado, *Elements of Filipino Ethics* (Tacloban City: Research Center, Divine World University, 1978), 62, 82; George M. Guthrie and Fortunata M. Azores, ''Philippine Interpersonal Behavior Patterns,'' *IPC Papers No. 6* (Quezon City: Ateneo de Manila University Press, 1968), 22–23; Frank Lynch, ''Social Acceptance,'' *IPC Papers No. 2* (Quezon City: Ateneo de Manila University Press, 1968), 15–19; Mary R. Hollnsteiner, ''Reciprocity in the Lowland Philippines,'' *IPC Papers No. 2*, 25–31 passim; Vitaliano R. Gorospe, ''Sources of Filipino Moral Consciousness,'' *Philippine Studies* 25 (Third Quarter, 1977): 278–301; George M. Guthrie, *The Psychology of Modernization in the Rural Philippines* (Quezon City: Ateneo de Manila University Press, 1970), 43; Maria Cristina Blanc Szanton, *A Right to Survive: Subsistence Marketing in a Lowland Philippine Town* (University Park: Pennsylvania State University Press, 1972), 127–31; and G. Sidney Siliman, ''The Folk Legal Culture of the Cebuano Filipino,'' *Philippine Quarterly of Culture and Society* 10 (1982): 232, 242; and my 1978-to-1979 and 1985 research in a central Luzon village.

Awareness of class and status differences is a second political aspect of villagers' political orientations. Not only are they highly cognizant of striking inequalities in living standards and life chances and aware that, in the main, they cannot compete well—which is one major reason they cultivate patrons—but they often believe that their impoverishment is a consequence of the minority who live noticeably better. Not all share this understanding. And even among those who do, many simultaneously think that their poverty is also a result of their own limitations. Moreover, while they can criticize those who live well, many envy such high standards of living. In short, peasants and agricultural workers have complex thoughts about the causes of poverty and wealth. Their assessments are not necessarily threatening to the upper classes; yet neither do they endorse the status quo.

One theme that is fairly clear is that villagers want a better life and think that they are entitled to a livelihood that permits them to live in dignity. Often this view underlies their demands for higher wages, job security, landownership, lower prices for farming expenses, and educational and other opportunities for their children. It is frequently the basis for their claims on the resources of those who live better. Even if they do not consistently believe that their poverty is the consequence of others' wealth, peasants and agricultural workers contend that people with higher socioeconomic status are obligated to help the poor to have a decent living standard and the means to achieve it. Such a contention typically underlies both efforts to build alliances with those in higher socioeconomic strata as well as acts of resistance and protest against the better-off.

Appropriate here is a word about their views of the United States. Generally, peasants and agricultural workers have little firsthand information about or dealings with Americans, American companies, or the United States government. But most do have favorable impressions about the United States. In particular, they commonly imagine that their American counterparts—workers and farmers—live reasonably well. In this view there are no or only very few poor Americans: everyone eats well, has sturdy housing, can go to school, and takes vacations. Villagers often dream about somehow going to work in the United States. More important, though, their image, along with other influences, contributes to an ideal about how people should live and their entitlement to a decent livelihood. It helps to nurture people's critique, however hesitantly put, of what they experience.

The third political view to highlight is that the peasants and landless villagers are cynical about government. They tend to see government as controlled by and for the local and national economic and other elites. Politicians' promises to help the little people are normally not to be taken seriously. It is more important, if poor villagers are to get anything positive from government agencies, to have some acquaintances among their networks who have personal contacts, patrons, and other direct access to those in office.

People do hold some minimal expectations. Government officials should leave them in peace, cause no physical harm to life and property, show respect to even the lowliest person, share the benefits of public office with those who helped them achieve their position, and exercise restraint when using public resources for the private use of oneself, relatives, and close friends. Most villagers do not demand much more from government even though many would like officials to use their position to make and implement policies that would improve villagers' living situations. When such individuals appear, they generally attract considerable support among rural people.

REBELLION

During the Marcos government, especially since the mid-1970s, rural unrest and rebellion grew, primarily in northern Luzon and much of Mindanao and to a lesser extent in parts of the Bicol and Visayas regions.

In central Luzon, the region of the Huk rebellion in the 1940s to the 1950s, the New People's Army (NPA) has not been nearly so prominent as in the areas just mentioned. One reason is that the government's land-reform program has been concentrated in central Luzon; the area is a major rice producer and the government hoped such a program would avert possible renewed unrest in this old "hotbed of revolt." For example, the four provinces (Bulacan, Pampanga, Nueva Ecija, and Tarlac) where the Huks were strongest had only 13 percent of the nation's tenants but in 1980 had 43 percent of all the nation's tenants who were approved by the Ministry of Agrarian Reform to begin payments on redistributed land.[7] Secondly, central Luzon has not been

---

[7] See figures in Philippines, Ministry of Agrarian Reform, "Summary Operation Land Transfer Program Accomplishment as of December 31, 1979."

affected by some of the worst aspects of agricultural and rural "development" programs that certain business interests and the government have imposed during the last fifteen to twenty years. Nevertheless, in recent years central Luzon has had signs of discontent, including peasant demonstrations against high costs of farming and considerable opposition to the Marcos government in the 1984 and 1986 elections.

What explains the strength of rural rebellion in Mindanao, northern Luzon, and some other parts of the country is a convergence of factors that typically cause rural revolt.[8]

In northern Luzon and Mindanao, greedy local elites, adverse state policies encouraged by transnational corporations, disruptive national and international market forces, scarce alternative means for livelihood, and rapid population growth in the last frontier areas of the nation have put tremendous pressures on land-use arrangements. Numerous first- and second-generation settlers, though they had title to their farms, have been forced by influential families and companies to leave or become tenants. The Marcos government's encouragement to Filipino and foreign companies to expand export crops (particularly bananas, sugarcane, and pineapple) gave additional incentives to these more powerful actors to accumulate land. Other small landholders have been lured (often through deception) to lease their lands to large owners and companies on terms that have proved exploitative.[9]

Meanwhile, uplanders—usually tribal communities—in both Mindanao and northern Luzon have been squeezed not only by expanding populations' encroaching on their fields and hunting grounds but suddenly by still other state policies. In decisions about how "public lands" are to be used, the Marcos government minimized if not absolutely denied the tribal people's rights. In both areas the government granted large concessions to logging and mining companies, who then employed government officials and the military to enforce their claims

---

[8]James C. Scott, *The Moral Economy of the Peasant* (New Haven: Yale University Press, 1976); Theda Skocpol, *States and Social Revolutions* (Cambridge: Cambridge University Press, 1979); John Walton, *Reluctant Rebels* (New York: Columbia University Press, 1984); Eric R. Wolf, *Peasant Wars of the Twentieth Century* (New York: Harper and Row, 1969).

[9]Randolf S. David, Temario C. Rivera, Patricio N. Abinales, and Oliver G. Teves, "Transnational Corporations and the Philippine Banana Export Industry," in *Political Economy of Philippine Commodities* (Quezon City: Third World Studies Center, University of the Philippines, 1983), 1–134.

against the hill tribes. In addition, dams and roads have destroyed or threaten to ruin many tribal communities' homes, lands, and waterways.[10]

On top of these adversities is the devastation in the coconut and sugar industries. After climbing to record highs in the mid-1970s, prices for coconut and sugarcane products dropped to practically all-time lows in the early 1980s. Meanwhile, the Marcos government's reorganization of the milling and marketing of these crops advantaged a tiny minority at the expense of most growers, workers, and millers. Both conditions exacerbated poverty and related problems for rural people in Mindanao, the Visayas, Bicol, and southern Luzon.[11]

People in many parts of Mindanao, northern Luzon, Bicol, and the Visayas have petitioned, resisted, and organized, hoping to get favorable attention from local elites and government officials. Instead, authorities, unable or unwilling to accommodate dissent and criticism, frequently dispatched soldiers who harassed, inflicted violence on, and extorted possessions and money from villagers and townspeople. So rampant were military abuses, says a 1984 report by the United States Congress, that "they are a key factor, if not the most important consideration, for . . . the degree of support people give to the NPA."[12] The NPA offers a recourse against lawless authorities and elites.[13]

[10]Interviews in Baguio and Cagayan de Oro City with people assisting tribal communities, August 1984.

[11]Dante B. Canlas, et al., "An Analysis of the Philippine Economic Crisis: A Workshop Report" (Quezon City: School of Economics, University of the Philippines, mimeographed, 1984); Rigoberto Tiglao, "The Political Economy of the Philippine Coconut Industry," in *Political Economy of Philippine Commodities,* 181–272.

[12]United States Congress, Senate Committee on Foreign Relations, "The Situation in the Philippines," 98th Cong., S. Prt. 98–237 (Washington, D.C.: Government Printing Office, 1984), 40, also 20, 22. Also see Guy Sacerdoti and Philip Bowring, "Marx, Mao, and Marcos," *Far Eastern Economic Review* (November 21, 1985), 54.

[13]United States Congress, Committee on Foreign Relations, "Situation in the Philippines"; Sacerdoti and Bowring, "Marx, Mao, and Marcos," Far Eastern Economic Review, November 21, 1985; Roland-Pierre Paringaux, "Philippines' Guerrillas Moving into the Towns" and "No Answer to Communist Challenge in the Philippines," *The Guardian Weekly,* May 12, 1985, 13, and May 19, 1985, 13; and interviews in Baguio, Cagayan de Oro City, and Metro-Manila, August 1984 and April 1985.

IMPLICATIONS FOR UNITED STATES GOVERNMENT POLICIES

1. A primary worry of United States policymakers regarding the Philippines has recently been the growing rebellion, which they have frequently and carelessly depicted as "spreading communism." Given the populist way in which the Marcos government has been deposed and the Aquino government has taken charge, I foresee a substantial decline in the rural rebellion provided the new leaders in Manila can make good their vow to listen to "the people," reduce poverty, and, perhaps most important because it must be done quickly, eliminate military abuses and reduce the military's power. Among several positive signs in these directions are the Aquino government's release of all political prisoners and restoration of civil liberties.

If after several months rebellion reappears, however, United States policymakers should examine carefully the causes. It may be easy to characterize the rebels as communists, especially if some are Communist party members, but that is too simplistic. Rural people, as I have suggested earlier, are not radicals. They do not seek revolution. In view of their dismal straits, they expect surprisingly little from elites and government. If they rebel, it is likely because they are forced to—not by "outside agitators" or by "communists" but because rapacious business people, military or paramilitary forces, and government policies have made their situation intolerable. Rather than concentrate on the rebels, as American policies have in the past, the United States government should be more introspective about and critical of its own priorities and actions as well as those of the elites and government officials with whom it does business in the Philippines.

2. The amazingly peaceful transition from an authoritarian government to a more democratic one has inspired people around the world, including Americans. The United States government has little to congratulate itself about for this turn of events and it should resist impulses to claim significant credit for the change. In the first place, for years noncommunist opposition to the Marcos government was growing in rural and urban areas, yet White House officials kept repeating that there were only two alternatives, Marcos or the communists. Most of the credit for the nonviolent overthrow belongs to millions of people in small and large groups throughout the country who have long criticized the Marcos rule and strove for changes. Their efforts culminated in the

February election and the events thereafter.

Second, although now it is easy for Americans to see how corrupt and disreputable the Marcos government was, the United States also has much to answer for. United States government officials and American business groups inside and outside the Philippines applauded Marcos when he imposed martial law in 1972 and, according to some evidence, may have helped him and his advisers plan and carry it out. And they certainly contributed, particularly through military aid, to perpetuating the regime whose political base was shrinking and thus had to rely on force and intimidation.[14] Top United States government officials persistently praised and defended not only the government but Ferdinand and Imelda Marcos themselves.

The United States government has no basis now for rushing into the Philippines with prescriptions for what Filipinos and their new government should or should not do. Neither its past record nor its role in February 1986 warrant that. Instead, the United States should treat the Philippines and its government with the full respect due to an equal, sovereign nation. It should give the new government a chance to organize and to prepare its own programs.

In addition to this reserved, more humble stance, the most direct help the United States government can give Filipinos now is to help the Aquino government to retrieve wealth that the Marcoses and others accumulated illegally.

3. A major long-term task facing not only the Aquino government but the entire country is to eliminate or at least drastically reduce poverty and underemployment. Peasants and landless laborers are eager to produce, feed and provide for themselves, improve their houses, and become better educated. A large percentage cannot, however, because opportunities are scarce, they control few resources, and they suffer from illnesses, malnutrition, and other adversities of being poor.

It would be marvelous if the United States government could contribute to this urgent project. I doubt, however, that policymakers know what to do. I can think of no place in the Third World where American policy has significantly served the poor and underemployed.

---

[14]Jim Zwick, *Militarism and Repression in the Philippines* (Montreal: Centre for Developing Area Studies, Working Paper number 31, McGill University, 1982).

"Solutions" that Washington policymakers are likely to generate, whether in the United States government itself or in the World Bank, which the United States government influences, will probably be similar to those they pushed in Manila during the 1970s and 1980s: export-orientated agriculture and industrialization that is capital-intensive, is more urban than rural-centered, requires foreign and joint-venture investments, and encourages if not demands low tariff protection for indigenous entrepreneurs and products. In part precisely because the Marcos government—in collaboration with the United States government, the World Bank, and other international business interests—pursued such policies, rural conditions worsened, urban and rural underemployment increased, and impoverishment deepened.[15]

More promising remedies and prescriptions for Filipinos to consider possibly could emerge from quarters other than United States government policymakers and their usual advisers drawn from Wall Street and Madison Avenue. People and organizations in the United States with innovative ideas and commitment to eliminating poverty should be consulted, as well as similar groups in other Western and Third World countries. Examples could include the Institute for Food and Development Policy in San Francisco, the Green Party in West Germany, Gandhigram in India, and communes and cooperatives in rural China. In addition, numerous Philippine groups and communities—some church-affiliated but others not—have been trying a variety of avenues to use local resources, including land and labor, for the poor's benefit.

Perhaps the best assistance the United States government can render in this regard at the present time takes two forms. First, stop pressuring the Philippines to follow conventional American prescriptions for economic development. This would create more room for other alternatives to be considered seriously. Second, help bring together the experiences and knowledge of an array of unconventional efforts that have had notable success with and innovative ideas about reducing poverty and enabling people to control and make better use of local resources. This might be done by organizing conferences, sending Filipinos to visit other places where exemplary projects are in progress,

[15]A number of analysts have made this argument. One of the most recent and best is Robin Broad, "Behind Philippines Policy Making: The Role of the World Bank and the International Monetary Fund," Ph.D. diss., Princeton University, 1983.

bringing people from there to interact with Filipinos, and assisting schools and other educational institutions to develop instructional programs in order to study these other experiences.

A "true land reform" is one promise that Cory Aquino repeatedly made during her campaign in January and February 1986. Her government has yet to come up with a policy, but she has appointed a new minister of agrarian reform and a special task force. The minister (Sonny Alvarez) and the task force members seem willing to consider seriously a broad range of possibilities—everything from significant redistribution of all lands regardless of crop within a capitalist context, such as what took place in Taiwan and South Korea, to the variety of cooperative and state farms found in the socialist approaches of China, Yugoslavia, Cuba, and Nicaragua. The United States could help this deliberation by funding the ministry and task force's research, seminars, missions to and from these various countries, and other preparatory work that is supposed to lead to a comprehensive agrarian program.

If that program involves, as is possible, taking thousands of hectares from a few owners (for example, the roughly 260,000 hectares of the country's 420,000-hectare sugar area controlled by the 11 percent of the sugar producers with farms exceeding 25 hectares), the government might need a large amount of money to compensate those landowners as well as to establish credit and other assistance for the new tillers.[16] Were the Aquino government to turn to the United States for financial aid for this program, the United States government should help.

Another likely need is assistance to the beneficiaries of the Marcos land reform—the roughly 400,000 tenants on rice and corn lands to whom the previous government gave assurances of permanent leasehold rights and, in about a fourth of those cases, promised that the tenants could eventually become owners of their fields. Having land, though, has in many cases proved insufficient to rise above poverty. High prices for fertilizers and other inputs required of modern agricultural procedures have consumed much of the increased yields, leaving little net gain for most small rice and corn producers. And now these peasants may face another threat to their livelihood.

---

[16]Figures for sugar area, farm sizes, and distribution come from Filomeno V. Aguilar, Jr., *The Making of Cane Sugar: Poverty Crisis, and Change in Negros Occidental* (Manila: La Salle Social Research Center, 1984), tables 3.2, 3.3, and 3.4.

Disgruntled former landowners who have been waiting for the day when they could challenge the constitutionality of the earlier land reform may coalesce and take their grievance to the courts. Among their arguments may be the claim that they have not been given the compensation promised by the Marcos government and that approximately three-fourths of the beneficiaries have not been paying rents or amortizements for the lands they have been farming during the last fifteen years. On these grounds, ex-owners might argue, the (limited) accomplishments of the 1970s land reform should be nullified. To counter this assault, peasants may need legal and financial assistance that the Aquino government may want to give but lack sufficient means. Again, United States aid could help.

4. Germane to the high priority of drastically reducing poverty is a contradiction of previous American policy in the Philippines. The United States favors democracy. This includes not only a political system that encourages citizens to elect officials and participate in making public policies. It also means that people have the right to organize, speak openly, and to advocate their particular interests. Consequently, democracy includes peasant organizations and labor unions pushing for redistribution of land and other resources and for better wages and working conditions. Indeed, in order for democracy to thrive, overall living conditions probably have to improve substantially for the majority.

The United States also has economic and security interests in the Philippines. The United States government helps to protect and perpetuate American companies as well as corporations from allied industrial countries such as Japan. These businesses have substantial investments in the Philippines. And the United States government has military bases, which it believes are important to protect American and allied economic interests not only in the Philippines but in Asia generally. American and Japanese transnational corporations tend to agree that their interests and United States military bases are interrelated.

But those economic/security interests and democracy are rather incompatible. In a political system that encourages democracy, organizations and movements are likely to emerge—as they have in the past—that threaten to make foreigners' economic returns less profitable, question the legitimacy of these business interests, and may even advocate the confiscation of their assets. In addition, democracies permit, indeed engender, nationalist movements that in the late twen-

217

tieth century are likely to be increasingly hostile to foreign military bases in the Philippines and critical of other aspects of how the United States in particular defines the world and its security/economic interests. Organizations pressing for better working conditions, the redistribution of land and other resources, and a higher standard of living for the majority at some, perhaps considerable, expense to the well-to-do majority and to foreign companies could also have alliances with nationalists who oppose American and other foreign involvement in their country.

This struggle could become a tremendous influence in Philippine political life. It is hoped that such a conflict will be confined to democratic methods.

In order for that to happen, one crucial factor will be the reaction of the United States government and American businesses. There may be strong pressure within the United States and even from certain sectors of the Philippines for the United States government to undermine the democratic processes in order to "protect" American economic and security interests. This could lead to imposing yet another authoritarian regime, to which the United States government becomes so wedded, as it did to Marcos, that it can see no alternative other than "communism."

In order to resist such pressures and avoid a scenario of repression and possibly (in the long run) revolution, the United States government should prepare now to give a higher priority to democracy than to economic/security interests, as currently conceived. Part of that preparation would be treating the Philippines as a sovereign nation, rather than as one to be manipulated. Another part should be to plan the removal of American bases so that those facilities will not hinder America's appreciation of the democratic possibilities in the Philippines.

12

The Urban Working Class in the Philippines: A Casualty of the New Society, 1972-1985

Robert A. and Beverly H. Hackenberg

URBAN WORKERS IN THE NEW SOCIETY: GOALS AND ACCOMPLISHMENTS

The martial law government, or New Society, established by Ferdinand Marcos on September 21, 1972, never lacked programmatic statements. These often included great expectations for the urban working class. Addressing the Interim National Assembly on July 28, 1980, he affirmed that the improvement of this group was essential to the objectives of the total development program:

> Industrialization and export expansion and diversification are essential components of our development strategies. They are made more urgent by the need to provide employment opportunities to new entrants to our labor force which number about half a million every year. . . . We also have to improve the capacity of our industry to absorb more of our abundant labor force per peso invested. . . . We have mapped out a program which forms part of the fundamental strategy in industrial development.

To achieve these linked objectives, the president advocated dispersed funding of investment in labor-intensive small- and medium-scale industries with backward linkages to raw materials producers. Mindanao was designated as a priority area for industrialization; several of its cities, including Davao, were listed as specific targets. This paper offers (1) a description of the New Society's efforts; (2) an analysis of its failure; and (3) an examination of some policy options for the future.

Elsewhere in the same speech, Marcos made it clear that the employment to be generated must provide income sufficient for households to enjoy financial security, adequate housing, health, nutrition, and education for their children. Realization of this vision requires the formal sector to create jobs, with emphasis on low- and mid-level positions. It also requires revitalized urban institutions (home finance and construction, technical and vocational schools, clinics and hospitals) to develop in parallel.

Assessment of progress toward these goals by the New Society can be made by reference to readily available indicators. Success must be spelled out in (1) an increasing rate of urbanization; (2) an expanded proportion of the labor force in industry; (3) a broadened base for income distribution; and (4) a substantial improvement in purchasing power linked to availability of local manufactures sold at moderate prices. Unfortunately, as is well known to all readers of the Southeast Asian press, these indicators during the past 15 years have described an unrelieved downward slide.

The Philippine population increased from 36.7 million in 1970 to 48.1 million in 1980; the national capital region expanded from 4 to 6 million over the same period. Still, across three separate census counts, the gauge giving the reading for overall urbanization remained stuck at 30 percent. From these two observations a third inference must follow: the 50 percent gain within the leading city means that urbanization rates throughout the regions into which industry was to have been dispersed must have declined. In fact, beyond Manila between 1970-1980, urban population grew at a substantially lower rate than total population in ten out of twelve regions (World Bank 1980a, 204).

The industrialization of the labor force described a corollary pattern. Even with Metro Manila *included*, there was a decline from 19 percent in 1971-1973 to 14.8 percent of total employed in 1983. Meanwhile, the percentage of workers in agriculture remained in the vicinity of 50 percent (Canlas et al. 1984, 41). Over roughly the same interval, 1972 to 1980, with 1972 = 100, the real wage of skilled workers in the industrial establishments of Manila fell to 63.7, and the real wage for unskilled workers dropped still further to 53.4. At the same time, the lower 60 percent of all households, which received only 25 percent of total income in 1971, suffered a further decline of their share to 22.5 percent in 1979 (Canlas et al. 1984, 36-37).

Urban industry in the Manila area experienced substantial growth during the 1970s; factory labor increased (1956-1976) at a rate of 6.7

percent per year (World Bank 1980b, 14), with emphasis upon three major exports: electronic components, textiles, and handicrafts. There was a parallel expansion of the "easy options" for import substitution in the domestic market (food processing, beverages, clothing, and housewares) and larger items with a more limited appeal, such as appliances and assembled vehicles. Were it not for these, the share of industrial workers in the active labor force would have fallen by more than the 4.2 percent reported for 1973 to 1983. Granted, this period includes several of the crisis years since 1980. But even over 1971 to 1976, when industrial growth was at its peak, the addition of workers was not all that impressive: 59.3 percent of the incremental growth in the labor force was added to agriculture, 33 percent to the services sector, and only 7.7 percent to industry (Callison 1981, 10). Outside Metro Manila, industrial growth was largely in the unorganized (cottage) sector.

RURAL BIAS IN ECONOMIC GROWTH UNDER THE NEW SOCIETY: 1972–1979

While these observations suggest that events befalling the urban working class during the past several years were calamitous, they do not examine the causal chain responsible for them. Stripped to essentials, the fate of those households that derive their income from the formal sector (government and corporately structured firms paying salaries and wages) appears to have been a consequence of the "rural bias" in the New Society's expansion plans, despite Michael Lipton's (1977) observations to the contrary. It was the collapse of the farm economy in the years around 1980 that doomed the working class to its present insecure status.

Beyond Manila, a primary task of the New Society was to keep rice cheap and plentiful; it was the price of political stability. Prices were supported at the farm gate for the grower, and controlled in the city for the consumer; but the emphasis, above all, was on production. The major expenditures of the martial law years were for rural infrastructure: roads, electrification, and expanded irrigation. The irrigated area was doubled from 0.73 million to 1.3 million hectares (1971–1980), and the rice crop increased from 5.1 million to 7.25 million tons. Rice self-sufficiency was attained by 1975; average yields were tripled (from thirty to ninety cavans per hectare) and the income of the average farm household, according to our survey data from Mindanao, increased 250 percent (in 1970 pesos), from P1,600 to P4,000 between 1970 and 1980. At the same time, the number of farm laborers employed in our sample municipalities of Davao del Sur also tripled in size. Furthermore, both the gains in yield and income, and the sharply increased labor absorption, were accomplished on a land base reduced by transfers of hectarage from rice to cash crops (Hackenberg 1985).

The other dimension to the expansion of the rural economy was in corporate farming. The new crop of the 1970s was banana (27,000 hectares planted in Min-Davao area by 1979), which, by 1985, had attained an export value equal to half that of the sugar crop (Asia Yearbook 1986, 225). While it generated a substantial additional amount of rural wealth and purchasing power, it supported a narrow segment of the population: in 1977, 28,000 workers and their dependents. The new production scheme of the 1970s was corporate rice farming. In 1974, all corporations employing more than 500 workers were made responsible for either growing or importing the rice requirement for their labor force. The program has been held partly responsible for the achievement of rice self-sufficiency (FEER 6/29/79, 56). Davao region in Mindanao was the site of 11,675 hectares, leased by 19 corporations, representing two-thirds of the total area planted by 1978 (IRTMS 1977). The corporate rice projects were capital intensive, employing equipment instead of labor. Jobs provided by these new corporations are not significant when compared with the estimated 320,000 laborers in the sugar industry (Lynch 1970), or the 675,000 who work in coconut plantations (Castillo 1979, 316). When indirect employment is added, these two crops are alleged to provide support for one-fourth or more of the total population of the Philippines.

The area allocated to both crops was sharply increased during the martial law period, as production was expanded at 3 percent to 4 percent annually. Coconut hectarage during the early Marcos years (1966-1973) grew from 1.6 million to 2.1 million hectares (31.3 percent); over the same interval, sugar expanded from .32 to .46 million hectares (a gain of 43.8 percent). The gains in farm labor were proportionate (Castillo 1979, 316). A striking geographical change was the emergence of Mindanao as the major coconut-producing area, accounting for half the total of 1974, compared with 26 percent in 1960 (World Bank 1976, 147). The increased absorption of labor in the rice fields was financed by P4.5 billion of rural bank credit in the peak years of "Masagana 99" in order to achieve the goal of self-sufficiency. The expansion of sugar and coconut was fueled by privileged access to the U.S. market; but these advantages ended for copra in 1974 and were reduced for sugar in 1982.

The first in a convergent series of devastating reversals occurred in 1980 when the price of copra dropped from 52¢ to 26¢ per pound on the world market. It continued downward to 16¢ in 1982 and 5¢ in 1985. Lagging only slightly behind, sugar in 1982 dropped to a four-year low of 6.7 ¢ per pound—about half its production cost. Like copra, it rode the commodities roller coaster downward to an all-time low of 3¢ in 1985. In 1982, rows of trucks filled with copra were parked along the roadside near Davao; they could not be unloaded because the dealers would not trade at the prevailing prices. The *Wall Street Journal* (April 3, 1986) notes that since 1984 in Negros 40 percent of the sugar land has remained unplanted, with a proportionate number of workers remaining unemployed. This year the usual six-month milling season will be reduced to three months.

Further losses were inflicted by the collapse of the mechanism for funding rice production. The Masagana 99 program extended loans through rural banks that were uncollateralized and frequently uncollected. The 1,041 rural banks were unable to repay their advances to the Central Bank and, by 1982, about half had been excluded from access to rediscounting facilities (World Bank 1983: i-iv). By the present year, according to the *Wall Street Journal* (April 3, 1986), *only about 60* remained solvent. In the mid-1970s, 68 percent of the credit received by rice producers came from government banks at subsidized interest rates. By 1980, this figure was reduced to 32 percent; the remaining two-thirds of credit was coming from "informal sources" at market rates. In 1982, once again, the Philippines was importing rice. In June of 1983, in the towns of Davao del Sur in which the rise to affluence was measured in 1980, it was necessary to distribute 19,000 sacks of National Food Authority (NFA) rice to alleviate starvation. Here, as elsewhere, those hit the hardest were former farm laborers.

URBAN CONSEQUENCES OF RURAL BIAS: 1980–1985

The urban sector reacted to these rural economic onslaughts as one organ of the body to another's illness. As rural consumer income desiccated, the demand for urban domestic manufactures also withered and the fragile framework of industry began to crumble. Inflation rose to 20 percent during the first half of 1980, and the same period was marked by the disappearance of 137,000 factory jobs—more than half of which were outside Manila! The Asia Yearbook (1981, 230) observed that the consequences could be compared with the havoc caused by the oil-price inflation of 1974. The attrition of the urban working-class members in industrial employment continued through 1981 with an average of 212 jobs lost per day, rising to 275 per day in 1982 and 290 in 1984. Over this four-year period, there was also an average of one new industrial strike for every working day (Asia Yearbook, 1983, 236).

As there was no respite from the deterioration of the farm economy, neither was there any deflection of the urban trend. From mid-1982, capital flight was measured at $2 million per day. Capital migration was the solution for the industrialists, and labor migration was the solution for the working class. In 1980 the trek to the Middle East began with 102,000 expatriate workers. By 1982 the volume had attained a crescendo of *671,000 emigrant jobseekers.* Most were skilled or semiskilled former industrial employees.

Contributing factors were the oil price hike of 1979, the U.S. recession, and, in the same year, the imposition by the International Monetary Fund (IMF) of conditions that curtailed growth and imposed import controls; these severely limited the output of manufacturers using nonindigenous materials, for example, textile producers. In each successive year, IMF constraints became more restrictive. Importers were put on a cash basis by foreign suppliers and paid a premium of 22 percent for their foreign exchange. By 1983 the major automobile assemblers ceased to operate; the closure of Ford Philippines alone resulted in the dismissal of 10,000 workers. The end came suddenly in October when the Central Bank was unable to make a payment on the outstanding principal to the private lenders. The major multilateral development projects ground to a halt because the government was not able to meet its counterpart requirements. Ironically, this same constraint restricted use of several World Bank structural adjustment loans which were intended to assist industries to overcome these problems.

By 1984, unemployment in the cities had reached 35 percent and estimates of the rate of underemployment were higher. No one took issue with claims that the inflation rate for that same year was 50 percent. For the first time, there were major strikes in the Bataan free trade zone. Planters Products, the primary provider of petrochemicals to small rice farmers at subsidized prices, was forced into bankruptcy by the government's failure to meet its share of the payments. While the World Bank proposed a third structural adjustment loan to meet credit and fertilizer requirements of rice producers, it imposed the new condition that both were to be priced at *market rates*. The national economy posted a *decline* in Gross National Product (GNP) of approximately 5 percent in each of the two preceding years, 1984 and 1985. Failure to obtain raw materials to maintain factory production was held responsible (FEER 1985, 84).

This review has sought to relate the declining position of the urban working class to evidence for unsound rural-based policies and programs. But a series of *urban* events *also* occurred from 1972 to 1980, such as the decision to build fourteen five-star hotels for the IMF Manila conference of 1975, the ill-fated eleven major industrial projects proposed in 1980, the "New City" plan to create a residential/commercial zone to parallel Roxas Boulevard by extending the foreshore into Manila Bay, and the endless series of special projects: the Cultural Center, Heart Center, Trade Center, Population Commission, Nutrition Center, University of Life, the Folk Art Center, Kapit Bahayan Housing Project and Children's City. These "enrichment projects," mostly proposed by the first lady, were augmented with the construction agenda of the individual ministries, for example, the Bureau of Internal Revenue building, the new National Housing Authority office, the massive Central Bank Building, the new Manila International Airport, and many, many more.

Enterprises of this sort, based in the Metro Manila area, had parallels throughout the country in the endless parade of building construction, falling in a descending cascade from the national capital to the twelve regional administrative centers, provincial capitals, and *municipios*. It was not unusual to find, at the lowest level of government, a new municipal hall, rural bank, and health center. The role of these projects in generating employment for both unskilled and semiskilled workers during the peak years of the New Society *must* have served (1) to soak up the surplus of Manila-bound migrants who were unable to find a place in the farm economy and (2) to retain thousands of workers and their families in regions receiving the inundation of heavy-infrastructure projects (roads, dams, bridges, power plants, and irrigation systems) that the dictatorship sought to establish as its hallmark of rural development.

Construction investments occupy a favorite place in development planning. Since the first World Bank mission to Colombia under

Lauchlin Currie in 1948, someone, somewhere (most recently Strassman 1985) has asserted that it gives the less developed country (LDC) economy a classic "quick fix." Construction projects are labor intensive, employ the uneducated and unskilled who are most likely to be unproductive, and generate huge wage payments distributed among a large number of poverty households. Almost the entire wage bill is translated immediately into consumer demand for basic goods (food, clothing, and construction material), which represent backward linkages to agriculture and small-scale manufacturing which is also labor intensive. The problem with construction investments is that they are self-limiting (one cannot continue to pour concrete endlessly) and their products—buildings—tend to generate rents rather than additional jobs. When they stop, a massive collapse may ensue. In the Philippines, they stopped after 1980.

Another urban dimension of the regime's economic activity must likewise be summarily dismissed. That is the dimension of government employment itself. The New Society created both supergovernments (Metro Manila and twelve other regional capitals throughout the country) and subgovernments (fifty-five provinces at the beginning of the Marcos years became seventy-three by 1980); the proliferation of municipalities cannot be enumerated here. There were entire new bureaucracies organized and represented at all levels of government, such as Ministry of Human Settlements and the Ministry of Local Government and Community Development. And there was duplication of old ones as, for example, in the impenetrable web of agencies involved in food production. These few examples could be endlessly extended to construct the image that gave rise to the ubiquitous beliefs that (1) government *was* the Philippines' basic growth industry and (2) all forms of opposition could be dealt with by co-opting the dissidents into government service.

Beginning in 1979, IMF curbs on budgeting placed the redundancy of Marcos's hiring practices in a harsh light. By 1981, a reduction of one-eighth in the government budget was intended to include a proportionate reduction in the bloated payroll. At last, agencies were to be merged and projects eliminated (Asia Yearbook 1983, 236). Staff reductions and failures to provide operating budgets crippled even such special projects of the first lady as the Philippine Heart Center for Asia, the first floor of which was rented out to commercial tenants and the research divisions of which were never equipped. Several wards to be used for the care of charity patients were never opened. Here as elsewhere, budget that could have been allocated to employment for provision of *services* was totally consumed for the more visible purpose of *construction*.

Dating the decline of status among urban workers from the Aquino murder of 1983, the IMF conditions of 1979, or even the establishment of the New Society in 1972 is illusory. Ranis (1974, 18) observes that even though growth rates following independence (1946) were satisfactory, there has been a persistent decline in real wages and income shares for those at the lower end of the scale since the early 1950s. Near the end of the seventies, economic writers noted that "GNP has risen by 50 percent since martial law. . .but real wages fell by one-third to March of 1979, and inflation adjusted farming incomes are only 60 percent of what they were in 1974. . . . The peso is worth only 40 centavos in 1972 prices and . . . the wages of nearly 90 percent of rural and urban workers in 1977 could barely meet their subsistence needs" (FEER 1979, 51). Five years passed and the Asia Yearbook (1984, 16) commented that Southeast Asian economies had managed to ". . . chalk up growth rates of 4–6 percent during the years of recession since 1979, *except for the Philippines*. . . . The majority of the Philippine population has failed to win a greater share of even a modest improvement in the country's GNP."

In the balance of this account, we will develop three analytic views of what has gone before. Each offers an explanation from a different perspective. First, the structure of Philippine industry will be probed to discover which features are responsible for the impoverishment of those who depend upon it for their survival. Second, we will interpret a decade of household-level income and employment data collected from Davao City to set forth the adaptive strategies of the urban working-class household for meeting the continuous erosion of its sources of support. Finally, we will use the entire discussion to evaluate the adequacy of the industrial elements in development policies proposed to extricate the Philippines from the present crisis.

THE STRUCTURE OF PHILIPPINE INDUSTRY: THE REALITY BEHIND THE STATISTICS

Three recent comprehensive studies contain the same conclusions concerning the major characteristics of Philippine industry: (1) it has a distorted and dualistic structure of employment and productivity and

(2) it has an asymmetric spatial distribution (Ranis 1974; World Bank 1976, 1980). These features tend to contribute to the impoverishment of working-class households and to contain the potential impact of modernization on the total economy.

The dualistic structure of industry in the New Society is set forth in the data contained in Tables 1 and 2. It is reflected in the heavy concentration of firms (97.1 percent) in the category represented by one to four employees (Table 1), which holds almost two-thirds of the industrial labor force but represents only 6 percent of the value added by manufacturing (Table 2). Conversely, a small number (2.9 percent) of firms with an average of fifty employees (Table 1) contribute 94 percent of the value added from manufacturing (Table 2)! The inescapable conclusion is that most of the urban industrial working class is found in household-level enterprises usually classified as the "unorganized" or informal sector (Hackenberg 1980, 396–401). More than half the employees in microindustries of this sort are unpaid family workers (Ranis 1974, 143). Wages paid to others fall outside the scope of regulatory agencies.

There is a critical mismatch also between the heavy concentration of two-thirds of all the value added in labor-intensive industries (food, clothing and furniture) with less than one-third of the manufacturing employment, and the output of cottage industries (Table 3). The elimination of the unorganized sector would be scarcely noticeable in terms of its impact on GNP, but its consequences for unemployment would be catastrophic. Similarly, more than half of capital investment in industry goes to heavy industry and mining. At the other extreme the capital investment required by *all* cottage industries is negligible (0.2 percent of total capital investment).

Since productivity is inseparably linked to both the size of the payroll (which represents the division of labor and level of operating efficiency) and to the level of wages payable, the future of Philippine employment generation and export promotion is linked to an increase in small and medium enterprises (SMEs) with more than five workers. Industrial studies (World Bank 1976, 233; Ranis 1974, 144) conclude that the SME with five to nineteen employees utilizes capital most efficiently, adding value at levels equal to firms with much heavier investment per worker. Despite this, the trend over the past several decades has not confirmed the expansion of SMEs in this size class. Between 1956 and 1973 the *number* of such firms increased while their average labor force *declined by one-third*, from 10.2 to 7.7 workers.

A World Bank (1976: 233) analyst noted ". . . proliferation of inefficient units as well as lack of normal consolidation and growth from smaller to larger units." In a favorable business environment the number of jobs will grow faster than the number of firms and the size of each enterprise will increase. Instead, in recent years employment in manufacturing declined as a share of total employment and grew by only 2.8 percent, creating a mere 40,000 jobs annually (1956 to 1976). During the same period, total employment in the economy grew by 660,000 jobs per annum. But factory jobs in enterprises with more than twenty workers increased by 6.7 percent per year, more than two times the rate of total manufacturing, including cottage industries. These export-oriented firms were favored by the Board of Investment with incentive packages that encouraged their capital-intensive development at the expense of the mass of urban industrial workers (World Bank 1980b, 13–14).

The second aspect of industrial structure that operates to the detriment of the urban working class is spatial segmentation. Industry has always been concentrated in the vicinity of Manila, and under the New Society it became more so. By 1975, 73 percent of manufacturing value added and 65 percent of employment was found in Metro Manila. Only in the resource-based food and wood industries is there any degree of dispersion; if these were excluded, the proportion of value added in Metro Manila by manufacturing would rise to 87 percent. Only sugar, copra, and plywood were processed in cities outside the core area. The World Bank (1980b, 50) noted that, ". . . certainly all the labor-intensive industry, on which the successful export drive has been based, is in the Manila area. For example, 91 percent of the clothing and 95 percent of electrical equipment." Projects listed under the Export Incentives Act were even more concentrated by 1977, with 132 of 160 projects in Manila and adjacent areas. Industries that are located beyond Manila are found only in the industrializing centers of Davao, Cebu, Cagayan de Oro, and Bacolod. Among them, they shared 19 percent of the total manufacturing value added in 1977.

If there is concentration in the metropolitan area by industry, there is also a parallel in the distribution of firms by size. More than three-fourths of all enterprises with twenty or more workers (77.2 percent) were found in Manila and its environs in 1970. This degree of segregation, both by industry and by size, was encouraged by the policies of the New Society, placing both smaller firms and their workers at an immense disadvantage. The explanation lies in the need for *complementarity* (or linkage) between smaller and larger firms if the industry to which they belong is to generate self-sustained growth. In a key passage, Ranis (1974, 559–560) observes:

> The dynamic program suggested for the development of SMEs assumes a close relationship between small and large factories. . . . Parts and components will be purchased by large firms from small. It is this type of complementarity which has the highest potential for growth in the Philippines. . . . All industrial countries . . . encourage subcontracting. It is most advanced in Japan.

It seems clear from these premises, based on the most recent facts, that the dualistic structure of manufacturing in the New Society can be traced to two sharply divergent tendencies. Industrial growth was selective, favoring the world market-oriented exports being produced only in Manila with the small fraction of the labor force retained by the factory system employing twenty or more workers. The urban industrial workers outside Manila were tied either *directly* to the trade in agricultural products, doomed by the decline in those same markets for commodities, or *indirectly* by involvement in production of domestic goods. If the export trade in T-shirts and transistors had been both large and sufficiently labor intensive, it might have overcome the rural collapse. However, as recently as 1984, electronics, the industrial growth leader in a generally bleak economic landscape, represented only 15 percent of total export value and employed only 50,000 persons in the Manila area (FEER 1985, 68).

In 1983, under a field-research contract from USAID/Philippines, both authors visited a representative sample of SMEs located beyond the metropolitan area in northern (Region I) and southern (Region V) Luzon. Firms were engaged in production of three potential exports: textiles, furniture, handicrafts. All were located in small cities: Laoag, Dagupan, Legaspi, San Fernando, Naga, and Sorsogon. Specifically, we were probing the limits to growth described above, and seeking to discover whether inputs of credit and technical support would permit these industries to expand production and create jobs in low-income communities. Our discoveries included the following:

1. The prevalence of household-scale firms in all types of production is an adaptive strategy. Market uncertainties, lack of sufficient working capital, and intermittent breakdown in raw materials supply make it necessary to spread risks over several types of income sources. Most entrepreneurs utilized networks of household producers who were also part-time farmers, buy-and-sell businessmen, or workers at a related trade. They could be mobilized on short notice to work on sewing, embroidering, mat making, woodworking, or weaving to fill an order before returning to other means of livelihood. Household workers, using hand tools and primitive machines, dispersed over an area rather than assembled in a workplace, have more income options. However, seasonal demands of better paid farm work (garlic harvest and curing tobacco in north Luzon, for example) impose discontinuity.
2. No production took place before an order was secured and a partial payment made to the entrepreneur. The funds were used to secure raw materials for the job, and to pay advances to workers. There were no regular hours worked for wages, and no inventories were ever produced against future orders before they were actually received. The labor mobilized when an order was received was compensated on a piecework basis. Neither entrepreneur nor worker household could anticipate income over any particular interval of time. Since all were working only part of the time, the judgment that they were "underemployed" is inevitable; but it is also a product of the structure of industry.
3. Government programs for securing loans and technical assistance were available through the Ministries of Trade and Industry (MTI) and Human Settlements and the Development Bank of the Philippines. Credit was too late, too little, or both. Technical assistance was well regarded, especially MTI's Small Business Advisory Centers (SBAC), but it consisted primarily of filling out loan applications for the other ministries. In general, resources were underutilized because the uncertainties concerning the market made entrepreneurs unwilling to accept loans that were heavily collateralized, unlike farm-production loans made under Masagana 99.

The SME environment was not supportive. There had been frequent business failures, losses of contracts, and reductions in commitments to workers in all three industries during 1983. Raw materials (yard-goods, timber and rattan, abaca fiber, paints, dyes, and chemicals) were subject to manipulation by government officials, the military, and their antagonists. Timber and rattan for furniture making, for example, could not be obtained without an "arrangement" with Bureau of Forestry personnel, the Philippine constabulary, or the New People's Army (NPA). Not infrequently, all three would be involved. Since the biggest source of textile and furniture orders was either the government or private schools (uniforms, school desks, office furniture), corruption in both placement of orders and payment for them was ubiquitous. By no coincidence, the entrepreneurs producing these goods were either present or former schoolteachers or government employees.

The clothing industry, the largest in the country (Table 3), incorporates all the features described above. It relies heavily upon "outworkers," who are part-time employees affiliated with a shop or factory, filling orders by working at home. There are 4 to 5 outworkers for every regular garment industry employee, that is, 400,000 to 500,000 in the entire country. They are mostly women, employed at piecework rates, with no employment benefits. This industry, like most others, has a "rurban" character (urban plant and rural outworkers). Because of poor quality, they sell to Middle East and African markets that have no import quotas, forcing producers into cutthroat price competition for their orders. To escape from constraints and produce goods for metropolitan sale or export, much higher uniformity and quality of output will be required. But these, in turn, depend upon assurance of standing orders that can be used to obtain lines of credit, purchase machines that turn out standardized products, and train and retain a permanent labor force. Without these, entrepreneurs in provincial cities will continue to sell cheap and imperfect goods to very limited local markets, or to Fiji.

ADAPTIVE STRATEGIES OF THE URBAN WORKING CLASS: DAVAO CITY

The typical urban household lives on its income. If its income is reduced it may accept diminished living standards, but if the trend continues it must resort to alternative sources of support. Davao Research and Planning Foundation (DRPF), our field station in Davao City, conducted citywide surveys at two-year intervals between 1972 and 1980 (Hackenberg 1983). These were linked to structural and historical observations. Our aim was to elicit adaptive patterns to the twin sources of income decline: (1) a 1970 to 1980 annual population growth rate of 4.5 percent and (2) the boom-and-bust pattern of the regional, national, and international economy.

Davao's industrial expansion under the New Society reflected the rural bias of the entire period. Its gains were primarily in commerce and service activity related to agribusiness expansion in the region: (1) the banana export industry (27,000 hectares); (2) a sugar central (18,000 hectares under contract); (3) corporate rice projects (12,000 hectares under contract); (4) green revolution rice farming by small-holders; and (5) the sawmill and plywood manufacturing center based on 500,000 hectares of timber concessions.

With the expansion of agribusiness came infrastructure and government. In 1967, old Davao Province was trisected and three new provincial capitals (Tagum, Digos, and Mati) were created. Davao City was upgraded to a regional center and, after 1972, acquired local offices of all major ministries established in Manila. Participation in the New Society was symbolized by construction of new urban infrastructure: regional hospital, a circumferential highway and several bridges, a new water system, city market and bus terminal, central bank building, and a massive slum-improvement and squatter-upgrading project.

Despite the expansion of business and government, median household incomes of Davao residents across the 1972 to 1979 interval *declined* 26.4 percent in real terms. For the subsequent high-inflation years, we know the decline has been much more precipitous, if unmeasured. The major concern in Davao under the New Society has been jobs. The demographic pressure of immigration plus fertility requires the economy to double its employment capacity every fourteen years at the 4.5 percent annual rate. But there is the additional stress imposed by declining household income. The only solution during the 1970s was the deployment of additional household members to the active labor force. These increased from 1.6 to 1.9 per household in seven years, an expansion of close to 25 percent (Table 4). There were 170 workers in 1979 for every 100 in 1972; male household heads remained fully employed across the interval, but the proportions of spouses at work almost doubled. And which sector of the economy expanded to absorb this explosion of new jobseekers?

It might be supposed that the expansion of agribusiness would generate a wealth of employment in the formal sector. While there were 28,000 new positions in the banana industry, and three-fourths within commuting distance of Davao City, the response was minimal. The explanation, once again, is to be found in the structure of the industry. Our DRPF survey of 1977, funded by the Banana Export Industry Foundation (BEIF), reported:

> The banana industry's payroll exceeds P66 million per year yet it uses primarily unskilled labor. The nine largest farms employ 14,724 people. Unspecialized field and packing house workers, earning the minimum of 7 to 9 pesos per day, comprise more than 7/8 of the labor force (88.5 percent), management included (Hackenberg 1977, 57).

The BEIF report also notes that the wages and job classifications in the banana industry match those of the urban manufacturing enterprises in Davao. Since they are part of the same contiguous labor pool, this is not surprising. Our survey revealed that, like the textile and furniture industries of Luzon, the workers in the banana industry are recruited from local rural villages in which they continue to farm or raise animals for sale on a part-time basis. It is not possible for them, nor do they expect, to support a household from plantation wages. Managers and technicians reside in Davao City and commute to work.

The factory system in the Philippines is the bottom step on the employment ladder. While Todaro and others have predicted that upward job mobility in the developing city will be from the informal sector (self-employment in trade or services within the bazaar economy) to the formal sector (employment for wages and benefits within a firm (Tadaro, 1976), many empirical studies (Hackenberg 1980; Hackenberg et al. 1984; Ogawa and Suits 1985; Teilhet-Waldorf 1983) show the reverse. Urban factory employment behaves the way Arthur Lewis or Fei and Ranis (rather than Todaro) predict: an unlimited supply of labor keeps upward mobility near zero and salaries at the subsistence minimum.

Not surprisingly, in view of the foregoing, it was the informal sector that expanded in Davao City between 1972 and 1979 to accommodate jobseekers (Table 5). While this category of employment grew from 36 percent to 46 percent of all jobs, the formal sector contracted from 64 percent to 54 percent. The major gain was in traditional sales (stall keeping, vending/peddling, shopkeeping); the major loss was in manufacturing employment (Table 6). The shift is self-explanatory when we add that the mean monthly income of households headed by market vendors and stall keepers was P2,026 in 1979; for households headed by factory workers it was P959, and for construction workers P1,017.

The events of 1980 to 1985 have caught the urban working class in a brutal squeeze that has reduced many Davao households to misery. Two blows have crippled the informal sector. First came the decline of the local small-farm economy with the collapse of the rice self-sufficiency program. At IMF demand, supports and controls were removed in 1979, lowering the price paid for rice at the farm gate and raising the price charged to the urban consumer. The drop in world copra and sugar prices struck at the same time. The loss of sales volume drove the peddlers from San Pedro Street in Davao, and forced half the Indian storekeepers to close their doors. The second blow came with vertical integration of retail sales; three major supermarket chains and two nationwide drugstores entered the Davao market between 1978 and 1980. Dealing in large stocks at low prices and paying subminimum wages, they quickly took the profit out of the much less efficient informal-sector trade in the same items. Superiority or inferiority of factory employment became a moot question when Alcantara and Sons plywood factory, the largest industry in Davao, was forced to close after its logging concessions were shifted to a "crony capitalist."

The new forms of adaptation should perhaps be called by another name. In the chaos resulting from the collapse of the rural *and* urban economic base of support, there were mass defections in both areas to the NPA. Through its widespread collection system, extracting regular payments from the plantation operators, transportation firms, storekeepers, and all accessible professionals and wage workers, it acquired a treasury sufficient to purchase and distribute grain to barrios and neighborhoods accepting its control. At the same time the NPA maintains "peace and order," protecting its areas against looters, scavengers, organized bands of hoodlums, and various military and paramilitary units (who may not be separable from the first three).

The advance of the NPA was made possible by the increasing venality, disorganization, and impotence of the Kilusang Bagong Lipunam (KBL) city government, which has been in office since 1980, coupled with the economic collapse. Crime grew to a crescendo after

1980, with an average of fifteen murders per week for 1984 and 1985 as the city police ceased to attempt to control the streets. A dangerous sign of the breakdown of political control has been the resurgence of widespread seizure of private land for the construction of squatter settlements within the city; now occupied by the unemployed recent arrivals from rural areas, they are quickly organized by NPA units. Basic urban services, fire protection as well as police, have long been inoperative. Brokenshire Hospital, the city's only full-service medical center, closed in 1984. People could no longer afford to use it. Regional Hospital has been without medicines for two years.

Convergence of these factors has prompted disinvestment and withdrawal of business leaders, managers, and professionals from the city; a Davao expatriate community has been formed in Vancouver. Many who are unable to legitimize migration to the United States have gone to the Middle East as guest workers, including the senior staff of the Davao Insular Hotel. Others obtain part or all of their support from the city's mushrooming underworld of smuggling, narcotics, and gambling. A new investment plan has begun among those who may still obtain profits from whatever source in the city. The financial and personal sense of insecurity in the rural communities has led to distress sale of large blocks of first-class rice land. Though formerly owner operated, they are now farmed by tenants for absentee landlords living in Davao.

CONCLUSIONS: TOWARD A TRULY NEW SOCIETY

A new government replaced the Marcos dictatorship in its fourteenth year. Generating employment is its most basic problem, although others will receive more publicity. The population machine continues to grind out between 0.5 million and 0.75 million new workers per year. It was estimated that 75,000 or more must be absorbed by urban industry, just to maintain the rural-urban balance of the 1970s in labor-force distribution. There are, in addition, the recent urban unemployed and substantial numbers of labor migrants returning from the Middle East as the oil economy continues its rapid descent; while there are no recent figures, Philippine remittance income from workers overseas dropped 25 percent in 1984. To relieve the increasing population burden on contracting agricultural employment would require an even larger number added to urban working-class households. While jobs are the key issue, wage levels and working-class income are closely related; as Davao's recent history confirms, inadequate support of household heads leads to the deployment of additional household members as jobseekers, adding aggravation to the employment problem.

Adequate employment generation must deal with the basic premise brought forth in the previous discussion: Philippine industry, as a source of support for the working class, is oriented in two directions: First, the domestic sector, which is aimed at the local consumer market, ". . . makes up 85 percent of manufacturing output and employment. If manufacturing as a whole is to contribute to Philippine development, improvements must be achieved by *home* industries" (World Bank 1980b, 3). Second, the residual 15 percent produces exports for the foreign sector, and the so-called "nontraditional exports" (textiles and electronic goods, primarily), which are the subject of most of the discussion, make up only one-third of the latter.

Conversion of each sector to more effective job production and placement requires us to confront a different problem. The domestic market in the 1980s confronts a crisis of *demand* for which the depressed state of the agricultural economy is responsible. The export market faces a crisis of *supply* for which the poor quality of goods and low volume of output is responsible. Since both are structural problems, neither can be solved by simple tinkering with prices, incentives, or tariff adjustments.

Agricultural analysts are not sanguine about the future of a farm economy based on two export crops that are becoming obsolete. Philippine copra is a poor competitor for Malaysian palm oil, and sugar is being replaced in major import markets with high-fructose corn. World demand for pineapple and banana, the other two Philippine plantation crops, is limited to present production. Basic changes in the sector are needed and will take time. Meanwhile, demand will lag as rural impoverishment deepens.

The Aquino government has already been presented with demands to get on with land reform by breaking up sugar plantations and converting them to small holdings for subsistence crops. This may feed the landless and unemployed *sacadas* of Negros, who have already become a high political risk for spreading radicalism. But it will not generate purchasing power to replace the wage bill formerly paid by the plantations. Even in the short run such moves, while attractive politically, are economically regressive.

Since foreign exchange earned by the export sector is a key factor in loan repayment, plans to restructure major industries to improve both quality and productivity must not be dismissed. However, currently recommended changes are focused on new machinery and related capital items. The transfer of current technology will tend to produce enterprises that are less labor intensive than before. To be precise, underemployment will be reduced within a smaller and better skilled labor force. Prospects for absorption of new and unskilled workers are not good. The resulting industries may add to gains in GNP but not to the share received by the workers.

The problems of agriculture and of manufacturing will not be resolved quickly, and may not be resolved in favor of the urban industrial worker. Paradoxically, it may be more effective to deal with both together than with either separately. Three thrusts in current development thinking are capable of being related in a more comprehensive model with great potential. These include (1) small and medium enterprise development; (2) creation of rural nonfarm employment through agro processing; (3) expansion of the service capacity of small urban places. Each of these has been pursued as a separate project within the Philippines, at least on a pilot basis, but the strengths of self-financing, reinvestment, and generation of backward and forward linkages are needed to obtain rapid growth (the critical element), and these can only be obtained from an integrated, local level approach.

In barest essentials, the strategy requires (1) selection of new crops with high marketing (probably export) potential to be raised by smallholders with (2) technical, financial, and support services from smallest urban places, which (3) are also the locus of small and medium labor intensive enterprises engaged in the processing of the farm products. The process, designated *microurbanization,* has been described at length elsewhere (Hackenberg 1984). The goal is to add value to farm crops while generating non-farm (industrial) employment in a semi-rural environment. As Oshima (1977, 1983) has argued, the trick lies in the selection of specialty crops (for example, nuts, fruits, and vegetables) that may be processed with light portable machinery using electric/gas technology. Ranis (1973) observes that with proper selection, suitable equipment can already be found on the more developed country (MDC) technology shelf.

If successful, the microurbanization strategy will supplement farm income, absorb surplus farm labor in rural-based industries, and retard further migration to overcrowded cities. And, for the urban working class it will generate demand, once again, for their industrial output. A key covert accomplishment of the strategy is its promise to promote political stabilization of the countryside while decelerating the expansion of squatter communities, which will be the sources of future destabilization in urban centers. The attraction of implementing the microurbanization strategy in the Philippines is that the one impediment, the creation of an expensive network of rural infrastructure (roads, electrification, and irrigation), has already been removed. This may be the best, and perhaps the only, lasting achievement of the New Society!

The microurbanization strategy requires research and demonstration. It is not readily embraced by development agencies because (1) it is a small-scale approach that promises no miracles and (2) it crosses sectors within which (but *not* between which) lending usually takes place. The U.S. government could make a very significant contribution by supporting research and demonstration projects with results to be communicated and explained to the leaders and policymakers within the LDCs. This was the successful strategy employed by, for example, the International Rice Research Institute. The example suggests that there is a major role for private agencies, both U.S. and Philippine, to play in this area. One of the tragedies of the New Society was the elimination of private groups from the fields of health, population, housing, and income supplementation as, one by one, they were co-opted or displaced by the Manila bureaucracy.

The Filipinos are organization minded. Capturing their energies, and some of their investment potential, for projects such as microurbanization would put this inherent tendency to good use. Those of us who were present in the Philippines in the late 1960s remember well the Free Farmers' Federation, the Associated Labor Unions of the Philippines, the Christian Family Movement, and the Cursillo, as well as the *Kabataang Makabayan,* the rural irrigation cooperatives, and the urban squatter associations. Newspaper accounts confirm that many of these groups have already begun to reconstitute themselves. If properly guided, some at least could provide vertical integration between class levels, to become a powerful agency for progress once again. Left to their own devices, they may represent the symbolic fracture lines separating the classes into opposing interest groups. No good will come from this.

Bibliography

Asia Yearbook. Hong Kong: Far Eastern Economic Review, 1981.

Asia Yearbook. Hong Kong: Far Eastern Economic Review, 1983.

Asia Yearbook. Hong Kong: Far Eastern Economic Review, 1986.

Callison, C. Stuart. *Economic Assessment of the New Society and Key Problems and Issues Facing the New Republic*. Manila: USAID/Philippines, 1981.

Castillo, Gelia, T. *Beyond Manila: Philippine Rural Problems in Perspective*. Ottawa: International Development Research Centre, 1979.

Canlas, Dante B., et al. *An Analysis of the Philippine Economic Crisis: A Workshop Report*. Quezon City: University of the Philippines School of Economics, 1984.

FEER (Far Eastern Economic Review). Ping, Ho Kyon. "The Mortgaged New Society" and "A Long Time Laying the Cornerstone." Hong Kong: Far Eastern Economic Review (1979) 6:29.

Hackenberg, Robert A. *The Economic Impact of the Banana Export Industry on the Economy of Davao del Norte*. Davao City, Philippines: Davao Research and Planning Foundation, 1977.

Hackenberg, Robert A. "New Patterns of Urbanization in Southeast Asia: An Assessment." *Population and Development Review* (1980) 6:3.

Hackenberg, Robert A. "The Urban Impact of Agropolitan Development: The Changing Regional Metropolis in the Southern Philippines." *Comparative Urban Research* (1983) X:1.

Hackenberg, Robert A. *Microurbanization: An Optimizing Strategy for Rural and Regional Development*. USAID/Washington, 1984.

Hackenberg, Robert A. "Upending Malthus: The Household Role in Philippine Food Gains and Fertility Losses, 1970–1980." in Carol Vlassoff, ed., *Household Demographic Behavior*. Ottawa: International Development Research Centre, 1985.

Hackenberg, Robert A., Arthur D. Murphy, and Henry A. Selby. "The Urban Household in Dependent Development." In *Comparative and Historical Studies of the Domestic Group*, edited by Robert McC. Netting, Richard R. Wilk, and Eric J. Arnould. Berkeley: University of California Press, 1984.

IRTMS (The Inter-Agency Research Team of Mindanao-Sulu). *The Corporate Farm*. Quezon City: National Grains Authority, 1977.

Lynch, Frank. A Bittersweet Taste of Sugar: *A Preliminary Report on the Sugar Industry in Negros Occidental*. Quezon City: Ateneo de Manila University Press, 1970.

Ogawa, Naohiro, and Daniel B. Suits. "An Application of the Harris-Todaro Model to Selected ASEAN Countries." In *Urbanization and Migration in ASEAN Development,* edited by Philip M. Hauser, Daniel B. Suits, and Naohiro Ogawa. Tokyo: National Institute for Research Advancement, 1985.

Oshima, Harry T. Review Article: New Directions in Development Strategies. *Economic Development and Culture Change,* 1977, 25:3, 555-579.

Oshima, Harry T. "The Industrial and Demographic Transitions in East Asia." *Population and Development Review* (1983) 9:4.

Ranis, Gustav. Sharing in Development: *A Program of Employment, Equity and Growth for the Philippines.* Geneva: International labour Office, 1974.

Ranis, Gustav. "Industrial Sector Labor Absorption." *Economic Development and Cultural Change* (1973) 21:3.

Strassman, W. Paul. "Employment in Construction: Multicountry Estimates of Costs and Substitution Elasticities for Small Dwellings." *Economic Development and Cultural Change* (1985) 33:2.

Teilhet-Waldorf, Saral. "Earnings of Self-employed in an Informal Sector: A Case Study of Bangkok." *Economic Development and Cultural Change* (1983) 31:3.

Todaro, Michael. *Internal Migration in Developing Countries.* Geneva: International Labour Organization, 1976.

The World Bank. *The Philippines: Priorities and Prospects for Development.* Washington, D.C.: The World Bank, 1976.

The World Bank. *Aspects of Poverty in the Philippines: A Review and Assessment.* Washington, D.C.: The World Bank, 1980.

The World Bank. *Philippines: Industrial Development Strategy and Policies.* Washington, D.C.: The World Bank, 1980.

The World Bank. *Philippines: Agricultural Credit Sector Review.* Vol. I and II. Washington, D.C.: The World Bank, 1983.

241

Table 1

MANUFACTURING SMEs BY SIZE OF LABOR FORCE: PHILIPPINES, 1974

Size of Labor Force	Number of Firms	Percent of Firms	Number of Employees	Percent of Employees
1– 4	356,319	97.1	890,798	62.6
5– 19	6,522	1.8	78,265	5.5
20– 99	2,358	.6	82,534	5.8
100–199	361	.1	54,074	3.8
200–	1,269	.4	317,329	22.3
TOTALS	366,829	100.0	1,423,000	100.0

Source: IBRD 1980, Statistical Appendix, 72.

Table 2

STRUCTURE OF MANUFACTURING ENTERPRISES BY TYPE:

Type of Enterprise	Value Added		Employer		Investment*	
	N	%	N	%	N	%
Capital-Intensive Industry (1)	4,472	19.4	94	6.7	22,580	45.0
Labor-Intensive Industry (2)	15,090	65.4	433	30.7	21,665	43.2
Cottage Industry (3)	1,350	5.9	844	59.8	125	.3
Mining (4)	2,154	9.3	40	2.8	5,822	11.5
TOTALS	23,066	100.0	1,411	100.0	50,192	100.0

Notes:
(1) Pulp and paper, chemicals, oil products, cement, mineral products, and basic metals.
(2) Food, beverages, and tobacco; textiles and clothing; wood processing; engineering and light industries.
(3) Establishments with fewer than five workers.
(4) Includes metal making other than basic metals.
* Millions of pesos
* Thousands of employees

Source: IBRD 1976, 210-11.

242

Table 3
HOUSEHOLD AND FACTORY EMPLOYMENT IN FIVE LARGE
INDUSTRIES: 1975

Industry Group	Household		Factory		Total No.
	N	%	N	%	
Clothing	363,207	89.6	42,219	10.4	405,426
Food Processing	86,514	43.6	111,693	56.4	198,207
Textiles	128,099	59.6	86,860	40.4	214,959
Wood	58,385	57.2	42,686	42.2	101,071
Furniture	28,410	71.1	11,533	28.9	39,943
All Industries	1,083,854	67.1	531,973	32.9	1,615,827

1. The factory designation applies to all firms with more than five
employees.

Source: IBRD 1980, 37.

Table 4
EMPLOYMENT OF HOUSEHOLD MEMBERS BY POSITION IN
THE HOUSEHOLD, DAVAO CITY, 1972 and 1979
(per 100)

	1972	1979
Male Household Head	93	94
Spouse	23	41
Children in the Household	24	31
Others in the Household	16	27
Total Household Members Employed per 100 Households	156	193

Table 5
METROPOLITAN OCCUPATIONS BOTH SEXES, DAVAO CITY
(Percent)

FORMAL SECTOR	1972	1979
1. Professional		
A. Teachers	6.3	3.3
B. Others	2.8	3.6
2. Retail Sales/Clerical		
A. Sales	6.9	7.8
B. Clerical	13.0	12.2
3. Trades		
A. Skilled	4.6	4.8
B. Semiskilled	18.3	16.8
C. Unskilled	12.5	4.6
4. Industrial Farming	0.0	.6
Subtotal	64.4	53.7
INFORMAL SECTOR		
1. Traditional Sales	16.7	22.3
2. Traditional Services	14.3	19.7
3. Agriculture/Fishing	4.6	4.3
Subtotal	35.6	46.3
TOTALS	100.0	100.0

Table 6
OCCUPATIONAL DISTRIBUTION: DAVAO CITY,
1972 AND 1979
(Percent)

	1972	1979
1. Sales		
Market Vendors, Peddlers, Buy-Sell		
Merchants	11.5	17.2
Owners, Small or Medium Business	6.3	5.1
Sales Representatives	2.5	2.2
Salespersons	1.9	2.7
Business Managers	1.2	1.3
Purchasing Agents, Collectors	.3	1.5
	23.7	30.1
2. Services		
Mechanics/Automotive	5.1	2.3
Tailors/Dressmakers	4.2	2.7
Maintenancemen/Security	4.1	3.5
Personal Services Workers	3.8	11.0
Food Services Workers	2.5	2.4
	19.7	21.9
3. Manufacturing/Construction		
Factory Workers	11.3	5.3
Building Trades Workers	6.4	6.9
Foremen/Contractors	1.3	0.0
	19.0	12.2
4. Clerical		
Office Workers	8.7	9.5
Accountants/Auditors	2.9	.8
Office Superintendents	.9	1.9
	12.5	12.2

5. Professional/Technical

Education Employees	6.3	3.3
Engineers	.7	.7
Lawyers	.6	.3
Clergymen	.5	.0
Medical Technicians	.4	.8
Doctors	.3	.2
Executives	.3	1.6
	9.1	6.9

6. Transportation/Communications

Drivers	7.5	7.8
Communications Workers	.8	.9
	8.3	8.7

7. Agriculture/Fishing

Farmers	3.2	3.6
Fishermen	.8	1.4
	4.0	5.0

8. Shipping

Stevedores	1.8	2.2
Sailors	.1	.9
	1.9	3.1

9. Unclassified

	1.8	0.0
TOTAL	100.0	100.0

13

The View from the Youth Sector

Benjamin N. Muego

It has been sixty-five days since Corazon C. Aquino, riding the crest of "people power," wrested power away from Ferdinand E. Marcos and his cabal of corrupt generals and cronies. While the initial euphoria which enveloped the Philippines after the ouster of the Marcoses has abated somewhat, it is clear that the Aquino government still has the support and trust of the majority of the Filipino people, despite recent anti-regime demonstrations organized and orchestrated by Marcos loyalists who insist that Ferdinand E. Marcos is still, technically and legally, the constitutionally elected president of the Republic of the Philippines.

The Aquino government has a grace period of at least one hundred days, according to a prominent Filipino educator,[1] to make its presence felt and to initiate reforms and come up with concrete and better alternatives to the programs of the deposed regime. If the Aquino government appears in the view of the general public to be incapable of decisively and efficiently addressing the Philippines' problems, the "honeymoon period" is likely to be cut short and the government, perhaps even Corazon Aquino herself, will begin to lose credibility. If and when this occurs, criticism will more than likely come first from the Philippines' large and militant youth sector.

About a million and a half of these potential critics are students in some fifty universities, colleges, and technical schools located in the

---

[1]Andrew B. Gonzalez, FSC, president of De La Salle University (Manila), in a speech entitled "The Role of the University in the Task of Social Reconstruction in the Philippines," given at the University of Toledo (Toledo, Ohio) on April 3, 1986.

Greater Manila area.[2] There are also over a dozen "convent schools," run by religious corporations and orders.[3] Other than the state-owned University of the Philippines, Polytechnic University of the Philippines (formerly known as the Philippine College of Commerce), Philippine Normal College, Philippine College of Arts and Trades, and the Philippine Merchant Marine Academy, all others are private institutions primarily operated by their owners for profit.

The majority of the students who reside in the area of Metro Manila known as the "university belt,"[4] are transients; *provincianos* sent by their parents to the big city to obtain a college education and hopefully, subsequently, to land a suitable and well-paying job. This is significant in that the same students usually return more or less politicized to their home towns and barrios during school breaks or after graduation and have become more sophisticated about the nature and ramifications of various political events. While it is true, therefore, that the "people power" revolution of February 24 was essentially confined to Metro Manila (in other words, an urban phenomenon), the students who manned the barricades at the approaches of Camp Crame (the headquarters of the Philippine Constabulary) and on Mendiola Street fronting Malacanang Palace, represent a good cross section of the national community.

Should the students, as some political observers predict, choose to rise against the Aquino government in the near future, it would be inaccurate to dismiss such an uprising as one of limited scope or in the

---

[2]There are at least twenty-nine major universities in the Metro Manila area, some, like Far Eastern University and the University of East, with enrollments in excess of 60,000 students. Other major universities in Metro Manila are: the University of the Philippines, University of Santo Tomas, Centro Escolar University, National University, University of Manila, Philippine Women's University, Mapua Institute of Technology, Arellano University, De La Salle University, Ateneo de Manila University, Manila Central University, FEATI University, Polytechnic University of the Philippines, Araneta University, Adamson University.

[3]Some of the better known convent schools are: Maryknoll College, St. Theresa College, St. Paul College, College of the Holy Spirit, Assumption College, St. Joseph College, and St. Escolastica.

[4]The "university belt" is a rectangular area bounded on the north by Espana Street, on the south by the Pasig River, and on the east by Malacanang Palace. Azcarraga Avenue intersects the "belt" from east to west. There are at least twelve major universities in the area.

same cavalier fashion that a key Aquino adviser treated a recent pro-Marcos demonstration at Rizal Park. The youth sector, usually spearheaded by students, tends to be more determined in the pursuit of its declared objectives. For instance, it was the youth who kept the opposition to the Marcos regime alive during the darkest days of martial rule. The *Philippine Collegian*, the official newspaper of the student body of the University of the Philippines, encouraged opposition to the Marcos regime, prompting the military authorities to arrest and detain the newspaper's editor.[5] The other members of the editorial staff were also threatened with physical harm if the newspaper did not stop printing anti-Marcos editorials and opinion columns. Undaunted, the students of the University of the Philippines fought on, employing such techniques of civil disobedience as beating on their plates with their knives and forks, in orchestrated "noise barrages" at the university's cafeterias and dining halls.

While it is true that the Filipino youth have not, by and large, been as forceful as youth activists in Indonesia (who were instrumental in bringing down the Dutch regime and, later, Sukarno himself) and in South Korea (where student riots forced the resignation of the Syngman Rhee government), or as adventurist and doctrinaire as the Revolutionary Red Guards of the People's Republic of China during the Great Proletarian Cultural Revolution, or as violence-prone as Japan's *zengakuren*, the youth of the Philippines do have a strong revolutionary tradition. The *ilustrados* who organized and carried out the Propaganda Movement against Spanish rule were men in their late twenties and early thirties; so too were the proletarian revolutionaries who constituted the bulk of the *Katipunan's* membership. In the mid-1930s, the youth leader Wenceslao Q. Vinzons organized a group called the "Young Philippines," which among other things, dreamed of a *Malaya Irredenta*, a supra-national union of all Asians of Malay heritage. In the 1960s and 1970s, other youth leaders followed in Vinzons' footsteps, rallying the general public on a number of key issues and questions such as excessive congressional allowances, Philippine involvement in the Vietnam War, and the ongoing call for a total

---

[5]The editor of the *Philippine Collegian* at the time was Abraham M. Sarmiento, Jr. He was placed under house arrest after having been released from detention. Not long afterwards, he died of a heart ailment (his associates at the University of the Philippines believed that this might have been aggravated by his arrest and detention).

reexamination of the Philippines' "special" relations with the United States. The youth sector was also the first to enthusiastically embrace the cause of Philippine nationalism which the late senator Claro Mayo Recto championed in the mid-1950s amidst overall public indifference. Several years later, this resurgent nationalism—a throwback to the fierce nationalism of Manuel Luis Quezon in the struggle for independence from the United States—would be embodied in an organization called *Kabataang Makabayan*, led by Jose Ma. Sison,[6] founder and putative leader of the revitalized Communist Party of the Philippines. Shortly after the declaration of martial law in 1972, the *Kabataang Makabayan* was outlawed by the Marcos regime and branded as a "front organization" for the Communist Party of the Philippines.

A KEY ROLE FOR THE YOUTH SECTOR

Undoubtedly, the youth sector played a major role in the events of February 7-25, 1986. Indeed, it was the youthful and idealistic young officers and men of the Reform the Armed Forces Movement (RAM), some of them barely out of their teens, who forced Ferdinand E. Marcos's vaunted military constituency to unravel. The Reform the Armed Forces Movement, credited by many as the crucial element that made "people power" possible, was dominated by young commissioned officers, recent graduates of the prestigious Philippine Military Academy (PMA).

These young military reformers became convinced soon after the brutal assassination of former Senator Benigno S. Aquino, Jr., in August 1983, that the only road to positive change within the Armed Forces of the Philippines (AFP) was the dismantling of the corrupt military network established by AFP Chief of Staff Fabian C. Ver. To these young men and women, the stakes were a lot larger than their own careers—the honor and integrity of the military profession itself. Thus, the defection on February 23, 1986, of Defense Minister Juan Ponce Enrile and AFP Vice-chief of Staff Fidel V. Ramos was not the coup de grace that signalled the collapse of the Marcos regime; the much earlier establishment of RAM was the crucial element. The

---

[6]Jose Ma. Sison, putative founder and chairman of the Communist Party of the Philippines, was taken into custody in 1978 and released in March 1986 by President Aquino. Sison was an instructor at the Lyceum of the Philippines when he founded the *Kabataang Makabayan*. Jose Sison is a graduate of the University of the Philippines.

Ponce Enrile-Ramos defection was merely frosting on the cake—a
culmination, as it were, of months of painstaking organizational work
by the leaders and supporters of RAM.

The civilian youth, on the other hand, were just as active. Unlike
previous anti-government uprisings, however, the events of February
22-25, described by a well known Filipino political scientist[7] as a
"global communications spectacular," was, oddly enough, led by
students from Maryknoll College, Ateneo de Manila University and
Assumption College, all Catholic institutions, not by students from the
University of the Philippines. Students at the University of the Philippines were reportedly torn between the "moderate" University Student
Council, on the one hand, and the more radical student groups on
campus, on the other. In the past, it was usually students from the
University of the Philippines and other state-run educational institutions like the Polytechnic University of the Philippines who were at the
forefront of student protest. A possible explanation for this role reversal of sorts lies in the class character of these disparate institutions.
While the majority of students at the University of the Philippines tends
to be predominantly upper-lower or lower-middle class (that is, children of government employees, teachers, military personnel, and academics), students at convent schools like Maryknoll College and Assumption College tend to be from upper-middle, lower-upper,
middle-upper or upper-upper class backgrounds; their parents for the
most part were never beholden to the Marcos regime for their survival.

As public opposition to Ferdinand Marcos and his regime intensified, however, and as it became clear that Marcos and his supporters in
the AFP and the Commission on Elections (COMELEC) were determined to thwart the will of the Filipino people (as expressed in the
presidential election of February 7, 1986), students from the University
of the Philippines became more vocal and militant. Dramatic and
political events such as the establishment of a "UP Hall of Shame,"
showcasing university alumni who have "sold out to Ferdinand E.
Marcos and American imperialism" created a lot of negative publicity
for Marcos and his "cronies." In addition, UP students boycotted their
classes and, with the cooperation of sympathetic professors and admin-

---

[7]Jose V. Abueva, director of the United Nations University's New York Liaison Office
from a presentation in the Graduate School and University Center of the City University of New York's Ralph Bunche Institute on the United Nations, March 24, 1986.

istrators, held "classrooms in the streets," to further dramatize the gravity of the situation as the students saw it and focus public attention on Ferdinand Marcos's blatant attempt to perpetuate himself in power.

Of course it cannot be gainsaid that the unusual militancy of the convent school students was spurred by the prominent and overt role the church hierarchy took vis-a-vis the Marcos regime. The archbishop of Manila, Jaime Cardinal Sin, personally broadcast appeals to the Catholic faithful on February 24 and 25 urging them to turn out en masse at pre-designated points to "protect" the mutinous troops from possible counterattack by Marcos loyalist forces. When students in Metro Manila's Catholic schools responded to Cardinal Sin's appeal, they were presumably doing so out of personal conviction as well as obedience to their spiritual leader. By this time, Sin and the rest of the ecclesiastical community had disavowed the legality of the Marcos government and openly advocated its overthrow. The central role played by the Catholic Educational Association of the Philippines (CEAP) was noteworthy as well in eliciting enthusiastic response from the usually conservative and apathetic convent school student population. Apparently the latter was not lost on Corazon Aquino, because when Jaime C. Laya tendered his "courtesy resignation" as minister of education and culture, Aquino was quick to appoint the president of Maryknoll College to head this important cabinet ministry."[8]

The student demonstrators rallied other youth to join the "revolution" and helped transport them to the various staging areas. A hard core of youth leaders and their followers—by then seasoned veterans of the so called "parliament in the streets"—manned the hastily built barricades, while still others performed various logistical chores, such as distributing food and other essentials to the mutinous forces and their civilian protectors. In like manner, thousands of young people helped secure radio and television stations after these strategic targets fell into rebel hands. At commandeered radio stations throughout Metro Manila and in the studios of Channels 4 and 9, students and other youth volunteers turned into instant cameramen, grips, script-writers, and even announcers.

[8]The new minister of education, culture, and sports is Lourdes Quisumbing, erstwhile president of Maryknoll College, vice-president of the Catholic Educational Association of the Philippines, and president of the Philippine Accrediting Association of Colleges and Universities, an institution which, although formally separate from CEAP, is made up of educators from the CEAP.

POTENTIAL FOR DISSENT IN THE YOUTH SECTOR

The first indication of the youth sector's discontent with the Aquino government surfaced soon after Ferdinand and Imelda Marcos (and their retinue of relatives, servants, "cronies," and bodyguards) arrived in Hawaii and the appointment of Juan Ponce Enrile as minister of defense was announced. Two prominent professionals, Edmundo Garcia and Carolina Galicia-Hernandez, with known ties to the left wing of the youth sector, openly criticized the Ponce Enrile appointment."[9] Garcia and Hernandez both warned that if this was a harbinger of things to come and if the new government did not demonstrate greater sensitivity to the youth sector's fears and concerns, "it may not be long before the youth returned to the barricades."

The opposition to Juan Ponce Enrile among the militant youth and elsewhere centers on his (Ponce Enrile's) role as the martial law regime's principal "hatchetman." Youth leaders point out that Ponce Enrile remained loyal to Ferdinand Marcos until his defection on February 23, 1986, the eve of the Marcos regime's collapse. Indeed, some youth leaders argue that Ponce Enrile defected only "after he saw the handwriting on the wall" and realized that his salvation lay in his severance of relations with his commander-in-chief of twenty years. Evidently, these youth leaders are not totally convinced of Ponce Enrile's sincerity.

The left wing of the youth sector sees Ponce Enrile as an unrepentant ideological hardliner while some long-time Aquino supporters still bristle at Ponce Enrile's unsuccessful attempt to tar Benigno Aquino, Jr. as a "CIA agent and stooge" in April 1978, in the midst of the campaign for seats in the interim *batasang pambansa*.[10] Other youth leaders on the right end of the spectrum question Ponce Enrile's

[9]Edmundo Garcia is a former Jesuit, while Carolina Galicia-Hernandez is the chairperson of the Department of Political Science at the University of the Philippines. Having done her doctoral dissertation at SUNY-Buffalo on the Philippine military Galicia-Hernandez is an expert on that subject.

[10]The late Benigno S. Aquino, Jr., headed a slate of candidates under the banner of "Laban" (the Filipino word for "fight") in the April 1978 election to the interim *Batasang Pambansa*. Although he campaigned from his jail cell at Fort Bonifacio, Aquino polled the largest number of opposition votes. In an effort to further discredit him in the eyes of the public, President Marcos, through his Defense Minister Juan Ponce Enrile, produced "documents" that purportedly showed Aquino's link with the CIA.

motives; many see him as an opportunist who switched his political allegiance only after it had become clear that Marcos was doomed and, conversely, that Corazon Aquino's succession to the presidency was all but inevitable.

Youth leaders from the convent schools, meanwhile, recall Ponce Enrile's pivotal role (along with former Minister of State for Political Affairs Leonardo B. Perez) in repeated clashes between the Marcos regime and the church's hierarchy on such matters as "unwarranted raids" on Catholic schools (including seminaries), custody of priests and nuns alleged to have committed "subversive acts," and the harassment and persecution of the leaders (both lay and clerical) of the Basic Christian Communities.[11] The Catholic Bishops Conference of the Philippines (CBCP), it will be recalled, voted unilaterally to withdraw from the Church-Military Liaison Committee (established in 1973 as a vehicle to monitor abuses by military personnel) in January 1983, partly to protest Ponce Enrile's high-handedness.

Other Aquino appointees to key cabinet positions so far, with the possible exception of presidential spokesman Rene A. V. Saguisag, Executive Secretary Joker K. Arroyo and Labor Minister Augusto Sanchez[12] are old-line politicians or representatives of the traditional economic and cultural elite. Many are beginning to wonder whether the Aquino government is serious about radically restructuring the Philippine polity. Indeed, there are even those who suggest that the so-called "changes" are merely cosmetic—a stylized *rigodon de honor* of new names and faces and of recycled names and faces.

In comparative terms, students from the University of the Philippines and other state-run institutions of higher learning and their non-student supporters appear to be more critical of the Aquino govern-

---

[11]For a good account of the church-state clashes in 1982 and 1983, including the persecution of laity and clergy involved in the Basic Christian Communities (BCC) or *kristianong katilingban*, as these were known in Panay and Negros, see Robert L. Youngblood, "Church and State in the New Republic," a paper presented at the 1983 Annual Meeting of the Association for Asian Studies in San Francisco, California, March 24-27, 1983. Juan Ponce Enrile, along with Minister of State for Political Affairs Leonardo B. Perez, led the attack on the church and on Jaime Cardinal Sin.

[12]Rene A.V. Saguisag, Joker K. Arroyo, and Augusto Sanchez are representatives of the so-called cause-oriented groups in the cabinet of President Aquino. All three were perennial defense counsels for persons arrested, detained, and tortured by the Marcos regime during and after martial law.

ment than their counterparts in the convent schools and other Catholic universities and colleges. The former suggest that for change to truly occur, the philosophical and ideological foundations of Philippine society must be seriously reexamined and, if necessary, altered. The convent school students, on the other hand, appear more willing to give the new government the benefit of the doubt; President Aquino needs more time than just a hundred days to search for alternatives and lasting solutions to the nation's problems.

With the schools scheduled to reopen in early June, the issue that is most likely to trigger nationwide student protest is the escalating cost of college education. Not only are tuition fees going up, but so too are related costs, such as books and educational supplies, board and lodging, and transportation. The hardest hit will be students in state-owned universities and colleges whose parents are by and large at the lower end of the economic scale, in contrast to the parents of those who go to expensive schools like Assumption College, Maryknoll College, Ateneo de Manila University, and the like.

In a paradoxical way, the spate of student protest expected in June may well be inspired by the "people power" phenomenon that cata-pulted Corazon Aquino to power. By deposing Marcos and restoring participatory democracy to the Philippines, President Aquino has cre-ated a totally new set of expectations—that the national government will listen to public protest, that the national government will provide, and that the national government will deal with all constituencies fairly and equitably. If only for this reason, the Aquino government cannot afford to appear less than resolute or to be perceived as lacking in compassion.

Yet whatever it does or however it proceeds to deal with the expected student unrest, the Aquino government will more than likely find itself in a double bind. If it chooses to do nothing (by letting the private colleges and universities raise tuition fees as planned), the Aquino government will be perceived to side with the rich and may even be suspected of paying off a campaign debt to the Catholic Educational Association of the Philippines (CEAP) and Opus Dei,[13] two sectarian

[13]Opus Dei supported and sponsored data collection and analysis by the Center for Research Communication headed by Harvard-trained economist Bernardo Villegas. The CRC helped formulate and develop arguments, and position papers which were later used by the Aquino campaign to counter claims of economic success by the Marcos regime.

organizations that played key roles in the Aquino presidential campaign. If, on the other hand, the Aquino government chose to freeze education costs at current levels (assuming that a legal mechanism to implement such a policy exists), this would be tantamount to government subsidization of private schools, a policy never before tried in the Philippines. Moreover, the impact of this policy on the Philippines' dismal fiscal and budgetary situation would almost certainly be catastrophic.

The issue of skyrocketing educational costs has the potential to polarize the youth sector and Philippine society itself. President Aquino's social and economic background, and those of her inner circle of economic advisers—Jaime Ongpin, Ramon del Rosario, Jr., and Jose Concepcion, all multi-millionaires—will be perceived by the general public, rightly or wrongly, as an obstacle to a fair and equitable solution of the problem. And it will not be at all surprising if as a group Catholic school students (especially in such expensive schools as Assumption College, Maryknoll College, Saint Paul College, and the College of the Holy Spirit, to name only a few) boycott or shun such anti-government demonstrations, and in so doing induce a class-based cleavage in the student-youth sector.

Ideological questions such as the role of the government vis-a-vis the economy, the nature of the relationship between the Philippines and the United States (including the matter of the military bases), the Philippines' relationship with countries of the socialist block, and the Philippines' twin insurgencies, temporarily relegated to secondary status, are bound to thrust themselves into center stage sooner or later. In the past, Catholic school students tended to take a conservative stand on these issues. In general, these students favored a strong relationship with the United States, particularly in matters relating to defense and security (and they therefore supported the retention of the military bases at Clark and Subic). As far as the economy is concerned, the position that Catholic school students are most likely to endorse is the total or nearly-total privatization of the economy, the current philosophy being promoted by Finance Minister Jaime Ongpin.

While by no means monolithic, students in secular educational institutions like the University of the Philippines tended in the past to take positions diametrically opposite that of their counterparts in sectarian schools. For instance, students from the University of the Philippines led the opposition to Philippine participation in the Vietnam war, supported a total reexamination of Philippine-American relations and urged the abrogation of the Parity Rights Amendment to the 1935 Philippine Constitution. Students at the University of the Philippines also enthusiastically supported the reorientation of Philippine foreign policy by the Marcos regime in the mid-1970s, that is, a strong accent on Asia and the establishment of commercial and diplomatic relations with nations of the socialist block.

These policy and ideological differences between the two student camps were effectively muted and set aside during the martial law period because of common opposition to Marcos. With Marcos, the common adversary, gone and his regime overthrown, it is possible that the old sectarian-secular dichotomy fueled by class and religious differences could resurface. If so, old stereotypes and myths, to a degree fostered by older Filipinos and the popular press—that the University of the Philippines is a "hotbed of communism and radicalism" or that the sectarian schools receive direct instructions from the Holy See and official Washington, D.C., or that all students at the University of the Philippines are communists or that all "convent school" students (the so-called "colegialas") are reactionaries—may well regain currency.

CONCLUSIONS AND OBSERVATIONS

Demographically, the Philippines is getting younger and younger, with over half of the population being under the age of thirty. This suggests that the current government in Manila has to pay greater attention to the concerns and needs of the youth sector. A sizable portion of this sector—about one and a half million—are enrolled in the nation's numerous colleges and universities and vocational-technical schools. Not surprisingly, therefore, the Philippines has one of the highest ratios of university students in relation to the total population in the whole world.

For well or ill, education has always been a passion to the Filipino. Even during the Spanish period when as a matter of state policy Filipinos (or *indios* as they were contemptuously referred to by the Spaniards) were denied schooling beyond the *caton* and catechism, some Filipinos, the *ilustrados* or *principalias*, somehow managed to educate themselves. The plebeian leader of the armed revolution against Spain, Andres Bonifacio, taught himself how to read and write and was familiar with such Western concepts as democracy, political freedom, and individual liberties. With the advent of American rule in 1901 and the institution of a system of free universal education, Filipinos sent their children to school in massive numbers, and came to view education as a means towards political and cultural emancipation as well as a ladder to upward social mobility.

Today, the same motivations continue to animate millions of parents and their children, and as a result the Philippines is honeycombed with thousands of institutions of higher learning offering a smorgasbord of degree programs and curricula ranging from the associate to the baccalaureate to the doctorate. And because over 90 percent of Philippine educational institutions are privately owned and administered and almost entirely dependent on revenues generated from tuition and other student fees, the quality of education offered often leaves a lot to be desired. Professors are for the most part poorly trained and woefully underpaid, and college graduates, except those graduating from the prestigious schools (University of the Philippines, De La Salle University, Ateneo de Manila University, Maryknoll College, Silliman University, and so on), are ill-prepared for the rigors and demands of the job market and the professions.

Yet because of the widespread belief that education is the key to economic success and social acceptance, the Philippines has a large pool of college graduates (the largest in Southeast Asia) who lack the requisite skills to secure gainful employment or make it on their own. Wittingly or unwittingly, Philippine society has created a "revolution of rising expectations," not only among the youth but in the larger society. Understandably, these graduates expect to find jobs and positions "commensurate with their skills" and academic training. If unable to find the jobs they feel their diplomas "entitle" them to, they become restive and angry—easy prey for charlatans who exploit the frustrations of the youth for their own selfish interests.

In the present case of the Aquino government, youth expectations are even higher. This is because young people played an instrumental role in the political movement that culminated in the overthrow of the Marcos regime with its surfeit of corruption, chicanery, and special privilege. Because they played such an active role in the "revolution" and were taught to expect better things under the new dispensation, the Aquino government will be well advised to listen carefully to the youth sector's concerns. The government cannot afford to alienate the youth or be perceived of as uncaring.

If the Aquino government is not able to produce instant results for whatever reasons, the new government will be in for a rash of student demonstrations in the future. Already there are signs that the youth sector is unhappy with President Aquino's initial cabinet appointments, especially of those individuals associated with the corruption and repression of the Marcos regime. The Aquino government, in the patois of the American mainstream, indeed "has its work cut out for it" in both the short and long term.

Because of the euphoria that enveloped the country in the aftermath of the dramatic overthrow of the much-despised Marcos regime, the general public, including the youth, are apparently willing to wait and afford the Aquino government an opportunity to establish the legal and physical infrastructure necessary to reconstruct the country. As soon as that euphoria wears off, however, and if the promised reforms have neither materialized nor are believed to be forthcoming, the honeymoon period will come to a halt and the Aquino government will be faced with public skepticism, if not outright hostility.

If and when this happens, expect the youth sector to once again play a vanguard role. The youth will spearhead anti-regime activity, as they have always done in the past, because they see their stakes in the system as greater than those of any other social sector. It is inevitable that the youth sector will be polarized, with one group (possibly the students in the convent schools) supporting the Aquino government or opting to remain neutral, and the other group reactivating the "parliament in the streets" that worked so well against the Marcos regime.

It will be interesting to see how the Aquino government responds to its first public challenge, especially if organized by the same elements that helped to put it in power. The manner in which the Aquino government deals with such organized and cause-oriented opposition may well determine whether it will survive or go the same way as the regime that it replaced. The irony of democracy, after all, is that it includes a full panoply of mechanisms and tools that could be used, depending on one's motives, to either assure its success or bring about its destruction.

14

Political Socialization, Filipino Values, and Prospects for Democracy

Justin J. Green

The recent change of regime in the Philippines from the martial law, quasi-authoritarian, semilegitimate government of Ferdinand Marcos to the millenarian redemptive government headed by Corazon Aquino contained many of the elements typical of Philippine revolutions and peasant movements of the past. Among these was the courage of Filipinos, who, as in the revolution of 1896, the Japanese occupation of World War II, the Huk rebellion, and other movements too numerous to mention, once again demonstrated their willingness to sacrifice their lives for a cause. In some of these rebellions the cause was secular nationalism, in others restoration of peasant lands and status, in others still the restoration of faith and/or the creation of a heaven on earth. All of these, as Ian Buruma has recently put it, have been characterized by the notion that "Mother Filipinas must be redeemed by faith and sacrifice, by death and resurrection. Such acts have been led by a succession of messiahs — promising paradise and freedom."[1]

That the above is true of Mrs. Aquino's accession can be illustrated by quoting one of the most secular of all Filipinos, Raul Manglapus, who upon his return to the Philippines following Marcos's departure said, "We have a new goddess in the pantheon of freedom and the name of that goddess is Corazon Aquino. I have come to pay homage to that goddess." Then reflecting more than half a century of American influence in the Philippines Manglapus said, "We are going to be the greatest democracy in the world."[2] While it is true that such hyperbole could be attributed to the emotions of the moment it is also probable that in his view of Mrs. Aquino and his vision of the future he may have

---

[1] Ian Buruma, "Who Can Redeem Mother Filipinas?" *New York Review of Books*, January 17, 1986, p. 16.
[2] *Philadelphia Inquirer*, March 1, 1986, p. 8A.

been speaking for many of his fellow Filipinos. It is Manglapus' uniting of two Filipino themes, the messianic and the democratic, that provides a focus for this essay.

There are of course many interesting issues regarding prospects for democracy raised by Mrs. Aquino's triumph. Among these are economic well being, reduction of economic inequalities, the growth of an autonomous bourgeoisie, the role of the United States, the role of the church, and the growth of the NPA—some of which are being examined by other articles in this volume. Our purpose here is to examine only one of these issues, the relationship of political culture to democratic prospects. In so doing we will attempt to answer two questions: (1) What values, attitudes, and norms do Filipinos, children or adults, learn that relate to political institutions and behavior? (2) Are the values Filipinos learn and the ways they behave supportive of past, present, and possibly future democratic institutions?

First a caveat: Despite almost thirty years of effort, political scientists have not yet reached universal agreement regarding the relationship between when, how, and from whom political norms are learned and what is learned. Nor do they agree on how what is learned, commonly called political culture, is translated into political behavior, nor how political culture and behavior patterns affect political institutions. This argument is lengthy as well as unresolved and it will therefore not be repeated here. Rather, this writer assumes that what people learn as children affects what they learn as adults. What is learned in childhood is mediated by adult learning, and thus a set of values, attitudes, and beliefs is inculcated that is held in common by a large enough group of people to be labeled a political culture. The resultant political culture provides a set of parameters which effectively limits an individual's range of behavior in such a way that certain kinds of social institutions are favored at the expense of other kinds. Once again the reader is warned that this model is not universally accepted. If agreed upon, however, the argument that follows has strong intellectual force.

One more issue remains before we begin examining Philippine values and their relationship to democratic institutions: how shall we define democracy or recognize democratic political institutions? There is a great deal of scholarly disagreement about the nature of democracy. Western and particularly American scholars have been accused and perhaps rightfully of attempting to impose their notions of democracy on other nations. Although scholars from many traditions might agree with the Greeks that democracy is government of the many, this agreement falls apart when each prescribes how participation by the many should be implemented. Despite this disagreement, in the Philippine context the resolution of this issue is easier. One of the legacies of a half-century of American tutelage is a rather broad agreement between Filipinos and Americans on many of the institutions and practices that are necessary for a democracy. Also, through the public educational system they implemented Americans made a special effort to reorient existing Philippine values and inculcate new ones that might best sustain the democratic institutions that Filipinos and Americans together were building. Given this agreement on institutions and the attempt to shape Filipino values to fit the American mold, it makes sense to compare Filipino values with American values as part of our attempt to understand the goodness of fit between Filipino values and democratic institutions.

In what follows we will consider three categories of Philippine values in relation to democratic institutions:

1. Values and attitudes that emerge from and reinforce the dominant Filipino social structure; patron-client dyads

2. Values and attitudes, both institutional and personal, that exist in the broader political culture, that is, separate from those explained by social strucutre

3. A set of psychological orientations whose roots, though poorly understood, are considered to underpin what Almond and Verba called the civic culture; that particular kind of political culture able to sustain a stable democratic government

Following this examination we will consider the relationships among socialization, value change, and prospects for democracy.

SOCIAL STRUCTURE AND VALUES

The literature describing Filipino social structure as made up of patron-client dyads or, in Eric Wolfe's terminology, vertical dyadic, multi-stranded relationships is so well known and understood that few would disagree that Philippine politics before martial law could be described as the interaction of patron-client-based factional networks.[3] What also seems clear is that Marcos since 1972 had attempted to replace autonomous local networks with one nationally integrated network. Regardless of whether he succeeded or not, some scholars are now saying that the victory of Corazon Aquino represents the triumph of pluralistic interest-group politics and/or of mass and symbolic politics over network politics. With this victory it is said the Philippines has a new opportunity to implement democratic institutions.

Does the Aquino victory mean the end of factional politics? On the one hand, Marcos's failure at the polls may have resulted from his failure to commit sufficient resources to maintain his national network. It could also be that over time many local leaders had withheld their own resources from network maintenance and had become totally dependent on Manila. With hard times Manila could not or would not provide, and thus KBL networks had begun to deteriorate. On the other hand, it could also mean that over time and with KBL ineffectiveness local opposition politicians may have begun to rebuild their own networks.

Lacking data, these explanations are mere conjecture. However, even if networks played only a minor role in Mrs. Aquino's victory, the theories that explain patron-client social structure suggest that network politics will remain important. Though patron-client dyads may have less meaning for middle-class Filipinos, it is likely they will remain important to those Filipinos who live at society's margin. As James Scott has pointed out, peasants (in my view poor workers as well) attempt to strengthen their dyadic ties when undergoing economic stress—surely the current condition of the Philippine economy.[4] Instead of disappearing, patronage pyramids may be at present in a state of flux, with many peasants and workers freed of old client obligations as patrons are unable or unwilling to provide the resources necessary to support their patron role. As a result, unattached clients, given the economic uncertainties of the times, are now seeking new attachments

[3]Eric Wolfe, *Peasants* (Englewood Cliffs, New Jersey: Prentice Hall, 1966). For example, see among others Carl H. Landé, "Networks and Groups in Southeast Asia: Some Observations on the Group Theory of Politics," *American Political Science Review*, 67: 1973 (pp. 103-127).

[4]James C. Scott, *The Moral Economy of the Peasant, Rebellion and Subsistence in Southeast Asia* (New Haven, Connecticut: Yale University Press, 1976).

to insure their survival. The mechanisms which attach patrons to clients, *utang na loob* (the debt without end), *Hiya* (shame), and *Compradrazgo* (joint parenthood) and its rituals, are still intact. And since networked clients translate into votes and votes lead to political power, which in turn has economic payoffs, it is likely that peasants and workers following well-understood and positively sanctioned behavior patterns will find new actors willing to accept the burden of patronship or old ones anxious to restore shattered ties. Though the possibility that networks have had their day cannot be ignored, it seems more likely that for the foreseeable future they will remain a major force in Philippine politics.

After making this argument the next question is, are patron-client politics antithetical to democratic institutions? After all, this kind of relationship has accounted for, and perhaps still accounts for, political behavior in the wards of some of America's great cities. The critique of patron-client politics and democratic institutions, whether in the Philippines or in an American ward, however, usually makes the following points:

1. The vertical nature of patron-client dyads leads to communication patterns (greater flow from top to bottom, limited horizontal communication, politeness language, and so on) which tend to preserve status gaps and class divisions.

2. The multi-stranded ties that bind patrons and clients together require attention and nurturing. This leads to exclusivity and the failure to develop meaningful cross-pressuring ties through which the compromises necessary for the stability of democratic institutions are fashioned.

3. The form that political demands take in a patron-client system are particular rather than universal. People seek personal rewards from government rather than the group rewards which tend to build interest group solidarity. In patron-client systems these particularistic rewards are not seen as a form of corruption, nepotism, favoritism, or cronyism, and unless they exceed some unstated norm are positively rather than negatively regarded. If a good patron provides whatever he can for his extended family, his close friends, and his followers before considering the needs of the larger society, then the pejorative content is emptied out of words like "corruption," "nepotism," and "cronyism."

4. The comparative values of things exchanged between patron and client are generally seen as unequal by objective observers. To the actors they appear more equal. Thus to outsiders the rewards that clients get may be seen as inadequate although clients themselves may deem them quite worthy. This tendency not only means that a vast number of people are relatively content with a highly unequal distribution of society's rewards but that there is not a great clamor for expanding the base of the distribution pyramid.

5. Clients in patron-client networks are highly mobilizable for political participation. The purpose of this participation is determined, however, by patrons; and when there is no patron stimulating participation, clients remain subdued and pursue their political interests only through their ties with the patron. Thus, public opinion, which is often an arbiter of outcomes in democratic systems, is articulated only by patrons in patron-client systems.

6. Finally, the multi-stranded nature of the ties that bind patrons to clients mean that the networks they form are highly stable so long as both patron and client meet their obligations. In fact, the more ties that bind the two together, the greater the brake on change and the more upsetting change becomes. Democratic institutions which depend upon an individual's ability to shift his loyalties from one group to another as his perception of his hierarchically ordered interests changes are thus incompatible with the behaviors that sustain patron-client networks. In networks such loyalty shifts would be seen as leading to alienation and anomie.

In summation, a good many of the values and behaviors embedded in patron-client dyads are at best nonsupportive of the kind of democratic institutions that have existed in the Philippines until now. At worst they undermine some of the critical foundations of these institutions.

In the pre-martial-law era, the democratic institutions that were a legacy of American colonialism did not perform very well. Since the elites who lead factions were reasonably well united in beliefs and purposes, elections were merely means by which access to political rewards changed hands, ensuring that no single family gained ascendancy over the entire Philippines.

Although the pluralism of interests the American system was supposed to accommodate never came into meaningful existence, the pluralism of factions did provide adequate rewards to those at the top and predictable, if inadequate, rewards to those at the bottom of the pyramid. Until martial law the factions were based on a small group of perhaps forty to fifty elite families, each with enough access to the political system to ensure sufficient assets to preserve and strengthen its base. With martial law Marcos was able to shatter the power of some of these families and divert their assets to both his and his wife Imelda's support bases. In some cases this was done by resegmenting other factions and attaching to theirs; in other cases growth came from providing cronies with sufficient assets to extend their factions. In both periods there was little social justice for the poor or weak, and little effort was made to shape an economic system in which enough wealth was created to make "trickle down" meaningful to peasants and workers. Land reform received lip service but little meaningful action. All in all, though many participated in the system, only a few received the rewards; and yet there was relatively little pressure from the bottom of society to overturn the oligarchy at the top.

NONSTRUCTURAL MAINSTREAM PHILIPPINE POLITICAL VALUES

Next we turn to a second set of values—those emerging from contact with the developed world and the Philippines' colonial history. These may overlap somewhat with social structural norms but are in the main independent from structural influences.

Drawing on the work of Hunt,[5] Lynch and de Guzman,[6] Jocano,[7] and Steinberg[8] we present in Table 1 fourteen mainstream values, of which seven are institutional and seven personal. What is meant by "mainstream" here is a set of values for which even those holding different

[5]Chester L. Hunt, Agaton P. Pal, Richard W. Coller, Socorro E. Espirito, J.E. DeYoung, and S.F. Corpus, *Sociology in The New Philippine Setting* (Quezon City, Philippines: Almar-Phoenix, 1976).
[6]Frank Lynch and A. deGuzman, eds., *Four Readings on Philippine Values,* IPC Papers, No. 2, 4th ed., enlarged, (Quezon City, Philippines: Ateneo de Manila University Press, 1973).
[7]F.L. Jocano, "Filipino Social Structure and Value System" in F.L. Jocano, ed., Filipino Cultural Heritage Lecture Series, 2 (Manila: Philippine Womens University Press, 1965).
[8]David J. Steinberg, *The Philippines, A Singular and Plural Place* (Boulder, Colorado: Westview Press, 1982).

*TABLE 1. PHILIPPINE VALUES**

Institutional Values

Welfare of Common Man
. . . Society's purpose is to protect the welfare of its citizens. Insensitivity to his (her) welfare is viewed as being deviant.

Nationalism
. . . Filipinos must struggle against the imperialist heritage of Spanish and American colonialism. A citizen's highest loyalty is to the nation; decisions should reflect primarily the nation's interest.

Pluralism
. . . Diverse ethnic and linguistic loyalties should be preserved. Preserving these loyalties is not incompatible with nationalism.

Judeo-Christian Values
. . . Appropriate behavior is defined in reference to the Judeo-Christian tradition. These values are the ultimate explanation for behavior.

Equalitarianism
. . . Deriving from the American tradition, equality of opportunity is emphasized in contradistinction to inherited status.

Economic Self-Sufficiency
. . . Emphasizes national self-sufficiency, even at the cost of an increased standard of living. Opposed to economic interdependence: Filipinos' interests prevail over those of any foreign nationality.

Constitutionalism
. . . A written constitution is the basis for legal and political institutions. This document can be amended only through official channels/responsible forums.

---

*Summary statements of each value.

Personal Values

Familism
    . . . The extended family is the unit for support and loyalty, rather than impersonal institutions. *Utang na loob* (reciprocity) and *hiya* (shame) are the social cement that bind group members.

Obedience to Authorities
    . . . Guidance is to be sought in authorities. Value is placed on deferring to others rather than on making independent decisions.

Personalism
    . . . Goals and rewards are based on personal rather than universal criteria. Uniqueness is valued; each group (individual) is treated in terms of its own particular values, which may or may not be shared with other groups (individuals).

Harmony
    . . . Emphasis is on a lack of conflict in interpersonal relations. Getting along with others, referred to as smooth interpersonal relations, is the preferred approach in contradistinction to conflict or disagreement.

Social Acceptance
    . . . A person is valued for himself. Filipinos desire to be accepted as people, to be treated as subjects rather than as objects.

Bahala Na
(God will provide)
    . . . Construed as optimistic fatalism, this value encourages modest efforts; outcomes are left to chance. It is opposite to the kind of approach favored in the West, namely, means to ends in the interest of efficiency.

Nonrationalism
    . . . Guided often by spiritualism, Filipinos believe that many events have no rational explanation; there are areas of life over which individuals have little control.

269

values will publicly provide lip service. At issue here are two aspects of these values. The first is, what kind of a fit is there between these values and democratic institutions? The second is, to what degree do powerful groups in society deviate from these values and in what way does their deviation affect democratic institutions?

If the institutional values appearing in Table 1 were dominant in the Philippines we would have a strong basis for optimism about democracy's future there. These sentiments, rooted in western liberal democratic thought, the Judeo-Christian tradition, and nationalist ideas, underpin the democratic regimes of Western Europe, the United States, Canada, and other nations whose governments are related to these. Older Filipinos were exposed to these views in the unquestioning atmosphere of the American-controlled educational system. Although younger Filipinos have had some exposure to values at odds with these views, they continue to dominate the educational system of the Philippines at all levels. Given the history of the Philippines over the last one hundred years and the universal exposure to these values, it is unlikely that many Filipinos would publicly disavow any of them. Indeed many of these themes were expressed in Corazon Aquino's election campaign, and all of them have appeared in the press in the post-election period as expressions of the goals of the new regime.

When we examine the depth of support for these values among key groups in the Philippines, we find less cause for optimism. Although the good of the common *tao* (man) is a part of every Filipino's public rhetoric, elites in the Philippines have rarely sought to implement this value, particularly if implementation would prove costly to themselves. Both before and during the martial law period elites resisted land reform and were strong supporters of the regime's no-strike policies. This is not to say that elites care nothing for the common man. He is not, however, their primary concern. When they act out this concern, they do so through traditional but antidemocratic network behavior. Nationalism and pluralism also have their enemies in the Philippines. Muslims, and to some degree Chinese, have never felt quite comfortable within the Philippine body politic. In the case of the Muslims, their strongly resisted demands for greater autonomy have led to the slow growth of Islamic fundamentalism, in itself an apparent opponent of democracy.

Among Christian Filipinos the ongoing strong support for ethnic and linguistic pluralism in regionally based subcultures is a double-edged sword. Though pluralism of well-integrated groups tends to diffuse conflict, the rather poor integration of subcultures into Philippine life makes the compromises necessary to sustain a democratic system difficult.

The value of egalitarianism will be considered later, and that of economic self-sufficiency may be unrelated to democracy. The belief in constitutionalism, however, may have lost its legitimacy due to a number of factors. The rewriting of the constitution by Marcos's martial law government to suit its own ends, the new constitution that will probably emerge from the Aquino government, the armed forces coup that played a role in Marcos's departure, and the reported growth of authoritarian beliefs within the army suggest that support for constitutionalism may be withering away along with the idea that such documents are the basis for legal and political institutions and can be amended only through official channels and responsible forums.

Overall, however, despite strong deviation from these institutional values by powerful groups in the Philippines, it would appear that these views still provide strong support for democracy and democratic institutions. To the extent that implementing these values becomes the overriding goal of all Filipinos, replacing or blotting out more traditional orientations, democracy will be strengthened.

When we examine personal values we have less cause for optimism regarding the future of democracy in the Philippines. There are strong inconsistencies between personal values and both institutional values and democratic ideals and institutions.

Familism, obedience to authorities, and personalism are to a large extent incompatible with the welfare of the common man, nationalism, and egalitarianism. Familism, as we have noted earlier, is an outcome of the patron-client social structure and, as we have argued earlier, fits poorly with democratic institutions. It also conflicts with the welfare of the common man. Obedience to authority tends to tilt the scale against equality and may undermine the degree of independence needed to preserve democratic institutions, while personalism conflicts with both nationalism and egalitarianism. The concept of *bahala na* (God will provide) and nonrationalism, while not contradicting any institutional values, together create an atmosphere of fatalism. Individuals may lack the sense of control over events necessary to support democratic institutions. Those Filipinos at the bottom of the social ladder often do not believe that instrumental participation delivers rewards.

In summary, our examination of these fourteen Filipino values suggests the following: As might be expected in a society where a traditional social structure dominates interpersonal relationships, personal values are often in conflict with modern institutional values. Where these conflicts exist it is likely that personal more than institutional values determine many behaviors, and particularly political behaviors. Thus, as long as the social structure persists those institutional values that support democracy are more likely to receive lip service than behavioral support. That these institutional values are in place, are taught in the educational system, and are supported at the cognitive level suggests that a transition to these values could take place rather quickly if existing social structural and personal values lost their usefulness. Whether this transition is happening or is likely to happen is a question we will turn to later.

PSYCHOLOGICAL ORIENTATIONS

To examine the psychological orientations of Filipinos I will draw upon research I have done in the past.[9] These past efforts were explicitly designed to measure a set of psychological orientations in theory related to the maintenance of stable democratic institutions. I interviewed members of a Filipina elite in 1966-67 and reexamined them in 1979 looking for evidence of change. I was also able to measure some of these attitudes in a population of young Filipino school children in 1966.[10]

Following the work of Almond and Verba,[11] Wendell Bell,[12] James Scott,[13] and Marvin Zonis,[14] I measured in my respondents levels of

[9]Justin J. Green, "Social Backgrounds, Attitudes and Political Behavior—A Study of a Philippine Elite," *Southeast Asia, An International Quarterly*, Vol. 11/No. 3/Summer 1973, pp. 301-336.

[10]Justin J. Green, "Children and Politics in the Philippines: Socialization for Stability in a Highly Stratified Society," *Asian Survey*, Vol. XVII, No. 7, July 1977, pp. 667-678.

[11]Gabriel Almond and Sidney Verba, *The Civic Culture — Political Attitudes and Democracy in Five Nations*, (New York: Little, Brown, 1965).

[12]Wendell Bell, *Jamaican Leaders — Political Attitudes in a New Nation*, (Berkeley: University of California Press, 1964).

[13]James C. Scott, *Political Ideology in Malaysia — Reality and the Beliefs of an Elite*, (New Haven: Yale University Press, 1968).

[14]Marvin Zonis, "Political Elites and Political Cynicism in Iran," *Comparative Political Studies*, Vol. 3, October 1968, pp. 351-371.

authoritarianism, innovativeness, political cynicism, faith in people, egalitarianism, and liberal-conservatism. In the sample of youth I looked at affect, political efficacy, and cynicism. The methods and the detailed findings of this research have been reported elsewhere, and I will only summarize them here.[15] As compared with American and other national elite groups, Filipina leaders controlled for level of education scored high on authoritarianism, rather low on innovativeness, low on cynicism (this perhaps more as a function of gender rather than being Filipino), opted for influencing government through personal rather than group activity, had average levels of trust, scored very low on a measure of egalitarianism, and ranked as very conservative on a conservative-liberal scale. On the whole these characteristics in the civic culture model mean that a stable participatory democracy is less likely.

Huntington has recently suggested that:

> political culture that values highly hierarchical relationships and extreme deference to authority presumably is less fertile ground for democracy than one that does not. Similarly, a culture in which there is a high degree of mutual trust among members of the society is likely to be more favorable to democracy than one in which interpersonal relationships are more generally characterized by suspicion, hostility, and distrust. A willingness to tolerate diversity and conflict among groups and to recognize the legitimacy of compromise also should be helpful to democratic development. Societies in which great stress is put on the need to acquire power and little on the need to accommodate others are more likely to have authoritarian or totalitarian regimes.[16]

If Huntington is correct, then an overall assessment of the prospects for democracy based on an analysis of social structural values, mainstream values, and psychological orientations is not a hopeful one.

Although we have noted that certain institutional values along with the low levels of cynicism and the medium levels of trust discussed

[15]Justin J. Green, 1973 and 1977, op. cit.
[16]Samuel P. Huntington, "Will More Countries Become Democratic," *Political Science Quarterly*, 99, No. 2 (Summer 1984), pp. 193-218, 207.

above provide limited support for democratic institutions, such support is being undermined constantly by the values emerging from patron-client networks, most mainstream personal values, and the high levels of authoritarianism, anti-egalitarianism, and change-inhibiting conservatism I have reported on in the past.

PHILIPPINE POLITICAL CULTURE AND SOME OTHER "ISMS"

If the values, norms, attitudes, and behaviors of Philippine political culture fit rather poorly with democratic institutions, our next question is, how well do they fit with other "modernizing ideologies"? Specifically, how much support does the political culture provide for Marxism and nationalism? Until now, only scholars interested in the Huk movement have considered these issues at all, and then only peripherally. Although this topic deserves its own full investigation, in the interests of symmetry I will briefly examine it here.

In theory Marxism's social structure is based on horizontal-polyadic ties as opposed to the vertical dyads which organize the Philippines. Thus, many of the values and behaviors that emerge from this structural clash contradict each other. It is interesting to note, however, that one analysis of the Huk movement ascribed both their power in central Luzon and their failure to expand much beyond the boundaries of Pampanga to their vertical dyadic organization as well as their common language ties. What this suggests is that Huk Marxism, rather than changing Philippine values, was itself changed by them. The Filipinization of Marxism, however, became an important restraint on the ability of the Huks to nationalize their revolution. It would appear that the Communist Party of the Philippines (CPP) and its military arm—the New Peoples Army (NPA)—as inheritors of Huk Marxism are making a conscious attempt to avoid the Huks' mistakes. The CPP claim to use Marxism to reorient Filipino values. Although such a conversion seems likely to have occurred among the hard-core leadership, the fact that these leaders downplay ideology and emphasize local economic and social grievances in their mass recruiting suggests that they have had little success in changing Filipino values to support Marxist structural forms. Another factor that limits the effects of Marxism on Philippine values is that Philippine Catholicism, an important prop of traditional Philippine social structure, has been antagonistic to communism. Although liberation theology and the development of Basic Christian Communities may have moved part of the church leftward, this movement has not yet reached a size where it has a serious effect on the values of many Filipinos.

The question of how nationalism affects Philippine values is more difficult to deal with. On the one hand, it is possible to graft nationalistic values to dyadic pyramids without disturbing either the structure or the values that hold them together. On the other hand, the persistence of that "special relationship" between the Philippines and the United States despite the growing pressures of anti-Americanism suggests to some observers that something more than self-interest binds the two together, and perhaps that something from a Filipino point of view is a shared *utang-na-loob* (debt without end).

POLITICAL SOCIALIZATION AND VALUE CHANGE

As noted earlier, the argument being made here depends on the acceptance of a model in which the attitudes that underlie a person's adult behavior are affected by what he learns as a child. If this assumption is incorrect then the connection between traditional Philippine values and unhappy prospects for democracy is broken. If adult values, attitudes, and norms are almost exclusively the result of adult socialization experiences, then the events of the last two years may presage a turning away from those values that have given meaning to Philippine life in the past and the adoption of a new set of orientations: one that fits better with democratic behaviors and democratic institutions.

Have Filipinos learned to put aside family and factional interests in the name of Philippine needs, or was the coalition that won the election held together only by a common desire to get rid of Marcos? Will Filipino elites encourage change, sharing power and wealth with other, less fortunate Filipinos for the good of all? Have enough Filipinos permanently acquired a sense of efficaciousness strong enough to keep them involved in the kind of interest groups and street politics that brought the Aquino campaign success? Have personal values undergone the kind of metamorphosis which will partially discourage the corruption, nepotism, and personalism that affected the ability of democratic institutions to function efficiently in the past? These and more are the lessons that Filipinos could possibly have learned in the years since Ninoy Aquino was shot down on the tarmac of Manila International Airport.

However much recent events have made Filipinos hopeful that these changes have taken place, I do not think expectations should be raised too high. For it is more probable that the cliche which underlies the socialization model assumed here, "the acorn does not fall far from the tree," remains true. My data, though admittedly collected before recent events, tends to support the more pessimistic view. In the 1960s the values of children in the Philippines were much like those of their parents, indicating that the mechanisms of intergenerational transmission were strong and efficient. Reinterviews of my leadership sample in 1979, thirteen years after the initial study, and a comparison of older leaders with a new generation of women leaders suggest the views of these Filipinas had changed very little over time. More important, the data indicate a similarity in values, attitudes, and norms of leaders across generations.

Gabriel Almond, responding in 1980 to those who criticized the civic culture model and noting Archie Brown's work on communist societies says:

> Among the more interesting findings of political culture research, these [Brown's] conclusions as to the intractability of these "pre communist" attitudes despite the awesome effort to transform them, stand in the sharpest contrast to overwhelming evidence that some humane and participant consequences flow from modern education wherever it is introduced. It would thus appear, not that political culture is an intractable variable, but that there are limits to its plasticity, and inherent-propensities of a modestly encouraging sort.[17]

Almond is of course trying to reconcile the findings of Brown which support the primacy theory of socialization, that what children learn affects what adults can absorb, with his own belief that adult socializa-

[17]Gabriel A. Almond, "The Intellectual History of the Civic Culture Concept" in G.A. Almond and S. Verba, eds., *The Civic Culture Revisited* (Boston: Little, Brown, 1980, pp. 1-36, 32. Almond is drawing on the work of Archie Brown in A. Brown and J. Gray, *Political Culture and Political Change in Communist States* (New York: Holmes and Meir, 1977).

tion experiences have greater importance than childhood learning.

A more pessimistic view of the relationship between traditional political culture and modern ideology was held by Scott in the sixties.

> A belief or value learned presumably during secondary socialization is being undercut or sabotaged, so to speak, by a more central belief internalized earlier. The discontinuity in political ideology permits central orientations that are often a part of the cultural tradition to seep through and affect the style and content of beliefs which are on the surface, more Western.[18]

My own view developed in the sixties is not of the immutability of political culture but rather that political culture is one of the mechanisms through which societies adapt to their changing environment. As such political culture is neither static nor revolutionary, it changes through a process whose pace avoids discontinuities within cohorts and across generations.

In the Philippines the complex mixture of particular and universal values held by Filipinos provides them with an opportunity to operationalize a broader set of goals and a potentially wider range of behavior than those which until now traditional society has sanctioned. This statement does not, however, permit us to predict the reemergence and stability of democratic institutions. Nor can we predict with much accuracy the values and behaviors that will affect future political, economic, or social life. Because other variables are operating, even a favorable change in Filipino values and behavior need not forecast a change in national goals or a reshuffling of the present order of society. Though changes may be occurring (documentation of these awaits the future efforts of researchers), it is probable that the kind of changes that take place will be those that will enable Filipinos to adapt to a changing world environment while preserving at the national level as much value stability as possible.

If the Philippines is to become "the greatest democracy on earth" it will be in this writer's view a long and painful process, and all the help and good wishes of democracy's friends both in the Philippines and in the United Sates are not likely to shorten the timespan or deaden the pain.

[18]James Scott, 1968, op. cit., p. 43.

15

Report on the Discussion:
Social Change, Social Needs,
and Social Policy

Daniel F. Doeppers

The essay which follows provides a general summary of the exchange which occurred following presentation of papers by Benjamin Kerkvliet, Robert and Beverly Hackenberg, Ben Muego, and Justin Green. The discussion was spirited and wide-ranging. It was marked by great interest in grappling with the religious symbolism of the February change of government in the Philippines and with the social-psychological requirements for participation in democratic, interest-group politics. In providing this summary, I have also felt free to add such material as seems germane to the confines of the discussion.

REDEFINITION OF THE SACRED AND THE PROSPECTS FOR A RATIONALIZATION OF PHILIPPINE ECONOMY AND SOCIETY

Reflecting on the many manifestations of labor surplus and poverty in Manila and the Philippines, on the quite evident need for fundamental change, the first discussant was moved to speculate more broadly on how some other countries have historically extricated themselves from such situations—in short with how they have modernized their societies and economies. Scholars interested in sociology and the history of religion have concluded that modernization did not simply come about as a result of the enhancement of the material resources of certain societies, or by some philosophic transformation, but, according to Max Weber's hypothesis, through a redefinition of the sacred. This redefinition, which took place in the Protestant Reformation, permitted the rationalization of economy and society in the West. Meiji Japan provides a parallel case. As Robert Bella has pointed out in his dissertation, the assertion of Shinto as the central state religious commitment also created a redefinition of the sacred. It permitted the

279

Japanese, for example, the lower Samurai bound by client-patron relationships to their immediate feudal lords, to find in this new set of religiously defined, religiously legitimated obligations, a way to override their old, feudal obligations and to participate in the new, centralized, and inherently rationalized society and economy which developed.

Struck by the Latin American-like religious background of the Philippines, the discussant went on to wonder if perhaps one of the things that is required is some kind of redefinition of the sacred if one is to develop attitudes which are appropriate for a rationalized modern economy. He cited the rise of fundamentalism in Islam as a reflection of the fact that in many parts of the Third World secular society does not have, in itself, the kind of legitimacy with which the political order can achieve any degree of stability. Is it possible for the Philippines to come out of a morass of an ever-increasing surplus population and an ineffective mechanism for creating and finding employment (or even bare subsistence for many) unless some kind of redefinition of the sacred helps to create and legitimize genuinely new attitudes?

This question proved a powerful organizing force in the subsequent discussion. One discussant noted that the redefinition of the sacred is something that happens despite governments, despite planning, despite even acute social criticism. It simply takes over and seizes a society at a certain point.

Some pursued the question of sacred symbols, not so much with an idea of useful redefinition, but more narrowly as an interpretive path for understanding both the outcome of the Philippine presidential election and the subsequent change of government. One discussant asserted that it was precisely sacred symbols that elected Cory Aquino. By this view, she didn't win because she had superior force, superior "pay-off" power, or because she had superior organization. She won because she had all the sacred symbols in her favor.

For this discussant, Mrs. Aquino is the sacred symbol of the bereaved widow, of the martyr, a modern madonna. She has suffered and, through her suffering, she has brought redemption, or at least a short-term chance for redemption for the Philippines. What becomes of the use of that symbol of the sacred is another matter, but at least it is there for the people and the politicians to fight over and claim in their favor. The madonna aspect of Mrs. Aquino's appeal was less powerful than the Christ-like, Passion-like quality of her husband's death. Like

Jose Rizal, Benigno Aquino willingly laid down his life for the country. By this light, Aquino's death foreshadowed and/or made possible the redemption of the Filipinos—a redemption which was accomplished by bloodlessly separating Ferdinand Marcos from the reins of state power. This argument was said to echo Ian Baruma's recent essay in the *New York Review of Books* (January 16, 1986). Referring to past revolutions, Baruma says that "Mother Filipinas must be redeemed by faith and sacrifice, by death and resurrection. Such acts have been led by a succession of Messiahs promising paradise and freedom." In this line of reasoning about symbols and Mrs. Aquino's assumption of power, little was inferred about a transformation, such as that in Meiji Japan or Reformation Europe.

Others wanted to link events to a redefinition centered around the idea of a nontheocentric "sacredness." For some years, political scientists have been trying to construct an interpretation of nationalism as a quasi-religion. At the same time, Philippine nationalism has often seemed to contain a somewhat negative referent. Indeed, one could say that the Marcos dictatorship created not only enormous discouragement, but also heightened this negative aspect, creating a crisis in Filipinos' perception of their national self-esteem. But suddenly, after February, Filipino nationalism is something else. It is something that is looked on with admiration. The Filipino has a new pride, Philippine nationalism has a new dignity. It has shed the undercurrent of apology. By this optimistic view, a national personality is being forged which represents the elevation of nationalism to a sacred category with this new dignity of Filipinism, this new optimism, this new pride that Filipinism has acquired after the February events.

In this view, the new nationalism may be seen as distinct from a national personality which is *attached* to a particular religion, but it is not without a religious context. Indeed, during February, the Filipino church asserted itself fulfilling the dreams of Jose Rizal and all the Filipino reformists. Finally, in this view, we have a Filipino church, staffed by native clergy, led by a native hierarchy, and being a basically conservative church, on the cutting edge of change, doing more things with its conservatism than the liberation theologians in more radical countries have been able to achieve, and doing it in the space of a few days and without bloodshed.

According to this passionately expressed, basically conservative view, one can see the elements of a new national personality, a new sacredness of nationalism, a sacredness elevated by the February events.

Still drawing on the definitions of the sacred theme, another discussant called our attention to the important interpretive work of Rey Ileto and, in particular, his *Passion and Revolution*.[1] Ileto's theme is that unorthodox religious ideas can be and have been powerful sources of inspiration in Philippine life. He argues that there are different interpretations of what Catholicism means and how to interpret the life of Christ. The interpretation that helped to stimulate and drive the Philippine revolution at the turn of the present century was one deeply rooted in peasant consciousness which allowed for a critique of the prevailing system dominated by the Spanish, as well as a critique of the elites that were working with the Spanish. This included a critique of the very elites that occupied leadership positions in the revolution itself. Just as peasants and revolutionary leaders differed in their interpretations of the life of Christ, you could say that within the Catholic church in the Philippines now, there is another kind of ongoing debate and dialogue about what Christianity is all about, what the life of Christ means here and now, how to live, how society should be organized, and what kinds of policies are just, fair, and legitimate. The more socially oriented side in this debate is sometimes called Liberation Theology, and it has been very important to the role of the church in the Philippines over the last several years, particularly in different parts of the country that are involved in the economic and social crises described in Mr. Kerkvliet's paper.

While no vote was taken among the thirty or forty persons participating in the discussion, there appeared to be general consensus on the importance of the Catholic symbol of the Passion of Christ and of the concept of redemption in the events of February. There was also fairly wide agreement that the actions of church people gave power to the idea that the public was doing something for the country and that God was behind them. The idea of a redefinition of the sacred is clearly a powerful one in the Protestant West and in Meiji Japan, but there was skepticism that such a redefinition is yet observable in the Philippines.

[1]Rey Ileto, *Passion and Revolution* (Quezon City and Metro Manila: Ateneo de Manila University Press, 1979).

SOCIALIZATION, ORGANIZATIONAL VALUES, AND THE SOCIAL-PSYCHOLOGICAL REQUIREMENTS FOR PARTICIPATION IN DEMOCRATIC POLITICS

The second major thread of the discussion was a debate taking off from a critique of the "socialization model" approach to Philippine politics. Discussion ranged widely to include an examination of organizational values and structures as these have affected and are likely to continue to affect Philippine economy and politics.

As presented in Justin Green's paper, the socialization model in the Philippine context suggests that if Filipinos are reared, or "socialized," in authoritarian, tightly knit, extended family structures, then they arrive at adulthood with values and models for action which tend to undercut educational and practical efforts to generate open, democratic, interest-group politics. This interpretation led Green to be pessimistic about the potential of the recent ouster of a dictatorial regime to lead to a democratic, popularly based kind of politics.

A number of others saw this model in application as being too static, as denying the possibility of fairly rapid value change brought on by immediate experience. By this critique, socialization is held to be extremely important, but generational experience often combines with socialization to create utilization of old things in new ways. In the Philippines, each living generation has had very different experiences —the World War II occupation, the ensuing period of electoral politics, and then martial law and the Marcos dictatorship. The Philippines now has a relatively large young people's generation—as outlined in the paper by Ben Muego—that has grown up during martial law with very little of the old politics-as-usual experience for background. Many young people instead participated in the "parliament of the streets," organizing and expressing popular opposition to the Marcos regime. Anyone who interviewed ordinary people during the economic and political crisis of the last three years, or who read the then-alternative press such as *Malaya* and *Veritas* heard cynical or very critical analyses of the dictatorship and observed people doing interest-group political organizing in ways that had little to do with dependent, client-patron relations. A number of discussants agreed that these generational experiences and this zeitgeist were of an order that would reasonably lead one to expect change in values and models for action, rather than continuity in political behavior to the degree predicted in Green's paper.

At this point, the discussion moved to focus on organizational values per se. An economist speculated that Filipinos lack, more than most other Asian nations, a commitment to organizational values. If you look at Japanese culture you will find several points of similarity with Filipino culture in terms of personal relationships. But a major value for the Japanese is membership in the organization and one's performance of a specific function in the organization. This loyalty and dedication is frequently seen to override personalistic concerns.

An example of these values is seen when the president of JAL considered resigning from the company because an airplane crashed. It never was shown that it was the fault of JAL; in fact, it may have been the fault of Boeing, and certainly not the fault of the president, so far as anyone could see. But he considered resigning. Another example is the man who would not drive through dangerously congested traffic because if he ever had an accident it would reflect poorly on his company. This discussant had difficulty imagining a Filipino expressing this degree of organizational commitment. This made it difficult for him to imagine organizing and mobilizing even a well-educated Filipino population for better economic performance.

Countering this negative contrast of Filipino and Japanese organizational values, another discussant pointed to differences in the economic and security benefits of being loyal. In Japan, it is said that company leadership tends to protect and stand up for its lower- and middle-level workers, especially its permanent workers. In the Philippines, one can point to many examples of workers, including landless laborers, whose wages were not fully paid, who were cheated out of their wages altogether, or who were otherwise abused by self-serving organizational superiors. According to this view, the possibility for developing stronger organizational loyalty of the kind seen in Japan rests as much with owners and management as with employees.

Others articulated variations on the same theme. One discussant cited studies indicating considerable similarity in the importance of vertical, patron-client ties in Japan and the Philippines. What is said to be different in this regard is that while Japanese tend to maintain a particular vertical relationship for a long period, Filipinos tend to switch more or less readily from one to another. Again, this was seen as being related to a more consistent material and security return to the Japanese dependent. The point is that the nature of the relationship while it lasts and the underlying values are not very different.

Whatever the similarities between Filipino and Japanese values, other discussants saw their resulting social structures as being quite different. Philippine structures tend to be bilateral (tending to connect to female kin as readily as to male kin), dyadic, open, fluent, recombinative. Japanese structures, by contrast tend to be unilateral, patrilineal, and closed, with the organizational strength that may imply. For the layman, this discussion reflects a larger literature which tends to see unilateral social structures as leading to quicker and less contested (not necessarily better) decisions, while bilateral structures lead to twice as many options and a greater likelihood of decisions being contested. Bilateral structures are common in Southeast Asia and virtually absent in China, Korea, and Japan.

Echoing this East versus Southeast Asian difference is the finding that Japanese partners in joint-ventures believe that Filipinos have very short time horizons. The Filipinos were seen as not being committed to the ongoing nature of the organization. Others saw this as more a problem of forming joint ventures with the spectacularly greedy cronies of the Marcos regime, rather than with the personnel of a stable, long-established Philippine corporation.

RECENT SOCIAL AND ORGANIZATIONAL CHANGE

The earlier speculative discussion about Filipino capacities to form and maintain organizations led into a more specific discussion of recent social and organizational change. The persons active in this part of the discussion disagreed strongly with those who doubted that Filipinos have organizational ability.

The Marcos dictatorship coopted, undercut, or drove underground a wide range of organizations. One of the first moves following the declaration of martial law was the elimination of the types of organization that were specifically formed by the lower class elements in the population for their own advancement. The labor unions were squelched. The student organizations were crushed. The promising Free Farmers Federation was abolished. And most importantly from the standpoint of the links between rural and urban, the squatter associations, which provided for the admission of the poorest rural people into the urban areas and gave them their first place in the urban society, were completely eliminated.

When we look at the advantage that was gained by the elite through the early years of the dictatorship in the 1970s, we see those advantages were organizational. Corporations were not basically interfered with, and a number of businessmen saw the new society providing them with a variety of opportunities for investment and advancement that they did not have before.

By contrast, the less affluent elements of the population, particularly the manual worker unions, the students, the squatters, and the farmers, were unable to match this because the organizations which they had formed in an attempt to protect their own interests were no longer possible to sustain in a nonclandestine way. Again, this effectively reversed the strong trend of the late 1960s, which was to pursue group interests through increasingly effective voluntary associations. One discussant concluded, "Those of us who were there in the years [just] before martial law and did battle with or for any of these organizations can testify to their viability."

While Marcos made it difficult or dangerous for many organizations to function, the years after 1972 were marked by both creative and reactive organizational change. Basic Christian Communities emerged in Mindanao and organizations were created in reaction to the human rights abuses that proliferated. One underappreciated change in the later years of the dictatorship was the terrific proliferation of organized interest groups of many kinds. The issue- or cause-oriented groups are perhaps the best known of these. Another is the rise of militant labor unions not affiliated with the federation fostered by Marcos and favored by some aid-giving organizations. One discussant, echoed by others who had worked in the Philippines during 1985, reported himself to be "incredibly impressed by the [union] organization that was going on—whole hierarchies of organizations." The ability to voluntarily form coalitions which come together and stay together for particular purposes is very important. All this is not a simple resurgence of the late 1960s. It appears to be a quantum change in Philippine society and will tend greatly to complicate old-school, personalistic, patron-client politics of the kind still pursued by Vice President Laurel. One early prospect is that as interest groups achieve higher levels of articulation, some of their interests will crosscut those of other groups and organizations. Coordination and mediating between such articulated interest-group claims will be a major task of the new government as it is in any democratic society.

The discussion took cognizance of the change in the organizational leadership of Cardinal Sin and the Conference of Bishops in the Catholic church—a very important change which seemed to crystalize suddenly, but which has been building for a number of years with both organizations of lay-persons and bishops in Mindanao taking the lead. In particular this reflects a growing tendency toward religious practice among the middle and upper classes. The discussion also took cognizance of new student organizations and their political role, and of the assertive political roles being played by women, not just in the office of president, but also in NAMFREL and at the barricades. This is not altogether new, but it is certainly promising.

Finally, in the perceptive papers of Mr. Kerkvliet and the Hackenbergs and in the discussion, we heard a great deal about the underside of provincial and poor urban life. There were reports of elderly Filipinos saying that the last three years have been much worse than the Great Depression. There were comments that in the face of economic hardship many Filipino families of modest means had been sustained by relatives working in Saudi Arabia, but that by 1985, most of these workers had been laid off. There were reports of enormous numbers of ambulant vendors and others in Manila trying desperately to eke out subsistence—of hardship that began to recall memories of the last months of the Japanese occupation during World War II. Clearly the now-prolonged depression has brought real hardship to the poor majority and also to the middle class. We ended with the realization that the inherited economic problems facing Mrs. Aquino's government are very great and that they have already caused considerable downward social mobility.

IV. Government and Politics

16

President Corazon Aquino: A Political and Personal Assessment

Guy J. Pauker

On February 25, 1986, at 10:45 a.m., at the Club Filipino in the Greenhills section of Metro-Manila, Corazon Cojuangco Aquino was sworn in as the seventh president of the Republic of the Philippines by Supreme Court Justice Claudio Teehankee. Five minutes earlier, Salvador H. Laurel had been sworn in as vice-president by Supreme Court Justice Vicente Abad Santos. The presence of these two respected judges was significant, as ten days earlier the national assembly had ratified the reelection of Ferdinand Marcos as president of the republic, an act that public opinion had viewed almost unanimously as fraudulent.

After the oathtaking, in brief speeches, Doy Laurel extolled the heroism of the Filipinos who had blocked the advancing army tanks with their bodies, while Cory Aquino called for national reconciliation, urging everybody to join in rebuilding the nation and declaring: "I am very magnanimous in victory." True to her word, in the month since President Aquino took power she has made no reprisals against persons associated with the Marcos regime, although vigorous efforts are being made to recover the enormous assets illegally accumulated by the Marcos family and their cronies.

For her inauguration Cory Aquino did not wear a new gown. She wore a simple yellow dress, one of the outfits in which she had appeared during the fifty-seven day electoral campaign that had galvanized the Filipino nation. The local press noted that the new president had only the barest trace of makeup and no jewelry except for the modest earrings that she usually wears. On arrival at the Club Filipino she was offered a bouquet of yellow flowers, but no pomp and pageantry marked that historical occasion.

About 500 persons had crowded into Sampaguita Hall, while thousands had been standing outside since early morning. In the presence of members of the Aquino and Laurel families, opposition leaders, journalists, and a few diplomats, Ninoy Aquino's mother, Dona Aurora, held the Bible on which her daughter-in-law took the oath of office, and Celia Laurel held it for her husband. After their respective speeches president and vice-president bussed each other lightly on the cheek, then all joined in singing the opposition's campaign song, "Bayan Ko." By 11:30 a.m. the ceremony was over.

The next morning some columnists expressed disappointment that no representatives of the working classes were seated at the head table, although the new government owed its victory to "people power." The failure to include a few symbolic workers and farmers may have been due to the elitism of the participants, but was more likely a result of the haste in which the ceremony had been organized. With Marcos still ensconced in Malacanang Palace, the victorious opposition leaders had no time or taste for stage setting. Actually, Cory Aquino's genuine honesty and simplicity, which had won her the heart of the Filipino people, was accurately reflected in her hour of triumph.

After having been sworn in, the new president promoted Lt. Gen. Fidel V. Ramos to full general and named him chief of staff of the armed forces. A Filipino reporter described the scene:

> Ramos gave his new Commander-in-Chief a snappy salute after he was promoted to full General's rank and appointed Chief of Staff. The new Commander-in-Chief, taken by surprise, returned the salute limply, and then flashed a rather embarrassed smile.

Less than a month later the *New York Times* published a three-column picture of the president, radiating authority, flanked by General Ramos and wearing the cordon of her high office, giving a crisp salute to her troops. An American correspondent reported from the graduation ceremony held on March 22 at the Philippine Military Academy in Baguio City:

> The President delighted the crowd with her easy adaptation to the military trappings of her new office as she strode in proper march step to the beat of the drum on the parade ground. Her yellow frock, as much a national uniform now as any in the ranks, gleamed as she stood in the vanguard of the plumes and brass of the armed forces. The military

wives and mothers in the crowd laughed then cheered as she calmly snapped off salute after salute and rode about in a white command jeep attended by the new Chief of Staff, General Fidel V. Ramos.

The metamorphosis of the fifty-three-year-old, shy and retiring housewife and mother of five into the confident chief executive of a nation of fifty-five million is an inspiring proof of the power of will and faith. In having been able to respond to the challenge of her country's deep crisis, Cory Aquino was motivated not by personal ambition but by a strong sense of mission that can be traced back to the heroic death of her husband. Knowing that he was risking his life, Ninoy Aquino had returned to the Philippines on August 21, 1983, in the hope that he might convince Ferdinand Marcos, who was seriously ill at that time, to manage a peaceful return to democracy. Ninoy had dismissed the pleas of family and friends to stay in the United States, out of harm's way, with the comment, "It is better to die a meaningful death than to live a meaningless life."

His widow was swept into her country's political life by the tidal wave of grief that had brought some two million people into the streets for her husband's funeral. She had to participate in the many street demonstrations invoking Ninoy's legacy. All opposition groups were soliciting her political support and, as she told an American friend in November 1983, she had to be cautious in letting her name be used.

Elections for a new national assembly were scheduled for May 1984, and Cory Aquino, showing superior political judgment and against the wishes of some of her close political friends who had decided to boycott the elections, campaigned for opposition candidates. Although Marcos managed to rig the elections so as to control a two-thirds majority in the new legislative body, the opposition made its first major breakthrough since the declaration of martial law in 1972 by getting sixty of its representatives into the national assembly.

In December 1984 Cory Aquino went one step further, joining octogenarian former Senator Lorenzo Tanada, a highly respected political leader, and Jaime Ongpin, a successful young business executive who had become an outspoken critic of the Marcos regime, in establishing a "Convener Group," which nominated eleven eligible presidential candidates. From their ranks a single presidential candidate was to be selected quickly were Marcos to die suddenly or leave office.

The Convener Group was criticized for not being broadly representative of the opposition. In March 1985 Cory Aquino, on behalf of the Convener Group, assumed the task of working out a formula for the selection of a single presidential candidate together with former Supreme Court Justice and opposition member of Parliament Cecilia Munoz-Palma, who as chairman of a National Unification Committee was attempting to forge an alliance of all national and regional opposition parties. Although these efforts were marred until the last moment by personality clashes and conflicting ambitions, Cory Aquino's stature among opposition leaders kept growing during those negotiations, and the view spread that she alone could rally broad enough support to defeat Marcos in a presidential election.

By the fall of 1985 Cory Aquino was beginning to act as a potential candidate, although she still had not declared her intentions and may have harbored serious doubts about her qualifications. Questioned about her availability she responded by asking: "What do I know about being president?" Yet she showed shrewd political judgment, as well as robust optimism. Addressing an international seminar in Singapore on the Philippines on October 1, 1985, Cory Aquino stated:

> In the past two years, I have become deeply involved in the struggle for the restoration of our rights and freedoms. I made a pledge to my husband, when I kissed him in his coffin, that I would continue his fight for the cause of justice and democracy. It would seem that many men and women from almost all sectors of society have been inspired by Ninoy's courage and sacrifice and have also committed themselves to the cause.

The cause was peaceful return to democracy. While in detention at Fort Bonifacio for seven years and seven months, Ninoy had outgrown traditional Filipino politics based on patronage, private armies, and empty promises. His religious faith had become a higher form of spirituality, with Gandhian overtones. Cory shared her husband's conviction that Marcos should be removed from office without spilling Filipino blood. In her talk to the Singapore seminar she discussed whether Marcos could be removed from power "without triggering the cycles of instability and suppression that his removal seeks to avoid" and concluded:

Those of us who believe in peaceful processes know that this is a difficult middle ground to take. But we have to hope. For the sake of our country we have to hope that a safe passage is possible. I am confident that a peaceful political situation is possible. I base my confidence principally on four factors: first, the capacity of opposition parties to unite; second, the electoral militancy of the awakened Filipino; third, the moral leadership of the Church; fourth, the reform movement of the military.

That remarkably accurate forecast, made one month before Marcos announced a snap election on November 3, 1985, and almost five months before her victory, was obviously ignored by those who questioned Cory Aquino's political acumen. In striking contrast, Marcos, who had been rated for decades by friend and foe alike as one of the most astute Filipino politicians, completely misjudged the situation that caused his downfall. President Aquino owes her present position precisely to the four factors that she had singled out as hopeful as early as October 1, when none of these factors had been tested.

Following the visit to Manila of U.S. Senator Paul Laxalt as a special emissary of President Reagan, the political tempo quickened. On October 22, while rumors circulated that Marcos was about to order a snap election, Cory Aquino indicated for the first time that she might respond to proposals she seek the presidency. She told a gathering of the Sigma Delta Phi sorority that she would make up her mind once Marcos called the snap election, but only if a million signatures were collected supporting her proposed candidacy.

She also told the sorority that she would not seek reconciliation with Marcos: "Ninoy came home on a mission for reconciliation but they killed him. . . . How can reconciliation be possible?" Initial, ill-advised White House comments after the February 7, 1986, elections ignored this statement, misjudging Cory Aquino's character and determination. The mission that she had reluctantly accepted was to remove Marcos from office, not to strengthen his hold on the country.

The following weeks must have been a period of intense soul searching for Cory Aquino. Her inner torment was revealed in an account in *Newsweek*, which dedicated its March 10, 1986, issue to President Aquino as "Woman of the Year"—significantly, without considering it necessary to identify her cover picture by name. She related that while trying to decide whether to accept the nomination, "she had a recurring dream of going to a church and seeing a casket that she expected to contain Ninoy's body. But the coffin was empty: Ninoy, she felt, had been reborn in her."

On Sunday, November 10, a week after Marcos had announced the snap election during an interview by satellite with David Brinkley, the PDP-Laban party nominated Cory Aquino as its official candidate, and the Convenor Group endorsed the nomination a day later. It took Cory Aquino another three weeks to finally accept the nomination, at the end of a climactic sequence of events and following a day of prayers and communion with her late husband.

On December 2 a special tribunal had acquitted all twenty-six accused conspirators in the assassination of Ninoy Aquino. The same day Marcos signed into law Cabinet No. 7, passed by Parliament that morning, allowing the holding of a snap presidential election, Cory Aquino was presented with 1,200,286 signatures urging her to run for president against Marcos while she was at a rally held at Santo Domingo Church, attended by some 15,000 people.

A week of political drama followed. On December 8 Doy Laurel surprised the opposition by announcing his candidacy for president, although Filipinos and some Americans hoping for a meaningful election were urging Cory and Doy to close ranks. After intense and heated debates and considerable pressure from a variety of sources at home and abroad, an agreement between them was finally reached half an hour before the December 11 deadline for filing candidacies. Laurel had agreed to step back and run as Cory's vice-presidential candidate, while she equally reluctantly consented to run under the banner of Laurel's UNIDO organization rather than under that of the PDP-Laban party, which had nominated her initially.

Once agreement was reached the two candidates campaigned together, and observers state that Doy truly campaigned for Cory: "Don't vote for me, vote for Cory," he said at rallies, telling the people that she had learned politics from the country's most eminent politician, her late husband. Despite very limited financial resources, no access to the government-controlled media, and with political organizations that were a pale shadow of the rich and powerful machine serving Marcos, Cory Aquino was able to generate massive and enthusiastic popular support. Throughout the fifty-seven day campaign the rallies grew bigger and emotionally more intense.

Experiencing again and again the spontaneously gathered crowds, cheerfully chanting "Co-ree, Co-ree" after standing for hours in the sun waiting to see and hear her, was bound to enhance the candidate's self-confidence. She became more aggressive in responding to the scurrilous lies and insults used by Marcos in his campaign. On January 23, addressing the Joint Rotary Clubs of Metro-Manila, an elite audience of some 1,500 persons who interrupted her twenty-six times with applause and gave her a standing ovation, she concluded by offering to set the record straight on some major issues raised by Marcos against her. Her memorable first point was: "I concede that I cannot match Mr. Marcos when it comes to experience. I admit that I have no experience in cheating, stealing, lying, or assassinating political opponents."

In the second month of the campaign Cory Aquino was ready to deliver carefully crafted program speeches in English before selected audiences, besides the innumerable campaign speeches in Tagalog delivered to outdoor audiences throughout the country. As the campaign progressed Cory became a political superstar both to the masses who gathered to hear her and to the foreign media who gave her the cover-story treatment that domestic media controlled by Marcos denied her. It was an amazing evolution for a woman who had told the Catholic Filipino magazine *Veritas* in December 1985 that she was more excited about being a grandmother than about becoming a president.

Actually, family background and life experience could have given Cory Aquino ample motivation to become politically ambitious. Her maternal grandfather, Don Juan Sumulong, had been a distinguished senator. Her father, Jose Cojuangco, and her younger brother, Jose (Peping) Cojuangco, Jr., had both been congressmen. Her late husband was a political powerhouse soon after they were married, and then became the most prominent victim of his ruthless enemy, Ferdinand Marcos.

Born on January 25, 1933, in Manila, Cory went to the United States to study at the age of thirteen. She attended Ravenhill Academy in Philadelphia for one year, finished high school at Notre Dame Convent School in New York, and then went to Mount St. Vincent College in the Bronx, run by the Sisters of Charity. There she majored in French and mathematics and was thinking of a teaching career. She became interested in Ninoy, whom she had known since their childhood in

Tarlac Province, while home for vacation after her third year of college. Although she had misgivings about the fact that they were the same age, she gradually became impressed by his maturity and intelligence, and they started writing to each other very often when she returned to New York. She told Nick Joaquin, the distinguished author who wrote *The Aquinos of Tarlac* in 1972, in preparation for the presidential elections, which were foiled by the proclamation of martial law, that she liked Ninoy's love letters: "Not mushy, for one thing."[1]

Back in Manila after graduating and now enrolled in the law school at Far Eastern University, Cory was going steady with Ninoy but responded that she thought it was best to wait when he repeatedly requested her to marry him. As for her graduate studies, she told Joaquin: "I was interested in law not as a profession but as a discipline." When she finally told her parents that she wanted to get married, the date was set for October 11, 1954, their own wedding anniversary, which was only ten days away. One can surmise that Cory had never been attracted to elaborate ceremonies. But President Ramon Magsaysay stood sponsor at her wedding and then sent the newlyweds to the United States for four months, where Ninoy observed training methods in intelligence schools, about which he wrote a report for Magsaysay when they returned in February 1955.

With their first child due in August 1955, Ninoy decided to buy land in his hometown, Concepcion, and to go into farming in order to earn more money than he could as a journalist. Cory stayed in Manila, where Ninoy visited her on weekends. "As a lover he is not an emotional person," Cory told Joaquin about her husband, back in 1972.[2] Soon after Ninoy had gone into farming, some of the local big landowners talked him into running for mayor of Concepcion, to help them settle some local political grudges. His widowed mother, Dona Aurora, and Cory joined in the campaign. Cory told Joaquin about her first campaign, at the age of twenty-two:

> I had to learn to adjust. I told myself that since I was in it I might as well make the most of it. Actually, I did little during that first campaign. I had just had my baby and that

[1]Nick Joaquin, *The Aquinos of Tarlac: An Essay on History as Three Generations* (Manila: Cacho Hermanos, Inc., 1983), p. 250.
[2]Ibid.

was a very good excuse. I would not have known what to do to begin with. It was his mother who did most of the campaigning.[3]

Thereafter Cory campaigned for Ninoy in Tarlac in 1959, when he ran for vice-governor, and in 1963, when he ran for governor and won 70 percent of the vote—the biggest majority a Tarlac governor had ever been given. "I just shook hands in the markets and did some house-to-house calls," she told Joaquin.[4]

By 1967 Ninoy had gained national stature as secretary general of the Liberal party and wanted to become a senatorial candidate. But on election day he would still be thirteen days shy of thirty-five, the required age for senators. The Commission on Elections approved his certificate of candidacy, and Cory, by then a mother of four, really stumped in earnest for the 1967 senate race. Under the 1935 Constitution, candidates for the senate had to campaign in the whole country. Ninoy told his biographer:

[Cory] went to all the factories in the Manila area. All the textile factories: 40,000 employees. All the cigarette factories: 30,000 employees. All the assembly factories, and Philamlife, and the markets. She did it quietly: "I am the wife of Ninoy Aquino. I'm sorry he can't be here, so I have come in his behalf." Every day, from eight to four. Sometimes with my oldest daughter. "Please vote for my Daddy." On the quiet. No fanfare. But that thing sewed up the metropolitan vote for me.[5]

Cory, in turn, told Joaquin about the 1967 senatorial campaign:

The farthest south I went was Cebu, to be godmother and shake hands; and the farthest north was La Union, where I flew for a day, to unveil a bell. I concentrated on the Greater Manila area, mostly the factories and nearby-town fiestas, shaking hands and giving out leaflets, but never going up on

[3]Ibid., p. 258.
[4]Ibid., p. 295.
[5]Ibid., p. 314.

the stage to talk or sing—never! I told Ninoy: "My goodness, you've won all your elections without my having to
sing. I don't want you to lose and then blame it on my
singing!"[6]

The night after the November 1967 election Cory was shaking Ninoy
in bed at one in the morning: "Wake up, wake up! You're leading!
You're leading!" She obviously really cared about his political career.
It could not have crossed her mind at that time that almost two decades
later, a widow and grandmother, she would draw larger crowds and get
more votes than Ninoy ever had the opportunity to garner.

Hundreds of thousands, who walked all across town without any
inducements or threats and waited for hours under a scorching sun to
hear Cory Aquino speak, came to the Luneta for her February 4 final
pre-election rally. Her post-election rally there on February 16 drew an
even larger crowd, to hear and obey Cory's appeal for nonviolent
protest the day after Marcos had proclaimed himself the victor in a
rotten election. Larger still was the victory celebration on March 2 with
Jaime Cardinal Sin celebrating a Thanksgiving Mass, then joining the
crowd in chanting "Cory! Cory!" and reading a message from Pope
John Paul II offering President Aquino "cordial good wishes."

Before a crowd estimated to exceed one million people, the new
president in her first public act read and signed Proclamation No. 1,
restoring the writ of habeas corpus. She then asked the assembled
citizens to make "people power" permanent and to become watchdogs
over government officials. She promised an uncompromising stand
against corruption, graft, nepotism, abuse of authority, incompetence,
and abuse of human rights—the whole repertoire of crimes rampant
during the Marcos regime.

Contrary to the misleading image of the housewife who became
president due to unusual circumstances, Cory Aquino was actually well
prepared for her current task. Her strong character, rooted in deep
religious faith, gave her impressive self-control. She shrewdly plays up
her stubborness, but she is actually willing to change her position when
she realizes that she was on the wrong track. This happened in 1984,
when she initially followed those who wanted to boycott the elections

[6]Ibid., p. 315.

for Parliament, and in 1985, when she initially came out against continued American use of the military bases at Clark Field and Subic Bay and admitted the possibility of including communists in her cabinet. In these instances she reversed her position.

Truly convinced that her fate is in the hands of God, who will protect her as long as she is the instrument of His will, she is oblivious to danger, a quality that people sense and appreciate in a leader. During the electoral campaign against a dangerous foe she had almost no visible security people, which augmented her image of calm and simplicity.

In retrospect her whole life can be viewed as preparation for her mission. Living in boarding schools in the United States and, deprived of the daily emotional support of an extended family from the age of thirteen to twenty-one, Cory had to become self-reliant. Married within a year after her return from schools abroad, Cory was for eighteen years a regular observer of the inner workings of Philippine political life. In September 1972 her role changed completely, when Ninoy became a political prisoner under martial law instead of a presidential candidate in the elections that Marcos canceled to maintain himself in power.

Years later while in the United States, Ninoy told an American friend that when she first visited him in prison Cory urged him to make no concessions in order to protect the considerable material interests of her family, but to follow exclusively the dictates of his conscience.

For seven years and seven months, eventually while he was under death sentence, Cory was Ninoy's political link with the outside world. She kept him informed about political events, memorized and relayed his messages to his political associates and friends at home and abroad, and helped organize the Laban party, under which Ninoy participated from his cell in the 1978 national assembly elections. While Ninoy was in jail Cory became his principal political aide, spending as much time with him in his cell as the authorities allowed, sustaining his morale, providing him with books, and leading an exemplary life that earned her the respect and admiration of all those who knew her. While living entirely for her family, Cory's hobbies were cooking, knitting, bonsai, movies, and especially reading.

In May 1980 her life changed again. Ninoy was set free by the Marcoses and rushed to Dallas, Texas, for triple-bypass surgery. The husband who had previously been under death sentence was now threatened by cardiac problems. For three years, till August 1983, Cory made a home for Ninoy and their five children in a suburb of Boston, while he was associated first with Harvard University and then with MIT. Although Ninoy traveled extensively to keep in touch with Filipinos in the United States and occasionally abroad, the family was very close during those years, and Cory has described them to friends as the happiest of her life. During that period, according to some of her relatives, Cory became her husband's real political partner, and he shared with her his plans and aspirations for the future of the Philippines. Her dream that Ninoy has been reborn in her has deep psychological validity. She knows what he would have done in her place.

Yet it would be misleading to assume that Cory Aquino is currently guided merely by her memories about what Ninoy would have done. She has stated repeatedly, in public as well as to personal friends, that she listens to many advisers but then ultimately makes her own decisions. The campaign speeches in which she outlined her program of government were drafted by a Committee of Seven, but Cory Aquino reviewed the texts word by word and edited them to reflect accurately her own views. Headed by Father Joaquin G. Bernas, president of Ateneo University, and including among its members three men who have since become cabinet ministers, the group prepared four major policy speeches: "Building From Ruins," her economic program; "Broken Promises in the Land of Promise," her social program; "Tearing Down the Dictatorship, Rebuilding Democracy," her political program; "Rescue from Disgrace in a Pharaoh's Prison," on external relations.

In the first speech, Cory Aquino told a prestigious business audience:

> While I share the general impatience to get on with the economic reconstruction and development of our country, I shall not, insofar as it lies in my power to prevent it, allow this to take place at the expense of social equity and justice. . . . I believe in the consultative approach. . . . My approach assumes that no one can know better what the people want and need, and what they are prepared to pay, than the people themselves.[7]

[7]Corazon Aquino, Speech delivered at the Intercontinental Hotel, Makati, January 6, 1986.

The private sector was described as "the engine of the economy," "the prime mover of the effort towards national recovery." Foreign investment was to be welcome, "but as a supplement to domestic capital." Outlining a path for economic recovery based on "common sense," Cory stated that "the firmest foundation for a stable economy is a motivated working force with the purchasing power to absorb the main part of a nation's productivity." This in turn required "the right of workers to organize, bargain collectively, and to exhaust all legal means for the redress of their legitimate grievances."[8] On the crucial issue of rural poverty, the candidate had this to say:

> We will review the allocation of our precious and limited arable land for domestic food crops and export crops. While we need export crops to generate foreign exchange, especially to pay the enormous debt that is Mr. Marcos's legacy to us, our first obligation is to provide for the basic food needs of our people. We are determined to implement a genuine land-reform program which will provide the beneficiaries of land reform with adequate credit and the marketing and technological support to enable them to become self-reliant and prosperous farmers.[9]

Land reform came up again, in a different context, in a later major speech Cory gave in Davao. She addressed the question, whether as a member of the wealthy Cojuangco family of sugar planters, who own some 15,000 acres of land in Tarlac Province, she could really be expected to act on land reform against her class interests:

> You will probably ask me: Will I also apply it to my family's Hacienda Luisita? My answer is yes; although sugar land is not covered by the land-reform law, I shall sit down with my family to explore how the twin goals of maximum productivity and dispersal of ownership can be exemplified for the rest of the nation in Hacienda Luisita.[10]

[8]Ibid.
[9]Ibid.
[10]Corazon Aquino, Speech delivered at the Ateneo de Davao, Davao City, January 16, 1986.

While holding his first elective office, as mayor of Concepcion, Ninoy had urged his mother to give their tenants the lots on which they lived. She told Nick Joaquin in 1972, "At first I was apprehensive, because of the other landlords: what would they say; and their tenants might demand the same thing." But she did it and "now they have this barrio where they themselves are the landowners."[11] Years later, in the early 1960s, while he was governor of Tarlac and land-reform efforts were being emasculated by the big landowners, Ninoy offered his own farm in Concepcion as a pilot area for land reform, seeking to liquidate tenancy and train the peasants to operate family-sized farms profitably.[12] These were only the first steps. According to Joaquin:

> Ninoy Aquino, with his nose for history, could not but smell the coming change in climate and, when he decided to run for senator, had sold his farm in Concepcion to his tenant farmers. "Another five hectares I owned, I had already subdivided among the tenants. So, I had no more land. I was really landless." He also advised his relatives and in-laws to unload their landholdings and go into industry. "The revolution is upon us," he warned them.[13]

Obviously his advice was not followed, as the Hacienda Luisita is still intact almost twenty years later. How Cory Aquino will cope with the land issue will have a determining influence on the future of the Philippines and on her own place in history. Her minister of agriculture, Ramon Mitra, is a highly respected opposition leader, but he is also an important rancher. In the wings, the communist party, which draws much of its appeal from land hunger and rural poverty, has already countered Cory Aquino's appeal for a policy of reconciliation with statements that they will wait and see how she handles land reform and the future of the American bases. The issue is, of course, not Hacienda Luisita, but the class survival of the big landowners, who are not only economically but also emotionally attached to lands that some of them have owned for many generations.

In outlining for the first time a comprehensive economic program,

---

[11]Joaquin, p. 260.
[12]Ibid., p. 298.
[13]Ibid., p. 321.

Cory Aquino listed as priority issues unemployment, the foreign debt, the coconut and sugar monopolies, investment priorities, rapid withdrawal of the government from private business, fiscal policies, budgetary priorities, and improved government service, stressing that all these issues would have to await consultations in order to be fleshed out.

Social problems were discussed in the second policy speech, delivered in Davao. After pledging "credibility, honesty, and integrity," Cory Aquino stated: "My government will be one of patient consultation and personal involvement. I will not ram reform down your throats. I will listen to you before I act." Curiously, a month later she is already criticized in the Manila press and by radical groups for moving too slowly, despite her persistent appeals for patience.

In listing her social priorities, "efficient utilization and equitable sharing of the ownership and benefits of land" came first, followed by the problem of labor. Third came housing and a reversal of the trend toward urban crowding, and fourth the place in society of the Muslim and tribal minorities. Health care and education were discussed next, leading, appropriately, to a major policy statement on the problem of insurgency. Mrs. Aquino promised the release of all political prisoners, which was promptly carried out in the first days after she took power. She also promised a cease-fire and dialogue with all insurgents in search of a peaceful termination of the communist and separatist armed insurrections. Her initiative has not been well received by the military and forces the Communist party to face the extremely different question whether they should renounce violence and pursue their goals within the democratic process in a society that has been dominated for centuries by an elite opposed to radical social and economic change. Cory Aquino expressed her views on the prospects of eliminating the communist threat as follows:

> As to the ideological aspect of the insurgency problem, I have no illusions that ideologies destructive of true democracy will easily die; but at the same time such ideologies will not flourish where people are happy and content. Such ideologies will merely stay in the periphery of national life.[14]

[14]Aquino, Davao speech.

During the election campaign Marcos had insistently accused Cory Aquino of being a communist, adding the equally shameless lie that her husband had been a founder of the Communist party of the Philippines, although Marcos also claimed that Ninoy had been murdered by a communist hit man. In fact, when the February 7 election was over and Marcos was manipulating the outcome in his favor, emissaries of the Bayan, the communist-controlled, openly leftist organization that had boycotted the elections, approached Cory Aquino, offering to discuss a joint strategy. Although it seemed, during those crucial post-election days, that she had lost, Cory Aquino decided, as she told an American friend, to reject any such discussions with the radical left.

The third policy speech was devoted to political issues. "My political program is simple," she told an audience of Rotarians. "I propose to dismantle the dictatorial edifice Mr. Marcos has built. In its place I propose to build for our people a genuine democracy." In the light of this and similar statements, Cory Aquino came under heavy criticism when on March 25, after being in power a month, she adopted a provisional constitution that gave her almost absolute power, and dissolved the national assembly, stating that she needed the extraordinary authority to "cut out the cancer in our political system." A new constitution was to be drafted within the next few months by appointed experts and then put to a vote by the people, and a new national assembly should be elected and in place within a year. Predictably, from exile in Hawaii Ferdinand Marcos lost no time telling reporters that the Aquino government is "just a plain and simple dictatorship," while Vice-President Salvador Laurel reassured the press: "Mrs. Corazon Aquino is not the type that will be a dictator."

Managing the transition from a deeply entrenched authoritarian system to democracy is a formidable and dangerous task. Even after the dictator had abandoned them, his supporters still controlled two-thirds of the national assembly and had vast personal and political interests to protect. At the provincial and local levels several thousand individuals had been allowed and supported by the fallen regime to consolidate their own power base to better be able to serve the rulers in Manila. Early elections at the national, provincial, and local level raised very serious practical problems at a time when the treasury was empty, the economy in shambles, participants in the February 7 presidential election exhausted, government services barely beginning to function again, and the Marcos machine still in place in most parts of the country.

Cory Aquino could only manage the transition if, with the people protected by a restored bill of rights and a credible judicial system, she assumed temporarily the power to govern by proclamation, perform legislative functions, and appoint new governors and mayors who had no vested interests in the defunct regime. Minister of Justice Neptali Gonzales, who wrote the provisional constitution, told a press conference that the present government is "democratic in essence" and "transitory in character." Asked what role Cory Aquino played in drafting the provisional constitution, Gonzales said: "You can be sure that the president went over this constitution line by line, sentence by sentence, paragraph by paragraph, and page by page." In presenting her political program on January 23, the candidate had said:

> The program I propose to you . . . is simple and straightforward: (1) We must break up the concentration of power in the hands of the Executive; (2) We must set up effective safeguards against abuse and misuse of power; (3) We must make the Executive and all who follow his directives answerable for their misdeeds. It is only thus that we can rebuild the nation from its ruin and redeem the honor and dignity of the Filipino people.[15]

To assume that a woman who is perceived by a whole nation as honest and sincere and who was the long-suffering victim of the fraud and deception of her predecessors in office could ignore her campaign pledge two months later strains credulity. The world has learned since the days of the Roman republic to distinguish between temporary dictatorship established for the purpose of managing acute crises and permanent dictatorship hiding selfish interests behind clever rhetoric. Cory Aquino will not betray the moral revolution that brought her to power.

Four days before the February 7 election Cory Aquino addressed the joint Philippine and foreign chambers of commerce, choosing that international audience for her final policy speech dealing with international issues. The thorny problem of American bases had not become a campaign issue, as the radical left, committed to the immediate removal of the bases, boycotted the election and consequently made no

---

[15]Corazon Aquino, speech delivered at the Manila Hotel, January 23, 1986.

campaign speeches, and Marcos was going overboard in seeking American support by suggested negotiations for an immediate extension of the base agreement beyond its present 1991 expiration date.

Cory Aquino started her foreign-policy address by confessing that she felt "pain and also shame" in facing an international audience, because her country had been brought to a "posture of humiliation and ridicule before the world" by defaulting on its debts, being unable to share its responsibilities in ASEAN, the Association of Southeast Asian Nations, consisting of Brunei, Indonesia, Malaysia, Philippines, Singapore, and Thailand, and being investigated for shady transactions in the disposition of foreign military aid, acquisition of real estate abroad, and cruelty and corruption at home. "We cannot renegotiate our foreign relations with dignity and honor," she said, "we cannot build solid bridges of international friendship, unless we can restore our self-respect as a nation." Therefore, she concluded, matters of foreign relations must take secondary priority, "after the process of purgation and purification has been firmly set in motion." She saw the Philippine nation at present "more deeply devastated than it was after the last great war":

> The devastation then was physical and it left the Filipino soul untarnished. The devastation today, wrought single-handedly by Mr. Marcos, is both physical and moral. It has debilitated the fiber of the the Filipino soul.
> Thus, as deep as my concern for regaining our self-respect and dignity in the family of nations, as strong as my desire to rise above the degradation and shame to which our political and economic plight has brought us, there is also in me a driving preoccupation with moral regeneration.[16]

In the same speech Cory Aquino also stated her position on the issue of the American bases, which had deeply divided the opposition in the previous two and a half years since the assassination of Ninoy Aquino had mobilized public opinion against the Marcos dictatorship:

[16]Corazon Aquino, speech delivered at the Intercontinental Hotel, Makati, February 3, 1986.

Concerning the military bases, let me simply reiterate the assurance I have already given that we do not propose to renounce the existing Military Bases Agreement or the Treaty of Mutual Defense with the United States. At the same time, however, I must state with candor that no sovereign nation should consent that a portion of its territory be a perpetual possession of a foreign power. The bases agreement expires in 1991. Before such date, a process of consultation will be undertaken—with the United States, with neighboring states, but above all with the Filipino people—so that an arrangement that will serve the best interest of the entire free world, but especially of the Filipino people, can be reached.[17]

This sensible, pragmatic policy statement, made on the eve of the election, and the prompt appointment of Vice President Salvador H. Laurel, a known supporter of the Philippine-American alliance, as foreign minister made it easy for the United States government to act without delay on the dramatic events of February 25, when Ferdinand Marcos fled the country and Cory Aquino assumed power. About two hours after the departure of the Marcos family from the Malacanang Palace, at 10:00 a.m. Washington time, Secretary of State George P. Shultz appeared in the White House briefing room and read a televised statement that said:

> With a peaceful transition to a new government of the Philippines, the United States extends recognition to this new government headed by President Aquino.
>
> We pay special tribute to her for her commitment to nonviolence, which has earned her the respect of all Americans. The new government has been produced by one of the most stirring and courageous examples of the democratic process in modern history. We honor the Filipino people.
>
> The United States stands ready, as always, to cooperate and assist the Philippines as the government of President Aquino engages the problems of economic development and national security.

[17]Ibid.

This well-advised early diplomatic recognition was followed in early March by an invitation from Speaker Thomas O'Neill, delivered by Representative Stephen Solarz, to address a joint session of the Congress, followed in late April by a phone call from President Ronald Reagan inviting President Aquino to a state visit to Washington, obviously signifying what could be called political recognition of the new regime.

Furthermore, both Secretary of Defense Caspar Weinberger and Secretary of State George Shultz, as well as other senior civilian and military officials, have called on President Aquino during her first hundred days in office, and were impressed by her inner strength. To review the staggering difficulties inherited by the new government and its initial achievements would go beyond the scope of this paper. As a first step in the transition from dictatorship to democracy the framework of the corrupt Marcos regime had to be dismantled by using discretionary powers. But civil liberties were restored, and serious efforts are being made to regain economic health, achieve more social justice, end the insurgencies peacefully, and adopt a new constitution.

Significantly, President Aquino's spokesman, Rene Saguisag, visiting Chicago during the Memorial Day weekend, told a Filipino audience: "She relishes every moment of her work. . . . She's having a real grand time discharging her duties. . . ." Cory Aquino's own views on her first hundred days in office were expressed in a nationwide TV speech on June 5, in which she said: "We have had a snap election, then we had a snap revolution, but I never promised you snap solutions."

By the time this assessment of President Corazon Aquino appears in print, many important new developments will have to have been taken into account. As anticipation of these is obviously not possible, one major event which casts additional light on her personality must be mentioned. Between September 16 and 23 President Aquino visited the United States, delivering nine major and at least fifteen other speeches to cheering audiences which included the Congress of the United States, Harvard University, the University of California at Berkeley, the United Nations General Assembly, and numerous business and civic groups. She displayed humor, toughness, quick judgment, stamina under pressure, and unfailing grace and self-confidence.

By all available accounts her meeting with President Ronald Reagan went well. After a 45-minute private conversation, which apparently focused primarily on the insurgency problem, the President of the

United States told the press, "I'm bullish on the Philippines." Secretary of State George Shultz, hosting the official dinner for President Aquino, praised her lavishly in his banquet toast and sported a yellow doll pinned to his tuxedo carrying an "I love Cory" logo. Congressional leaders were equally emphatic in their praise of the address they had heard. Senator Robert Dole told her, "You have hit a home run," to which President Aquino answered instantly, "I hope the bases were loaded." The consensus of all commentators was that her visit to the United States had been successful beyond all expectations.

Yet only the future can tell whether President Aquino's popularity at home and abroad will produce political stability and economic recovery. Without a political organization of her own she is not likely to control the lawmakers and regional and local officials to be elected next year. It is entirely possible that the first democratic elections in almost two decades will result in political paralysis, as contending factions might block each other's initiatives. Even more disturbing is the prospect of an economy which will lack for a long time to come the capacity to generate employment and even a modest measure of welfare for a population that has experienced long years of painful deprivation.

Although President Aquino views the nonviolent transition from dictatorship to democracy as a miracle which fulfilled the dream for which her husband Ninoy had given his life, a miraculous economic recovery is less likely. Inexplicably, the United States and the other democracies, which have many reasons to want to see Philippine democracy consolidated, are not providing the material resources which the Philippines desperately needs to remedy years of mismanagement and outright plunder by the Marcos dictatorship. It is as if the world expects the former housewife to have the secret of baking cakes without flour, sugar, eggs, and butter, in a stove that cannot be lit because gas and electricity have been cut off. But unfortunately faith healing has not been mastered by economic planners and managers.

There is still time. If the friends of Philippine democracy would grasp that it is in their enlightened self-interest to help make the Philippines the living proof that democracy is possible in developing countries, President Aquino may be remembered by future generations as a major figure in the endless struggle for human dignity and freedom.

17

The Political Legacy of Marcos;
The Political Inheritance of Aquino

Ross Marlay

Philippine politics is changing very fast now, after years of stagnation and atrophy. President Corazon Aquino's seemingly miraculous triumph over former President Ferdinand E. Marcos in February 1986 was greeted with euphoric celebration all over the Philippines, but her accession to power did not mark the end of her nation's problems.[1] Her inheritance from Marcos is daunting: a $26 billion debt, a factionalized military, a growing communist insurgency, and a newly awakened polity bursting with energy after fourteen years of one-man rule. As a new era of Philippine politics opens, it is appropriate to analyze the political system as it exists today, and to hazard some guesses about where it is going.

HOW TO CONCEPTUALIZE THE MARCOS REGIME

Marcos himself is unique, in some ways the product of a culture not duplicated elsewhere, but he has been variously compared to Anastasio Somoza, Jean-Claude Duvalier, Huey Long, Adolf Hitler, the Shah of Iran and Mayor Richard Daley. In some ways he was cleverer than any of these men, but in the end his regime seemed simply pointless.

Political scientists and pundits have been searching for the proper term to describe Marcos' regime. At least eight have been suggested: (1) military dictatorship, (2) clubhouse politics, (3) traditional Filipino politics, (4) corporatism, (5) totalitarianism, (6) monarchy, (7) reformist authoritarianism, and (8) kleptocracy. In fact, there is some truth to each of these characterizations, but none by itself is sufficient.

---

[1]Cardinal Sin made it explicit: "With the grace of God—and I must be honest with you and tell you that I know no other explanation for it—we toppled the dictator."

Military dictatorship. Because his vehicle for indefinite office was martial law, Marcos' regime at first seemed similar to that in Indonesia or a Latin American dictatorship. The military tripled in size during martial law, but Marcos himself was a politician, not an officer, and the mutiny that finally pushed him from Malcan'tang was started by another civilian, Minister of Defense Juan Ponce Enrile. Marcos' regime was somewhat militarized, but it was not a military dictatorship.

Clubhouse politics. It is tempting to view Marcos' party, the *Kilusang Bagong Lipunan* (New Society Movement), as a nationwide Filipino version of Mayor Daley's Chicago Democratic party machine, and indeed there are similarities, the most prominent being corruption and electoral fraud. Other parallels are a pyramid of power presided over by one "boss," the machine's patronage function, and the bending of police and judges to the imperatives of staying in power. But this analogy cannot be pushed too far, for Daley's machine was limited to Cook County, his actions were circumscribed by a constitutional Bill of Rights.

Traditional Filipino politics. Some analysts deny that Marcos transformed Philippine politics. They see continuity or, at most, gradual evolution. In this view, Marcos is a modern Quezon, a brilliant political maneuverer who pushed everyone else to the sidelines. This formula, too, is unsatisfying. Marcos' use of what Filipino pundits laughingly called the "three G's of Philippine politics, *guns, goons and gold*" was nothing new, but his middle-class Ilocano background differed significantly from that of the landed aristocrats who dominated the pre-1972 Philippine Congress. In 1972 he completely upset the rules of the game by throwing all of his enemies in jail and destroying the political system under which they and he had been elected.

Corporatism. In the early years of martial law, Professor Robert Stauffer of the University of Hawaii characterized Ferdinand Marcos' rule as "corporatist." Stauffer saw parallels between Marcos' plans to integrate all lawyers into one guild, all broadcasters into one association, and so on, and fascist political theory, which saw the polity as an organic body.[2] Stauffer was right, but Marcos never succeeded in forging unity out of the extraordinary diversity of Philippine society

[2]See Stauffer's provocative "Philippine Corporatism: A Vote on the 'New Society,'" *Asian Survey* Vol. XVII (April 1977), pp. 393-407.

and culture. Filipinos are not Germans. The most Marcos could do was to silence his opposition. He could never unite Filipinos, and he soon gave up trying.

Totalitarianism. Leftists often called Marcos a "totalitarian dictator" but from a political scientist's perspective this was strictly hyperbole. A real totalitarian regime seeks total control over the individual and total control over society. Its hallmarks are pervasive, ceaseless propaganda and a secret police to deal with people who still are not brainwashed. Marcos' propaganda was half-hearted and unconvincing. It owed more to Madison Avenue than to the really effective propaganda machines of Hitler, Stalin, or Mao. Similarly, General Ver's National Intelligence and Security Agency (NISA), evil as it was, was simply not in the same league as the KGB or the SS. Marcos never achieved total control over society, though he cowed it for eleven years, from 1972 to 1983. His control over people's thoughts was, in the end, weaker than that of the Catholic church.

Monarchy. This analogy is tempting. Filipinos have no heritage of monarchy, no ancient empire or kingdom to hark back to, and they had every reason to hate the king of Spain. Furthermore, most middle-class Filipinos assimilated the American bias against monarchs. Still, Ferdinand and Imelda put on a good show out in the barrios and she (more than he) saw herself as "a star" for "her people." Perhaps because Marcos never favored the displays of jewelry and clothes that obsessed his wife, it was not until February 1986, when Filipinos got their first look inside the palace, that they spoke of the president and the first lady as "king and queen." But monarchs stay in power through legitimacy, not fraudulent elections. Monarchs also pass their thrones to their children. The Marcoses were unable to do so.

Reformist authoritarianism. This is how Marcos saw himself. He was very acutely aware of deep flaws in Philippine society and wanted to correct them. In his own eyes he was the stern but kindly father, and the common mass of Filipinos were his children. They were still irresponsible, but he would provide the discipline and guidance they needed to reach adulthood. So his propaganda went, and he seemed to believe it himself, at least at first. Although Marcos sometimes likes to call himself a revolutionary, his political goals were reformist, until finally power and greed so encrusted him that he had no goal at all beyond staying in Malacan'tang at all costs. The terrible irony is that his "reforms" made the patient sicker, and he was never authoritarian enough with his own supporters or his own wife to stop the bandwagon of theft. This leads naturally to an eighth way to look at Marcos' regime:

Kleptocracy. Representative Stephen Solarz has said that Marcos' rule "can only be characterized as a kleptocracy, a regime which existed for the sole purpose of plundering the wealth of the country it governed."[3] This conclusion seems reasonable. Documents released to Solarz' committee by U.S. Customs prove that Marcos' larceny was on a truly grand scale. The resources of the nation—its timber, coconuts, sugar—all were his. *Part* of the fortune of *one* of his cronies (Roberto Benedicto) was equal to the *entire* fortune of Nicaragua's Somoza. Marcos is thought to have put more than $800 million in a *single* Swiss bank account. Thus, Solarz' imaginative term "kleptocracy" is appropriate, but we must qualify it. Theft was never Marcos' "sole purpose" —he had others, too, and labelling a regime a kleptocracy tells us nothing about how it acquired and held power, or what political legacy it left behind. For that, we must look more closely at the Marcos political machine.

THE KILUSANG BAGONG LIPUNAN

President Marcos called his personal political organization a "movement," not a "party," but in fact it was neither. Movements are mass-based and voluntary, while the KBL was elitist and forced—the only game in town, so to speak, for local leaders who wanted to rise by distributing largesse from above to "their people." In competitive polities, parties exist to contest elections, but from 1972 to 1984 all elections were rigged. Perhaps the KBL is best characterized as a *machine for regulating the downward and upward flow of resources and power*.

Perhaps only Ferdinand Marcos could have built such a machine. He emerged from a traditional Filipino political milieu, but transcended and transformed that milieu. He was so successful in Philippine political culture that he dominated it and bent it to his own will. Marcos' personal qualities of high intelligence, caution, patience, shrewdness, a capacity to suffer and endure, an obsessive drive to be number one in everything, and, above all, a brilliant sense of timing combined to

[3]*Associated Press Dispatch*, March 23, 1986.

enable him to rise straight to the top and to stay there for twenty years. Tragically, once he had amassed monumental power, he did little with it but enrich himself, his family, his friends, and hangers-on.

In a seminal work published before Ferdinand Marcos became president, Carl Landé used an anthropological approach to describe the structure of Philippine politics as one permeated by vertical dyadic ties.[4] The political struggle was seen as continuous with, and an extension of, the ceaseless jockeying for social prestige among prominent local families. Kit Machado later modified Landé's analysis, noting that "new men" were emerging as political brokers, men who "lacked the kind of family prominence and ties that would assure their position of leadership" if they were voted out of office. Machado saw that these "new men" had "more compelling reasons than notables from old leading families to make a career of officeholding."[5]

Landé's research was done about twenty-five years ago, and Machado's about sixteen years ago. A scholar building on their work today would have to start by recognizing that Marcos himself was the quintessential "new man," and that Marcos' KBL machine was staffed very heavily by "new men" because the old landed elite were largely disenfranchised and stripped of national power by Marcos' 1972 closure of Congress. The Laurel family in Batangas and the Osmenas in Cebu are cases in point.

Marcos' KBL did not entirely dispense with "old society" aristocrats, however, for he had forged alliances with some of them during his years in the Senate and during his first term as president. But most aristocrats were expendable as far as Marcos was concerned for he always followed the logical strategy of assembling a minimum winning coalition.[6] Marcos liked to sneer at the "oligarchs" he had outsmarted. His power seizure:

[4]Carl Landé, *Leaders, Factions and Parties: The Structure of Philippine Politics* (New Haven, Yale University Southeast Asia Studies Monograph No. 6, 1965).

[5]Kit G. Machado, "Continuity and Change in Philippine Factionalism," in Frank P. Belloni and Dennis C. Beller, (eds.), *Faction Politics: Political Parties and Factionalism in Comparative Perspective* (Santa Barbara, California: ABC-Clio, 1978), pp. 193-217.

[6]David F. Roth, "Towards a Theory of Philippine Presidential Politics," *Philippine Journal of Public Administration* 13 (1969), p. 42.

represented a breakthrough by a coalition of the central Executive and new social forces that had emerged from the Philippines' transition to modernity against the constitutional restraints on presidential power. The new coalition, in which the military, the technocracy, and foreign economic interests were important components, succeeded in destroying the old balance of power, which had rested on the adversary relationship between the Chief Executive and Congress. The disbanding of Congress by emergency fiat reflected the decisive flow of power towards the executive.[7]

Philippine political parties before martial law had no ideology at all, and there was frequent party-switching. The two parties were really nothing more than constantly shifting coalitions of leaders who could deliver blocs of votes, but who had to earn those votes by sending money and resources down to the barrios. Martial law changed all that. The old Liberal and Nacionalista parties went dormant, and Marcos personally selected all governors and mayors. His KBL was not an ideological party. It was not even a personal following. Rather, it was a pyramid of opportunism and necessity. A local leader would have been foolish not to join, for his town quickly would have been deprived of all government aid, and his people would soon have found another leader, one who could produce, one who was KBL. At the same time, some of those local leaders were firmly entrenched and probably could not have been ousted easily, even if Marcos had chosen to make the effort. Particularly after August 1983, Ferdinand Marcos dared not push any of his supporters into the arms of the growing opposition, and so chose to tolerate even the most vicious provincial warlords, such as Armando Gustillo in the Visayan sugar country.

Marcos claimed in the early 1970s to have an ideology uniquely suited for Philippine development, and had several books ghostwritten to propound his "ideology." On close inspection, however, it was neither left nor right and was not even coherent. It seemed to stress discipline and a preference for reform from the top down. It was

---

[7]Amando Dornila, "The Transformation of Patron-Client Relations and Its Political Consequences in Postwar Philippines," *Journal of Southeast Asian Studies* 16 (1985), p. 99.

explicitly opposed to class struggle, but beyond that there was little more than a collection of platitudes praising technocrats. In retrospect, it seems likely that the prime intended audience for Marcos' ideology was not the Filipino public, nor even KBL members, but rather the American government, the World Bank, and the International Monetary Fund. After a few years even those diplomats and bankers who wanted to believe in Marcos came to see the "ideology" as a thin facade.

When Marcos declared martial law in September 1972, and made it clear that this was no temporary measure, but rather a condition that would last until Philippine society was entirely reformed, he created the KBL as the vehicle for that national transformation. It seemed that Marcos had taken a leaf from Hitler's book, or Mao's. The KBL would create barrio organizations that would turn unemployed youth into "New Filipino Men." A youth group, the Kabataang Barangay, even held night-time ceremonies on Mount Makiling that had a flavor of mysterious fascist ritual. But the use of fascist trappings faded as fast as it started. Perhaps the large dose of public ridicule that the Kabataang Barangay elicited made Marcos go back to more traditional ways of influencing the political behavior of Filipinos: bribery and intimidation.

Marcos "rationalized" his government's delivery of services to the provinces by dividing the country up into twelve regions, consisting of an average of six provinces each, plus the National Capital Region, Metro-Manila. The KBL organizational structure corresponded precisely to this scheme. (So did the new military chain of command.) There were KBL regional bosses, kingmakers like Eduardo "Danding" Cojuangco, cousin of Cory Aquino. Cojuangco became probably the richest man in the Philippines after Marcos himself, and maintained a private army trained by Israelis. He fled the Philippines on the same United States plane as Marcos. Each regional boss oversaw provincial governors and national assemblymen. Regional bosses, governors and assemblymen could all be warlords. In this respect, the KBL resembled nothing so much as the Mafia. Roberto Benedicto in the *Western Visayan* sugar region supplemented his private army with troops from the Philippine Constabulary and Integrated National Police. Arturo Pacificador, warlord of Antique Province and KBL assistant majority floor leader in the Batasang Pambansa (National Assembly), gunned down his rivals in broad daylight. He is now in hiding. Eighty-year-old Ramon Durano, who so terrorized Danao City that the Aquino forces could not find a single pollwatcher, held Cebu for the KBL.[8]

Some KBL leaders were bound to Marcos and his wife by blood ties. Some were long-time political allies. Some (Benedicto, Cojuangco, and Antonio Floirendo, the banana king) were "business" partners, who later proved fair-weather friends when they abandoned Marcos in exile and extended feelers to the new Philippine government. Others may have hated Marcos, but saw no choice. On paper, it all looks perfectly pyramidal and highly centralized. The governors and assemblymen controlled the mayors, and each mayor was supposed to control the barrio (renamed *barangay*) captains. The barangay leaders were responsible for delivering the vote. A similar pyramidal structure of Marcos supporters could be discerned in the bureaucracy, particularly in those agencies such as the Bureau of Customs and the Bureau of Internal Revenue, where there was a lot of money to be made; the Commission on Immigration and Deportation (for putting the squeeze on Chinese businessmen); and of course the military and intelligence services. As with the politicians, however, the bureaucrats who aligned themselves with Marcos did so for purely instrumental reasons, not from undying loyalty or ideological affinity. They all proved willing to dump Marcos with nary a tear when the time came. One suspects that as Marcos aged, lost his sharpness, got bogged down in the trappings of his office, spent more and more time inside Malacan'tang, and saw his own legendary physical toughness sapped by kidney disease, the whole KBL structure started coming unglued.

What happened in 1986? First, the KBL broke down. All else followed from that: The election returns had to be so blatantly rigged that the whole world knew Marcos had lost, Mrs. Aquino refused to concede, the military deserted Marcos, and Americans had to help him escape. It all started with the breakdown of the KBL, and that accelerated on August 21, 1983, when Benigno Aquino, Jr. was shot through the back of the head by General Ver's men. There is a moral and a psychological dimension to politics. Quite simply, after August 1983, most decent local leaders were *ashamed* to be part of the KBL. When Mrs. Aquino ran against Marcos, local KBL leaders started deserting. Anthony Spaeth described what was happening out in the provinces in

[8]James B. Goodno, "Aquino vs. the Marcos Machine," *In These Times,* February 5, 1986.

a remarkably prescient article in the *Asian Wall Street Journal* published three weeks before the climactic 1986 presidential election:

> Former Marcos loyalists are abandoning the KBL, for a variety of reasons. Some are genuinely disappointed with Mr. Marcos. Others have lost control of their provinces or towns to other KBL politicians and have nothing to lose by switching sides. Still others hope to ally themselves with the opposition in time for the gubernatorial and mayoral elections scheduled for May.
>
> Each KBL defector could take with him the loyalties that he has built up in his province or city. In Philippine politics, local officials are often beholden to higher officials who have passed favors along to them or their *barangays*. These *utang na loob*, or debts of gratitude, are powerful forces in politics.
>
> In the past few weeks, KBL defectors have been hustling to realign those loyalties. They're traveling their local turfs, asking *barangay* captains and town councilmen to join them in Mrs. Aquino's camp—and to bring villagers with them. In this way, the opposition is, in varying degrees from province to province, eating away at the base of Mr. Marcos' political pyramid.[9]

When election day came, all the KBL money (uncountable, but reliably estimated in the hundreds of millions of dollars) and all the KBL guns could not produce a convincing victory for Marcos. What is the likely shape of the new political system that will emerge from the ruin of the New Society and the New Republic?

THE POLITICAL INHERITANCE OF AQUINO

Under the new "Freedom Constitution" proclaimed in March, President Aquino can make laws, set election dates, appoint and dismiss mayors and governors, appoint new judges to all courts, reorganize government commissions and name all forty-eight people to a commis-

---

[9]Anthony Spaeth, "Marcos' Well-Oiled Political Machine Starting to Break Down in the Provinces," *Asian Wall Street Journal*, January 20, 1986, p. 2.

sion to write a new constitution. She set about dismantling or remaking the three "unjust structures" of Marcos rule: the National Assembly, the Supreme Court, and the Commission on Elections. Armed Forces Chief of Staff Fidel Ramos and Defense Minister Enrile have taken apart two other "unjust structures," the Presidential Security Command and the National Intelligence and Security Agency. Meanwhile, the new Justice Minister Neptali Gonzalez carefully formulated an official statement on the nature of the present government. It is "revolutionary in origin and nature, democratic in essence and essentially transitory in character."

At first glance it appears that President Aquino has a golden opportunity to wipe the slate clean and start fresh. Her popularity is still extremely high and those members of the Marcos-Ver clique not in exile are lying low. Her actual ability to reshape the polity is a great deal more limited than the "Freedom Constitution" would suggest, however. She will be constrained by foreign debt, continuing factional and ideological fights, and above all by the stubborn problems of rural backwardness, overpopulation, unemployment, and resource depletion —in short, by Philippine "underdevelopment." Some would add to this list of woes the observation that Philippine society is still semi-feudal and that the nation is at the mercy of richer and stronger nations.

The future of Philippine politics hinges on answers to four questions: (1) Can the present Aquino coalition hold together? (2) What is happening politically out in the villages? (3) What is the status of Philippine political parties today? (4) Can really programmatic or ideological parties emerge in the Philippines? Let us consider these questions one at a time.

Can the Present Aquino Coalition Hold Together?

Officials in Washington were greatly relieved when they learned of Mrs. Aquino's cabinet choices. There were many familiar faces and no radicals. Some cabinet members had been allied with Marcos in the past (notably Defense Minister Juan Ponce Enrile, Natural Resources Minister Ernesto Maceda and Central Bank Governor Jose Fernandez). Some had been senators before martial law (Agriculture Minister Ramon Mitra and Jovito Salonga, chairman of the Presidential Commission on Good Government). Many had close ties with the United States (Enrile, Salonga, Maceda, Aquino herself, and of course her running-mate, Salvador Laurel). Two are regarded as financial reformers (Trade and Industry Minister Jose Concepcion, Jr., and Finance Minister Jaime Ongpin). All in all, it is a talented and reassuring group. However, it contains the seeds of factionalism.

For one thing, at least four members of the Aquino cabinet are themselves openly ambitious to become president one day: Laurel, Salonga, Enrile and Local Government Minister Aquilino Pimentel. Only two of the four (Salonga and Pimentel) are fully trusted by Aquino backers. Salonga is a bible-quoting Protestant in a nation of Catholics, and is regarded as trustworthy and perhaps not political enough to make trouble. Pimentel, by contrast, is supremely political and may be setting himself up for future campaigns, but for the present he seems firmly committed to Mrs. Aquino.

Vice President Salvador Laurel presents something of a problem. He wants very badly to be president, and nearly torpedoed the effort to unseat Marcos by refusing until the eleventh hour to accept the vice-presidential slot. Finally, he acceded to the pleas of Jaime Cardinal Sin who pointed out that only Mrs. Aquino possessed the potent symbolic force of being a martyr's widow. Laurel temporarily swallowed his pride and joined Mrs. Aquino, but throughout the campaign his supporters and hers distrusted each other and acted independently. Laurel is a scion of an old, wealthy political family, and reform-minded Filipinos see him as only slightly more progressive than Marcos. Laurel was shocked that Aquino gave "his men" only two slots in the cabinet (Maceda, and Luis Villafuerte, the chairman of the Presidential Commission on Government Reorganization).[10]

If Laurel's loyalty to Mrs. Aquino is dubious, that of Defense Minister Enrile is even more so. Philippine culture stresses forgiveness and reconciliation, but it strains credulity to think that Mrs. Aquino could be comfortable with a defense minister who kept her husband in jail for seven years. Enrile has said that if his critics are willing to give him a chance he will show them "just what kind of man I am," but that is precisely what they fear. He cannot move against Aquino now because of her immense popularity, and she cannot move against him because of the real danger that he might do to her what he did to Marcos. Enrile has become more assertive lately, and the Aquino government has not had time yet to promote its own supporters to

[10]Cherie M. Querol-Moreno, "President Aquino's Cabinet," *Philippine News* (San Francisco), March 12-18, 1986.

positions of command. There are intriguing signs that Enrile is already attracting strong regional (Ilocano) support. It is possible that after their experience with Marcos, other ethnolinguistic groups in the Philippines might be leary of another Ilocano president.

Mrs. Aquino has no experience as a politician and that was part of her attraction. She was, above all else, clean and honest, but that was Jimmy Carter's strong point in 1976, too. Like Carter, President Aquino now must show that she can exert political muscle to rein in an all-star cabinet with strong centrifugal tendencies. Mrs. Aquino is deeply religious, like Carter. That can make compromise difficult. Some critics believe she is in thrall to a "Jesuit Mafia," particularly to Father Joaquin Bernas, president of Ateneo de Manila University.[11]

What is Happening Politically Out in the Villages?

President Aquino has set herself three tasks, and has moved strongly and decisively to complete them: (1) disarm the warlords, (2) remove KBL governors and mayors, and (3) prepare for the local elections to be held next year. Rapid progress has been made in disarming the warlords. Little has been heard of Eduardo Cojuangco's private army, which was based in Central Luzon, Negros, and Bugsuk Island. Likewise, the local hoodlums who comprised Armando Gustilo's army in Negros have been quiet since the Aquino takeover. Residents of Antique, no longer terrorized by Arturo Pacificador, danced in the plaza where hired guns killed his rival, Evelio Javier, an Aquino supporter. Much depends on General Fidel Ramos' success in re-introducing professionalism to the Philippine Constabulary and the Armed Forces of the Philippines.

Mrs. Aquino has also shown determination, even ruthlessness, in ousting former Marcos supporters from local offices all over the country. This is perfectly legal. The Philippines was never a federal state, and local officials remain subordinate to national officials. The terms of office of all local officials expired March 3. Mrs. Aquino has designated Aquilino Pimentel as her broom to sweep the country clean of Marcos men. Pimentel has been busy naming his and Aquino's supporters to mayorships and governorships all over the islands.

---

[11]Francis X. Clines, "Aquino Makes Some Moves, But Still Seems in Low Gear," *New York Times,* March 30, 1986.

They have met some resistance. In Pampanga, Vice-governor Cicero Punsalan barricaded himself in the provincial capital, and in its capital city San Fernando the mayor barricaded himself in the town hall. In San Juan (part of Metro-Manila) Mayor Joseph Estrada "hunkered down inside City Hall, refusing to leave, while hundreds of people massed at the front door to prevent [his replacement] from entering."[12] Olongapo Mayor Richard Gordon also rallied his supporters and tried to stay in office despite the fact that Pimentel named a replacement. The Aquino people are unsympathetic. Pimentel called the holdouts "free-loaders" and Executive Secretary Joker Arroyo defended their replacement by saying that "they are the very people who cheated in the elections—the ones who caused this abnormal situation."[13]

Local resistance cannot last long because the provinces and towns have no way to raise local revenue and so are almost completely dependent on Manila. At least until a national legislature is elected local officials will be as beholden to Aquino and Pimentel as they were to Marcos. Nor will it be easy for local anti-Aquino leaders to get elected next year, because they could only draw national support from opposition members of the new legislature, and *those* offices will not be filled until next year either.

Of course, there is another political actor in the villages, which exists outside of, and at war with, the "normal" electoral system—the New People's Army. Its role in future elections is impossible to predict as the NPA itself is in crisis because of its disastrously wrong strategy of boycott in February 1986. The NPA could play a spoiler role by disrupting local elections, it could back certain candidates, or it could adopt a "hands-off" strategy.

What Is the Status of Philippine Political Parties Today?

First, KBL members are down but not out. Mrs. Aquino was surely wise to do to the *Batasan* what Marcos did to the old Congress—completely disband it. As long as it remained, President Marcos would have had a lever for exerting influence, even from exile. Incredible as it may sound, Marcos has not given up hope of returning someday. That is why he had himself sworn in before he departed. The likelihood of

---

[12]Clyde Haberman, "Manila Regime With Two Mayors," *New York Times,* March 30, 1986.
[13]*Christian Science Monitor*, March 10, 1986.

his ever returning is near zero, however, although if he runs true to form he will never stop trying. His series of telephone calls to the Manila Hotel during Arturo Tolentino's failed coup attempt clearly shows Marcos' intent, but also clearly shows how little Marcos can now accomplish. The very blunt U.S. State Department "political obituary" for Marcos, delivered by spokesman Bernard Kalb, signals Washington's determination to clamp down on Marcos' meddling in the still-delicate situation in Manila. It read, in part: "The United States considers Ferdinand Marcos a persona from the past—past tense and so forth." That is hardly the language of diplomacy, and must have been intended to get the message to Marcos' allies, as well as to Marcos himself.

More immediately, Minister Enrile controlled a bloc of thirty-one KBL assemblymen, and the loyalties of the rest were divided between Blas Ople, Leonardo Perez and Jose Rono. Arturo Tolentino and Cesar Virata each had followings, too, but in the executive branch rather than the legislature. The ingratitude of KBL men was breathtaking. Orlando Dulay (suspected of killing Aquino followers in Quirino Province) praised the new openness KBL members displayed after Marcos' flight: "Our caucus was different—everybody can talk now. When we used to meet in caucus, everything was precooked."[14]

The KBL tried nearly everything to preserve itself. It offered to switch loyalties and proclaim Aquino president, even though it had already obediently proclaimed Marcos president. It made overtures to Minister Enrile, asking him to lead it from within Mrs. Aquino's cabinet. It toyed with changing its name to "Partido Nacionalista ng Pilipinas." Blas Ople, formerly one of Marcos' most abject sycophants, whined that Marcos had "betrayed the trust not only of his nation but also of his own political party." But there is little hope that the KBL can hold together as a party. It is already splitting, crumbling, breaking down into discrete factions. Depending on the fortunes of particular factional leaders, some KBL factions may be able to rejoin the political process next year in opposition to the Aquino government. Some KBL factions may actually be decimated by revenge killings carried out by local rivals persecuted during the reign of the KBL. This is already happening in provinces with a long record of political

[14]*New York Times*, March 4, 1986.

warfare, such as Tarlac and Ilocos Sur. The biggest long-range threat to Aquino and Pimentel is that former KBL elements may join Laurel's United Nationalist Democratic Organization (UNIDO). Such a combination would have wealth, political savvy, experience and an immense network of connections.

The future of UNIDO is an open question. On the one hand, many of its members may be co-opted into Pimentel's party. On the other hand, UNIDO represents more than just the Laurels of Batangas. It stands for all the "old society" legislators who refused to fade away under martial law. As such, it is in a better position than the weak and divided Liberal party survivors (Jovito Salonga and Eva Estrada Kalaw) who were unable to challenge Marcos in 1984 or 1986. UNIDO has done surprisingly well in the selection of "officers in charge" (OIC's), probably because Pimentel's initially overt favoritism of PDP-Laban drew such loud protests from UNIDO that the "Cory coalition" threatened to come undone. Of sixty-eight OIC governors picked by Aquino and Pimentel as of June 1986, fifty-six were UNIDO, eleven were PDP/Laban, and one represented a regional party named Panaghiusa. Of fifty-four OIC mayors named, thirty-eight were UNIDO, eleven were PDP/Laban, and five represented minor parties. Seemingly irrelevant at this point is the Social Democratic party organized around Kit Tatad of Catanduanes. Little is likely to be heard from the Pusyon Bisaya, defunct since the late 1970s.

For now, the party to watch is the Pilipino Democratic party, also known as PDP-Laban. Its chairman is Pimentel, and since he has been given carte blanche to name local officials all over the country (except Batangas), it is likely that only PDP-Laban will be well-organized when local elections are held. Thus, it will have a head start in the Philippines' new political system, and will probably elect many members to whatever legislative body the new constitution will establish. Jose Cojuangco, President Aquino's brother, is secretary-general of PDP-Laban, so the party is unlikely to stray too far away from the president. If Corazon Aquino is to be more than a transitional figure, she must build a real party, and PDP-Laban does differ in some important ways from the agglomerations of personal factions that were called "parties" before 1972. It has an ideology (social democratic, mildly left of center), it is a cadre party (special training is required for anyone who wants to join), and it has tried something only underground parties have tried before: organizing the urban and rural poor.[15] The most likely prospect for the future is a two-party system pitting PDP-Laban against UNIDO plus discrete defectors from the KBL.

Can Really Programmatic or Ideological Parties Emerge in the Philippines?

We need first to remember that no political system is ever autonomous; it is always profoundly affected by a nation's economic and social systems, and by the national culture. This is especially true when an entire political system is starting from scratch. Whether or not the new Philippine political system can contain the nation's bitter and deep social and economic cleavages remains to be seen. The actions of key extra-political actors (church, army, labor unions, business) will be critical. All played important roles in bringing down Marcos, and all believe they have a right to be heeded by Aquino. The same is true for many so-called "cause-oriented groups" composed of smart, young, Manilenos who were activists but who despaired of traditional political participation. These groups could well be absorbed into PDP-Laban, if that party remains programmatic and does not slip into old-society ways.

One dilemma remains: The people interested in ideology and activism are concentrated in Manila, whereas most of the voters are still poor peasants out in the countryside. They are largely unable to view politics as a long-term effort to achieve national goals; their needs are much more immediate—money or, better yet, a job. Their orientation toward political action is wholly different from that of urbane Manilenos. They still rely on patron-client ties for security in a harsh environment.

The old factional politics described by Landé and Machado met the immediate needs of the poor, especially outside of Manila. The new ideological politics appeals to those who brought Marcos down. The future will belong to that party which most successfully unites the two.

---

[15]See Paul Quinn-Judge, "Power Struggle in Aquino Ranks," *Christian Science Monitor,* March 10, 1986.

18

The Changing Structure Of Philippine Government from Marcos To Aquino

David A. Rosenberg

INTRODUCTION

On February 25, 1986, Philippine President Ferdinand E. Marcos was forced out of power in the Philippines, ending nearly twenty years of rule. During that time, the country was transformed profoundly. Marcos changed the institutions of Philippine government to centralize and personalize his control over the main sources of power and wealth in the country. "Crony capitalism" left deep structural flaws in the economy. The "green revolution" benefited some Filipino farmers, but it also led to the creation of a large and durable class of landless peasants and urban squatters. They have lost their traditionally local and conservative orientations and have become ripe for radical mobilization. The role of the church changed drastically from having been the staunch supporter of the status quo to being the constant critic of government. Liberation theology led some in the church into organizing Basic Christian Communities and other social and political action groups to seek redress for popular grievances. Patron-client ties—the fundamental building blocks of Filipino political power—were torn apart. The military became highly politicized and tainted by frequent reports of abuses. A new generation of rebel leaders has succeeded in attracting supporters of armed struggle for national liberation throughout the country.

This essay provides an analysis of how and why the structure of Philippine government has changed in the past twenty years. It describes how Ferdinand Marcos established and maintained his "constitutional authoritarian" government. It attempts to identify the basic political dynamics that account for the rise and fall of the Marcos government. It also describes the enduring problems that now confront the government of Corazon Aquino and the "people power" which provides her popular legitimacy.

FROM DEMOCRACY TO DICTATORSHIP

On September 23, 1972, the Philippines ended its long experiment with Western-style democracy. On that day, President Marcos proclaimed martial law throughout the country and began a drastic transformation of Philippine political institutions. He rapidly began to dismantle the superstructure of constitutional government which had been transplanted to the Philippines under American colonial rule. Congress was dissolved, civil liberties were sharply curtailed, and the constitution of 1935 was replaced. A "New Society" was proposed by President Marcos to be implemented by a new style of government, "constitutional authoritarianism."

Why was martial law deemed necessary? The official explanation provided by Marcos in Proclamation No. 1081 stated that the country was in "urgent danger of violent overthrow, insurrection, and rebellion." Communist subversives, right-wing oligarchs, Muslim rebels, urban terrorists, student demonstrators, labor unrest, economic setbacks and natural disasters—all these, said Marcos, necessitated the regrettable but temporary imposition of martial law to restore order to the country. Marcos emphasized the immediate right-wing and left-wing threats to the Philippines. No change of government was intended. To the contrary, Marcos stated explicitly that martial law did not mean a military take-over of civilian government and that he was acting strictly in accordance with the existing constitution and laws of the Republic of the Philippines.

Other presidential statements, however, offered a long-term justification for authoritarian government, namely, that it was necessary to make drastic changes in government to achieve urgent socio-economic reforms. It was necessary to create the "New Society." The "Emancipation of Tenants from the Bondage of the Soil" was one of the earliest and most publicized of these early martial law reform proposals.[1] "The land reform program is the only gauge for the success or failure of the New

---

[1]Presidential Decree No. 27, "The Emancipation of Tenants from the Bondage of the Soil," October 21, 1972.

Society," said Marcos. "If land reform fails, there is no New Society."[2]

Marcos also proposed drastic changes in the government structure, including the creation of a new system of popular representation based on barangays or "citizens' assemblies," and extensive administrative and economic reforms. These bold new proposals were important in winning the support of the domestic and foreign business community.

However, there is now considerable evidence to dispute the official justifications for the imposition of authoritarian government. The precipitating incident for the declaration of martial law was an assassination attempt against Defense Secretary Juan Ponce Enrile as he was driving home on September 21, 1972. But Enrile, still the defense secretary in the new Aquino cabinet, has now confessed that the incident was a hoax, staged to provide a pretext for the Marcos take-over.[3]

Marcos claimed that the loss of civil liberties and representative government was the regrettable but temporary price that Filipinos would have to pay for political stability, economic growth, and social reform. But there is also considerable evidence to indicate that Marcos was not willing to implement the necessary policies to achieve these objectives. To the contrary, his government ultimately failed because it could not provide political stability, economic growth, or social reform. In many ways, the country is now worse off than it was before Marcos' rule.

CONSEQUENCES OF MARTIAL LAW AND AUTHORITARIAN GOVERNMENT

Concentration of political power

The New Society produced a sharp increase in the concentration of political power within the central government, especially in the urban areas. President Marcos shared this power with his wife, Imelda Romualdez Marcos, and his close allies. These included Eduardo Cojuangco and Roberto Benedicto, chief among the crony capitalists, as well as a few "technocrats" or other government policy makers, such as Cesar Virata, finance minister and later prime minister in the Marcos government, who together increasingly controlled and directed the economy.

[2]Reported in David A. Rosenberg, "Introduction: Creating A 'New Society,'" in David A. Rosenberg, ed., *Marcos and Martial Law in the Philippines* (Ithaca, N.Y.: Cornell University Press, 1979), p. 22.
[3]*New York Times*, February 25, 1986.

Imelda Romualdez Marcos had an increasing share of national power and wealth. Initially, she was concerned with various beautification campaigns and the building of national monuments. In 1975, she was appointed governor of Metro Manila. In 1978, she was the leading candidate for the president's ruling party, the KBL (Kilusang Bagong Lipunan or New Society Movement), in the interim national assembly elections. She also became head of the Ministry of Human Settlements, thereby gaining discretionary control over vast expenditures at the local level. In addition, she served on numerous occasions as a special ambassador and presidential emissary to the United Nations, the United States, the Soviet Union, China, the Middle East, and many other countries. Many other members of the Marcos and Romualdez families obtained high positions in the government and the economy.

The military acquired other important political roles in this new, contracted ruling elite group. At the outset, a dozen military leaders, the president's "Twelve Disciples," agreed to support Marcos and his martial law rule, including almost all the top-ranking officers of the military.[4] By detaining thousands of real and potential dissidents and taking control of all national and international communications, the military provided the essential coercive force necessary to impose martial law. Many military officers were appointed ambassadors and presidential envoys, directors of government agencies and corporations, members of military tribunals, officials of local and provincial government, and other administrators of martial law. The Presidential Regional Officers for Development, or "PRODS," in charge of administering development programs, were mostly drawn from the military. The management of several corporations taken over by the government as well as the National Investment Development Corporation was turned over to the military. Marcos gained control over the military through selective promotions and transfers as well as a dramatic increase in the power and prosperity of the "integrated" national armed forces. The size and budget of Philippine Armed Forces increased rapidly. Base pay rates, living allowances, and housing allowances

---

[4]A detailed analysis of the changing role of the military, along with a list of the "twelve disciples," may be found in Carolina G. Hernandez, "The Extent of Civilian Control of the Military in the Philippines: 1946-1976" (Unpublished Ph.D. dissertation, State University of New York at Buffalo, 1979), available through University Microfilms, Ann Arbor, Michigan.

were increased considerably. Investment opportunities for military officers were opened up, such as the Veterans' Investment Development Corporation.

Marcos tightened the chains of command in the hands of his most loyal supporters. The most notable example of this was Fabian Ver, a relative and once a personal bodyguard and chauffeur for Marcos; he became chief of staff of the Philippine Armed Forces, director of the National Intelligence and Security Administration, and chief of the Presidential Security Command at Malacantang Palace. His last presidential assignment was "to ensure the safety and honesty" of the February 7, 1986 presidential elections.

To summarize, according to a leading authority, "the scale of such penetration of the military in practically every aspect of government and society, from housing to postal services to transportation, from stevedoring to janitorial services, is unprecedented in the nation's history."[5]

All these Marcos supporters were bound together in a governing coalition based on traditional kinship and ethnic loyalties, regional alliances, patronage, graft and corruption, and coercive force.

Initially, the restoration of law and order was widely cited as the major achievement of the New Society. Private armies and crime syndicates were disbanded, and thousands of unlicensed guns were confiscated. A government shake-up led to the dismissal of many corrupt officials. Government revenues increased through improved tax collections. The rate of inflation declined. Foreign investment increased substantially, as did domestic capital formation. Tourism increased. At the outset, the New Society had considerable support from the business community, the urban middle class, landlords, and the military and civilian bureaucracies.

Concentration of Economic Power and Increased Dependence on the World Market

The short-run gains of authoritarian rule were offset by problems due to the growing concentration of power and wealth within the economy

[5]Carolina G. Hernandez, "The Military and the Future of Civilian Rule in the Context of the Prevailing Political Crisis," in Alexander R. Magno, ed., *Nation in Crisis: The University Inquires into the Present* (Diliman, Quezon City: University of the Philippines Press, 1984), viii, 251 pages (Distributed in North America by University Press of Hawaii).

similar to that within the political system. The crucial units of capital accumulation and economic power were the elite families and their allies who enjoyed the patronage of Ferdinand and Imelda Marcos. Many of these "crony capitalists" enriched themselves, their firms, and their families through concessionary government and "public enterprise" loans and licenses. Nepotism, patronage, and pork-barrel politics, often present in Philippine politics, became systematic and comprehensive during the Marcos years.

While the Marcos administration was praised by some for increasing economic growth, it was criticized by others for not distributing the benefits of this growth widely enough. Despite the prominent themes of discipline and austerity in the New Society, there was ample evidence of conspicuous consumption and extravagant affluence. Economic reforms or social welfare policies such as land reform were implemented only to the extent necessary to avoid open rebellion and secure at least passive acquiescence to the New Society.

By actively pursuing policies to create "an attractive environment for foreign investment," the Marcos administration greatly favored large firms in the industrial and trade sectors of the economy, many of which became the local junior partners of multinational corporations. As a consequence, the Philippines has increased its already high dependence on the world market to sell its major exports—copper and other minerals, sugar, coconut products, palm oil, and timber—and to obtain the necessary inputs—oil, technology, and capital—for the New Society development program. Indeed, many of the economic successes and reversals of the martial law government may be more accurately attributed to changes in world market prices for key Philippine exports and imports rather than to any improvement in government management of the economy.

Decline in Political Participation: Elections and the National Assembly

The concentration of economic and political power greatly reduced political activity in the New Society. Initially, congress was disbanded, political parties and many interest groups were restricted, and their leaders were arrested. Due process was denied to many Filipinos, who were detained without charges for indefinite periods. The role of local and provincial government was sharply reduced. Strikes and other job actions by labor unions were banned. The right to organize rallies, public meetings, or other political activities was denied. The news media were censored. Licenses were required for all publications. Even mimeograph machines had to be registered with military.

With the imposition of martial law, party politics and electoral competition were suspended. Elections were held to be "costly, divisive, counter-productive and destabilizing."[6] Whatever electoral exercises were held between 1972 and 1978 were in the form of plebiscites and referenda carefully staged to demonstrate popular consent to the policies of the martial law regime.

After six years of consolidating his rule, Marcos resumed elections for the new institutions of participatory government. Elections were held in 1978 to elect an interim national assembly, in 1980 to elect local government officials, in 1981 to elect the president, in 1982 to elect the officials of the barangay or village government, in 1984 to elect the regular national assembly, and lastly, in February 1986 to elect the president. In general, these elections were "neither fair nor clean."[7] Many government employees openly worked for Marcos and his designated candidates in these elections. Many more were paid spectators at pro-Marcos and pro-KBL rallies. From the printing and distributing of ballots, to the tabulation and transmittal of the tallies, to the adjudication and declaration of the final voting results, these "demonstration elections" were controlled by Marcos and his appointees on the Commission on Elections, the Commission on Audit, the Civil Service Commission, and other agencies of the government.

The Batasang Pambansa or National Assembly, the ostensible legislative body of the Philippines, was widely viewed as a "rubber-stamp" legislature. Proposed at the outset of martial law in 1972, it was not convened until after the 1978 elections to the interim Batasang Pambansa. From mid-1978 up to 1986, it remained firmly under the control of Marcos and his supporters in the KBL. Abraham Sarmiento, an opposition Liberal party official, conducted a study of the legislature and concluded that it was ineffective, expensive, and unnecessary

---

[6]Carolina Hernandez, "Constitutional Authoritarianism and the Prospects of Democracy in the Philippines," *Journal of International Affairs*, Winter 1985 (38:2), pp. 243-258.
[7]Ibid., p. 248.

compared to the president's formidable decree powers.[8]

The president's decree powers were vast and were exercised widely to set policies, create or abolish institutions, and manage the government civil and military bureaucracies. Dissent was stifled through Presidential Commitment Orders (PCOs) and subsequently, preventive detention actions (PDAs), which authorized the arrest and detention of anyone suspected of intending to commit a subversive act.

Amendment No. 6 of the 1973 constitution further strengthened the powers of the president by providing that "whenever in the judgment of the President (Prime Minister), there exists a grave emergency or a threat or imminence thereof, or whenever the interim Batasang Pambansa or the regular National Assembly fails or is unable to act adequately on any matter for any reason that in his judgment requires immediate action, he may, in order to meet the exigency, issue the necessary decrees, orders, or letters of instruction, which shall form part of the law of the land."[9]

Amendment No. 6 was objectionable on several grounds, according to Carolina Hernandez:

> It authorizes the president to issue decrees and orders on any subject. It can lead to abuse and enables the president to issue the dreaded "secret decrees." In addition, it violates the principle that all laws are repealable. Even if the assembly issues a law repealing a PD, presidential approval is required for it to become valid. Finally, the assembly is reduced to a subordinate body under the primacy of the president.[10]

The few mass organizations that were created—the system of citizens' assemblies, the national assembly, as well as the KBL, Marcos's political party—clearly were not genuine representative or deliberative bodies. They were instrumental, however, in the distribution of material and status benefits allocated by Marcos. Indeed, the political structure of the New Society was so personalistic that no provisions for

---

[8]Abraham Sarmiento, Speech at the Symposium on Women in Media Now (WOMEN), National Heritage Art Center, Quezon City, January 21, 1984.

[9]Amendment No. 6, Constitution of the Philippines, January 17, 1973, as amended October 27, 1976.

[10]Hernandez, op. cit., p. 247.

presidential succession were announced until 1981, when martial law was formally lifted and an executive council was created to govern in the president's absence or incapacity. In June of that year, Marcos permitted a presidential election which he won with eighty-eight percent of the vote against token opposition in an election marked by voting abuses and a widespread boycott.

The Decline of the Courts and Constitutional Legitimacy

Immediately after the declaration of martial law in September 1972, with his critics in jail and the press muzzled, Marcos moved quickly to consolidate his rule. He manipulated the constitutional convention that had been called in 1971 to draft a new constitution which gave him combined executive and legislative powers. It also gave him sole authority to appoint and remove all government officials—civilian and military, in all branches of government. In January 1973, Filipinos were convened in the newly established citizens' assemblies and were asked to raise their hands in support of the 1973 constitution. A compliant Supreme Court ruled that, although this was an unconstitutional method of ratification, the new constitution was in full force and effect. In June 1973, as Marcos approached the original two-term limit on his incumbency, he conducted another referendum which asked Filipinos: "Shall President Marcos continue in office and finish the reforms he has initiated under Martial Law?" Under these intimidating circumstances, it is not surprising that the censored press reported overwhelming approval for continued Marcos rule. In this manner, Marcos clothed his power grab in constitutional garb and gave his New Society an appearance of legitimacy.

The Supreme Court, once an independent and highly respected institution, lost public esteem as it became a willing accomplice in the removal of civil liberties and democratic procedures which had been guaranteed in the 1935 Constitution. Raul de Guzman economically summarized the Supreme Court decisions which legitimized Marcos rule by martial law:

(1) Validity of the suspension of the privilege of habeas corpus; (2) Power of the President to call a plebiscite for the ratification of the Constitution; (3) Validity and effectivity of the new Constitution; (4) Constitutionality of martial law; (5) Constitutionality of the Referendum of 1975 (reorganizing local government); (6)

Validity of the creation and jurisdiction of military tribunals; (7) Power of the President to propose amendments to the Constitution; (8) Validity of the Judicial Reorganization Act of 1980; and (9) Power of the President to exercise legislative power even after Martial Law.[11]

The Supreme Court remained compliant to Marcos and his authoritarian rule until the assassination of Benigno Aquino, Jr., in August 1983 after which it began to assert its independence in a series of rulings granting greater freedom of assembly.

After the initial shock of martial law wore off, there were signs of a growing disillusionment with the government's policies. Strikes and demonstrations, although illegal, still occurred. Crime and corruption surpassed pre-martial law levels by the mid-1970s. Underground resistance and open protest against the Marcos administration grew slowly but steadily.

The New Society dealt with dissent in a number of ways. Centralized control over the economy and all government agencies as well as a submissive mass media were sufficient to ensure widespread compliance with the regime's peace and order policies. In order to control his own government bureaucracy, President Marcos resorted to a system of informants, frequent dismissals, and personnel changes. Outside of government, he attempted to win and maintain friends and allies through the strategic distribution of economic rewards, culminating in the system of "crony capitalism." As long as economic performance was high, this brand of pay-off politics and coercive intimidation was adequate to reinforce the ruling alliance and minimize significant dissent. Nevertheless, as inequalities increased and as popular grievances accumulated, the costs of repression also increased.

Arbitrary arrests and intimidations increased steadily, but large-scale coercion was used only selectively. However, local military units, often beyond the effective control of the central government, were frequently accused of committing arbitrary violence. Amnesty International documented numerous charges that prisoners were tortured and

---

[11]Raul de Guzman, "The Evolution of Filipino Political Institutions: Prospects for Normalization in the Philippines," Paper presented at the Joint Seminar on U.S.-Philippine Relations, Georgetown University, Center for Strategic and International Studies, Washington, D.C., September 11, 1982.

executed.[12] With an expanding military and increasing military aid, Marcos was able to pay the increasing cost of maintaining rule without submitting his government to any genuine test of popular legitimacy.

CHALLENGES OF THE 1980s

By the 1980s, the Philippine government had accumulated so many vested interests and had insulated itself from popular concerns to such an extent that it was unable to respond to the major external and internal challenges of the decade.

Economic Decline

In part, the general problem of the Philippine economy is a familiar one for developing countries pursuing an export-led growth strategy. Import costs increased significantly in the 1970s, especially oil prices. A major recession in the industrial countries and a decline in world trade decreased demand for Philippine exports. The result was a steady increase in the balance of payments deficit. Rising interest rates and new protectionist policies in industrial countries exacerbated the problem into a major debt crisis.

During the Marcos years, these external problems were compounded by financial mismanagement and corruption. The full extent of the plunder of national resources has yet to be calculated, but some well-documented cases indicate the dimensions of the problem. For example, in 1984, IMF auditors discovered that the total foreign debt had been understated by over $7 billion for most of 1983 due to "accounting errors." That debt is now estimated at over $25 billion. The Philippine Central Bank had overstated its foreign exchange reserves in 1983 by about $600 million. To make matters worse, the money supply had been inexplicably expanded by about thirty percent during the last quarter of 1983 after the assassination of Benigno Aquino, Jr. The result of this mismanagement and corruption was a surge in inflation, up to fifty percent per year, and an alarming outburst of capital flight. Foreign reserves dropped drastically—from $2.28 billion on June 30, 1983, to $430 million on October 17, 1983—until the IMF imposed an economic austerity program. This resulted in the

---

[12]See *Report of Amnesty International Mission to the Republic of the Philippines, November 11-28, 1981,* Amnesty International, 1982.

devaluation of the currency, cuts in government spending, tight credit controls, factory closings, and job layoffs. As a result, real gross national product fell by 5.5 percent in 1984 and by an estimated 5 percent in 1985.

This economic contraction added to the country's poverty. High unemployment, declining real wages, widespread malnutrition, and high infant mortality rates are all symptomatic of one of the most unequal distributions of national income in Asia.

The economic crisis had three major political consequences. First, President Marcos lost the support of a large part of the domestic and international business community. Many Filipino business groups organized an active opposition to the Marcos government. The chief cause of the economic crisis, they said, was not the sagging international market for Philippine exports; rather, it was the incompetence of the Marcos administration. The best way to cure the problem, they said, was to remove the Marcos administration, not by armed struggle, but by international financial pressure against the system of "crony capitalism."

A second major political consequence of the economic crisis was that it became much more difficult for Marcos to continue his well-practiced techniques of payoff politics. Under the conditions of increasing economic austerity, there just were not enough material benefits to go around. This had long been evident to the bottom half of the Philippine population, where real wages for farmers and workers had been dropping for two decades. By the 1980s, the scarcity of material benefits had reached the middle class and upper class as well. This was evident in declining savings rates, bank deposit withdrawals, capital flight, and the high number of bankruptcies and mergers. Many Filipinos, in particular skilled workers and professionals, left the country to seek better opportunities abroad.

Third, serious conflicts within the ruling elite were revealed in the scramble to assign the blame for the economic difficulties of the country. Imelda Marcos publicly criticized Cesar Virata, prime minister and finance minister, for pursuing policies which made the economy so vulnerable to downturns in the world market. Virata, in turn, accused Mrs. Marcos of wasting scarce national resources on luxury projects and other inessential activities. In the meantime, Eduardo M. Cojuangco and other Marcos cronies built up their own private armies to protect their lands and vested interests.

Rebellion

For the second time since World War II, radical movements are challenging government authority in the Philippines. As in the case of the Huk rebellion of the 1940s and 1950s, the current radical insurgencies are rooted in poverty and injustice. They were fueled during the Marcos years by the combination of economic deterioration, political repression, and military abuses.

The first armed opposition to the martial law government came from Muslim rebels in the southern Philippines. The Moro National Liberation Front (MNLF) was founded in 1969 by young radical Muslim leaders to "re-acquire the Bangsa Moro people's political freedom and independence from the clutches of Filipino terror and enslavement."[13] Its first leader was Nur Misuari, a Tausug Muslim and graduate in Asian studies at the University of the Philippines. The MNLF began its armed struggle for secession after Marcos declared martial law. Warfare was intensified for at least three reasons: Marcos consolidated power within almost exclusively Christian groups; he rejected MNLF demands for autonomy; and he sent in government forces to disarm the Muslim population. After several years of hostilities and thousands of fatalities, a cease-fire was arranged with diplomatic pressure from some Arab League nations. With much of its leadership in exile or divided over strategy, the MNLF rebellion became dormant, although it still conducts occasional raids on government outposts.

In the late 1960s, a new Communist Party of the Philippines (CPP) broke away from the old, largely discredited Parti Komunista ng Pilipinas (PKP). It was revived during the Marcos years and has spread its influence widely throughout the country. The New People's Army (NPA), the military arm of the CPP, has grown slowly but steadily during the Marcos years. Current estimates of NPA strength range from 15,000 to 30,000. According to Philippine military estimates, there were 3,000 violent incidents involving the NPA in 1984 and nearly 5,000 in 1985, most of which were initiated by the NPA.

The revolutionary movement was not strong enough to make any serious challenge during the Marcos succession struggle. However, under authoritarian rule, it was successfully revived from near-extinction. It benefited enormously from the lack of other institutional outlets

---

[13]Abdurasad Asani, "The Bangsamoro People: A Nation in Travail," paper presented to the Philippines Studies Conference, University of Michigan, Aug. 2, 1984.

for popular grievances. It demonstrated a capability to shape the issues of political debate and to work with other opposition groups in extra-parliamentary efforts. It is also well prepared to survive in the turmoil of transition following twenty years of one-man rule.

Declining Government Legitimacy; Rising Popular Insurgency

During the Marcos years, the basic issue of legitimacy was government performance itself. The New Society of Ferdinand Marcos was not producing its promised benefits of political stability, economic growth, or social reform. Instead, there was increasing instability, persistent poverty, and more violence than there had been before Marcos. Increasingly, Filipinos were looking for, and demanding, alternatives to it. One Filipino who tried to provide leadership for this popular anti-Marcos movement was Benigno Aquino, Jr., a longstanding political rival of Marcos and his most likely successor until martial law was declared.

More than any other single event, the assassination of Benigno Aquino, Jr., undermined the legitimacy and credibility of the Marcos government. Aquino had been arrested at the outset of martial law in September 1972 and had been kept under arrest for the next seven and a half years. Aquino had returned to the Philippines after three years of exile in the United States to try to unify opposition groups which had been fragmented and ineffectual throughout most of the preceding decade. His objective was to lead a united opposition in contesting the May 1984 national assembly elections.

Aquino's death precipitated storms of protest against the Marcos government. Millions of Filipinos turned out to mourn Aquino's death and to demand Marcos' resignation. Many individuals previously uninvolved in politics held demonstrations, silent vigils, prayer rallies, candlelight processions, noise barrages, confetti parades, mill-ins, and many other forms of protest with their neighbors, co-workers, class-mates, and other social or religious groups to demand "Justice for Aquino, Justice for All."

NAMFREL, the National Citizens Movement for Free Elections, was revived to help get Filipinos to restore democracy through elections. Established over thirty years ago with CIA help to elect Ramon Magsaysay president, NAMFREL became accredited as an official election supervisory committee. Under the direction of Jose Concepcion, Jr., a businessman and chairman of the Bishops and Businessmen's Conference on National Reconciliation, NAMFREL rallied thousands of Filipinos to serve as poll-watchers to promote free and honest elections. It played a crucial role in minimizing and exposing fraud in the 1984 national assembly elections and the February 1986 presidential election.

In the new outspoken political environment, Filipino intellectuals were quick to formulate a diagnosis and prescription of the "nation in crisis." The causes of the crisis, according to Carolina G. Hernandez, were:

(1) the concentration of political power in the hands of one man, (2) the absence of institutionalized mechanisms for effective government accountability to the people, (3) the consequent tendency to set aside people's rights including political participation in the face of declared national policies, (4) inadequate mechanisms for political succession, (5) the general decline of civilian political institutions outside of the Presidency, (6) the emergence of the military as a major political force, and (7) the polarization of Philippine society.[14]

Ledivina V. Carino, dean of the University of the Philippines College of Public Administration, explained with candor in "Why We Accepted Martial Law"—a combination of fear of repression, hope for eventual improvement, and intellectual paralysis. She described how Ferdinand Marcos manipulated the laws of the land to justify his continued rule, and she listed the possible ways for Marcos to leave power. She outlined possible constitutional arrangements for the post-Marcos period as well as the major interest groups which would seek to

[14]Shortly after the assassination of Benigno Aquino, Jr., in August 1983, as crisis after crisis engulfed the Philippines, Alexander R. Magno of the University of the Philippines Political Science Department proposed a university colloquium to "reflect and deliberate on the present national situation, investigate those conditions that have managed to distress and torment the Filipino people, look into the root causes of the people's discontent, explore viable alternatives for meaningful social transformation and arrive at a People's Agenda for popular intervention towards a genuine New Society. . . ." The result was a soul-searching discussion among leading Filipino intellectuals on the "nation in crisis." See Alexander R. Magno, ed., *Nation in Crisis: The University Inquiries into the Present* (Diliman, Quezon City: University of the Philippines Press, 1984), viii, 251 pages (Distributed in North America by University Press of Hawaii.)

influence the outcome.[15] Through intellectual analysis and popular clamor, the Marcos government facade of legitimacy was unmasked.

The Aquino assassination marked an important turning point in modern Filipino politics. The "people power" which put Corazon Aquino in power was schooled in this "parliament of the streets." These new "cause-oriented" or "sectoral" political activist groups are now an important feature in the new Philippine political milieu. They are a more militant and a more urbanized version of the nationalist and reformist groups who initiated the 1971 constitutional convention.

Marcos charged that a lone assassin, Rolando C. Galman, had been hired by the Communist party to kill Aquino; but on October 23, 1984, the independent, government-appointed Agrava Commission reported no evidence to support these charges. Instead, it blamed Aquino's death on close Marcos allies in the military, including General Fabian Ver, chief of staff of the Philippine armed forces.

All the military officers and security forces implicated in the assassination were indicted. But the trial became a cover-up. Marcos gave instructions to court officials to clear the case expeditiously. Witnesses against the accused disappeared. Crucial evidence was ruled inadmissible. Some charges were dropped on technical grounds. Finally, on December 2, 1985, all the defendants were acquitted. Within hours, Marcos reinstated Ver. His forces were charged with providing security for the February 7 elections, despite previous Marcos pledges that the military would be kept away from the polls. The next day, December 3, 1985, Corazon Aquino declared her candidacy for the presidency.

The final and ultimately fatal challenge to the legitimacy and authority of the Marcos government came on November 1, 1985, in a charge made by U.S. Senator David Durenberger, chairman of the Senate Select Committee on Intelligence, who quoted a staff report that the communist insurgency and the economic situation were rapidly worsening, and that "democracy was doomed" unless drastic reforms were carried out. He added that the Marcos government was incapable and unwilling to carry out these reforms and he therefore urged Marcos to resign and make way for free and fair elections to choose the next Philippine president. Two days later, on November 3, 1985, in the course of a Sunday morning news interview on American network

---

[15]"The Succession Issue and the Continuity of the Present Order," in Magno, *op. cit.*

television, Marcos announced that, despite previous assertions, he would call for an early "snap election" to demonstrate his popular support and his ability to handle the growing insurgency. After some indecision about exactly when to set the election date and whether or not to include vice-presidential running mates, Marcos decided on February 7 as the election date and chose his former foreign minister, Arturo Tolentino, as his running mate.

Up until then, the opposition had been fragmented and ineffective, and Marcos was probably expecting them to remain divided. He thought he could continue to get United States support as he had done previously, by claiming to be the only one who could control the government and combat the rebels. He thought he could control the electoral machinery to produce the desired results as he had also done previously. But he miscalculated on all three issues. On December 11, Corazon Aquino and former senator Salvador Laurel agreed to run on a unified opposition ticket. American support was publicly hedged while others in the United States government openly backed the Aquino campaign. And no amount of government bribery and intimidation of voters or manipulation of the electoral machinery could hide the overwhelming popular mandate given to Cory Aquino.

Mrs. Aquino was the catalyst for unifying "people power" into a new coalition for political change, one with strong support from the church, the business community, and almost every socio-economic group in the country. Her campaign rekindled the democratic spirit of the country and gave her an electoral victory which could not be denied by the rapidly dwindling Marcos forces. She won over important allies in the military, including Secretary of National Defense Juan Ponce Enrile and Deputy Chief of the Armed Forces Fidel Ramos. Abandoned by all but his most faithful supporters, Marcos gave up power and left the country with a minimum of violence. He left with two of the most prominent targets of opposition criticism, Fabian Ver, chief of the armed forces, and Eduardo Cojuangco, the richest of the crony capitalists.

The rebels also made a grave miscalculation in underestimating popular support for Aquino's bid for power. Communist party officials said the election was "largely irrelevant" to the problems of the Philippines. They chose to boycott the election as they had in the 1984 national assembly elections. The only way to remove Marcos, they argued, was through armed struggle. Despite Mrs. Aquino's enormously popular campaign for nonviolent civil disobedience, the left was unable or unwilling to support her effort to oust Marcos. Hence, the election not only forced Marcos out of power; it also split the previously combined, moderate and radical, anti-Marcos opposition into two separate political forces, one in power and the other in disarray.

PROBLEMS AND PROSPECTS FOR THE AQUINO GOVERNMENT

Corazon Aquino, popularly acclaimed as the leading opposition candidate to challenge Marcos, has vowed to redress the grievances at the root of the popular and radical insurgencies. She said she would investigate Marcos' links to the assassination of her husband, Benigno Aquino, Jr., and to government corruption. She called for military reform and an end to "crony capitalism." She also said she would call for a six-month cease-fire in the government's counter-insurgency campaign and invite the rebels to lay down their arms and pledge support to the government in exchange for the legalization of the Communist party. She promised amnesty to all political prisoners of the Marcos regime. Former Philippines President Diosdado Macapagal also proposed that the Communist party and the New People's Army be legalized to bring them "into the democratic political mainstream" of the country.

Mrs. Aquino began her government by fulfilling her campaign pledges of political reconciliation. Her first proclamation was to abolish the government's power to detain people without charge, a practice that Marcos had used widely in purported cases of subversion, sedition, conspiracy, and "other offenses against the requirements of public safety."

Over five hundred political prisoners were released by the Aquino government, despite some objections from top military officials. These included Jose Maria Sison, founder of the Communist Party of the Philippines and a former English professor at the University of the Philippines, and Bernabe Buscayno, also known as Commander Dante, son of a poor farm family and reportedly the former head of the New People's Army. Both had been imprisoned for nearly ten years. Also released were Alexander Birondo, alleged chief of the Armed City Partisans in Manila, and Ruben Alegre, who had been captured in a shoot-out with police in Manila in June, 1985.

Mrs. Aquino's economic goals aim to reduce the country's poverty, unemployment and underemployment, an essential task to defuse the communist insurgency. Finance Minister Jaime Ongpin calls his economic program "private enterprise with a social conscience." It gives top priority to increasing domestic food production and only secondarily to export promotion.

Land reform, however, was not addressed in the first few months of the new Aquino government. This will be a crucial challenge to the new government, especially in the economically depressed sugar-producing regions of Negros and Panay Islands and northern Mindanao, where the NPA and CPP continue to be active. Firefights and general strikes occurred with regularity before the election and have slowly resumed since then. Shadow governments continue to operate in the hinterland villages. The first "powderkeg" of the country's communist rebellion could explode on Negros Island, where CPP spokesmen predict a strategic stalemate by 1987. CPP and NPA members now enter and leave the seaport capital of Bacolod under cover and freely roam sugarcane fields just outside city limits. Masses of unemployed peasants and workers remain ripe for the rebels, many residents believe.

One of the major problems inherited by the Aquino government is the extremely centralized system of control by Manila authorities over local governments and the rural economy. In theory, every governor and mayor needs Manila's permission even to come to the capital. Small expenditures and employee hiring must first be approved in Manila. Marcos further fragmented local authority and rewarded the faithful by increasing the number of provinces from fifty-four in 1965 to seventy-four in 1986.

Many officials in the Aquino cabinet have called for "more provincial control," "regional autonomy," or even "local self-determination." According to Dodoy Villareal, governor of Capiz, "the only solution to the insurgency and poverty is local autonomy."[16] Members of the Constitutional Commission are considering ways to grant more powers to the seventy-four provinces and sixty large towns of the Philippines. In the meantime, Mrs. Aquino exercises control and supervision over

[16]Quoted in James Clad, "Power to the Provinces?" *Far Eastern Economic Review*, July 3, 1986.

all local governments. With the advice of her minister of local government, Aquilino Pimentel, she has appointed over one hundred interim governors and mayors, known as "officers-in-charge" or OICs, displacing KBL and other pro-Marcos officials.

Without electoral legitimacy, local autonomy, or revenue-raising authority, OICs can do little to deal with the enormous problems they face. Regional development and rural industry plans are made in Manila, not the provinces. The long-term trend toward the centralization of power in the Philippines still has momentum. Fears remain strong that decentralization of control will lead to more separatism, especially in the southern provinces. "Centralism is the dominant theme . . . in Philippine history," remarked Gaudioso Sosmena, a senior Local Government Ministry official. Every constitution since 1935 "did not gamble the future of Philippine independence by espousing local autonomy."[17] While there is widening agreement on the need to hold local elections as soon as possible, it seems likely that the Constitutional Commission and the Aquino government will be slow in granting a genuine decentralization of power.

If political reconciliation and economic recovery are inadequate to stop the communist insurgency, then Mrs. Aquino will use military force where necessary to put down armed rebellion. Unfortunately, the Philippine armed forces are ill prepared for this, according to many reports. The defense budget equals only one percent of GNP, the lowest in Southeast Asia. Shortages of supplies and equipment—trucks, aircraft, uniforms, food, fuel—are endemic. Pay is poor and medical care is often nonexistent. A disproportionate number of units are concentrated in Manila rather than sent into the field against the NPA. Equipment maintenance is inadequate and there is no logistical system worthy of the name. Morale and mobility are both low. Perhaps most important, leadership is often poor and there are no central training facilities, with the result that troops are frequently sent into the field with inadequate training. Many of the best officers and technically skilled personnel have left the armed forces to take higher-paying jobs as mercenaries with armies in the Middle East.

All these problems are magnified for the Civil Home Defense Force —the government-sponsored local militia. Frequently, CHDF forces

[17]Ibid., p. 33.

have thrown down their arms and fled when challenged by the NPA. As a consequence, they have been a major source of weapons and ammunition for the insurgency. Ill-trained CHDF are also a source of many abuses of the civilian population. The *Asia 1986 Yearbook* contrasts the "exceptionally disciplined NPA" with government armed forces "involved in kidnappings, torture, 'salvaging' (or summary execution), intimidation of the rural population and frequent drunken binges at night with indiscriminate firing."[18]

These and other perceived abuses have been a major factor in many Filipinos' choosing to join the insurgent ranks. This is especially true of Catholic clergy and nuns who support the rebels. Some, such as Conrado Balweg, a rebel priest and a popular Filipino folk hero to some, was an NPA commander until he broke away to form the Cordillera People's Liberation Army in Northern Luzon.

Abuses perpetuated by corrupt officers and undisciplined personnel and a general breakdown of peace and order have severely shaken popular respect for the military and the police. Many Filipinos still question the government's ability to protect them from lawless elements and to dispense justice equitably.

Mrs. Aquino has said she will dismiss all generals eligible for retirement, which would include nearly all senior commanders. She has also said she will cut the military intelligence budget and demobilize the Civilian Home Defense Forces.

Given the persistent threats to internal security, the military is likely to remain a powerful national institution in the post-Marcos period: it has a Regional Unified Command (RUC) over the country; it is directly controlled from the top in a unified way; it has many members who have acquired civilian-oriented skills and governing experience and who believe they can manage society as well as any civilian. The military does have "legitimate corporate interests" to protect and promote; that is, internal autonomy in organization, promotion, strategy, and logistics.[19]

Despite the severe problems she faces in reforming the military, and despite the differences of opinion within her cabinet on how to deal

---

[18]*Asia 1986 Yearbook* (Hong Kong: Far Eastern Economic Review, Dec. 1985), page 222.

[19]Carolina G. Hernandez, "The Military and the Future of Civilian Rule in the Context of the Prevailing Political Crisis," in Magno, ed., op. cit.

with the military and the rebels, Mrs. Aquino can rely on a few major assets. She can count on the support of many of the officers who are concerned about restoring the professionalism of the armed forces and the supremacy of civilian authority, and who gave her strong support at a crucial moment in her postelection bid to take power. She is also very determined to seek justice in her case against the military officers she believes were responsible for the murder of her husband.

19

Church and State in the Philippines: Some Implications for United States Policy

Robert L. Youngblood

CHURCH AND STATE IN THE PHILIPPINES: SOME IMPLICATIONS FOR UNITED STATES POLICY

For all who watched the February 7, 1986, presidential campaign in the Philippines, it was clear that the hierarchy of the Philippine Roman Catholic church was not only deeply committed to a free and honest election, but also favored the candidacy of Corazon "Cory" Aquino. Jaime Cardinal Sin, the archbishop of Manila and the titular head of the Philippine Catholic church, was credited with having helped Mrs. Aquino and Salvador "Doy" Laurel forge a united opposition ticket in December 1985; and on January 19, 1986 the cardinal issued a pastoral letter widely publicized throughout the Philippines condemning "a very sinister plot by some people and groups [meaning the Marcos regime] to frustrate the honest and orderly expression of the people's genuine will."[1] Immediately after the election, when it became obvious that President Marcos intended to remain in office by manipulating the election returns, the Catholic Bishops' Conference of the Philippines (CBCP) issued a statement branding the election as "unparalleled in . . . fraudulence" and saying "a government that assumes or retains power through fraudulent means has no moral basis." The bishops went on to recommend a "non-violent struggle for justice,"[2] and following the revolt of Minister of Defense Juan Ponce Enrile and Vice-Chief-of-Staff Fidel Ramos, Cardinal Sin asked Filipinos to go to Camp Crame

---

[1] Jaime Cardinal Sin, "A Call to Conscience," January 19, 1986, reprinted in *Bulletin Today,* January 19, 1986, p. 10.
[2] Catholic Bishops' Conference of the Philippines (CBCP), "Post Election Statement," February 13, 1986. (n.p., Claretian Publications, February 1986).

and Camp Aguinaldo in support of the military dissidents. Thousands responded and within days Ferdinand Marcos was forced into exile, ending a twenty-year rule that had become increasingly corrupt and abusive.

The role of the church in the February 7th election was but a dramatic manifestation of a growing dissatisfaction among church leaders with the Marcos regime, and it reflected a shift already taking place within the church toward more activism among conservative and moderate bishops, who comprise the majority in the CBCP. Not only did Cardinal Sin, a moderate, and, to a much lesser extent, Antonio Mabutas, the conservative archbishop of Davao, step up their criticism of the Marcos regime after 1975, but also after 1979 the CBCP issued a number of pastoral letters admonishing the Marcos government for a variety of shortcomings and failures.[3] An intensified publicity campaign in the government-controlled media beginning in 1982 and repeated assertions by government officials that the church was infiltrated by communists exacerbated church-state relations to the point where in January 1983 the CBCP withdrew from the Church-Military Liaison Committee (CMLC), established in November 1973 to resolve conflicts between the Catholic and Protestant churches and the military. A month later, on February 20, 1983, the CBCP issued a pastoral letter accusing the government of graft and corruption, economic mismanagement, and repression, and the bishops indicated that without the Marcos regime's making fundamental reforms, which accepted a "certain pluralism of positions in the way . . . people strive for justice according to their faith,"[4] tensions were unlikely to ease.

Given the inability of Marcos to reform the system, the breach with the Catholic bishops was never repaired. In fact church-state relations became increasingly acrimonious, notwithstanding intermittent attempts at reconciliation, from 1982 until Marcos' departure from the Philippines. At the root of the conflict was the right of the church to engage in social justice activities as an integral part of preaching the

---

[3]CBCP, "Pastoral Letter, Exhortation Against Violence," reprinted in *The Bishops Speak (1968– 1983)*, ed. Richard P. Hardy (Quezon City: Maryhill School of Theology, 1984), pp. 207-212.

[4]CBCP, "Pastoral Letter, A Dialogue for Peace," reprinted in *The Bishops Speak (1968 –1983)*, ed. Richard P. Hardy (Quezon City: Maryhill School of Theology, 1984), pp. 232-238.

gospel versus the regime's economic programs—usually justified in terms of national development and national security—that favored close associates of the president at the expense of peasant farmers, tribal minorities, and the urban poor. That a preferential option for the poor and government repression were key ingredients in unifying the church behind the Aquino candidacy and free and honest elections, however, masks major divisions within the Roman Catholic and Protestant churches in the Philippines. An awareness of the political and ecclesiological orientations as well as the capabilities of the various major groups within the churches —especially the Roman Catholic church—is necessary in order to better assess the evolving role of the churches in Philippine society.

MAJOR DIVISIONS WITHIN THE PHILIPPINE CHURCHES

Of the approximately 87 percent of the population that are Christian, 84 percent are Roman Catholic and 3 percent are Protestant. In 1983, the Roman Catholic church had sixteen archdioceses, forty-one dioceses, five prelatures nullius, and five apostolic vicariates, and had an active clergy that consisted of two cardinals (the archbishops of Manila and Cebu), fifteen other archbishops, seventy-seven bishops, and 4,954 secular and regular priests. There were also thirty-nine religious congregations of men, with 3,326 religious men; ninety-six religious congregations of women, with 7,130 sisters; and nearly 5,000 students in fifty-five major and minor diocesan seminaries.[5] Among the major organizations of the Catholic church are the CBCP, the Association of Major Religious Superiors of the Philippines (AMRSP),[6] the Philippine Priests, Incorporated (PPI), and the National Secretariat for Social Action (NASSA).

The Protestant population, by way of contrast, was divided among approximately two hundred denominations. A number of the more prominent Protestant denominations, however, have close ties with

---

[5]Figures taken from Pedro S. De Achuategui, "The Catholic Church in the Philippines: A Statistical Overview," *Philippine Studies* 32 (First Quarter, 1984): 77-106.

[6]The AMRSP is made up of two organizations established in 1955, the Association of Major Religious Superiors of Men in the Philippines (AMRSMP) and the Association of Major Religious Superiors of Women in the Philippines (AMRSWP). Since the boards of the AMRSMP and AMRSWP were joined in 1975, both are now simply referred to as the AMRSP.

churches in the United States, which provide economic assistance and missionary personnel, and with the Christian Conference of Asia (CCA) and with the World Council of Churches (WCC) in Geneva.[7] These linkages, along with the fact that some congregations draw their membership disproportionately from the middle class, gives the Protestants more influence than their numbers would ordinarily suggest. The single most important interdenominational Protestant organization is the National Council of Churches in the Philippines (NCCP), which is composed of the Iglesia Filipina Independiente (Philippine Independent Church), the Convention of Philippine Baptist Churches, Iglesia Evangelica Unida de Cristo, the Lutheran Church in the Philippines, the Salvation Army, Iglesia Evangelica Metodista en las Isles Filipinas, the Philippine Episcopal Church, the United Methodist Church, and the Church of Christ in the Philippines.

MAINSTREAM DIVISIONS

President Marcos' elimination of institutional opposition with the declaration of martial law in September 1972 left the Catholic and Protestant churches in the unique position—among legal organizations—of still having enough autonomy, authority, and power to question the policies of the government. Such a distinction, however, was insufficient to mask significant political divisions within the churches on socioeconomic and political issues as well as on questions of ecclesiology. Among major Catholic organizations, the CBCP is considered to be the most conservative, but even within the Bishops' Conference there are at least three identifiable divisions—conservatives, moderates, and progressives—in terms of attitudes toward the Marcos regime and the role of the church in modern society. Elsewhere I have described the CBCP factions as follows:[8]

> The conservative group is the most supportive of martial law and government reforms in the new society and, if critical of the regime at all, it has done so in moderate terms,

---

[7]Nena Vreeland et al., *Area Handbook for the Philippines* (Washington, D.C.: U.S. Government Printing Office, 1976), p. 171.

[8]Robert L. Youngblood, "Structural Imperialism: An Analysis of the Catholic Bishops' Conference of the Philippines," *Comparative Political Studies*, 15 (April 1982): 35-36.

disagreeing, for example, most notably with government programs, such as the taxation of church schools, legalization of divorce, and family planning, that affect vital church interests. The ecclesiological outlook of the conservatives stresses the sacred mission of the church in providing a refuge for the fulfillment of religious needs and favors and an avoidance of involvement in temporal affairs.

The moderates also criticize government programs that threaten vital church interests, but, in contrast to the conservatives, they reserve the right to criticize specific injustices of the regime, while not going to the extent of attacking martial law in principle. Moderate opposition is characterized by what . . . Cardinal Sin . . . has termed "critical collaboration." The ecclesiology of the moderates is similar to that of the conservatives, but because of the influence of Vatican II and recent social encyclicals coupled with gross inequities in Philippine society, the moderates recognize, with reservations, that the church must become more responsive to the needs and demands of contemporary society.

A third group, considered progressive or liberal, joins with conservatives and moderates in defending vital church interests against undesirable government programs, but differs from the other two groups in speaking out repeatedly against what it considers a wide array of abuses by the government and military as well as by condemning martial law as immoral. The progressives adhere to the "community of liberation" model of the church and agree with Antonio Lambino . . . a Filipino theologian, that "effective Christian love is manifested in solidarity with the poor and the oppressed, in sharing their struggle to liberate themselves from the unjust structures of society."[9]

[9]Antonio B. Lambino, "Justice and Evangelization: A Theological Perspective," in *On Faith and Justice: Contemporary Issues for Filipino Christians*, ed. Pedro S. De Achuategui (Quezon City: Loyola School of Theology, Ateneo de Manila University, 1976), p. 32. See Brian H. Smith, "Religion and Social Change: Classical Theories and New Formulations in the Context of Recent Developments in Latin America," *Latin American Research Review*, 10 (2): 3-34, for a discussion of the "distinction of planes" and "community of liberation" models within the Roman Catholic church.

Although distinctions among the three groups remain, it was evident that by 1981 a significant number of conservative and moderate bishops were moving toward the position of the progressive bishops vis-a-vis the Marcos regime and the need to defend more forthrightly the social justice activities of the church. No other bishop dramatized the shift more than Cardinal Sin. In 1976, for example, Sin, along with other conservative and moderate bishops, avoided protesting strongly the deportation of Father Edward Gerlock, an American Maryknoll missionary, for his social justice activities in support of the rights of peasant farmers and tribal minorities in northeastern Mindanao and, subsequently, the urban poor in metropolitan Manila. In response to a letter from Gerlock's mother, who asked the cardinal why he had not come to the defense of her son, Sin maintained that had he "chosen to engage the government in direct confrontation" President Marcos "could have ordered all churches closed and all priests arrested." Thus, in order to preserve the interests of the Philippine church, Sin concluded that it was best that he remain silent on Gerlock's summary deportation.[10] Sin's response was characteristic of the conservatives and moderates toward the deportation of priests in the early years of martial law.

Within two years of writing Mrs. Gerlock, however, Cardinal Sin assumed a much more critical stance toward the Marcos regime, increasingly warning of revolution and civil war if the corruption and abuses of government officials and the military continued; and by the termination of martial rule in January 1981, he found himself repeatedly at odds with the government on a wide array of issues. Sin labeled the June 1981 presidential election as a "farce reminiscent of one-candidate elections in totalitarian countries," averring that the "uncounted millions of pesos" spent on the election could be put to better use on underfinanced government projects;[11] and in 1982, he suggested that Marcos, who had "lost the respect of the people," should step down in order for "new leadership" to tackle the nation's problems and blunt the growth of the Communist Party of the Philippines (CPP) and its military arm, the New People's Army (NPA).[12] The cardinal also questioned the morality of using national security as a justification for

[10]Jaime Cardinal Sin to Mrs. Angela C. Gerlock, August 15, 1977 (Typewritten).
[11]*Foreign Broadcast Information Service* (FBIS), IV, April 24, 1981, p. 5.
[12]*Philippine News,* July 28 —August 3, 1982, pp. 1-2, 8.

the derogation of civil liberties, and he dissented vociferously from the regime's decision to screen pornographic films to underwrite the cost of the 1982 Manila International Film Festival.[13]

Following the assassination of Benigno Aquino, Jr., in August 1983, Cardinal Sin's castigation of the regime increased. Sin indicated that he felt the government was at least partially responsible for the murder, since Aquino died in the custody of the military, and Radio Veritas, the church's radio station, provided the most accurate and comprehensive information about the assassination and the subsequent mass demonstrations of anguish and outrage over the murder. He also refused to participate as a member of the commission established by the president to investigate the Aquino killing as he considered that his presence would be nothing more than a "dissenting voice in the wilderness,"[14] and he approved the organization of a new newspaper, *Veritas,* in the interests of reestablishing a free press in the Philippines. Similarly, Cardinal Sin called for fair and honest national assembly elections in May 1984, adding his blessings to the organization of the National Citizens' Movement for Free Elections (NAMFREL). According to Alfred McCoy, the cardinal also played an instrumental part in behind-the-scenes negotiations with President Marcos which resulted in a political settlement, arrived at in June 1984, to the murder trial and deportation cases against two Columban missionaries, Brian Gore, an Australian, and Nial O'Brien, an Irishman, falsely charged with complicity in the assassination of Mayor Pablo Sola of Kabankalan, Negros Occidental, in March 1982.

Cardinal Sin's metamorphosis from a mild to a trenchant —though circumspect— critic of the government and military was duplicated by other moderate as well as some conservative bishops, while the progressive bishops continued, as they had since the beginning of martial rule, to condemn regularly the chicanery and abuses of the Marcos regime. A few examples are instructive. In 1979, Bishop William Brausseur, a moderate, asserted that the abuses by government and military officials were driving the Kilingas and Bontocs in the Moun-

[13]Jaime L. Cardinal Sin, "The Climate of Fear Has Stifled Dissent," Speech delivered at the eighth anniversary of the Cheers Executive Club, Cheers Restaurant, February 3, 1983.

[14]FBIS, August 29, 1983, pp. P4-P5, and August 30, p. P2; and Maryknoll Justice and Peace Office, *Newsnotes,* September 1983, p. 7.

tain Province area to embrace the NPA,[15] while Antonio Mabutas, a conservative, issued a sharply worded pastoral letter condemning the execution of two church leaders and others suspected of "subversion" by the military.[16] In 1981, Bishop Claver, a progressive, pointed out numerous inconsistencies in the government's version of the assassination of Father Godofredo Alingal, S.J., in Bukidnon. Many believe the unsolved murder was committed by the military.[17] That same year Bishop Pedro Dean, a conservative, denied government charges that Fathers Ralph Kroes and Edward Shilleto, Maryknoll missionaries who were expelled and then allowed to return to the Philippines, were engaged in subversive activities.[18] Similarly, in 1982, Bishop Alberto Van Overbeke, a conservative, issued a strongly worded pastoral letter asserting that two arrested priests, Theodore Bandsma and Herman Sanderinck, C.I.C.M., were "neither criminals nor subversives,"[19] and Bishop Antonio Fortich, a moderate, consistently maintained the innocence of Columban missionaries Brian Gore and Nial O'Brien, and a diocesan priest, Vincente Dangan, and of six lay leaders accused in the murder of Mayor Pablo Sola.[20]

Church-state conflict involving bishops escalated after 1982 with military raids on two bishops' residences in 1983 and 1984 and with the killing of an Italisted stronary in 1985. In 1983, Bishop Miguel Purugganan, a progressive, protested strongly the simultaneous military raids on his residence and on the nearby convent of the Franciscan Sisters of the Immaculate Conception of the Mother of God (D.F.I.C.),[21] while in 1984, Ireneo Amantillo, a moderate, denounced a military assault on his residence and an adjacent pastoral center, and he warned that continued military repression against the church would eventually destroy the government's credibility.[22] Finally, the entire nation joined Bishop Orlando Quevedo, a moderate, in condemning

[15]*Bulletin Today*, June 19, 1979, pp. 1, 10.
[16]*Asiaweek*, September 7, 1979, pp. 22-23.
[17]*Filipino Reporter*, April 24-30, 1981, pp. 1, 4.
[18]*Far Eastern Economic Review*, July 17, 1981, p. 6.
[19]*Political Detainees Update* (PDU), October 15, 1982, p. 7; and *National Catholic Reporter*, October 1, 1982, pp. 1, 15.
[20]Alfred W. McCoy, *Priests on Trial* (Ringwood, Victoria: Penguin Books Australia, Ltd., 1984).
[21]PDU, September 15, 1983, p. 1; and *NASSA News*, Special Issue, September 1983.
[22]*MIPC Communications*, November 1984, pp. 4-7.

the April 1985 murder of Father Tullio Favali, P.I.M.E., by a unit of the Civilian Home Defense Forces (CHDF) in the province of North Cotabato.[23]

A lack of agreement with the Marcos government and with the prescribed role of the church in society has also characterized other Catholic organizations, but the AMRSP, NASSA, and a number of religious orders, such as the Maryknoll Fathers, the Society of St. Columban, the Society of Jesus, and the Missionary Sisters of the Immaculate Heart of Mary, are considered much more progressive than the Bishops' Conference. Since the early 1970s all of these church organizations have been on the cutting edge of experimentation with church social justice programs that periodically resulted in clashes with the Marcos government. The same was true for the PPI, which, prior to martial law, published highly critical articles on the Marcos government in its journal, the *Philippine Priests' Forum;* but since 1972, it has assumed a much lower profile with respect to questions of social justice. The PPI is no longer considered an activist group, although the leadership still professes to be committed to reforms within the church and society.[24]

Among Philippine Protestant denominations a major distinction exists between a group of non-ecumenical, often fundamentalist Christian sects and the nine member churches of the NCCP. The fundamentalists are conservative on social issues and were viewed as passive toward, or supportive of, the Marcos regime, while churches belonging to the NCCP are considered more progressive. Yet just as within the Roman Catholic church, there are divisions among the NCCP-affiliated churches with respect to the role of the churches on social and political issues. Individual pastors and laymen, such as former Senator Jovito Salonga, the son of a minister and now head of the Commission on Good Government in the Aquino administration, and some programs and sub-groups of the NCCP, namely the Philippine Ecumenical Action for Community Development (PEACE), the Wednesday Fellowship, and the Commission on Development and Social Concerns, have consistently supported Protestant social justice activities, but they are

---

[23]Orlando B. Quevedo, "Message of the Bishop of Kidapawan on the Killing of Fr. Tullio Favali, P.I.M.E.," April 12, 1985, reprinted in *Simbayan* 4 (March 1985): 19.
[24]See Robert L. Youngblood, "Church Opposition to Martial Law in the Philippines," *Asian Survey,* 18 (May 1978): 505-520.

in a minority. Although adumbrated by the much larger Catholic church, the efforts of progressive Protestants are nevertheless significant because of their willingness to work in an ecumenical context—frequently with Catholics—and because of the support they receive from abroad, especially from the mother churches in the United States.[25]

OTHER DIVISIONS

Two other organizations—the Christians for National Liberation (CNL) and the Mindanao Interfaith People's Conference (MIPC)—add additional complexity to the divisions within and among the Roman Catholic and Protestant churches in the Philippines. The CNL is an illegal, underground organization not recognized officially by any church, while the MIPC, although not an official body of any denomination, receives support from both Catholics and Protestant churches in the Mindanao region of the country. Of the two organizations, the CNL is the oldest and most radical. It was established in February 1972, held its first national convention in August 1972, and immediately thereafter was forced underground by the declaration of martial law. In early 1973, the CNL joined with other nationalist groups, many of which were community or marxist-influenced, to establish the National Democratic Front (NDF), an umbrella organization of the CPP. The CNL adheres to the ten-point program of the NDF, and embraces the CPP's notion of an armed struggle as the most efficacious method for bringing about "liberation" in the Philippines.[26]

The MIPC is a small ecumenical group of priests, nuns, pastors, and laypersons that was organized after the Mindanao-Sulu bishops of the Catholic church withdrew support in 1981 from the Mindanao-Sulu Pastoral Conference (MSPC) because of a belief that the MSPC Secretariat was inordinately under the influence of the NDF and, as such, was becoming too closely associated with the policies and goals of the CPP in Mindanao and Sulu. Others felt that a good part of the reason for the separation had to do with a dispute over authority in the church,

[25]See Robert L. Youngblood, "The Protestant Church in the Philippines' New Society," *Bulletin of Concerned Asian Scholars,* 12 (July-September 1980): 19-29.
[26]See, *inter alia, Christians for National Liberation: 2nd National Congress Documents* (n.p., n.p.).

wherein the bishops were unwilling to allow the Secretariat a freer hand in developing and administering programs within the individual dioceses.[27] What is clear, however, is that the MSPC and its successor, the MIPC, were and are at the forefront of a move in Mindanao to make the churches more relevant to the needs of the people. Such a commitment included an emphasis on addressing questions of social justice as an integral part of preaching the gospel. The result was increasing conflict during the Marcos regime between church activists, most of whom were left-of-center nationalists but non-communists, and the military, which generally viewed social justice activities, including criticism of itself and the government, as "subversive."

SOCIAL JUSTICE AND CHURCH CAPABILITIES

Like churches elsewhere in the Third World, the Roman Catholic church in the Philippines has been profoundly influenced by the deliberations of the Second Vatican Council and by a series of papal encyclicals issued since the early 1960s addressing questions of the role of the church in the modern world. In the mid-1960s the Philippine Catholic church began to emphasize the importance of social action in the ministry. This led to the establishment of NASSA and, between 1969 and 1974, the organization of three regional social action secretariats to help coordinate nationwide the social action programs of the Catholic church. Simultaneously the NCCP and various Protestant denominations were active among the urban poor in Manila, especially in the squatter area known as Tondo.

The imposition of martial law in 1972 accelerated a move away from self-help social action programs that had failed to benefit the very poor to an emphasis on social justice, *conscientizacioan* (consciousness raising), and the establishment of Basic Christian Communities (BCC). This new orientation, which stressed more people's participation in the decisions that affected their lives within the church and the community, received strong support from the AMRSP, has been an essential part of NASSA's program since 1975, and was endorsed by the CBCP in a

---

[27]Ben Verberne, "What Happened to the Mindanao-Sulu Pastoral Conference?" *MSPC Theological Articles*, July 1983, pp. 1-6; and personal correspondence with Mindanao-based priest familiar with the conflict, February 20, 1986.

1977 pastoral letter.[28] Although not all dioceses were equally enthusiastic, a large number had established some kind of a social justice program by the late 1970s; and by 1983 Bishop Claver estimated that BCCs nationwide numbered in the thousands.[29]

Guided by the notions "total human development" and "integral evangelization" set forth by Pope Paul VI in *Populorum Progresso* and *Evangelli Nutiandi,* the creation of Christian communities was aimed at the "liberation of the whole man rather than [just] 'saving souls.'"[30] To accomplish this, stress was placed on lay leadership and lay participation in the activities of the church, and although the lay leaders operated under the direction of the parish priest (and ultimately the local bishop), the creation of BCCs resulted in a decentralization of church structures as parishes were divided into small units of approximately thirty families and in a greater sharing of responsibility and power between the local priest and the laity. This, in turn, helped undermine the traditional view of leadership as naturally authoritarian in favor of a more participatory leadership style that emphasized dialogue, sharing, reconciliation, and social justice, and, as Patricia Licuanan found, frequently led to a conviction that the BCC was "an effective instrument for mutual assistance among group members as well as a force against oppression from power groups in the community."[31]

The establishment of BCCs, coupled with concomitant leadership training programs, thus provided both the context and the means by which the local churches were able to address more adequately problems of concern within the church and community. Nowhere was the emphasis on BCCs more pronounced than in the MSPC, where social

[28]CBCP, "Position Paper on the Synod Theme Catechetics in our Time with Special Reference to Catechetics for Children and Adults," reprinted in *The Philippine Bishops Speak (1968– 1983),* ed. Richard P. Hardy (Quezon City: Maryhill School of Theology, 1984), pp. 149-164.
[29]Francisco F. Claver, "Who's Afraid of the Basic Christian Communities?," *Solidarity,* No. 95 (1983), pp. 23-27.
[30]Nial O'Brian, "Basic Christian Communities –A Six Year Parish Experience," *St. Columban's Mission Education,* as quoted in Jose T. Deles, Jr., Asian Institute of Management, (Typewritten), p. 5.
[31]Ibid., pp. 5-6; and Patricia B. Licuanan, "Basic Christian Communities as a Force for Social Change," paper presented at the 9th Bishops-Businessmen's Conference General Assembly, June 30, 1985, pp. 2, 6.

justice and BCC formation became a major theme of the tri-annual MSPC assemblies between 1971 and 1980. Since those speaking out against abuses by local government officials and the military were frequently leaders or members of BCCs, the Marcos regime quickly came to view church social justice programs and the organization of BCCs as subversive activities, and, suggesting that they were manipulated and/or infiltrated both by the CPP/NPA and the CIA, Marcos attempted through the military to suppress them. To be sure, some BCCs fell under the influence of the CPP/NPA, which saw them as a vehicle for opposing the Marcos regime; but much more significant was the fact that the BCCs were largely independent of government control and thus represented a formidable challenge to the authority and power of the Marcos government.

The Marcos regime made a critical error in attempting to control the churches' social justice and BCC programs, for while there were (and are) ecclesiological differences among Catholic and, to a lesser extent, Protestant church officials about the proper role of the churches in contemporary society (which in part translated into conflicting views of martial law and Marcos' use of constitutional authoritarianism to remain in power), the CBCP progressively viewed harassment by government and military officials as repression, pure and simple. This change in view by some of the most powerful and influential conservative and moderate members of CBCP shifted much of the vast resources and capabilities of the Roman Catholic church to support the position of the progressive bishops, who, since 1972, as indicated above, had been outspokenly critical of martial law and the policies of the New Society and the New Republic.

The move by the conservative and moderate prelates to a more critical stance vis-a-vis the Marcos regime was important because they form a majority within the Catholic hierarchy. In 1979, they numbered sixty-four bishops and comprised 81 percent of the CBCP, while fifteen progressive bishops made up only 19 percent of the Catholic hierarchy. Of even greater significance is the fact that the conservative and moderate bishops control most of the material and manpower resources of the church. As Table 1 demonstrates, more than 85 percent of the Catholic population and of the children enrolled in parochial schools are within the administrative jurisdictions of conservative and moderate bishops, as are a similar percentage of the church's priests, nuns, and educational institutions. These statistics are only indicative, however; for the conservative and moderate Catholic bishops either control or have access to other resources (for example, radio stations, printing presses, mimeograph machines, vehicles, buildings) which they were able to employ to counteract the Marcos regime's attempt to discredit the church.

Table 1
RESOURCE CAPABILITIES OF THE PHILIPPINE CATHOLIC
BISHOPS BY GROUP MEMBERSHIP[a]

Total Resources	Conservative/ Moderate	Progressive
Size of Religious Area (sq. km)	252,705	65,913
Population	35,385,810	6,025,727
Catholic Population	29,793,651	4,111,778
Priests	4,112	516
Brothers and Sisters	7,133	587
Schools	1,444	198
Enrollment	817,672	115,912

[a]Data adapted from Robert L. Youngblood, "Structural Imperialism: An Analysis of the Catholic Bishops' Conference of the Philippines," *Comparative Political Studies*, 15 (April 1982), Tables 3–6.

The capabilities of the conservative and moderate Catholic bishops, together with those of the progressive bishops, as well as the resources of other progressive institutions in the Catholic and Protestant churches, posed a formidable challenge to Marcos. This was clear in the February 7, 1986, presidential election in which the churches, especially the Catholic church, not only called for a fair and honest election, but also used their personnel and resources in an attempt to protect the sanctity of the ballot, generally working closely with NAMFREL both at the national and local levels. Reports from throughout the country indicated that the clergy was a crucial factor in the outcome of the election. Among the measures of their effectiveness were accusations by President Marcos that some bishops were communists and that priests and nuns "overwhelmed" his supporters in many precincts.[32]

[32]*Christian Science Monitor*, February 18, 1986, pp. 1, 10-11.

364

By contrast, the influence and capabilities of the CNL appear to be much less formidable than recently reported. Ross Munro, in a widely quoted article published in December 1985,[33] asserted that the CNL consisted of 1,200 priests and nuns who form a network of secret cells within the Philippine "Catholic Church and its many organizations" and that Task Force Detainees (TFD), an arm of the AMRSP, which, by 1984, had forty units throughout the country and over one hundred human rights workers, is a creature of the CNL.[34] Unfortunately, Munro's analysis suffers from a number of serious shortcomings. To be sure, there are a small number of priests, nuns, and pastors who are sympathetic to or have joined the CPP, but there is no hard evidence that the CNL represents 1,200 clergy dispersed into a honeycomb of secret cells within the Catholic church. Second, Munro's suggestion that TFD was organized by the CNL is false. TFD was one of several task forces established by the AMRSP in 1974 to facilitate the work of the church under martial law, and although TFD took upon itself the task of monitoring government (and military) violations of human rights, since atrocities of the CPP/NPA were widely publicized by the Marcos-controlled media, such an admission of bias does not mean the organization is perforce communist. TFD is, however, a highly nationalistic, left-leaning organization which opposed the Marcos regime, yet the extent to which its personnel are communists or sympathetic to the CPP is a matter of dispute within the church.[35] In this regard it is interesting to note that Sister Mariani Dimaranan, C.F.I.C., the head of TFD, has assumed a post in the Aquino government.

The fact that the overwhelming majority of Filipinos heeded the call of the churches for participation in the February 7, 1986, election was a clear repudiation of the boycott stance of the CPP and its front organizations, among which is the CNL. This is an indication of the limited influence of the CNL within the Catholic and Protestant churches as well as among the population in general. There are also suggestions that many left-of-center clergy, who Munro would probably categorize as CNL or CPP sympathizers, supported the February 7th election and the candidacy of President Aquino.

[33]Ross H. Munro, "The New Khmer Rouge," *Commentary,* December 1985, pp. 19-38.
[34]Ibid., p. 26.
[35]Confidential correspondence, February 11 and 20, 1986, from two priests familiar with the work of TFD.

THE AQUINO ADMINISTRATION AND THE CHURCHES

Cardinal Sin's close relationship with President Aquino, coupled with the highly critical posture of the CBCP toward graft and corruption, abuse of power, and failed government development programs over the past several years, suggest that the Roman Catholic church will play a more significant role in Philippine politics during the Aquino administration. First, church leaders other than Cardinal Sin and personnel from church-related organizations have regularly assisted the Aquino government. Among the most visible have been Father Joaquin Bernas, president of Ateneo de Manila University and Jesuit provincial superior; Bernardo Villegas, an economist affiliated with the Center for Research and Communications, an organization with close ties to Opus Dei; and Lourdes Quisumbing, former head of Maryknoll University. Bernas, the most visible of the so-called "Jesuit Mafia" advisors close to the president, has reportedly written or contributed to a number of Mrs. Aquino's major speeches on political and social justice issues since her inauguration; and Villegas, who is frequently quoted in the Manila press, is perceived as an influential economic advisor, although just how close he is to the president or Minister of Finance Jaime Ongpin is unclear. Both Bernas and Villegas received presidential appointments to the Constitutional Commission (Concom) charged with writing a new charter for the Philippines, while Quisumbing was appointed to the cabinet as minister of education.

Second, and perhaps most important, the Roman Catholic church will continue to stress the necessity for higher standards of honesty and integrity in politics and will support President Aquino's attempts to make the government more responsive to the needs of the people.[36] Protestant church leaders will assume a similar position. Given the personal nature of Philippine politics, the churches' emphasis on morality and performance in government may translate into unofficial approval of certain political candidates in future elections, much as Sin favored Aquino over Laurel for president; but at the same time, church leaders will be cautious about being perceived as too involved in partisan politics. Already, on March 16 and 17, 1986, approximately

[36]In a speech to the Manila clergy on May 20, 1986, President Aquino indicated a desire to see the Philippine churches continue to play a prominent moral role in support of government programs of social reform. I appreciate John Carroll, S.J., pointing this out to me.

twenty bishops met at Ateneo de Manila University in Quezon City to discuss the problem of office seekers attempting to obtain the church's seal of approval, and in an effort to assist the clergy from becoming political power brokers, the bishops established guidelines that emphasized the endorsement of "qualities rather than persons as such" for office.[37]

Third, the impetus toward greater social justice and the organization of BCCs will continue, and may accelerate.[38] Although BCC formation will provide additional opportunities for CPP infiltration, a more important development will be increased pressure for democratization within the church and within Philippine society, for a key element of the BCCs is to encourage participation and responsibility within the local church. Already BCC participation has resulted in heightened demands for a role in local planning and decision making and in greater resistance to harassment and intimidation by local elites, including government and military officials. Accordingly, the BCCs are assisting in breaking the dependency syndrome of the poor by helping them become the instruments of their own liberation. The Christian communities, as the CPP realizes, are formidable agents for social change. Given the colonial heritage of the Philippines and continued governmental paternalism, both at the national and local level, democratic participation in local decision making is revolutionary. The result will be continued tension within the Catholic church and between the church and the government as various elements within the church and Philippine society adjust to the increase in participation.

The United States government should attempt to understand the nature of the qualitative changes taking place within the Philippine churches and avoid overreacting to the rhetoric of nationalist clergy. Clearly, conservative and moderate church leaders have the capability of responding to the challenge of the left, including the CNL, as recent pastoral letters of the CBCP have demonstrated. By condemning graft and corruption, military misconduct, and fraud in the recent election, the Catholic hierarchy has not only moved to the forefront of those calling for peaceful change, which is what the overwhelming majority

[37]*Philippine News and Features,* April 21, 1986, p. 13.
[38]This assertion is supported by John J. Carroll and Francisco F. Claver, "The Pastoral Priorities of the Bishops: Conclusions to A Survey Report," *Ministry Today* 1 (January-March 1985): 19-34.

of Filipinos want, but in the process it has also undercut leftist clergy sympathetic to the use of the armed struggle to transform Philippine society. Cardinal Sin has indicated he (and the church) will continue to speak out on issues of morality relevant to the conduct of the Aquino administration.

That the leadership of the Philippine churches—especially the Roman Catholic church—are actively supporting peaceful change is important, for the churches represent a powerful voice outside of the government that can function as a brake on political excesses both inside and outside of the government. In contrast to the arguments made by Samuel Huntington about the necessity of strengthening the government bureaucracy to process the demands of rising expectations,[39] it may be more efficacious in the long run for United States policy in the Philippines to encourage the development of pressure groups that are democratically oriented and committed to the notion of political pluralism. Thus the United States should be supportive of Philippine church leaders, asking them how we can best be of assistance in their effort to establish a more just and democratic society,[40] and in this regard American officials should pay particular attention to the views of progressive church leaders, since, as a group, their analysis of Philippine society over the past fifteen years has been the most accurate.

[39]Samuel P. Huntington, *Political Order in Changing Societies* (New Haven: Yale University Press, 1968).

[40]This point was evidently made to Secretary of State George Shultz during a meeting on May 9, 1986, with representatives of the CBCP. *Philippine News and Features,* May 12, 1986, p. 7.

20

A New Philippine Political System

Richard J. Kessler

From the time former President Ferdinand Marcos first declared martial law in 1972 until his overthrow on February 25, 1986, at the hands of the "people power" revolution, research on the evolution of pluralistic politics in the Philippines to all intents and purposes came to a halt.

During the 14 years of martial law, field research, analysis of voting behavior, and public opinion polling all were virtually moribund. The quality of the information that was gleaned is tainted by the martial law period and Marcos' almost obsessive manipulation of the electoral processes through a series of stage-managed referenda and elections.

There now exists an opportunity to renew research where it broke off in 1972, to analyze the present situation in the country and suggest possible future political analysis. Few specialists, for example, predicted that Marcos would have been able to declare martial law and then continue to rule for 14 years, although many observed that the political balance of power in the Philippines was not conducive to social reform, and thus political and economic instability would ensue.

These issues are not irrelevant to understanding the possible evolution of the present situation into a pluralistic democracy capable of resolving problems peacefully.

Today, the question is not whether or not there will be opposition parties but what the nature of all the parties will be. Will they evolve out of their historical clientelist framework or will they remain rooted in the past and thus perpetuate the problems of the past?

Prior to 1972 the Philippine political system was noted for its clientelist framework. Leaders derived support by satisfying the particularistic demands of their followers. Leaders were patrons and followers were clients. Leaders, too, had patrons. Thus, the society was vertically integrated from the *barrio* through municipalities and provinces to the national level. Philippine culture, which emphasizes the value of a set of mutual obligations, provided the continuing basis for this system.

The system had a number of negative effects on national development. First, it did not reward rational or normative policies. National leaders had few direct ties to the voters at the base although in the early 1950's Ramon Magsaysay's popular forays among the populace created the myth that similar displays were needed in order to be elected. To be elected to national office—that is, the presidency—politicians in a very basic way depended on the equivalent of the *barrio* ward heeler who through the dispensation of certain rewards was able to command the loyalty of a voting bloc.

There was very little party loyalty, except in a small way, among elites who identified themselves as *Nacionalistas* or Liberals. This was not because the parties had distinct ideological identities, but because in a medieval sense the Liberal or *Nacionalista* escutcheon provided a rallying point for their families' supporters.

Thus the second negative effect of the system was a lack of party loyalties and with it party identity. Parties were really an amalgam of separate fiefdoms. National leaders either came out of these fiefdoms or were directly supported by one. As Carl Landé has shown, parties had no formal affiliation procedure; candidates were selected by other politicians rather than through one primary or convention system; parties lacked advisory councils of private citizens; and party platforms were nonbinding.[1]

FEW DIFFERENCES

Parties were essentially indistinguishable. Politicians campaigned on broad issues but not on programs. In fact, as Francisco Araneta and John Carroll have observed, a party with a strong program of social reform would destroy itself because those reforms cut across the system of alliances and particularistic rewards that are the basis for power. The usual campaign issues were graft and corruption, public works and human services, the economy, and peace and order.[2] Campaigning on

---

[1]Carl H. Landé, "Party Politics in the Philippines," in George M. Guthrie, ed., *Six Perspectives on the Philippines* (Manila: Bookmark, 1971), pp. 85-132.
[2]Francisco Araneta and John J. Carroll, "Politics and Government," in Carroll, et al., eds., *Philippine Institutions* (Manila: Solidaridad Publishing House, 1970), p. 147.

issues meant promising change but not providing a program for change.

Leaders lacked a stable constituency or political organization beyond that provided in the short term through rewards or during an election. Success at retaining political power was founded on creating individual and shifting coalitions of supporters. This in turn provided national leaders, primarily the president, with little or no support for national programs.

While national politics was a game of elite competition, power was founded on local voting blocs controlled by local leaders and sustained by the ability of elites to distribute scarce resources to the local leaders.

At the local level, political factions replicated the national system in that the basis of their conflict was not programmatic but particularistic: individual rivalries for power and the prestige power conveyed.

The importance of local politics is clearly indicated in one of the last pre-martial-law political studies. Then, a survey of voting behavior since Philippine independence showed consistent trends: Local elections attracted more voters than national elections. Voter turnout was higher in rural areas and not positively correlated to socio-economic variables or mass communication facilities (including the radio).[3] The study confirmed the independence of local political leaders from national and provincial elites and thus the continued importance of the reward system in sustaining elite political ambitions.

There were signs that this system was breaking down or evolving into a more rational approach to politics when Marcos declared martial law.

The increasing size of the Philippine electorate made the distribution of sufficient benefits necessary to ensure loyalty more difficult. Scarce resources were becoming scarcer. Ando attributes the rising importance of coercion in the 1969 presidential election to this factor.[4] The rise of urban voters, especially the urban middle class, and an increase in the importance of associational groupings, such as new cause-oriented groups and the more traditional organizations such as the Jaycees and Rotary, were also contributing to a change in voter decision-criteria toward normative values. In fact, it was the urban middle class which finally made possible Marcos' overthrow.

One interesting question, which will be answered in the next few

[3]See Hirofumi Ando, "Elections in the Philippines: Mass-Elite Interaction through the Electoral Process, 1946-1969" (Ph.D. dissertation, University of Michigan, 1971).
[4]Ibid., p. 113.

years, is whether the Marcos years accelerated or impeded the evolutionary process to a modern, reason-based political process in the Philippines.

What appears evident on cursory examination is that Marcos tried to perfect the clientelist system, controlling all the rewards, replacing local leaders down to the *barrio*, or *barangay*, level with individuals personally loyal to himself, and destroying the economic basis for political power of potential elite competitors. The system began to fall apart when a collapsing economy made it more difficult to distribute rewards and Marcos's health and continued support from the United States became questionable.

Corazon Aquino's victory, on the other hand, was based on a coalition of both traditional and non-traditional political forces. The traditional politicians included many prominent holdovers from the pre-1972 period whose basis of power is rooted in traditional politics. The non-traditional forces included, most prominently, the Catholic Church, the urban middle class, and the cause-oriented groups.

Marcos' abrupt departure left his political machine in shambles and with no real successor. It is possible that out of the remnants of his KBL Party (*Kilusang Bagong Libunan,* or New Society Movement) a vital opposition party will emerge, but this is unlikely.

The KBL split almost immediately into several camps. Blas Ople, former minister of labor, with 17 former KBL members, announced the formation of the *Partido Nacionalista ng Pilipinas* (PNP). Another faction formed under the former leader of the National Assembly, the aging Nicanor Yniguez, and the younger former minister of local governments, Jose Rono. It was suggested that the former prime minister, Cesar Virata, might even try to lead a faction. Another group of approximately 53 members led by Alejandro Almendras renounced its KBL membership.

Circling about these men were groups of young and not-so-young "Turks," one of whom is Manuel Garcia, former deputy minister of justice. They were now men without a party. Younger members of the KBL suggested a compromise would involve a party with an older titular head and a younger secretary-general.

FROM THE ASHES

It is conceivable that out of the ashes of the KBL a modern opposition party will emerge with a pronounced conservative ideological orientation. Certainly, it is the only way because none of the KBL survivors have sufficient economic power to sustain a strong party on their own. Even those who are wealthy will likely find their fortunes under attack as the investigation continues into corruption during the Marcos period. They will also lack access to the *"barrio* barrel," having lost the presidency. Finally, they suffer from the Marcos stigma. Creating a modern party on the basis of an alternative program would be the only way for a KBL "look-alike" to survive.

There is some basis for that possibility among former KBL provincial strongholds. The Aquino government's initial efforts at wholesale replacement of KBL appointees to local government positions with its own appointees has been frustrated by outcries of protest from these same officials who, in some cases, can legitimately argue they were duly elected by popular vote. When local elections are again held, these officials might be responsive to joining an opposition "KBL" party if they cannot join the government's party. But in order to gain access to government largesse, these officials will have to argue programs and policy rather than personal loyalties. Given past Philippine political behavior, this seems unlikely. Instead, local "KBL" leaders will play turncoat, and bargain their control of bloc votes in exchange for their own political future unless a strong national opposition party can be formed from individuals disenfranchised by Aquino's victory or formerly pro-Aquino forces who do not feel sufficiently rewarded for their past support.

Attacks by Minister of National Defense Juan Ponce Enrile against Aquino's government in late 1986, which ultimately led to Enrile's dismissal on November 23rd, were part of the new correlation of political forces in the post-Marcos period. Enrile, one of the richest men in the Philippines with his own presidential ambitions, had long been frustrated in his position in the Aquino cabinet. A close associate of his, Rey Cayetano, had been reorganizing the old Nacionalista Party and Enrile had begun actively campaigning for support among the Marcos "loyalists" and others who had felt disenfranchised by Aquino's victory. With his resignation, Enrile became free to take the helm as leader of the anti-Aquino opposition, articulating a conservative program closely attuned to the anti-communist sentiments and pro-economic protectionist views of the traditional oligarchy. Enrile has the wealth, personal charisma, and political aptitude to become the leader sought by the new political outcasts.

Some "KBL" leaders may even have sufficient provincial strength to remain in control of their provinces. Reuben Canoy, former deputy minister of information, and recently ousted Lanao Del Sur governor Ali Dimaporo have formed their own Mindanao People's Democratic Movement. Previously Canoy had co-chaired the Social Democratic Party until a split with Francisco Tatad and before that even had split with Homobono Adaza's Mindanao Alliance. Other Marcos-era political warlords such as Ramon Durano in Cebu and Armand Gustillo in Negros remain sufficiently influential in the Aquino-era to ensure retention of their personal regional political power bases.

Regional parties, however, do not represent a break with the past. The only area where third parties have been relatively successful before is Central Luzon. It can be argued that conditions which made such movements possible in Central Luzon are now apparent in Mindanao.[5] Still, such breakaway groups will ultimately have to form explicit or implicit alliances with the ruling party to sustain themselves. Or, again, they will have to argue policies and programs, not personalities.

More likely the party framework will emerge out of the present forces governing the Philippines. Within that framework, the former KBL members will find their home. Differences are already evident within the Aquino government.

Corazon Aquino is a member of the *Laban (Lakasa ng Bayan)* Party co-founded by her late husband, but she ran under the banner of UNIDO (United Nationalist Democratic Organization), the party of her vice president, Salvador Laurel. *Laban* itself had previously formed a coalition with the Pilipino-Democratic Party (PDP) under Aquilino Pimentel, Aquino's first minister of local government. The secretary-general of PDP-Laban is Jose Cojuangco, Corazon Aquino's brother. Also members of PDP-Laban are Minister of Agriculture Ramon Mitra and Teofisto Guingona (Commission on Audit).

Mrs. Aquino resisted pressures in 1986 to form her own political party. In response, Jose Cojuangco focused his efforts at making PDP-Laban a national party, co-opting former members of UNIDO. He was also a behind-the-scenes actor in a new party, *Lakas ng Bansa*, established in late 1986 mainly by members of the Aquino cabinet who had spent much of the martial law period in American exile, during which their political roots in the Philippines had atrophied.

[5]See Landé, Ibid., p. 104.

UNIDO, headed by Laurel with Rene Espina as secretary-general, is also a loose coalition, consisting of elements of the old *Nacionalista* Party, the Mindanao Alliance of Homobono Adaza, and several associations (the National Organization of Women, the National Union for Liberation, the Concerned Citizens Aggrupation, the Interim National Assembly Association, and the *Kabataang Pilipino*). UNIDO began to fragment in 1986 because Laurel, as vice-president, did not have control of as large a "pork barrel" as President Aquino's forces.

UNIDO also has ties to the Minnie Osmena and Eva Kalaw wing of the Liberal Party (LP) while PDP-Laban is close to the Jovito Salonga and John Osmena wings of the LP.

Other traditional politicians include former senators Jose Diokno, now chairing the newly created Commission on Human Rights, Ambrosio Padilla and Lorenzo Tanada, who were titular heads of the leftist group *Bayan,* and recently returned exile Raul Manglapus who heads the Christian Social Movement.

BLOOD TIES

Related to all of these individuals either by blood or organization are a host of cause-related groups. These include moderate groups such as the Makati Businessman's Club and Butz Aquino's *Bandila*; women's organizations such as *Gabriela*; groups on the far Left such as *Bayan* and the National Democratic Front; and student organizations such as *Samsa* and *Tugon*.

There are almost as many organizations as Filipinos, representing all sections of the economy and society. In many instances these are only affiliates of larger groups. For example, *Tugon* is affiliated with *Bandila* and *Samsa* with *Bayan*. Others are loose umbrella organizations. *Gabriela* envelops a number of these. Finally, there is a series of implicit interlinked directorates with groups loosely allied through family relationships.

The *Partido ng Bayan*, for example, was formed in 1986 by Jose Sison, the founder of the communist party. While Sison eschewed a visible role in the party's leadership, instead promoting Rolando Olalia as the PNB's secretary-general, he remained as the new party's driving force, basing it on many of the same groups which had formed *Bayan*. PNB is a legal party but in tacit alliance with the Communist party, although communist leaders remain suspicious of Sison's intentions, viewing it as his vehicle to regain control of the Community party. Olalia's brutal assassination in November 1986 gained the party a martyr which may help it become the most visible party of the left, promising to field candidates in the 1987 national and local elections.

Many of the cause-oriented groups exist because of the popularity of their leader rather than their cause. Some are only fronts behind which other organizations can try to broaden their support base. These organizations form and re-form according to directives from above—the Communist Party of the Philippines (CPP) most often engages in this type of activity. Many of these organizations will disband if the Aquino government is successful in co-opting their leadership by bringing them into government service or co-opting their issue by making it part of government policy. The mobilization capacity of many of these groups was always limited.

Some will survive, however, either through the charisma of their leadership or by being able to focus on particular issues neglected by the government. The traditional example of this is the Philippine labor movement which Marcos tried to control in 1975 with the formation of the Trade Union Congress of the Philippines (TUCP). Despite his efforts, an active union movement continued, most notably Bonifacio Tupaz's Trade Union of the Philippines and Allied Services (TUPAS) with 153,000 members, Rolando Olalia's leftist Kilusang Mayo Uno (KMU, or May 1st November) with 650,000 members and even the TUCP, the largest with 1.5 million members, which has been able to differentiate itself somewhat from its original pro-Marcos image. By focusing on equity issues in both rural and urban areas, labor movements may be able to become important political actors. For this reason, the CPP has focussed a large part of its organizing efforts through the KMU and its affiliates.

The continued importance of labor unions and cause-oriented groups will be dependent upon the degree to which Philippine politics continues previous patterns. A key test will be the local and national elections which are to be held in 1987.

These elections will decide Aquino's political future. She has three choices: remain with the existing PDP-Laban Party, withdraw from party activities, or form a new party. The last option would be most promising for the country's political future.

POSSIBILITIES

Having come to power by melding traditional contending factions together with support from her base, an urban middle class, and the church, Corazon Aquino has the opportunity to create a more modern political party in the Philippines. In essence, this would institutionalize "people power" and would have the advantage of providing a basis for disregarding the traditional elites in formulating national policy. In effect it would disenfranchise these elites unless they developed their own modern party to compete.

Obviously this would be a contentious approach. By remaining with PDP-Laban and developing a *modus vivendi* with UNIDO over selection of candidates, Aquino would reduce (but not eliminate) friction between the two ruling groups. But this is also likely to accelerate intra-governmental rivalries and ultimately affect legislative initiatives. It will encourage the return to traditional political practices.

If Aquino refrained from political activity in the upcoming elections, the same rivalries would still emerge—and probably sooner and more virulently, as forces within her own group would be forced to compete for party leadership.

By establishing a new party along modern lines (with membership, primaries, offices, etc.) Aquino will be able to tap the roots of popular participation that made her victory possible and bring new leaders into the political process. The support she received from the church indicates that this is possible. It will break up the current ruling coalition as individuals feel their personal ambitions have been frustrated. This, however, is encouraging, as it will force these individuals to create a similar apparatus if they are to gain power.

The new constitution will also promote modernization of the political system. With the nation-wide election of 24 Senators, a premium will be placed on the ability to raise funds, identify voters' concerns, and publicize candidacies. This will mean the importation of some of the sophisticated techniques now used in American elections. Once one candidate adopts this approach, others will too. The expense of a national campaign will make it difficult for a candidate to be identified with a specific interest group or family.

The Philippines has not yet shown that it has emerged out of the Marcos period into the bright light of progressive politics. In retrospect the problems that made Marcos declare martial law are apparent. In retrospect the problems that made his downfall and Aquino's rise inevitable are apparent. What is not yet apparent is whether the problems of Philippine political maturation are resolved.

21

Report on the Discussion: Government and Politics from Marcos to Aquino

Linda K. Richter

Free-flowing discussions among scholars, former diplomats, and current policy holders are difficult to synthesize under the best of circumstances. Add the general enthusiasm occasioned by the flight of President Marcos, the new presidency of Corazon Aquino, and the luxury of discussing such events over more than two days, and the task in the case of the Philippines becomes richer but immensely more complex.

What this chapter seeks to do is not only to capture the essence of the discussion and debate but to order it in such a way that it is clear what the points of consensus and disagreement are. Further, as the rapporteur, this writer also includes her own analysis of these topics and an appraisal of subject areas deserving further evaluation.

If there is one dominant impression that emerged from the conference it is a sense of exhilaration in having a new, dynamic and incredibly more complicated political canvas to study. For twenty years President Marcos and his wife Imelda dominated most examinations of Philippine politics and United States policy making toward the Philippines. After the 1972 declaration of martial law the increasingly personalistic nature of the Marcos government intensified the preoccupation of scholars and policy makers with the president, his political instincts and health, and the web of associates surrounding him. Political institutions became correspondingly less important. Some, like the national Congress, the vice-presidency, and the constitution, were simply abolished. Others, like the mass media, the courts, and local governments, were tamed, co-opted, and reorganized to maximize presidential power. Rule by presidential decree became the norm. New institutions were designed expressly for President Marcos. An example was the constitution (ratified by voice vote) establishing a parliamentary system. It illustrated that even without martial law the government would be designed to the president's specifications. It not only did not limit presidential tenure as the 1935 Constitution had, but it also provided for continued rule by presidential decree. After martial law was lifted in 1981, or "facelifted" as critics charged, the new national assembly and the president's personally controlled KBL party continued his domination of the formal political process. The president's power to rule by decree, use the economy and military for personal needs, and curtail civil liberties remained largely unchecked.

Thus, the same variables in Philippine politics and the United States-Philippine relationship remained. Whatever optimism scholars or policy makers may have had in the early years of President Marcos' tenure had largely evaporated in the last ten years. This left scholars chronicling *ad nauseum* the banality and greed of the regime, the deteriorating economic and political situation, the rise of radicalized groups, and the plummeting standard of living of the average Filipino. American policy makers argued inconclusively and with increasing despair as they sought guarantees of future access to Clark Air Force Base and Subic Bay Naval Base from a government unable to ensure its own control in over half of the nation's provinces. The radicalized and Communist-dominated New People's Army grew rapidly despite increased American military and economic aid during the martial law era. Philippine immigration to the United States soared following martial law even as capital flight accelerated. The debate over how much the United States could or should do was aggravated by a growing anti-American sentiment in the Philippines that fed on the continued association of the United States with the unpopular Marcos regime. For years, scholars and policy makers have debated these themes or their variations.

Thus there was among the conference participants a palpable sense of relief and an enthusiasm for exploring the unassessed and generally unexpected victory of Corazon Aquino and its implications for the Philippines and for United States relationships with that nation. Discussion centered around five topics. They were (1) the nature of the new leadership, most importantly the personality and expertise of Corazon Aquino, but also that of her key associates; (2) the new roles assumed by several of the prominent Philippine institutions, specifically the military and the Catholic church; (3) the potentially most critical new development—the evolution of a new constitution and the process of its construction; (4) new parties and interests; and (5) an assessment of Aquino's new policy directions and their likely impact. While discussion centered on President Aquino's first two months in office, this analysis includes a general assessment of the first hundred days of her government.

THE NEW LEADERSHIP

The media hype proclaimed that a timid housewife had wrested control of the Philippines from an aging and ailing despot. It made good copy, and clearly many in the Reagan administration and among the general public considered her victory a fluke. Conference participants were also candid in acknowledging their surprise at how well her campaign had fared. Their reaction was, however, less a reflection on her ability— which many had come to respect even before the campaign began —than their expectation (which proved accurate) that the election would be bought or rigged and the results improperly tallied by Marcos supporters.

Of course, what was fascinating about the 1986 presidential elections was that, while the expected electoral scenario unfolded with few surprises beyond the enormous crowds for Aquino, what followed the corrupt election was totally unanticipated.

Consider the bizarre sequence of events: Aquino refused to concede. NAMFREL, the independent electoral monitoring organization, denounced the government cheating. Official American observers convinced a reluctant President Reagan that the election had further discredited the Marcos regime. Demonstrations massed against Marcos despite his threats to unleash government troops. Key members of those troops, Defense Minister Juan Ponce Enrile and General Fidel Ramos dramatically defected and set up opposition headquarters which other military units subsequently joined. Cardinal Sin of Manila rallied hundreds of thousands via the Catholic radio station broadcasts to encircle opposition headquarters to "protect" the mutinous soldiers —which the people did. Both Aquino and Marcos held separate inaugural ceremonies, but within hours American planes flew Marcos and his 80-person entourage out of the country to exile in Hawaii, ending his 20-year rule. Cory Aquino took control of the Philippines in an almost bloodless revolution. No one at the conference took credit for anticipating a victory for Aquino, let alone the implausible string of events that had preceded it. Most participants echoed Cardinal Sin, who called it simply "a miracle."

Following such a series of improbable circumstances, it is perhaps understandable that even those doubtful about Cory Aquino's political savvy were not eager to write off her coalition government. While one person was heard referring to hers as "a Kerensky government," alluding to the short-lived Russian democracy that existed between the overthrow of the tsars and the installation of Soviet rule, a general aura of positive expectations was reflected in the comments of most.

Optimism was particularly characteristic of those in the gathering that knew Aquino personally. All cited her stunning transformation following the 1983 assassination of her husband Benigno Aquino upon his return to the Philippines from exile. Others, who had known the Aquino family for years, saw her self-discipline, personal control, and ethical commitment as going back to her youth, her convent education, and her rigorous study of mathematics, French, and law. The development of her political understanding is attributed less to her upbringing in a prominent family and the early years of her marriage to a politically successful spouse, than it is to her experiences during the nearly eight years her husband was imprisoned by Marcos under martial law. During those years she had been his political conduit and spokesperson to the outside world, as well as the family manager and disciplinarian. The division of labor in the family between wife and husband blurred. He became dependent on her as she had to take over the leadership of the family. At no time would either compromise with President Marcos for Aquino's release or for the economic security of their extended family. Co-opting—the favorite tactic of the Marcos authoritarian era—did not work on the Aquinos. Others commented that Corazon Aquino is a good judge of character and a woman in total control of herself.

Given the media reports about her being just a housewife it is striking that in Singapore on October 1, 1985, at a seminar on risk assessment of the Center for Research and Communication—still two months before she became a candidate—Aquino presented a paper outlining how peaceful political change could occur in the Philippines. At the time, it appeared only a pipe dream since it would have required the unification of the democratic opposition, the active involvement of ordinary Filipinos, the moral leadership of the church in that direction, and a reform movement of the military. In fact, it was just this unlikely coalescence that five months later brought victory for Corazon Aquino.

The Aquino presidency, however, by its very nature shares power with others and so cannot be summarized, as the Marcos regime was, solely in terms of the president. The Marcos cronies were just that—individuals whose power derived almost exclusively from their association with the president. Aquino's close advisors and cabinet officials have power bases and ambitions of their own. Much of the debate at the session and in informal discussions hinged on assessments of their temperament, loyalty, competence, and political ambitions.

Specifically, the acknowledged ambitions of Vice President and Foreign Minister Salvador Laurel and Local Government Minister Aquilino Pimintel were evaluated. Still more problematic are the personal and professional allegiance of Defense Minister Enrile and General Fidel Ramos, chief of staff of the New Army of the Philippines.

Both these men were loyal to President Marcos until a few days before his exile. Both are hated and distrusted by many of Aquino's close advisors. Indeed, Enrile had been the "gatekeeper" who determined if and when Cory Aquino was allowed to visit her imprisoned husband during his long ordeal. Nevertheless, the defection of Enrile and Ramos was the catalyst that ended the Marcos era.

Participants debated whether the Aquino government was an "unholy alliance" doomed to stalemate and drift at best, vicious in-fighting and threats of coups at worst. While few were sanguine about the mix, some saw Aquino's portfolio decisions as balanced and probably an attempt to co-opt rival centers of power that might otherwise challenge a more ideologically consistent administration. Pragmatism is characteristic of Filipino mainstream politics; and the present cabinet, while diverse, offers practical advantages for all who are willing to work within it, while holding out the possibility that many of the key figures can use their bases for future political advancement.

Sabotaging the Aquino presidency at this point in time would probably hurt rather than advance a rival candidacy. Indeed, Aquino's charisma and integrity are such that even conference participants spoke of Cory Aquino as "a Madonna figure," a "Joan of Arc," and so on.

This does not mean, however, that Aquino or her cabinet has much freedom to maneuver. There is much "old business" with which to wrestle, including (a) a $26 billion debt, (b) a devastated economy, (c) a growing communist-led insurgency, (d) a demoralized military,

(e) discredited political institutions, and (f) daily demonstrations and at least one coup attempt by pro-Marcos elements reputedly on the payroll of the exiled ex-president.

OLD INSTITUTIONS IN NEW ROLES

The "People Power Revolution" politicized a broader stratum of Filipinos than any other political movement in memory. Businessmen and students, union leaders and nuns, shopkeepers and soldiers were all represented in the demonstrations that eventually broke the Marcos political hold on the nation.

Perhaps the major surprise of the "revolution" was that it was led at the last by some of the most conservative establishment elements: Makati businessmen, convent-educated students, the top hierarchy of the Catholic church, and once-loyal military leaders. Keeping such conservative class interests working with more traditional sources of political activism will be a major challenge.

The church is a preeminent institution that played a pivotal role in bringing Aquino to power and legitimizing her unorthodox accession to the presidency by dint of its own moral authority. Cardinal Sin remains a regular advisor to the Aquino government. Aquino herself has tried to use the influence of the church as a tool of national reconciliation, holding a thanksgiving mass after her inauguration and observing a pious and deliberately spartan lifestyle. Refusing to live in lavish Malacañtang Palace, she has instead made it a museum of the excesses of the Marcos years. The contrast between the Marcos "evil" and her own "saintly" behavior as widow of a martyred nationalist reinforces the church's relationship with her.

Most of the participants approved of Cardinal Sin's and the Philippine church's courage in participating in moves both to reform the political process and—when that failed—to promote elections and struggle for the defeat of President Marcos. The church had acted at great risk, particularly given the Vatican's reluctance to see priests and nuns directly involved in politics. Many of those present who were praising the church's new political activism are probably appalled by similar religious activism by conservative groups like the Moral Majority in this country. Several acknowledged that being Philippine specialists did not make them immune to applying double standards.

There were some cautionary notes. Can a politicized church exert extraordinary power and then after such a heady and successful undertaking return to a preoccupation with only spiritual matters? Has Aquino been "captured" by the activist church hierarchy? What happens to policy issues like the legalization of divorce or abortion, or efforts at family planning, when the church becomes a dominant *political* as well as moral force? It was noted that on most if not all of these issues the Aquino government was unlikely to forge ahead—with or without church involvement. Moreover, it was noted that at the local level the church could be quite lax about challenging family planning efforts.

The more serious long-term issue of church conflict with the state was sidestepped in the general approval of the church's new activism on behalf of social justice issues. It was recognized that the church has never been monolithic and that activist, even radical, elements had always been present. What *was* new was that, for perhaps the first time, there were reports of aspiring politicians' seeking endorsements from local priests! Several priests have even met with their bishops to consider backing certain honest and acceptable candidates. This would allow voters a chance to know which candidates the church felt were capable, without getting the church involved in individual candidacies. This is a major new flexing of church muscle.

There are also indications that the progressive elements in the church have been strengthened by recent events and that therefore social justice issues may figure more prominently in the future. United States policy makers as a consequence were advised to monitor, understand, and avoid overreacting to the nationalist rhetoric. Since it is just these progressive elements that have proved most relevant in the last fifteen years, it is imperative that the United States listen rather than attempt to dictate to them.

There was considerable interest in and discussion of the church's relationship to the Marcos regime (from which it received tax-exempt status and cooperation on its opposition to divorce and family planning), to the new Aquino regime, and to the possible ascendancy of either the military of the leftist groups.

The military's role in the new government was alluded to several times. As one of the discredited weak spots in the Marcos regime, the military has, through the exile of General Fabian Ver and the sudden defections of General Ramos and Defense Minister Enrile to Cory Aquino, acquired a new veneer of respectability. The improbable protection of the defecting military by the general populace in Manila also forged symbolic though probably transient links between the people and the once-despised military. Cory Aquino is caught in a similarly unfamiliar embrace with the very institution that slaughtered her husband. How much of past military abuses can she, the public, and the church forgive? How much reform can be implemented and how rapidly? Commentators seemed hopeful that, given particularly the limited reforms already undertaken, and General Ramos' moves to retire "overstaying" military brass, a new ethical base could take root that would further Aquino's and the church's genuine search for national reconciliation. The military leadership has so far given no hint of disloyalty to the Aquino government despite deep misgivings about her release of all political prisoners, including leaders of the Philippine Communist Party and the New People's Army (NPA).

The military has pursued the president's initiatives toward amnesty for NPA rebels, instigated intensified ethical training for its officers, and generally sought a refurbished image as reflected in its title, "The New Armed Forces of the Philippines."

In recent weeks, the military has been reported to be discouraged by the growth of NPA control in the provinces, the slow disarming of some rebels, and the reputed heavy casualties that continue to be suffered on all sides in this guerrilla struggle. The conference participants remained, however, cautiously optimistic.

NEW VARIABLES IN PHILIPPINE POLITICS

A third theme in the discussions was the emergence of new groups, interests, and political parties and their anticipated impact on the future constitution and formal institutions of government.

While some traditional institutions like the military and the church have assumed new political roles, there are also several other elements that are anticipated to have a strong impact on Philippine politics. Foremost of these will be the post-Marcos constitution now being drafted.

Currently President Aquino is operating under a temporary "Freedom Constitution" which allows her sweeping powers but permits most civil liberties that had been denied during the years of President Marcos' authoritarian rule. The National Assembly, which had been predominantly filled with Marcos supporters elected in earlier, fraudulent, elections, has been dissolved. By September 2, 1986, Aquino expects the constitutional commission to have a constitution drafted to submit to the voters.

Forming a new constitution will be no easy task. The 1935 Constitution that governed the Philippines until 1972 was modeled in many respects on that of the United States, but it provided for greater centralization and far more presidential authority. In retrospect, it is acknowledged by its provision for emergency executive powers, to have given the initial aura of legitimacy to President Marcos' declaration of martial law. As a consequence, that constitution has been discredited. A simple retreat to the 1935 Constitution is impossible, though many including Aquino favor a bicameral legislature and a presidential system.

During the martial law years another constitution based on a parliamentary system was adopted by voice vote. It conveniently established a system without tenure restrictions on the president or prime minister so that Marcos could be assured of no barriers to his indefinite rule so long as he could control the election of representatives to the National Assembly. This constitution lacked legitimacy both because of the circumstances under which it was formulated and ratified and because it was routinely amended to suit the President's needs after martial law. The power to rule by presidential decree continued.

Given such a history, the task before the constitutional commission was considered by participants to be a daunting one. Two problems dominate: the legitimacy of this constitutional process and the subsequent structural decisions.

The legitimacy issue is based on the fact that Aquino, herself an irregular successor to the presidency, chose all but five of the forty-nine members of the constitutional commission. They were not elected representatives of the people. Five were chosen by Marcos loyalist and former labor minister Blas Ople to represent Marcos supporters. Aquino attempted to cover many interests in her selections, including one general, two Muslim leaders, three Catholic leaders, two former judges, a journalist, a labor leader, a peasant leader, and six women. Still, the resulting composition includes twenty-five lawyers and virtually no leftist labor leaders or communists.

That may reassure Western observers already nervous about the nationalist rhetoric and debate over the military bases and restrictions on foreign capital which may be included in the constitution. Still, the

New People's Army and the left may find little reason to cooperate with the Aquino government, given their lack of representation. A central factor in the constitution's perceived legitimacy will be whether it is seen as an independent outcome of a cross-section of Filipino interests or whether it is considered to be drafted to United States specifications. The Philippine press has raised the specter of American intervention in the process, which will surely continue to be controversial.

At the time of this conference, delegates to the constitutional commission had not yet been selected, so participants focused attention primarily on the type of system needed. Primary concern revolved around the issue of how much power the central government should have vis-a-vis the local and provincial levels of government. Despite the Philippines' heritage as a Spanish and then American colony, and while the Philippines adopted a political system at independence resembling in many ways the American one, it never seriously considered federalism. Though the country is composed of thousands of islands and possesses great ethnic and linguistic diversity, federalism's chief supporters were Muslims. Thus, federalism came to be associated with the fear of a Muslim separatist movement. Ironically, it has been a unitary form of government that has grappled with Muslim political opposition for over three hundred years.

While federalism is unlikely to emerge with the new constitution, many of the conference participants and certainly many groups within the Philippines are insisting that the constitution needs to provide for greater local autonomy. There was debate over whether the center or the local level of political control is the more effective for pursuing the social justice issues that all felt needed to be addressed. Some argued that the local level had proved to be critical for social and political organization, that it had been innovative and active over especially the last five years, while the center's plans had historically burned out like wild grasses after a short burst of flame.

Others insisted "people power" was largely an urban, indeed Manila-based, phenomenon without roots in the largely feudal hinterlands. They felt that the credibility and security of the central government hinged on dramatic initiatives which would restructure political power in the countryside, defuse the appeal of the NPA and prevent regional turf battles from challenging the national government.

President Aquino feels this dilemma most keenly. When governor of Tarlac province, her husband was constantly frustrated by the feeble powers entrusted to his office. In 1976 this writer had the chilling experience of hearing President Marcos tell three hundred Philippine mayors that he could "make them or break them." Though that was during martial law, legal powers explicit in both of the earlier constitutions permitted the central government a fiscal tyranny over all lower political levels. Still, in the absence of assured support in all regions, it is difficult for President Aquino or her cabinet to look with much equanimity upon the possibility of significant local autonomy.

NEW PARTIES AND INTEREST

The emergence of new political parties and factions was also the topic of several commentators' remarks. There was much debate as to whether the Philippines had seen the last of pragmatic, personality-led parties built on patron-client ties. Would the old formula of guns, goons, and gold —honed to a fine art by President Marcos —re-emerge to keep feudal relationships in place? Or would the numerous cause-oriented interests serve as the organizing nucleus for more ideologically-oriented parties?

Some thought that President Marcos' personal instrument of party rule, the KBL, would reorganize (perhaps as Blas Ople has already attempted) into a new, more policy-oriented form of conservative party. Then President Aquino would proceed to develop her own political party organized in support of liberal reforms and based on the rapidly growing urban population. As was pointed out, however, there is no historical base for classic conservatism in Philippine politics. One might add that social justice issues have also been rarely addressed except in rhetorical terms in the old mainline Philippine parties.

The importance of political parties for organizing diverse interests was seen as critical in the Philippine context. No one advanced any sympathy for or expectation of "partyless democracy." Still, it was recognized that Aquino's support was unique in modern Philippine politics. She came to power not on the basis of a single party and its patronage machinery but as a result of a diverse coalition of parties and interest groups, some with quite modern political objectives, others with more traditional orientations.

Governing with such a coalition will be, several argued, far more formidable than forging an electoral coalition. However, after having overcome the obstacles Marcos placed in their way one can hardly call the Aquino victory coalition naive or inexperienced with the "political hardball" of Philippine politics.

One participant commented that Marcos' heavy-handed subversion of the election was a blessing in disguise. By holding an election to provide a veneer of legitimacy for his own continued rule and then corrupting the electoral process, he in fact guaranteed the perceived legitimacy of his *opponent*, who despite Marcos' best efforts made an incredibly strong showing. Secondly, by holding most of the power and money and blatantly buying votes, Marcos forced his opponents, who could not compete for such traditional resources, to campaign on a high moral plane totally unparalleled in Philippine politics. Thus, Marcos gave the Aquino camp a cloak of respectability that has brought Aquino to office with unprecedented moral authority.

It was suggested that several facets of the Aquino political coalition may not be understood by foreigners but are not unusual in the Philippine or broader Asian context. Many outsiders were amazed that after years of squabbling among the opposition, when the opportunity arose, the two chief contenders for the presidency could reconcile themselves to places on the ticket as well as to the party label, rally other opposition groups, and mount a formidable nationwide campaign in a mere two months. This pattern of delay, debate, and division, followed by sudden closure and intense organizational zeal is not unusual in the Philippines.

Nor is the notion of national reconciliation with enemies on the left or the right after a bitter election unrealistic in that cultural context. Philippine culture places a high value on consensus and harmony and does not recognize confrontation, competition, and aggressiveness as either natural or inevitable. Politics has been historically an area where conflict has been perceived as legitimate, but the culture itself can appreciate political amnesty for NPA guerrillas or "forgiveness" toward Marcos loyalists. The reconciliation strategy may not work, as military leaders fear, but it is not considered bizarre or timid. Instead, it is seen as the generous gesture of a confident leader.

A critical test for the new government which outside observers may underestimate will be transcending traditional regional politics. Historically, home provinces of Philippine presidents have been favored during their brief terms of office. The unprecedented twenty-year tenure of President Marcos was a time of unparalleled largesse and patronage for his home province of Ilocos Norte and for adjacent

Ilocano-speaking areas. Wooing this region without further impoverishing other areas will be an important task for Aquino.

This effort has taken on even more importance as the small but persistent pro-Marcos, anti-American demonstrations continue in Manila. Whether these are financed by Marcos, as many claim, they are clearly encouraged by the exiled leader and have in their ranks many from Marcos' home province. At the time of the conference, these demonstrations were not taken seriously, and they pose no significant threat to the Aquino government. However, they are a chronic irritant tempting the government to overreact, and they continue to nourish probably misplaced hopes in the Ilocos Norte region that cooperation with Aquino is unnecessary. A similar and more serious threat exists in the south of the country, where Reuben Canoy has announced an independence movement embracing the mineral-rich center of Muslim strength, the island of Mindanao.

Beyond constitutional structure and presidential initiatives, there was also discussion of the group politics that emerged in the last few years of the Marcos era. The number of such ad hoc groups and the incredible variety of their concerns are impressive. They also reflect the availability of leadership and initiative, as well as a politicizing of the society channeled toward collective, organized civic action. This is a new element in Philippine politics, which has been perhaps in large part stimulated by almost a generation of authoritarian rule.

Many of these groups, discussants suggested, are likely to be sympathetic to the Aquino government or at least united in their opposition to Marcos and thus might operate to blur the urban-rural political divisions others saw as divisive.

One new institution that clearly proved able to mobilize support in urban and rural areas was NAMFREL, the independent group of over 500,000 Filipinos that monitored the presidential election. Some participants saw it as a particularly important political factor in the post-Marcos Philippines. NAMFREL field precinct observers faced intimidation and violence in their efforts to ensure that election laws were followed, and in attempting to deliver a clean election or document lapses from a fair contest. It was also remarked that NAMFREL demonstrated an amazing sophistication about the electoral process. Filipinos know well how an election can be stolen and as a result astutely monitored every stage of the election from the production of ballots and voting lists to the transfer of computer tallies and the delivery of election results to the National Assembly. The reality of a neutral organization, not co-optable, not expecting patronage or favors, is without precedent in the Philippines. Its ability to organize quickly and to provide a check on the Marcos-controlled election commission gave it a commanding presence in the presidential election. International observer teams and Filipino citizens looked to it for authoritative information. Its future in what is hoped will be a more democratically run nation is still unclear, but the example it provided of all types of individuals working a precinct together has surely been a constructive one.

Bayan, a leftist cause-oriented group, was another element many participants felt was destined to keep the pressure on Aquino to respond to nationalist and social justice issues. It was considered the largest and most important of such groups.

ISSUES

A final general area that the session on Government and Politics explored was the "Where does she go from here?" issue. As Aquino herself has warned, she may have won a "snap election" and emerged victorious from a "snap revolution," but there are no "snap solutions" to the problems facing the Philippines. Despite the general high regard in which she is held by the participants, few disputed the assessment of one commentator who warned that she has at most a year to make decisive headway in improving the standard of living.

Aquino's cabinet is divided on how to proceed. The minister of finance prefers a mixed economy with incentives for foreign investment. His approach is popular with the business sector and the United States, which has encouraged American investors to be bullish on the Philippines. Her labor minister, on the other hand, has favored a higher minimum wage as a deterrent to strikes and as a tangible recognition of the plight of workers, even if such moves make the Philippines less attractive as a site for cheap labor.

Land reform has been called for by Aquino and others. However, for land reform measures to seem credible and be effective for a populace jaded by earlier attempts, which were undercut by landlord resistance and executive timidity, strong, concrete steps must be taken. Moreover, they must be taken immediately, *before* the restoration of a democratic legislature, which may become stalemated over such an issue, as it has been in the past. In one sense the timing is perfect. The insurgency is strongest in sugar- and coconut-producing areas, which heretofore had not been subject to land reform. The argument was made in the past that land producing such commodities should not be considered for land reform because of the need for stable export production. That is no longer the case. The world prices for both sugar and coconut are severely depressed, with sugar unlikely to recover as artificial sweeteners and changing diets cut demand.

Now is precisely the time to convert such lands to subsistence crops. Such a move would defuse the appeal of the NPA and directly confront the serious malnutrition in the area. Moreover, it would be a way for President Aquino to personally set an example among area elites as her family estate is a major coconut producer. Ironically, hers is one of the more efficient estates, but often the maximization of economic rationality must be sacrificed to the establishment of political credibility. Land reform is not a panacea. It rarely works. It needs continued monitoring and in the Philippine context land is simply too scarce for mere division of lands or resettlement to be the answer to Philippine agriculture. It does, however, buy time for political leaders, something Aquino desperately needs. It may also be effective on a regional basis as a counterinsurgency tool. It also has the merit of being something the Philippines can do for itself, without IMF, World Bank, or United States involvement.

The Philippines will of necessity be compelled to accommodate, cooperate, or at least seek assistance from capitalist nations. All such actions will provide ammunition for groups on the left to cry "sell out." Land reform is designed to offer something to the left ideologically while encouraging tenant farmers and landless agricultural workers in practical terms.

Actions taken to recover billions reputedly smuggled abroad by the Marcos family and associates as well as domestic tax amnesties have been designed with both economic and political goals in view. Aside from the monetary relief such income may garner, there are also the twin political messages of a new ethic in government from which scoundrels cannot hide and a spirit of forgiveness for those who come to obey the law. Stiffer taxes generally for the middle class fall on a very important component of Aquino's political coalition, but the reality of lower inflation and less corrupt politics may make the new policies palatable.

"People Power" brought a new politics to the Philippines. After six months it is still unclear whether "people power" can forge an enduring government. Yet, if good wishes within the Philippines or abroad can translate even partially to political power the Aquino presidency will be very strong indeed.

V. Internal War and Defense

22

The Communist Party of the Philippines and the Aquino Government: Responding to the "New Situation"

Larry A. Niksch*

BACKGROUND

In November 1985, the Senate Foreign Relations Committee published a study of the communist insurgency in the Philippines. The study profiled the state of the insurgency up to the middle of 1985.[1] It also analyzed the strategy of the Marcos government in dealing with the communist movement. The study found that the insurgency had made major gains since 1980 due to a combination of factors including (1) the weakness of local government and law enforcement at the level of the Philippines' 1,534 towns; (2) worsening living standards in the towns, particularly falling real incomes, unemployment, lack of medicine and medical care, and malnutrition; (3) the breakdown of traditional social structures and support systems in places like Mindanao and Negros; (4) communist organizations at the local level that are skilled in penetration, establishing links with people in the *barangays,* and convincing people that the government at various levels is responsible for their problems and worsening conditions; (5) military abuses of civilians, which alienate civilians from the government and armed forces; and (6) the political unpopularity of the Marcos government with key groups in the cities.

According to the study, the Communist party of the Philippines (CPP) has a three-pronged strategy consisting of building up party organizations in the rural towns and barangays, forming armed guer-

---

*The views expressed in this chapter are those of the author and do not necessarily reflect those of the Congressional Research Service.

[1] U.S. Congress, Senate, Committee on Foreign Relations, *Insurgency and Counterinsurgency in the Philippines.* S. Prt. 99–99, 99th Congress, 1st Session (Washington: U.S. Government Printing Office, 1985).

rilla units of the New Peoples Army (NPA), and increasing its influence among the politically aware segments of urban society through the National Democratic Front (NDF). By mid-1985, the CPP had become adept at organization building and projecting its influence despite problems such as shortages of arms and the weak ideological commitment among rank-and-file guerrillas and other supporters.

The study contended that the CPP's successes depend to a large degree on the mistakes and weaknesses of the Philippine government. It concluded that the government and the armed forces (AFP) faced severe problems which they must overcome in order to defeat the insurgency, including (1) the lack of security in the towns and barangays; (2) the strained relations between the military and civilians because of military abuses and corruption; (3) the severe deficiency of material resources in the AFP; (4) inadequate training of AFP personnel; and (5) the lack of noncommunist political unity.

The study noted that many of these problems were similar to those of the Huk rebellion of the 1940s and 1950s. These were solved, under the direction of Ramon Magsaysay, by policies that combined reform of the AFP, including leadership changes, with a major upgrading of resources for the units in the field. This combination bolstered morale in the AFP, significantly altered the AFP's relations with the civilian population, and enabled the AFP to initiate and intensify its military operations, programs to encourage Huk defections, and civic action projects aimed at civilians.

The study asserted that the Philippines needed two ingredients to deal successfully with insurgency: leadership and resources; that is, a political and military leadership that would give a much higher priority in the shaping of policies to the impact of such policies on the insurgency and the spread of communist political influence. Immediate tasks defined were training and retraining the AFP in counterinsurgency tactics and strategy; a revitalization of basic training for new military personnel; an increase in AFP transportation and communications assets; a reconsideration of the Civilian Home Defense Forces (CHDF), including the option of abolishing them; a strengthening of regular police forces at the local level as an alternative to the CHDF; a strengthening of town governments, including a revival of political participation and electoral politics; a combination of actions to improve AFP conduct toward civilians; a major improvement in the pay, feeding, and medical care of AFP personnel; economic reforms, including an end to the bias toward Manila and central and southern Luzon in the allocation of development programs; and political policies designed to reduce the CPP's appeal and create an anti-CPP front between the government and noncommunist opposition groups.

RECENT TRENDS IN THE INSURGENCY

Military Capabilities

NPA military capabilities since the spring of 1985 show a more mixed pattern than in the previous period. Regular forces have continued to grow, but the variance between United States and Philippine estimates has widened. American officials gave an estimate of 20,000 in NPA regular forces early in 1986, but the Philippine government estimated 13,000 about the same time.[2]

The growth in numbers of NPA regulars may not mean a corresponding increase in military effectiveness to the same degree as in the 1980–1984 period. The pattern of NPA attacks since the spring of 1985 shows a reduction in the number of big-unit assaults (two hundred to five hundred men). Platoon- and company-sized operations composed of thirty to one hundred men have been the recent norm. The NPA has concentrated on ambushes; attacks on police stations, small military outposts, and the CHDF; and assassinations.

A mounting inadequacy of resources appears to be the key obstacle to the NPA's ability to form permanent battalion-sized units or to use units of this size more frequently. CPP and NPA leaders admit difficulties in securing sufficient weapons and ammunition.[3] The NPA, too, lacks heavier weapons that would give it greater potential for assaults on bigger AFP units and posts. Current weapons consist mainly of rifles and smaller quantities of grenade launchers and machine guns. The lack of mortars presents a crucial limitation. Thus, the insurgency remains in a stage in which NPA main-force activity drops significantly in areas where the AFP can concentrate forces.

The NPA appears to suffer from shortages of food and medicine. Statements from CPP/NPA officials and CPP literature acknowledge that the "mass bases"—that is, the populace—are impoverished and

[2]*Business Day* (Manila), December 26, 1985.
[3]*Washington Post*, November 11, 1985; *Business Day*, March 19, 1986; *The New Philippine Daily Express,* March 27, 1986.

cannot supply all the needs of the insurgency.[4]

The Communist party receives no material assistance from outside the Philippines except for money from leftist groups in Western Europe and the United States. The CPP apparently does have contacts with the Soviet government, but it reportedly has turned down a Soviet offer of arms aid.[5] The leadership of the CPP reportedly is debating the question of outside support; but so far those who advocate total reliance on indigenous resources have prevailed.[6] Nevertheless, the internal debate suggests that CPP policy could shift in the future if the resources problem worsens.

The NPA, nevertheless, can launch effective smaller-unit operations. The recent pattern shows increases in small-unit attacks, ambushes, and assassinations. Moreover, these activities have spread or accelerated in central Luzon, Negros Occidental, the western part of Region X in Mindanao, Bohol, and Bicol. NPA strength in the last three years has risen from one hundred to eight hundred in central Luzon and from practically zero to over six hundred in Negros Occidental province, according to Philippine intelligence estimates.

A possible conclusion from the recent pattern is that the rate of growth of NPA armed regulars may start to slow. The formation of permanent battalions, moreover, may not be possible without a significantly larger inflow of weapons and supplies. The reverse side is that the NPA still could expand its smaller-unit operations quantitatively and geographically. This in turn would increase the strain on AFP resources, as evidenced by the AFP's moves in late 1985 to add new combat battalions.[7] The key is that the NPA can ration resources more successfully in small-unit assaults and assassinations. Of even greater importance, the growing political base of the CPP can support it—if growth continues.

The CPP'S Political Surge

The CPP's greatest success in the last two years has been in the expansion of its political influence, and this continued and probably

---

[4]*Ang Bayan,* October 1985. *Ang Bayan* is a CPP publication. See also *Washington Post,* November 11, 1985, and August 3, 1985.

[5]*Christian Science Monitor,* November 26, 1985.

[6]Ibid. *Bulletin Today* (Manila), December 25, 1985, and September 10, 1985.

[7]*Business Day,* November 6, 1985. Statement by General Fidel Ramos.

accelerated in the latter half of 1985. The CPP has established political organizations in over twenty percent of the country's 41,000 barangays, and it exercises varying degrees of political influence over twenty- five percent of the population.[8] As a result, governments at the barangay and town levels have started to disintegrate in regions such as northern and eastern Mindanao, Samar, Bicol, and Negros Occidental.

As of the end of 1985, communist influence and infiltration of key groups in the society and institutions appeared to be more extensive than many had believed. This reflected the success of the CPP's strategy of exploiting the hostility toward Marcos in the cities, the worsening economic conditions, and reactions to military abuses.

The emergence of Bayan in early 1985 probably stemmed from a decision by the CPP leadership to accelerate the united front strategy. The CPP probably had at least two purposes in mind with respect to Bayan. First, Bayan was to act as an umbrella group in order to draw more noncommunist elements into the CPP's united front network. Bayan, in fact, brought in many noncommunists. By the end of 1985, Bayan was estimated to influence politically three million to five million people. Most surely are not communists. Nevertheless, the national leadership and many local chapters are dominated by CPP/NDF cadres. This situation led to the publicized walkout by Butz Aquino, Joker Arroyo, Jose Diokno, and others in May 1985.

Second, the CPP intended Bayan to further the movement of the anti-regime united front toward greater militancy and eventually violence. The CPP sees in this the final merger of the "legal struggle" and the "armed struggle" into one violent, convulsive revolutionary movement, probably first in the provinces and then in Manila. One of Bayan's major activities in the provinces in 1985 was the general strike. Bayan mobilized thousands of people in a number of provincial capitals and literally shut these towns down for days on end with general strikes.[9]

---

[8]General Headquarters, AFP, Letter, Subject: AFP Action, January 26, 1985; *Congressional Record,* May 15, 1985. Statement by Senator John Kerry describing an intelligence briefing at Subic Bay Naval Base.

[9]For descriptions of the Bayan-led general strikes in the provincial capitals of Bacolod and Iloilo, see *Times Journal* (Manila), December 9, 1985; and *Agence France Presse* (Hong Kong), December 9, 1985; October 23, 1985. For general strikes in Davao and Cebu, see *Agence France Presse,* September 21, 1985.

The CPP also has gained adherents and influence in midlevel social-action organizations of the Catholic church. Organizations such as the Task Force on Detainees and Basic Christian Communities appear to be heavily infiltrated.[10] Even Catholic Relief Services has not escaped. Knowledgeable Filipino sources report that leftist elements have used the church's food distribution centers in Negros Occidental province for pro-CPP propaganda and political agitation.

The situation with regard to the parish priests is less clear. Knowledgeable church leaders such as Father Joachim Bernas estimate that only a handful of priests nationwide actually have joined the insurgency.[11] Conversely, a substantial minority of priests in certain regions sympathize and/or cooperate with the insurgents.[12] The trend has appeared to be one of increased cooperation by grassroots clergymen with the NPA.

The CPP has penetrated local labor organizations, including groups in Manila's industrial belt. The CPP no doubt has been aided by the leftist May First labor union, which has ties with the party. Communist influence probably contributed to the growing number of strikes and incidents of labor violence in 1984 and 1985, although this is not the only factor.

The CPP has continued to recruit in the universities in Manila and the provinces. The League of Filipino Students and other leftist campus groups have provided the party with a sophisticated front network on the campuses. As observers in the United States praised the commitment of thousands of young people to NAMFREL during the February 7 election, Philippine press reports cited a large outflow of youth from Manila and other cities into the countryside apparently to join the insurgents.[13]

The Repression Issue

Throughout the 1970s and well into the present period, outsider perceptions of the NPA—Filipino and foreign—often emphasized the

[10]Guy Sacerdoti and Phillip Bowring, "Marx, Mao and Marcos," *Far Eastern Economic Review*, November 21, 1985, p. 55.

[11]*Washington Post*, April 6, 1985.

[12]In Negros, for example, clergymen in significant numbers have cooperated with the NPA or have been involved in Bayan. See *Agence France Presse* (Hong Kong), October 15, 1985; and *Le Monde*, March 19, 1986.

[13]*Bulletin Today*, December 26, 1985.

insurgency's action to redress people's grievances against the ruling government and other oppressive forces in the society. The codeword "NPA justice" became established. This usually consisted of direct action by the NPA, including assassinations and executions of corrupt or abusive people who were hated by the local populace. The target could be a criminal, an abusive or corrupt official, or a rich landowner. NPA action against a rustler who steals a farmer's carabao is a commonly told example. Additionally, the NPA has gained popular support by warning plantation owners on Negros not to interfere with sugar workers who use land previously planted with sugar cane to grow needed foodstuffs.

In 1985, however, greater attention was paid to the terroristic and repressive nature of CPP/NPA policies and practices. Part of this grew from the perception of a broadening pattern of executions and assassinations of local officials. The CPP/NPA also reportedly began to tax common people such as farmers and small shopkeepers. Moreover, it seemingly extended the definition of "enemies of the people," subject to assassination or execution, to include those who are suspected of cooperating with or being sympathetic to the government, who resist social controls, or who express opposition to the new organization.

An inkling of this trend in CPP policy came from an internal document on CPP activities prepared by the security office of a business firm in Davao for the managers of the firm. This analysis, made available to the author, gave the following categorical breakdown for people killed by the NPA in Davao from January through March 1985:

Category	Number killed by the NPA
Individuals regarded as pro-government or indifferent, if not hostile, to the insurgents (mainly women and old people)	12
Government officials	30
Suspected government informants	90

Bishop Frederico Escaler of Mindanao, a frequent critic of the Marcos government, gave a similar portrayal of this trend in a speech of July 2, 1985. He stated that the NPA on Mindanao was forcing common people to pay "taxes" and was executing suspected government informers and local officials "just because they happen to be on the government side."[14]

A CPP document captured in February 1986 in northern Samar listed sixty two "counter-revolutionaries"—all civilians—who were summarily executed in 1985. A separate table listed seventy-nine civilians who were assassinated during the year. CPP records for Leyte showed the names of sixty civilians, mainly suspected informers, who had been executed in the first half of 1985. Another 129 were listed as having been assassinated.[15]

Several other developments point to a growing pattern of murder and coercion in CPP policy. In late March 1985, an NPA unit attacked a religious group, described as anticommunist, in the town of El Salvador in northern Mindanao. The NPA killed twenty and wounded fifty. Nearly all of those killed and wounded were civilians, and a large percentage were children, women, and old people.[16] In Negros Occidental province, social workers from private agencies involved in organizing self-help projects for sugar workers claimed that the NPA had begun to harass them in the southern part of the province.[17] Bishop Antonio Fortich, an outspoken critic of the Marcos regime, subsequently cited what he described as a growing trend of rural people in Negros Occidental telling him that they were terrified of the NPA because of increased NPA killings of civilians and heavier taxation of the rural populace.[18] On Luzon, in the province of Pampanga, the CPP/NPA reportedly assassinated some fifty people from the beginning of 1985 to March 1986.[19]

In December 1984 and early 1985, six officials of the moderate Trade Union Congress of the Philippines (TUCP) were murdered. Several of these officials were involved in union organizing in locales where the CPP was attempting to infiltrate workers. TUCP officials and officials of the AFL-CIO's Asian-American Free Labor Institute, which

---

[14]*Agence France Presse* (Hong Kong), July 2, 1985.
[15]*Asian Wall Street Journal Weekly,* May 5, 1986.
[16]*Agence France Presse* (Hong Kong), March 28, 1985; *Manila Times Journal*, March 29, 1985.
[17]*Business Day,* June 12, 1985.
[18]*New York Times,* February 28, 1986.
[19]*Washington Post,* March 17, 1986.

supports TUCP projects, believe that the CPP was responsible for most and probably all of the killings.

With the changeover to the Aquino government, reports from several regions described large-scale torture and executions of suspected informers. Some observers interpreted this as a sign that the movement was going through a purge of people who were beginning to question CPP policy in the wake of the new Aquino government.

Observers in the Philippines and the United States have given two broad explanations for CPP/NPA repression. One emphasizes CPP/NPA repression as a phenomenon of the unique social conditions of the island of Mindanao, which, they assert, have produced an insurgent movement that is much more prone to repression and terror than are the organizations on the other islands. A second explanation states that repression is integral to a communist-controlled movement like the CPP/NPA and that it is a forerunner to conditions that would exist if the CPP should take over the country.

The second explanation is more plausible than the first. The pattern of executions and assassinations is not confined to Mindanao. It may be more pronounced there, but it has come to light on the other islands and appears to be growing.

The real pattern seems to be that repression expands as the CPP organizations grow in influence in individual areas. As a CPP organization becomes more powerful and/or dominant in a given locale, the forms of individual conduct acceptable to it shrink; thus, the targets of assassinations and summary executions broaden in scope to include not only "bad people" but also people who criticize or try to remain independent of the organizations, people within the organization suspected of having deviant ideas, and people whose social conduct differs from the CPP standard. On the issue of social conduct, a CPP political cadre in Quezon province on Luzon testified that the organization warns people who engage in drunkenness, gambling, and extramarital sex to cease such conduct; if the warnings are unheeded, execution follows. As the cadre put it, "By the third warning, it's a simple question: Which do you prefer—above or below ground?"[20]

In short, if repression is more severe on Mindanao, it is more likely because CPP organizations there are stronger and/or more dominant

[20]*Agence France Presse* (Hong Kong), March 24, 1986.

than on the other islands. The same pattern, however, has appeared in Negros, Samar, Leyte, and Cagayan province in Luzon, where the organizations have expanded significantly in recent years.

THE COMMUNIST PARTY AND THE AQUINO GOVERNMENT

Despite CPP political successes going into 1986, the communist leadership miscalculated badly in its assessment of and reaction to the emergence of Corazon Aquino as a political leader. It also failed to foresee the coalescing of those forces that overthrew Ferdinand Marcos in February 1986 and paved the way for Aquino to assume the reins of government. CPP leaders appear to be aware of their errors and recognize the threat that the Aquino government poses to the CPP's hard-won gains. Since the end of February, the CPP has tried to develop a strategy for what it admits is a "new situation." Differing views within the leadership have been reported, but the outlines of a future approach appeared by mid-April.

Communist strategy in the immediate future undoubtedly will constitute a reaction to the problems the Aquino government creates for the CPP. The first and most pressing problem is the threat to the CPP's united front strategy, especially in the cities. The Aquino government is attractive to many well-educated urban Filipinos who, under Marcos, had become involved in CPP/NDF-sponsored activities through front organizations or groups that the CPP had infiltrated. The primary motive of many of these people, however was anti-Marcos sentiment. Leftist ideology, though felt to various degrees, often was secondary. These people, therefore, have felt a strong bond with the Aquino movement. Such a bond could become permanent if the Aquino government is able to establish political credibility with Filipinos beyond the immediate post-Marcos period. If so, the CPP may find in jeopardy its strategy of enlarging its front network and pushing united front activities in the cities in a more militant and violent direction.

The possibility of disaffection of united front elements became apparent over the issue of whether or not to support Aquino in the election. The CPP Central Committee reportedly decided on December 23, 1985, to boycott the election.[21] Later CPP statements made clear

---

[21]*Agence France Presse* (Hong Kong), January 6, 1986.

that the leadership assumed that Marcos would crush Aquino in a fraudulent election. The CPP's decision to boycott thus would be validated, and the base would be laid for more militant united front actions and continued expansion of the insurgency. The CPP voiced disdain for Mrs. Aquino and her supporters, describing them as "local reactionaries" and accusing her of "vacillation and equivocation" on the issue of United States-operated military bases.[22]

In order to justify the boycott to noncommunists in Bayan and other front organizations, the leadership of Bayan put forth conditions for supporting Aquino, including demands that she promise to abrogate American military base rights and reject ties with the International Monetary Fund and the World Bank. The CPP undoubtedly expected that Aquino would not accept such terms, and this proved to be the case.

Substantial dissent against the boycott arose, however, in Bayan and reportedly even within the NDF itself.[23] Bayan officials reported "stormy" debates over the issue. Some NDF members argued against the pro-boycott stance of party leaders Rodolfo Salas and Rafael Baylosis. Local Bayan chapters in some places subsequently broke with the national organization and campaigned for Aquino.[24]

The Communist party moved quickly to recover when Aquino made a strong showing in the election in the face of widespread fraud. Front spokesmen offered the Aquino camp support in what CPP leaders no doubt believed would be a protracted period of escalating struggle against the regime. The February 22 revolution intervened with such suddenness that the communists were unable to take part in it or gain advantage from it.

A CPP analysis of the postrevolution situation, written in mid-March and published in *Veritas* (April 3), spoke of new difficulties in building the united front in the cities where "counter-revolutionary sentiment is strongly felt" among the "middle forces." The cracks of disunity within Bayan widened, and the organization praised Corazon Aquino and announced at the end of February a moratorium on street demonstra-

[22]Ibid., and January 15, 1986.
[23]*Washington Post*, December 22, 1985; *Agence France Presse* (Hong Kong), January 9, 1986; *Times Journal*, January 14, 1986.
[24]Margaret Scott, "The Mood in Mindanao," *Far Eastern Economic Review*, January 30, 1986, p. 12.

tions and other forms of protest. Bayan reached this decision despite an NDF pronouncement of February 27 urging "the people to continue mass actions and surge on to establish a genuine people's democratic government." One Bayan official criticized CPP hard-liners for their unshakable adherence to "armed struggle," and he stated that the political left should participate peacefully in a "liberal democratic transition."[25]

Bayan and other front groups remain in some degree of disarray. They were unable, for example, to turn out sizeable crowds to protest the visits to Manila of American cabinet officials George Shultz and Caspar Weinberger. Bayan has ceased general strikes but so far lacks any clear alternative strategy.

Some members of Bayan and other front groups, such as the Nationalist Alliance for Justice, Peace, and Freedom, are advocating that the "nationalist left" form a political party to operate in a multiparty system. Jose Sison, the founder of the CPP recently released from prison, is pushing the idea of a legal party on the left.[26] Such a development could influence many of those who are presently associated with the front groups to move away from militant action and toward participation according to the rules of a constitutional, democratic system. Unless it were controlled by the CPP, a political party on the left could find itself torn between pressure from the CPP for greater militancy and the need to moderate its views and conduct in order to broaden its electoral appeal.

The second problem faced by the CPP is the threat of erosion among the rank-and-file insurgents and even among local party and NPA leaders. Spokesmen for President Aquino have set forth a goal of weaning the "soft-core" and "socially discontented" segment of the insurgents away from the CPP. Indeed, the "soft core" exists, as factors other than Marxist-Leninist ideology are responsible for the insurgency's appeal to people in the rural towns and barangays.

Officials of the new government, however, are likely to be wrong in their predictions that the insurgency will collapse in a few months. This

---

[25]*Business Day,* February 27, 1986.

[26]It is uncertain whether Sison's views reflect those of the current CPP leaders, but it appears that he is laying out his own agenda. Sison is an attractive figure to the political left and always has been personally ambitious. His actions could have an important influence on the future political course of elements with the front organizations.

view does not appear to take adequately into account the sophisticated organizational structure which the communists have built, the discipline among the political cadre and the armed units, the social and economic conditions in the countryside that fuel the insurgency, the complex motives for people in the barangays to join and remain in the organization, and the ideological commitment of the CPP leadership and political cadre.[27]

Consequently, the government is not likely to succeed in its offer to negotiate a political settlement with the CPP unless it is prepared to make far-reaching concessions which could endanger its political position. The negotiation of Aquino's proposed cease-fire with the CPP could weaken the possibility of a successful strategy to attract the rank-and-file insurgents if a cease-fire allowed the CPP to consolidate its political and military positions in those regions it presently dominates or where it is strong.

Nevertheless, some elements of the new government's thinking could form the basis of an effective attractions program. These include the idea of an amnesty for insurgents who surrender and lay down their arms (President Aquino's postrevolution statements have given greater emphasis to the necessity of insurgents' laying down their arms). President Aquino's proposal for job training and resettlement of those who accept amnesty also could be effective if put into practice. Magsaysay installed similar programs during the Huk insurgency. The government and the AFP too have offered amnesty to the NPA in specific locales, with local civil and religious leaders and former guerrillas acting as intermediaries. The use of local intermediaries could be a productive tactic, given the greater familiarity, and presumably trust, that local guerrillas and members of CPP "mass organizations" in the barangays would have with such people. Finally, the AFP has begun to use leaflets to disseminate the amnesty offer to the insurgents.

The government and AFP have had little success so far in inducing guerrillas to surrender, but a comprehensive attractions program implemented over a longer period and combined with other counterinsurgency measures and general reforms could begin to produce results— possibly mass surrenders of entire units or, more likely, actions by

[27]Senate Foreign Relations Committee, *Insurgency and Counterinsurgency in the Philippines*, pp. 14-27.

individuals and small groups to give up the "armed struggle." Social reforms, including land reform in some areas and measures to generate greater rural income and social services to rural people would help address grievances held by rank-and-file NPA members. Military reform is also essential in this regard. Successful programs of this nature eventually would create a sense among the insurgents that their cause is lost. When they begin to think in those terms, many will look for other options, including surrender. Successful counterinsurgency campaigns against communist-led guerrillas in other countries have included these kinds of measures.[28]

The CPP appears to be worried about the future. The CPP's March analysis, cited earlier, suggested that divisions exist within the party over "the necessity of armed struggle." It stressed the need for "propaganda and political work" in the NPA and warned against the "falsehoods and intrigues of the enemy." CPP leaders have stated that only the CPP's Central Committee can conduct negotiations with the government, thus possibly revealing a fear that local party officials and NPA local commanders might begin to talk with the government and AFP.

Reports persist of pre-election and postelection disagreements within the CPP leadership over how to deal with Corazon Aquino. Reports have surfaced that insurgent leader Conrado Balweg has contacted the government about the possibility of negotiations. Moreover, the leadership of the Kabataang Makabayan (Nationalist Youth), a member organization of the NDF, has proposed a separate dialogue with the government. Leaders of the Kabataang Makabayan earlier had stated that they disagreed with other CPP/NDF leaders over the way to deal with Corazon Aquino.[29]

The CPP leadership, however, is not a soft core. It is ideologically committed, and disagreements are largely over tactics. For example, Sison (who reportedly maintains communications with current CPP leaders), may favor more emphasis on the "legal struggle," but the totality of his statements portray a man who remains a doctrinaire communist. There eventually may be defections of CPP leaders, or

[28]Larry A. Niksch, *Case Studies of Counterinsurgencies* (Washington, D.C.: Congressional Research Service, 1985).
[29]*Philippine Daily Inquirer*, March 4, 1986.

some may decide to abandon the armed revolution. However, government spokesmen probably are correct in saying that the "hard-core" leadership probably won't give up the struggle.[30]

A third problem for the communists lies in President Aquino's stated commitment to reform and revitalize the armed forces and her threat to make it an effective instrument against the CPP if the communists refuse to end the insurgency. She has given General Fidel Ramos the primary responsibility for this. Ramos has made numerous personnel shifts and has disbanded key military organizations that were bastions of support for General Fabian Ver. The task ahead is still formidable. More personnel changes undoubtedly will be required down into the middle ranks of the command structure. The government will have to address the severe resources deficiencies of the AFP and upgrade training considerably. The AFP will have to create a mechanism to deal effectively and sternly with incidents of military abuse of civilians. The police in the rural towns are badly in need of training and new equipment.

Any improvement in AFP performance is bound to hurt the insurgency. It would not only hurt the insurgents in individual tactical situations, but it would also strengthen the AFP as an institution. Given the lack of material support from foreign governments, the insurgents cannot hope for a victory unless the military disintegrates from within. The CPP reportedly expects that the United States will provide greater amounts of military assistance to the Aquino government and that this will fund a military reform program similar to that in El Salvador.[31]

THE COMMUNIST RESPONSE

The Communist party has not yet finished the formulation of a response to the new situation as of this writing. CPP spokesmen, however, have enunciated certain views toward the Aquino govern-

---

[30]Balweg, a former priest, heads a component of the insurgency that is based on ethnic considerations. The NPA under Balweg is located in the Cordillera mountain range of northern Luzon. It is composed primarily of Igorot tribesmen who have resisted encroachments of the central government and lowland business firms. Thus, given the unique character of the situation, Balweg's surrender or defection from the CPP probably would not have a broad impact on other elements of the insurgency.

[31]*Agence France Presse* (Hong Kong), April 3, 1986, and March 18, 1986.

ment, which likely will form a large part of the response.[32] The CPP appears to see as its immediate tasks the minimizing of losses, consolidating its present position, and laying the groundwork for a future surge. Its tactics in the short term likely will be intended to buy time until—as the CPP assumes—the Aquino government loses popularity. The CPP then can resume the full confrontational strategy that it conducted during the Marcos era.

Three objectives seem to be forming: (1) maintain access to urban politics through the front organizations as the basis for future building of the united front; (2) isolate the Aquino government from public opinion and influence the development of splits among its members: military versus civilians, "progressives" versus "reactionaries," capitalists versus representatives of the "masses," and so on; (3) make permanent the party's position in the rural areas and maintain strategic and tactical flexibility in pursuing the insurgency.

Future CPP strategy likely will seek these goals and include the following elements:

1. Do not attack Corazon Aquino personally: CPP pronouncements indicate an awareness of her enormous popularity. Party spokesmen now praise her, and they try to identify the CPP with her "democratic ambitions." The CPP apparently sees little political gain at this time from branding her a reactionary.

2. Develop the "nationalist issues" (American military bases, the IMF and World Bank, multinational corporations, land reform, workers' rights, and so on), using the front groups, in order to stimulate or restimulate "nationalist left" attitudes among urban elite groups and industrial workers and put the Aquino government on the political defensive. The CPP undoubtedly will escalate criticism on these issues if, as expected, the government cooperates with the United States and the international financial institutions. A ranking CPP/NPA official, in an interview March 21, stated that the Aquino government had two choices: "service to U.S. imperialism" or a nationalist stand. Only the second, he

---

[32]Besides the CPP's March analysis, informative pronouncements can be found in *Veritas,* March 30, 1986; *Kyodo News Service* (Japan), April 1, 1986; *Agence France Presse* (Hong Kong), March 28, 1986; *Business Day,* March 25, 1986, and March 19, 1986; *Le Monde,* March 19, 1986; and *New York Times,* March 15, 1986.

said, would put the Filipino people behind the government.[33]

3. Attack politically the "reactionary" elements in the government and seek to influence the "progressive" elements to adopt "nationalist" and other positions in line with those of the CPP. The CPP's March analysis identified certain factions within the government: the military under Enrile and Ramos; the "big capitalists" (businessmen and economists) who currently direct economic policy; UNIDO (a "conservative if not outright reactionary" element); the Catholic church leadership; and the "progressive liberals" of the LABAN coalition. The analysis predicted "that the struggle between the reactionaries and the liberals in the government will grow more intense."

Communist political attacks so far have concentrated on the military, which the CPP accuses of conspiring against Aquino and which is dedicated to continued counterinsurgency.[34] One should expect the CPP to broaden its targets in the future when the Aquino government develops clear policy choices on issues.

4. Cease direct action against the government in the cities, such as the Bayan-led general strikes and antigovernment demonstrations, but try to influence confrontational actions by sectoral groups, especially strikes by industrial workers against nongovernment targets. Observers predict turbulence in the labor sector as workers seek higher wages. This would give the CPP a means of fomenting confrontation in a more indirect role and not against the Aquino government. The effects of industrial unrest, however, would hurt the government's plans for economic recovery.

5. Enter into negotiations with the government: As of this writing, the CPP leadership has not made a final decision on whether to accept the government's offer of negotiations, but recent statements suggest that it may do so. A decision to negotiate would serve several tactical ends. It would give the CPP greater political legitimacy and prestige. It would display a political flexibility to the recent critics in the front organizations. It would preclude

[33]*Ang Pahayagang Malaya* (Manila), March 31, 1986.
[34]*Ang Bayan,* an official CPP publication, for example, has denounced Enrile and Ramos for forming a military clique in the government. It asserted that despite the military's role in overthrowing Marcos, it remained "reactionary if not fascist."

local NPA commanders or the party cadre from negotiating separately.

The CPP likely would use negotiations to play up the alleged divisions between Aquino and her military advisers. The CPP also could be expected to publicize the "nationalist" issues in a negotiating forum. CPP/NPA pronouncements on a cease-fire have emphasized conditions that first must be negotiated, including the role of "U.S. imperialism," the institution of "democratic reforms," and "fundamental economic and political changes." The CPP might press for a maximum tactical goal: inclusion in a coalition government.

CPP leaders have stated that they will not accept an amnesty offer and surrender their arms. Some CPP pronouncements indicate an interest in a cease-fire if it created zones of control by the opposing sides. CPP officials have stated, for example, that the first step in a cease-fire should be the withdrawal of the AFP from contested areas back to their barracks.[35]

A cease-fire based on zones of exclusive control would pose great dangers for the Aquino government. It would allow the CPP to consolidate control over locales where it has a significant organizational presence or even dominance but where control is still being contested. It would help the CPP prevent any serious erosion of rank-and-file members of the NPA and the rural "mass organizations," at least in the areas of control.

The CPP undoubtedly would try to utilize such a cease-fire to continue its political organization-building in the government's zones. It still would likely employ intimidation of local officials and possibly assassinations and other low-level violence as part of organization building—on the assumption that the government would not react to such low-level activity.[36]

Finally, this kind of cease-fire likely would lead to a de facto

[35]*Veritas,* March 30, 1986; *Agence France Presse* (Hong Kong), March 18, 1986; *Business Day,* March 19, 1986; *Le Monde,* March 19, 1986.
[36]The CPP's March analysis, for example, argued against an "unconditional cease-fire" and for a "continued and defensive armed struggle against fascism." Such a defensive armed struggle would stress "military operations that have political effects" and would cease bigger-unit operations and attacks aimed at seizing arms. Antonio Zumel,

situation of two administrations in the Philippines: the Aquino government and a "revolutionary" government/administration in the communist zones. The CPP would gain new political status through establishment of a counteradministration. Its bargaining position would be strengthened in any negotiations with the Manila government. A de facto government holding permanent geographical zones could also facilitate any arrangements for the movement of arms and weapons to the NPA from foreign governments.

6. The issue of a political party: A critical decision for the CPP leadership may be whether or not to lead or associate the party with the formation of a legal political party on the left, possibly through Bayan or the creation of a new organization. The present CPP leaders (Salas, Baylosis, Rivera, and others) may not favor the idea, fearing that a legal political party would dilute support for violent revolution and result in a rival leadership under Sison and others. On the other hand, the dissent within the CPP itself over future strategy could influence the leadership toward a "two-track strategy" (a legal party and continued insurgency) in order to restore unity.

The purpose of a political party on the left would be to develop the "nationalist" issues and woo Filipino "progressives"; in short, the united front strategy at a higher level. The extent of its influence, however, probably would depend on whether it adopted a straight Marxist line or whether it turned toward a democratic socialist program within the existing political system. Given a free choice, most Filipinos currently would reject an orthodox Marxist party. The issue, therefore, is a difficult one for the CPP, for it holds the possibility of deeper splits in the party and political left.

reputed head of the National Democratic Front, stated in late March that even in a cease-fire, the NPA would launch assaults on "fascist leaders, elements and units who owe blood debts to the people and who continue to assault the countryside." The NPA command in northern Mindanao also issued a statement that in a cease-fire, the NPA would continue "its struggle against class enemies—those who have owed the people blood debts and continue to cause undue misery on the people."

CONCLUSION

A CPP strategy along the above lines would be essentially defensive, and the CPP would view it as lasting only until the "balance of forces" began to turn against the Aquino government. This would depend, however, on the Aquino government's squandering its present advantages over the CPP. The government may do just the opposite. It may build a lasting political credibility with Filipinos by instituting a constitutional, democratic political order, demonstrating a commitment to solving the country's economic and social problems, and building a professionally competent AFP. If it accomplishes these tasks, the communists would find themselves permanently on the defensive with declining prospects.

23

Muslim Grievances and the Muslim Rebellion

Lela Garner Noble

Whether there is now a widespread, organized Muslim insurgency in the Philippines is debatable. Both Philippine military and Muslim spokesmen have claimed that there is or threatened that there will be. Others point to the fact that even those Muslims organized in armed bands do not agree on leadership, goals, or tactics, and suggest that it is more accurate to talk of anarchy than of insurgency. It is clear, however, that a Muslim insurgency did occur in the Philippines between 1972 and 1976 on a scale far greater than anything yet achieved by the New People's Army, as measured by any indicator except geographical scope. Reasons for the Muslims' resort to armed rebellion can be identified, and the Marcos regime's handling of the insurgency, while superficially successful, left its own legacy of policies and problems.

The purpose of this paper, then, is to review the reasons for the rebellion and the legacy left by the Marcos regime in order to define an agenda for the Philippine government in the post-Marcos era, and to discuss the implications of that agenda for United States policy. First, however, it is necessary to establish the limits of our information.

There simply are no reliable numerical data on Muslims in the Philippines. Most sources assume that Muslims constitute five percent of the Philippine population, which is approximately 55.6 million. This assumption produces an estimate of 2.8 million Muslims. Yet many—certainly many Muslims—believe that figure is too low and assert five to six million is a more accurate range. Numbers and distribution of Muslim subgroups are also problematic. Thirteen different Muslim groups have been identified, distinguished by language, territorial identifications, economic activities, social and political structures, art forms, and hierarchies of value. There are four main groups: the Maguindanaoan of the Cotabato region, who number about 674,000; the Maranao-Ilanun of the Lanao region, about 670,000; and the Tausug and Samal of the Sulu archipelago, together about 694,000.[1] However, because of Christian migration, Muslims do not necessarily constitute a majority in the areas with which they are identified. Professor Cesar Majul identifies only three provinces where the population is over ninety percent Muslim—Lanao del Sur, Sulu, and Tawi Tawi; two where the population is about seventy percent Muslim—Basilan and North Cotabato; and three where it is between twenty and fifty percent—Lanao del Norte, Maguindanao, and Sultan Kudarat.[2]

As for the insurgency itself, numbers of armed participants generally ranged from 15,000 to 30,000 during the height of the rebellion. Yet David Steinberg cites a number of 50,000 to 60,000 as being the estimate of Rear Admiral Romulo Espaldon, presumably at a time when the military budget was being debated, or when government figures for Muslims "returning to the fold of the law" were totalled.[3] A Bangsa Moro Army commander in 1974 estimated that perhaps fifty-five percent of Muslim Filipinos supported the insurgents, fifteen percent supported the government, and the rest were neutral.[4] Casualties are estimated as being from 50,000 up to hundreds of thousands; refugees may be half a million, with at least 200,000 in Sabah. Approximately two-thirds to three-fourths of Philippine military forces were stationed in the area between 1973 and 1977, and they used the full range of their arsenals. Geographically, the fighting included the Lanao, Cotabato, Zamboanga, Sulu, Basilan, and Tawi Tawi provinces.

Other significant data—on land holdings, income, literacy, and nutrition, for example—are either nonexistent or so obviously unreliable as to be useless. Numbers do, however, reflect perceptions on which Muslims and the government have acted, or have wished to appear to be acting.

---

[1]These figures are derived from Peter G. Gowing, *Muslim Filipinos—Heritage and Horizon* (Quezon City: New Day Publishers, 1979), p. 2.

[2]Cesar Adib Majul, *The Contemporary Muslim Movement in the Philippines* (Berkeley: Mizan Press, 1985), p. 74.

[3]David Joel Steinberg, *The Philippines: A Singular and Plural Place* (Boulder: Westview Press, 1982), p. 107.

[4]Frank Gould, Interview with Commander Ulangutan, April 1974.

Some specific data about perceptions have been collected. Among the most meaningful in this context are those collected by a research intern at the Gowing Memorial Research Center in Marawi City, who asked five hundred Muslim students about their "self-images and intergroup attitudes." Of his sample, 54.6 percent listed their "primary citizenship" as Muslim; 28.6 percent, Bangsa Moro (Moro people— the designation promoted by the Moro National Liberation Front); 12 percent, ethnic name; 4.2 percent, Muslim Filipino; 3.8 percent, Fili-pino; and 2.6 percent, not stated. When asked to indicate if "Filipino" was an appropriate designation for Muslims, a strong majority (89.4 percent) disagreed that "Filipino" was accurate. The results, then, are startling in their manifestation of alienation from Philippine/Filipino identifications; they are equally startling in the revelation of differences among Muslim ethnic groups.[5]

MUSLIM GRIEVANCES

The foregoing is a summary of the kinds of limited information with which Philippine specialists are accustomed to cope. The lack of information, along with limitations of time and space, suggest why a summary of causes of Muslim discontent, and hence rebellion, is necessarily general.

Muslim grievances had been expressed in and derived from centuries of warfare against the Spaniards and their Filipino converts to Catholicism. Muslims in the southern Philippines intended to be neither conquered nor converted, and fought exhaustive battles to preserve freedom and Islam. They ultimately succumbed to American rule because the Americans had superior weaponry and tactics, but they continued to protest incorporation into a centralized, and in their perception Christian, Philippine government by whatever means they had at their disposal: running amok, organizing a rebellion, presenting petitions or legislative proposals, retreating into depression and/or isolation.

By the 1960s and early 1970s a combination of circumstances inside

---

[5]The thesis is the master's thesis of Abdulsiddik A. Abbahil, "The 'Bangsa Moro': Their Self-Image and Inter-Group Ethnic Attitudes," University of San Carlos (Cebu City), May 1983. For a full summary of his data see Lela Garner Noble, "The Philippines: Autonomy for the Muslims," forthcoming in John L. Esposito, ed., *Islam in Public Life in Asia*, Oxford University Press.

and outside the Philippines had led Muslims both to a clearer articulation of their grievances and to mobilization to redress them. Government programs designed to defuse agrarian unrest in the north and to increase economic productivity resulted in resettlement programs which challenged Muslims' economic and political dominance in the south. Muslims tended to perceive the challenge as also threatening religious identity and practice.

Events during the first and second Marcos administrations increased Muslim feelings of comparative disadvantage and vulnerability. Most pivotal were the Corregidor massacre of twenty-eight Muslim recruits who by Muslim accounts had been duped into participating in a planned invasion of the Malaysian state of Sabah, in Northern Borneo, and the escalating violence of the 1971 elections, which pitted Muslims against Christians in campaigns in areas where the population balance had been shifting. Because these developments coincided with a worldwide Islamic resurgence in which Philippine Muslims participated, they had access to newly created and wealthy Islamic organizations. Islamic states such as Malaysia and Libya had their own reasons for concern about Philippine government actions, and hence for supporting Muslim protests. The Islamic Conference sent teams to investigate charges of genocide.

But the declaration of martial law, and the ensuing policy of collecting guns from civilians, ultimately provoked the resort to full-scale rebellion. Filipinos elsewhere in the Philippines (and scholars outside the Philippines) saw the regime as authoritarian, and analyzed its participants and beneficiaries by sociological categories or classes; Muslims saw it as exclusively Christian. The collection of guns threatened whatever potential for self-assertion of beliefs and interests remained, and incited resort to armed resistance. Armed and provided refuge by Libya and Malaysia (or Sabah, which acted independently during the period when Tun Mustapha was chief minister), protected against massive onslaught by the Islamic Conference and its members' control of the Philippine oil supply, Muslims moved into rebellion under the leadership of the Moro National Liberation Front.

That the rebellion flared as intensely as it did and then subsided is reflective of the MNLF's strengths and weaknesses. Having initially succeeded in building a team of leaders representing all Musulim groups and bound by discontent with the rule of Christian and traditional Muslim politicians, and then in recruiting followers with more diffuse discontents who were bound by a protostructure and by weapons supplied from overseas Islamic contacts, the MNLF dominated Muslim areas and absorbed and justified an expanding Philippine military establishment during the early years of martial law. It lost its dominance because it succeeded in extracting at least nominal concessions, which satisfied many of its war-weary supporters at home and abroad, and because it lacked the ideology, organization, or support necessary to prolong a struggle for the more radical objectives its founders had envisioned.

THE MARCOS LEGACY

Of equal importance were the tactics used by the Marcos regime. Whatever one's stance on Ross Marlay's general description of Ferdinand Marcos as a political genius, one must at least conclude that with regard to Philippine Muslims he was uncannily clever. In the early years of martial law he pitted a growing military establishment against young Muslims "in the hills," involved their more moderate brothers and sisters in developing legal, economic, or political schemes, and proclaimed their fathers or uncles sultans and/or invited them to peace conferences. The turning point, however, was the Tripoli Agreement of 1976 and the measures taken to "implement" it.

Briefly, the agreement—reached among representatives from the MNLF, the Islamic Conference, and the Phililippine government, after direct conversations between Imelda Marcos and Colonel Muammar Kadafi—provided for an "autonomy for the Muslims" in thirteen provinces. The "autonomy" was to have Muslim courts, a legislative assembly and executive council, an administrative system, special regional security forces, and representation in the central government; control over education, finance, and the economic system; and a right to a "reasonable percentage" from the revenues of mines and minerals. The central government was to maintain responsibility for foreign policy and national defense affairs. The role of the MNLF forces in the Philippine armed forces and relationships between structures and policies of the "autonomy" and those of the central government were to be discussed during further talks. In the meantime, there was to be a cease-fire, supervised by a committee representing the Philippine government, the MNLF, and the Islamic Conference's committee of four (representatives of four states who had been appointed to investigate and oversee negotiations).[6]

The agreement was significant for two reasons. It was accompanied by a cease-fire which was responsible for an almost total cessation of fighting for several months. When fighting subsequently resumed, it was at a greatly reduced level, though one of the worst incidents of the war occurred on Pata Island, off Jolo, in early 1981.[7] Military aid from Sabah had ceased with Tun Mustapha's ouster in 1975; Libyan aid apparently was also greatly curtailed after the Tripoli meetings. Of equal importance was that the terms of the agreement were subsequently used by the Marcos regime and by various Muslim organizations, states, and factions to legitimize their goals and actions.

That participants at the Tripoli meetings had divergent interpretations of the agreement became apparent immediately, and negotiations to reach a consensus foundered. Marcos then proceeded to "implement" the agreement as he saw fit, modifying its provisions regarding territorial scope, structure, authority, and the role of Muslims and Islam by plebiscites and decrees. Hence, the thirteen provinces originally included in the "autonomy for the Muslims" were reduced to ten and divided into two regional governments with limited powers and considerable fiscal constraints. Some positions in the governments were to be filled by elections, others appointment—by Marcos.

The result, I argued in an article in 1981, was that "government" in the southern Philippines was provided by three parallel structures:

The first is an "official" government structure, dominated by civilians; divided into regional, provincial, and local levels; and integrated into national structures by elections, representation in parties and planning bodies, and implementation of programs. The second structure is the Philippines Armed Forces, divided into two commands containing in total about three-quarters of the country's military manpower. The third structure, rudimentary but dominant in certain areas and/or for certain functions, consists of a number of armed bands, some affiliated with the MNLF or with factional groups linked loosely with the MNLF and some

[6]The text of the agreement is found in *From Secession to Autonomy: Self-Government in Southern Philippines* (Manila: Republic of the Philippines, Ministry of Foreign Affairs, 1980), p. 157.
[7]Richard Vokey, *Far Eastern Economic Review*, May 8, 1981.

assuming whatever identity or allegiance best legitimizes their schemes for extortion.[8]

Five years later, as the Marcos era was drawing to a close, the situation had only become more complicated. Michael Mastura described participants in the government structure as themselves divided into three groups. The first was a Muslim leadership, recruited by Marcos, whose concern was "how best to maintain the political conduit to Malacanang without need to seek mandate from below." Mastura's description was not clear, but this group appeared to combine some new people with those chosen "from the ranks of old society politicians." The second was former MNLF commanders who Mastura believed represented concessions to social mobility and who he thought were perceived of "by the masses" as being of a different mold from that of the traditional leaders. The third group included Muslim intellectuals, the *ulama* (religious leaders), student activists, and second-generation Muslim professionals. These he described as predisposed toward radicalism, politically disaffected, but potentially a source of a better-informed leadership.[9]

Mastura's analysis was insightful and surprisingly honest, given his position as deputy minister of Muslim affairs; it was perhaps also excessively optimistic. Jumada Al-Oola, for contrast, described MNLF commanders who surrendered in 1974: "Some of the tough Moro 'returnees' returned to Sulu to begin new careers as government officials, assemblymen, mayors, and privileged businessmen, and generally reveled in the generosity of a relieved government."[10]

The problem, as I see it, was that both structures and programs were increasingly perceived by the Marcos regime as tools for cooptation: they were designed to buy support. While some participants had goals that transcended immediate personal interest, most did not, and those programs that were well conceptualized and administered toward the

[8]Lela G. Noble, "Muslim Separatism in the Philippines, 1972-1981: The Making of a Stalemate," *Asian Survey*, XXI:11 (November 1981), p. 1104.
[9]Michael O. Mastura, *Muslim Filipino Experience: A Collection of Essays* (Manila: Ministry of Muslim Affairs, 1984), pp. 132–133. Mastura's book also contains useful explanations of the rationale behind programs of the Ministry of Muslim Affairs and, in some cases, the frustrations involved in implementing them.
[10]"Jolo Kidnap Highlights Moro Fight," *Arabia*, February 1985.

achievement of general goals were rare. Politics was a contest for spoils; participants vied for positions in order to get funds or other government-provided benefits, such as subsidized housing. The result was not simply the tensions Mastura describes, or even factionalism, but something more like atomism, with splits within families and among former political allies producing particularly intense passions. In this context, the resumption of "opposition" politics seemed significant primarily because it allowed an outlet for those who were disgruntled because they had not been appointed to a regional council or included on the Kilusang Bagong Lipunan (KBL) slate for an election.[11]

This situation resembled, of course, that prevailing before martial law was declared. It was different, and worse, because even more of the underlying social structure had been shattered, and because governing structures themselves had become more fluid. The system had also become more expensive, both economically and psychologically. Particularly marked was the increase in greed, opportunism, and cynicism, as government funds flowed into the south.

As for the military, while both command structures and commanders changed and many soldiers were shifted from Muslim areas to other areas of Mindanao or to other islands where the NPA had been more active, the number of armed Civil Home Defense Units and other paramilitary bands increased markedly. Even more disorganized and undisciplined than the regular military units that preceded them, they became participants in a pattern of violence which seemed endemic. When linked with particular officials, they practiced thuggery with impunity.

Antigovernment Muslim armed bands seemed, however, to have declined. Many "rebels" surrendered, and the loyalties of those who remained in the field were difficult to identify. In Sulu those with either ideology or loyalty apparently remained linked with Nur Misuari, the original and more radical MNLF leader. In Maguindanaoan areas, there seemed to be some degree of identification with Hashim Salamat, though most of those loyal to him had surrendered. In Maranao

---

[11]During the parliamentary elections in 1984 there is evidence from the Muslim areas that suggests government support for some "opposition" candidates. This provides another reason to curb optimism about idealistic/ideological reasons for dissent.

territory the situation was even less clear. Dimas Pundato, Salamat, and Misuari appeared to have some support.

Equally difficult to gauge was the significance of those loyalties. After the Tripoli agreement, the MNLF overseas leadership disintegrated into endless factionalism. Misuari maintained the official recognition of the Islamic Conference and apparently still received limited support from the more militant Islamic states. However, MNLF newsletters, which at one time reported fully on events "in the field," became markedly more intermittent. The organization's most recent publications were a collection of Misuari's speeches made between 1980 and 1983 and a compilation of articles and letters by pro-Misuari Philippine Muslims appearing in the Saudi press.

When Salamat split with Misuari, it was ostensibly over leadership styles and ideology (Salamat was more "Islamic"; Misuari, "Marxist," it was said), but ethnic differences probably were also important: Misuari was Tausug/Samal, Salamat Maguindanaoan. In any event, Salamat's leadership was apparently nominal; virtually all that was known was that some people claimed to be his spokesmen, others his followers.

Two of the founders of the rival Bangsa Moro Liberation Organization, Raschid Lucman and Macapanton Abbas, Jr., had personal reasons to oppose Misuari (he had accused them both of corruption and had broken with them for ideological reasons before the MNLF emerged in 1972); both were Maranao. The third founder, Salipada Pendatun, was, like Lucman, a pre-martial law "traditional" politician, and was related to Lucman (and to Salamat). Pendatun, however, returned to the Philippines; then Lucman and Abbas split, each charging the other with corruption. Meanwhile, Dimas Pundato had left Misuari's group; after Lucman's death he and Abbas began to issue joint press releases, many filled with claims that were at best implausible.

It was, in short, difficult to identify either leaders or followers. Certainly the unity the MNLF leadership had originally achieved had vanished. While armed bands remained, they had neither organizational structure nor clear goals. Instead, the NPA emerged as the primary challenge to government authority in some areas of central and southern Mindanao where the MNLF had been active earlier.

The issues posed by the existence of parallel "governing" structures, all of which lacked internal coherence, authority, and a shared notion of the common good, were exemplified by reports from Marawi City regarding the "snap election." The primary actors, Ali Dimaporo—governor of Lanao del Sur, acting president of Mindanao State University, sole Muslim member of Marcos' Executive Council—and Omar Dianalan—former mayor of Marawi and currently an assemblyman—were married to daughters of former Governor Dimacuta. Both also were members of the KBL, until Dianalan left the KBL in December 1985 after an incident he described to *Veritas:*

> Dianalan left the KBL last month because "he 'could no longer stand being treated shabbily by Dimaporo and the ruling party.'" He contested the post of Batasan speaker protempore with Macacuna Dimaporo, brother of Ali, but President Marcos picked Macacuna.

> "Since then, all my men, including those whose appointments I had a hand in, have been fired. Not even those with qualifications and civil-service eligibilities were spread. What they merely lacked was Ali-gibilities and Ali-fications," Dianalan charged.[12]

Then Dianalan, his father-in-law, and his younger brother joined forces with the Lucmans and Alontos ("Politics makes strange bedfellows. This is our first time to work together with the Alontos," he said), and switched their support to Corazon Aquino ("after Cory said she'll give the Muslims meaningful autonomy under the Tripoli Agreement"). His action of course, exacerbated relations with Dimaporo, whom he accused of "forcing government employees to swear before the Koran that they'll vote for President Marcos and that each of them will deliver 10 more votes to the ruling party."[13]

The employees, he said, had no choice because they were afraid of Dimaporo's armed men and of being fired.

> "The Mindanao State University, of which Ali is the president, has a 450-man security guard, which Ali has converted into his own private army. Can you imagine, a campus which used to have only a handful of security guards, now guarded by 450?" Dianalan said.

---

[12]*Veritas,* January 29, 1986.
[13]Ibid.

He added that Ali also has 300 special action men, 200 provincial guards, 250 security guards in his different business interests, and 1,500 CHDFs distributed in 37 towns. "All these men are armed with high-powered guns," he said, in stressing why it is very urgent that the Comelec [Commission on Elections] place the province under its control.[14]

He also asked the Comelec to purge the voters' lists of ghost voters in Lanao del Sur (40,000) and Lanao del Norte (30,000).

At least one of Dianalan's fears was misplaced—the voters' lists *were* purged, but of eligible voters, and many people apparently behaved with courage and integrity despite the pressures on them. One Muslim, for example, persuaded his barrio captain to return the 1,000 pesos of KBL money given him and to let the people express their will freely; the result was a vote of 170 for Aquino, 30 for Marcos. Nevertheless, the returns for the province were hotly contested, and on February 24 Dimaporo's armed men ringed the campus of one of Marawi City's Islamic schools, causing a prayer rally to be cancelled. Dianalan himself was reported to be on a "hit list" of six drawn up by Marcos men (others were Antonio Cuenco, Aquilino Pimentel, Ramon Mitra, Juan Ponce Enrile, and Fidel Ramos).[15]

After Marcos left the country Dimaporo retreated to the MSU campus with hundreds of armed men, declaring, "I will fight and protect the 'MSU-ans' to the last drop of my blood. We are going to protect this republic. We are going to protect this university from any forces that will attack."[16] He and his men finally left the campus March 1, apparently having surrendered some guns; in mid-March he still claimed to be both governor and president of MSU, though others had been appointed to both posts.

AGENDA FOR THE POST-MARCOS ERA

If this account helps define the legacy of the Marcos era, it also helps define an agenda for the post-Marcos era. Dianalan took the initiative in convening the Islamic Conference of the Philippines, with partici-

[14]Ibid.
[15]*San Jose Mercury,* February 23, 1986.
[16]*Veritas,* March 12, 1986.

pants described as representing UNIDO, PDP-Laban (Pilipino Democratic Party), and academicians, to draft resolutions urging immediate attention to (1) immediate and full implementation of the Tripoli Agreement and renegotiation with the MNLF; (2) appointment of qualified Muslims to government positions under a scheme of equitable representation; (3) release of all Muslim political prisoners; (4) appointment of MP Omar Dianalan to the Ministry of Agrarian Reform; (5) repatriation of Muslim refugees; and (6) Muslim representation in the commissions on good government and reorganization.[17]

Then, reportedly at President Aquino's request, Dianalan made further proposals. He called for the creation of a panel to be composed of five representatives from the government, five members from the Quadripartite Ministerial Commission of the Islamic Conference, five from civic-religious-educational groups, four from the MNLF rebel factions, and seven from ex-rebel returnees. Meanwhile, four MNLF factions based abroad and thirteen local zone commanders would be given fifteen days, starting March 16, to make contact with their forces on a cease-fire and to negotiate. The military would then take all necessary steps to issue safe conduct passes to the groups joining the negotiations in Manila, tentatively scheduled for April 1 through 15.

These proposals were promptly denounced by Macapanton Abbas' sister, who said the "Bangsa Moro Islamic Party, an affiliate Pundato-Abbas faction," would not recognize any representation made by Dianalan on behalf of the Muslim people. Abbas' brother Firdausi had, however, participated in the conference producing the earlier resolution. In any event, Sultan Panangan Pangandaman, the secretary-general of the Muslim Association of the Philippines, promptly declared the negotiation efforts of the Pundato-Abbas faction "a lot of hogwash" and accused Macapanton Abbas of being responsible "for every splinter event in the MNLF."[18] Dianalan, at least ten of the fifteen listed as attending the Islamic Conference of the Philippines meeting, the Abbas family, Dimas Pundato, and Pangandaman are Maranao.

Under the circumstances it is not surprising that the Aquino administration itself has a Muslim policy consisting, at best, of notions. Senator Benigno Aquino had met with both Misuari and Lucman and

[17]*Bulletin Today*, March 5, 1986.
[18]*Midday*, March 13, 1986.

was sympathetic to the Muslim demand for autonomy. Before the UNIDO decided to boycott the June 1981 presidential election, there was talk of including in the UNIDO candidate's platform a proposal that the two existing southern regions be reorganized to include only provinces with Muslim majorities and to grant them genuine autonomy. After that election there was a report that Salvador Laurel had left the country to meet with Aquino and Misuari. The Aquino-Laurel "minimal program" for the February 1986 election included the following provisions:

The new Constitution should provide for . . . effective local political units which will lodge the power and make political and economic decisions as close to the people as possible. . . .

The economic, social, and cultural rights of the people must be safeguarded, especially those of members of ethnic minorities. Meaningful participation in the country's development should be insured in the context of a free and united Philippines . . .

The rich diversity of customs, traditions, languages, cultural heritage, and ways of life of our Muslim brothers and other tribal Filipinos [should be recognized and respected] to the end that they may have equal rights as other citizens.[19]

During the election, Agapito ("Butz") Aquino, Benigno Aquino's brother, was reported to have met with Misuari in Spain. After Marcos left, the Aquino government initiated talks with various Muslim groups, offered a cease-fire from April 1 to September 30, and proposed negotiations within the framework of the Tripoli agreement.[20] However, the Aquino-Laurel campaign was launched and its victory celebrated with Catholic masses, and no Muslims were appointed to cabinet posts.

Basic issues, then, remain unresolved. Three can be identified:

---

[19]*Philippine News* (San Francisco), January 15-21, 1986.

[20]*Manila Times*, March 13, 1986. The text in the *Times* makes reference to "the 1978 Tripoli Agreement, which binds the government to grant autonomy to the two Muslim regions (IX and XII) without conceding territorial integrity and autonomy." Since the agreement was signed in 1976 and provides for one autonomous region, one hopes that the Aquino administration has a clearer understanding than the writer of the article.

1. Political structures. The announced intent to negotiate regional political structure within the framework of the Tripoli agreement is an appropriate response to Muslim wishes, but negotiations will not be easy. Whatever chicanery was involved in the process which reduced the provinces from thirteen to ten, divided the "autonomy" into two regions rather than one, and reduced (if not eliminated) the Islamic/Muslim identity of the undertaking, the decisions reflected both Muslim and Christian realities which any negotiation must confront. Muslims represent a majority of the population in only five provinces. In Region IX, where Muslim influence is strongest, rivalry between Maranao and Maguindanaon Muslims has produced considerable friction. Marcos, during his state visit to Saudi Arabia in 1982, and subsequently during the 1986 election campaign, agreed to move toward merger of the two regions. This may or may not be what Muslim and Christian inhabitants of those regions want.

   In short, the Tripoli agreement represents compromises among a particular group of participants at a particular point in history. Neither the participants nor the perceptions of reality will be identical at future negotiations. The mandate must be that negotiations continue among relevant parties until agreement on implementation is reached among the majority. There are clear trade-offs between geographical scope and Muslim influence, and the ambitions of all will never be satisfied.

2. Policies and programs. Both domestic and foreign policies toward Muslims were better developed during the Marcos era than they had ever been before; that they were inconsistently pursued or subverted should not diminish their potential value. Many programs—particularly those initiated by Alejandro Melchor's task force and by the Ministry of Muslim Affairs under Michael Mastura's instigation—deserve full support. Of particular importance were efforts at developing a Muslim law code and provisions for administering it, at improving *madrasah* schools and addressing issues affecting Muslims in public schools, and at promoting foreign policies which recognized both Muslim contacts with Muslim states and the mutual advantage of good relations between the Philippines and Muslim states. The Philippines has considerable economic reasons to pursue good relations with Muslim states; I suspect it will find them grateful to recipro-

cate if they can count on honesty, forthrightness, and sensitivity.
3. National identity. Among the issues confronted and unresolved by the Marcos regime is that of forging an inclusive national identity. To the extent that the regime attempted to supersede all forms of ethnic, religious, or ideological orientation, substituting instead the "common patrimony of nationality [shared] with all Filipinos," it was doomed to failure. What is needed instead is a notion of nationality which assumes, in David Steinberg's words, that the Philippines is indeed "a singular and a plural place." Celebratory masses bind the majority of Filipinos, and the role of the Catholic church in recent events warrants recognition and respect by all who take religion seriously; yet the identification of government with masses and a dominant role for Catholicism can only leave isolated and alienated those whose faith has other rituals, structures, and prescriptions for conduct.

Islam and Muslims have much to offer the Philippines. Muslims need to be assured that their faith is also recognized and respected, their holy days set aside for observance, and their definitions of ethical conduct affirmed—and that they are valued as equal participants in the Philippine polity.

At the same time they need to be challenged to rise above the ethnic, factional, and personalistic loyalties which have prevented cooperative action and achievement in the past. Perhaps all that is needed is an administration which demonstrates to all that the purpose of government is not individual enrichment but collective well-being, but I suspect that a Muslim leadership which calls Muslims to ethical conduct is a necessary supplement. There are Muslims ready to play this role, given support and encouragement.

As for the United States, there seems little it can or should do, other than to be aware of our own history, which demonstrates that minority issues are difficult to deal with, and to be wary of being used by particular factions of Muslims. For this we should be grateful.

POSTSCRIPT

In the months since this paper was originally written, there have been few developments giving cause for optimism. Dimaporo and his armed men were forced out of Marawi by the end of April, but continued to cause trouble. Certainly Dimaporo's relatives and followers were responsible for the kidnaping of Father Michel de Gigord on June 4 from the campus of Mindanao State University in Marawi, and probably also for that of Brian Lawrence on July 12. Probably they were not involved in the kidnaping of ten nuns in Marawi on July 11, though the actors seemed to have identical motives: revenge against the government, which had taken away power and positions, and extortion. In Father Michel's case there was an additional, personal motivation: he had been outspoken in his criticisms of the Dimaporo era at MSU.

In Zamboanga a meeting of Muslims in April apparently produced no more than a platform for a series of speakers to threaten armed action. Soon thereafter, Macapanton Abbas and some of his colleagues left the country, claiming to be exasperated at the government's failure to initiate negotiations. The kidnaping on July 19 from an island near Zamboanga of a Swiss tourist and his Filipino traveling companion was subsequently attributed to pirates. Skirmishes in Basilan, Jolo, and Tawi Tawi, however, were apparently linked to Muslim groups loyal to Nur Misuari.

Meanwhile the Aquino government seemed to have moved little beyond its initial notions. It named Muslim Officers in Charge (OICs) in a few areas in the south, appointed three respected Muslims to the Constitutional Commission, and chose a former "rebel" to be minister of Muslim affairs. Agapito ("Butz") Aquino spoke to the Zamboanga City gathering, and General Magno met with Abbas to discuss a cease-fire. President Aquino announced that Vice President Laurel would form a negotiating panel—when leaders of the various groups in the MNLF decided who would represent them. Other government officials expressed their frustration that Muslim factionalism made negotiations difficult; some admitted that thus far they had given Muslim issues low priority, assuming that the factionalism encouraged by Marcos would prevent insurgency of the kind experienced in the 1970s.[21]

Finally, after intense diplomacy in Southeast Asia and the Middle East, President Aquino arranged to meet MNLF chairman Misuari in Jolo on September 5. They agreed to continue and formalize the

[21]*Los Angeles Times,* April 23, 1986.

informal, localized cease-fire accords already in existence and to select panel members for later talks to be held under the auspices of the Islamic Conference. Guaranteed safe conduct, Misuari then began to travel around the southern Philippines to consult with other Muslim leaders.[22]

Reports of that consultation are both confusing and contradictory. Obviously the MNLF is divided internally on its goals, and has not yet reached an accommodation with either Salamat's and Pundato's factions or with other Muslim leaders. Thus the Aquino government is likely to remain frustrated by Muslim factionalism.

Yet arguably factionalism and the anarchy it produces should be considered an imperative for action rather than a reason for inaction. Continued delays in the development of an explicit Muslim agenda and the commitment to it of government attention and resources will only corroborate Muslims' suspicions that the Christian (and, more specifically, Catholic) government will not respond to their interests and needs until forced to do so by violence. The Jolo meeting was an important, if belated, first step.

[22]*Far Eastern Economic Review*, September 11 and 18, 1986.

24

The Philippine Military After Marcos

William M. Wise*

From the 1983 assassination of Benigno Aquino to the 1986 presidential election, United States Department of Defense officials spent countless hours before congressional committees discussing the Philippines military. Three distinct themes emerged from their testimony during this seemingly endless series of hearings:

- The communist insurgency posed an increasingly serious threat to the Philippine nation;
- The Armed Forces of the Philippines (AFP) would not be capable of meeting the military component of that threat without sweeping reforms; and
- There existed within the AFP a solid core of competent, professional officers who were capable of reforming the military and subduing the armed insurgency, if given the opportunity and resources to do so.

Implicit in DoD's characterization of the Philippine military was a warning that whoever inherited political authority in Manila would find the AFP a seriously weakened, though no less essential, national institution. DoD's strong urging that Congress continue to provide significant levels of military assistance to the AFP during that period reflected not only a belief that United States aid could act as a stimulus for reform, but also a deep concern that the continued weakening of the AFP as an institution could cripple its ability to defend the nation when the opportunity to perform that function inevitably arrived.

---

*The opinions expressed in this chapter are the personal views of the author and not necessarily those of the Office of the Secretary of Defense.

While the events of February 1986 may have in some measure vindicated the Defense view of the Philippine military, the change in government did not solve the problems of the AFP. At most, the demise of the Marcos regime created conditions under which the AFP's urgent problems might finally be addressed. The solutions—and the restoration of the military as an effective institution in Philippine society and an instrument of national policy—remain for the new government to find. Considering the nature and immediacy of the Communist military threat, the Aquino government may have less time than it would wish in which to fashion those solutions.

THE LEGACY OF THE MARCOS YEARS

Whether the AFP was ever truly "professional" may be arguable, but the deterioration of its military professionalism during the Marcos years is clearly not. During the martial law era (1972–81) the AFP underwent a rapid expansion in size, authority, and perquisites. Among the by-products of these changes were a decline in the quality of the officer corps and an increase in the political responsibilities of AFP officers. Active-duty officers, for example, were assigned to positions in the civil sector, both in government ministries and agencies and in government-controlled corporations. In some parts of Mindanao, military officers were given responsibility for running local governments. Additionally, Marcos, acting through General Ver, tended to promote, assign, and then extend the terms of senior officers who demonstrated personal and political allegiance to him. He ensured that these officers occupied the most significant positions in the AFP, thus stifling the development of professional military leadership. He constructed a command system that would permit him, again through Ver, to direct the AFP from Malacanang and focused the AFP on preserving the security of the seat of government rather than the security of the countryside.

Despite the increased involvement of the AFP in nonmilitary activities during the Marcos years, there were substantial limits to its politicization. Traditionally, the AFP had not been an independent political institution in Philippine society. During the Marcos years the AFP as an institution retained its traditional role of serving the central government, and its loyalty was to Marcos as legal civilian authority rather than to Marcos the man. Although some of its senior leaders played important and highly visible political roles under Marcos, the

AFP did not become an independent actor in the political system until the election crisis of 1986. Even then, it can be argued that the personal actions of a few key leaders and their immediate subordinates, rather than the military as an institution, produced the dramatic events of February.

Politicization at the senior levels adversely affected the AFP, but was not by itself the principal negative aspect of the Marcos legacy. The most damaging elements of the Marcos legacy were the decline of the AFP's capability to perform its military missions and the loss of respect for the military as a guarantor of national security and independence. These two elements were in fact connected by a common thread: the AFP's lack of leadership, training, and resources. The AFP's failures in these critical areas gave rise to abuses and corruption, which strained civil-military relations; an inability to provide the security environment necessary for local governments to deliver services; and disaffection within the military institution itself. Specifically:

- Severe underfunding and resource neglect denied the AFP the matériel to accomplish its missions. Shortages of mobility and communications equipment, food, clothing, medicines and medical care, and low pay not only eroded morale and reduced operational capabilities, but also left soldiers largely dependent on the population for support, contributing to corruption and misconduct toward civilians.

- Deficiencies in personal and unit training impaired the AFP's ability to use its relatively meager resources to best military advantage. The general absence of standardized personal training and a coordinated unit rotation and retraining program restricted the preparation of soldiers and units for counterinsurgency operations and the imparting of new operational concepts and techniques.

- Leadership failures exacerbated the problems deriving from insufficient material resources and training. Military organizations can often, through sacrifice and creative employment of available resources, make up for shortages in matériel and limitations in training opportunities. They cannot, however, substitute resources and training for leadership. Nor can strong leadership at the end of the chain of command compensate for its absence in the middle or at the top. Leadership failures left the AFP defensively oriented, undisciplined, and lacking direction and unity of purpose.

The AFP's deteriorating capability to perform its military missions and the loss of popular respect for the military as protector and defender had a profound influence on elements of the officer corps, an effect not fully grasped by many observers who had not shared the experience of military service. The AFP Reform the Armed Forces Movement (RAM) evolved from a small group of field grade officers— most assigned to the Manila area—who began meeting informally in the 1983-84 period to share growing concerns over the Communist insurgency and stagnation of the armed forces. This original group— often referred to as the RAM "core group"—was composed of PMA graduates, many from the class of 1971. As political and security conditions deteriorated, the group gradually took on a more activist posture, and began seeking ways to demonstrate widespread military frustration, promote military reforms, and plan for worst-case scenarios in which the military might be forced to intervene in the political system. The launching of RAM in 1985 was one of a number of tactics devised by the core group to mobilize military disaffection, pressure the armed forces leadership, and provide a cover for their detailed contingency planning. Using the expanding RAM organization as a front, the core group began quietly building a network of individuals, in and out of the armed forces, who could be tapped for political and military support in a crisis situation, or if a move against Marcos and Ver became inevitable.

The core group, soliciting guidance and support from senior officers and even retired generals, apparently devised a number of tactical plans to meet various contingencies. The actual course of events of the February revolution, however, was probably for the most part unplanned. Nevertheless, the support network developed by the reformists over the previous year probably accounted for much of the immediate support for Ramos and Enrile's sudden break with Marcos. In addition, there were many spontaneous defections.

In retrospect, given the AFP's decline under Marcos, neither the emergence of a military-reform movement in early 1985, nor that movement's instrumental role in the February revolt that brought down Marcos, should have been surprising. What was surprising, however, was the initial sight of masses of unarmed people encircling Camp Crame to protect the minister of national defense, AFP vice chief of staff, and a small force of AFP officers and men inside. The event forged a bond of solidarity between the Manila populace in the streets and a faction of the professional military, both of which sought an end to the Marcos regime. Attitudes toward the military changed almost overnight, and the AFP gained popular support for the first time in years. At the height of the rebellion, General Fidel Ramos appealed to members of the AFP to join "the *new* AFP . . . in the service of the people." The Philippine military thus has a unique opportunity to achieve those reforms that constituted the basic platform of the military-reform movement: professional leadership, a new sense of dedication to service, and an enhanced capability, which, if achieved, should enable the AFP to perform more ably its military missions in countering the Communist insurgency.

REFORMING THE NEW AFP: THE FIRST SIXTY DAYS

As NAFP chief of staff, General Ramos acted swiftly to promote reconciliation and reform within the military. Twenty-three "overstaying" generals, including Ver, the commanders of the army, navy, and air force, and several key operational commanders, were retired on March 1. In place of the "extendees" and other politically connected officers who were removed, Ramos named a group of respected military professionals to key positions. Brigadier General Salvador Mison, a highly regarded former commander in the eastern Visayans, was named vice chief of staff. The former head of the AFP Civil Relations Service, BG Eduardo Ermita, was appointed to the number three position, deputy chief of staff. Ramos also designated new service chiefs—BG Rodolfo Canieso for the army, Commodore Serapio Martillano for the navy, BG Ramon Farolan for the air force, and Colonel Brigido Paredes for the marine corps—new headquarters staffs, and many new field commanders. Collectively, these new appointees represent the best of the NAFP and indicate Ramos's intention of attacking the NAFP senior leadership problem head-on.

Another appointment of great significance for the Philippine military was retired Lieutenant General Rafael "Rocky" Ileto as deputy minister of defense. General Ileto enjoys wide respect in the NAFP and is close to both Minister of National Defense Juan Ponce Enrile and General Ramos. Ileto is a former Philippine army commander and AFP vice chief of staff. He was exiled by Marcos in 1975 as ambassador to Iran and then Thailand because he opposed martial law. Press reports indicate that he played a key role during the military revolt, acting as intermediary between Ramos and Ver. He told the press in March that Minister Enrile has given him a free hand "to a large extent" to help reorganize the armed forces, trim the "excess fat," and remove political influences.

Within a week of the rebellion, General Ramos had identified three problem areas for reform: the low credibility of the NAFP in the eyes of the people, lack of discipline in the ranks, and the low combat effectiveness of many military units. Credibility can only be regained over time, but the "four-day revolution" itself, as well as the speed with which the majority of extendees were retired and the quality of the new appointees to senior command and staff positions, did much to improve the NAFP's image. So, too, did Ramos's early pronouncements of respect for civilian authority work to allay fears of military intentions. To begin the task of shoring up discipline, Ramos issued directives to safeguard public order and to establish strict disciplinary standards for AFP personnel. Since discipline is a function of command, Ramos's appointment of military professionals to key command positions may also be seen as a positive influence on NAFP behavior.

Likewise, the retirement of more politically oriented commanders should help Ramos in the task of raising the combat effectiveness of the NAFP. The subsequent retirement, rather than extension, of officers whose terms of service concluded on April 1, 1986, served notice that personnel actions would be constrained by law and regulation instead of political influence or patronage. In a similar vein, among General Ramos's first actions was the return of NAFP personnel assigned to government agencies and government-owned corporations to their parent units. Press accounts indicate that the chief of staff is now contemplating reductions in the size of the NAFP to create a smaller, better-trained, and better-equipped force. He is also studying proposals to reorganize the armed forces to reduce duplication and streamline operations. Two organizational changes announced in early March were the reduction of the Presidential Security Command—Marcos's large, praetorian guard—to a single battalion with ceremonial responsibilities and the dismantling of the National Intelligence and Security Authority (NISA), which, under the command of General Ver, served as Marcos's personal counterintelligence apparatus. Additionally, Ramos has also begun moving units and personnel from garrison positions in the Metro Manila area to the provinces threatened by increasing New People's Army (NPA) activity.

General Ramos has also indicated that the Civilian Home Defense Forces (CHDF), a principal source of human-rights abuses and corruption problems, will undergo extensive reform. Apparently, the plan is to reduce the size of the CHDF while instituting a personnel-screening-and-evaluation system to weed out undesirables. The tenure of personnel appointments to CHDF units has also been reduced from one year to three months. Although many Aquino supporters had hoped that the CHDF would be abolished, military leaders have concluded that the CHDF is necessary to provide local security in areas where NAFP presence is negligible.

It is probably safe to say that the reforms of the first sixty days were intended to provide visible evidence of "newness" in the "New AFP." However, the first sixty days also contained evidence of strains not only within the NAFP but also between the NAFP and the Aquino government. The initial military resistance to the release of imprisoned communist leaders prompted concerns among President Aquino's advisers about military attitudes toward civilian control. The reported intention of the new Presidential Human Rights Commission to investigate alleged military human-rights violations from the Marcos era raised suspicions in the military concerning the political agenda of Mrs. Aquino's advisers. Hanging over these mutual suspicions is the question of how to handle the communist insurgency that has continued unabated. It is here, on this fundamental issue, that the greatest risk of a breach between the Philippine military and its civilian masters exists. It is here that the Aquino government's political prescription of cease-fire, amnesty, and rehabilitation meets the reality of an armed communist insurgency led by hard-core ideologues whose objective of a violent seizure of power is unchanged. For the NAFP to overcome the legacy of the Marcos years and cope with the military arm of the Communist Party of the Philippines (CPP), the NPA, will require a defense policy that provides the license and resources to reorganize, equip, train, and employ government forces effectively.

PRESIDENT AQUINO'S DEFENSE POLICY

That President Corazon Aquino harbored deep suspicions about the Philippine military was evident during the 1986 presidential campaign. These suspicions were firmly rooted in the belief that the AFP bore responsibility for the murder of her husband, former senator Benigno

Aquino. They were manifested in part in her campaign pledges to release Communist leaders from jail and to call an immediate cease-fire in the battle with the NPA. The implication of her campaign statements was unmistakably to place blame on President Marcos and the AFP for the existence of an armed insurgent movement. So, while the surprising manner by which she finally assumed the presidency may have influenced her views of General Ramos and, perhaps, Minister Enrile, it was unlikely to overcome long-standing mistrust of the military institution. Still, a candidate borne to the presidency on the strength of a military rebellion as well as "people power" needed to ensure the support of the armed forces for her concept of the proper role of the military in Philippine society.

Mrs. Aquino's first major presidential policy statement on the military and the insurgency came on March 22 at the Philippine Military Academy (PMA) graduation ceremonies. In that speech, she called for a full accounting of past military wrongdoings in order to rebuild the NAFP's image. She pledged to punish military personnel found guilty of illegally enriching themselves or who were responsible for human-rights violations. Democracy, she said, depends on civilian supremacy over the military, adding that "a soldier's role is not in politics, but rather to serve as guarantor of the people's security and protector of the people's government." She also made clear that she would exercise fully her authority as commander in chief to impose high standards of professionalism and commitment on the NAFP. She noted that General Ramos and the service commanders would report directly to her and that Minister Enrile's function would be to monitor their performance. And she warned that "neither errors of policy nor gross misconduct will long escape my attention and rebuke."

On the insurgency, President Aquino reiterated her policy of "national reconciliation." She called on the insurgents to stop waging war and to join in rebuilding the nation. She emphasized that, in order to end the insurgency, it was necessary to heal the divisions that had given rise to its growth. A key factor in this process would be the forging of a special relationship between political leaders and the NAFP. The policy of national reconciliation would not be pursued unilaterally, however. She warned that those who refused to heed her call for peace would "face a reformed and reinvigorated fighting force." Absent from her remarks, however, was any indication as to what resources the financially pressed government would devote to the achievement of this capability.

In the ensuing weeks, the Aquino government seemed to be struggling in its effort to develop and articulate a cease-fire and amnesty program that would induce the NPA to lay down their arms and return to the fold. The NAFP appeared to assume a defensive posture that in some instances produced a de facto cease-fire with the insurgents. Tensions between President Aquino's advisers and military officers, including members of the reform movement, spilled over into the press. For their part, the CPP/NPA responded by establishing an elaborate set of preconditions for a cease-fire that the government would be certain not to meet, by increasing political activities, such as recruiting and propaganda meetings, and by escalating military operations against selected NAFP targets. The CPP/NPA used the lull in the NAFP operations to improve its own political and military situation, but an ancillary objective seemed to be to sow discord between the Aquino government and the NAFP.

With NAFP frustration increasing in the face of mounting casualty reports, President Aquino readdressed the problem of the military and the insurgency a month later at the University of the Philippines graduation ceremony. She promised a cease-fire for a definite period during which the government would negotiate only with the top CPP leaders. She said that the NAFP had honored her cease-fire pledge "even as the insurgents continued to strike in order to recreate conditions conducive to successful armed struggle." But, she warned, Communist aggression would not be allowed to continue. She stressed that the "soldiers of the Republic are under my wing; I have obligations to the people's security, the stability of their new democracy and the New AFP's new-found honor, and I will not renege on any."

Thus, while she offered the CPP peace, the President said, "I shall prepare for the eventuality that my offer will be rebuffed." If peace efforts fail through no fault of the government, "it will not be the old dispirited Marcos army that insurgents will face, but a new army and a new government that they must deal with now." She announced what the press called radical changes in military strategy, including more discriminating and effective application of force, as well as better-trained, better-equipped and more mobile units. This was apparently a reference to the NAFP's new counterinsurgency plan, "Mamamayan," which was announced a few days earlier. The focus of the new plan, according to NAFP deputy chief of staff BG Ermita, will be security, development, and national reconciliation. Comments by General Ramos suggest that this plan will emphasize security of the rural population rather than of the political and economic leaders and their properties and will utilize psychological warfare and civic-action techniques more extensively.

CHALLENGES FOR THE FUTURE

While the NAFP has not announced a specific agenda for the reorganization and reform promised by President Aquino and General Ramos, some indications of the direction of military thinking have appeared in the press. Additionally, previous assessments of the NAFP's problems suggest what a reform agenda might contain. At the same time, these problems will challenge military leaders' efforts to rebuild a military establishment that can both perform its military missions effectively and regain the support and respect of the Philippine people.

Organization

The question of reorganizing the NAFP will undoubtedly stir some controversy, perhaps raising long-standing differences, such as between the Philippine army and the constabulary, and stimulating competing proposals. Although the outcome of the organizational debate is unknown, it appears likely that some regional unified commands will be consolidated and that a more rational distribution of responsibilities among RUC's, army infantry divisions and brigades, and Philippine constabulary units will be proposed. Air-support assets may be organized more flexibly, so as to make them available on the basis of operational commanders' needs. The overall strength of the NAFP may decline also. NAFP vice chief of staff BG Salvador Mison favors a small, highly trained, and well-equipped force, but is concerned that a reduction in NAFP size might have adverse social and economic consequences. Changes are also due in the organization of the CHDF and its relationship to the NAFP.

Leadership and Management

Replacing the extendee generals and politically oriented commanders, while a necessary first step, only brushes the surface of the NAFP's leadership problems. It is likely that General Ramos will expect his top echelon of command to extend the housecleaning to the mid-levels of the NAFP. While this may produce some dislocations in the short term, stronger leadership at all levels of command remains an NAFP imperative. General Ramos is also likely to seek improvement in NAFP management practices, particularly in the personnel and logistics fields, in which management systems are weak or nonexistent. Old customs and habits die slowly, but strong initiatives must be taken to begin the process of change. The ability to manage people and resources professionally, without corruption and political favoritism, will be vital to the reinvigoration of the NAFP.

Training

NAFP leaders recognize the extensive training needs of their forces, but resource constraints imperil the attainment of training objectives. In the past, consideration has been given to developing a network of national training centers for individual and unit training. Unit counter-insurgency training, in particular, would appear to offer immediate returns in improved combat effectiveness, reduced casualties, and enhanced civil-military relations. Despite the cost in time and re-sources, it seems unlikely that a substantial improvement in NAFP military capability can be obtained without resort to a massive training effort.

Resources

The Philippines spends a lower percentage of its GDP on defense and devotes less of its national budget to its military than almost any of its East Asian neighbors. According to a November 1985 Congressional Research Service study, Philippine defense expenditures—expressed in dollars spent per individual member of the armed forces—have been at or near the bottom regionally. The result of severe underfunding has been chronic shortages of mobility and communications equipment, logistics support, food and personal equipment, and medicines and medical care. These resource constraints have contributed directly to declining combat effectiveness and produced frustration in an officer corps forced to cope with an increasing security threat on a severely curtailed budget. Low pay and frequently dismal living conditions add to the low state of morale in the NAFP. Solving the resource shortage will be General Ramos's most vexing problem in the near term, for it is unlikely that the NAFP can achieve its operational goals without an infusion of funds, and finding those funds in the midst of the Philip-pines' financial crisis will be difficult.

Counterinsurgency Plans and Operations

Leadership, training, and resources must be brought together in a coherent plan to combat the military component of the Communist insurgency. In saying this, it is well to bear in mind Colonel Harry Summers's dictum in *On Strategy: A Critical Assessment of the Vietnam War* that "military forces are designed, equipped, and trained for a specific task: to fight and win on the battlefield." They can complement political and economic policies, but they cannot substitute for them. The principal counterinsurgency mission of the NAFP is to destroy the NPA's armed forces. A renewed Philippine military must be capable of fighting and winning against the NPA, but it must be only one element in a counterinsurgency strategy that integrates political, economic, *and* military elements. Press reports indicate that Minister Enrile has been urging the reactivation of the National Security Council to coordinate the efforts of various ministries and agencies in combatting the insurgency. The presence of democratic institutions—elections, a national legislature, local governments responsive to the people, courts of justice, and so forth—the ability to engage freely in economic activities, and the attention of government to the social needs of the populace are as important to counterinsurgency as the development of combat-effective military forces.

The Role of the Reformists

The members of the "Reform the Armed Forces Movement" (RAM) constitute a force in the NAFP with influence beyond what their status as mid-level officers would imply. In early March, RAM leaders said in an interview with the Philippine newspaper *Business Day* that the organization would continue until wide-ranging and substantial reforms are implemented in the NAFP. Although Minister Enrile indicated that the organization would disband and navy captain Rex Robles, RAM spokesman and policy-planning assistant to Enrile, labeled it "redundant" in the face of the reforms being made, RAM has indeed continued to play an informal role in military affairs. Its leaders have attended meetings with senior officials, including President Aquino, and generally maintained vigilance over government and military policy making. A few reformists have publicly criticized some of President Aquino's advisers for failure to understand and respond appropriately to the CPP/NPA threat. They have also been critical of the refusal of the Presidential Human Rights Commission to investigate abuses perpetrated by the CPP/NPA as well as the NAFP. These outbursts have been curbed by strong warnings from General Ramos, but they serve to remind that RAM will remain vigilant. Within the NAFP, RAM leaders seem to sense that their special situation carries with it the potential for sowing disunity.

As a result of the revolution, some of the core group officers have become well-known; others have remained out of the spotlight. The overt RAM organization, while remaining officially intact, has become less active due to the pressing requirements of rebuilding armed forces capabilities and installing new leadership. RAM nonetheless remains a forum for keeping reformist spirit alive and for unofficially monitoring progress. Despite the close association of some RAM leaders to Enrile, it would be inaccurate to conclude that RAM was—or is—merely an Enrile instrument; they have played mutually supportive roles.

THE ROLE OF THE UNITED STATES

Only the Aquino government and the NAFP leadership can rebuild the Philippine armed forces. Restoring the NAFP's military professionalism and capabilities and reestablishing its role as guarantor of Philippine national security will require a substantial investment in national will and resource support for the NAFP. As a long-standing treaty ally and special friend of the Philippines, however, the United States can play a supportive role in this process.

During this period of internal reconciliation and reconstruction, the United States can assist the Philippines by continuing its contribution to external defense and regional security under the terms of the Philippines-United States mutual security treaty of 1951 and the military bases agreement of 1947. The United States can also aid in the task of reinvigorating the NAFP through our security-assistance program in the Philippines. For Fiscal Year 1986 the U.S. Congress has appropriated $40 million in Military Assistance Program (MAP) grants and $15 million in Foreign Military Sales (FMS) credits. President Reagan has also proposed an FY 1987 program of $50 million in MAP and $50 million in FMS. This aid will support the long-term NAFP rebuilding program developed by General Ramos.

Additionally, the United States will make available, through the International Military Education and Training Program, more than $2 million in grant aid this year for Philippine military students to attend professional military-education and technical-training courses in the

United States. Some MAP grants and FMS credits can also be utilized for in-country training, including mobile training teams from the United States and on-the-job technical training at United States military facilities in the Philippines.

Shortly after the events of February that brought Mrs. Aquino to power, a United States assistance team, which included DoD officials, visited Manila to confer with senior Philippine leaders on how the United States might be helpful in supporting the new government's efforts to address economic and military problems. Only a few weeks ago, Secretary of Defense Caspar W. Weinberger became the first United States Cabinet member to meet with President Aquino. In the course of their discussions, Mrs. Aquino emphasized that the economy was her immediate priority. "She also made clear," the secretary reported, "that she understands that economic and military assistance go hand-in-hand—that a revitalized and professional Philippine armed force must be capable of dealing with the hardcore (NPA) elements . . . which refuse to change their goals."

Based on these assessments of Philippine economic and military needs and the desires of the Philippine government for additional assistance, President Reagan announced on April 23 a major program of economic and military support for the Philippines. The military component of this program includes a request for an additional $50 million in MAP for FY 1986, conversion of approximately $29 million of prior years' unused FMS credits to MAP grants, and replacement of $50 million in FMS credits with MAP grants in the FY 1987 budget request. These funds will be used for basic military requirements: logistics support, communications and transportation equipment, and troop support, and to help promote military reforms.

Thus, the role of the United States is to be supportive in those areas of defense cooperation in which our resources can help provide for external defense and build military professionalism and technical capabilities in the NAFP. It is the task of the Aquino government to achieve the ultimate goals of rebuilding military effectiveness and restoring the proper relationship between the military and the people. These are great challenges, but President Aquino has demonstrated a determination to meet them. Secretary Weinberger has indicated his appreciation of the problems facing the new President, recognizing that "she has difficult days ahead, and she needs our support and the support of other democratic countries to realize in full measure the promise of the new democracy in Manila."

25

The Philippine-American Defense Partnership

Alva M. Bowen, Jr.*

THE PHILIPPINE-AMERICAN DEFENSE PARTNERSHIP

The military aspect of the Philippine-American relationship has varied in character over the years, but it has always been a major consideration since Commodore George Dewey's victory over the Spanish Fleet at Manila Bay on May 1, 1898. That event crystallized attitudes in the United States that eventually led to the acquisition of the Philippine Islands as an American colony on December 12, 1898. Strategic thinking at the time recognized a need only for a coaling station and naval base to provide a "home" area from which we could operate in the Orient. But the whole archipelago was acquired to deny "unfriendly powers" (at that time thought to be Germany) a nearby countering position.

By 1906, Japan had displaced Germany as the perceived threat, and many Americans, including President Theodore Roosevelt, came to view the Philippines as our "Achilles' heel," hostage to Japanese imperialist designs and likely to involve the United States in a war in the Far East. The strategy adopted to guard against this threat—keeping the Philippines largely defenseless so the Japanese would not feel threatened and would leave the islands alone—sufficed for thirty years, but finally failed in 1941.[1] The war was fought, and Japan defeated (and eventually allied to our side).

*This essay contains the opinions of the author and does not purport to be the view of the Congressional Research Service.

[1] On November 11, 1909, President Taft approved a recommendation by the Joint Army-Navy Board that no major base be established west of Hawaii and that Subic Bay be restricted to a repair base without military value during wartime. This policy, in modified form, was eventually codified into international law by the Washington Naval Treaties of 1922, which contained a provision that none of the signatories would fortify any of the Pacific islands north of the latitude of Singapore or west of the longitude of Guam.

When the Philippines was granted its independence on July 4, 1946, both Filipino and American defense planners felt a need to continue a military relationship. From the Filipino standpoint, their newly independent island country needed time to rebuild after the war. With the memory of the Japanese occupation still fresh, the Philippine government welcomed American willingness to continue to underwrite their defense needs. From the American standpoint, the ongoing Chinese civil war, the uncertain outcome of the postwar attempt by the European powers to reassert sovereignty over their former colonies in the region, the need to oversee Japanese reconstruction, and an already-developing distrust of Soviet motives argued for continuance of an American military presence in East Asia. For both countries, geopolitical circumstances, a genuine liking for one another, and the shared wartime experiences of military adversity and victory led naturally to a defense partnership arrangement that has endured. Initially the Philippines was very much the junior partner in this relationship, with the United States carrying most of the burden and privileged to make most of the decisions.

This essay examines the status of that partnership today in light of the international power structure that has evolved in the region and the progress the Philippines has made toward self-sufficiency.

LEGAL STRUCTURE OF THE PARTNERSHIP

Forecast by the treaty that granted independence to the Philippines in 1946, the Philippine-American partnership is given legal status by two treaties and two executive agreements. Listed chronologically, they are:

- The Agreement Between the United States of America and the Republic of the Philippines Concerning Military Bases, signed at Manila on March 14, 1947, and amended from time to time;
- The Agreement Between the Government of the United States of America and the Government of the Philippines on Military Assistance to the Philippines, signed at Manila on March 21, 1947, and amended from time to time;
- The Mutual Defense Treaty Between the United States of America and the Republic of the Philippines, signed at Washington on August 30, 1951; and

- The Southeast Asia Collective Defense Treaty (Manila Pact), signed at Manila on September 8, 1954.

Under the bilateral treaties and agreements the United States and the Philippines each recognizes that an armed attack in the Pacific area on either of the parties would be dangerous to its own peace and each would "act to meet the common danger in accordance with its constitutional processes."[2] The United States is granted the use of military bases in the Philippines, rent free, and is obligated to provide military assistance to the Philippines in amounts, according to a schedule, and for purposes to be negotiated between the parties and in accordance with United States laws.[3]

Under the Manila Pact, "if the inviolability or the integrity of the territory or the sovereignty of any of the parties, or political independence of any party to the treaty" in the general area of Southeast Asia "is threatened in any way *other than by armed attack* or is affected or threatened by any fact or situation which might endanger the peace of the area, the parties shall consult immediately to agree on measures to be taken for the common defense."[4]

This legal structure has served the partnership well over the years, providing an underlying basis for cooperation in the security sphere while proving flexible enough for adaptation to the changing security environment and needs of the two countries. The next sections of the essay will examine the security goals for each country that the partnership is perceived as serving today.

---

[2]The Philippine government has, from time to time, sought an understanding from the United States as to the actual commitment defined by this wording. See the copy of the Bohlen-Serrano Agreement of October 12, 1959, and the letter from Cyrus Vance to General Romulo dated January 6, 1979, both in the appendix, for examples of replies by United States officials to Philippine government inquiries on this point.

[3]The naval base at Subic Bay and Clark Air Base are tangible evidence of the defense partnership, as are the military-assistance funds loaned or given to the Philippines annually ($1,075.9 billion from 1946 to 1983).

[4]Emphasis added. The Manila Pact was invoked to justify intervention in Vietnam's insurrection and presumably could be invoked in the Philippines if the situation justified it.

PHILIPPINE SECURITY GOALS

Homeland Defense

As has been the case throughout the military relationship, homeland defense against external threats is one need of the Philippine government served by the partnership. Sea and air defenses are the primary means of defending this island nation against invasion. United States military-assistance funding pays to equip Philippine military forces intended for self-defense. U.S. naval and air forces based at Subic Bay and Clark Air Base have defense of the Philippines as one of their missions, and, theoretically, all the resources of the United States armed forces could be committed to defense of the Philippines if the threat warranted.

Most observers believe invasion of the Philippines is not a serious threat, not least because the United States is known to be the guarantor of Philippine security. But there are a number of territorial issues between the Philippines and other countries in the region that have been suppressed. These issues might surface again if United States protection were removed.[5]

There has been a concern among Filipinos, openly expressed from time to time, that United States global interests might drag the Philippines into a war originating in some other part of the world that is not particularly relevant to Philippine national interests. This concern was eventually addressed in the Bohlen-Serrano agreement of 1959, in which the United States promised to consult with the Philippines before using the American bases there for military combat operations other than those conducted in accordance with the mutual defense treaty or the Manila Pact. This promise was repeated in the 1983 amendment to

[5]The Philippines has territorial disputes with China, Taiwan, and Vietnam over ownership of the Spratley Islands in the South China Sea, and with Malaysia over ownership of Sabah on the island of Borneo. To support their overlapping claims, Taiwan, Vietnam, and the Philippines have garrisoned the Spratleys, which are believed to have oil deposits offshore. The mutual defense treaty clearly would apply if Taiwan or Vietnam attacked these Philippine forces without provocation. There have been no Philippine forces involved in the Sabah dispute to date. See U.S. Congress, House Committee on Foreign Affairs, Subcommittee on Asian and Pacific Affairs, *United States-Philippine Relations and the New Base and Aid Agreement,* Hearings, 98th Cong., 1st sess., June 17, 23, and 28, 1983 (Washington, D.C.: Government Printing Office, 1983), 208.

the bases agreement, which returned the bases to Philippine control, with the United States facilities on the bases becoming tenant activities. (See the appendix for the wording of this promise in both documents.)

Internal Security

Some kind of insurrection has been ongoing in the Philippines since early in the period of their independence. In 1986 two insurrections are in progress, one involving Muslims in the southern islands and the other, more widespread, led by Marxists. Observers believe these insurgencies have been stimulated by economic hardship, exacerbated by tyrannies of the Marcos government, but the leaderships of the insurgencies are known to have other goals besides improving economic conditions. The Muslims seek autonomy for their adherents from central government control. The Marxist-led insurgency has been credited by observers with the potential to threaten the central government itself if not checked.

United States military aid helps equip and train Philippine counterinsurgency forces. Economic aid and the direct input of about $300 million annually to the Philippine economy from wages and other expenses related to operation of the military bases address the economic hardship underlying the insurgencies.[6]

American aid for the established government is seen, of course, as counter to their cause by insurgents. And United States domestic politics sometimes focuses on this aspect of military aid. The line between legitimate counterinsurgency measures and unacceptable human- or civil-rights violations by the established government is fuzzy, but clear enough for the citizens of the country and the international community to make a judgment. The onus is on the established government to justify its counterinsurgency measures. Failure of the Marcos government to meet this test contributed to the downfall of that government. How the Aquino government will fare in this regard has not been demonstrated.

Nuclear Deterrence

A third Philippine security goal affected by the partnership is deterrence of nuclear attack on the Philippines. The presumption was

---

[6]A major criticism of the Marcos government in the United States was that American aid was misused, and even stolen, while the insurgencies grew.

established in the early years of Philippine independence, when the United States enjoyed monopoly or overwhelming superiority in the nuclear field, that the American "nuclear shield" covered the Philippines. With the advent of nuclear parity between the two superpowers, United States administrations have occasionally been asked for reassurance on this point, and those reassurances have been forthcoming.[7] But, as is the case with other United States allies, these assurances have not entirely erased doubts whether, in the moment of truth, an American president will respond to a nuclear attack on the Philippines by launching nuclear weapons against the Soviet Union, thereby calling down Soviet retaliation on the United States homeland. Uncertainty on this point leads some Filipinos to search for other solutions to nuclear deterrence.

Whether a nuclear threat would exist if the Philippines were not allied with the United States is a sometimes emotional domestic issue raised by Filipino critics of the partnership. The Bohlin-Serrano agreement of 1959 addressed this concern by providing a United States promise to consult before "the establishment by the United States of long range missiles (IRBM, ICBM) on United States bases in the Philippines." And this promise was repeated in the 1983 amendment to the bases agreement, but without the parenthetical definition of "long range missiles." This promise has not completely laid to rest concerns of those Filipinos who fear the "lightning rod" effect of the security partnership (that the United States use of bases in the Philippines will someday attract a Soviet nuclear attack).

UNITED STATES SECURITY GOALS

United States security goals served by the defense partnership with the Philippines are more complex than those of the Philippine government because of the global security concerns of a superpower with coalition leadership responsibilities. This disparity, along with the disparity in military capability between the two partners, leads to perceptions of unequal benefits and risks that have plagued the rela-

---

[7]For example, see the letter from Secretary Vance to General Romulo included with the 1979 amendment to the bases agreement (included in the appendix to this report).

tionship from the beginning.[8] This section examines the United States security goals and benefits from the relationship.

In the Pacific Basin, as elsewhere, the two major American goals are continued access to valuable trading and resource areas and the continued maintenance of a global strategic balance. These goals could both be threatened by radical change in either the political or economic structure of the region. Hence "stability," by which is meant the absence of radical, adverse political and economic change, is frequently given as the primary United States goal for the region, passing as surrogate for the two, more fundamental, goals. It will be so used in the discussion that follows.[9]

How American military strength affects regional stability has been at issue since the Vietnam War. A subissue is whether United States military strength must be on display in the Far East, or if having it available in home territory will suffice. Despite some occasional disagreement, United States governments over the years since World War II have consistently held that U.S. military presence in East Asia is necessary to promote confidence among the peoples and governments of the region in our ability to counter military threats from the Soviet Union and their clients, currently North Korea and Vietnam, all of whom maintain larger military establishments than they need purely for self-defense. U.S. military forces stationed in the Philippines, Japan, and Korea are positioned to come to the aid of South Korea in the event of a border crossing by North Korea and to maintain control of sea and air lanes needed for commerce and strategic support of American allies and friends in the region.[10]

---

[8]Philippine national independence might be at risk if the partnership were terminated, though that risk is currently assessed as small. On the other hand, the Philippines might become involved in a nuclear war they could otherwise avoid if they continue to permit the United States to use their bases. Most observers assess that risk as small also. The risk to the United States from terminating the partnership, loss of face and military effectiveness and having to pay for a more expensive basing arrangement, is not as apocalyptic, but inevitable.

[9]For a more detailed treatment of this theme see "Stability in the Pacific Basin," in U.S. Congress, Joint Economic Committee, *The U.S. Role in a Changing World Political Economy: Major Issues for the 96th Congress,* Joint Committee Print, 96th Cong., 1st sess., June 25, 1979 (Washington, D.C.: Government Printing Office, 1979).

[10]For the most recent restatement of this position see U.S. Department of Defense, *Defense Posture Statement for FY 1987,* Annual Report to the Congress, February 5, 1986, 275-80.

This "forward defense" in East Asia ensures the Soviets will have to plan for an Asian theater if they contemplate any military venture against the United States, and demonstrates United States intention to fulfill alliance obligations toward the Japanese, Koreans, Filipinos, Thais, and Australians. It also encourages the mainland Chinese, Indonesians, Malaysians, and Singaporeans to continue their political and economic independence from the Soviets.

The key to "forward defense" in East Asia, as in the European theater, is the availability of bases in the region for United States military forces deployed there and security of the sea and air lanes over which these forces can be sustained. United States security planning is based on this set of perceptions.

THE PHILIPPINES IN UNITED STATES SECURITY PLANNING

Strategically, East Asia is divided into two subregions, each with an enclosed sea formed by offshore archipelagos. The Sea of Japan, enclosed by the Japanese Islands, is shared with them by the Soviets and Koreans on the mainland. A fundamental United States strategic goal is to keep the Soviets from breaking out of the Sea of Japan. The South China Sea, enclosed by Taiwan, the Philippines, Brunei, Malaysia, Indonesia, and Singapore, is shared with them by China, Vietnam, Thailand, and Kampuchea on the mainland. The United States strategic goals for the South China Sea are to keep its sea and air routes open for our use and that of our friends and allies and to prevent its use by adversaries in wartime.

Bases in the Philippines have the primary mission to support deployment of American military forces in Southeast Asia, and thereby contribute to sea and air lane defense in the South China Sea and in the region to the east of the Philippines where pass some of the most important oil routes to Northeast Asia.

The Philippines also are a welcome stepping-stone on the long southern route from the United States West Coast to Northeast Asia. (The shorter great circle route, which passes near Soviet bases in Kamchatka, would probably be unsafe during wartime.) (See map 1.) In addition, the Philippine bases would be a secure rear base, not far removed from the scene of active combat, in any future war that threatened the security of American bases in Japan or Korea.

456

Philippine bases support United States security interests in other ways. Map 2 shows that bases in the Philippines, geographically a part of Southeast Asia, are well located to support military operations both in East Asia and in the Indian Ocean. Because the sea and air routes from America through the Pacific to the Persian Gulf have seemed more secure, militarily, than alternate routes via the Mediterranean or the Cape of Good Hope, American military planning for Persian Gulf security has come to rely on the Pacific route. Accordingly, keeping open the sea and air routes through the South China Sea has significance beyond East Asia.

The Indian Ocean security requirement is separate from, and in addition to, the East Asia requirement. For reasons beyond the scope of this essay, stationing U.S. forces permanently in the Indian Ocean region is not desirable. In peacetime, the commander in chief, Pacific command (CINCPAC), who is responsible for the Indian Ocean, meets his "forward defense" needs there from his resources in the Western Pacific, using the Philippine bases as a way station along the route.[11] Clark Air Base is particularly well located for this purpose, providing near-optimum distance-payload factors for flights to the United States advance base at Diego Garcia.[12]

The bases in the Philippines played a major role in supporting United States ground, sea, and air operations during the Vietnam War. During that war control of the sea and air routes to the combat zone was not contested. After the war, the Soviets began to use the former United States base at Cam Ranh Bay, Vietnam.

In 1986 the Soviets were maintaining a permanent force in Southeast Asia of about thirty ships, including submarines, and eight Bear, sixteen Badger, and fourteen MIG 23 aircraft. These forces could be augmented in time of rising tension. Soviet units based in Vietnam are outside the geographic barriers and ice that inhibit operations from their home bases in Siberia. In a sense, they are a functional counterpart to the United States Seventh Fleet, "forward deployed" to a region of Soviet national interest. (For comparison, the Seventh Fleet has thirty-

[11]Occasionally CINCPAC has to "borrow" from the Atlantic theater commander to meet his requirements in the Indian Ocean.
[12]For more detail on how Clark Air Base figures in airlift planning see U.S. Congress, Congressional Research Service, *Philippine Bases: U.S. Redeployment Options*, Report No. 86-44F, February 20, 1986, 21-22.

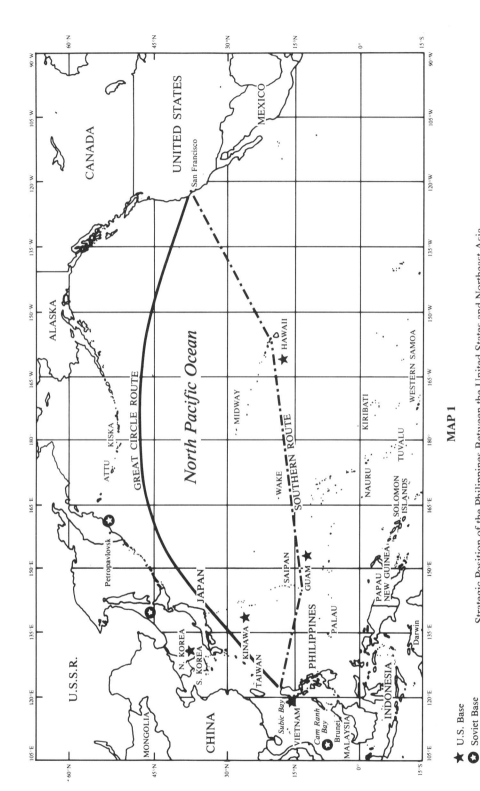

MAP 1

Strategic Position of the Philippines Between the United States and Northeast Asia.

★ U.S. Base

◉ Soviet Base

MAP 2

The Philippines in Southeast Asia

Source: Clifford R. Krieger and Robert E. Webb, *Strategic Importance of U.S. Military Facilities in the Republic of the Philippines*, U.S. Army War College, Carlisle Barracks, Pa., May 20, 1983.

459

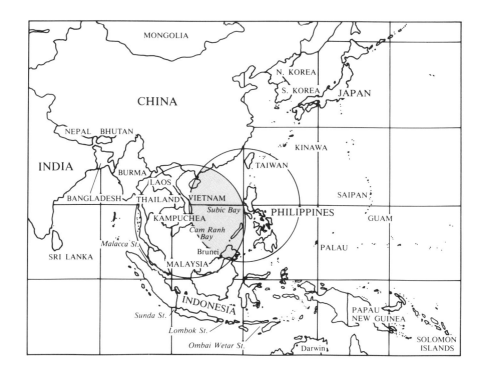

MAP 3

Overlap of Equal-Radius Operating Zones Centered on Subic and Cam Ranh Bays

This map shows the current situation, in which U.S. forces have the use of the Philippine bases while the Soviets use bases in Vietnam. It graphically portrays the fact that two opposing nearby military bases tend to offset one another. Within the area circumscribed by the intersection of the two circles of equal radius, equal-capability forces should be able to fight at comparable levels of efficiency. The 600-nautical mile circles are schematic; they could be larger or smaller, depending on the aircraft or ships represented. However, the center of gravity of the intersection lies in the South China Sea as long as we retain the present bases. Outside the intersection one side pays a significant time-distance penalty.

460

four warships, including two aircraft carrier battle groups, six submarines, seven amphibious-warfare ships, nearly two hundred aircraft, and a sizable logistics train.)

Having Soviet aircraft and ships stationed in Southeast Asia on a continuing basis has changed threat perceptions throughout the region, particularly regarding the safety of the sea and air routes. The importance of the Philippine bases as an offset to the new Soviet presence, both militarily and psychologically, has therefore increased greatly. (See map 3.)

In conjunction with United States forces based in Japan, Guam, and Hawaii, forces using the Philippine bases protect the trans-Pacific and Western Pacific sea lanes for our own use and the use of our friends and allies. American forces based in Japan and the Philippines also threaten Soviet lines of communication with their Vietnamese client. Therefore, the Soviets cannot count on the wartime use of their bases in Vietnam, while the United States bases in the Philippines, with longer but more protected lines of communications, would more than likely continue to be useful to us.

The ways in which the Philippine bases figure in U.S. military planning are summarized in Table 1.

THE PHILIPPINE-AMERICAN DEFENSE PARTNERSHIP TODAY

In the preliminary maneuvering that led to the downfall of the Marcos government in February 1986, concern that United States military and economic aid was being misused to tyrannize the Philippine people challenged the Philippine-American defense partnership. Most Filipinos opposing the Marcos regime saw United States economic and military assistance to Marco's government as support of tyranny. This presented a difficult policy issue for the moderates, who wanted United States help for Marcos to cease but were unwilling to cast aside the defense partnership entirely. To do so, they felt, would have alienated many Filipino citizens who believe the relationship with America continues to benefit the Philippines in the long run and whose support the moderates needed to gain control of the government. More radical opponents of the Marcos regime, particularly the communists, were willing to abrogate the partnership. After some equivocation, the moderates resolved the issue by promising to keep the partnership in

TABLE 1
U.S. Military Benefits from the Philippine Bases

Area Suported	Operation Supported By Philippine Bases
Southeast Asia	1. Offset peacetime Soviet military presence
	2. Threaten Soviet lines of communication to Southeast Asia from the Soviet Far East
	3. Support ground warfare in defense of United States allies
	4. Defend Southeast Asian sea and air routes
Northeast Asia	1. Defend Southeast Asian sea and air routes
	2. Defend trans-Pacific sea and air routes
	3. Threaten sea routes from Europe to the Soviet Far East
	4. Rear-base support of ground warfare in defense of United States allies
Indian Ocean	1. Defend Southeast Asian sea and air routes
	2. Way station on the air route from United States to Diego Garcia
	3. Rear-base support of combat operations in defense of Persian Gulf oil fields

United States defense planners agree that the Philippine bases provide the most effective and efficient support for current United States "forward defense" posture in East Asia and that any other basing arrangement will be less efficient and would have a range of other drawbacks.[13]

force at least until the bases agreement expires in 1991.

Although opposition to President Marcos developed in the United States, general approval of the basic United States-Philippine defense partnership remained. In particular, continued access to the bases was one of several major goals of United States policymakers dealing with

[13]These disadvantages are explored in some detail in U.S. Congress, Congressional Research Service, *Philippine Bases: U.S. Redeployment Options*, Report No. 86-44F, February 20, 1986.

the instability in the Philippines prior to the fall of the Marcos government. The perception developed that President Marcos was unable or unwilling to deal with the causes of this instability and this ultimately would threaten access to the bases.

The United States Congress indicated disapproval of the Marcos regime's human-rights policies by varying the composition of the annual economic-aid package in FY 1985 and 1986. In October 1984, Congress approved legislation (P.L. 98-473) that "delayed" military aid and expanded economic aid in an attempt to signal that Congress wanted democracy and improved human-rights conditions in the Philippines. The FY 1986 foreign-aid bill was similarly modified. Upon the ascent of the Aquino government the president promised more economic aid.[14]

Removal of President Marcos from office and the ascendancy of the moderates, led by Mrs. Aquino, has not settled the issue in the Philippines concerning their need for the defense partnership. It can be said, however, that Marcos's departure makes possible a resolution of the issue on the merits of the partnership, rather than on the acceptability of President Marcos.

The communists, who would terminate the American presence in the Philippines, are continuing their insurgency. And not all moderates favor retention of the United States-Philippine defense partnership. Some, for reasons of nationalism or concern about being dragged into a superpower war, would prefer to disengage.

Mrs. Aquino has promised to honor the bases agreement until its 1991 expiration date, and then submit the issue to a plebiscite. And she has declared her intention to renegotiate the foreign-aid package before then, with an eye to increasing the United States economic aid linked to base access despite the "rent free" provision of the formal agreement.

This position highlights the significance of the economic aspects of the defense partnership at a time when the crying need of the government of the Philippines is for economic aid. In many respects the performance of the United States government in helping the government of the Philippines to meet its need for economic aid could determine the perception of the Filipinos of the value of the defense partnership to the Philippines.

[14]For more details on United States foreign aid to the Philippines see U.S. Congress, Congressional Research Service, *Philippines: Foreign Aid Facts*, Issue Brief No. IB85077 (updated regularly).

The bases agreement and its associated aid package are scheduled for review in 1988, according to the amendment of 1979, which provided for a review every five years. The likely emphasis of the Philippine government on the economic aspects of the partnership, coupled with the fiscal stringencies facing the United States government, necessitate understanding of the strategic and economic trade-offs involved for the United States in doing without the Philippine bases. Where the forces go would determine the particulars of these trade-offs.

REDEPLOYMENT OPTIONS[15]

The possibility that United States forces might need to redeploy from the Philippine bases has arisen from time to time over the years of the relationship, and a number of redeployment options have been studied. Since the "forward defense" strategy is not likely to be dropped, even if a move out of the Philippines is decided upon, all options assume redeployment somewhere in the Western Pacific. These options can be summarized under two headings:

(1) *Redeployment to other existing United States bases in Japan (including Okinawa), Guam, and Hawaii.* Some new military construction would be required to partially relieve overcrowding that would result from moving forces into bases sized for smaller contingents, but this option is the most readily available because the bases are there already. A variant of this option adds refurbishing and expanding some of the unused World War II facilities in Micronesia to overcome most of the overcrowding. Relocation costs have been estimated at between $5 billion and $12 billion, depending on the extent of new construction. Strategically, this option is a withdrawal from the South China Sea. To fully overcome the time/distance disadvantages incurred, a United States force expansion by about one-third to one-half would be needed. This force expansion could cost up to $100 billion if undertaken. But the likelihood of Congress's funding such an expansion in peacetime is very low. Without this expansion the option adds significant military risk to the United States force posture in the Pacific.

---

[15]This section summarizes the principal findings in U.S. Congress, Congressional Research Service, *Philippine Bases: U.S. Redeployment Options*, Report No. 86-44F, February 20, 1986.

(2) *Redeployment to new bases on the South China Sea.* This option would not be a strategic withdrawal, but requires a new host country, or countries, from a short list of potential hosts: China, Taiwan, Thailand, Malaysia, Indonesia, Brunei, or Singapore. Diplomatic difficulties, some formidable, abound in this option. How economic aid to the new host country would compare with that required to keep the bases in the Philippines is uncertain, but it could be as high or higher. Base-relocation costs, including military-construction costs, would be higher than in the first option. Time/distance factors from Taiwan or the south China coast are similar, though less favorable, than from the Philippines. For other sites, time/distance factors are considerably less favorable for most tasks, and the new base could be cut off by Soviet forces based in Vietnam. This option would take several years of preparation and may not be feasible politically.

The probable outcome of American forces' vacating the Philippine bases would be their initial redeployment to other existing United States bases in the Western Pacific without the acquisition of the additional forces needed to compensate for this less effective basing arrangement. The peacetime consequences of such a move would be acceptance of more military risk, particularly to the ability to defend the sea and air routes in Southeast Asia that are of great importance to United States strategy for defense of the Persian Gulf and to United States allies and associates in East Asia.

Wartime consequences would depend on specific circumstances. In some cases, the remaining forces may be sufficient to meet the challenge. In others, consequences could well involve delays and costly battles while sufficient United States forces and active military staging areas were acquired to deal with an initially adverse strategic situation.

FUTURE PROSPECTS FOR THE PARTNERSHIP

Many observers believe the Filipinos will choose to continue the defense partnership when the issue is put to the test as the bases agreement approaches its 1991 expiration date. This perception is based on several favorable assumptions:

- that the moderates who succeeded Marcos will be able to govern the Philippines, sufficiently overcoming the economic adversity they inherited to meet at least the minimum expectations of the people;

- that the new government will be able to defuse the communist-led insurrection and reduce its appeal to the people of the Philippines;

- that the United States will be perceived by the Philippine government and people as part of the solution to the economic problems facing their country, and not part of the problem;

- that the people of the United States and their government will continue to believe that the defense partnership with the Philippines is worth the cost; and

- that the United States will be successful in maintaining a stable balance of military power in the region, and the threat of nuclear war remains remote.

Although the assumptions do not appear to be unrealistic, failure of any of them to materialize would place the defense partnership in jeopardy. Both parties face severe penalties if that happens. Filipinos face an increase in the economic hardship and political instability they have long suffered. In turn, the United States position in Asia might be severely eroded if the partnership failed. This might be destabilizing for all of east Asia.

The challenge facing policymakers in both countries is to find ways to enhance the likelihood that these favorable assumptions come to pass. As in any partnership, this will require cooperative endeavor by both sides. This analysis suggests that the goal is well worth the effort.

Appendix to Chapter 25

Extracts from Military Bases Agreement, March 14, 1947, and Selected Amendments

MILITARY BASES AGREEMENT

Agreement with annexes and exchanges of notes signed at Manila March 14, 1947
Entered into force March 26, 1947
Ratified by the President of the Philippines January 21, 1948
Implemented by agreements of July 1 and September 12, 1947; October 12, 1947 (as supplemented by agreements of January 2 and 3, 1948, and February 19 and 29, 1948); October 3 and 14, 1947; December 18 and 19, 1947; December 23 and 24, 1947; March 31 and April 1, 1948; May 14 and 16, 1949; December 29, 1952 (as amended by agreement of January 15 and February 9, 1953); May 29 and June 17, 1953; and April 7 and 22 and July 7 and 22, 1953
Amended by agreements of May 14 and 16, 1949; August 10, 1965; and September 16, 1966

61 Stat. 4019; Treaties and Other
International Acts Series 1775

467

AGREEMENT BETWEEN THE UNITED STATES OF AMERICA AND THE REPUBLIC OF THE PHILIPPINES CONCERNING MILITARY BASES

WHEREAS, the Governments of the United States of America and of the Republic of the Philippines are desirous of cooperating in the common defense of their two countries through arrangements consonant with the procedures and objectives of the United Nations, and particularly through a grant to the United States of America by the Republic of the Philippines in the exercise of its title and sovereignty, of the use, free of rent, in furtherance of the mutual interest of both countries, of certain lands of the public domain;

ARTICLE I
GRANTS OF BASES

1. The Government of the Republic of the Philippines (hereinafter referred to as the Philippines) grants to the Government of the United States of America (hereinafter referred to as the United States) the right to retain the use of the bases in the Philippines listed in Annex A attached hereto.

2. The Philippines agrees to permit the United States, upon notice to the Philippines, to use such of those bases listed in Annex B as the United States determines to be required by military necessity.

ARTICLE II
MUTUAL COOPERATION

1. It is mutually agreed that the armed forces of the Philippines may serve on United States bases and that the armed forces of the United States may serve on Philippine military establishments whenever such conditions appear beneficial as mutually determined by the armed forces of both countries.

2. Joint outlined plans for the development of military bases in the Philippines may be prepared by military authorities of the two Governments.

3. In the interest of international security any bases listed in An-

nexes A and B may be made available to the Security Council of the United Nations on its call by prior mutual agreement between the United States and the Philippines.

ARTICLE III
DESCRIPTION OF RIGHTS

1. It is mutually agreed that the United States shall have the rights, power and authority within the bases which are necessary for the establishment, use, operation and defense thereof or appropriate for the control thereof and all the rights, power and authority within the limits of territorial waters and air space adjacent to, or in the vicinity of, the bases which are necessary to provide access to them, or appropriate for their control.

2. Such rights, power and authority shall include, *inter alia,* the right, power and authority:

(a) to construct (including dredging and filling), operate, maintain, utilize, occupy, garrison and control the bases;

(b) to improve and deepen the harbors, channels, entrances and anchorages, and to construct or maintain necessary roads and bridges affording access to the bases;

(c) to control (including the right to prohibit) in so far as may be required for the efficient operation and safety of the bases, and within the limits of military necessity, anchorages, moorings, landings, take-offs, movements and operation of ships and waterborne craft, aircraft and other vehicles on water, in the air or on land comprising or in the vicinity of the bases;

(d) the right to acquire, as may be agreed between the two Governments, such rights of way, and to construct thereon, as may be required for military purposes, wire and radio communications facilities, including submarine and subterranean cables, pipe lines and spur tracks from railroads to bases, and the right, as may be agreed upon between the two Governments to construct the necessary facilities;

(e) to construct, install, maintain, and employ on any base any type of facilities, weapons, substance, device, vessel or vehicle on or under the ground, in the air or on or under the water that may be requisite or appropriate, including meteorological systems, aerial and water navi-

gation lights, radio and radar apparatus and electronic devices, of any desired power, type of emission and frequency.

3. In the exercise of the above-mentioned rights, power and authority, the United States agrees that the powers granted to it will not be used unreasonably or, unless required by military necessity determined by the two Governments, so as to interfere with the necessary rights of navigation, aviation, communication, or land travel within the territories of the Philippines. In the practical application outside the bases of the rights, power and authority granted in this Article there shall be, as the occasion requires, consultation between the two Governments.

ARTICLE IV
SHIPPING AND NAVIGATION

1. It is mutually agreed that United States public vessels operated by or for the War or Navy Departments, the Coast Guard or the Coast and Geodetic Survey, and the military forces of the United States, military and naval aircraft and Government-owned vehicles, including armor, shall be accorded free access to and movement between ports and United States bases throughout the Philippines, including territorial waters, by land, air and sea. This right shall include freedom from compulsory pilotage and all toll charges. If, however, a pilot is taken, pilotage shall be paid for at appropriate rates. In connection with entrance into Philippine ports by United States public vessels appropriate notification under normal conditions shall be made to the Philippine authorities.

2. Lights and other aids to navigation of vessels and aircraft placed or established in the bases and territorial waters adjacent thereto or in the vicinity of such bases shall conform to the system in use in the Philippines. The position, characteristics and any alterations in the lights or other aids shall be communicated in advance to the appropriate authorities of the Philippines.

3. Philippine commercial vessels may use the bases on the same terms and conditions as United States commercial vessels.

4. It is understood that a base is not a part of the territory of the United States for the purpose of coastwise shipping laws so as to exclude Philippine vessels from trade between the United States and the bases.

ARTICLE XXIX
TERM OF AGREEMENT

The present Agreement shall enter into force upon its acceptance by the two Governments and shall remain in force for a period of ninety-nine years subject to extension thereafter as agreed by the two Governments.

ARTICLE XXV
GRANT OF BASES TO A THIRD POWER

1. The Philippines agrees that it shall not grant, without prior consent of the United States, any bases or any rights, power, or authority whatsoever, in or relating to bases, to any third power.

ANNEX A

Clark Field Air Base, Pampanga.

Fort Stotsenberg, Pampanga.

Mariveles Military Reservation, POL Terminal and Training Area, Bataan.

Camp John Hay Leave and Recreation Center, Baguio.

Army Communications System with the deletion of all stations in the Port of Manila Area.

United States Armed Forces Cemetery No. 2, San Francisco del Monte, Rizal.

Angeles General Depot, Pampanga.

Leyte-Samar Naval Base including shore installations and air bases.

Subic Bay, Northwest Shore Naval Base, Zambales Province, and the existing Naval reservation at Olongapo and the existing Baguio Naval Reservation.

Tawi Tawi Naval Anchorage and small adjacent land areas.

Canacao-Sangley Point Navy Base, Cavite Province.

Bagobantay Transmitter Area, Quezon City, and associated radio receiving and control sites, Manila Area.

Tarumpitao Point (Loran Master Transmitter Station), Palawan.

Talampulan Island, Coast Guard #354 (Loran), Palawan.

Naule Point (Loran Station), Zambales.

Castillejos, Coast Guard #356, Zambales.

Mactan Island Army and Navy Air Base.

Florida Blanca Air Base, Pampanga.

Aircraft Service Warning Net.

Camp Wallace, San Fernando, La Union.

Puerto Princesa Army and Navy Air Base, including Navy Section Base and Air Warning Sites, Palawan.

SEPTEMBER 16, 1966 AMENDMENT

Agreement amending the agreement of March 14, 1947, as amended.
Effected by exchange of notes
Signed at Washington September 16, 1966;
Entered into force September 16, 1966.

The Secretary of State to the Philippine Secretary of Foreign Affairs

DEPARTMENT OF STATE
WASHINGTON
September 16, 1966

EXCELLENCY:

I have the honor to refer to the Military Bases Agreement of 1947 between the Republic of the Philippines and the United States of America and the Memorandum of Agreement of Foreign Secretary Serrano and Ambassador Bohlen of October 12, 1959. In this regard, I have the honor on behalf of my government to reaffirm the policy of the United States regarding mutual defense expressed in the 1959 Memorandum.

I have the honor, further, to propose that agreements reached between Ambassador Bohlen and Secretary Serrano in that Memorandum regarding consultation be confirmed, and that Article XXIX of the Military Bases Agreement be amended by substituting for the present provisions of Article XXIX the following:

Article XXIX—Term of Agreement. Unless terminated earlier by mutual agreement of the two governments, this Agreement and agreed revisions thereof shall remain in force for a period of 25 years from September 16, 1966 after which, unless extended for a longer period by mutual agreement, it shall become subject to termination upon one year's notice by either government.

If the foregoing proposal is acceptable to your government, I have the honor to propose that Your Excellency's reply indicating such acceptance shall constitute an agreement between our two governments on this proposal, which will enter into force on the date of Your Excellency's reply.

Accept, Excellency, the renewed assurances of my highest consideration.

DEAN RUSK

His Excellency
 NARCISO RAMOS,
  Secretary of Foreign Affairs,
   c/o Embassy of the Philippines,
    Washington, D.C.

JANUARY 7, 1979, AMENDMENT

Agreement amending the agreement of March 14, 1947, as amended.
Effected by exchange of notes
Signed at Manila January 7, 1979;
Entered into force January 7, 1979.
With related notes and letters
Signed at Washington and Manila January 4, 6 and 7, 1979.

The American Ambassador to the Philippine Minister for Foreign Affairs

No. 7   MANILA, *January 7, 1979*

EXCELLENCY:
 On December 7, 1975, at the conclusion of U.S. President Gerald R. Ford's state visit to the Philippines, a Joint Communique was issued by Philippine President Ferdinand E. Marcos and U.S. President Gerald

R. Ford. The Joint Communique stated, *inter alia,* as follows:

"They agreed that negotiations on the subject of United States use of Philippine military bases should be conducted in the clear recognition of Philippine sovereignty. The two Presidents agreed that there should be an early review of the steps necessary to conclude the negotiations through the two panels already organized for that purpose."

Also, on May 4, 1978, at the conclusion of U.S. Vice President Walter F. Mondale's official visit to the Philippines, a Joint Statement was issued by Philippine President Ferdinand E. Marcos and U.S. Vice President Walter F. Mondale, in which it was agreed that representatives of their governments would negotiate amendments to the Military Bases Agreement reflecting certain principles.

Copies of the Joint Communique of December 7, 1975 and of the Joint Statement of May 4, 1978 are appended hereto for reference.

Representatives of our governments have since met and agreed on modification to the Philippine-United States Military Bases Agreement of 1947, as previously amended. Our representatives have agreed that:

1. The bases subject of the Agreement are Philippine military bases over which Philippine sovereignty extends;

2. Each base shall be under the command of a Philippine base commander; and

3. The United States shall have the use of certain facilities and areas within the bases and shall have effective command and control over such facilities and over United States personnel, employees, equipment and material. Consistent with its rights and obligations under the 1947 Agreement, as amended, the United States shall be assured unhampered military operations involving its forces in the Philippines.

In implementation of the above, the two governments have agreed on the attached implementing arrangements with annexes and accompanying maps.

They have further agreed that:

1. Only the Philippine flag shall be flown singly at the Bases. The United States flag, together with the Philippine flag which shall at all times occupy the place of honor, may be displayed within buildings and other indoor sites at the United States facilities, and in front of the headquarters of the United States Commanders and, upon coordination

with the Philippine Base Commanders, for appropriate outdoor ceremonies such as military honors and parades on the facilities.

2. Development of base lands subsequent to this Agreement, for other than military purposes, shall be accomplished in such a manner as to ensure that Philippine and United States military operations will remain unhampered and effective security of the bases will be maintained. The parties shall see to it that any such development will not limit the use of the facilities or in any way obstruct military operations, the safety of flight, navigation or the efficiency of communication or transportation.

3. The provisions of the military bases agreement of 1947, as previously amended, regarding grant and definition of bases, as set forth in Article I, Article XXVI and Annexes A and B of such agreement are hereby superseded.

4. In every fifth anniversary year from the date of this modification and until the termination of the Military Bases Agreement there shall be begun and completed a complete and thorough review and reassessment of the agreement including its objectives, its provisions, its duration, and the manner of implementation to assure that the agreement continues to serve the mutual interest of both parties.

The two parties take note of the economic and social conditions in the areas surrounding the bases and express their joint interest in developing programs designed to upgrade them.

The two parties also take note of the decision by the Government of the Philippines to assume responsibility for perimeter security at the bases. This should significantly decrease contacts between Filipino civilians and American servicemen on official duty involving security. The parties also note the decision of the United States to retain accused personnel in the Philippines for a reasonable time, and to prevent their inadvertent departure, in order to provide opportunities for adequate discussions between the two governments relating to the jurisdictional question in official duty cases.

If the foregoing is acceptable to the Government of the Philippines, I have the honor to propose that this Note and Your Note in reply confirming acceptance constitute an agreement between our governments.

Accept Excellency the renewed assurances of my highest consideration.

RICHARD W. MURPHY

His Excellency
   CARLOS P. ROMULO,
      Minister for Foreign Affairs,
      Manila.

Arrangements Regarding Delineation of United States Facilities at Clark Air Base and Subic Naval Base; Powers and Responsibilities of the Philippine Base Commanders and Related Powers and Responsibilities of the United States Facility Commanders; and the Tabones Training Complex

The Governments of the Republic of the Philippines and the United States of America have, with respect to the above-mentioned issues relative to the Philippines-United States Military Bases Agreement of 1947, as previously amended, this date agreed to the following:

I. The boundaries of the Philippine military bases known as Clark Air Base and Subic Naval Base and their extensions, as well as the boundaries of the United States Facilities therein, their extensions and depicted areas, and the special arrangements for the use thereof by Philippine and United States forces are contained in Annexes I and II hereto. The boundary lines represented on the maps and charts attached to the annexes are symbolic, and joint surveys to be conducted by representatives of the Philippine-United States Mutual Defense Board, are required to delineate precise boundaries.

II. The powers and responsibilities of Philippine Base Commanders (hereinafter referred to as Base Commanders) and the related powers and responsibilities of United States Facility Commanders (hereinafter referred to as United States Commanders), in addition to those contained in Annexes I and II hereto, are set forth in Annex III hereto. In the performance of their duties, the Base Commanders and the United States Commanders shall be guided by full respect for Philippine sovereignty on the one hand and the assurance of unhampered United States military operations on the other.

III. The Philippines and the United States, with respect to the United States Facilities, shall have the rights granted to each in relation to what heretofore were known as "United States bases" under the provisions of the Military Bases Agreement of 1947, as previously amended (other than Article I, Article XXVI and Annexes A and B thereof) and as modified this date.

IV. The boundaries of the Tabones Training Complex and the special operating arrangements for its use by Philippine and United States forces, pursuant to the exchange of Notes of December 22, 1965 between the Governments of the Republic of the Philippines and the United States of America, are contained in Annex IV.

V. The Philippine Government assures that United States forces access to, egress from, and movement between United States Facilities, depicted areas, other areas of the Philippine military bases which are made available for use by United States forces in this Agreement and related agreements, and the Tabones Training Complex shall be unimpeded.

ANNEX III

Powers and Responsibilities of the Base Commanders and the Related Powers and Responsibilities of the United States Commanders

1. The bases covered by this Agreement are Philippine military bases and shall be under the command of Philippine Base Commanders.

2. The United States Commanders shall exercise command and control over the United States Facility, over United States military personnel, over civilian personnel in the employ of the United States forces, over United States equipment and material, and over military operations involving United States forces.

3. In the performance of their duties, the Base Commanders and United States Commanders shall be guided by full respect for Philippine sovereignty on the one hand and the assurance of unhampered United States military operations on the other. They shall maintain close contact and coordination to ensure that the activities of the Philippine and the United States forces within the bases are conducted in a manner consistent with the provisions of this Agreement. They shall promote cooperation, understanding and harmonious relations within the base and with the general public in the proximate vicinity thereof.

4. The Base Commanders shall formulate and issue plans, policies and implementing directives concerning security, administration, maintenance of order and related matters applicable throughout the base. However, on matters affecting the United States Facility, United

States military personnel, civilian personnel in the employ of United States forces, dependents of those personnel, operations of United States forces, or United States equipment or material, such plans, policies and implementing directives shall be agreed upon with the United States Commanders. The United States Commanders shall likewise issue such plans, policies and implementing directives to United States forces, to civilian personnel in the employ of United States forces, and to dependents of those personnel.

5. The Base Commanders and the United States Commanders shall create such instrumentalities as may be necessary to assist them in the formulation and coordination of such agreed plans, policies and implementing directives mentioned in paragraph 4 above.

6. The Base Commanders shall be responsible for the overall security of the base; however, the United States Commanders shall be responsible for the security of the United States Facility and certain depicted areas as provided for in this Agreement. The Base Commanders shall be responsible for control of base gates in accordance with mutually agreed rules and procedures. The United States Commanders shall participate in the security activities at the base gates and may provide security personnel to assist in the conduct of such security activities in accordance with mutually agreed rules and procedures. The United States Commanders may participate in security activities within the base but outside the United States Facility and off the base in accordance with mutually agreed procedures. The Base Commanders and United States Commanders shall contribute security forces to carry out the agreed security plan.

7. Except as otherwise provided, to the extent that a matter or issue concerns dealings by or with Philippine authorities relating to the responsibility of the Philippines with respect to the administration, security, operations and control of the base, the Base Commanders or their duly designated representative shall be the initial point of contact. The United States Commanders or their duly designated representative shall be the initial point of contact on matters or issues relating to United States forces, United States military personnel, civilian personnel in the employ of United States forces, or dependents of those personnel, and on matters or issues relating to the United States Facility or United States equipment or material.

8. The Base Commander of Clark Air Base shall station a Liaison Officer at Clark Radar Approach Control and shall designate a repre-

sentative who shall have free access to the Clark Air Base Control Tower. The Base Commanders of Clark Air Base and Subic Naval Base shall each station a representative at the respective Base Operations Offices of the United States Facility at Clark Air Base and Subic Naval Base.

9. The Base Commanders shall coordinate the activities of officials of the Philippine civil agencies performing functions at the base or at the United States Facility. Appropriate administrative arrangements for these officials at the United States Facility shall be agreed upon between the Base Commanders and United States Commanders.

10. The Base Commander and United States Commander shall undertake engineering consultations on any major construction or major alteration which results in substantial changes to existing construction within the bases and shall see to it that such construction or alteration will not hamper the operations of Philippine or United States forces.

11. An inventory listing of buildings and other permanent constructions within the United States Facility will be provided by the United States Commanders to the Base Commanders. This inventory listing will be jointly reviewed on an annual basis to ensure its accuracy.

12. The Base Commanders and the United States Commanders shall cooperate in the prevention and control of drug abuse and trafficking in dangerous drugs and other contraband within the base.

[RELATED NOTES AND LETTERS]

JANUARY 4, 1979

DEAR MR. PRESIDENT:

I was pleased to learn that our negotiators have reached agreement on an amendment to the 1947 Military Bases Agreement.

In light of this development, I wish to state that the Executive Branch of the United States Government will, during the next five fiscal years, make its best effort to obtain appropriations for the Philippines of the following amounts of security assistance:

	Millions
Military Assistance.	$50
Foreign Military Sales Credits.	$250
Security Supporting Assistance.	$200

In addition, the United States will give prompt and sympathetic consideration to requests for specific items of military equipment to be provided under these programs, and to requests for the sale of other military equipment which your Government may wish to purchase through U.S. Government or commercial channels, consistent with the world-wide policies of this Government with respect to the transfer of conventional arms.

In closing, let me state once again that I appreciate your personal efforts in bringing these negotiations to a successful conclusion. I believe that the amendment to which our two Governments have now agreed will strengthen the security not only of the Philippines and the United States but also of the entire western Pacific region.

Sincerely,

Jimmy Carter

Jimmy Carter

His Excellency
  Ferdinand E. Marcos,
    President of the Republic of the Philippines,
    Malacanan,
    Manila.

January 6, 1979

Dear General Romulo:

I was delighted to learn that negotiators for our two governments have reached agreement on a comprehensive amendment to the Military Bases Agreement. I believe much significance will be attached to this Amendment, which places our use of facilities in the Republic of the Philippines on a new and long-term basis that fully recognizes Philippine sovereignty over the bases. It will be symbolic in Asia, as well as in our two countries, of the importance which the United States attaches to continued close relations with the Philippines. It provides tangible assurance of the strong desire of the United States for close cooperation with its friends and allies.

I should like to reaffirm our obligation under Article IV of the Mutual Defense Treaty to act to meet the common dangers in accordance with our Constitutional processes in the event of an armed attack in the

Pacific area on the Republic of the Philippines. I also reaffirm our obligations under Article III of this treaty, which provides for consultations between our two governments regarding the implementation of this treaty and whenever in the opinion of either party the territorial integrity, political independence or security of either of the parties is threatened by external armed attack in the Pacific. This assures that either party will be able to consult the other on any matter which it believes falls within this Article.

Article V of the Mutual Defense Treaty states that for the purposes of Article IV, an armed attack on either of the parties is deemed to include an armed attack on the metropolitan territory of either of the parties or on the island territories under its jurisdiction in the Pacific or on its armed forces, public vessels or aircraft in the Pacific. All elements of this definition are of equal validity in terms of US commitment under the treaty. Metropolitan territory is defined below. However, as provided in Article V, an attack on Philippine armed forces, public vessels or aircraft in the Pacific would not have to occur within the metropolitan territory of the Philippines or island territories under its jurisdiction in the Pacific in order to come within the definition of Pacific area in Article V.

"Metropolitan territory of the Philippines" means all of the land areas and all adjacent waters subject to the sovereignty of the Republic of the Philippines, in accordance with international law, lying within the area delineated by Spain and the United States in the Treaty of Paris of December 10, 1898, and in the Treaty of Washington of November 7, 1900, and subsequently amended in the Treaty concluded by the United States and Great Britain on January 2, 1930.

At the same time, the United States will support Philippine plans and efforts to achieve military self-reliance, within the guidelines of President Carter's letter. We will support those efforts by means of our security assistance programs, including the important training component. We remain receptive to discussing new ideas or concepts that might improve the capability and self-reliance of Philippine armed forces and enhance our mutual contribution to regional peace and stability.

The provisions regarding criminal jurisdiction for United States forces in the Philippines incorporate the substance of comparable arrangements applicable to United States forces in member countries of the North Atlantic Treaty Organization and in Japan. Moreover, in those cases where official duty is at issue between the United States and Philippine Governments, United States forces have developed procedures to retain accused personnel in the Philippines for a reasonable time, and to prevent their inadvertent departure, in order to provide opportunities for discussions between the two governments relating to the jurisdictional question. I welcome the assumption by Philippine forces of responsibility for perimeter security at the bases. These new arrangements should contribute greatly to easing the problems of criminal jurisdiction.

With respect to base lands outside the United States facilities and the surrounding areas, the United States Government is ready to consider the question of economic assistance and other United States Government programs for suitable projects as well as projects that might appropriately be undertaken by private enterprise. The United States Government stands ready, for example, to work with the Philippine Government to determine what could be done to help small farmer agriculture provide more food of the type and quality which the U.S. facilities, along with other buyers, might purchase. In addition, the United States Government is prepared to consider appropriate assistance, subject to the approval of the Congress, for improving economic and social conditions in Angeles City and Olongapo City and surrounding areas and to relate these U.S. efforts to Philippine Government plans for utilization of returned base land areas.

In the negotiations leading to the present Amendment, a number of questions have arisen regarding the Mutual Defense Treaty and the proposal to conduct a review of the Military Bases Agreement five years after the entry into force of the present Amendment. I should like to set forth the positions of the United States Government with respect to those questions as follows:

In the context of the Mutual Defense Treaty, we would define "aggression" as external armed attack. The provisions of the Mutual Defense Treaty most relevant are Articles IV and V. Article IV provides that "each party recognizes that an armed attack in the Pacific area on either of the parties would be dangerous to its own peace and safety and declares that it would act to meet the common dangers in accordance with its constitutional processes." Article V provides that "an armed attack" is deemed to include "an armed attack on the metropolitan territory of either of the parties, or on the island territories under its jurisdiction in the Pacific or on its armed forces, public vessels or aircraft in the Pacific." An external attack on any part of the metropolitan Philippines would make the Treaty applicable and would, accordingly, obligate the United States to "act to meet the common dangers in accordance with its constitutional processes."

The reference in the Treaty to "constitutional processes" serves to make clear that the Treaty could not, and was not intended to, alter those processes for either party. In the case of the United States, the powers of the President under our Constitution as Chief Executive and Commander-in-Chief are extensive and remain unimpaired by the Treaty. It should be noted that the War Powers Resolution provides that it is not intended "to alter the Constitutional authority of the Congress or of the President, or the provisions of existing treaties."

Mutuality in our relationship shapes the United States approach to all issues between the United States and the Philippines. The Mutual Defense Treaty is the most explicit statement of this mutuality. The Mutual Defense Treaty has force and effect independent of the Military Bases Agreement. In fact, the Mutual Defense Treaty, which entered into force four years after the Military Bases Agreement, states in its preamble that ". . . nothing in this present instrument shall be considered or interpreted as in any way or sense altering or diminishing any existing Agreements or understandings between the United States of America and the Republic of the Philippines." The Mutual Defense Treaty and the Military Bases Agreement have their own separate provisions for termination.

By "review" of the Military Bases Agreement after five years, we mean a complete and thorough process which would address any outstanding issues between our governments regarding the Military Bases Agreement, including its provisions, its duration, and the manner of its implementation, to assure that the Agreement continues to serve the mutual interests of both parties.

In closing, let me say that I deeply appreciate the vital role you have played in bringing these significant talks to a successful conclusion.

In this new year, I look forward to a continuation of the cooperation which has so long marked relations between our two countries and our personal relationship.

Sincerely,
CYRUS VANCE

His Excellency
   CARLOS P. ROMULO
      Minister of Foreign Affairs
         of the Philippines
            Manila

JANUARY 1, 1983 AMENDMENT

Memorandum of agreement amending the agreement of March 14, 1947, as amended.
Signed at Manila June 1, 1983;
Entered into force June 1, 1983.
With related note.

MEMORANDUM OF AGREEMENT

The Exchange of Notes between the Government of the United States and the Government of the Philippines amending the Military Bases Agreement, dated January 7, 1979, provides: "In every fifth anniversary year from the date of this modification and until the termination of the Military Bases Agreement, there shall be begun and completed a complete and thorough review and reassessment of the agreement, including its objectives, its provisions, its duration, and the manner of implementation, to assure that the agreement continues to serve the mutual interest of both parties."

Accordingly, discussions between representatives of the Government of the United States and the Government of the Philippines were conducted in Manila from April 11, 1983 to June 1, 1983. Pursuant to the understanding reached during the Review, the Government of the United States and the Government of the Philippines agree to the following:

I. OPERATIONAL USE OF THE BASES:

Within the context of Philippine sovereignty, the operational use of the bases for military combat operations other than those conducted in accordance with the Philippines-United States Mutual Defense Treaty and the Southeast Asian Collective Defense Treaty (Manila Pact), or the establishment by the Government of the United States of long-range missiles in the bases, shall be the subject of prior consultation with the Government of the Philippines, notwithstanding the provision of the 1979 Amendment to the Military Bases Agreement assuring the United States of unhampered military operations involving its forces in the Philippines.

II. ACCESS AND INFORMATION:

With a view to keeping the Government of the Philippines fully informed about the activities of the United States forces in the Philippines, the following shall be established:

1. The Base Commander and his designated representative shall have access to all areas of the United States facilities except cryptographic areas and areas where classified equipment or information is located. Access to areas where classified equipment or information is located shall be in accordance with mutually agreed procedures.

2. The Government of the United States shall, within a reasonable period, inform the Government of the Philippines of the current level of the United States forces permanently stationed in the Philippines, and their equipment and weapons systems. Thereafter, the United States Government shall notify the Government of the Philippines of any major change in United States forces permanently stationed in the Philippines, and major changes in their equipment and weapons systems.

TEXT OF PRESIDENTIAL LETTER

THE WHITE HOUSE
WASHINGTON

May 31, 1983

Dear Mr. President:

I was pleased to learn that our representatives have completed the review of the Military Bases Agreement which was agreed to during your state visit to the United States last year.

In light of this development, I wish to state that the Executive Branch of the United States Government will, during the five fiscal years beginning on October 1, 1984, make its best effort to obtain appropriation of security assistance for the Philippines in the following amounts:

Military Assistance. $125,000,000
Foreign Military Sales Credits. $300,000,000
Economic Support Fund Assistance. $475,000,000

In this connection the United States Government will seek to provide the Foreign Military Sales Credit on the basis of a grace period of ten years and a repayment period of twenty years. As you are aware, under our constitutional system, the Congress has sole authority to appropriate funds.

I was also pleased to note that the Military Bases Agreement review confirmed that the Agreement continues to meet our mutual needs and interests. I believe that this review has again underlined the close and historic ties linking our two countries, and will contribute to further strengthening the peace and security of the western Pacific region.

Sincerely,

Ronald Reagan

His Excellency
Ferdinand E. Marcos
President of the Philippines
Manila

BOHLEN-SERRANO AGREEMENT OF 1959

MEMORANDUM OF AGREEMENT

1. In accordance with the understandings reached during our discussions in: August, September and October 1959, the following is agreed:

(a) *Consultations.*—The operational use of United States bases in the Philippines for military combat operations, other than those conducted in accordance with United States-Philippines Mutual Defense Treaty and Southeast Asian Collective Defense Treaty, will be the subject of prior consultation with the Government of the Philippines.

The establishment by the United States of long range missiles (IRBM, ICBM) on United States bases in the Philippines will be the subject of prior consultation with the Government of the Philippines.

(b) Duration and Termination.—Article XXIX of the Military Bases Agreement of 1947 will be amended in order to reduce the duration of the agreement from 99 to 25 years together with a proviso for renewal at the expiration of the 25 year period, or earlier termination by mutual agreement of our two governments. The period of 25 years will commence from the date of signature of the formal documents giving effect to the agreements reached.

(c) Mutual Defense.—The policy of the United States with regard to armed attack on the Philippines is contained in the Mutual Defense Treaty. Further the United States reaffirms the policy set forth in the statement of September 7, 1954 of then Secretary of State Dulles which reads as follows:

Under our Mutual Defense Treaty and related actions, there have resulted air and naval dispositions of the United States in the Philippines, such that an armed attack on the Philippines could not but be also an attack upon the military forces of the United States. As between our nations, it is no legal fiction to say that an attack on one is an attack on both. It is a reality that an attack on the Philippines is an attack also on the United States.

and in the joint communique issued on June 20, 1958 by President Eisenhower and President Garcia the pertinent part of which reads as follows:

President Eisenhower made clear that, in accordance with these existing alliances and the deployments and dispositions thereunder, any armed attack against the Philippines would involve an attack against United States forces stationed there and against the United States and would instantly be repelled.

(Signed) CHARLES E. BOHLEN,
Ambassador of the United States.
(Signed) FELIXBERTO M. SERRANO,
Secretary of Foreign Affairs.

MINUTE OF UNDERSTANDING

It is agreed that the general aspects of the military assistance rendered by the United States to the Philippines under existing agreements will be referred to the Mutual Defense Board for consideration and discussion.

(Signed) CHARLES E. BOHLEN,
Ambassador of the United States.
(Signed) FELIXBERTO M. SERRANO,
Secretary of Foreign Affairs.
October 12, 1959.

PRIOR CONSULTATION PROVISION IN BOHLEN-SERRANO AGREEMENT

Question. Why did the Filipinos insist on this prior consultation provision for the Bohlen-Serrano Agreement, and what was our response at that time? Did we vigorously resist this limitation or not?

ANSWER

The origin of the prior consultation provision goes back at least to the Bendetsen Mission Base Negotiations of 1956 when the Philippines proposed that war time utilization and development of the US bases in the Philippines be subject to prior consultation and agreement between the governments. The Bohlen-Serrano talks two years later readdressed the issues (particularly criminal jurisdiction) unresolved in the recessed Bendetsen talks.

Foreign Secretary Serrano, when raising the subject of consultations in December 1958, set forth the following explanation: 1) the Philippine base system is primarily and expressly intended by both governments to be for their mutual defense and as a logical consequence of this assumption the Philippines believes that the US cannot use the bases in pursuit of its own unilateral policy or its own defense commitments with other countries without Philippine consent; and 2) to the extent Philippine bases are used for regional defense, the use of the bases would be determined on the basis of obligations the Philippines and the U.S. assume under SEATO and as SEATO shall decide. Serrano explained that by the phrase "use of bases" he had in mind military operations in terms of emergencies of war that he did not conceive of the phrase narrowly or limiting in our actions or activities needed to maintain our defense position in the area.

At the same time, Serrano asked Bohlen whether it might be possible in connection with these talks to formalize in a statement our orally expressed policy that the bases would not be used for the establishment of offensive missile launching sites without the consent of the Philippine government.

Returning to the subject in September 1959, Serrano noted to Ambassador Bohlen that certain uses by the U.S. of Philippine bases could create "real danger of Philippine involvement" in hostilities and "in view of such risks the Philippines must insist on consultation."

We reached agreement regarding prior consultation with comparatively little difficulty once we had established an understanding that logistic or staging activities were excepted from that requirement.

Published in U.S. Congress. Senate Hearings: United States Security Agreements and Commitments Abroad. September 30–October 20, 1969. 91st Congress, First Session. Washington, D.C. U.S. Govt. Print. Off. 1969. p. 24

26

Report on the Discussion: Philippine Insurgency and the American Bases Question

Robert N. Smith

This report is divided into two parts. The first summarizes three papers delivered at the conference, as well as two other papers that have a bearing on our topic. The second part presents a brief review of the discussion.

THE PAPERS

Three papers were presented at this session of the conference: "The Communist Party of the Philippines and the Aquino Government: Responding to the New Situation," by Larry K. Niksch of the Congressional Research Service of the Library of Congress; "Muslim Grievances and the Muslim Rebellion," by Lela Garner Noble, professor of political science, California State University; and "The Philippine Military After Marcos," by Colonel William Wise, Office of the Secretary of Defense, the Pentagon. A fourth paper, "The Philippine-American Defense Partnership," by Captain Alva M. Bowen, also of the Congressional Research Service, was commissioned after the conference had been held and is included in this book. In addition I shall refer to an earlier paper written by one of our contributors but not included in this book, "The Military Bases in the Philippines: the Past and Future," by Ambassador Emmanuel Pelaez. I have also drawn on my personal knowledge of the military bases to help bring the panel papers into sharper focus.

Two conclusions can be drawn from the papers. The first is that the Muslim insurgency and the New Peoples Army (NPA) are internal insurgency problems that can probably be resolved by Corazon Aquino's achievement of a stable, honest, and clean government, beyond suspicion and corruption. Second, there is a high probability that the Military Bases Agreement will be renewed, though with modifications and at considerably higher rent.

The Philippine Insurgencies

Philippine insurgency is, in reality, two separate and distinct insurgencies—one, a Muslim insurgency confined to the Muslim provinces in the south, and the other, a nationwide communist insurgency. Muslim insurgency goes back to the conquest of the Philippines by the Spaniards; it continued during the American occupation until it was subdued but not broken by the American military.

Noble states in her paper that under Ferdinand Marcos, the Muslim armed insurgency participants were reported to number from 15,000 to 30,000 during the 1974-1975 rebellion. Other estimates indicate that 50,000 to 60,000 is more accurate. Casualties were estimated from 60,000 up to hundreds of thousands, refugees from one million, with 100,000 to 200,000 in Sabah. Most of the Philippine military was stationed in that area between 1973 and 1974. Fighting occurred in seventeen of the Mindanao provinces.

According to Noble, it is generally believed that there is not now a significant Muslim insurgency in the Philippines. She delineates the historical basis for the Muslim rebellion and its relatively disorganized state. While grievances remain, in spite of the Tripoli agreement of 1976 (in part due to the Philippine government's reluctance to fulfill its obligations under that agreement), organized Moro National Liberation Front (MNLF) resistance is expected to be sporadic unless the (CCP) and the MNLF can find common ground to join forces. That would be very unlikely in view of the fundamental objectives of each, one being religious and the other ideological.

The CPP insurgency is relatively new and had its origin during Marcos' presidency. It became a factor in Philippine politics after the declaration of martial law in 1972. Although outlawed by the Philippine government, the CCP and its armed force, the NPA, have been a growing force to contend with since that time.

In his paper, Niksch provides an overview of the CCP and the NPA in terms of strengths and objectives. While the actual strength of the NPA is estimated at between 15,000 and 20,000 armed insurgents, it is also estimated that CCP sympathizers number in the hundreds of thousands. Most of these are not communists in the traditional sense but persons who have been dissatisfied with their lot under Marcos. The CCP offers a change for the 70 percent of the Filipino population that live below the poverty line.

Niksch lists six reasons for the insurgency's major gains since 1980:

(1) the weaknesses of local government at the level of the Philippines' 1,534 towns, (2) worsening living standards in the towns, (3) the breakdown of traditional social structures, (4) skilled communist organizations at the local level, (5) military abuse of civilians, and (6) the unpopularity of the Marcos government. As opposed to the gains by the CCP, the government and the Armed Forces of the Philippines (AFP) were, and still are, faced with severe problems in order to defeat the rising insurgency: (1) lack of security in towns and barangays, (2) strained relations between military and civilians because of military abuses and corruption, (3) the deficiency of material resources and inadequate training, and (4) the lack of noncommunist political unity.

In his paper, Wise states that U.S. Department of Defense officials discussing the Philippine military before congressional committees gave the following impressions: (1) the communist insurgency posed an increasingly serious threat to the Philippines, (2) the AFP would not be capable of meeting the military component of that threat without sweeping reforms, and (3) there existed within the AFP a solid core of competent, professional officers who were capable of reforming the military and subduing the armed insurgency if given the opportunity and resources to do so.

While a revitalized military is only one of the factors needed to suppress the gains made by the CPP and the NPA during the last five years of the Marcos regime, it is fundamental to the defeat of the NPA if the Aquino amnesty program fails.

Wise takes note of the declining military capability of the AFP and its loss of respect among civilians during the Marcos years. He finds not surprising, therefore, the emergence of the Reform of the Armed Forces Movement (RAM) and its part in the overthrowing of the Marcos government. Unpredictable only was the massed people power that helped to protect the Camp Crame rebels against the still loyal elements of Marcos' forces. In the aftermath of this shared achievement, public respect for the military improved dramatically. This gives the New Armed Forces an opportunity to reform itself and become an effective counter-insurgency force.

The Question Of American Bases

Bowen discusses the American military bases. He traces the place of the Philippines in American strategic thinking since 1898, when it was seen mainly as a coaling station and base for the operation of American naval power in the Orient, through the early decades of the century when it was perceived as an achilles heel that could threaten the United States with involvement in a war with Japan, to its post-independence place in American thought as a partner in mutual defense. The author then examines the two treaties and the two executive agreements that underly that postwar defense partnership in detail. This legal structure provided a basis for cooperation in the security sphere and still proved flexible enough to adapt to the changing security environment and the needs of the two countries.

A Philippine view of the military bases arrangement is presented in an article by Pelaez, now the Aquino government's ambassador to the United States. While Pelaez has contributed another paper to this book, the aforementioned article is not readily available in the United States. Therefore I shall summarize parts of it below.

A particularly sensitive aspect of the bases arrangement from the Filipino point of view relates to the issue of extraterritoriality. In a speech of July 7, 1975, quoted by Pelaez, President Marcos addressed the question directly:

> The word is out, and I confirm it, that we want to put an end to the practice of extra-territoriality in our country in keeping with our dignity as a sovereign republic and in keeping with the developments of our time. We want to assume control of all bases and put them to a productive and economic, as well as military use. At the same time, we are willing to enter into new arrangements that would help the United States maintain an effective presence over the air and sea lanes of the western Pacific.[1]

As Pelaez put it: "President Marcos had reached the conclusion, as many among his people had, that amending the MBA from time to time to remedy its deficiencies was futile. It had to be scrapped entirely; and a new, less onerous, more reciprocally beneficial treaty was imperative, if the Americans would continue to have a substantial military presence on Philippine soil."[2]

The new talks opened in Washington, D.C., on April 12, 1976. This was after President Ford's visit to the Philippines on December 7,

[1]Emmanuel Pelaez, "The Military Bases in the Philippines: the Past and the Future," *Foreign Relations Journal* (January 1986): 19.
[2]Ibid., p. 19.

1975, and the United States' announcement of its "clear recognition of Philippine sovereignty" in its use of Philippine military bases. The talks resulted in nothing of substance in agreement other than to hold another round of talks during June. Secretary of State Henry Kissinger, who headed the U.S. team, expected to come up with a new treaty by July 1976. However, the subsequent meeting in Manila from July 1 to August 31, 1976, ended with no new agreements. Eduardo Z. Romualdez, the Philippine ambassador to Washington at the time, described the session as follows: "Thus ended two and one-half months of talks. It was not entirely useless, as it had clarified some issues. But it brought out no major breakthrough. At the end of two months, we still had 25 unresolved issues."

The Philippine representatives wanted to assure that there was no derogation of Philippine sovereignty, that the Philippine laws would be applicable on the bases, and that the Philippines would participate in formulating the policies concerning the use of the bases. The Americans, however, wanted to retain the authority they had under the 1947 MBA, without participation by Philippine authorities. Some progress was made. The United States agreed to rename the bases as Philippine military bases, to fly the Philippine flag alone over them, and to appoint a Philippine base commander. However, the American negotiators insisted on the right to unhampered operational use of the bases within the American facilities. The question of nuclear weapons was raised, and the Americans proposed the "Spanish base solution," that is, not to store nuclear weapons on Philippine soil. The matter of rental also became an unresolved problem as Marcos wanted it to consist entirely of military assistance, instead of a fifty-fifty, military-economic assistance split. During the Carter administration, the proposed amendments to the 1947 MBA were pursued through diplomatic channels, and five agreements were formalized in an exchange of diplomatic notes on January 7, 1979. Most importantly, the agreements acceded to the Philippine demand for sovereignty over the bases but recognized that the United States was to have, within these bases, certain facilities and areas over which it would have "effective command and control" and "unhampered operations." Also, the Philippine government assumed responsibility for perimeter security of the bases, with a review of the agreement to be undertaken every five years.

As for rental payments, President Carter sent a letter to Marcos dated January 4, 1979, in which Carter stated that the "executive branch of the United States government will, during the next five years, make its best effort to obtain appropriations for the Philippines of the following amounts as security assistance: military assistance—$50 million; foreign military sales credits—$250 million; security supporting assistance—$200 million."[3]

The five-year review of the 1979 amendments took place in Manila between April 11 and June 1, 1983. Along with some minor concessions by the United States, the pledge of security assistance was increased to $900 million for the second five-year period, to $125 million in grant military assistance, to $300 million in foreign military sales credit, and to $475 million in economic assistance. The pledge was made in a letter to Marcos by President Reagan, dated May 31, 1983. The American president also pledged that the use of the bases for military combat operations other than those conducted under the Manila pact would be subject to prior consultation with the Philippine government.

Currently, under the Aquino government, the question of American bases is on hold until 1988, the next year for review of the 1983 agreement. While the 1983 agreement is valid until 1991, considerable official comment indicates that it will be a subject of major Philippine concern. The Aquino government does not want to create another problem in the face of almost insurmountable economic chaos. The Filipinos have raised such questions as the bases being targets in a nuclear exchange between the major powers and whether full respect for Philippine sovereignty over the bases and effective Philippine participation in the use and operations of the American forces can be expected. Many Filipinos believe that the real danger to the Philippines is internal, not external, aggression, while the bases are needed by the United States as part of a global and regional defense strategy to have a visible military presence in view of Soviet expansion in the region. However, as a member of the Association of Southeast Asian Nations (ASEAN), the Philippines must take into account its relationships with its ASEAN neighbors. Admittedly, the United States needs the bases. As has been reported many times in the American press, the cost of relocating the bases, even to less advantageous locations, would be in the billions; and the effectiveness of the deployed forces from the ASEAN area would be reduced.

[3]Ibid., p. 25.

Bowen reports that as of 1986 the Soviets maintain a force in Southeast Asia of about thirty ships, including submarines, eight Bear, sixteen Badger, and fourteen Mig-23 aircraft. With Soviet aircraft and naval vessels stationed in Vietnam, the question of the safety of the sea and air lanes of the region becomes important and has increased the value of the Philippine bases to offset the Soviet presence.

What are the possible courses of action that the Aquino government can consider during the 1988 review of the Military Base Agreement? There is no question of the desirability of the United States retaining bases. According to Pelaez, three options have emerged: "dismantle the bases immediately; call for a national plebiscite on whether or not they should continue; or allow the amended 1947 MBA to run its full term, to September 16, 1991, and either adopt a permanent policy against military bases in the country or renegotiate entirely new mutual defense and base treaties with the United States."[4] The new constitution deals with the question of bases by requiring that any extension of the bases agreement must take the form of a treaty concurred in by the Philippine Senate and, if the Congress so requires, ratified by the people in a referendum.

Dismantling the bases seems to be out of the question. This would bring about grave social, economic, and political repercussions that would seriously damage Philippine efforts for national economic recovery. It must be borne in mind by responsible Filipinos that economic recovery may well depend on foreign investments—hardly encouraged by the loss of American base rights, a stabilizing influence in the area. Further, the annual dollar income from the bases, Clark Air Force Base and the Subic Bay Naval Base, has been estimated to be between $250 and $300 million. That, coupled with the $900 million security assistance pledge through 1991, may well be more persuasive than the vocal minority of communists and ultra-nationalists.

The Philippines' stature among its neighbors will be a factor for mature consideration by the Philippine Senate. As one of the ASEAN countries, the Philippines must recognize that the loss of American bases in the area would jeopardize a major goal of the member states—to counter the spread of communism.

[4]Ibid., p. 31

THE DISCUSSION

In the discussion following the presentation of the papers many participants felt that the United States should now maintain some distance from Philippine military affairs. Insurgencies at some level have been endemic in the Philippines as in other parts of Southeast Asia. Such insurgencies have been debilitating but rarely fatal. Effective governments such as those of Thailand, Malaysia, and Indonesia have managed to contain them. Marcos evidently did not regard the NPA as a serious threat. A popular new government and a respected military can deal with the present communist and Muslim insurgencies in their own way, without intrusive, if well-meaning, American advice. Similarly it was argued, the United States should not presume to advise the Philippine government on the proper combination or timing of offers of peace to the rebels and threats of resumed military action.

The employment of military force, it was pointed out, is one of the attributes of sovereignty. Its use on the advice of a foreign government undermines the sovereignty and political legitimacy of the home government. American involvement in anti-insurgency planning could only strengthen the nationalist credentials of the rebels, and weaken those of the Aquino government. Furthermore, the fear of revolution was seen as a healthy stimulus for governmental and social reform. A seeming foreign guarantee of help to combat a revolution could produce domestic complacency.

In the same vein, General Ramos is in no need of public American support. An embrace by the United States would only make him a target for ultranationalist attack. Furthermore, it was pointed out, it is always risky to base policy on a heavy reliance on a particular foreign leader whose sudden disappearance from a position of power is likely to leave policy in confusion.

The impoverishment of the Philippine armed forces elicited general concern. All agreed that their funding level per man had fallen during the Marcos years and now is the lowest in the region: one-third that of Thailand, one-twelfth that of the Republic of Korea, and one-sixteenth or one-seventeenth that of Malaysia. There were different estimates as to the extent of this decline in funding. One author stated that, in real terms, the AFP budget now stands at less than half of its value in 1977, when the Muslim rebellion was winding down. Another discussant stated that the real value of the resources available to the military remains roughly equal to that of 1970. But both agreed that, in view of the rapid increase in the size of the AFP, the amount available per individual had dropped to less than half of that during the Marcos years.

The result, it was agreed, was inadequate supplies, equipment, communications, mobility, rations, and pay. The last two of these helps to explain the troops' habit of living off the land, which in turn has contributed to the unpopularity of the military among the rural people. This situation must be corrected. For half a year, it was suggested, some funds previously committed to Marcos' praetorian guard can be shifted to combat forces in the field. After that, new funding will be needed. Improvements can also be made through the building of a smaller, better equipped and better trained force, with an improved "tooth to tail" ratio. General Ramos was reported to be considering such a plan.

Differing views were expressed as to the desirability of providing increased American aid for the Philippine armed forces. Many thought such additional aid to be important for their rejuvenation. The United States, it was pointed out, has long-standing treaty security commitments to the Philippines. The Philippines has asked for security assistance. Such assistance cannot properly be denied. For these reasons, President Reagan's proposal in April 1986 to increase military aid by $50 million beyond the regularly programmed security assistance and other aid already promised under the bases "best efforts pledge" was noted with approval. But other participants warned that such an offer of financial aid for the military could distort the Philippine government's priorities and divert funds from needed reforms. Further, it was suggested, the human rights violations that inevitably accompany anti-insurgency campaigns, become less damaging to the United States if it is not paying for them.

With regard to the communist and Muslim rebellions, it was suggested that in both cases there may be less internal unity among the rebels than is assumed from afar. It should not be taken for granted, a discussant suggested, that the Philippine communist leadership is united. Some top leaders may have personal agendas of their own. Similarly, it is a mistake to see the NPA, the National Democratic Front (NDF), and various leftist mass organizations simply as communist-inspired, and communist-controlled operations. While the party exercises dominant influence over many leftist organizations, influence may run in two directions. Thus CCP and NPA leaders may prefer to continue the guerrilla war. But they appear to be under some pressure from the NDF, *Bayan,* various communist-influenced sectoral, and cause-oriented groups (and now perhaps from *Patrido ng Bayan*) to take the legal route of electoral participation, strikes, and nonviolent street demonstrations instead. Some organizations of *Bayan,* Larry Niksch noted in his paper, rejected the CPP call for a boycott during the February elections and campaigned for Aquino instead. Similarly, *Bayan* has ignored the NDF call for a continuation of demonstrations since Aquino's accession to office.

Still, communist leaders know that no communist party has come to power through elections alone, nor can they be sure that the military would allow them to take power if they won a national election. Thus they are not likely to adopt a purely legal, non-violent course in the Philippines. Their strategy, it was concluded, is likely to be a Nicaraguan one instead of the purely Maoist, peasant-based strategy adopted in the 1960s by CPP founder Jose Maria Sison.

While communist control of the NPA was recognized, it was stressed that serious and widely held grievances have made possible the NPA's rapid growth. Unless these grievances are addressed by the Aquino government, it cannot hope to win away the NPA's followers among noncommunists. Thus, a participant from the Philippines described the situation in Negros, the heart of the once flourishing sugar industry as follows:

> Twenty years ago, the NPA movement was unknown in the Philippines. Negros was the richest province and was enjoying tranquility. Now it is in the grip of economic crisis. Because of the closing of many sugar mills and the lack of financing for sugar, many farmers simply pulled out and abandoned their farms. The dislocated sugar workers have no jobs, and their children are hungry. They live in the hills, where newspapers cannot reach them. They are ignorant of what is going on. They know only that they are hungry, that their children are sick, and cannot go to school. They complain about injustice, about military abuses.
>
> Now here comes the New Peoples Army, with a new ideology, whose soldiers promise to defend the poor as Marcos' soldiers never did. They have teach-ins, they give medicine. Up in the

mountains they provide doctors, nurses and priests. They support themselves with forced donations from the rich. They will not disperse their movement until they see that the peasants and working class acknowledge that they have received justice and freedom.

In this connection, an American participant criticized the bureaucratic inertia that, he observed, has slowed American aid to Negros. Because the Philippines is classified as a middle-income country, it does not qualify for the type of emergency food assistance that clearly is needed in this starvation-affected province. Special efforts should be made to get around this obstacle to American assistance.

Discussants took note of the new government's effort to win over the Muslim region. President Aquino had promised to raise the economic condition of the Muslims to the level of other Filipinos within ten to twenty years. If the government failed in that promise, she has said, it should allow the predominantly Muslim provinces to secede from the republic.

The Muslim rebellion reached its high point between late 1972 and mid-1975 but since then has been in decline. In its heyday, the principal rebel group, MNLF, had displayed a fairly high degree of cohesion throughout the Muslim region. Since then, unity has eroded and local groups increasingly have engaged in kidnapping and assassination, seemingly a common feature of Philippine insurgencies in decline.

That the Muslim movement, both legal and revolutionary, has been weakened by ethno-regional divisions among its leaders has been a matter of common knowledge. There have also been divisions, it was suggested, due to differences in social status among the leaders of rival groups. Leaders in Lanao del Sur: Pendatun, Lucman, Dimaporo, and Abbas, are members of the traditional Maranao nobility. Salamat of Maguindanao and the Tausug MNLF leader Misuari, are not members of the old elites of their regions. But while the old nobility has lost much of its influence among the Tausug, Salamat has not been successful in preempting leadership from the established Maguindanao elite. Status considerations appear to have influenced new local government appointments. A number of key officers in charge, appointed in Lanao del Sur, are from relatively little-known, nonelite families. Their selection may have been designed to avoid taking sides among the rival elite claimants to provincial leadership.

CONCLUSIONS

Much remains to be done in the Philippines under the mandate that propelled the Aquino government into power. In spite of the departure from the cabinet of former Defense Minister Juan Ponce Enrile and of several ministers who had been criticized by him, there remains the possibility of cabinet friction that could hinder a smooth and effective transition to the "stable, honest and clean government, beyond suspicion and corruption" advocated by Enrile.

However, under President Aquino's Chief of Staff, General Fidel Ramos, the writer believes, the New Armed Forces of the Philippines (NAFP) has its best chance for the reform that is necessary in order to make it capable of checking the communist insurgency that now finds the NPA in control of parts of many provinces. If and when President Aquino decides that the amnesty program is not effective and that negotiations will not end the insurgency on terms the government can accept, the NAFP should be able to make a substantial showing in restoring order out of the present chaos. Certainly, the two thousand killings so far during the Aquino presidency should be reason enough to expedite the retraining and refurbishing of the NAFP. Surely, the $125 million USD in grant military assistance and $300 million in military sales credits, if properly controlled and spent for the required equipment (mainly communications and transportation), should go a long way in transforming the NAFP into a force Filipinos can trust and of which they can be justly proud.

VI. United States Policy
and the Philippines

27

United States Policy in the Period Leading to the Declaration of Martial Law and Its Immediate Aftermath

William C. Hamilton*

American policy toward the Philippines during 1971 to 1973, when the author served as deputy chief of mission in Manila, was intended—as, indeed, both before and since—to serve our national interest, though accented by the special relationship that had developed through the colonial period and then annealed in the fires of World War II.

After Ferdinand Marcos's unprecedented second election in 1969, the Philippine scene was marked by:

- an impending constitutional crisis as the struggle sharpened between the administration's reform movement led by young technocrats and the entrenched power of the landed oligarchs;
- endemic poverty and excessive population growth, accentuated by sharp crises brought on by natural disasters;
- failure to meet economic targets and a slowing in the rate of growth in foreign investment;
- deterioration of law and order in Manila and in the countryside, with violence directed against Philippine authority and, sometimes, Americans;
- an increase in the communist insurgent threat, with the New People's Army (NPA) reaching into many new areas;
- an increasingly costly rebellion in the Muslim south;
- American frustration and uncertainty about continued use of military bases; and
- deepening Filipino disquiet about United States purposes and reliability in the Pacific.

*The opinions expressed in this chapter are the personal views of the author and not necessarily those of the Department of State.

However contemporary they may sound, these were the onditions prevailing in the Philippines as the decade of the 1970s opened.

PRE-MARTIAL LAW POLICY

American policy and purposes were, as is usual, multifaceted, and the principal problems were those of blending and balancing various aspects. It is easy to begin but difficult after that to prioritize.

While the Indochina war continued, preservation of the mutual security relationship and access to and unrestricted use of the military bases was foremost. Conduct of the war would have been much more difficult (some, at the time, said impossible) without the bases. Ship replenishment and refit, air force training and transit, munitions storage, and crew rest would all have been more awkward and inefficient some 1,500 miles farther from the battle.

Without our defense relationships, it would also have been even more difficult to secure Philippine participation in the Indochina effort. United States policy, as we all recall, emphasized multilateral, particularly Asian, aspects of the war. Participation had been controversial in the Philippines for reasons of both principle and cost, and few Americans at the time questioned the suitability of subvention to ensure the dispatch of medical and engineering teams.

There were, however, many problems. Working-level negotiations for modernization of the bases agreement faltered over questions that by now seem rather minor and most of which had been easily conceded by the United States in arrangements for the use of bases in Thailand. These included aspects of criminal jurisdiction, immigration control, and taxation—all of which could have been swept away at minor cost to enduring American interests. Absent a solution, the pre-martial law years witnessed recurring labor difficulties and sharp issues about base security and criminal jurisdiction. And later, allegations of financial irregularities blurred somewhat the record of Philippine participation in Vietnam.

A second, emerging American interest in the security field concerned the Association of Southeast Asian Nations (ASEAN), which American policy strongly though quietly supported. ASEAN was then a tender plant, nourished by the goodwill of many, and, in contrast to earlier regional cooperation initiatives, rooted in strong personal rapport and trust between its principal founders, Indonesia's Adam Malik and Thailand's Thanat Khoman. Without any inclination at that stage toward military cooperation within ASEAN, its leaders recognized the need for a security umbrella and looked to the United States to continue to provide it. Maintenance of a credible deterrent and of stability in the region would have been impossible in the short run without the Philippine bases.

Even so, the credibility of United States deterrent strength deteriorated. The Filipinos had been edging toward the establishment of relations with the People's Republic of China and, forty years behind the United States, with the Soviet Union; but the Philippine government and people, along with other Asians, seemed stunned by the American opening to China in 1971. Surprise made the shock more acute, especially when news of the Kissinger visit to Beijing broke on the opening day of the annual ministerial meeting of the old Asian and Pacific Council (ASPAC), presided over in Manila by Carlos Romulo —who was generally viewed by the other Asians as an outlet for, or at least an informed interpreter of, American policy.

But it was more than that. Announcement of the Nixon Doctrine had sent a tremor through the Philippines as through the rest of the region. The prospect that the American role would be reduced to maintenance of the strategic umbrella, relying on friendly nations to carry the primary load in assuring their own internal and external security, intensified Philippine interest in all aspects of our defense relationship —the mutual defense treaty, the mutual defense assistance program, and the duration and content of the bases agreement—as well as the Southeast Asia Treaty Organization (SEATO). These developments revived an intermittent dialogue on security policy and regional as well as bilateral relations that has continued to the present. And the bottom line for many Filipinos was the bases, which represented some 25,000 jobs and the annual injection of some $300 million into the Philippine economy.

There was no appreciable difference in attitude toward security policy for the Philippines between United States officials in Manila and in Washington. But there were voices of disagreement at each end of the line, with views varying in rather direct relationship to the holder's attitudes toward the Indochina war and a proper postwar Southeast Asian policy. Some Americans (as well as some Filipinos) questioned whether the bases would remain necessary or appropriate. Some military planners considered that growing Soviet and American interest in the Indian Ocean added a new element to the important historical functions of the bases.

Similar differences emerged within the Philippine polity. Marcos said in 1971, "While I am president, the Philippines will be a friendly ally." But some politicians and nongovernment figures began to advocate deliberate distancing from the United States—a reflection of what they saw as American moves toward disengagement. Except for the volatile student community and opposition politicians, for many of whom criticizing the American relationship was a convenient device for attacking Marcos, however, Filipinos seemed to retain their attitudes of affection for Americans and their excessive zeal to follow American folkways in many—not always the most laudable—fields.

A second general American objective in the pre-martial law period was to continue to contribute to Philippine economic development and to support Filipinos in moves toward greater political and economic democracy. A mix of motives underlay these goals: (a) our general stress on development in the Third World; (b) a wish to continue to play our part in progress that had been interrupted by World War II and the Philippine desire for speedy independence; and (c) pursuit of trade and investment opportunities.

Basic to the Philippine-United States relationship was the beneficial two-way market access provided under the Laurel-Langley Agreement and special related arrangements. Two-way trade had reached $800 million. But Laurel-Langley was due to expire after 1973, and early in the second Marcos term the United States began steps to persuade both the American business community and Philippine authorities of the need to arrange a smooth transition to a successor regime—through a treaty of friendship, commerce and navigation (FCN) or a simple treaty of amity and economic relations, under which the Philippines would have access to the United States market on a basis similar to that of other developing nations. The educational and preparatory effort consumed a great deal of time and effort in the ensuing years.

In addition to several complementary unilateral programs—grant developmental aid, technical assistance, P.L. 480 commodity programs, and Export-Import Bank loans—the United States was the largest single contributor to both the World Bank (IBRD) program and the increasingly important Asian Development Bank (ADB). Between them, the two banks greatly enhanced available resources including, significantly, sound fiscal and economic advice.

Those who were involved in the field, as well as policymakers in Washington, considered the infusion of private capital a major benefit, side by side with government efforts. American private investment reached a billion dollars, in such traditional areas as shipping, mining, and agriculture but also in banking, insurance, and high-technology areas. The United States Mission supported these activities though recognizing that some Filipinos and outsiders viewed certain enterprises—particularly plantation agriculture—as exploitive. I considered the existence of company housing, stores, schools, clinics, and credit institutions less significant than the press of people who wished to move onto, rather than away from, these plantations. Schooling, medical care, and physical security were better than in surrounding barrios; I was impressed by one "company" health center staffed by nursing sisters that featured a bravely painted sign: "Family Planning Clinic."

The United States Diplomatic Mission was one of the largest in the world (450 Americans and 1,500 national employees) and represented more than twenty government departments and agencies—several of which had regional responsibilities. There were socially and economically important programs in drug enforcement, social security and veteran-benefit distributions, a widely dispersed Peace Corps contingent, and many more. Those programs that involved travel or residence in outlying provinces had special value in the overall scheme of things, due to the ethnically and linguistically fractured characteristics of the archipelagic Philippine Republic.

It was impossible for official Americans to avoid a high posture, because Filipinos propelled them forward—in social settings, in charitable endeavors and, unfortunately, even in activities heavily accented with politics, when they could. The American ambassador to the Philippines was considered by Filipinos to be one of the most important persons in the country, and he deliberately sought to limit presidential contacts of the sort that would attract widespread attention or that were plainly political. Any presidential activity is apt to have a political component, but we tried to eschew those that were dominantly so. At the same time, we thought travel at all levels was important—not only to know people and conditions, as in any country of diplomatic assignment, but because Filipinos enjoyed it and wanted us to share in their lives. In that sense, officials complemented the substantial working American presence in business, education, the professions, and missionary activity. Almost all of this was good, although I regretted the large number of foreign parish clergy, because it seemed to signal the failure of the heavily Catholic Filipino population to produce enough of their own priests and nuns.

To sum up the situation, the mood, and the policy lines during the pre-martial law period, it may be useful to recall several sharp ambivalences in Filipino attitudes: complaints of too much direct American economic involvement but also of too little investment; criticism of the large military presence and its social consequences (though reductions were beginning from the Vietnam high), but anxiety also about the extent and reliability of defense guarantees; chafing under American paternalism, but simultaneous longing for frequent and tangible evidence of American affection. There were countervailing ambivalences on the American side: a desire to be involved and helpful, but distress and disgust with the corruption and waste that afflicted or threatened even some of the best-conceived programs; a conscious wish to attenuate the historic "special relationship," but recognition of the numerous aspects of Filipino life in which help was still needed; disenchantment with the stand-off between the Philippine executive and congress and with the sometimes-irresponsible posturing of the constitutional convention—and concern about increasing indications that Marcos intended to prolong his tenure beyond the constitutional limit in 1973—but at the same time a judgment that Marcos was more likely than other visible leaders (including Aquino, who by mid-1972 was increasingly viewed as a maverick even within the Liberal party) to be able to help the country progress.

MARTIAL LAW AND ITS IMPACT ON AMERICAN POLICY AND ACTION

The declaration of martial law on September 22, 1972, was a tactical but not a strategic surprise. Rumored and occasionally threatened by Marcos for months, and favored by some of the technocrats as a way to get on with reform, the declaration was sprung after a series of crescendoing acts of violence. Many of these were genuine and vicious, in contrast to the attack on Defense Secretary Ponce Enrile, which was suspicious at the time and since acknowledged to have been staged. Marcos received neither encouragement nor tacit approval from or through the embassy in Manila. To the contrary, stories that were floated in Manila saying that Ambassador Henry A. Byroade had been privy to Marcos's decision were incorrect. He had repeatedly gone as far as a foreigner could to paint a discouraging picture of the probable negative reaction, within and outside the Philippines and especially in the United States Congress, to what officially remained only a hypothetical possibility. If there was some direct communication between the White House and Marcos, as some have alleged, the ambassador had no knowledge of it. Our surmise in Manila afterward was that Marcos had deliberately refrained from privately signaling his intent in order to avoid any confrontation.

It is also important to one's image of the events of early 1986 and to our purpose here of anticipating policy issues to recall the initial actions after the declaration of martial law and how they were greeted by Filipinos, foreign residents, and friendly governments. "Martial law" was probably a misnomer. In the initial period, the army went back to barracks, except for its responsibility for conducting trials of those detained before military tribunals and for continuing anti-insurgent efforts. Controls, which in fact were minimal, were applied by the civil police and by the Philippine constabulary—the latter at that time a small force of lightly armed units with internal-security functions, similar to the French gendarmerie.

Martial law was chosen by Marcos as a control device because it was a constitutionally sanctioned route to his principal objective: authority to suspend the privilege of the writ of habeas corpus and thus to detain active or too-vocal regime opponents as well as suspected subversives without the delays of due process. The American image of martial law, with tanks in the streets and the displacement of civilian politicians and executive managers by the military, is inapt. There was, thus, little comparison with the conditions that followed a declaration of martial law in the Republic of Korea soon afterward. Marcos's opponents— those politicians or journalists who declined to knuckle under to the severely curtailed right of public discussion of public policy—and well-documented criminals were quickly affected. In the first months, some 500 Filipinos went summarily to jail, and their supporters and foreign friends were dismayed; most of the rest of the country, at first, breathed deeply in relief.

Except for those under arrest and those who feared it, the changes in lifestyle were minor. The midnight to four o'clock curfew was welcomed by many, who could leave the incessant parties in time for their drivers (and *their* bus drivers) to get home in time. The young in heart stayed through till morning in clubs and casinos. Those who placed the highest value on free expression and/or mischievous gossip were disturbed, but General Romulo was probably right when he observed that the average Filipino would rather have security and a full belly than a choice among eighteen daily newspapers.

The effects of the decree were swift, however, and evident to almost everyone. Farmers stopped taking turns watching the barrio carabao all night out of fear they would be stolen. Crime statistics dropped dramatically. The government claim to have collected a half million illegal firearms was probably exaggerated, but the piles were huge; and the cattle rancher whose estate had been guarded by his private tank—only the most dramatic example of landlord lawlessness—was put out of business. The physical condition of Manila and provincial cities improved, and bureaucratic performance in many fields was at least temporarily spruced up. A number of police and constabulary personnel were investigated and charged, and some were punished for past transgressions.

The political atmosphere also changed dramatically, however. Deprived of access to the media, opposition members of congress and others became ineffectual. The constitutional convention, which Marcos had already controlled, became more efficient in completing its work, including settlement on the transitory provisions that became the vehicle for the extension of his power.

It was embarrassing when some private American businessmen rose to congratulate Marcos publicly for his seizure of power. United States officials nevertheless shared their hopes for greater predictability in governmental action and for improved economic performance. Foreign diplomats and private observers shared our judgment that the vast majority of Filipinos initially welcomed the stabilization and tranquillity that followed the declaration of martial law.

The Marcos regime set out to elaborate the reform program that the technocrats had developed and to which his administration had already been committed but that too frequently had been undercut or obstructed by entrenched economic and family-group interests. Skeptics doubted his sincerity, labeling Marcos first among the oligarchs who were the targets of reform. Many considered the plans to be too ambitious even if well intended. But the objectives addressed the real problems:

- Peace and order
- Increased investment and production

- Land reform, beginning with grants to tenant rice farmers
- Government reorganization
- Educational reform to emphasize economic development
- Fair labor policies
- Adequate health and social services

Many of these goals became the subjects of prescriptive presidential orders in the ensuing months. Many would require injections of economic or technical aid from donor governments or the international lending institutions, and these were to become the United States-Philippine agenda.

How did the martial law regime affect the range of policies summarized in the first section of this paper? It affected the tone of the dialogue. For a time it altered American public behavior, leading to a kind of standing apart. It led to some reexamination of existing programs and more careful scrutiny of new proposals, during which there was understandably some discernibly greater caution in Washington than in the mission in Manila, but no dispute arose over goals. Despite misgivings, the embassy favored continuing to do business with Marcos, but more directly with the technocrats, and this was the course followed. After a time, the course of American policy continued without significant change of direction, though with new program content in response to Philippine initiatives. Policy goals had been directed not to support of the Marcos administration, but to the benefit of the Filipino people and, of course, to American security interests.

The first tangible demonstration of policy continuity appeared in the relief and rehabilitation efforts after the catastrophic flooding that had preceded and may have contributed to the martial law decision. In July, 180 inches of rain had fallen in thirty days—inundating the entire Luzon plain, changing the course of rivers and ruining agricultural land with silt, and menacing millions of people and their animals. The Philippine economy and the government's mandate were shaken to the foundations. American diplomatic wives had worked alongside Imelda Marcos and her coterie of socialite ladies stuffing rice and bread from big sacks into small bags for helicopter delivery and airdrop. Such activities were not controversial to anyone. The United States ultimately gave transportation and commodities totaling $80 million.

In Washington and Manila, United States officials refrained from publicly characterizing the martial law regime and, therefore, from any endorsement. United States Mission officials kept lower profiles. A brief statement by Vice President Agnew during a four-hour stopover during travel throughout Southeast Asia in February 1973 contained no endorsement, and I recall none until March 1973, when Assistant Secretary for East Asian Affairs Marshall Green told Reuters in an interview, "We support Marcos." This affirmation sustained the ongoing work of diplomatic and foreign-assistance officials with the technocrat ministers and their staffs.

Even then it was muted endorsement. In his annual policy report in April, the secretary of state noted that the Republic of the Philippines was moving away from the prior special relationship, but averred that the United States "will continue to contribute to development and security programs." Recalling the unrest and violence of 1972, with the flood and, later, severe drought in the southern corn belt, he welcomed the stress in the martial law program on land reform, reform of the civil service and armed forces, and the drive against corruption and crime, including narcotics. The report approvingly noted Philippine participation in expanding ASEAN activities as well as continued support for SEATO.

Despite the promise of the regime's declarative statements, there was uncertainty and some discomfort in workaday efforts to support the reform programs. Marcos had referred to his method as a "revolution from the center" and, more than once, as "constitutional authoritarianism." Each phrase was ambiguous enough to permit embellishment by both admirers and detractors. Some similarities to other dictatorships were disturbing, and particularly disturbing to Americans after the period of colonial tutelage. The martial law regime had, generally speaking, failed to attract Filipino academics, and there were three obvious power centers:

- presidential (including the military, which followed out of personal loyalty and/or the constitutional principle of subordination to established civilian authority, and the technocrats);
- political (regionally influential oppositionists and dissenters); and
- economic (the entrenched oligarchs and some American business interests).

On the other hand, there was an extensive Filipino history of resilience against inadequate administrative performance, injustice, and corruption. Well into the mid-1970s, Marcos and his coalition of modernizing forces offered the best discernible chance for progress toward the goals of most Filipinos and toward American policy preferences.

United States military activities and force levels were geared to post-Vietnam regional strategy, that is, somewhat downward. Total security assistance to the Philippines gradually increased under the stimulus of the seriously eroded security situation in southern Muslim areas. Economic grant and loan assistance concentrated on support for land reform, population planning, power development and rural electrification, and modernization of economic management. Cultural exchanges and a somewhat reduced Peace Corps effort continued.

By the mid-1970s the portents were definitely mixed and could easily have presented a policy dilemma. The ostentatious lifestyle of Malacanang increasingly offended foreigners and exceeded the tolerance of Filipinos (in common with many other cultures) for a degree of splendor at the top. Some of the technocrats left and others were sent away. Military performance did not improve enough, and some of the anticorruption efforts backslid. More and more businessmen, officials, and military officers were allowed to siphon off shares from public expenditures and from the earnings of controlled public and private enterprises—forming the expanding cadre of "crony capitalism."

Given the historic and future American stake in the Philippines, however, it seemed prudent, Washington and Manila agreed, to emphasize the positive, to continue program support but noticeably without political enthusiasm. This is the legacy, and perhaps the lesson, of the pre- and immediate post-martial law period.

28

Moments of Truth in Philippine-American Relations: The Carter Years

Lee T. Stull

There follows a preliminary attempt to look ahead to the maturation of United States-Philippines relations based largely on the perspective of 1975 to 1978, when the author was deputy chief of mission at the United States embassy in Manila. During this period most, if not all, salient issues and trends of the current crisis in the Philippines were evident, voiced, and passed over in the customary inertia of state.

There are moments in the life of nations as of individuals when circumstances not necessarily new are seen in a new light, illuminating turning points, freshening insights, and opening options. Responses are neither inevitable nor unpredictable. The interrelated crises of Philippine nationalism and Philippine-American relations have been long coming. They might not have erupted at all, or in very different form, were it not for the economic, political, and moral injury wreaked upon the Philippine nation over the past decade. Disillusionment of the Philippine middle class, business and professional; distress of impoverished farmers; disgust of church leaders, educators, and more than a few soldiers were heightened by the assassination of Benigno Aquino and climaxed by the stealing of a decisive election from his widow. Something had to happen and did. Now the prospect is protracted struggle to shape the political and economic future of the Philippines. The United States needs to understand that struggle and to recognize and defend its stake in that future.

THE SETTING

To understand where to go, it helps to remember where we have been. The Philippines and the United States have a long and much-scrambled history. It is basic to recognize that there are widely different perceptions in each country about that history and its implications.

Most Americans assume that the United States

- liberated the Philippines from the Spanish and again from the Japanese,
- tutored and generously assisted the Philippine people until they graduated into independence, and
- lived happily together ever after, until recently, in a beneficial, special relationship.

Significant numbers of influential Filipinos think that the United States:

- hijacked their revolution in 1898,
- left them defenseless in World War II, to return with parsimonious relief and demands for special privilege, and
- failed generally to appreciate and give them their due.

The subliminal question is: "How much better off might the Philippines have been if the Americans had never come?" An equally trenchant one is: "How much better off might the Americans have been:

- if President McKinley had not talked to God?
- if Teddy Roosevelt had not been secretary of the navy?
- if Admiral Dewey had gotten lost?
- if the resolution in the United States Congress against annexing the Philippines had received two fewer votes, and been defeated?"

Such musings underline the differing and sometimes contradictory perceptions that inform Filipinos and Americans. Both certainly agree that roughly the periods 1898 to 1903 and 1941 to 1946 were fateful junctures with lasting implications for their relations. We are now at yet a third such juncture, of comparable long-run impact. For there can be little doubt that the restructuring of Philippine-American relations, conceptually and concretely, over the next few years, will shape their quality through the turn of the century.

The Philippine-American special relationship rests upon its psychological dimension, upon the personal, emotional, human experiences of fifty years of colonialism, four years of World War II, and forty subsequent years of intensive interaction. "Which two other nations could be closer than America and the Philippines?" a well-known Philippine politician asked, and answered that "the interweaving of our histories has been so powerful and lasting that we cannot tell the story of our own people without telling also part of your own." It is right that Filipinos and Americans should recall their history of common sacrifices and achievement. But we should not allow such recollections to obscure untoward dependencies and inequities; and we should not permit the past to inhibit the development of a more truly mutual, self-respecting, and beneficial future relationship.

A president of the University of the Philippines characterized the Philippine-American association as "too close for comfort and too special for self-respect." Key concepts helpful to understanding the Philippine-American complexity are transition and interpenetration. Transition seems to be particularly apt in the current revolutionary environment as we reexamine Philippine-American relationships characterized by:

- historical transition in the interpretation of the Philippine-American experience,
- strategic transition in the Pacific Basin and the perception of Sino-Soviet and regional communist preoccupations,
- political transition from "constitutional authoritarianism" to participatory democracy,
- psychological transition from "little brown brother" and "Made in U.S.A." to self-identity—national, regional, and Asian,
- economic transition from privileged foreign and capital-intensive import substitution to people-intensive agroindustrial development.

There is also much continuity shaping and limiting change in an abiding network of expectations and obligations derived from the Philippine-American association over ninety years. This interpenetration is the other key and it includes such manifestations as:

- more than a million Philippine immigrants in the United States, including 25,000 doctors and nurses,
- scores of thousands of Americans resident in the Philippines, including 30,000 United States military personnel and their dependents,

- major air and naval bases for United States forces, which employ some 40,000 Philippine civilians and generate $500 million annually in direct and indirect benefits,
- half a million Filipino-American veterans with disbursements since World War II totaling significantly more than $2 billion.

This makes the United States a major attraction, point of reference, and easy target in the Philippines. It also makes for vestiges of dependency, of imbalance in scale, of lack of symmetry in the Philippine-American relationship that can be politically volatile and psychologically wearing.

HUMAN RIGHTS

Already by 1977, the wear and tear of Philippine-American interaction was increasingly evident across a range of interrelated issues, among which human rights and military bases figured large. There may have been only two people in the United States government at that time who really believed in human-rights diplomacy. One was the president of the United States, and he soon evidenced a lack of staying power and of the close attention necessary to motivate and control an apathetic bureaucracy.

In the Philippines, Ferdinand Marcos, who had successfully manipulated several previous American administrations, did not at first know what to make of the new policy. He, of course, was aware of the central importance of human rights in American political thought and constitutional law, and perhaps assumed that he might have to take seriously a president who, as a candidate, stated that he would link American friendship and support to a nation's respect for the human rights of its people. Then, too, there was President Carter's inaugural pledge that, "Because we are free, we cannot be indifferent to the fate of freedom elsewhere. . . . Our commitment to human rights must be absolute."

Accordingly, the American embassy, early in 1977, initiated a concerted effort to persuade Marcos that he should take seriously the American rediscovery, renewal, and reassertion of human-rights policy. These efforts included:

- several in-depth discussions with Marcos setting forth the moral and philosophical importance of human rights in the thinking of the new president, noting the strong support for human rights among key American public-opinion and legislative groups, and concluding that it was our respectful duty to observe that, if Marcos wanted to get along with the new administration, he might improve the human-rights environment in the Philippines;

- confirming in the above discussions embassy knowledge of various recent and egregious human-rights violations to imply that we were well informed about such violations generally;
- making several measuredly strong speeches on human rights to selective conveyor audiences (American Legion, Navy League, Defense Educators);
- maintaining extended contact with the spectrum of opposition, religious, and other activists for human rights, and advocating and programming private meetings of Vice President Mondale with those personages during his visit to Manila in April 1978;
- privately over luncheon presenting to, and discussing with, Mrs. Marcos a human-rights action plan for study and possible implementation as appropriate;
- mounting major fence-mending initiatives, including revival of Philippine-American Friendship Day, with President and Mrs. Marcos as guests of honor, and otherwise seeking to make the firm human-rights dialogue palatable.

It was obvious that the embassy could not hope to identify, let alone effect the release of, thousands of political detainees, and that we could not reform piecemeal the system of oppression established over many years. We could, however, seek to motivate Marcos in his own interest to reform, or at least mitigate, what he himself had created. This we set out to do, with little guidance other than the high-level rhetoric already cited.

There were early results, but in late May Washington backed down from an advertised threat to question an $18 million International Bank for Reconstruction and Development (IBRD) loan to the Philippines because of fresh allegations of severe torture. By late June, Washington was exhibiting nervousness about even the phased and deliberate human-rights approach being pursued by the embassy. Marcos, reading the signs, was able to conclude, only six months into the new administration, that he could be reasonably confident of deflecting the American human-rights thrust with little more than the cosmetic changes of which he was a master. Thereafter, when we cited cases in the private office of the president, he would summon General Ver from behind the curtains to witness at stiff attention, feign surprise, and hurry off "to set things right."

This is not to say that human-rights diplomacy was without significance. In the beginning, at least, that policy rang alarm bells in the presidential palace. Embassy representatives were personally invited by Marcos to visit a tortured nun, and did so. Hundreds of detainees reportedly were released at our instigation. As late as April 1978, Marcos, while still at the airport following the departure of Vice President Mondale, summarily ordered the immediate release of numerous opposition activists arrested during the vice-president's visit. The compelling argument then was that such arrests invited unfavorable foreign press. Marcos listened and acted—when he believed it was in his interests to do so. There also probably was some easing of detention conditions, certainly for Ninoy Aquino, who later was permitted to leave the Philippines for medical treatment. Elections, perhaps better than none, were held. A credible signal of hope that Americans cared was sent to the growing cadres of active and silent opposition. We might have done it earlier and better, but what was done from 1977 to 1978 to reach out to the Philippine people in distress was perhaps useful to the more discrete, subtle, and effective American reaction to events in 1985 and 1986.

MILITARY BASES

It was difficult to maximize human-rights initiatives in 1977 and 1978 because of Washington's concurrent preoccupation with the United States military bases in the Philippines. Policymakers on both sides labored under the misguided notion that the choices could be reduced to Marcos or communism and democracy or the bases. The real issue was, and remains, democracy and the bases, without Marcos and without communism. For it was clear that in the long run it would not be Marcos but the emerging opposition that would decide about the military bases, and in the short run Marcos had no practical alternative but to maintain the existing agreement while manipulating maximum benefit from the United States for doing so. This he had managed most skillfully and to great personal advantage for more than ten years.

United States military bases in the Philippines are major repair facilities, technical-training centers, subcontractors, and, as we have seen, foreign-currency generators of extraordinary importance to the Philippine economy. Marcos was not about to kill the golden bases. What might have killed the bases, however, was the violence, radicalism, and prospective civil war brewing even then. History is prologue and not mere hindsight. By the period 1977 to 78, Marcos's "kleptocracy" was manifest and middle-class bitterness evident. Church leaders were alarmed, military officers were muttering, and the New Peoples Army was expanding.[1]

As early as President Ford's much-sought state visit to Manila in December 1975, Marcos asked him and accompanying Secretary Kissinger for discussion and possible renegotiation of the Philippine-United States military bases agreement (to run until 1991). Through 1976, there were extensive negotiations to write, in effect, a new bases agreement. Principal issues were the perennial ones of sovereignty, jurisdiction, and security; that is, issues of nationalism and, of course, money. Human rights did not figure. A final end-of-term meeting failed to reach agreement despite a reported Kissinger offer of $1 billion over five years as quid pro quo. Marcos then shifted his focus to doing better with the next administration. Meanwhile, Philippine public pressures against the American presence increased, in a variety of forms—from allegations of imperial style at the American embassy to charges of insulting treatment in the visa line at the American consulate general. Also, resumption of base negotiations in September 1977 was accompanied by a series of incidents at those bases involving United States servicemen and Filipinos. These incidents were featured in the Manila press and exploited by the Philippine government to bolster its negotiating position. A joint task force was organized by both governments to deal with such incidents and other base-related issues in an effort to improve the negotiating environment. Thereafter, both sides began anew to discuss the issues of sovereignty, jurisdiction, security, and money. By late 1978, a substantial amendment to the previous agreement conceded the forms and appearance of management while protecting the substance of operational control. And so it went—an interrelated dialogue of nationalism and dollars within and between governments and their constituencies.

[1]The 1977 and 1978 files of the Department of State are filled with reports in this vein.

ASSISTANCE

Related issues of importance during the 1977 to 1978 period included the philosophy and composition, as well as the amount, of economic and military assistance. Was it assistance or was it rental for military real estate? Were the kinds of hardware, technology, and training appropriate to the principal perceived threat of two insurrections: one Maoist/Marxist, then simmering in the north, and the other a chronic Muslim insurrection then under cease-fire in the south? Large sums were involved; how much was enough? Issues were raised and unresolved. (Early in 1978, for example, the American embassy recommended increasing the economic content of military assistance by making funds more fungible and reducing big-ticket military hardware.)

Economically, a development miracle was predicted for the Philippines from the late 1970s. By then, however, the Marcos regime was reexporting multiples of foreign assistance into private accounts, and fast losing the support of the most important civilian elements in Philippine society. Any assistance program that did not address such underlying issues was bound to fail, and did.

> The real problem and the real solutions for the Philippines and the Philippine ecology lie, it seems to me, not so much between the United States and the Philippines as within the Philippines itself. The necessity clearly exists to come to grips with such questions as population, conservation of resources, distribution of income, energy policies—fundamental issues. Whether the Philippine management will do the necessary and push the "economic miracle of Manila" out into the provinces in the form of middle-level technology, labor-intensive for farm boys, and thereby realize an all-Philippine miracle, remains to be seen.[2]

It didn't happen, of course. Rather, migrants from rural misery crowded more than a million strong, under increasingly appalling conditions, into the 250 slums of metro-Manila. "Economic develop-

[2]Remarks by charge d'affaires concerning the economic ecology of the Philippines at the annual meeting of the board of directors of the Manufacturers Hanover Trust Company, Manila, May 16, 1977.

ment is the best human rights," United States Agency for International Development (USAID) representatives used to say, and they had a point.

One memorable development scene from the late 1970s: Arkansas engineers using bulldozers constructed oversize rice paddies in the Philippines, intended for seeding by aircraft, while unemployed laborers watched.

OTHERS

There were other issues, of course—reliability of our defense commitment; areas of disputed sovereignty and responsibility; the Spratly Islands and Reed bank, where an American company was drilling for oil; issues of the Third World. One nonissue that deserved to be treated with some importance was the scale of the United States government's presence there. Simply put, we had too many people. With twenty-three United States government agencies and arguably the largest diplomatic mission in the world, our presence was much too cumbersome. A major effort was made, initially encouraged at high levels in the State Department, to reduce staff and dismantle colonial trappings, but without follow-through and with minimal effect.

Then there was ex-president of the Philippines Diosadado Macapagal, a vocal opposition spokesman and author of a critical tome, *Democracy in the Philippines*, who sought political asylum at the American embassy in anticipation of arrest and remained as a guest until assurance of his safety could be obtained from Foreign Minister Romulo. The incident itself was of little moment, but it makes an important point about United States policy in the Philippines from 1976 to 1978: that the American embassy, for all its limitations during that period, was in contact, often close contact, with a variety of actual and potential members of the Philippine opposition—political, religious, economic, intellectual, and military.[3,4,5] The common ground usually

---

[3]Aquino, before his fateful return to the Philippines, told the author that he owed the circumstances of his reprieve, and indeed his very life, to United States pressures on his behalf.

[4]Cardinal Sin manifested his appreciation for the human-rights efforts of the embassy by hosting an unprecedented farewell dinner, as did also the usually fragmented opposition.

[5]Principled senior military officers, in an especially difficult position, maintained close personal relations throughout.

was human rights. To those Filipinos, human-rights diplomacy was a valued sign of American concern and a source of hope. Subsequently, many of the same people were in the forefront of the Philippine people's revolution. Several lead the Philippine government today.

IN SUM

If the years 1976 to 1978 represented a period when most issues and trends of the gathering crisis in the Philippines already were evident, then the recollection that those evidences were largely ignored at the time counsels a measure of humility concerning the American capacity to understand at the policy level what is transpiring in the Philippines, what is really required there, and how we might most effectively respond. The symbiotic Philippine-American association rewards close and discriminating analysis and punishes inattention and neglect. There has been much of both. Attention spans can be short, priorities different, and disproportions in scale great.

Recently a national news magazine carried a cover story about Mrs. Aquino entitled "Now for the Hard Part." The riveting political drama of early 1986 in the Philippines has introduced a far-reaching social, military, and, especially, economic crisis comparable in scale, duration, and impact to the American conquest at the turn of the century and to the trauma of Japanese occupation in World War II. We must recognize the psychological liberation and end to self-colonialization of the Philippine people's revolution. We should expect more vigorous Philippine nationalism and aspirations for greater equity. We need to respond sensitively to this powerful revival of democratic energy following the political cynicism of the Marcos era. And we might as well enjoy the current resurgence of pro-American sentiment while it lasts.

President Reagan is profoundly correct that it is up to the Philippine people to shape their future. It is their business, their responsibility, and their opportunity. The United States, however, is inescapably part of both the problem and the solution. History wills it. We wish to treat the Philippines as a respected and equal sovereign nation. Respect they certainly have earned; sovereign they indeed are. Equal? There's the rub: how to respond sympathetically and effectively across the many differences in scale and culture. Most Americans would agree that the Philippines must lead in shaping its own priorities, programs, and institutions. As the Filipinos proceed to do so, we Americans may think that we have much to contribute conceptually and prescriptively to the resolution of their problems. However, the American record throughout the 1970s would suggest otherwise. During that period, most of the American policy establishment was generally sanguine about the achievements of the Marcos regime. One need only recall the uncritical accommodation to martial law, the streams of high-level political and military visitations, the glowing reports of World Bank president MacNamara, of AID and the international banking community. American misperceptions were almost inherent:

- We believed what we wanted to believe especially as it might relate to the military bases.
- Almost nobody wanted to question conventional wisdom, to dig down to bedrock interests and rethink policy.
- Our sense of underlying trends was impeded by preoccupations with stability and by limited contacts with such harbingers of change as university youth, local churchmen, disaffected military, and, increasingly, opposition and dissident groups.
- We were preoccupied with getting our message across, mostly in regard to short-term goals in Vietnam, the UN, ASEAN, etc.
- As a corollary of the above, we were not listening, certainly not listening with the necessary attention and sensitivity.

Modern democratic, bureaucratic government may be largely incapable of transcending laundry-list policy revision in the absence of immediate crisis. But we need to try harder in the face of a protracted crisis in the Philippines, where the best American policy response might well be:

- to avoid crowding the new Philippine government with United States initiatives and eager American counselors;
- to allow the Filipinos to formulate their own plans and set their own priorities while we focus on mechanisms for allocating international resources and alleviating external pressures;
- to be sensitive to the mitigation of fundamental Philippine problems that are seemingly beyond resolution—for example: expanding agricultural proletariat, rapid population growth, dependency relations, and extreme poverty (all warranting emergency attention on political as well as humanitarian grounds);
- to be careful not to distort again the Philippine policy-formulation

and decision-making process with the presence and prospect of excessive American resources.

We want United States influence and resources to facilitate necessary reforms, not to avoid them, and to support independence, not to perpetuate dependency.

Regarding United States military bases in the Philippines:

- We should talk as little as possible at this time, since the subject is emotionally loaded, and both sides need to reassess longer-term interests in changing circumstances.
- We should, however, think a great deal about those bases quietly and in depth, to include possible modifications in such marginal privileges and practices as admissions policy at the American golf course in Bagio and guard-dog management around Clark Air Force Base, and to press the search for significant changes in strategic perception. For example, most Pacific Rim countries, including Japan and the People's Republic of China, favor maintaining the strategic presence at Subic Bay and Clark Airfield. This perception of interests could include the Philippines to the extent they recognize the economic benefits, the strategic value, and the worth of regional consensus.

Predictably, the Philippines will need much assistance from the Pacific Rim countries, including the United States, over the next years. Concurrently, the Philippines will be in a position to make a significant reciprocal contribution to security in the region by continuing those bases on Philippine soil. Call it a mutual debt of gratitude, *utang na loob*; rename the bases Philippine Pacific Security Resources; and insulate them from the issues and differences of economic and military assistance.

In sum, the United States, however inadvertently and briefly, pursued a low-cost human-rights policy during the late 1970s that succeeded in conveying a message of concern and hope to then-opposition, now-ruling elements in the Philippines. The lesson: soft policies can have durable results. As Philippine ambassador Pelaezes put it in Washington recently, "It is important to the Philippines to know that human rights and social justice still matter in United States policy."[6]

[6]Remarks by Ambassador Emmanuel Pelaez at the conference on the "Crisis in the Philippines" of the Washington Institute, April 30-May 1, 1986, Washington, D.C.

29

United States-Philippine Relations in the 1980s

John F. Maisto*

First of all, I'd like to say that there's an old Foreign Service tradition that the youngest Foreign Service officer present in the group picks up the tab for lunch or for dinner. I'm happy that I don't have to pick up a tab, but I feel that I am the youngest here amid a great group of former ambassadors, DCMs, and political officers, and it's really a privilege.

I'm going to talk about U.S. policy toward the Philippines from 1981 to May 1986. I'd like to start with the focus that the new administration, elected in November 1980, brought to Southeast Asia policy. That focus was simple and straightforward. It can be summed up as follows.

In Southeast Asia the new administration sought to strengthen our relations with our friends and allies. In the first months of Reagan administration policy toward the Philippines this effort included visits of U.S. officials such as the secretary of defense and other highly placed government officials and clear statements of reaffirmation of treaty commitments. Also, it involved state visits to the United States by the five chiefs of state or heads of government of all five ASEAN nations. These visits took place between 1981 and 1983, including the state visit of President Marcos in September 1982. The most important task in bilateral relations in 1981 and 1982 was preparation for the five-year review of our military bases agreement, which took place in 1983.

In turn, this assumption of a new administration in Washington was planned for by President Marcos. He announced the lifting of martial law on January 17, 1981. We should recall that there were two events in early 1981 of political importance to the Marcos government: President Reagan's inauguration January 20 and Pope John Paul II's

---

*The opinions expressed in this chapter are the personal views of the author and not necessarily those of the Department of State.

visit in February. Both events clearly figured in the Marcos decision to end martial law.

Subsequently, President Marcos also announced he was seeking a new constitutional order in the Philippines. By midyear, there was constitutional change—back to a strong presidential system, with a presidential election and inauguration. The name of the game in the first months of the Marcos administration was to project a sense of movement, a change, action toward, in the jargon of that time, "political normalization." Looking back, that policy served the Marcos administration well, not only in terms of its relationship with the United States but also in terms of Marcos's manipulation of the internal political scene.

I remember clearly the last six months of 1981, in which the political opposition in Manila (I was stationed there) was in the doldrums. They didn't quite know how to deal with this new phenomenon. Remember, they had thought very seriously about contesting the 1981 presidential election, but then decided not to. That was a very controversial issue among the opposition; there were very strong arguments for and against. It was the influence of former senator Gerry Rojas that, in the end, carried the policy day for the opposition. That political decision rested on the principle of refusing to provide Marcos a legitimating electoral process.

In 1982, U.S. policy toward the Philippines was focused on the review of the military bases agreement that was to begin in 1983. One event of importance that year in this regard was the state visit, the objective of which was to underline the bilateral relationship and the alliance, that is, to set the stage for the 1983 review.

There was a collateral objective, too: human rights. It was a low-key, quiet diplomacy, human-rights objective, the thrust of which was to attempt to convince the Marcos government that an improved human-rights record and true political normalization were in its best political interests. As one who was on the scene there, I can assure you that day by day and case by case our interest in the human-rights area in the 1980s in the Philippines continued to be strong.

The 1983 military bases agreement review took place in a record seven weeks. The result was quite acceptable to the United States overall. It was a workmanlike negotiation, behind closed doors and quiet. It avoided extraneous issues. The compensation package agreed to was for $900 million in military and economic assistance over five years. The discussions concerning the compensation issue usually continue until the end of a negotiation, and it is often the toughest issue to work out.

Following the completion of the bases review in June 1983, the United States focus on the Philippines turned to another important area. If you read the transcripts of the Solarz hearings of June 1983 on the military bases agreement review, you will see in the testimony of assistant secretary Paul Wolfowitz that the United States was very much interested in political transition in the Philippines. Those remarks contained the policy foundations for reform and strengthened institutions that we hoped would see the Philippines through the transition to the post-Marcos period, whenever the post-Marcos period was going to begin.

We saw transition coming. We put our policy emphasis on institutional reforms early on. Our policy objective was to see the Philippines move safely, without violence, into the post-Marcos period.

A very important Philippine political figure, Ninoy Aquino, saw the coming transition as well. Sitting in Boston in exile, Aquino announced in June 1983 that he was returning to the Philippines. He looked toward the May 1984 parliamentary elections as a very important step in the transition process.

Aquino, a pragmatic politician, returned for two reasons: first, to convince the opposition that it was a good idea to participate in those elections; and second, to take on Ferdinand Marcos, and get Marcos to agree to appropriate ground rules that would give the opposition, whose campaign Aquino expected to manage, a fighting chance in that election.

You know what happened when Aquino returned to Manila. Without doubt, his assassination marks the beginning of the train of events that led to the post-Marcos period.

Our policy, set forth in 1983, was to promote three types of reform, which those of you who have been following U.S. policy toward the Philippines have heard repeatedly. The first was political reform, that is, strengthened political institutions to see the country through the transition. The most important political institution was the electoral system and everything that goes with free, fair, open, and credible elections: access to the media, freedom of assembly, freedom of the opposition to participate in the political process.

This particular objective became increasingly important for the

United States for one simple reason. It is a very straightforward issue, one that is quite easy for the American people to understand, and one that is quite easy to explain to the Congress. There was strong bipartisan support in the Congress for such a political solution, as attested in several congressional resolutions on the Philippines. Also, there was very strong support within the administration for just that type of resolution to the nagging political problem in the Philippines, with the Marcos regime approaching twenty years in power.

Our second objective was economic reform, the end of crony capitalism. Crony capitalism is not "capitalism"; it is "cronyism," blatant favoritism toward family, friends, and loyalists that over time becomes more deeply entrenched and wide in scope. It gives capitalism a bad name. Our objective was a return to a free-market economy. This was another objective easily understood in Washington in the 1980s.

The third reform area was on the military side: an end to military cronyism and return to a functioning professional military institution once more.

The issue in which these three elements came together was the security problem, manifested in the rapid growth in the 1980s of the communist New People's Army (NPA). Insurgency growth fed on all three factors: a corrupt military that could not or would not fight, an economy that was in trouble, and a deteriorating political situation, with flawed political institutions that were not credible to Filipinos.

What was the response of President Ferdinand Marcos to this U.S. policy of pushing for reform? It was a typical Marcos response: Deflect. Say, "Yes, I couldn't agree more," and then proceed to engage in the same old policies. Pay a lot of attention to public relations. Make a lot of speeches. Treat American visitors very well when they come to Manila—and the Marcos government did this very well.

With the Aquino assassination came a very strong U.S. reaction. Within the framework of institutional policy change, U.S. officials in Manila and Washington spoke privately and publicly about the changes that Filipinos began to emphasize themselves. Large numbers of Filipinos who had acquiesced to/or supported the Marcos regime, many having welcomed the declaration of martial law in 1972, began to speak out, take public positions, and become politically active. The United States immediately supported their efforts in Manila, and in Washington, for a new presidential succession formula. We supported their efforts for new ground rules for the parliamentary elections in

1984. We supported their efforts for a free Philippine media. And we supported their clamoring for a credible investigation of the Aquino assassination.

The immediate policy issue confronting the administration during this period was President Reagan's visit to Southeast Asia in the fall of that year. As you recall, it was canceled in October 1983. That decision deeply disappointed Ferdinand Marcos. These events were taking place on the backdrop of public statements by the American ambassador in Manila and in Washington emphasizing the need for political, economic, and military reform.

The May 1984 parliamentary election turned out much better than most Filipinos thought it would, including some of my Filipino friends sitting in this audience who, as I recall, were advocates of a boycott. One third of the new parliament was opposition. Following that election, from mid-1984 to October 1985, U.S. reform policy crystalized within the administration into a compact set of incentives and disincentives linked to various aspects of American economic and military assistance.

This was a time when the Philippines was having tremendous troubles with the International Monetary Fund, the NPA was growing in strength, and there was increased interest in the Philippines on Capitol Hill.

You recall in October 1983, after the Aquino assassination, there was condemnation of the Marcos regime on the part of the U.S. House of Representatives; the vote was 414 to 3 to condemn the Marcos government for Aquino's murder and demand that the guilty be identified and punished. These events mounted and contributed to an atmosphere of much more U.S. concern about "whither the Philippines."

Beginning in early 1985, a steady stream of Washington visitors carried the policy reform message, publicly and privately, to Manila. These included assistant secretaries of state and defense; the under secretary for political affairs; the commander of the Pacific fleet, soon to be named chairman of the Joint Chiefs of staff; the director of the Central Intelligence Agency; members of the U.S. Congress, both Republicans and Democrats, including such members as Stephen Solarz and Jack Kemp. What is important is that all of these visitors delivered the *same* policy reform message.

Come the fall, October 1985, the administration came to the conclusion that the U.S. policy message was not getting through to President

Marcos. At that point, Senator Paul Laxalt was asked to convey the personal concern, the unequivocal personal concern, of the President of the United States about the Philippines, and to assure Marcos that the message Marcos was hearing about needed reform came from the top of the U.S. government. He did that. It was a successful mission. Marcos got the message.

Two weeks later a typical Marcos move—"Operation Deflect"—began. President Marcos called a snap presidential election.

Why did Marcos call a snap election at this time? Some contend that the United States leaned on Marcos to call an election. That is not so. One magazine alleged that CIA director Casey had urged Marcos to call a snap election. The State Department has denied that report. There was a report that Senator Laxalt leaned on Marcos to call a snap election. That was not correct.

One does not have to be much of a student of Marcos to understand what motivated him to call a snap election (which, in retrospect, was a bad political decision). Marcos saw the opposition as weak. He saw communism as an issue. He saw that he had a strong party. He had lots of money, which the opposition did not have, to spend on an election. And there was some question about the state of President Marcos's health.

When the election was announced, the U.S. policy response was to welcome it. We felt that an election was a good way to resolve political issues—providing the elections were free, fair, honest, and credible. We pledged to do what we could to help make the elections free, fair, honest, and credible.

We organized observer teams. We explored the nature of elections in the Philippines in congressional hearings. The role of the U.S. Congress was tremendously supportive. The Philippines was a unique foreign-policy problem in terms of effective executive-legislative relations and bipartisan support.

Boston University's Center for Democracy sent a team of Republican and Democratic election specialists to the Philippines in December. That team put together the best analysis of the Philippine electoral system during the Marcos years ever written. It examined what observers should look for and be aware of in the Philippine politicocultural context. The Republican and Democratic party International Institutes sent observer teams. And Senator Lugar and Representative Murtha headed the President's Election Observer Mission.

We went quickly from the election strategy to the postelection strategy. The Philippines was paralyzed after the flawed February 7 election. The immediate response in Washington was to get the clearest possible reading of exactly what was going on.

Our embassy reporting, as Senator Lugar has stated publicly, was superb, and was giving us a very clear reading. Nevertheless, the President and the secretary thought it a good idea to send a veteran diplomatic observer and ambassador with experience in the area, Ambassador Phil Habib, to go out and take a look, to assess the situation. Ambassador Habib sought answers to two questions following the February 7 election: first, did the Marcos government have the ability to govern, and second, what was the state of the opposition?

After eight days in Manila and consultations with many Filipinos and our embassy, Ambassador Habib came back to Washington with the view that there was no question at all with regard to the strength of the Marcos government—it had lost support almost completely because of election fraud. By the time he got back to Washington, the revolution broke out.

I will now summarize some conclusions about the Philippine transition and U.S. policy. A very vital first point: this was a Philippine undertaking. It flowed from the shock of the Aquino assassination. The revolution was a Philippine solution, in the Philippine manner, in Philippine time, unique in its style. What emerged was a Manila-based, Catholic church-influenced, middle-class, moral, nationalist, popular, noncommunist, nonradical revolution against the existing order. It was a reaction against the blatant, brazen attempt of the Marcos political machine to steal the presidential election. The cry was *Basta Na.* Enough. Too much. No more.

Secondly, the transition occurred because of the Filipinos' deep, genuine democratic roots. Those roots exist. They make the Filipinos unique as Asians. Those roots are, in part, our contribution, part of our political legacy. That is something that Americans must remember when we deal with the Philippines.

The third point, without question, is that the Aquino assassination was the first cause of the transition. That murder was too much. The urban population reacted, the Catholic church reacted, businessmen, professionals, and elites reacted. The same people who simply accepted things following the declaration of martial law in 1972 came out against the government and became active.

Fourth, the United States' role was important in this transition because the Filipinos see the United States' role as important. But it was not the dominant factor. The United States played a catalytic role. We were either with the power curve or ahead of the power curve in the transition. We were never behind it. We were able to move very rapidly in policy decisions because we knew and understood what was happening.

Fifth, the NPA issue was also a catalyst. There was real concern in the Philippine body politic about the growth and strength of the NPA capitalizing on the Marcos government's weakness.

The sixth vital point is the U.S. congressional role, which I have already talked about, combined with the role of the U.S. media in the transition. American media reporting got back to the people in the streets and to the military in Camp Crame. That same reporting disheartened the Marcos loyalists.

All things considered, our Philippine policy was relatively easy for Americans of whatever political party to comprehend. It was based on the notion that political problems are best resolved through open, free, and credible elections in a country where elections really mean something. By recognizing that fact and aiming our efforts at clean elections, our policy was successful—because that is what the huge majority of Filipinos wanted for themselves.

I want to address one final word to those of the view that the United States could have or should have exerted pressure on Marcos to step down years ago, and that the unwillingness of both Democratic and Republican administrations to do this has hurt our relations with the Philippines.

The notion that the United States can make or break Philippine governments has been the staple of Manila coffee shops (as well as among some U.S. academics) for many years. In the abstract, the United States possesses such power. However, in the concrete, brokered, foreign-policy-making process of a democracy, and in particular the U.S. democracy, such a scenario could take shape only in the event of strong national consensus, and probably only following provocation. The United States is not a country that deposes the governments of friendly allies. Rather, the United States looks to the citizens of other nations, particularly friendly ones, to take the primary responsibility to bring about their own political change.

Our Philippine policy was—and is —based on the notion that only

Filipinos can resolve Filipino problems. Millions of Filipinos determined that they themselves were responsible for their own political fate during the events of February 1986. The United States watched closely, lent strong moral support to the notion of free elections, spoke out forcefully and in very timely fashion, facilitated some communication, and provided helpful logistical support for Marcos's evacuation at a key moment.

However, these efforts were peripheral. The power of determined people in the streets, risking their lives and knowing it, was the force that brought Marcos down and Corazon Aquino to power. Bringing that power to bear was exclusively a Filipino decision.

30

The United States-Philippine Strategic Relationship

William H. Sullivan

The strategic relationship of the Philippines to the United States has been anything but static. When Theodore Roosevelt and his Washington cronies positioned Commodore Dewey's ships for action against the Spanish in Manila Bay, they were motivated more by hubris than by strategy. The archaic Spanish ships presented the opportunity for a cheap but spectacular victory in a conflict that was really centered in the Caribbean rather than in the South China Sea.

Yet Roosevelt and his friends were strongly influenced by the writings of Captain Alfred Thayer Mahan, whose views on naval strategy were congenial to their aspirations for the advancement of American power. The use of the Philippine islands as coaling stations for the "Great White Fleet" that they were developing fitted into a concept that was generally accepted as "strategic" at the time. It was a concept for projection of military, economic, and political power in an imperial pattern. In that epoch, power and empire were accepted as desirable ends in their own right.

However, the American political ethos at the end of the nineteenth century was not all that comfortable with "empire." It is true that Manifest Destiny had carried the nation across the continent and had sublimated any feelings of remorse about the Indians. It is also true that the same spirit had tolerated the filibustering in Texas and the Mexican-American War of 1848. But, to cross a vast ocean and to establish a colony in the Philippines was something else again.

President McKinley, faced with his young hawks on the one hand, and the reluctant conservatism of his countrymen on the other, did not enjoy his dilemma. He was being told by the hawks that Aguinaldo, whom Dewey had brought to Manila, was incapable of forming a Filipino government. He was advised by intelligence services that the

Germans, and perhaps the Japanese, were planning to stimulate the collapse of Philippine independence and to take over the islands for their own imperial purposes. And so, according to his own account, he fell on his knees and asked God for divine guidance.

History does not record whether God was considered a strategist, but the divine guidance provided to McKinley was positive. He got up from his knees convinced that it was an American duty to take over the Philippines, and, among other things, to "Christianize" the Filipino people. Since that was one of the few objectives that the Spanish had successfully accomplished in their 300-year reign, it seems fair to assume that strategic considerations must have ranked higher than spiritual in McKinley's mind. From what we know of McKinley's political processes, it also seems likely that preemption of rival empires was a more compelling motivation than extension of the American imperium.

Nevertheless, once the United States had taken the islands, public attention was concentrated far more on the tutorial task of uplifting the "little brown brothers" than it was on matters of strategic concern. In the early years, this was certainly designed as a shrewd way to forestall moral opinion that might otherwise be offended by the brutalities of a pacification campaign and the utter disregard for traditional American attitudes toward national independence. As time went on, it also reflected the priorities of a remarkable series of governors general, such as William Howard Taft and Francis B. Harrison, for whom the Philippines became both a "noble experiment" and a political stepping stone.

By the advent of World War I, with the ebbing of the Imperial tide in the American political scheme, the strategic aspects of the Philippines had nearly evaporated, at least in the United States Congress. The Jones Act of 1916 reflected the willingness of Washington to regard strategic matters of such little consequence that the United States was prepared to grant the Philippines its independence and abandon a U.S. stake in Southeast Asia.

American entry into the war in 1917 and the consequent emphasis on military and strategic considerations combined with economic and other factors to restrain the drive for independence that was inherent in the Jones Act. The Republican administrations of the 1920s slowed down, but did not reverse, Washington's policies. However, during World War I and in the "disarmament" years that followed it, there is precious little record of any systematic consideration of the Philippines as a strategic asset for the United States.

In fact, as the world entered the 1930s and the era of totalitarian expansion, official Washington seemed to look upon the Philippines as a strategic liability rather than an asset. When General Douglas MacArthur was recalled from retirement and sent to Manila to train the "Philippine Scouts," his mission was designed as a token of belated responsibility for giving the Filipinos some sense of self-defense before the United States cast them loose on the seas of independence. As confrontation with the Japanese grew closer, Washington did not look on MacArthur's command as a source of strength to the United States' position in the Pacific, but rather as a burden that was a drain upon its military resources.

When war came, the Japanese attack on the Philippines was swift and effective. But, it does not appear, from the records of that war, that the Philippines was a prime Japanese strategic objective. Indeed, the principal reason that the Japanese attacked the Philippines was because the Americans were there and because they could not afford to leave American forces and bases in their rear as they proceeded to consolidate their Greater East Asian Co-Prosperity Sphere.

By the same token, the United States, in pursuing its victory against Japan, did not regard the Philippines as a prime strategic objective. The basic strategy devised for that victory drove straight across the Pacific, heading for the heart of the Japanese homeland. Even MacArthur, fighting his way up from the South Pacific, had developed island-hopping tactics that deliberately avoided head-on confrontations with Japanese troop units and left large enemy concentrations in his rear destined to be starved out as their supply lines were cut and as they were subjected to attrition by air power.

Admiral Nimitz considered MacArthur's plan to invade the Philippines a costly political gesture and opposed it. He was sustained in this opposition by King and Marshall, who would have bypassed the Philippines if they had had their way. It was only when MacArthur went directly to President Roosevelt, who sympathized with Mac-Arthur's political purposes, that the Philippines became a major military objective in the Pacific campaign.

After World War II, the Philippines took on greater strategic importance to the United States as U.S. global responsibilities took shape. The air and naval bases there were maintained after the Philippines regained independence and the two countries entered into a mutual defense agreement. As the American confrontation with communist expansion grew rapidly, these bases began to assume greater importance. They became part of the structure erected in the Western Pacific as a result of the Korean War, the Off-Shore Islands crisis, and the French involvement in Indochina.

It was in the Vietnam War, however, that the Philippines took on a major strategic significance for the United States. The Clark Air Force Base and the Subic Naval Base, with their facilities, were essential to the United States for the conduct of the campaigns on the Indochina peninsula from 1965 to 1972. Even in 1975, when the United States withdrew all its personnel from Vietnam and Cambodia in the wake of their humiliating collapse, the military facilities in the Philippines proved necessary for the success of that evacuation.

The Vietnam experience was a traumatic one for the United States. Its effects upon the American domestic body politic are still being felt. Much has been written about the "lessons of Vietnam" on matters of relations between branches of our government, on decisions concerning the use of force in the conduct of international relations, and on the role of the media in policy matters. But not much has been written or spoken about the effect of Vietnam on the strategic posture of the United States.

Indeed, the legacy of Vietnam is ultimately a paradox. Four presidents of the United States led this country into combat in Vietnam because they were convinced, with much justification, that the strategic balance in Asia was turning inexorably against the interests of the United States, its allies, and its friends. This conviction stemmed not only from the tenacious purpose of the Lao Dong leadership in Hanoi to take over all of French Indochina, but from the combination of that effort with the Chinese effort to conduct subversion in Thailand, Malaysia, the Philippines, and, above all, in Indonesia. Successive American administrations saw these actions as a coordinated move to sever the lines of communication between Japan and its energy sources and as an intention to bring all of Southeast Asia, down to Australia, within the scope of communist military control.

The failure of the Chinese-sponsored 1965 military coup in Indonesia can, in retrospect, be seen as the turning point in this strategic threat. At the time, its significance was probably not adequately appreciated in the United States because of U.S. fixation on events in

Vietnam. There was not even much public awareness in the United States that as many as 300,000 ethnic Chinese and their associates were slaughtered in retribution for the attempted coup.

Moreover, the collapse of this Chinese-inspired effort did not seem to have had an immediate effect on the radicalization of Chinese leadership, which continued through the era of the Cultural Revolution and the Gang of Four to proclaim a "lips and teeth" policy with Hanoi and a virulent antagonism toward the West. However, it must be weighed as one of the factors that convinced more sober Chinese leaders that there were practical limits to the revolutionary goals frenetically proclaimed for their system.

Other factors surely had their effect. One of them must have been the willingness of the "paper tiger" Americans to commit themselves to military intervention on the Asian mainland so close to China's frontiers and to sustain significant casualties there. The risk that a frustrated Washington leadership might use nuclear weapons must certainly have put a strain on the measure of enthusiasm that Peking could muster for the leaders in Hanoi.

Whatever the motivating factors, the Chinese leaders, under Chou En-lai, were ready in the early 1970s to make a historic change in strategy that would ultimately reach cosmic proportions. They were able to shift their position between the Soviet Union, on the one hand, and the United States, on the other, for reasons too complex to enumerate here. But certainly two of those reasons had to do with the condition of the United States. First, in President Nixon, there was a chief executive who could accommodate to China without domestic political revolt. Second, by having failed to win in Indochina, the United States was prepared to remove its troops from the Southeast Asian mainland. Had the United States won, it is predictable that its forces would have had to remain in Vietnam, that China would have had to maintain some sort of "lips and teeth" support of Hanoi, and that China and the Soviet Union would have had to continue some sort of logistical alliance in support of that policy. In the absence of those U.S. troops, China has been able to effect a sweeping realignment of forces that has changed global strategy.

China is not an ally of the United States, but its international posture is congenial to our interests. To all practical effects, the line of confrontation for the United States and its allies has shifted from the Western shores of the Pacific to the Soviet-Chinese frontier. There is a certain limited strategic cooperation between the United States and its allies, on the one hand, and China, on the other. The conditions that China has posed for normalization of its relations with the Soviets seem destined to maintain the Sino-Soviet impasse indefinitely. For the first time in centuries, the Pacific is in a state of strategic equilibrium, and it seems unlikely that any of the major powers sees any advantage in upsetting it.

Clearly, this overall strategic shift has altered once again the strategic relationship of the Philippines to the United States. As a member of ASEAN, the Philippines joins with the other Southeast Asian nations as one of the elements maintaining the basic equilibrium. In that sense, it asserts its own valence in the overall strategic equation.

As the host for American military facilities, it enables the United States to project a measure of military power into an important quadrant of that equilibrium. However, the purpose of this power has changed. No longer is it deployed primarily as a buffer against Chinese expansion, but rather for some rather specialized capabilities affecting the Soviets. And, given these purposes, its presence is openly welcomed by the Chinese, officially supported by Japan, and tacitly endorsed by the ASEAN governments.

In large measure, the United States military facilities in the Philippines have been oriented toward the containment of Soviet threats into the Indian Ocean and the Persian Gulf. They are first of all part of a strategic logistics line that reaches through Diego Garcia into the Arabian Sea. They are also in excellent position to service the United States fleet as a counterpoise to increasing Soviet surface and submarine activity in the China Seas. Their primary characteristic, aside from the advantage of their location, is the availability of highly skilled, hardworking technicians who are able to service U.S. aircraft and ships at a fraction of our domestic costs and at enormous savings, especially in steaming and station time for its naval vessels.

In this sense, the whole Pacific community is a beneficiary of the current Philippine-American strategic relationship. But, on balance, given the broader scope of American interests, it must be stipulated that it is the United States that benefits more than any other nation from the current arrangements. Those benefits can certainly be expected to endure at least for the current life of the United States' bilateral security arrangements with the Philippines and probably for a long period after that.

544

On the other side of the strategic ledger are the problems that are inherent in the New People's Army insurgency in the Philippines. This militant guerrilla movement reflects some fundamental social, economic, and political problems that have not disappeared with the Marcos regime. It seems probable that the insurgency will endure for some time and will require major attention from the Philippine armed forces. What can be hoped is that it is now less likely, under an Aquino presidency, to degenerate into a civil war.

However, it still has the capability to become a nuisance by inviting Soviet, Vietnamese, or North Korean interference. If that were to happen and if the United States were to feel obligated to respond by a more active American involvement against the guerrillas, the Philippines could become the destabilizing element in the Pacific state of equilibrium. It is the prospect that was altogether too compelling in the last stages of the Marcos era, and should not be dismissed lightly in the new euphoria.

In sum, if there is one lesson that we can draw from the historical relationship between the Philippines and the United States, it is that the pattern of that relationship is subject to change in its strategic dimensions. It is not like the relationship between the United States and the Caribbean or the United States and Western Europe. It is one that is subject to the ebbs and flows of great international forces that are still in flux.

Therefore, when Americans and Filipinos look at their strategic relationship, they should be prepared to view it with a certain flexibility. This means that there is some value to the periodic examination of all its arrangements, whether with respect to United States use of Philippine military facilities or with respect to United States obligations with regard to the protection of Filipino territorial claims, or with respect to the provision of United States military assistance to Philippine counterinsurgency efforts.

Given the emotional content of the long and complex ties between the two countries, it is probably too much to ask that these periodic reviews be conducted without the political rhetoric that has always characterized them in the past. But it would not be unrealistic to suggest that they be conducted in the context of an open-minded assessment of the larger strategic contexts in which both countries find themselves as history unfolds.

The maturity of the United States' association with the Philippines, which has now endured for eighty-eight years, demands that it try to place that association on a new basis. It would be fatuous to suggest that the United States and the Philippines are strategic equals, since the disparities in global position are enormous. But it would be useful to draw up some objective balance sheets to measure the interests that each nation has in the continuation of a strategic association. These will be valuable assets for both Washington and Manila to have in hand when the current bilateral agreement expires in 1991 and the two governments must decide how to address the future.

31

The Case for Ending the Special Relationship and Leaving the United States Bases in the Philippines

Paul M. Kattenburg

A notable and admirable series of events took place in the Philippines at the end of February and the beginning of March 1986. Backed by massive popular support, "people power" as she termed it, Cory Aquino was able to overcome President Marcos' massive electoral fraud and establish her own government. This peaceful revolution culminated in the departure into exile of Ferdinand and Imelda Marcos and of their closest cronies. Democracy was restored to the Republic after 20 years of Marcos misrule, including many years of martial law and the curtailing of civil liberties. With Cory Aquino's accession, the rebellion led by the new Communist party of the Philippines (CPP) and its military arm, the New People's Army (NPA), has been dealt a severe if perhaps not yet fatal setback. Assuming that the proper steps are taken, the Philippine economy—disastrous in 1984-86—stands at least a chance of recuperating some if not immediately all of its former strength and vigor.

This might seem, then, to be an ill-chosen moment for the United States to disengage itself from the Philippines. It may also seem strange for me to argue the case for ending the special relationship and leaving the United States bases. I was a strong proponent, both in and out of the State Department, of close Philippine-American relations, and for several years I actively supported Ninoy Aquino and the anti-Marcos struggle.

Nevertheless, far-sighted United States statesmanship would recognize the present moment as providing precisely that "exquisite watershed" in which fundamental rethinking of our long-standing special relationship should take place. Rethinking would lead us to the conclusion that United States interest would now and in the future be best served by gradual and substantial disengagement from special economic relations and, more important, from our long-held though increasingly less vital strategic posture, including the United States military bases, in the archipelago.

The Philippines' foreign-policy orientation, if left to Philippine decision making, is likely to take a natural shift to an increasingly Southeast Asia-oriented type of non-alignment. At the same time, our own East Asian interests should compel us increasingly toward concentration of our economic and military power in the Northeast Asian portion of the Pacific Basin, and toward de-emphasis and in fact demilitarization of the vast oceanic realms south of the equator, both in the eastern portions of the South Pacific and in the Indian Ocean.

It is moreover essential that a period of "psychological maturity" now enter into our relations with the Philippine Republic. Filipinos must at last assume full responsibility for their own defense and future, and not remain wards of the United States. For its part, the United States must seek to refrain from its frankly outmoded mentor and "nation-building" propensities. These propensities have led us to patronizing and frequently incorrect policies and attitudes, both under the pre-Marcos democracy and during the last dozen or more years since Marcos established his dictatorship. The worst thing the United States could do now would be to strangle Cory Aquino's newly formed democracy with an embrace "made in the U.S.A."

The United States is already overextended in the Third World. The moment has come to cease exaggerating the Soviet threat in the world's less developed regions, to abandon areas of relatively peripheral or remote concern, and to address instead the pressing problems facing us at home and in the vital regions of Europe, the Middle East and Japan.

UNITED STATES BASES IN THE PHILIPPINES

There is a significant and intimate connection between what many Filipinos still call their "special relationship" with the United States, and the presence of an extensive and important United States military-base complex in the Republic of the Philippines. U.S. military forces have been deployed in the Philippines since the turn of the century, well before Philippine independence (July 1946). But it was clearly understood when the Military Bases Agreement (MBA) was negotiated and signed in 1947, that the *quid pro quo* for these first quasi-permanent United States bases obtained abroad (except for those at Guantanamo and the Canal Zone), would be a privileged position for the Philippines in United States foreign policy and specifically United States foreign economic relations. The 1951 bilateral Mutual Security Treaty (MST), the only one signed by the United States with any Southeast Asian nation, was a logical follow-up to the MBA.

Before the stationing of United States military forces in Northeast Asia (Japan, Korea, Okinawa) following World War II, the Philippine bases signalled (as they continue to do today) the relative permanence of the United States presence in East Asia after approximately 1900. They also symbolized the obligations assumed by the United States toward its adopted wards in the Far Pacific, however ineffectual the United States may at times have been (as in 1941) in discharging these obligations. A United States military presence in bases on Philippine soil, combined with United States defense of the Philippines, implied some clear-cut policies on both sides—however much tinkering there may have been after 1947 with specifics about the bases arrangements or the special economic and political ties. The heart of these policies always involved an American willingness to shoulder ultimate responsibility for the fate of the democratic Republic of the Philippines; as well as Philippine willingness to allow the United States a reasonable measure of unhampered access to and use of its military bases. (The determination of "reasonable" was allowed to fluctuate.)

United States bases in the Philippines are intimately related with the fate of the Philippines. If either side ends the special relationship, there is no intrinsic reason for the presence of bases, regardless of broader United States strategic considerations. The question sometimes being asked in the United States may well be: "How important are the Philippine bases and what are they really worth?" A more crucial question is: "What is the worth and future of the Philippine-United States special relationship?" New generations coming into leadership roles on both sides are quite ignorant of the depth of this "love-hate" relationship—and of the significance of the defense partnership which the bases made possible for so long.

It is probably symbolic that the wartime episode that remained etched in the minds of postwar Philippine leaders was not the Japanese defeat of United States forces at the onset of the Pacific War (though leaders like the Laurels, Marcoses and Aquinos all owe their postwar prominence largely to reputations made under the Japanese occupation), but rather General MacArthur's somewhat bombastic promise, "I shall return." In the first 20 or more years after the war, there was a considerable outpouring of American largesse and generosity, as in the settlement of so-called guerrilla war claims.

In the future, however, Philippine security and national interests may well be governed by considerations quite alien to those which seem to govern American concerns. The Filipinos' interest will be governed by their proximity and vulnerability to present or potential power centers in Japan, China and Vietnam; Philippine involvement in the oceanic and archipelagic realms of the South China Seas, South Pacific and Indonesia; and, most of all, Philippine nearness to and ethno-cultural affiliation with Southeast Asian countries and specifically to the Indonesian-Malaysian sphere. Similarly, rationales for United States bases in the Philippines are global-strategic and relate only remotely to the Philippines.

What is the intrinsic worth of the Philippine-United States special relationship to the United States? There is no obvious, geopolitically based answer. Indonesia, for example, is far larger as real estate, three times more populous as a potential market, infinitely more replete with all types of resources, and much more strategically located because it commands the straits into both the South Pacific and Indian Oceans. Yet the United States has no military bases in Indonesia (or in Malaysia, which includes all North Borneo except Brunei), and no known intention of acquiring them.

There was something other than strategy and resources which made the Philippines so significant to the United States in the past: its United States training in democracy and its legacy of working democratic institutions. For those Americans who knew the Philippines in the first quarter century of its independence, there was no doubt that a genuine "showcase of democracy" (as it used to be called) had been built in Southeast Asia, and one not doing all that badly on the economic front.

With the Rusk-Ramos revision of the Military Bases Agreement in 1966, the United States committed itself to genuine consultations on the uses of the bases for the first time. This was coupled with a United States repudiation of vestiges of Philippine economic dependency on the United States, in the so-called parity amendment to the Philippine Constitution and in a similar provision of the 1955 Laurel-Langley

Trade Agreement. The United States then began to lose interest in the purposes for which it had originally acquired the Philippine bases. Simultaneously, the Filipinos were continuously demanding greater and more genuine political and economic independence, although at first they did so rhetorically and without fully believing in the ultimate consequences of complete independence.

Almost overnight, it seemed, a lot of things changed. American leadership in the Nixon administration, obsessed with the last phases of the Vietnam War and uninterested in what seemed to Kissinger a peripheral backwater, allowed Philippine democracy to perish without a whimper of protest. The administration encouraged Marcos in the fraud that he perpetrated on his people through the imposition of martial law on flimsy pretexts in September 1972. It suddenly appeared, judging by the administration's pronouncements, that Philippine democracy had never been real; more important, democracy there did not seem to matter much anyway.

The one thing that did seem to matter, in the wake of Vietnam, was that the bases permit the United States to demonstrate a symbolic surviving presence near mainland Southeast Asia, regardless of the character of the polity surrounding the bases or of its intimacy with us. Abjuring its responsibility for the fate of Philippine democracy, the United States crossed a watershed in 1972 by encouraging Marcos' imposition of martial law. The Philippines also crossed a watershed just a few years later, when Marcos ignored largely rhetorical United States demands for the restoration of human rights. The trends thus set in motion may permanently influence the future United States-Philippine relationship.

It is true that in the late sixties and early seventies, the United States continued to depend on the Philippine bases for support of its Vietnam War effort. The Philippines, however, in the grips of rising nationalism and conscious of the ongoing United States repudiation of the special relationship, never climbed fully "on board" behind the United States effort in Vietnam. Conversely, the United States never fully trusted or utilized its old ally for Vietnam backup. For example, runways long enough for B-52's were not built at Clark AFB, although the United States flew KC-135's from Clark for mid-air refueling of Guam-based B-52's. The United States did make use of Subic Naval Base, Clark AFB and the temporarily opened Mactan Air Base on Cebu, but this was for staging and logistical purposes only, not for combat use, and it was done at considerable cost in terms of additional assistance to the Philippines.

The old postwar special relationship was already ending. Everything the United States did from the Philippines to backup Vietnam, it exceeded in places and countries that seemed either better suited or more responsive to American wishes: Okinawa, Korea, Thailand, Japan, Guam. Loath as it was to provide even one battalion of non-combat engineering troops for Vietnam, and that at a prohibitively high price, the Philippines did not have its heart set on serving United States needs in Southeast Asia. And the United States was unwilling to pay an excessive cost merely to make full use of what it was gradually ceasing to regard as an exclusive unilateral asset in a former United States dependency.

UNITED STATES-PHILIPPINE RELATIONS

Today, it is most doubtful that the Aquino government will give the United States unhampered use of the bases, even if it allows us for a period to maintain installations at Clark, Subic and subsidiary points. The vast majority of the Filipino people have not forgotten that the United States gave near total support to the hated Marcos regime until at least Ninoy Aquino's assassination in 1983. Despite their awareness of positive United States support for Philippine democracy in the ultimate stages of the Marcos dictatorship, they may oppose any permanent foreign (including United States) military presence on Phil-ippine soil. Many of the moderates—not to mention a few extremists —in charge of the new government, are against foreign bases in principle and have long struggled for nationalistic policies of non-alignment. President Cory Aquino and her chief aides pay at least lip service to the maintenance of United States bases until the expiration of the MBA in 1991, but it is very uncertain whether they will maintain the bases in the Philippines in the long run.

We should therefore be encouraged by today's healthy United States official trend of thinking less about the future of the bases in the Philippines and more about the situation likely to arise in the country if radical changes do not promptly occur to permit rescuing the rapidly failing economy. There is also more concern about giving the govern-ing moderate politicians, backed by reform-minded military commanders, a real chance to prevent the takeover for which the new CPP and the NPA have been working for so long. Such a takeover, especially if it were brought about without any external assistance, would certainly create an entirely new situation in Southeast Asia and the Western Pacific.

But even if non-communist moderates backing Cory Aquino succeed in holding the communist threat at bay, Philippine-American relations are likely to undergo fundamental change. The more so if prestigious, reform-minded nationalist elder statesmen like Diokno, Salonga and Tanada continue to support the present leadership. These statesmen tend to view the United States as following outmoded policies of cold war confrontation and neo-economic imperialism. American multinational corporations in the Philippines are particularly unpopular. But the end of the military bases after approximately 1991 and greatly diminished United States aid are likely to be the most important manifestations of change in the United States-Philippine relationship.

(There is, of course, the possibility of adopting some harebrained scheme like the so-called "enclave strategy," which has been mentioned in United States policy discussions. In such a strategy, Clark AFB [which is in any case not a vital but rather a redundant United States installation] would presumably be given up, while Subic Naval Base would become a sort of Guantanamo: The United States would presumably carry out the relevant portion of its anti-communist and anti-Soviet global strategies from an enclave within a communist-controlled, or even conceivably a non-aligned, Philippines. This scenario is a *reductio ad absurdum* of the kind of thinking which in time turns the instruments of policy into the objects of the policy itself.)

CONSEQUENCES OF WITHDRAWAL

In order to adapt realistically to present and foreseeable circumstances, the United States should carefully weigh the risks and consider the advantages of adopting the following course of action:

(1) End the special relationship by abrogating the 1951 MST and whatever vestiges remain of special economic ties. Even though the Aquino regime should be assisted as necessary to help it avert a recrudescence of communist activity, this should be done "at a distance," with reserve, and in any case only in response to direct and even insistent Philippine requests. The worst possible thing to do

would be to strangle Aquino in too tight a United States embrace, not permitting her to develop a nationally rooted, firmly *sui generis* way of ridding the country of the communist menace.

(2) Withdraw from and permanently close the bases at Clark and Subic, as well as subsidiary communications facilities and other support installations too large to be conveniently handled from the confines of a much smaller, more modest U.S. Embassy in Manila. The vice-regal edifice on Roxas Boulevard, so long a symbol of pro-Marcos support, should be shorn of all extra and unnecessary activities reminiscent of United States proclivities for taking on so-called "counterinsurgency warfare."

(3) Proclaim loudly that the United States is in no way abjuring its interests in East Asia; but nonetheless pursue a radically modified regional strategy under altered political conditions in the Southwest Pacific and Indian Oceans, which would obviate the need for United States bases in the Philippines while seeking to obtain maximum advantage in terms of global diplomacy from the voluntary relinquishment of such facilities.

A decision made now to withdraw from the bases, to seek new alternative facilities as necessary, and above all to plan a new regional strategy within the context of a global diplomacy fitted to new circumstances in the Philippines and Southeast Asia, would have the essential advantage of not being made under pressure. The United States would not have been forced out of its bases; it would have made a conscious decision to adjust to circumstances which are bound to change drastically in Southeast Asia and the Southwest Pacific once the Philippines decides to leave the United States defense orbit. At the same time, the United States should be able to obtain something in return for an early voluntary decision; even if it does not, considerable loss of prestige might be averted.

Why are these bases regarded as vital today, and what would be lost under the circumstances described above? First, the Philippine bases signal and symbolize the presence of fairly large United States forces and support facilities in the general area of the South China Sea. Other than bases at Guam, the United States has no other permanent facilities south of a line drawn through the Pacific and Indian Oceans between Hawaii and Diego Garcia in the far western Indian Ocean. This is not to suggest, of course, that no possible alternatives exist. Islands such as Palau and others in the Western Pacific could be used for the construction of a new naval base, but at considerable expense. Facilities could be leased at Singapore, in North Borneo (Malaysia), or in Western Australia, but these would presumably not be bases in the sense Subic was. A base could conceivably be obtained at Trincomalee in Sri Lanka, though the country is unstable and such United States action would no doubt raise serious diplomatic problems with India.

Nowhere could the extremely cheap and productive labor pool available for ship repair and support at Subic be duplicated. There would be serious impairment of the outward projection of American naval power into the Indian Ocean—and even into the Indonesian straits and the Southwest Pacific, where Western military resolve may increasingly be tested by growing pacifist and neutralist sentiment (as in New Zealand). But is the outward projection of American naval power in these zones still really important? Is there any validity to the dubious "choke-point" theories often propounded by geopoliticians in the administration and outside?

Second, the Philippine bases enable the United States to counter directly what is regarded as a significant and still-growing Soviet military build-up in the South China Sea. There are reasons to believe, however, that the Soviets continue to view this area as one of secondary importance in their scale of priorities, and that aspects of the Soviet build-up may be more defensive than offensive in nature. These may be concerned mainly with the countering of United States anti-submarine warfare (ASW) capabilities in the Philippines and with the long-range defense of Indochina and the containment of China. It is at least possible that the withdrawal of American forces and bases from the Philippines, consequently decreasing the United States capability to project power into the Indian Ocean, would decrease the need for Soviet naval presence in the South China Sea. (But this should not be assumed without verification through explicit negotiations.)

Third, United States bases in the Philippines are at least theoretically available as a back up for offensive or counter-offensive operations designed to contain the really strong Soviet naval and air capabilities in the straits and potential combat zones of the Sea of Japan and Northeast Asia, where these Soviet forces pose a genuine threat to Japan, Okinawa, South Korea and—under wartime conditions—to the sea lanes linking these areas to the Persian Gulf and Middle East. Associated with this, the Philippine bases provide an ancillary but important potential backup zone to support anti-Soviet Chinese combat potential, especially in terms of staging United States logistics support to the People's Republic of China (PRC). Although the role of the bases is ancillary, it is nonetheless significant enough potentially to confer bargaining leverage if part of an explicit negotiation with the Soviets.

Finally, United States bases in the Philippines continue to provide means to defend the Philippines against indeterminate external threats. They generally make life in the Far Pacific easier, less costly, and more comfortable for the United States Navy and Air Force. (For example, they include the John Hay Golf Club Air Base.) But this is a waning asset; in the future, the Philippines is most unlikely to opt for a United States defensive system, while the United States itself long ago ceased thinking of a special relationship and keeps the bases for purposes of global strategy only remotely related to the Philippines.

RECOMMENDED UNITED STATES STRATEGY

The United States might at least support if not partially design a new grand strategy for the South Pacific/Southeast Asia/Indian Ocean region, not entailing bases in the Philippines. This could be done in association with some of its closer partners in the region and in possible consultation with Japan, and even with the PRC. What might be the general shape and some of the key elements of such a strategy?

(1) The Philippines, as a member of the Association of Southeast Asian Nations (ASEAN), would look first to that association for its security now and into the 21st century. ASEAN, however, is not a military organization but only a loose association of countries in Southeast Asia with a basically similar outlook. The Philippines is the only one among them to have maintained a formal treaty of alliance with a superpower (although Thailand has frequently expressed a desire for a similar United States tie). It would be expected that the basic security orientation of ASEAN as well as its individual members would remain one of neutrality and reasonably genuine non-alignment with the superpowers. The United States would in due course inform the Philippines of its decision to abrogate the 1951 MST, as well as to withdraw from the military bases, thus leaving the Philippines free for a foreign-policy reorientation which would more fully conform to ASEAN's long-standing (and thus far largely rhetorical) objective of establishing a Zone of Peace, Freedom and Neutrality (ZOPFAN) in Southeast Asia, which at least in theory excludes the presence of

superpower military bases in the region.

(2) As part of the above, the United States and others would expect the Philippines with the other members of ASEAN to explore with the members of the Indochina bloc in Southeast Asia—as well as in due course with the Soviet Union itself—the possibility of a Soviet withdrawal from their naval and air bases at Danang and Cam Ranh Bay. Soviet presence in these bases derives at least in part from the presence and activities of American forces at Subic and Clark. There is, however, no guarantee that the Soviets, who are undoubtedly engaged in a significant and worldwide naval build-up, would agree to withdraw from Indochina, even at the price of United States withdrawal from the Philippines. To make the result of mutual withdrawal more likely, the ASEAN powers might consider proposing an Indochina settlement which would essentially ratify Vietnamese hegemony—at the price of military withdrawal—in Kampuchea, including recognition of the Heng Samrin regime. The present ASEAN policy of sponsoring a change of regime in Kampuchea and supporting guerrilla warfare there, largely by Khmer Rouge elements, has demonstrably failed and is unlikely to be sustainable.

(3) Further, a worldwide re-proclamation and recognition of a ZOP-FAN in Southeast Asia would probably accompany the unilateral withdrawal of United States forces from the Philippine bases. This might be broadened to encompass a nuclear free zone. Under such a concept, ASEAN would ban the presence of Soviet, American or other nuclear weapons throughout Southeast Asia including (one would hope) Indochina. It would be difficult to see how the Indochinese communist states would be able to resist joining such a nuclear free zone; its proclamation might be a further incentive for the Soviets to join the United States in withdrawing from military bases in a region to which they have traditionally accorded low priority. Moreover, it is quite conceivable that Australia and New Zealand would be willing, if invited, to join what would then become the Southeast Asia/Southwest Pacific Nuclear Free Zone. The United States and Australia would have to draw the consequences for their alliance from such a new situation; New Zealand's current defection invites them to do so. Appropriate means of verification would have to be established to ensure respect of the nuclear-free status of this zone by all nuclear powers and by nuclear-armed vessels of all states.

(4) In return for this complete departure from the prevailing *status*

quo in Southeast Asia and the Southwest Pacific, entailing above all the United States withdrawal from military bases heretofore considered vital in as strategic a country as the Philippines, the Soviet Union would be expected to make considerable concessions—in addition to withdrawing from its relatively small military presence in a traditionally low-priority area. Specifically, the United States would seek a negotiated agreement under which the Soviets—assuming changes in the *status quo* as projected in (1), (2) and (3) above—would accede to limiting the units in the Soviet Pacific Fleet (except in Southeast and Northeast Asian waters) to only those types of units which in the view of both superpowers could be considered vital for the legitimate protection of Soviet strategic nuclear deterrent forces (i.e., submarines and ASW vessels and aircraft). No other Soviet surface, underwater or air units would be expected to prowl the eastern Pacific Ocean. Western Pacific zones such as Southeast Asia and Northeast Asia would, as indicated, remain at least for a period open to all units of the Soviet fleet.

(5) Further, the United States would in the same agreement expect a minimum of one-third reduction of Soviet naval presence in the Indian Ocean. Its own naval presence there would be expected to decrease commensurately as well. The Indian Ocean never did assume the strategic importance that an over-eager United States Navy sought for it in the sixties and seventies, when the United States was involved in Vietnam and potentially in the Horn of Africa, and sought back-door entry to the Middle East. Persian Gulf oil has almost totally lost its significance as a world fuel resource, except perhaps to Japan. But Japan can secure mid-east oil just as well, if not better, under conditions of demilitarization as under circumstances of tense superpower confrontation in the Indian Ocean. Nor is Persian Gulf oil likely to regain its significance. The idea of back-door entry to the Middle East has proved futile and counter-productive and has enhanced South Asian and Near Eastern tensions.

(6) The proposals of (4) and (5) above could be rejected by the Soviets, especially if they were presented under the conditions of tense superpower confrontation which now prevail worldwide. Even with better superpower relations, the Soviets might still refuse to make concessions to obtain conditions they think would naturally arise if the United States were forced out of its Philippine bases. United States withdrawal from the Philippine bases, and the proclamation of a

genuine ZOPFAN and possibly a nuclear free zone in Southeast Asia and the Southwest Pacific, might be sufficient to bring about Soviet withdrawal or at least significant reduction from bases in Indochina— but not necessarily a reduction of fleets in the Pacific and Indian oceans. The proposals under (4) and (5) would therefore have to be merely offers made under conditions of explicit negotiations. If the Soviets showed interest, they could expect a commensurate reduction of tensions in these regions; if they did not, the United States would in any case withdraw unilaterally from its Philippine bases, but without diminishing its pressure, vigilance and presence in the Pacific and Indian Ocean regions, which could be ensured through the use of alternative facilities and basing arrangements.

(7) Finally, it is hard to see how proposals for mutual disarmament of the United States and USSR in the southern oceans could be objectionable to the PRC, provided it was assured of the surviving and continued effective presence of strong United States forces elsewhere in the region. The withdrawal of Soviet elements from Vietnam might in itself benefit the PRC, while an effectively neutralized and possibly denuclearized Southeast Asia/Southwest Pacific should be acceptable to China so long as the United States maintains strong army, naval and air forces and a major effective Soviet-containing presence in Northeast Asia, supported by strong elements of the United States Pacific Fleet based on Hawaii and points in between.

UNITED STATES-SOVIET AGREEMENT

The days of long and intimate United States association with the Philippines, marked by the notion of mutual defense and special economic ties, and by the presence of large American military bases in the Philippines, are drawing to a close. A new strategy is necessary for the United States in the region. The new situation can best be accommodated by an explicit agreement of the two superpowers looking for mutual reduction of their presence in the Southeast Asian region along the lines detailed in the previous section.

Under its new strategy, the United States would move to facilities and installations in Korea, Okinawa and Japan, those elements of the Thirteenth Air Force and of its major communication facilities in the Philippines which play a vital and effective role in the worldwide superpower confrontation. (The possibility that Taiwan might again become available should not be ruled out, though it is unlikely.) Similarly, major naval and marine units used primarily in the global strategic confrontation would move from Subic to existing facilities in Northeast Asia, backed as required by refurbished, enhanced or new facilities in the western Pacific islands.

At the same time, the strategy of United States power projection in the further South China Seas, the Southwest Pacific, and, above all, the Indian Ocean would be gradually reduced and eventually eliminated in favor of a diplomacy of reduced superpower tensions in these regions. The United States would in no sense abdicate its ruling power position in Northeast Asia and the Central Pacific and Micronesia, but the Far South Pacific and Indian Ocean zones would increasingly be allowed to become regions of neutrality and reduced confrontation, under mutually agreed-upon, explicit terms. The United States would not abandon its facilities at Diego Garcia, but the signal would be clear that it would not seek to intervene in South Asia, the Persian Gulf or the Near East by the back door. Such intervention in South Asia or the Persian Gulf would be futile in any case, because of the future lack of capabilities for the United States, given its preoccupations elsewhere (Central and, probably later, South America, for example). As to the Near East, it is an area of such major intrinsic importance to both the United States and its NATO allies, that a policy enabling entry from the Mediterranean and Southeast Europe is the only possible route of intervention.

America's new strategy in the Asia-Pacific region would not be adopted as a result of the haphazard play of events following upon an uncertain period of Marcos succession in the Philippines. Rather it would be the planned result of realizing the impossibility of maintaining military presence in the Republic of the Philippines and responsibility for its fate into the 21st century.

32

Report on the Discussion:
United States Policy and the Philippines

Francis T. Underhill

In their oral presentations beginning the afternoon's session, three of the five discussants offered the following outline of United States policy towards the Philippines from 1970 to 1986:

- United States policy priorities in order of importance were (1) western Pacific military security needs and the unhampered use of the United States military bases; (2) economic, political, and social development of the Philippines; and (3) use of the Philippines as a centrally located, low-cost, efficient, and hospitable site for the regional operations of United States government agencies.
- The United States Embassy in Manila had no foreknowledge of Marcos's proclamation of martial law. We suspected he might try to extend his tenure by some extra-constitutional action, and Ambassador Byroade had attempted to discourage such a move.
- Deterioration in law and order, general social disintegration, and the catastrophic floods of July and August of 1972 offered some justification for martial law.
- The United States government did not endorse martial law but accepted it. We regarded Marcos as the best agent for reform and development.
- During the Carter years, our human-rights diplomacy played a major role in softening martial law excesses.
- Our policy establishment from 1976 to 1983 was strongly pro-Marcos.
- The United States helped to bring an end to martial law in 1981.
- We continued low-key pressure in support of human rights.
- During the early 1980s, we became concerned about transition and the need for political, economic, and military reform. The murder of Aquino in August 1983 was a turning point, and United States pressure for action in these three areas was intensified.
- Marcos stonewalled. He would agree with the ambassador or

high-level American visitor. A flurry of speeches and public relations ploys would follow, but no real reform. We concluded that the message was not getting through, and Senator Paul Laxalt was sent to convey the personal concern of President Reagan.

- Marcos's tactic to satisfy the United States was to call a snap election. He was confident that he would win and reestablish his legitimacy. We did not urge an election, but once he had made the decision, we sought to ensure that it would be fair, honest, and credible.

- The people's revolution that swept Corazon Aquino into power was purely Filipino. It sprang from the Philippine people's deep love for democracy, which we had helped to instill. Our role was that of a catalyst.

This summary of United States policy received no major challenges from the participants. There were, however, some minor demurrals. One participant charged that much of the breakdown of law and order prior to September 1972 was staged or encouraged by Marcos to provide justification for dictatorial rule. He pointed out that while there was no official American statement of approval of the martial law proclamation, there was also no official condemnation of this suspension of democratic freedoms. The American government acquiesced, and the American business community through its Chamber of Commerce sent a telegram of support to Marcos. In sharp contrast, when President Park Chung Hee declared martial law in South Korea three weeks later, the United States government issued a statement of strong disapproval.

American criticism of the structure and functioning of the Philippine government was commonplace during my tour in Manila from mid-1968 to early 1971. Colleagues serving in our embassy in earlier years have told me it was equally prevalent in their day. It came from United States officials, both civilian and military, in private conversations. It was voiced in the easy intimacy of the Filipino-American social relationship in late-night, beer-drinking "bull sessions" with Filipino congressmen, newspapermen, and government officials.

The Americans would say things of this sort: "The checks and balances you've adopted from our system work too well. Your president can't get anything done. Executive and legislative power is too evenly shared. Your country is too disorderly and democratic. Your press is too free. See what Park Chung Hee and Lee Kwan Yew have been able to accomplish in South Korea and Singapore with order and discipline. What this country needs is a man on horseback to take charge and get the show on the road."

Filipinos have had three-quarters of a century of experience in reading Americans and judging their true desires. There was every reason to feel confident that martial law would be welcomed by the United States government. Marcos as a young congressman must have heard his American embassy friends praise Park and Lee on many occasions. Filipinos were also aware that our overriding policy priority in their country was strategic. A Marcos ruling by edict was in a better position to provide untroubled use of our bases than a Marcos beset by an obstreperous congress and an independent judiciary.

For the remainder of the afternoon, the conference concentrated on the future of American bases, acknowledging tacitly as we did so the overriding importance of the strategic and security aspects of our relations with the Philippines. The two major areas considered were the attitude of the Philippines' Association of Southeast Asian Nations (ASEAN) partners to the bases and the future of the bases themselves.

Congressman Steven Solarz during his luncheon address had said that anything threatening the future of our bases in the Philippines would sent a shock wave through Asia and that he was certain that at the ASEAN meeting on Bali the other foreign ministers would be telling Foreign Secretary Laurel of the importance they attached to the base presence.

The congressman's view was strongly endorsed. A participant noted that Jusuf Wanandi, the director of the Centre for Strategic and International Studies (CSIS) in Jakarta, had addressed the Cincinnati Council on World Affairs in mid-April. Wanandi had said, "We are not alarmed about the Soviet military presence in Southeast Asia because of your presence. As long as you remain, the nations of ASEAN can concentrate on putting our political, economic, and social houses in order." The speaker reminded the group of the influence of the CSIS and the closeness of Wanandi to the Indonesian government. He noted that Wanandi was often the spokesman for positions the government did not wish to take publicly. Directors of strategic studies institutes of similar stature in Singapore and Kuala Lumpur had made it clear in recent conversations with him that they opposed unilateral United States withdrawal from the bases. He acknowledged that the Zone of Peace,

Freedom, and Neutrality (ZOPFAN) was still a long-range ASEAN goal. He admitted there was ambivalence and perhaps hypocrisy in the ASEAN partners' unwillingness to state in public what they said in private. Nonetheless he felt they attached great importance to the bases.

A Filipino participant supported these views. His remarks also reflected resentment that the other ASEAN countries were prepared to let the Filipinos face the Third World sneer that their country was, in his words, "the last remaining outpost of American imperialism." They were also quite content to have the Philippines bear all of the other political, social, and economic costs of the bases while they kept their nonaligned credentials clear.

Another participant noted that he and his wife had conducted an extensive series of interviews with Filipinos in recent months. The bases were seen as the main point of friction in United States-Philippine relations. Their respondents had told them that friends from other ASEAN countries had said they were very happy to have the American bases in the Philippines. Their Filipino respondents were resentful of the "better in your country than in ours" implication of this comment.

UNITED STATES-ASEAN RELATIONS

ASEAN attitudes towards our bases in the Philippines are an aspect of each nation's perception of its overall relationship with the United States, its view of the superpowers, and its perception of the threats to its national survival. It is a complex, subtle judgment and we would be simplistic and naive if we accepted at face value their statements about the bases. The United States suffers from a handicap in communicating with the nations of Southeast Asia. We have difficulty in distinguishing between true feelings and what is said to preserve harmonious interpersonal relations and avoid confrontation. Asians are acutely aware of the tremendous disparities in power, of their vulnerability, of what we can do to them or for them. This awareness often accentuates the differences between what the Japanese call *tetemae* (explicit statements) and *honne* (private intentions and beliefs).

The United States connection is critical for all the countries in ASEAN. The health of their economies depends to a major degree on the health of our economy. Access to our markets is essential, and they are begging for executive branch support in fighting the rising tide of protectionism in the U.S. Congress. We are the principal source of the technology and the capital needed for continued industrial growth. We are their main source of military supplies, equipment, and training. The military-based regimes in Thailand and Indonesia have close historical ties with our defense establishment and look to the United States for military assistance and logistic support for their United States-equipped armed forces. American goodwill and cooperation are central, in short, to their economic development and internal political stability.

We have made it clear that we consider our military presence in the Philippines to be of the utmost importance. We describe the bases as "vital to our national security" and "the linchpin of our strategic position in the Western Pacific." We say that the bases "guard choke points lying athwart or astride vital trade routes." We pay the Philippines a substantial rent for base rights.

Considering the strength of these views, unilateral withdrawal from the Clark and Subic bases could only come as part of a broader American disengagement from Southeast Asia—a disaster for the nations of ASEAN. Therefore, when an ASEAN leader is asked by an American official for his views on the bases, simple prudence would require him to say that his government favors an American military presence in the area and would oppose our unilateral withdrawal from the bases. Why do anything that might jeopardize the critical agenda with the United States?

Such a statement, voiced in a private conversation, can furthermore be made without cost. The United States was not asking that a base be accepted on his country's soil, nor suggesting that his country contribute to the costs of maintaining the bases in the Philippines. Why cavil about a free insurance policy?

Threat perceptions in ASEAN differ of course from nation to nation, but there are some common general themes. The ASEAN nations emphasize the internal dimension of national security. They are concerned about dissidence and insurgency. They are worried about the political consequences of flagging economic growth and the difficulties of finding jobs for the flood of young people entering the job market each year. They feel threatened by trade barriers and protectionism in the developed world. Most have economies in which large sectors of the population depend for their livelihood on agricultural raw materials. (In Malaysia, an estimated 20 percent of the population are immediately affected by changes in the price of rubber.) These commodity prices have been falling. Several ASEAN countries are troubled by the rise of religious fundamentalism.

All of the ASEAN countries, Thailand especially, would like to end the Vietnamese occupation of Kampuchea, but the Hanoi regime does not loom as a threat to the degree it did a decade ago. Thailand looks to the China connection and the Chinese armies on the Vietnamese border, not American naval and air power in the Philippines, as the counterweight to Hanoi's ambitions.

The Soviet Union does not figure prominently in the ASEAN perception of the threat. An American Fulbright scholar wrote in a monograph published in 1985 by the Malaysian Institute of Strategic and International Studies: "Living in Malaysia gives the impression that the USSR is almost a non-factor in the region. There simply seems not to be a great deal of attention paid to it."[1]

Noordin Sopiee, the director-general of ISIS, in a monograph published by his institute, states: "We should not be overly concerned about the Soviet threat, firstly because the Soviets do not have the capability, and secondly because they do not have the intent."[2] Sopiee argues that the Soviet Union is "an incredibly unidimensional power" in Southeast Asia. It has no economic clout, it has no psychological or cultural levers of power, and it has no significant political influence. All it has is military power. He finds it difficult to imagine any circumstance in which this military power could be brought to bear to any effect. In his analysis of Soviet intent, Sopiee states that Moscow has limited objectives in the ASEAN community: prevent Chinese hegemonism and reduce American influence. Soviet military pressure against any ASEAN state, he argues, would defeat this policy of denial and drive the ASEAN nations into the embrace of the USSR's rivals.

If it is difficult to translate military power into political influence, why have the Soviets increased their Pacific military power to such a degree? According to Sopiee, the increase is the result of the USSR's global strategic rivalry with the United States, its desire to contain China, its need to defend Siberia, and its need to honor its commit-

---

[1]Robert C. Horn, *The Soviet Threat in Southeast Asia: Illusion or Reality?* (Kuala Lumpur: ISIS, 1985), p. 1.
[2]Mohamed Noordin Sopiee, *The Russian Threat: Between Alarm and Complacency* (Kuala Lumpur: ISIS, 1985), p. 4.

ments to Vietnam. The ASEAN nations are all peripheral to these objectives.

American strategic thinkers find a serious threat to the sea lines of communication in the Soviet military buildup in the Pacific. The Strait of Malacca is often cited as a major choke point. An Indonesian perspective on this threat appears in an article in the January 1986 issue of a quarterly published by Jusuf Wanandi's Centre for Strategic and International Studies. J. Soedjati Djiwandono argues that an expanded Soviet Pacific fleet, far from suggesting a Russian desire to disrupt international shipping between the Indian Ocean and the Pacific, instead indicates a greater Soviet interest in having international passage remain open. He notes that the USSR was one of the first to oppose the Indonesian and Malaysian 1971 declaration which applied the twelve-mile limit of territorial waters to the Strait of Malacca. (He might have noted also that during law-of-the-sea negotiations, the United States and the Soviet Union were usually on the same side on the matter of straits, archipelago seas, and innocent passage of naval vessels. Soviet admirals and American admirals tend to think alike on freedom of the seas.)

Djiwandono argues that Soviet rivalry with the United States and a desire for surveillance over United States deployments in the Indian Ocean and the Pacific suggest a Soviet interest in unimpeded passage through the straits. He adds that Russia's need for increased trade with the area, its support of Vietnam, and its confrontation with the People's Republic of China all indicate a Soviet desire for peaceful access to the sea lanes in Southeast Asia. Finally, he joins his Malaysian colleague in maintaining that the Soviet military buildup in the Pacific is not to achieve superiority, but rather to redress an imbalance created by United States dominance and supremacy in the region over past decades.[3]

In mid-February and early March 1986, I led a group from the World Affairs Council of Northern California on a study mission to the Philippines' five ASEAN partners. The Philippine crisis was at its height during our travels. Philippine developments were on the front pages of the local newspapers, and there was much press speculation

---

[3]J. Soedjati Djiwandono, "The Security of Sea Lanes in the Asian-Pacific Region," *The Indonesian Quarterly,* vol. XIV, No. 1, January 1986 (Jakarta), pp. 53-54.

about the possibility that the United States might be forced out of its bases. In each of the ASEAN capitals, we met with host government officials, United States Embassy officials, and community leaders. In Kuala Lumpur, Singapore, and Jakarta, we spent mornings at the strategic studies institutes conferring with scholars. The bases and the host-country view of the American military role in the area was a central element in our discussions. These are the salient elements of my impressions of local attitudes:

- Government officials said that the question of American military bases in the Philippines was a bilateral matter between the United States and the Philippines. They dodged questions on the role they saw the bases playing in their own security. They and the scholars were prepared to say only that an American military presence "over the horizon" was appreciated.

- I saw no editorials or other expressions of concern in the press that their security might be adversely affected if the United States were forced to leave Clark and Subic bases.

- When asked by the press about their country as an alternative site for United States bases, local officials rejected the idea out of hand. In Bangkok, Air Marshal Paniang, the deputy defense minister, said that it would be difficult to relocate the bases in Thailand "because they had been asked to leave by the Thai government. The United States has learned a lesson here—that they are not wanted." In Singapore there were half-humorous evasions that they could not take the bases because Clark Field was as large as the entire island of Singapore.

- In the strategic institutes, I found no locally produced studies defending or supporting prevailing American strategic doctrine about the bases or our military role in the area.

- A Zone of Peace, Freedom, and Neutrality (ZOPFAN) actively continues to be sought as an ASEAN goal. Withdrawal of all foreign military bases from the ASEAN area is one of the long-range objectives of ZOPFAN.

I have therefore reached the conclusion that the ASEAN partners find our military bases in the Philippines to have little relevance to what they perceive as the main threats to their national security. The tough, sophisticated, experienced men who rule these countries are neither impressed nor intimidated by growing Soviet military power in the area. They find it hard to see how this military power can be converted to political influence, or used to coerce them. Singapore feels comfortable enough with the Soviet presence to provide repair services to Soviet naval units passing to and from the Indian Ocean.

The ASEAN partners accept the American military presence as nonthreatening. In the face of a clear American determination to maintain this presence, they are prepared to say that they value it to avoid jeopardizing their broader agenda with the United States. American trade and investment policy, interest rates, and the health of our economy are vastly more important to them than American air and naval power in the Philippines.

CLARK AND SUBIC BASES

The American bases as a factor in bilateral United States-Philippine relations occupied the remaining time in the discussion period.

I was the only participant who supported Professor Kattenburg's proposal for disengagement and a gradual and negotiated withdrawal of our bases. My principal argument was one of utility. In a time of crisis, we cannot be sure that we will be permitted unrestricted use of the bases. The 1979 and 1984 revisions of the bases agreement incorporate a fundamental contradiction. The United States is guaranteed "unhampered military operations." At the same time, the United States acknowledges Philippine sovereignty over the bases. Sovereignty is inherently unconditional, and the Philippine government could assert a right to limit use of the bases if it seemed in its interest to do so. We faced such restrictions during the Vietnam war, and are certain to face them in any future crisis situation.

With Marcos, we knew we could have our way if we met his price. We are now, however, dealing with a woman of principle. The restrictions on military operations imposed by our European allies during the Yom Kippur War and the recent bombing of Libya illustrate the unreliability of foreign bases. We are, in effect, paying half a billion dollars in annual premium on an insurance policy that can be cancelled unilaterally at any time.

Strong objections were voiced to a withdrawal from the bases, particularly Subic. Subic, it was argued, affords our navy enormous savings, not only in upkeep and maintenance, but also in capital costs. Its repair facilities and skilled labor force are available to us at a fraction of the cost of similar services in Hawaii or on the West Coast. Without Subic, we would need half again as many surface vessels in the Seventh Fleet to maintain the same level of naval force in the western Pacific. Clark, while somewhat less essential, is important for logistic support of Diego Garcia. Alternatives to Subic and Clark could be found, but the cost of poor substitutes would be enormous, in the range of $12 billion.

Professor Kattenburg's suggestion that our withdrawal from Philippines bases might be linked with negotiations for a Soviet withdrawal from Cam Ranh Bay provoked some discussion. There was general agreement that the Soviets wanted us out of Clark and Subic, and several participants thought it likely that the Soviets might be ready to give up their current use of the American-built facility in Vietnam if it would bring an American withdrawal from the Philippines. There were strong questions raised, however, on whether the Soviet *quid pro quo* would be adequate.

While there was little support for the idea of withdrawal from the bases, several spoke in favor of some measure of disengagement. President Aquino should be given elbow room and not smothered in an American embrace. We should allow the new government to deal in its own way with the problems confronting it and not overwhelm it with well-meaning advice. We should help, but not encourage patterns of dependence.

In the discussion of the bases there was one theme which I believe may have been the most important aspect of the afternoon's discussion. All of the speakers, whether for or against withdrawal, urged that the strategic rationale for the bases, the impact of the bases on our bilateral relations with the Philippines, and the question of alternative sites be given the most careful scrutiny and reevaluation during the five years before the expiration of the bases agreement in 1991.

It is my fervent hope that the Washington Institute's conference will stimulate both in the academic community and at policy levels in our government such a critical examination of our base presence. Clark and Subic are so firmly established, so glitteringly efficient, and in place for so many years, that they have become a permanent, immutable "given" in our relations with the Philippines. Protected by popular support for national defense and military confrontation of communism, they have come to be seen as an essential element in our global deployment of military power. Immune from critical examination of missions and costs, the bases have become the dominant element in our relations with the Philippines. As a consequence, policy has become the servant of its instrument.

INTIMACY AND CONDESCENSION

In the decades since the end of World War II, the rationale for our military presence has changed constantly. The bases were initially to protect the Philippines from foreign invasion, and the mutual defense aspect of our relationship was uppermost. As this threat became gradually less credible, defense of the Philippines faded as an objective, and the bases became an element in the American strategic confrontation with the Soviet Union. The sense of a shared defense goal disappeared, and the Filipinos came to regard the bases as potential targets in conflicts not of their making or concern. Instead of enhancing their security, the bases were seen as endangering it. Feelings of vulnerability and alienation have produced an explicit Philippine demand that we pay rent. The Filipinos now want money for what they used to give for love.

We are well aware of the financial costs of the bases. We should also give serious thought to the psychological costs. Our historical ties, our huge civilian government presence, and above all the military bases have perpetuated colonial attitudes and created between our two countries an excessive intimacy, an intimacy poisoned on both sides by love-hate, unreasonable expectations, and hypocrisy. The intimacy has existed for so long and has increased so much that we seem hardly aware of it.

During the conference, I described our relationship as "pathological." During the coffee break, a participant told me the term was too strong. My perceptions are influenced by service in Indonesia and Malaysia prior to my posting to Manila. I found Americans ready to accept Malaysians and Indonesians as Asians. Filipinos on the other hand were measured against other standards and condemned as failed Americans. Robert Pringle, a Foreign Service officer with a similar background of service in Indonesia prior to assignment to Manila, writes: "Emotionalism pervades all aspects of United States-Philippine relations. . . . Special treatment is expected, slights and insults are magnified, motives are suspected. There is much warmth and frank talk in the relationship, but they yield quickly and unpredictably to alienation and misunderstanding."[4] If this is not pathological it is certainly unhealthy.

The ASEAN partners are conscious of this excessive intimacy. During my visit to Southeast Asia mentioned above, a major focus of attention in the other capitals was on the role of the United States in the drama of Marcos's downfall. A Habib mission's passing judgment on the legitimacy of the election, the pathetic "say-it-isn't-so" phone calls to the White House, Marcos's acceptance of the *coup de grace* at the hands of an United States senator, and the flight from Manila on United States military aircraft seemed in their eyes an inappropriate level of American involvement in the internal affairs of a nominally independent Asian country. A Malaysian friend remarked that the Philippines had behaved like a small country in the Caribbean. An Indonesian friend said that the manner of Marcos's departure confirmed their view that national independence can be threatened as much from the embrace of one's friends as from the machinations of one's enemies.

While usually well-intentioned in communicating with Filipinos, Americans are often condescending, patronizing, and proprietary. Affection is present but is often mixed with exasperation and contempt. We are compulsive head-patters. We feel that it is our proper role to offer advice and guidance and theirs to accept it. One of the Filipino conference participants seemed to find overtones of this overbearing attitude in the conference agenda when he said we "overdid it" in our examination of Philippine society and our personal analysis of President Aquino.

Americans move customarily to an anglicized diminutive of Filipino Christian names, a freedom we would never take with other Asians. In our conference, both in formal papers and in the discussions, the Philippine president was usually referred to as "Cory." If our conference had been on relations with the United Kingdom, would we have routinely said "Maggie?" If Philippine scholars had met in Manila to discuss the United States, would they have routinely said "Ronnie?"

When they deal with Americans, Filipinos resort to the tactics of the weak. They are seen as devious and indirect, difficult to pin down. An

---

[4]Robert Pringle, *Indonesia and the Philippines: American Interests in Island Southeast Asia* (New York: Columbia University Press, 1980), p. 61.

agreement reached today often evaporates during the night, and the issue must be addressed from the beginning on the next day. Their manner swings from engaging friendliness and pliability to prickly sensitivity and stubbornness. Forty years of post-colonial intimacy have generated in the Filipinos a neurotic, manipulative, psychically crippling dependency.

Following independence in 1946, our two governments agreed to continue to allow Philippine citizens to enlist in the United States Navy as stewards. Filipino stewards on detail from the Navy now staff the White House Mess and the vice president's residence. A Filipino steward serving as a valet was with President Ford on his state visit to Manila in 1976. Presidents Reagan and Marcos during the summit meetings in Cancun, Mexico, in 1981 posed for a photograph with the Filipino stewards in the Reagan party. A Foreign Service friend heard President Eisenhower remark at a White House meeting, "I understand the Filipinos. I've had a Filipino messboy most of my adult life."

The Philippine government allows its citizens to enlist in the armed forces of a foreign power as officers' servants. The United States government permits aliens access to the highest and most sensitive areas of our government and to the persons of our highest officials. That neither government regards this situation as anomalous reveals the persistence of colonial attitudes on both sides.

The Filipinos are sharply ambivalent about the bases. On the one hand, they feel that the base presence makes their independence and nationhood flawed and incomplete. It rankles to have to ask permission of a foreigner to go on their own soil. Filipinos are acutely conscious of this colonial stigma in their dealing with other countries of the Third World. They are resentful about the sordid interface of the two cultures in the cities at the gates of Clark and Subic. The order and efficiency on on side of the perimeter fence and the crime and squalor on the other contribute to feelings of inadequacy and poor self-image.

On the other hand, they value the substantial benefit to the economy that flows from base operations. The United States is the largest employer after the Philippine government in this poor Asian country. It is difficult for Filipinos to imagine life without the bases. Of equal importance is the hold they give the Philippines on the United States. We proclaim that the bases are vital to our national security, and this admission of need has put a ring in our nose that the Filipinos use to bring us into line.

A time-honored tug on the ring has been to hint that they might turn the bases over to the Soviet Union if we refuse to meet their demands. Marcos resorted to it often. A Filipino conference participant gave a ritual, almost automatic tug on the ring when he said that if the Americans should withdraw from the bases "we'll probably sleep with them [the Soviets]. No hard feelings." But our need for the bases means more to them than mere bargaining leverage. It demonstrates also that we still love them, that we will be sympathetic and responsive to their needs, that we still regard the relationship as "special." It would be a terrible emotional wrench to confront a distant, disinterested United States.

Thoughtful Filipinos and Americans have been concerned about the emotionally unhealthy aspect of our relationship for some time. An unnamed American official at the Symington Committee hearings in 1969 said: "Dr. Spock should be the Ambassador in Manila. The United States has a father image in the Philippines, and like most fathers we don't understand the problem." When I was posted to Manila in 1968, the embassy's orientation program for new arrivals included a lecture by a Filipino psychologist who was also a Jesuit priest on the emotional aspects of the Philippine-American relationship. The excessive intimacy and its adverse consequences have been accepted as one of the costs of our base presence, a sacrifice we have been willing to make in the service of broader regional and global security interests.

A restudy of the strategic rationale for our bases should therefore include an equally rigorous examination of their impact on our bilateral relations. We have long described our role in the Third World as "nation building." Have we in fact been retarding maturation and encouraging dependency in the Philippines? The United States has also suffered from the intimacy. Our concern for the stability of base operations put us on the side of the status quo and made us an apologist for the regime during the Marcos years. Base rent payments became political support and economic subvention, which linked us to the excesses of the regime. We should be attempting to open some decent distance between ourselves and our former colony in our own interest as well.

Pentagon files are full of studies and cost estimates on alternative base sites. Every island and atoll in the western Pacific has been considered, and the conclusions have been the same. Even if we spent billions on airfields, drydocks, fuel storage tanks, ammunition maga-zines and all the other necessary facilities, we would never approach the combination of location, labor force, convenience, and utility that we have in the Philippines. In simple terms, say all the studies, there are no real alternatives to Subic and Clark.

The question has been, "How can we do elsewhere what we are now doing at our Philippine bases?" We should instead be asking ourselves, "Could we be doing it at greatly reduced levels?" and "Do we need to be doing it at all?" If the bases did not exist, would we see today a need to establish such a military presence in a foreign country in Southeast Asia? Considering the levels of political maturity and economic growth in Southeast Asia, is there any longer any justification for our assuming the responsibility for area stability? Southeast Asia ranks last among Third World regions in terms of Soviet aid. Soviet trade with ASEAN represents 0.5 percent of Moscow's total trade turnover. Soviet politi-cal influence is equally negligible. Are current levels of surveillance of Soviet naval activity really necessary? William P. Bundy writing in 1971 asserted that America's only *vital* geopolitical interest in South-east Asia is that it should remain an area where *none* of the super-powers, including ourselves, regards its interests as vital.[5]

We must also look carefully at the utility of a military base on foreign soil. We cannot assume a permanent identity of security interests with any foreign country, nor can we assume unrestricted use of military facilities not entirely under our sovereign control.

FUTURE NEGOTIATIONS

If we should decide to give up control, we would have to negotiate a gradual withdrawal providing time for adjustment. An abrupt unilateral pullout would be harmful. The Filipinos are hooked on the bases, and the more we seem ready to leave, the more they will be inclined to cling to us. When the British government decided to give up its naval dockyards in Singapore, Prime Minister Lee fought the decision and there were dire predictions of economic hardship. Yet Singapore, with far fewer natural resources, weathered the crisis. The physical facilities at Clark and Subic would remain if they were no longer American

[5]William P. Bundy, "New Tides in Southeast Asia," *Foreign Affairs* 49 (January 1971): 198.

bases. We should give serious thought to privatization with Filipino or Philippine-American joint-venture contractors operating the facilities as private contractors now do in Brooklyn and Newport News. Logistics and maintenance are the most important function of the bases today, and private contractors could provide these services.

In February and March 1986 the extraordinary courage and great political sophistication of the Philippine people produced a miracle in Manila. Instead of the chaos, bloodshed, and civil war that seemed almost inevitable, we have instead civil order, communist insurgents divided and politically isolated, a corrupt ex-dictator holed up in Honolulu, and a responsible, legitimate, democratic government in control. The United States has been far luckier than it deserves, and we now have the opportunity to work out with this new government the future course of our relations. President Aquino has made it clear she wants to shelve the base problem for the time being and "keep her options open." There are five years until 1991. We should nevertheless be preparing for the time when she says, "Now I'd like to talk about the bases."

INDEX

Numbers in **bold face** refer to pages written by the person indexed. A number in a bracket [ ] following a page number refers to the footnote with that backeted number on that page; there may be other references to the topic on a page bésides that shown in a footnote.

Dutch regime 249
Duvalier, Jean-Claude 313

East Asia 53, 445, 450, 455-457, 466, 540, 554
Economic Research Service 155
economic self-sufficiency 268
economics
    decline 339-341
    Philippine nationalism and 126-135
    policies of nationalism 131-135
    recovery 174-175
EDSA (Epifanio de los Santos Avenue) 187
education employees 245 (table)
Eisenhower, Dwight D. 487, 573
El Salvador 66, 404, 411
elections (1978-1985) 19-24
    February (1985) 19-24
Embassy, U. S. 39
emotionalism 571
employment by industry (table) 243
En-lai, Chou 543
enclave strategy 553
engineers 245 (table)
Enrile, Juan Ponce xvi, 15, 23, 29 [6], 32-37, 42, 43, 57, 253 [10], 254 [11], 314, 322-326, 331, 345, 351, 373, 381, 383, 385, 413 [34], 427, 438-440, 442, 446, 447, 502, 510
environment, decline of Philippine 171
equalitarianism 268
Ermita, Eduardo 433, 439
Escaler, Frederico 403
Espaldon, Romulo 418
Espana Street 248 [4]
Espina, Rene 375
Espirito, Socorro E. 267 [5]
Estrada, Joseph 325
Europe 548, 560, 569
    liberalism in 73
    power in 450
European Economic Community 27 [5]
Evangelista, Cristanto 82
Evangelli Nutiandi 362
executive-legislative relations 534
executives 245 (table)
Export Incentives Act 229
Export-Import Bank 508

factionalism 424, 432, 433
factory workers 245 (table)
familism 269
family planning clinic 509
Far East 449, 455
farming 245 (table), 329
    occupations in 244 (table)
    See also agriculture

fascist leaders 415 [36]
Favali, Tullio 359
FBIS 357 [14]
FCN See friendship, commerce and navigation
February Revolution 8, 20-24, 438
federalism 388
Federation of Free Farmers 92
FEER See Far Eastern Economic Review
Fermin, Patria N. 207 [5]
Fernandez, Jose 322
Fertilizer and Pesticide Authority 171
Filipino American veterans 520
Filipino Democratic Organization 374
fishing workers 245 (table)
flags, United States and Philippine 474
Floirendo, Antonio 320
Florida Blanca Air Base (Pampanga) 472
FMS See Foreign Military Sales
Folk Art Center 225
Food Aid Authority in the Food Security Act 1985
food industry
    food system, Philippine 173-174
    processing 243 (table)
    resources and common property 183-184
    services workers 245 (table)
    See also individual foods, e.g. corn, rice, etc.
Food Security Act of 1985 149, 150, 154
Food Security Inprovements Act of 1986, The 154
Ford, Gerald R. 473-474, 494, 523, 573
Foreign Broadcast Information Service 356 [11]
foreign military sales 447, 448
foremen 245 (table)
forfeitures and sugar industry 149-150
Fort Bonifacio 253 [10]
Fort Stotsenberg 471
Fortich, Antonio 358, 404
four-day revolution 440
Franciscan Sisters 358
Free Farmers Federation, or Free Farmers' Federation 239, 285
"Freedom Constitution" 27, 125, 321, 322, 386
French 511, 542
    colonies 17
French Fifth Republic 13
Friend, Theodore ix, 8, **69-86,** 74 [7]
friendship, commerce and navigation (FCN) 508
furniture industry 243 (table)
future of Philippines, leadership in 444, 445
    challenges for 444-447

Paul VI 362
Paz, Octavio 86 [37]
PD-27, 162, 175-181, 186
PDP-Laban party 20, 296, 327, 328, 374, 375-377, 428
PDU 358 [21]
Peace Corps 509, 515
PEACE **See** Philippine Ecumenical Action for Community Development
peasants and agricultural workers 205-218, [3]
peddlers 244 (table)
Peking 543
Pelaez, Emmanuel M. ix, 38, 43, **45-55,** 81 [24], 491, 494 [1], 497, 528 [6]
Pendatun, Salipasa 425, 501
People Power Revolution 384, 394
"people power" 24, 36, 57, 442, 547
People's Party (*Partido ng Bayan*) 26
People's Republic of China 82, 249, 507, 528, 556, 559, 567
Perez, Leonardo B. 254 [11], 326
Persian Gulf 462, 465, 544, 555, 558, 560
    oil fields 462
personal services workers 245 (table)
Petropavlovsk 458 (map)
Philippine Accrediting Association of Colleges and Universities 252 [8]
Philippine-American Association 7, 45-55, 111-121, 53, 449, 491, 505, 519, 521, 526, 544, 547, 574, 576
    See also treaties; United States
Philippine-American Defense Partnership, The 491
Philippine-American Friendship Day 521
Philippine Armed Forces 332, 333
Philippine Bases 457 [12], 462 [13], 464 [15]
Philippine Central Bank, The 339
Philippine College of Arts and Trades 248
Philippine Commission on Good Goverment 168, 180
Philippine Council for Foreign Relations 45
Philippine Ecumenical Action for Community Development 359
Philippine Exchange Company 145
Philippine Heart Center for Asia 226
Philippine Military Academy 97, 438, 442
Philippine National Bank 194, 196
Philippine Scouts 541
Philippine Sugar Commission, The 145, 151, 154
Philippine Sugar Marketing Corporation 151
Philippine Trade Act of 1946 46, 50, 154
Pimentel, Aquilino Q. 35, 374,383, 427
PKP **See** *Partido Komunista ng Pilipinas*
PMA **See** Philippine Military Academy

PNB 375
PNP 372
Politburo 17
Populorum Progresso 362
Pot, Pol 64
power
    economic 333-334
    political 331-333
PRC **See** People's Republic of China
President's Observer Mission 534
Presidential Human Rights Commission 441, 446
Robles, Rex 15, 446
Presidential Security Command 14, 23, 440
Pringle, Robert 571, 572 [4]
Proctor and Gamble 96, 100
Protestants 361-366
Pundato, Dimas 425, 433

Quadripartite Ministerial Commission 428
Quezon, Manuel 9, 46, 82, 72-77, 76 [11], 77 [12, 13, 14], 78 [15], 79 [17], 80, 82 [28], 83, 84 [31], 85, 158, 405
"Quezon Commonwealth" 72 [4]
Quirino, Elpidio 46, 75
Quisumbing, Lourdes 366

Ralph Bunche Institute on the United Nations 251 [7]
RAM **See** Reform the Armed Forces Movement
Ramos, Fidel 14, 15, 23, 25, 32, 34, 42, 57, 381, 383, 385, 386, 400 [7], 411, 413 [34], 427, 433, 438-440, 442-447, 493, 496, 498, 499, 502, 550
Ranis, Gustav x, **111-121**
Reagan, Ronald 27, 39, 41, 42, 52, 58, 59, 98, 381, 448, 526, 533, 562, 573
    administration 40, 51, 529
Reed Bank 525
Reform the Armed Forces Movement 15, 23, 34, 493
Reinah, David 14, **141-154**
Republic of Korea 498, 511
Republic of the Philippines 548, 549, 560
Republican administration 533-536, 540
Richter, Linda K. xii, 12, **379-394**
Rizal, Jose 46, 79
Robles, Rex 15, 446
Rojas, Gerry 530
Roman Catholic **See** Catholic
Roman republic 307
Romualdez, Eduardo Z. 332, 495
Romulo, Carlos 451 [2], 454 [7], 507, 512, 525
Rono, Jose 326, 372
Roosevelt, Theodore 449, 518, 539, 541

Rosenberg, David A. 12, 330 [2], **329-350**
Rotarians 306, 371
ROTC 15
Roxas, Manuel 46, 75 [9]
RUC 444
Russian democracy 382

Sabah 418, 420, 422, 452 [5], 492
Sacerdoti, Guy 402 [10]
Saguisag, Rene A. V. 33, 254 [12], 310
St. Escolastica 248 [3]
St. Joseph College 248 [3]
St. Paul College 248 [3], 256
St. Theresa College 248 [3]
Salamat, Hashim 424, 425, 433, 501
Salas, Rodolfo 407, 415
Salonga, Jovito 322, 323, 327, 359, 375,
   553
Salvation Army 354
Samal 375, 406, 418, 425
Sampaguita Hall 291
San Juan 325
San Jose Mercury 427 [15]
Sanchez, Agusto 33, 35, 254 [12]
Sanderinck, Herman 358
Santos, Bienvenido 78
Santos, Vicente Abad 291
Sarmiento, Abraham M. Jr. 249 [5], 335,
   336 [8]
Saudi Arabia 287, 430
Saudi press 425
Sayre, Francis 74
Scott, James 264 [4], 272 [13], 277
Scott, Margaret 407 [24]
Sea of Japan 456, 555
SEATO **See** Southeast Asia Treaty
   Organization
Second Philippine Revolution 8
Second Vatican Council 361
Security Agency 14
Senate Foreign Relations Committee 397,
   409 [27]
Senate Select Committee on Intelligence 344
Shah of Iran 39, 313
Shilleto, Edward 358
Shinto 279
Shultz, George P. 309-311, 368 [40], 408
Siberia 457, 566
Sigma Delta Phi 295
Sillman University 258
Sin, Cardinal 19, 23, 85 [35], 95, 252, 254
   [11], 287, 300, 313 [1], 351 [1], 352,
   355, 356 [10], 357 [13], 366, 368, 381,
   382, 384, 525 [4]
Singapore 9, 49, 294, 308, 449 [1], 456,
   465, 555, 563, 568, 569, 575, 73
Sison, Jose Maria 25, 250 [6], 346, 375,

408 [26], 500
Sisters of Charity 297
Smith, Brian H. 355 [9]
Smith, Robert **491-502**
Society of Jesus 359
Society of St. Columban 359
Sola, Pablo 357, 358
Solarz, Steven J. 38, **57-67**, 61, 62-65, 310,
   316, 531, 533, 563
Somoza, Anastasio 39, 313, 316
Sopiee, Mohamed Noordin 566 [2]
Sosmena, Gaudioso 348
South China Sea 452 [5], 456, 460, 464,
   465, 539, 550, 555, 555, 5605
South Korea 91, 92, 249, 555, 562, 563
South Pacific 541, 548, 556
Southeast Asia 10, 30, 43, 69, 70, 94, 258,
   285, 438, 456, 457, 461, 465, 497, 498,
   507, 514, 522, 529, 533, 540, 542-544,
   548-559, 563-566, 572, 575
Southeast Asia Collective Defense Treaty,
   The 451
Southeast Asia Treaty Organization 507, 514
Southeast Asian Nations 466, 496, 497,
   506, 507, 514
Southeast pacific 554-555, 558, 559
Soviet Union 17, 43, 47, 51, 52, 332, 450,
   454-456, 460-462, 465, 496, 497, 507,
   543, 544, 545, 548, 556-559, 566, 570,
   571, 574
   air force 555
   military 555, 567, 569
   navy 558, 567
   rule 382
   trade 575
Soviet-Chinese frontier 543
Spaeth, Anthony 320, 321 [9]
Spain or Spaniards 8, 53, 73, 83, 249, 257,
   268, 282, 257, 315, 388, 419, 429, 449,
   492, 495, 518, 539
   colonial rule 8, 9
   surrender 45
Spanish American relationship 90, 97
Spanish Fleet 449
Spock, Benjamin 574
Spratly Islands 525
Sri Lanka 555
Stalin, Josef 315
State Department 40, 525, 534, 547
Stauffer, Robert A. 85 [34], 314 [2]
Steinberg, David Joel 73 [5], 267 [8], 418
   [3], 431
Strait of Malacca 567
Strassman, W. Paul 241
Stull, Lee T. 38, **517-528**
Subcommittee on Asian and Pacific Affairs
   452 [5]